Authors
and Illustrators
of Children's Books

Authors and Illustrators of Children's Books

Writings on Their Lives and Works

Miriam Hoffman and
Eva Samuels

R. R. BOWKER COMPANY, New York & London 1972

Published by R. R. Bowker Co. (a Xerox company)
1180 Avenue of the Americas, New York, N.Y. 10036
Copyright © 1972 by Xerox Corporation
All rights reserved.
International Standard Book Number: 0–8352–0523–1
Library of Congress Catalog Card Number: 76–38607
Printed and bound in the United States of America

Contents

Preface

FOR SOME TIME we have felt the need for a book of readings which would bring together information about authors and author-illustrators of children's literature. A popular assignment in our courses in this field is to find out as much as possible about one author or illustrator and his contributions. The results of a recent questionnaire sent to college and university professors of children's literature throughout the U.S. indicate that this is a frequent requirement.

We feel that it is important for students to be acquainted with the personalities behind children's books in order to better understand these books. By providing students with background material on authors and author-illustrators, we hope to make children's books more meaningful, not only for the students, but most especially for the children with whom they will be working.

Those of us who have taught in the elementary school know, for instance, how much more children relate to and understand Robert McCloskey's books when they are able to recognize his home, his family, and his children in *Blueberries for Sal* and *Time of Wonder;* when they can identify with his youthful experiences in *Homer Price* and *Lentil;* and when they hear his funny stories about his adventures with ducks while writing and illustrating *Make Way for Ducklings.* Not only does the child begin to understand that books are written and illustrated by real people, but he also begins to realize how much of himself the author or illustrator reveals in each of his books.

A rather common belief of college students as well as youngsters seems to be that children's books are written overnight. In reality, however, many children's books take a year or more from start to finish, a fact which college students can immediately appreciate when they try their hand at writing their own books. A casual examination of the articles in this volume should indicate to students the painstaking research, dedication, and devotion that are involved in creating many of the excellent books for children.

Many fine articles about these creators of children's books have been written in various periodicals, newspapers, and journals, but these are often difficult to locate due to limited library resources or overburdened library facilities. Our primary aim in compiling this volume is to make these articles permanently accessible by bringing them together under one cover, thus saving the time and energy usually consumed in locating and reviewing this type of material.

Limitation of choices was necessary, so we regrettably had to narrow down our selections. In books for older elementary-school children, content is of prime importance — thus, in that category, we have chosen articles dealing principally with authors. For younger children of picture-book age, we have selected primarily articles about author-illustrators, since in books on this level the pictorial statement complements the written one. However, a few of the author-illustrators included address themselves to both groups. We realize that this is an artificial limitation and necessarily excludes many fine artists and writers, but in any single volume no one could possibly include the many deserving craftsmen in the field of children's books.

Due to space limitations, we have omitted authors who write only poetry and illustrators who have not authored books of their own. The writers selected are contemporary. Some have been popular with children for more than twenty-five years; others are relative newcomers to the field. All share in common the ability to talk directly to children, in a personal and uncondescending way.

Another important consideration which determined selection was the quality of the article. In situations where we found two or more articles about the same individual, we generally chose the most recent one, unless the writing was significantly better or the content more relevant or complete in an earlier one.

The fifty articles finally chosen are from various sources, their dates of publication ranging over a twenty-one year period, from 1950 to 1971. No changes have been made in the articles. Our contribution has been in the choice of material and in the editors' notes following each selection. In the latter, where necessary, we have included awards and honors received, updated and added biographic information, and noted recent books. Included also is an Appendix which lists the books, both in and out of print, that have been produced by the subjects of this volume.

It is our hope that this book will be an invaluable aid, not only to students of children's literature in schools of education and library science, but also to children's librarians in elementary schools and public libraries. Elementary-school teachers and youngsters should find the selections interesting as well as useful. The older child will be able to find out more about a particular author and his books, whether for class booktalks, units revolving around particular writers, or just to satisfy his curiosity. For the younger child, reading time can be much more enjoyable; the teacher can provide background material and recount anecdotes and other human-interest items which add a personal touch to the books she reads.

We wish to express our appreciation to the authors and publishers who have graciously given us permission to reprint the articles, and to the many publishers who helped us to locate authors. The task of finding and reproducing materials was greatly lightened by the assistance of Hofstra University Education Librarian, Mrs. Dorothy Hallborg, and Mrs. Roseann Rybak of her staff. A debt of gratitude is owed to Mrs. Jo Sadowski, who helped with some of the necessary paper work associated with this type of undertaking, and to our editors J. A. Neal and Cary Bynum, who made many helpful suggestions along the way.

M.H.
E.S.

Edward Ardizzone:
An Autobiographical Note *

I WAS BORN IN THE YEAR 1900 of a French father and a Scottish mother in the town of Haiphong situated in Tonkin, a province of Indo-China. When five years old I was brought to England and England has been my permanent home ever since.

I was the eldest of a family of three boys and two girls and our upbringing and schooling followed the traditional pattern of the middle classes, viz. a series of governesses, then the private and the public school.

My birthday falling towards the end of the year, being 18 in the year 1918, I was fortunate, though I remember being bitterly disappointed at the time, to escape military service in the Great War, and early in 1919 I started my rather chequered career in the city of London.

I had various jobs in quick succession, till finally in the early twenties I joined the Eastern Telegraph Co. and was to remain with them for six years.

My position was that of Statistical Clerk and it had two advantages which, like my escape from military service, I was not aware of at the time. These advantages were first that it was a job ineffably boring and secondly that there was very little work to do, with the result that I was able to spend hours doodling and I had plenty of surplus energy left over after the day's work to attend evening classes in drawing at least three times and sometimes four times a week.

I was fortunate too to find as a master that fine artist and great teacher,

* By Edward Ardizzone. Reprinted by permission from *The Junior Bookshelf* 14 (March 1950), 39–45.

Mr. Bernard Meninsky, doubly fortunate, as these evening classes were the only form of Art Education that I was to have.

In 1926 my father gave me the sum of £500 and on the strength of this, and I am afraid to my father's displeasure, I left the Telegraph Co. and decided to become a professional artist, a thing I should have hesitated to do if my job had been more congenial, and if I had known the difficulties that lay ahead.

My next three years were thin ones indeed, but in 1929, though I made little money, I at least achieved some sort of recognition, and it was in this year that I held my first small exhibition of water-colours, and illustrated my first book, and though I did not sell a picture both the show and the book were well received and obtained the right sort of notices in the right sort of papers.

It was in 1929 also that I was married.

The years that followed were, I suppose, of much the same pattern as that of any young married painter. The children arrived, and to begin with there was very little money. Show followed show, with a few but increasing number of pictures sold. There was the occasional job and the odd book to illustrate.

In 1935 and 1936 respectively were published my first two children's books. They were *Tim and the Brave Sea Captain* and *Lucy Brown and Mr. Grimes*. These were followed fairly soon by *Tim and Lucy Go to Sea*.

Now when I wrote these books I had no theories as to the right form that children's books should take. I have plenty now admittedly, but then, one usually theorises after the event. However, to repeat myself, at the time I had none. The books were written and illustrated with one object only, that of amusing my two eldest children, and it was only when these books were done that I had any thought of publishing them, and nobody could have been more surprised than I was at their success. The stories used for these books were the favourite ones of many that I used to tell and they did not achieve their written form in a day, but grew and were modified by constant re-telling. In a sense they were composite works, being as much the result of the children's promptings as of my own imagination.

It is this method of letting a story grow by telling and re-telling, before committing it to paper, that I have also used for my later children's books, the only difficulty being the supply of children of the right age to tell them to. Alas, they will grow up. However, I have been lucky as my youngest child was not born till 1939. Now even he is getting too old.

However, to go back to the late thirties. These years were only eventful for me on account of an increasing amount of work and more sales of pictures, with the Tate Gallery and provincial Galleries among the purchasers. Also for the fact that it was during this period that I joined the Territorial Army.

Now I joined the Territorials because I was at the time convinced, and rightly so, that there would be a war. However, I had another reason for joining and that was a mistaken one. It was that there would be no work for artists in wartime.

I was called up in August before the outbreak of war and for the next seven months held in succession the various ranks of Gunner, Bombardier, Sergeant and Lieutenant, and had experience that may not always have been pleasant, but which was of the greatest use to me later, for on the 31st March, 1940 I was given the job of Official War Artist and was sent to France.

Now it was the inside knowledge of Army life gained from serving in the ranks which helped me enormously. I knew something about the Army before I had to draw it and therefore my task was the easier.

I spent the war years, on the whole, happily, following the fortunes of the Army in France, Egypt and North Africa, Sicily, Italy, France again and then Germany, always being conscious of my incredible good fortune in being able, unlike so many others, to follow my own profession.

Once the war in Europe was over and I out of the Army, I found myself inundated with work and enjoying once again the task of book illustration.

My first job was to illustrate Walter de la Mare's *Peacock Pie,* a job which could not be more delightful to one like myself, who after the best part of four years abroad was still suffering from an acute nostalgia for England. This was followed by perhaps my major work to date. It was the making of 125 drawings for the Faber edition of Bunyan's *Pilgrim's Progress,* a book that I have loved since a schoolboy and one that I have always wanted to illustrate. For months I lived in it and even dreamt of it.

Again I feel that like the children's books it was in a way composite work, Bunyan's sense of imagery and vivid prose almost making the illustrations for me.

However, to go back to my own children's books. It was about this time that I invented and illustrated *Nicholas and the Fast-Moving Diesel* for my youngest son. In it the cottage and the countryside depicted are real, being taken from the small house in Wales and the surrounding landscape where we lived at the time. Even the dog is a portrait of our own son's small Hunt terrier.

Paul, the Hero of the Fire, written for my small nephew, came out within a year of this, while now there is on the market my latest book, though I hope not my last, called *Tim to the Rescue*.

The fact that three of my books have the sea and ships as a background has been commented upon, but in truth this is not very surprising. First I have a love of the sea which may to some extent be inherited, as both my paternal and maternal great grandfathers were seamen. The former owned and sailed a steamship trading between the Mediterranean ports, while the latter was captain of one of the great sailing ships engaged in the China trade, my grandmother being born at sea off the Cape.

As to my knowledge of ships, I began to acquire this early, on my long voyage home from China at the age of five, and then added to it as a boy in Ipswich where I used to spend days in the docks playing about in the small coasting steamers and barges that moored there and making friends with the sailors.

Since then a short visit to America and my journeys on troopships during the war have added still more to my knowledge, but have also confirmed me in my preference for the small ship—the coast vessel, the tramp steamer and the barge—rather than the liner.

Now having mentioned before that I have ideas about children's books, I feel that it is only fair that I should describe them.

Firstly let me say that my main difficulty in writing and illustrating for children is not to please the children, but to please the parents. To please the children is easy; one has only to give them the bare bones of a story and then go on re-telling it. In the course of time the children will elaborate it for you, adding those details, taken from their own imagination and experiences, which give it life.

Alas, here is the difficulty. These details, a blend of ruthlessness and sentimentality so peculiar to little children, have to be pruned for the parents' consumption. To give an example. A story of mine, and a favourite one with my children, contained a death-bed scene. They loved it, but it had to go. The publishers objected, saying that no parent would like it.

Now children are by nature very imitative and they will usually take and like what their parents admire but for a book to become a Classic it must contain more than just adult whimsey, however prettily done. It must contain something of that gangster world which is the child's. Also, and this to my mind is the most important, it should contain a moral.

After all, morals are of the very stuff of the nursery. Punishment for wrong-doing and rewards for goodness are everyday things for the child and are really understood by him. His delight is unbounded when the villain gets his deserts and the good boy his reward.

To sum up, I think the following ingredients go a long way towards making a book for little children a Classic. Firstly plenty of excitement and a touch of ruthlessness; secondly a little sentiment and thirdly, a good and simple moral. Children are like adults in that they enjoy having their feelings harrowed by the misfortunes of a fictitious character; and they have a strong sense of justice which the author must satisfy if his work is to be appreciated.

EDITORS' NOTE

Since the success of *Tim to the Rescue,* Edward Ardizzone has delighted children with more of Tim's adventures in: *Tim and Charlotte* (1951), *Tim in Danger* (1953), *Tim All Alone* (1956), *Tim's Friend Towser* (1962), *Tim and Ginger* (1965), and *Tim to the Lighthouse* (1968), all published by Walck.

This prolific author-illustrator has written other books for children, such as: *John, the Clockmaker* (1960—Walck), *Peter, the Wanderer* (1963—Oxford University Press; 1964—Walck), *Diana and Her Rhinoceros* (1964—Walck), *Sarah and Simon and No Red Paint* (1965—Constable; 1966—Dial), and *The Wrong Side of the Bed* (Doubleday). To date more than 120 books bear the name of Edward Ardizzone as either author-illustrator or illustrator. Some of the authors for whom he has illustrated are familiar names, such as Eleanor Farjeon, James Reeves, Eleanor Estes, Walter de la Mare, and John Symonds—to name only a very few.

Ardizzone has also won the Kate Greenaway Medal, in 1956, for *Tim All Alone* (given annually since 1955 by the British Library Association to the most distinguished work in the illustration of children's books published in the United Kingdom during the preceding year).

In 1962, his illustrations for *The Island of Fish in the Trees* (World) by Eva-Lis Wuorio won an award and a place on the New York Times Choice of Best Illustrated Children's Books of the Year (an annual selection since 1952 of best illustrated children's books by a panel of three judges).

Ardizzone's "Autobiographical Note" mentions his assignment between 1940 and 1945 as Official War Artist, which took him to France, North Africa, Sicily, Germany, and Italy. Some three hundred of his paintings from this period can now be viewed in the Imperial War Museum.

In the article written in 1950, Mr. Ardizzone says that "England has been my permanent home" since the age of five. Twenty some years later, we find him still residing in England—London, to be exact.

The Children's World of Ludwig Bemelmans *

LUDWIG BEMELMANS BECAME a recognized figure in the field of children's books almost immediately after the publication of his first attempt at writing in 1934. As his long-time editor put it, *Hansi* "established Ludwig as an important writer-artist or artist-writer with a cosmopolitan genius all his own" (19). The *Children's Catalog,* an authoritative arbiter of quality in children's literature, in quick order indicated this book was deserving of the highest regard. They soon gave it their ultimate sign of approval, a two-star ranking. Thus the world of *Bemelmania* for children was launched.

What kind of man was this suddenly successful writer for children? What was in his 36-year background that could bring him to such eminence on a very first try? Who was this artist-writer whom *Time* later called, "Raoul Dufy, James Thurber and Peter Arno tossed in a salad and marinated in strong dark beer?"

Ludwig Bemelmans was born just before the turn of the century in the Austrian (now Italian) Tyrols. From what is known of his parents and his early upbringing, one could have predicted a boyhood full of personal difficulties. First, there seems a strong likelihood the boy was indulged. His father was a "rather ne'er-do-well" Belgian painter who apparently took little hand in the discipline of the young Ludwig (16). Moreover, his mother (the daughter of a wealthy Bavarian brewer) and his father were soon divorced, and young Ludwig was sent to be raised by his maternal

---

* By Patrick Groff. From *Elementary English* 43 (October 1966), 559–568. Reprinted with the permission of the National Council of Teachers of English and Dr. Patrick Groff.

grandfather. Being born in and living much of his early life in hotels, and moving from country to country must certainly have given him a lonely life away from children his own age. When asked later, "Did you always want to make pictures?" Bemelmans' answer was, "Yes, I always did" (14:86). But he was even discouraged in this one early interest, thought by his grandfather to be an inexcusable occupation.

After learning all this it is not surprising to see the young boy became more than difficult to manage. He rebelled not only against his parents and grandfather, but against his teachers as well. He adjusted so poorly to the public school of the time that he was enrolled in a private school for retarded boys (of all places!) which proved even less acceptable to him, of course. Before he was sixteen, Bemelmans was what we now refer to as a school "dropout."

One must say that Ludwig was luckier than many present-day dropouts, however, since he had an Uncle Hans who owned a string of hotels and who was willing to give him another chance to make his way. So Ludwig became an apprentice hotelman, to begin at the bottom with not a few but many to tell him what to do. The pattern of his behavior toward authority seen above came to the fore, as could be expected. He grew increasingly intolerable to all those put in his charge. This situation worsened until at the age of sixteen he was involved in the almost fatal wounding of one of his supervisors. Bemelmans claimed later that this was justified assault on his part since this headwaiter was cruel and threatening. In any event the police must have thought otherwise since they gave his Uncle Hans the option of whether his charge would be banished from the country (how characteristic a punishment in pre-World War I Europe!) or be sent to reform school.

While this was hardly an enviable choice for either Ludwig or his uncle, America in 1914 probably did hold out exciting possibilities for this rambunctious young man. And very likely his uncle had had his fill of the troubles that seemed to surround Ludwig wherever he went. So it was decided he would immigrate to America. Ludwig went armed with more than the letters of introduction to hotelmen given him by his uncle. His penchant for firearms would put him in good stead in this exploration, or so he thought. He recalled later how in preparation for coming to the U.S. he armed himself with pistols and the appropriate ammunition to fend off the hostile Indians whom he had learned from James Fenimore Cooper roamed America in wild abandon (23).

He found no such adventure, of course. Instead there awaited him in America only hard work in hotels as a waiter and such. Even here his troubles persisted. He lost a series of such jobs for very similar reasons, *e.g.*, he broke too many dishes, he reported for duty in one white and one yellow shoe, he dropped an ambassador's breakfast tray, he was caught more absorbed in the hotel's music than in his duties, he stepped (literally) on the toes of a famous actor, and he was involved in the surreptitious disappearance of a hotel's fancy foods. As a waiter his life was a succession of tragedies.

"Anything is better than this," the young Bemelmans must have thought. Enlistment in the Army in the middle of World War I thus should provide an easy escape. Again his service proved to be totally unheroic — he was an attendant at a mental hospital and an instructor of German-speaking recruits. This did not dull Bemelmans' sense of humor, however, as his later very humorous book on army life indicates.

The drawing of pictures the young Bemelmans had done during his pre-World War I life in America was continued after his demobilization. During the 1920's and the early 1930's to support himself he also continued to work in restaurants. Finally in 1925 he broke through with a measure of success by rising to a part ownership of one. More important to Bemelmans obviously was that he was gradually gaining more and more recognition and success as an artist.

In spite of this complicated childhood and youth Bemelmans grew to become a warm and appealing adult. His best photograph shows a broad face with rosy cheeks, engagingly open eyes, and an infectious smile. A very bald head tilted in an inviting manner toward the viewer sits on top of a body going heavy towards its middle. The entire demeanor is one of zest for life. As *Time* (January 20, 1941) put it: "Ludwig Bemelmans has the face and physique of a divinely inspired, slightly intoxicated baby . . . a fey genius whose private life was as original as his books." To his editor he was "an impossible combination of the most sophisticated European and a nice straightforward small boy with a glint of mischief in his eye" (18:484). His speech was equally charming. He spoke several languages — all with an accent. Although he was born in a German-speaking country, he lived in hotels whose guests spoke a dozen different languages. It was fashionable to be taught French, which he was, as well as German. When questioned about his ubiquitous accent in whatever country he traveled or lived, he remarked, "It has its advantages. It's like being a gypsy, belonging everywhere and nowhere" (23:73).

BEMELMANS THE WRITER

The first turn in Bemelmans' life of interest to followers of children's literature came during a visit by May Massee, a children's book editor, to his apartment. Bemelmans had been feeling very homesick for his

native Austria. To compensate for this he had painted Tyrolean landscapes on his window shades so that with the flick of a wrist he could
transfer the view of New York from his apartment to these longed-for
scenes. Equally impressive to Miss Massee were Bemelmans' other decorations in his room. He had painted all the furniture he held appropriate
for the space, but which he did not own, on the walls of the room so that
it was transformed into a stately salon. At dinner that night "with the
help of a folded napkin she [Miss Massee] showed him how a book should
go; he could have colored pictures on the cover and here, here, and here;
black and white pictures would go anywhere he liked" (8:1509).

From this meeting came Bemelmans' first book (for either adults or
children): *Hansi* (1934). It started him on a long and profitable relationship with Viking Press. Following *Hansi* came *Golden Basket* (1936)
and *Quito Express* (1938). And then *Madeline* (1939)! While he was
moderately successful with his first three children's books, it was only
with the latter book, which became the first of a very popular series, that
his fame was assured, however. Unbelievably, there were reservations
by publishers about *Madeline*. As Bemelmans tells it to *Newsweek*
(October 15, 1962): "Nobody wanted to publish it. They said it was too
sophisticated for children. Of course, I never in my life wrote for children.
I write for myself." Simon and Schuster first bought *Madeline*, according
to Bemelmans, and kept it for five years before deciding it was not for
them, and deciding to sell it to Viking Press.*

If this was the case, what mistakes publishers can make! For one of the
two top favorites among Caldecott Award books seems to be *Madeline's
Rescue*, according to Irene Smith (22); and this book reflects the "change-
less popularity of its predecessor, *Madeline*" (22:94). As Bemelmans
noted later, "The *Madeline* books are my old-age insurance" (6:115).
And he was not making a light witticism, for the *Madeline* series of books
have sold well over a quarter of a million copies. Each has been a selection of the Junior Literary Guild and each has been selected for inclusion
in *Children's Catalog*. *Madeline and the Bad Hat* (1957) won the New
York *Herald Tribune* Children's Spring Book Festival Award (as did
Sunshine — in 1950). While they were not up to Bemelmans' usual standards, *Madeline and the Gypsies* (1959) and *Madeline in London* (1961)
have remained favorites among many readers.

At this point we should remind ourselves that Bemelmans moved from
children's books *to* adult literature. His *first* book was *Hansi*. There is
little doubt, however, that the style with which he captivated the adult
audiences of his fifteen books also came through in his books for children.

* A curious statement since the book's title page says "Simon and Schuster."

His books for adults represented so unique a facet of life that he was said to have created a *Bemelmania*. This was a "world of childlike wonder and continental sophistication" (*Saturday Review,* August 29, 1953) full of travel, hotels, boats, trains, restaurants, bright colors, and peopled with noble dogs and innocent yet powerful children. The major industry of its heroes was eating and drinking. They were served by equally civilized waiters of major importance to the plots of the stories. The only villains of this romance were petty officials determined to dampen this frivolity, and those of the upper social class who tended to prize their possessions too much. Everything in *Bemelmania* looked slightly fantastic. The most ordinary subjects became faintly ridiculous, if not ludicrous.

From the above description of Bemelmans' background, it would be expected this strange mixture of reality and fantasy that he chose for his writing would have come to him quite easily. To the contrary Bemelmans protested many times that he really hated to write, and that it was difficult for him. He told *Time* (March 31, 1952), "I walk around a typewriter for hours with cramps in my stomach." In his acceptance speech for the Caldecott Award for the best illustrated book for children of 1953, *Madeline's Rescue,* he insisted, "I am not a writer but a painter and secondly, I have no imagination" (1:270). Perhaps he felt this way because he did not consciously write specifically for children. He simply wrote stories that he himself liked and wanted to write (8). Of his responsibilities in writing for children Bemelmans said, "For the children I feel that . . . first of all . . . is owed a story. If this story is robust enough, it will, to the best of my ability and endeavor, hold their interest, be liked for its own sake . . ." (20:5).

Perhaps he held these misgivings because of the feeling he had that writing served him as occupational therapy (4). Three or four hours of sleep a night was his average. He seldom slept more according to his calculations. In fact, he claimed he took to writing because of this insomnia and remarked, probably facetiously, on one occasion that if he could sleep well, he would never write again (16). While lying awake he made a habit of writing in his mind, but unlike so many of us who do such musing, he could recall these key phrases and even the fillers between them at a later time.

Perhaps it was because he thought certain gimmicks brought out his best ideas. For example, he was highly attached to an old silver-plated typewriter. He claimed he did most of his best writing on it and most of his best writing and drawing while soaking in a tub of hot water. A photograph in *Newsweek* (July 24, 1937) shows the artist-author in this highly unusual writing position.

Perhaps he held this belief in his lack of imagination because he found his stories too familiar. But after all, they should have been since he took them exclusively from his own experiences. *Hansi* is based on his life in the Tyrols as a child. The hero of *Quito Express* he met on a real train during an actual trip in Ecuador where he had gone to gather some writing material. He traced the beginnings of *Madeline* to an early visit to a convent, and to his own early life in a boarding school in Rothenburg. "We walked through that ancient town in two straight lines" just as Madeline and her classmates did later (2:271). As the result of being knocked over by a bakery truck, a "breadbasket on wheels," while on vacation, Bemelmans found himself in a hospital where the same stout nurse brought him his tray that later brought a similar one to Madeline in her hospital stay. In this hospital Bemelmans also saw:

> A little girl who had had an appendix operation, and standing up in bed, with great pride she showed her scar to me. Over my bed was the crack in the ceiling "that had the habit of sometimes looking like a rabbit." It all began to arrange itself. (1:272)

> One day I had a meeting with Leon Blum, and if you take a look at the book (*Madeline's Rescue*) you will see that the doctor who runs to Madeline's bed is the great patriot and humanitarian Leon Blum. (1:274)

BEMELMANS THE ARTIST

Bemelmans was often asked, "When did you first feel the urge to be an artist?" To this he replied, "Never—and I wish there were a simpler word for it" (14:85). For he strongly believed on the basis of his experience that anyone could be taught to draw pictures—even teach himself to do so. Too, there is little doubt Bemelmans believed that formal training in art was unnecessary. This feeling may have been conditioned strongly by his difficult earlier years in America—when wearied by his long working hours as a waiter, the class routine of art school easily bored him. He decided then that formal instruction in art would be of little help. It is remarkable, but one must say his lack of training actually emphasized his natural talents. In fact, as the editors of *Design* magazine say, Bemelmans was:

> A man in whom lack of academic talent is so far offset by the charm and verve of his work that the critic has to invent new standards in order to begin to criticize. (5:106)

With Bemelmans' art it is true "some might judge at first glance that the pictures are too sophisticated for small children's choice. The truth is, however, that they could not please the audience better" (22:94). Perhaps children are attracted by what may look like aimless daubing— but it is far from that. As with children's art little of the anatomy of Bemelmans' figures are correct or in proportion. It is useless to protest, therefore, as did one critic, that the legs on his horses do not look right. As with buildings drawn by children, Bemelmans' buildings will collapse if you look at them too severely. The great mass of detail he puts on them and the putting of important things in greater perspective also remind one of the child artist. It is as if Bemelmans was saying, "I will use my mature artistic talent but I will use it as a child."

As Bemelmans did put it, "I wanted to paint purely what gave me pleasure, scenes that interested me; and one day I found that the audience for that kind of painting was a vast reservoir of impressionists who did very good work themselves, who were very clear-eyed and capable of enthusiasm. I addressed myself to children" (1:271). In his paintings of New York for *Holiday* magazine he recalled the influence of children on his art. "I wanted to paint New York as soon as I arrived at Ellis Island." The best champagne and expensive cigars he could buy could not act as the agent for getting him started to a gratification of this desire, how-ever. "Then, one day I came upon a child painting in Gramercy Park— he was painting in the spirit of sheer fun. I had discovered the secret" (2:64). These drawings are a fine example of how little Bemelmans changes his painting style and content for the adult readers of *Holiday* and for the child readers of *Madeline*. They remind one why it is said adult readers get as much enjoyment reading *Madeline* as do the children for whom she was intended.

This does not mean that Bemelmans was not a hard-working artist without definite ideas about his craft. His long-time editor, May Massee, called him a "prodigious worker of tremendous energy." She noted that in spite of the rather careless appearance of Bemelmans' final drawings, they were the result of the discarding of dozens of sketches in order to get the right one (18). He particularly loathed the patronizing, cute, or overly whimsical illustrations he found in some children's books. He was careful never to read these to his daughter Barbara. His illustrations never make these mistakes.

Too, he worked hard to plan well the order of his books. While he usually planned the book as a whole, sometimes the pictures, as they came along, actually added to the story line. Watercolor was his best medium as one sees so clearly from the *Madeline* books. This medium lends itself to pictures on a large scale. It is not surprising to learn, therefore, that the novice Bemelmans tried to convince his editor that his first book should be about three-foot square! (6) As with many artists we have seen, he was self-critical of his work. This might explain why his editor on one instance had a most difficult time getting him to return a pasted-up dummy of what a finished book was to look like. On the other hand, some have criticized Bemelmans as being "an artist by inspiration and not by craftsmanship" (17:243). It seems true he cared little for the rather tedious finishing up of his art work. For example, he would not do the labor necessary to separate his work into the four colors needed for printing *Hansi*. This was done for him by his good friend, Kurt Wiese, an artist in his own right, who copied the drawing onto the four zinc plates needed. The emergence of modern technology undoubtedly saved Bemelmans from this chore in his later work.

THE QUALITY OF BEMELMANS' WORK

There is little doubt that Bemelmans' talent was a large and exceptional one. We have previously noted that for *Madeline's Rescue* he won the Caldecott Award. It should also be remembered that *Golden Basket* was a runner-up for the Newbery Award and that *Madeline* was a runner-up for the Caldecott Award. Of the latter one critic was moved to say, "Anyone who does not adore this book would poison wells" (*Saturday Review*, August 29, 1953). Dora Smith lists *Madeline* among her "Significant Books of 1910–59" (21) as does Eakin (3). *Hansi*, written in 1934, was still in print at the time of Bemelmans' death in 1962. In 1941, *Time* said of his writing for adults, "Bemelmans seems to be as incapable of writing a sentence that lacks beauty as was Mozart."

Coupled to this recognition from the critics is Bemelmans' obvious appeal to children. For it is in its approach to the child that the art of Bemelmans has its greatest strength (24). As seen before, Bemelmans depended greatly on the child artist for his inspiration. In the pictures of *Madeline's Rescue* (and in the other picture books) there is a casualness, a carefree spirit, and a childlike approach to the representation of details. It is this immediacy, simplicity, and directness of approach to the subject that beckon the child's spontaneous approval. The child feels akin to the pictures because of the "sudden" approach of the painter. Like Bemelmans, the child is also a dauber with the consequent boldness and freedom of effort. In Bemelmans the child gains an imaginative, visual communication, given with a vigorous and even an anxious manipulation of the artist's tools. The paintings say, "First a slap, then a splash, and then a quick stroke to finish up." The colors used are rich and satisfying—which renders a note of security. As a series of illustrations unfolds, it expresses to children a symbol of their rejection of academic art or that of scientific severity.

Beyond this, Bemelmans makes himself comprehensible to the child. The total effect of his painting adds to the intimacy of his words and pictures. His illustrations are full of hidden details that appeal to the child, that stimulate his curiosity, and that help to improve his span of attention. And all this is done without the hazards of overstatement or excessive complication.

And yet, despite this relationship to childlikeness, Bemelmans' illustrations are not vague and unrehearsed. He has firm aesthetic convictions. His pictures as they come to light are quite intentional and methodical in spite of their shroud of childlike naivety and comicalness.

We have undoubtedly witnessed in Bemelmans a major influence upon the art of children's picture books. To prove this, one need only page through an early *Madeline* book to henceforth instantly recognize on all occasions this unique and compelling talent. One must also say and rather regretfully, however, that the latter *Madeline* books failed to maintain the forceful promise of his earliest efforts. Thankfully this was only in the text. It seems true that *Madeline* in her later days exhibited various and serious textual weaknesses. One must agree with *Horn Book* that in *Madeline and the Gypsies* the "verse seems inexcusably limp." Without doubt, *Madeline and the Bad Hat* "is contrived and overlong, and the text awkwardly rhymed" (*Booklist*). It is observable in *Madeline in London* that "the sentiments and their versification are often strained, sometimes strange . . ." (*Library Journal*). Thus while Bemelmans' visual artistry remained at a consistently high peak throughout his books, his writing, which hit its peak with *Madeline's Rescue,* fell to an embarassingly mediocre level after 1953.

The reasons for this eclipse are probably complicated by the press of his other writing interests and perhaps even by a relaxation of effort that sometimes comes with success. It is important to say, nevertheless, that as a visual artist he was undiminished.

Hansi. New York: Viking Press, 1934.

> Hansi is the average, vigorous boy from anywhere—in this story from the Austrian Tyrols. His uncle invites him to his remote mountain home during the winter school vacation. On Hansi's trip we see the old-fashioned trains and trainmen, and the picturesque mountain

villages and landscapes. The plot thickens when Waldl, the dachs-hund, is lost on a skiing outing. After his recovery at a colorful woodchopper's house, a visit is made to a "society shack" of the mountain climbers. There Hansi finds the Christmas celebrations and entertainments of the mountain people beautiful and exciting. He returns home promising to return soon. (Mostly half-page illus-trations for an extended text.)

Golden Basket. New York: Viking Press, 1936.

Two English girls and their father visit the Hotel of the Golden Basket where are seen some of the eccentric hotel guests Bemel-mans knew as a boy. Here the girls meet Jan, whose father is the proprietor and chef. After playing with Jan, they visit a carillon and learn how it operates, and a cathedral where they meet Madeline who is visiting with her school class who march sedately two-by-two, except of course, Madeline. They learn the wonders of French cooking, and go boating on the canal. The boat tips over in front of a museum which they enter to dry off. And from here to home. This is a child's guide to Bruges, Belgium of the middle 1930's. (Half-page illustrations on some pages. Mostly text.)

Quito Express. New York: Viking Press, 1938.

Pedro, a baby, is taken to the market place in Otavalo, Ecuador, by his mother and big sister where they will sell the pots his father makes. Pedro crawls aboard a train stopped nearby. He is dis-covered miles from Otavalo by the conductor who out of despera-tion takes him home for the night in Quito, and to Guayaquil the next day to get his brother's opinion of the dilemma. Finally, the conductor makes a return trip, inquiring at each stop, "Whose baby is this?" At the Otavalo stop Pedro is reclaimed. (Pictures take up most of every page.)

Madeline. New York: Simon and Schuster, 1939.

Madeline, though the smallest of the twelve little girls in her school in Paris, is not afraid of anything including mice, snow and ice, or tigers in the zoo. "And nobody knew so well how to frighten Miss Clavel" her schoolmistress nun. Even Madeline has pains, however, which turn out to be appendicitis. After visiting Madeline in the hospital and seeing her pretty flowers, toys, candy, *and* her scar, her classmates went home to bed—but—"In the middle of the night Miss Clavel knows something is not right." She finds the children crying, "Boo-hoo, we want to have our appendix out, too!" (Full page pictures and a slight text.)

Madeline's Rescue. New York: Viking Press, 1953.

Madeline, whom we know now to be excessively adventuresome, is rescued from a fall in the river by a dog. Genevieve, a very smart dog indeed, is promptly adopted by the girls of the school. But the school's trustees turn her out. An unsuccessful search for her across Paris is conducted. Finally she reappears and the girls continue their contention as to whose bed she will sleep under. The dilemma is resolved when Genevieve has enough pups to go around. (Full page pictures and a slight text.)

Parsley. New York: Harper and Brothers, 1955.

Parsley, a stag deer who got his name from the aromatic herb he loved so well, acts as a vigilant scout for any danger to his herd. The inevitable hunter appears. Just as he is about to shoot Parsley, *the* tree of which Parsley is so fond is whipped about by the wind and knocks the hunter over a precipice. His binoculars, left hanging on the tree, are then used by Parsley to better scout for other threats to the herd. (Full page pictures and a brief text.)

Madeline and the Bad Hat. New York: Viking, 1956.

Pepito, the son of the Spanish Ambassador to France, moves next door to Madeline's school. As Madeline says, "It is evident that this boy is a Bad Hat!" He is an imp, all right. He terrifies the girls, animals, and passersby. A present of a tool chest he uses for a *guillotine* for the cook's chickens. His worst stunt is to let a cat out among a pack of vicious dogs, who instead chew him up badly. He learns his lesson so well Madeline can now say, "You are the world's most wonderful boy!" (Full page pictures and a short text.)

Madeline and the Gypsies. New York: Viking Press, 1959.

Pepito (seen before) invites Madeline and her classmates to the Gypsy Carnival. They are mistakenly left behind when the classmates leave. The gypsies take them away—quite willingly—and teach them circus tricks. Miss Clavel rushes to rescue Madeline after receiving a card from her. The crystal ball tells the gypsies of this, and they hide the children by sewing them up in an old lion hide. Inside the pelt the two children wander away, scaring all they meet. Finally they rejoin the circus just in time to be taken home by Miss Clavel. (Full page pictures and a short text.)

Madeline in London. New York: Viking, 1961.

(The last of the Madeline series. Bemelmans died the year after this book's publication.)

Pepito's Ambassador father is transferred to London. Madeline and her classmates set out to visit him upon learning he is lonely for them. On the way to the Embassy they pick up an English "retired" horse for his birthday. The horse runs away with Pepito and Madeline. The girls and Miss Clavel rush all over London in pursuit of the three before they are found. The horse eats up the garden and trees at the Embassy, and thus cannot be kept, so the girls take him to Paris with them. (Full page pictures and a brief text.)

REFERENCES

1. Bemelmans, Ludwig, "Caldecott Award Acceptance," *Horn Book,* 30 (August, 1954), 270–276.
2. Bemelmans, Ludwig, "Bemelmans Paints New York," *Holiday,* 25 (June, 1959), 65.
3. Eakin, Mary K., *Good Books for Children.* Chicago: University of Chicago, 1962.
4. Editors, *Current Biography.* New York: H. W. Wilson, 1941.
5. Editors, *Design.* "Ludwig Bemelmans," 63 (January, 1962), 106–108.
6. Editors, *Newsweek,* October 15, 1962.
7. Editors, *Newsweek,* July 24, 1937.
8. Editors, *Publisher's Weekly.* "Ludwig Bemelmans," 134 (October 22, 1938), 1508–1510.
9. Editors, *Saturday Review,* August 29, 1953.
10. Editors, *Time,* January 20, 1941.
11. Editors, *Time,* December 15, 1941.
12. Editors, *Time,* November 14, 1949.
13. Editors, *Time,* August 31, 1953.
14. Ferris, Helen (Editor), *Writing Books for Boys and Girls.* Garden City, N.Y.: Doubleday, 1952.
15. Fuller, Muriel (Editor), *More Junior Authors.* New York: H. W. Wilson, 1963.
16. Kunitz, Stanley J. and Howard Haycroft, *Twentieth Century Authors.* New York: H. W. Wilson, 1942.
17. Mahoney, Bertha, Louise P. Latimer, and Beulah Folmsbee, *Illustrators of Children's Books: 1744–1945.* Boston: Horn Book, 1947.
18. Massee, May, "Caldecott Award to Bemelmans," *Library Journal,* 79 (March 15, 1954), 2184–2185.

19. Massee, May, "Ludwig Bemelmans," *Horn Book,* 30 (August, 1954), 263–269.
20. Root, Shelton, "Ludwig Bemelmans and His Books for Children," *Elementary English,* 34 (January, 1957), 3–12.
21. Smith, Dora V., *Fifty Years of Children's Books.* Champaign, Illinois: National Council of Teachers of English, 1963.
22. Smith, Irene, *A History of the Newbery and Caldecott Medals.* New York: Viking Press, 1957.
23. Viguers, Ruth Hill, Marcia Dolphin, and Bertha Mahoney Miller, *Illustrators of Children's Books: 1946–1956.* Boston: Horn Book, 1958.
24. Comments on Bemelmans' art are taken partially from those of Dr. Gerald Gates, Professor of Art Education, San Diego State College.

EDITORS' NOTE

Many of Bemelmans' books have won awards: *Golden Basket* (1937 — Viking) was a runner-up for the John Newbery Medal; *Madeline* (1940 — Viking) was a runner-up for the Randolph J. Caldecott Medal; *Sunshine: A Story About New York* (Simon & Schuster) won the 1950 Book World Children's Spring Book Festival Award (given annually since 1937 to children's books in four categories — Y for Younger Children, P for Picture Books, M for Middle Ages and O for Older Children. It was in the Y category that the award was won by Mr. Bemelmans). *The Happy Place* (1952 — Little) was recognized as one of the books on the list of the New York Times Choice of Best Illustrated Children's Books of the Year (an annual selection since 1952 by a panel of three judges); *Madeline's Rescue* (1954 — Viking) won the Randolph J. Caldecott Medal; and *Madeline and the Bad Hat* (Viking) won the 1957 Book World Children's Spring Book Festival Award, again in the "Younger Children" category.

Margaret Wise Brown, "Laureate of the Nursery" *

WHAT DO WRITERS CARE most about? My answer would be two simple things: first, that they continue to feel a joy in the act of writing; second, that their work be published so that possibly it may live. Margaret Wise Brown was one whose joy in writing was most obvious to all who knew her. She wanted her books published even more than most writers because she conceived them as picture books and couldn't wait to see the picture part completed. She had that satisfaction to a remarkable degree, with the added joy of huge sales which told her she had delighted many children.

Her success was almost fantastic. To date, about one hundred books by her have been published, with total sales probably over fifteen million. She collaborated on, or contributed to, a dozen more books, including some school primers. She wrote a children's page for *Good Housekeeping* and helped make several Victrola records. She was given an illustrated write-up in *Life,* for which she and the interviewer concocted a rather fantastic picture of herself. Probably humor or fantasy is all one can use who is asked to explain what drives one to publish from four to eight books a year, when it is not financial need. Her inner ambition was to write adult poetry, of which she left a great hoard, all unpublished. More or less secretly, she kept trying to be a painter. She was adult and sophisticated in many ways, yet she never lost the special sensory acuteness

* By L. S. Bechtel. Reprinted by permission from *Horn Book* 34 (June 1958), 172–186. Based on a speech opening the Margaret Wise Brown Collection in the Westerly (Rhode Island) Public Library.

of childhood nor a present sense of the real and the dream worlds of her childhood.

How can I describe this engaging friend, to make her come alive to you? She was medium tall, slim, with flying flaxen hair, and never a hat upon it. I saw her most often in winter, in a worn old fur coat, holding the leash of one or both of her big Kerry Blue dogs. Her pale face had a golden glow to match her hair. Her large, light blue-green eyes were quiet, watchful, often lit with fun; when she talked they became most luminous and expressive. She had an odd, gentle, high-pitched voice; she talked slowly, often hesitantly, hinting at a complex emotional make-up.

Margaret Wise Brown was born in Brooklyn, New York, on May 23, 1910. Her father, Robert Bruce Brown, was a prosperous manufacturer. Both he and her mother came from Kirkwood, Missouri, where his father had been a governor and a United States Senator. Early in her childhood they moved to Whitestone Landing on Long Island where she had the freedom of woods and beaches. She had many pet animals: the thirty-odd rabbits and "one dog of my own plus six borrowed dogs" foretold the many animal heroes of her books. Her brother being a bit too old and her sister a bit too young for close companionship perhaps bred an independence in play and friendships. Very early she showed that special love for and need of privacy that never left her.

She attended Dana Hall, in Wellesley, Massachusetts, after spending two years at school in Switzerland where, she insisted, she learned "French *and Scotch.*" She went to Hollins College, Virginia, where she won her Bachelor of Arts degree in 1932. At school and college she was chiefly interested in experimental writing and in reading "new" writers. After college she took a short story course at Columbia but said she gave it up because she "couldn't think up any plots." That she was more a poet than a storyteller is obvious in most of her children's books.

Chance suddenly led her into a field of writing she had never considered. She heard of a truly experimental writing group, a class conducted by Lucy Sprague Mitchell at the Bank Street School, then called "The Bureau for Educational Experiment." Her very first work there made her happy. She said, "Experimenting in writing for children is so much less *precious* than doing it for grownups."

The brilliant Mrs. Mitchell who ruled over "69 Bank Street" was the sort of creative person who analyzed writers shrewdly and helped many besides Brownie to find themselves. I often visited her writing classes to criticize or to advise about publication. After one of them Mrs. Mitchell said to me, "That Brownie bears watching. She is a poet, and really knows small children."

At Bank Street, Brownie could tell stories to various age groups of children. She could watch them through those windows at which they cannot see you looking in. She was put on the school's publication staff, and helped through the press Mrs. Mitchell's second *Here and Now Story Book* to which both she and I contributed, and in meetings about it we became friends. She took down stories told by children at the Little Red Schoolhouse and said they were "a revelation of spontaneity, of imagination and of language." So she studied lower age levels "to find how and when this creative vitality started." She found that Mrs. Mitchell had already studied the same problem and written upon it.

Soon she met young William Scott and his partner John McCullough, who were starting a new firm to publish new kinds of books for the "neglected" nursery-age child, the age of their own children. She was their first official editor, and author of their first book *Bumblebugs and Elephants* (1937). Printed on stiff cardboard, its "big and little" creatures still delight the very youngest. A bit before that, Harper published *When the Wind Blew,* a fantasy based on a story by Chekhov. Then in 1938, Dutton issued *The Fish with the Deep Sea Smile,* and Scott, *The Little Fireman.* Altogether, she had seven books in those first two years and was well started on her extraordinary career.

In 1939 came Brownie's and Scott's first big sales success, *The Noisy Book.* We met the little dog Muffin, with his bandaged eyes, guessing at city things about him by their sounds. A child must guess, as Muffin does, before you turn the page. Thousands of parents found out how their youngest children were all attention for a book they had to talk back to. The brilliant flat-colored modern art by Leonard Weisgard fascinated them. So a series was started which now has seven titles, all nursery classics. Harper published the last three and have now taken over also the first four. When interviewed about them, Brownie once said that they were intended "to make children give honest sensory responses, not take them from a page without thinking."

Brownie's greatest editorial excitement, while still an editor for William Scott, was in persuading Gertrude Stein to write a children's book for them. She loved to tell about the day the manuscript arrived, how she and Mr. Scott and Mr. McCullough gathered at her apartment that evening, forgetting dinner, to read it aloud. A huge birthday cake in the shape of a ship stood there, intended for a friend. They sat up most of the night, reading and rereading *The World Is Round, or Rose Is a Rose* (Scott, 1939) and gradually ate up the cake. The book caused a tremendous stir; some adults were "against" it, but lots of children loved it and saw the fun of the style. I wrote a vigorous bit of praise for it in *The Horn Book.*

With four books a year, and half a dozen more contracted for, Brownie left her editorial job. During the war, I once met her for lunch at the Museum of Modern Art where she introduced me to that great Mexican artist, Orozco. I told her I was against her using pseudonyms — "Golden MacDonald" and "Juniper Sage" — that they didn't hide her real name from anyone. She gleefully announced a third one, "Timothy Hay," but *he* had only one book, *Horses.* She claimed that each name had a different personality, and publishers didn't like having so many books a year under one name. Probably I told her that success was ruining her.

Be that as it may, "Golden MacDonald" wrote some of Brownie's best books for Margaret Lesser at Doubleday. What child could resist *Red Light, Green Light* (1944)? What adult could fail to buy *Little Lost Lamb* (1945) for which Leonard Weisgard created that appealing small shepherd and of course a *black* lamb? Then in 1946 he illustrated *The Little Island,* which won him the Caldecott Medal, and of which more later. Whatever the "alias" used on them, these books surely will live as Brownie's.

As "Juniper Sage" she collaborated with Edith Thacher Hurd, a friend of the Bank Street days, on that startling book *The Man in the Manhole: and the Fix-it Men,* illustrated by Bill Ballantine (Scott, 1946). A new edition has appeared recently, taking children again under city streets to see the mysteries that bring them light, heat, and water. Brownie and Mrs. Hurd also did together the Little Golden Books about firemen, miners, policemen, etc., bringing those heroes to the level of very small children, weaving facts into brief, amusing stories.

Brownie's first Simon and Schuster book was a "big" one, *The Golden Egg Book* (1947), with truly gorgeous color by Leonard Weisgard. It was the essence of spring and a most welcome new version of the Easter bunny idea. It was a great success, and of course they offered her further contracts. This got her into trouble with her other publishers. Simon and Schuster's children's books were sweeping the country, and other countries, too. Publishers of the "regular" trade editions were apprehensive and wanted to keep their authors to themselves. But Brownie would sign no contract restricting her output, and she won. As a matter of fact, she had books with nine publishers by 1952.

Well I remember the day when she received her first huge check from S. & S., huge because they paid in advance on the printing of the first edition, which might be 50,000 to 75,000. She was dazed, and decided to spend it at once before it proved untrue. New cars were hard to get that year so she took her one remaining Kerry Blue on a plane to Florida where she had heard there were lots of new cars. "I'm going to buy a big station wagon," she said. "A dog like a Kerry isn't comfortable in a little car." It was the same spirit in which, ten years before, she had taken her first advance royalty check from Dutton straight to the steamship office to buy passage to Ireland.

Her eighteen titles with Simon and Schuster have sold, up to this writing (February, 1958), almost twelve million copies. The best seller is *Five Little Firemen,* over two million. All have had foreign editions, mostly in European countries, some in the Argentine and Australia. The delightful *Color Kittens* wins with nine foreign editions. Brownie's editors here were Georges Duplaix, Dorothy Bennett, and Lucille Ogle.

My own firm favorite of these books is *Mister Dog,* "the dog who belonged to himself." He is named Crispin's Crispian, after Brownie's big black poodle who succeeded the Kerry Blues. What a lovably ragged, characterful person Garth Williams made of him! He appears again in *The Sailor Dog,* a fine story told her by the eight-year-old neighbor, Austin Clarke, whom she credits as collaborator. Dog lovers of all ages chuckle at the details in *Mister Dog* and at the very essence of dogginess in this lovable book. The touch of genius is in creating a small boy who also "belongs to himself," as all little boys realize they do, while they laugh at the pretend boy who lived with a dog.

Brownie could write anywhere and on any old scrap of paper, in an airplane, in the station wagon in front of her grocer's. But of course her homes were important to her books. When I first knew her, she lived in an apartment on West Tenth Street, a conventional, well-kept home, with lovely old furniture, many books, unusual paintings. There was nonsense around, too, possibly gifts from members of her "Bird Brain Club" which held Christmas at any time of the year they wished.

Later she bought an old house on the Maine island called Vinal Haven, twelve miles out to sea from Rockland. There she had spent several summers in childhood. She named it "The Only House," because it was the last of a group built long ago by granite cutters. In its attic studio, she told me, she felt as if living in treetops, wonderfully alone with the sounds of the sea, "wanting to think hard but happy just in being." The magic of the place, its dramatic changes with mists and tides, seeped into her. No words or ideas about it seemed worthy of it; she waited and waited. "Suddenly I had the thought that it is such a relief, when we are adults with the bewilderingly gigantic world around us, to remember that we knew, as children, that the world is as big as the part of it we really know."

So she slowly wrote and rewrote *The Little Island,* with its kitten who learns that the island is both part of the great world and a world of its own. Mr. Weisgard came to the attic studio to make the pictures, and later wrote of it all vividly for *Junior Wings:* about the window opening on a sheer twenty-foot drop to the sea; apple blossoms in another window; bees and bats coming in and out; the odor of fish chowder rising from the kitchen. Together they made an outstanding book, which Doubleday gave very fine color printing. It captures the magic of all islands.

Now let us put the pail of clams we have just dug, some flowers, a big basket of books, and the dog, into the station wagon and head for New York. We go home to "Cobble Court," way up on York Avenue. We ring the bell of a shabby old brick house, go through its dark hall, and out onto a sunny courtyard, neatly set about with clipped trees in tubs and perhaps potted daisies or chrysanthemums. There stands a tiny old white ginger-bread house, a storybook house, built in 1810, miraculously left among factories and skyscraping apartments, and still heated only by wood fires.

In the hall hang Brownie's big brass beagle-horn and velvet beagling cap. There are fur rugs, a big fur-covered chair, and in the bedroom a fur rug on the bed. You go upstairs for the living-dining room and galley-size kitchen. Here sun pours in over plants in bloom and a row of big shells. A typewriter looks incongruous, and you note with surprise that Brownie knows how to use it. On an outer balcony you see piles of oil paintings, "all beginnings," says Brownie, "no good, but I can't stop doing them." She tells of an illustrator, whose work she criticized severely, who said, "You're really a frustrated painter."

One day she showed me her "Diary," kept in an old book with a worn Florentine leather cover. "What's in it," she said, "isn't facts of my life, but other matters. Dreams—I have wonderful dreams—and I put down interesting colors, and faces, and places. A few stories—here are some told me by children at a school in Harlem. Maybe I'll use them some day, but not as they are here, the children wouldn't like that. They want words better arranged than their own, and a few gorgeous big grownup words to bite on. Most children are so wonderful. After being with them I decide that almost no stories they have are good enough for them. I mean, of course, very small children. One can keep trying new ways to release their own feelings and imaginings."

It is odd to think that I jotted down these words in 1946, meaning to write a *Horn Book* piece about Brownie. Little did I know that soon I would be reviewing her books each season. How difficult it is to choose a few more to mention here! First I turn with satisfaction to the Harper books, where her first editor (1937) was Louise Raymond. Ursula Nordstrom, her assistant, was soon to be head of the department. Harper has published thirty-two of Brownie's books, more than any other publisher, proving Miss Nordstrom's very special understanding of, and friendship for, this unique writer.

The Runaway Bunny (Harper, 1942), with its beautiful pictures in five colors by Clement Hurd, is a treasure for young mothers to read aloud and for young eyes to look at over and over. Brownie said she was "using the repeated cadences of an old French love song, transferred to the real world of a small child." It has sold on and on. Less popular, but still being reprinted, is *The House of a Hundred Windows* (Harper, 1945), introducing fifteen modern paintings to children. Each was a window in a magical house where lived only a cat. At the end, "It was up to the cat!"— whether or not he would go out the door and never return, a mind-stretching question. The talented young architect De Veyrac created this house and helped make the book one of rare distinction.

And oh! the fun I had with *The Little Fur Family* (Harper, 1946). Do you remember it, all bound in rabbit skin, in a little box with a hole to show that little fur stomach? That box alone made a kindergarten class roll on the floor with laughter. I had to read it to them over and over, and pass it around for loving pats, and for squeals of joy at Garth Williams' entrancing, tiny pictures. After over 100,000 were sold, and it had appeared "in fur" in three other countries, it turned out that rabbit skins were sadly prone to worms and moths. So a new edition appeared in more normal book format.

Of thirty-eight illustrators of her work, Mr. Weisgard has been her most frequent collaborator, with twenty-two titles. His are the books with the most varied styles and moods — he can be funny, real, magical; he can evoke beautiful places, create appealing children and creatures; he used a striking poster style in *The Noisy Books* and a brilliant, Dali-like exactness in *The Important Book*. Clement Hurd, with his power to make the present world both real and touched with magic, and his special understanding of small children, comes next with ten titles. Garth Williams, in nine books, brings to life unforgettable creatures, expressive, wonderfully funny and appealing, always real animals. All three artists were superbly able to fulfill Brownie's book plans and to supplement them with their own different sorts of imagination. But she was in a very real sense a collaborator with each artist, discussing her own layout, their sketches, and all details. When a picture was finished, sometimes she changed some words in the text to fit it better. She generally "pulled out" the best work of every artist. She was always eager for collaborators with "new" styles, such as Lucienne Bloch, Dahlov Ipcar, Symeon Shimin, E. Slobodkina, Marc Simont, Remy Charlip.

An artist whose work Brownie greatly admired and was proud to have illustrate her words was the French-Mexican Jean Charlot. He did *A Child's Goodnight Book* in 1943 and made a larger, revised version of it in 1950. With all his forceful strength and bold design, he still captured the humor and tenderness of the text and took the poetic suggestions a leap further. His handling of *Two Little Trains* (1949) is superb. In fact, all five of his books for Brownie's texts are masterpieces of modern children's bookmaking. All were published by her old friend William R. Scott, who since those early days has done twenty of her books. He has cleverly revived some of the first in new editions, such as *Willie's Adventures* and *Sneakers*.

Mr. Scott wrote in 1938: "The tremendous success of her books is due to a rare quality: sure emotional insight into the realities of a young child's world bounded by the here and now." With equal discernment, he wrote in 1955: "All her books have an elusive quality that was Margaret Wise Brown. . . . [They have] simplicity, directness, humor, unexpectedness, respect for the reader, and a sense of the importance of living."

In years to come, publishers will be able to rediscover and reissue books by Brownie for a most fortunate reason. They can turn to the permanent collection of her work at the Westerly (Rhode Island) Public Library. To date, they possess all but four of the ninety books of which she was author, the eleven which she adapted or edited, the seven story collections in which she appeared. They have some of the artist's originals and the author's book layouts; records, filmstrips, and much other fascinating material.

In the early days a publisher once asked Brownie, "Have you another manuscript you can show us?" She replied: "I have a big drawer full of them. I dream them up in twenty minutes, then polish some of them for a year." A person who is creative in this way (and I think most truly creative people are prolific) is not apt to be self-critical, that is, as to relative values of separate pieces of writing. Brownie believed in the criticism given her by children themselves. She would often try out manuscripts and finished books on children she knew in various homes and in schools. This way of testing books is far from infallible. But anyone who has seen small children make a beeline for her books knows that, with her, it worked.

I suspect that she enjoyed the wide arena of her publishing world in the same sporting spirit as that which took her off to hunt with the Buckram Beagles on Long Island. She enjoyed any contest of wits in a publisher's office, whether over binding or punctuation (her idea of this was, the less the better). She seemed shy in public but she was very curious about people and interested in editors she felt were truly creative. As to the business end of it all, she was far from reliable. She kept no proper record of her sales and royalties. I find a letter which tells me one firm paid her 40 per cent on a book! It is said that once she claimed she *couldn't* have to pay an income tax because that year she had spent more than she had earned. One list she sent me that I fully believed in is headed "Books Under Construction." Some of these you will see in 1958 and 1959.

To her host of friends, news of her death in France on November 13, 1952, was a terrible shock. She was extra happy that year, for she was planning to be married. How could she, the adventurous, strong one who could chop wood, ski, skate, do so many things well, just suddenly go, after a normal appendicitis operation? It couldn't be true. She had had fun in Paris, celebrating the appearance of *Mister Dog* in French. She was staying at the Château Barlow, near Eze, the magical little ancient castle town on its steep hill above the Grand Corniche. She died suddenly, in the hospital at Nice, thinking she was well and ready to go home.

Once she said to me, "In the back of my head, I keep busy; in the front of my head, I am slow and stupid." I love to think of her at Eze, seeping in impressions of that beautiful old world and the sea spread out below, wondering whether she would now, in a new life at home, turn at last to writing for adults. The last words should be her own:

> A book can make a child laugh or feel clear-and-happy-headed as he follows a simple rhythm to its logical end. It can jog him with the unexpected and comfort him with the familiar, lift him for a few minutes from his own problems of shoelaces that won't tie and busy parents and mysterious clock-time, into the world of a bug or a bear or a bee or a boy living in the timeless world of story. If I've been lucky, I hope I have written a book simple enough to come near to that timeless world.

EDITORS' NOTE

Margaret Wise Brown has written over 100 books for children. *A Child's Goodnight Book,* illustrated by Jean Charlot, was runner-up in 1944 for the Randolph J. Caldecott Medal. In 1955, another of Miss Brown's books, *Wheel on the Chimney* with illustrations by Tibor Gergely, was again a runner-up for the Caldecott Medal. Her book, *The Little Island,* published under the pseudonym of Golden MacDonald and illustrated by Leonard Weisgard was the 1947 Caldecott winner.

Clyde Robert Bulla:
Master Story Weaver*

IN A SMALL ALASKAN VILLAGE above the Arctic Circle an Eskimo boy sits in a warm, well-lit school room reading *The Sword in the Tree* by Clyde Robert Bulla. Outside, even though it is just past noon, darkness drops silently over the treeless, wind-swept tundra and over the cluster of nondescript houses huddled together around the school. The boy remains oblivious to all this. Through the magic of words creatively used he is experiencing life in another place and another time.

Some fifteen years earlier Clyde Robert Bulla wrote this story at his desk in his comfortable home in a Los Angeles suburb. These colorful, sunny California surroundings where the author has chosen to live and work stand in sharp contrast to the bleak, barren arctic just referred to. A similar sharp cultural difference separates author and reader and one might rightfully ask, "What special knowledge of the creative process does this quiet, unassuming man possess which enables him to step across cultural and experience background barriers and to stimulate the imaginations of his young readers so that they can in turn identify with young people of other cultures, in other places, and in other times?"

To properly evaluate the contribution Clyde Robert Bulla has made to the field of children's literature we must, besides studying the quality of his writing, take note of both the number and variety of his works. Since his first book *The Donkey Cart* was published in 1946 he has

* By Arnold A. Griese. From *Elementary English* 48 (November 1971), 766–778. Reprinted with the permission of the National Council of Teachers of English and Arnold A. Griese.

written over forty books. The list of his works given at the end of this article suggests the breadth of his writing. Few authors have the depth of background, or are willing to do the painstaking research, required to write with accuracy and feeling about children living in both past and present and in other lands. Much of his writing is historical fiction which must not only fulfill the usual criteria for good literature but must also present an accurate picture of life in an earlier time. The soundness of his works in this category is indicated by the fact that Huck and Kuhn, in their textbook *Children's Literature in the Elementary School,* cite his works as models in five separate instances in their chapter dealing with biography and historical fiction. Also, his book *Squanto, Friend of the White Man* won a Boys Club of America Junior Book Award for the year 1955. Perhaps the best expression of Clyde Bulla's contribution to the field of historical fiction is contained in Margaret Warren Brown's review of *Viking Adventure* in the August, 1963, issue of *Horn Book.* She states:

> Once again Mr. Bulla writes a good story with strong plot inter-
> est, which is also very easy to read. This one will be particularly
> welcome because its subject is perennially interesting to younger
> readers — yet, most of the best books about Vikings have been writ-
> ten for older boys and girls. . . . The tale and its telling are mature
> enough to hold the interest of older boys who find reading difficult.

But, before studying his writing more closely, what about Clyde Bulla himself? Even a few minutes conversation confirms his quiet, unassuming nature. Humility, a trait not commonly ascribed to those possessing ar- tistic talents, is evidenced mostly by his genuine openness to new ideas. The viewpoints of others are considered not as threats, but rather as vehicles for his further growth. It may well be that in this way his humility serves as a wellspring for his creativity — a creativity which seems to have been strengthened rather than diminished by over a quarter century of writing.

Artists appear to possess an inborn creativity expressed through an active imagination. Clyde Bulla is no exception, but his early days spent on a farm near King City, Missouri, did much to both nurture and dis- courage his creativity and his innate curiosity. These circumstances resulted also in the development of determination — another attribute of successful writers. Being brought up among brothers and sisters in a family where music and reading were actively encouraged undoubtedly contributed to his competence as a writer. But other factors in this isolated rural environment may well have worked to oppose this development. Farm life during Clyde Bulla's boyhood required long hours of physical labor of all members of the family including the children. Only after the work was finished could attention be given to the pent up demands of a curious and creative mind. Under these circumstances determination became an important attribute. It was determination to become a good writer that moved young Clyde Bulla to stay up after everyone else had gone to bed in order to write. The time and privacy needed to write were scarce but determination found a way.

An incident that happened to Clyde Bulla while in first grade in a one-room school illustrates at once his early determination to be a writer and his willingness to stand up for his choice even to the extent of being laughed at by others. In answer to the teacher's question to the class as to what each would ask for if given one wish, young Clyde replied, "A desk." This response was greeted with general laughter and when asked why, he responded with, "So I'd have something to do my writing on." This prompted another boy who typified the practical orientation toward material possessions of that farm community to reply, "Gee, I'd get me a good mare."

Placed in an environment which gave priority to physical labor and in which no TV existed to break the barrier of physical isolation, Clyde Bulla made good use of his imagination to extend and enrich his world. Books available in his home became a natural pathway to new experiences; but other people, unknowingly, played a part too. His life-long interest in opera, travel, and history were indirectly stimulated by his fertile imagination's interaction with the ideas and actions of those close to him.

His initial interest in opera developed from hearing his sisters practice on the piano excerpts from familiar operas. This led to a study of his older sister's scrapbook which contained pictures of opera figures in exotic costumes. These glamorous figures acted as a further stimulus to his imagination. Always present, as a goal to experience more, was the unanswered question, "Will I ever get to see these figures perform in real costumes on an actual stage?" Listening to opera on the radio followed naturally and again, when engaging in this activity tended not to be totally accepted by the community, he did not let this deter him. However, in this instance it did lead him to go underground; that is, he only listened to opera when those who might make fun of him were not present.

This determined interest in opera, and in music generally, led to a continued enrichment of his personal life and led him eventually to author the various books dealing with the stories of famous operas. This long interest in opera allowed him to see that many operas contained the strong theme and simple plot which is so characteristic of the myth and folktale, and to translate these literary essences in a manner that encourages young people's interest in this rarely appreciated art form. The following Kirkus review of his *Stories of Favorite Operas,* published in 1954, suggests the effectiveness of his contribution:

> Written with enthusiasm and clarity, Clyde Bulla has managed to give a clear picture of the often somewhat confused action of the operas in brief summaries which maintain the glamour of the original. Interesting in themselves these condensations should encourage the reader to investigate this rich repertoire of music.

The study of history too has been a lifelong interest of Clyde Bulla and, as has already been indicated, has had a pronounced influence on the content of his writing. Again, both reading and people close to him played their parts in stimulating initial interest. As one of the younger children in his one-room school he would escape the drudgery of his assigned lessons by listening in on the older students' discussion of long ago times and faraway places during their history lessons. This talk of different times, people, and places interacted with his own reading and, again, proved a powerful stimulus to his imagination. Frustrated for many years in not being able to travel, his imagination provided a substitute. A substitute which in most instances was much more romantic and glamorous than the actual.

This practice of identifying with characters — both fictional and historical — as they traveled and adventured in faraway places and faraway times developed into a habit which he uses to an advantage in preparing to write a story. His writing procedure from the very beginning has been to carefully research the people, time, place, and cultural setting of his proposed story. If the plot and story problem have not been completely arrived at before research is begun, the reading done during research helps finalize this aspect. Next, he makes every effort to identify with the main story character — to sense the emotional reactions and motives of this person. To accomplish this, and to obtain a more vivid and concrete picture of the setting in which the story character lived, he visits the place involved whenever possible. For example, before writing *White Sails to China* he traveled to Salem and placed himself on one of the wharves which he then conceived of as the spot where the main character, Nat, stood as he watched the sailing ships come in to unload their cargo. In the story, Nat longs to go back to China where he had lived with his father. In this instance it was not difficult for the author to personally experience the emotional reactions of Nat since he, too, as a boy had longed to leave King City, Missouri, and visit distant lands.

The fact that he was unable to travel when he was young other than through his imagination did not reduce his determination to do so. The time and money needed to make this possible did not become available until he reached manhood, and his first trips were to the Southwest and to California to get a glimpse of the ocean. During one of these trips he traveled to Hawaii and worked there briefly as a linotype operator. He returned to the Mainland at Los Angeles with only fifty dollars remaining. At this point he had just begun publishing, and it seems that his zest for travel was outdistancing the revenue from royalties. His practical nature told him to return as quickly as possible to his home in Missouri; but a long-standing desire to see the Golden Gate Bridge, which he had so often pictured in his mind enshrouded in mist, won out over prudence. Fortunately, a royalty check for six hundred dollars – an unheard of amount at that time – awaited him on his return to Los Angeles and this happy event, along with a desire to write a story about California's past and his sister, Mrs. Gilbert's, encouragement, persuaded him to remain in Los Angeles. His next book was *The Secret Valley,* a story with the California gold rush as its setting. He has traveled extensively since then to all parts of the U.S., Mexico, and Europe but has made Southern California his home.

Clyde Robert Bulla lives on a quiet street, but within a few short blocks lies a bustling freeway which places him only minutes from downtown Los Angeles. Bringing to his attention that most children's authors prefer a rustic setting in which to do their creating, he was asked whether the availability of opera performances kept him close to this large city. For a moment a quiet smile appeared as he replied, "Perhaps." Then in a more serious vein he pointed out his dependence on the presence of others to aid and enrich his work. Although he needs physical isolation when actually writing, even then this isolation must not be complete. Background sounds such as a door slamming in the house next door, which suggests the presence of other humans going about their daily tasks, have a supportive influence and are welcome. Thus, a small studio in a quiet neighborhood is to Clyde Bulla an ideal working environment; and here, sitting in his favorite rocking chair with only pencil and paper as aids, he makes a small, lonely boy named Torr, of another time and place, come alive for young people of today who too at times experience loneliness. Torr is the main character in *The Moon Singer,* and Ethel Heins in her review of it in the December, 1969, issue of *Horn Book* says:

The author's recent stories have a mystical element which the artist perceived and underscored in her block line drawings. . . .

Many of us who are familiar with both his past and present works would agree that Clyde Bulla appears to be achieving even greater depth as he continues his writing. And, although modesty would not permit him to concur, he would willingly admit his indebtedness to those around him for stimulating him into continued creativity. And this indebtedness is not limited to merely having people nearby, as was suggested above, but involves also active interchange of ideas. Here the Southern California environment offers an advantage. Residing in this same area are other authors and illustrators, such as Conrad Buff, Taro Yashima, Julia Cunningham, Sid Fleischman, Bill Peet, and Don Freeman, with whom he has developed a personal relationship which allows him to share with them ideas as well as common problems. Thus, the roots he has established combine with his travels to nourish and enrich his writing background.

A closer look at the content and structure of some of Clyde Bulla's books will give evidence of the quality of his writing — the degree to which it successfully meets the criteria for good children's literature in regard to content, plot, characterization, setting, theme, and style.

Part of his success in dealing with a variety of story content appears to stem from adroitness in managing plot. His story problems emerge and develop naturally from the story setting, and its characters — what they do, what they believe, etc. This happens only because he already has, or first researches for, information on the people involved and their physical and cultural setting before he begins a story.

For example, *The Sugar Pear Tree* is a story of a modern family — the main character, a boy named Lonnie; his mother, a nurse who must work because there is no father to provide; and a grandfather who lives with them and is supposed to keep an eye on things while Lonnie's mother is working. This family faces the problem of having to move from the home they all love because the state has condemned the land to make room for a freeway. The problem is obviously a natural one stemming from our modern technology (in this instance no research was required, since Clyde Bulla was personally involved in an almost identical problem). In real life, however, dramatic story content would not evolve because the family would quietly search for, and find, another house and go on with living. How then does a master plot weaver such as Clyde Bulla create an interesting story out of this basic problem? He obviously knows he has the right to choose a fictional set of circumstances — one which will suit his needs — and does so. He must also have the practical background and creative imagination to choose the right combination of circumstances. In *The Sugar Pear Tree* he does this subtly by characterizing the grandfather as a blend of zealous altruism and genuine human stubbornness. Although Gramp does play an important role in the family, he deludes himself into believing that, as he says to Lonnie, "I'm the head of this family, and I'll take care of things." This commendable but unrealistic attitude of a very old man leads naturally to a wish to protect Lonnie's mother from unnecessary worry. Thus, when the eviction notices are served he simply destroys them, leaving the mother to believe that all is well. But good intentions are not enough; and defiance of the law brings its inevitable consequences. One evening Lonnie's mother comes home to find Lonnie, Gramp, and all the family owns out on the sidewalk with the doors and windows of the house boarded up. Gramp sits in his chair, face in his hands, crushed by what has happened.

Clyde Bulla continues to demonstrate his mastery of plot structure in the story ending. At the very beginning Lonnie has created his own problem of sorts when he wins an essay contest in which the prize is a tree which he becomes very attached to but which he cannot plant for lack of a suitable place. Clyde Bulla uses this situation to make Lonnie the unsuspecting resolver of the problem. Earlier in the story when Lonnie tried to carry the potted tree home it was really too big a job for him, so Nick, the owner of the nursery (a bachelor, apparently the age of Lonnie's mother) who had awarded the prize, takes Lonnie and the tree home in his truck. In this way Nick relates to the family and eventually plays an important part in resolving the problem.

Thus we see how the problem arose out of a natural setting and how it was at once heightened and finally resolved by the very human and logical actions of the story characters. This should not imply, however, that Clyde Bulla's plots do not include coincidence. For example, Lonnie's mother happens to be home when Nick brings Lonnie and the tree home. This is a fortunate circumstance, since Lonnie's mother and Nick might otherwise not have been brought together. But even here the incident is not contrived since the mother, as a nurse, takes care of private cases and keeps no regular hours. The point being that a good plot — as in real life — finds a proper balance between accidental events and events caused by the actions of the character, and Clyde Bulla is a master at finding such a balance.

Using the usual in an unusual way to advance the plot is also used in his historical stories. *The Valentine Cat,* although more a folktale than a work of historical fiction, contains carefully researched facts. One of these was the practice in earlier times of chimney sweeps lowering cats tied to a string down chimneys so that, as the cat struggled furiously to escape the frightening situation, the chimney was cleared of its soot. In the story a lonely, homeless cat is taken in by a lonely, unsuccessful artist. This happens early in the story, and there appears to be no further problem. At this point Clyde Bulla introduces an unscrupulous chimney sweep who steals the cat to use it as just stated, and so the plot has been advanced in a natural but original way.

A final point regarding plot. Reviewers and librarians frequently praise Clyde Bulla's stories for the swift action and adventure they contain and which is so appealing to children. There can be little doubt that his stories do contain fast moving action, but the above discussion of plot should also prove that, unlike the series stories, his books do not rely solely on actions and happenings. Certainly *The Sugar Pear Tree* is completely void of action taken in the usual sense, but it is nevertheless a moving story which children find satisfying and interesting to read.

Characterization, too, plays an important part in making Clyde Bulla's books satisfying and interesting reading. His humane portrayal of people as possessing both strengths and weaknesses makes it easy for the reader to recognize his own human traits and to identify with the story characters as they are confronted with suffering as well as good fortune. Clyde Bulla's rigorous efforts to become one with the characters as he writes leads to a portrayal of more genuine emotional reactions in these characters and helps the reader identify and respond to these emotions. His simple, straightforward writing, especially as it is used in dialogue, allows characterization to develop without slowing down the story itself. This brief conversation from *The Sugar Pear Tree* between Gramp and Lonnie's mother concerning the need to move illustrates how Clyde Bulla uses dialogue to delineate in greater depth the nature of these two individuals and the relationship between them, while at the same time intensifying the story problem (at this point the mother is unaware of Gramp's deception in not telling her about the eviction notices).

"You couldn't do that," said Lonnie's mother. . . . "One of these days everything on this street will have to go."

"Why will it?" asked Gramp.

"To make way for the freeway," she said. "You know that."

"No, I *don't* know that!" said Gramp. "They'd better not try to take our house."

"Grandfather, please don't talk that way," she said. "This house is not ours. We only rent it from the state. When the state tells us to go, we'll have to go."

"Oh, no, we won't," said Gramp. "They can't push us around."

Clyde Bulla's treatment of setting is also both unusual and effective. His terse style is nowhere more evident. Few adjectives and no literary devices are used; nevertheless, a feeling for both time and place are quickly established as evidenced by these opening passages from one of his earlier books, *The Sword in the Tree.*

The boy sat up in bed. A sound in the night had awakened him. His room was so dark he could see nothing, but he could hear footsteps outside his door. He held his breath and listened.

"Shan!" said a voice.

He let his breath go. It was his mother, calling his name. "Yes?" he said. "What is it?"

Lady Marion came into the room. She had a candle in her hand, and the light moved over the stone walls.

"Shan, I'm glad to find you here," she said. "I was afraid you had gone with your father."

"Where has my father gone?" asked Shan.

"One of the servants just awakened him and they went away together," she said. "I heard them speak of a wounded knight."

"A wounded knight?" said Shan.

"Yes," said Lady Marion. "Shan, what does it mean? Is someone making war on us? Are there enemy soldiers outside?"

"Don't be afraid, Mother," said Shan. "Our good King Arthur has beaten all our enemies. And even if there were enemies, we would be safe here. There is no stronger castle in England than ours."

In these few opening words Clyde Bulla has established a mood of suspense, a possible problem, insight into Shan's character, and the medieval setting. Children are taken into a suspenseful situation while at the same time they are being supplied with vital information needed to add realism to these exciting events. This is additional proof that Clyde Bulla's simple, easy-to-read style, which makes his books sought after by reluctant readers, does in no way compromise the quality criteria demanded in good children's literature, nor does it limit his books to the very young and to older children who find reading difficult.

Theme is a singularly important criterion in judging a children's book since its absence tends to make a story "escape reading" while mishandling it is apt to make the work a moral tract. After arbitrarily defining theme as the ideas in an author's story which have to do with people — what they are like, what they should be like, etc. — Clyde Bulla was asked whether he was conscious of any themes in his stories. His answer was a thought-provoking one. No, he didn't think about theme as he prepared to write a story or while he was actually writing. But he felt if the story problem is real in the sense that it is something that could happen to any child simply because he is a child, and if the characters are realistically depicted in the sense that they act like children with all their subtle — and not so subtle — faults and strengths, then theme will be present in that story. He ended by adding, "I suppose things a writer believes will inevitably find their way into his stories." They apparently do in his books. It is true, his characters possess the capacity for both good and evil, but underlying it all is a life-affirming belief in the dignity and basic goodness of people. His empathy for the special problems of minority groups — especially the Mexican-American and the Indian of the Southwest — is evident in such books as *Benito* and *Indian Hill.* The latter, dealing with the relocation of a Navajo family from their reservation to the city where job opportunity awaits the father, moved Priscilla Moulton to make the following comments in her review of the book in the February, 1964, issue of *Horn Book:*

> Though less exciting than the other simply written stories by Bulla, this has an added dimension in its brief and realistic treatment of the psychological and emotional problems of a family moving into a foreign situation. . . . The youngest reader can gain appreciation for frictions inherent in change, for the sadness, and for the goodness. An unusually gentle and sincere story with deft handling of complex tensions experienced by so many children.

Children intuitively sense and undoubtedly find security in Clyde Bulla's subtle affirmation of human living and it would thus appear that his books fully satisfy the criteria regarding the treatment of theme.

Style is perhaps the most misunderstood aspect of Clyde Bulla's writing. This is partly due to his simple, direct style which has quite naturally placed his writing in the simplified and easy-to-read category. This movement in children's literature began in earnest in the early 50's and was severely, and it would seem justly, criticized for its overemphasis on linguistic simplicity and for the failure of its writing to fulfill the criteria for good children's literature. As the above examples and discussion have attempted to demonstrate, Clyde Bulla's simple, direct style is not achieved by ignoring the other qualities found in good children's literature.

Clyde Bulla's own response to this aspect of his writing is best expressed in this statement, "I think the young need simply written stories since this might encourage them to go on to other types, but I don't feel any limitations while writing. I feel that each story is meant to be written in that particular way." The fact that he has maintained a life-long interest in the study of words may help explain his ability to unconsciously select words that forthrightly express his story ideas.

A point that is usually overlooked in commenting on Clyde Bulla's style is its similarity to poetry—especially to Haiku and other short-form verse.

Poetry—and much literary prose—claims to communicate meaning more effectively by reaching the mind through the emotions. It attempts to communicate a total experience by emphasizing the feelings that accompany that experience rather than by emphasizing exact, objective information. Of the various literary devices used to communicate this total experience, imagery figures as most important. Imagery is here defined as the use of words that appeal to the senses and which thus convey feelings and meaning concretely by evoking images in the reader's mind. The latter then uses these images to attempt a recreation of the original experience as intended by the writer.

Imagery defined in this way involves essentially use of concrete words and figurative language—especially simile and metaphor. Literary prose and poetry both use these devices, but poetry uses words more sparingly and is thus noted for its careful selection and organization of these words. Haiku and other short forms of poetry are especially noted for their terseness and simplicity (which allows the reader's imagination greater freedom in dealing with what has been suggested but left unsaid) and Clyde Bulla's style is most closely related to these forms of poetry.

The following excerpt from *Benito* is used to illustrate this relationship. Benito is about to leave with his uncle who lives some distance away. This is the second family that has taken him since his mother died and his sick father returned to Mexico.

He looked down the road at the house that had been his home. No one lived there now. The windows were broken, and weeds grew in the yard.

Far to the south he could see the hills of Mexico. "Some day we will go there," his mother had said. But they had never gone.

"Come," said Uncle Pedro.

Benito got into the truck, and they drove off.

The passage contains an informal rhythm created by the alternation of long and short sentences but more important are the experiences the author chose to communicate; seeing, perhaps for the last time, the home he loved and an unfulfilled dream promised by another. Both of these experiences a child has either had or has had occasion to think about. Thus children can readily relate to Benito's experience. But to make certain that the meanings and feeling of this experience are conveyed concretely the author follows up the more abstract statement "No one lived there now" with brief, concrete words that stimulate the reader's imagination to create visual images of broken windows and high weeds and thus to place himself in Benito's situation. In the case of the promise, the author stressed concreteness through use of the mother's exact words, then placed these in opposition to painful reality.

How much more effective is this treatment than the sentences "Benito was sad. He would never see his home again," which an unskilled writer— one who did not have an intuitive grasp of poetic expression—might attempt in producing an easy-to-read book for reluctant readers.

Thus it would appear that Clyde Bulla's style which uses poetic expression in its most elemental form to convey concretely both feeling and meaning, does more than just encourage the reader to go on to more complex forms of writing but introduces him, at an earlier age, to universal ideas which help him better understand human living and in this way gives greater meaning to his own life. This is the ultimate goal of all good literature.

In closing this article, as in opening it, an episode is cited showing Clyde Robert Bulla's writing at work enriching the lives of children and also suggesting what for him must be a source of satisfaction even greater than that obtained from awards and plaudits of reviewers.

The Moon Singer was originally written in response to a request from the editor of "Expectations," an annual magazine published in Braille by the Braille Institute of America. Just before Christmas the first copies of the publication were delivered to a school for the blind, the Frances Blend School in Los Angeles, and Clyde Bulla was invited to the school to help distribute them to the boys and girls. A buzz of excitement filled the room as each child explored the pages of his copy with his hands and reacted to the ideas with his mind. One girl found *The Moon Singer* and after a brief moment began reading it aloud. Slowly the general commotion died down as one by one the other children stopped to listen. Together they responded to the young boy Torr's experience in a time gone by and empathized with him for they knew he was different and understood fully what this meant.

Experiences such as this must be what stimulates Clyde Robert Bulla to put all his energies and talent into each new book and try to make it the very best he is capable of.

EDITORS' NOTE

Clyde Robert Bulla has received much recognition for his artistry in creating fine children's books. In 1961, he received the Southern California Children's Literature Award (given in seven categories since 1961 to an author or artist who resides in Southern California, by the Southern California Council on Literature for Children and Young People) in the category of "Distinguished Contribution to the Field of Children's Literature."

In 1968, *White Bird* (Crowell) was recognized for its capacity to arouse in children an awareness of the beauty and complexity of their expanding universe. It was also awarded the George G. Stone Center for Children's Books Recognition of Merit Award (given annually since 1965 by the Claremont Reading Conference).

The Commonwealth Club of California Literature Award (given annually since 1939 to the finest juvenile on any subject by a Californian) was presented to Mr. Bulla in 1970 for *Jonah & the Great Fish* (Crowell).

Virginia Lee Burton's Dynamic Sense of Design *

WHEN VIRGINIA LEE BURTON CREATED her final book, *Life Story,* published in 1962, she was in total command of her ability to combine design, illustration, and text in a manner distinctively her own. But the student of illustration, book production, or design can learn much by seeing how she developed her theories from the time her first book, *Choo Choo,* was published in 1935.

At that time Virginia Lee Burton had moved with her husband, George Demetrios, to Folly Cove, between Rockport and Gloucester, Massachusetts, on Cape Ann. When her first son, Aristides, was old enough to be intrigued with the sounds of trains, his mother was just as fascinated with their shapes and their energy. The strong black-and-white patterns of the trains racing across the pages of *Choo Choo* are bursting with motion. Choo Choo never waits placidly at the station; the engine always looks ready to spring out along the track.

This sense of movement, whether derived from the action inherent in an illustration, or from the changes and contrasts in a design, is an essential quality in all Virginia Lee Burton's work. She studied art at the California School of Fine Arts in San Francisco, but she also studied ballet and even planned at one point to become a professional dancer. Her love for and appreciation of dancing was an important part of her whole life. In Folly Cove, parties with the Demetrioi usually included square-dancing in the barn or Greek dancing on the lawn. When she was in her

* By Lee Kingman. Reprinted by permission from *Horn Book* 46 (October 1970), 449–460; 46 (December 1970), 593–602.

early fifties, she still took great joy in participating in a dance class given by Ina Hahn, a well-known dancer, teacher, and choreographer who lives on Cape Ann and whose group in recent years has given programs choreographed around spatial concepts in dance. This use of the shapes of spaces, while a new concept in a modern dance technique, had long been an important factor in Jinnee's own theory of design.

To one so kinesthetically motivated as Jinnee, drawing must have seemed an extension of dance, the capture of motion on paper. But another vital element in her work, the clarity of her drawing, certainly came from her study with her husband, George Demetrios, one of the few great teachers of Life Drawing. It is revealing to read *Illustrators of Children's Books: 1957–1966* and see how many of the artists mention in their biographies that they had studied with George Demetrios. His classes are a stimulating experience, for he has the rare ability of teaching how to see as well as how to draw. As he urges his students to draw "Faster, faster, faster!"—sometimes making the model change poses every minute—they must learn to see the figure in its entirety and put it on the paper rapidly. His own drawings of nudes are a perfection of pure line.

Jinnee met George when she was twenty-one and a student in his class at the Boston Museum of Fine Arts School. They were married only a few months afterward in 1931. In later years, even when Jinnee was extremely busy with her books, she always enjoyed finding an hour to run up the hill to the big studio where George held his summer classes and to refresh her eye and hand through his perceptive criticism.

Given these two qualities, the exuberant sense of movement and the clear ability to depict it, Jinnee had to find a way to hold them down on a page. With her second book, *Mike Mulligan and His Steam Shovel* (1939), she began to use the double-spread pages as a unit and also began to place the lines of text in a specially shaped area. She felt that the illustrator should be allowed by the publisher to command all the elements on the page—the type and unit of text as well as the pictures. While her illustrations for *The Fast Sooner Hound* by Arna Bontemps and Jack Conroy (1942) are delightful—a more energetic, ecstatic hound could never be found—she was dismayed by the amount of type in proportion to illustration, and from then on she was not interested in illustrating any book in which she could not control the length of the text.

Mike Mulligan was written for her second son, Michael Burton Demetrios, and the sturdy blond little boy racing up to see the arrival of Mike Mulligan and Mary Anne in Popperville was definitely drawn from life. There is a relaxed freedom in this book, even though the vitality of its many figures depends upon the organization of each page, an indication of things to come in her later work. Mike and Aris were fortunate in having an artist-mother who could not only create books for them but who could paint scenes from *Mike Mulligan* around the walls of their room.

In 1941, Jinnee was distressed by the influence of comic strips and comic books on children. She deplored the bad drawing and meaningless themes, and took great delight in offering her boys a substitute — *Calico the Wonder Horse or the Saga of Stewy Stinker*. Whether she would have cared to admit it or not, the comic-strip format of squared-off sequences influenced the development of her design techniques in *Calico*. The book was originally published on very poor wartime paper. There was a controversy, too, as a most proper librarian of the period felt Stinker was not an appropriate name for children to utter. Jinnee, always a forthright woman and knowledgeable about small boys' utterances, did not care for the librarian's criticism. The book was reissued in 1950 on better paper, with the name Stewy Stinker triumphant.

My copy of *Calico,* a 1950 reprint, is quite battered, worn out by my children and their friends, but one of its delights is its end papers. Prebound or rebound library copies may have lost this feature, and the loss is unfortunate, for the end papers tell a lot about Virginia Lee Burton's methods of working. They show the complete design of the whole book in quick sketches of the action appearing in the black-and-white pattern of each page. Of course, almost every artist works out a dummy before beginning any finished illustration. But Jinnee always lived in the middle of hers. Once the dummy was made, up went the sketches for each page, tacked in sequence around the studio, gradually replaced by "finished" illustrations still in sequence. One of her habits in criticizing her own work — illustration or linoleum block print — was constant visual criticism of that segment of work by itself and in relation to anything before it or after it. Suddenly looking up, she might see, in a page supposedly completed days ago, an area or a line she knew needed changing. To do one book, she filled wastebaskets full of what other artists might well have considered completely satisfactory work. This practice could be extremely disconcerting to her own students in her design classes, many of whom were not primarily artists and drew laboriously and slowly, taking many minutes to depict an object or a figure which she could draw in seconds. She could never understand why our design homework, a necessary part of her Folly Cove Design course, was often limited in volume, and why some of us could not produce many pages of experimental drawings of our chosen subject for a design between the monthly meetings of the group. It would have been a lifework just to do the complete chart of mathematical combinations and permutations that she worked out for five sizes of lines, plus five changes of tone from black to white, in developing her Folly Cove Design theories.

The illustrations for *Calico* were done in black and white on scratchboard, the perfect medium for an artist who keeps enriching and changing the black-and-white areas as the illustration emerges. A black line in a white area can be quickly eliminated by scraping it off the surface. A white line in a black area can be easily incised. Black dots are quickly penned for tone and texture, or white dots cut out of the black. Compared to the precise and exquisite work Virginia Lee Burton did for *Song of Robin Hood* six years later, *Calico* is an early stage in both her design and her use of the medium. But the quickness and dash of the illustration excitingly carries out the comic-strip feeling she obviously used and transcended. The double-spread on pages 6 and 7 of *Calico* carries a continuing flow of design, yet is a good example of how each illustration can stand alone. Even the distant cattle are contributing to the motion of the whole as they stand in swirling loops that grow in size. After the subject of her designs or illustrations—here the cowboys—the next important element in her design theory was called "sizes." The contrast in size of the subject—the cowboys and horses being larger on the left-hand page than they are seen in perspective on the right-hand page—helps to build a sense of motion. The third important element of her design was "tones" —the black, white, and gray areas being used, in this case, to emphasize each other. A far too simple definition of her theory, which became internationally known as Folly Cove Design, is that it is based on the interplay of the subject in contrasting sizes and tones.

Calico reflects these theories as Jinnee worked them out. She had already taught her version of design to a class which met in her barn during the years 1939–1941. Where "Watch those sizes!" might indicate to most people an admonition to diet or exercise earnestly, the phrase was actually a watchword for the designers group. It meant squinting hard, with an honest second look at the design being criticized, to see where a larger or a more varied constrast in the sizes of lines, or a contrast in tones, would make that design come alive. From her first group of students came the original block-printers, later known as the Folly Cove Designers, who, with some changes in membership over the years, sold their hand-printed textiles beginning in 1941 and maintained their own shop in Folly Cove from 1948 to 1969. The shop has closed its doors permanently, since the demand for textiles that must be laboriously printed by hand became too great for the few active members left in the group. However, a permanent collection of the fabrics is now on display and will be continually available to students at the Cape Ann Historical Association in Gloucester, Massachusetts.

After Virginia Lee Burton's death in October, 1968, I asked her former editor and friend through the years, Grace Allen Hogarth, about her special memories of Jinnee, and she wrote:

> I started to work for Houghton Mifflin just after *Mike Mulligan* was published. There was a long pause then, when Jinnee said she hadn't any other ideas at all. I knew that as a new editor I should be getting something out of this very talented person, but I was at a loss. After quiet nagging, which I think she rather enjoyed, I had a telephone call and a hint that an idea had come. I instantly asked her to come into Town and lunch with me which she did. I shall never forget the exact look of some sunlight on the wall-paper at the Women's City Club just behind her head — I think because the head was so sculpturesque and beautiful. She was very diffident, but bit by bit the idea for *The Little House* emerged. She needed, as she always did, immense encouragement and I had no hesitation whatever in giving it to her. After that day we became firm friends and I went often to Folly Cove to watch each step of the work as it progressed. We worked together also on the type-setting about which she was most particular. I don't think that I have ever enjoyed working with any author or illustrator as much as I did with Jinnee. We both had the feeling that we were necessary to each other and the book which emerged seemed to be the special property of both of us! I can hear myself calling it "My" book and this particular kind of pride pleased Jinnee because she was the most generous-hearted person about her work that I have ever known. This modesty and what, at first sight, appeared to be lack of self-confidence in her was most touching. Each book required a great deal of encouragement, each idea was a fledgling that had to learn to fly and all editors realize the excitement of these first flights. After I left I think I missed Jinnee more than any one else.

With *The Little House,* the Caldecott Medal winner published in 1942, Virginia Lee Burton's name was permanently established in children's literature, and this book is so known and loved around the world that it does not need to be described here. It is probably also well known that the idea for the book came from the Demetrioi's experience of buying a piece of land in Folly Cove and moving the small house on it back from its original position too close to the street. In the book Jinnee made her Little House small and simple and gave her a traditional shape, to emphasize her survival through decades of change. But the country setting, as seen in the cycle of the seasons, is very close to the appearance of the Demetrioi yard itself.

Jinnee was strongly influenced by her physical surroundings and while there has been criticism of her using the same theme more than once — *Life Story* recapitulates some of *The Little House* in its last twenty pages — it was only natural for her to use what she saw and felt around her. A basic tenet she always upheld to the Folly Cove Designers was: *Draw what you see and what you know. Don't copy, but draw from nature itself.*

Since nature is omnipresent, yet ever-changing, she apparently felt no limiting sense of repetition in using the theme of small home and changing seasons more than once. Not long before she died, she was discussing a book with her editors at Houghton Mifflin, which would have been about the actual building of a little house, and she planned to accompany the text and large illustrations with diagrams to show the fine points of structure and carpentry. Since she found writing more difficult by far than drawing, she always needed a strong simple theme, and apparently did not feel at ease with a conventional story having a child or animal for a hero. At one point when she was searching for an idea, I suggested using Lefty, her very large, very present, part-Newfoundland dog, in a story. But while she loved Lefty, who always accompanied her to the cove where she swam and he chased sea gulls, she could not see him as the protagonist in a plot — possibly because she was not subjective, as a writer can be, but was naturally an observer, an objective illustrator.

If you want to see Virginia Lee Burton at home, as her environment looked in recent years, do enjoy pages 51 to 58 of *Life Story* in all its detail. She even introduces this section, Act V of the book, by changing the little figure on stage left from the professor-lecturer of the earlier pages to herself, and in the text she invites:

> Twenty-five summers have passed quickly since we bought the old orchard, meadow, and woodland and moved a little house and my barn studio into the middle of it. The old apple trees have been trimmed, the woods cleaned up, and in the meadow we have put sheep to keep the grass down. Evergreens and flowering plants have been planted. Ferns and mosses grow by the running brook. Here is where we raised our children until they grew old enough to begin living a life of their own.

And it is her own environment that she shows, beginning on page 56, in realistic detail. In Folly Cove there really is a driveway curving in and up hill to the house with its yellow blinds—and this is just how the house looked before part of it was damaged in a fire and later enlarged by the addition of a kitchen wing. There really are forsythia bushes on the left and a sheep meadow behind the fence on the right. There is a small sheep shed, featured not only in her book, as on pages 66 and 68 of *Life Story,* but also on one of her family Christmas cards; and there is one of her procession of Siamese cats, usually named Zaidee, on the shed roof. The sheep in the meadow came and went over the years—some dignified ewes becoming distinct personalities; some rams troublemakers; all lambs spring delights. Jinnee and George often took the time and trouble to raise a cosset lamb—one abandoned by its mother and so bottle-fed. One of the textile designs she most enjoyed printing was her "Spring Lambs," where the solidity of the heavy ewes contrasts strongly with the dancing leaps of their offspring.

Her friends have their own memories of the meadow. For many years the Demetrioi gave a picnic for an enormous group of people at the end of August, when the birthdays of Jinnee and Mike came on the same date. During the afternoon there was always a baseball game in the meadow, and, of course, we remember the year when my husband's home run drove the ball through the studio window, and I, who hated baseball but was assured by all that I could not possibly get hurt, connected with a surprise hit, dashed for first base, and was promptly stung by a bee.

These were marvelous parties, largely because of George's ebullient personality as host and cook. He usually roasted a sheep over an open fire. Then there was the crisp tenderness of salad greens fresh from his incredible garden. There was Jinnee's insistence that everyone dance, and George's fondness for songs in many languages. The Greeks learned Finn songs; the Finns sang Greek songs. The Russians and Italians and Yankees joined in. And Jinnee always sang a song from her English heritage about the Captain's daughter who could only say, "Oh, No, John, No, John, No-o, John, No."

In Decembers, the barn-studio was the scene on Christmas Eve of a carol-singing party. Jinnee had a small spinet which was placed in the middle of the barn. Green boughs were tied with red ribbon and hung around the walls between books and paintings. Hundreds of Christmas cards from friends, with special attention going to those done by hand, brightened the walls. And in recent years, spectacular large paper ornaments in brilliant red, sent by her sons from San Francisco's Chinatown, added to the evening's spirit. The huge oval table held a buffet of ham and cheese and good Greek homemade bread. George kept busy passing out mugs of half-stout-half-beer and glasses of cool white wine. Generations mixed easily and contentedly: the eight-year-old boy who loved to sing and knew all the words by heart to the shame of elders who had forgotten many of them; the new neighbor whose heritage was Hanukkah, but who had specially learned the words to the carols so she could join in the singing. And the high point of the evening was the rendition of "The Twelve Days of Christmas" with soloists, duets, and trios, and whenever Mike could be there, his special part, "Five—gold—en rings," with embellishments that a singer of *bel canto* would have admired.

There are other personal notes in *Life Story*. In the autumn illustration, there is the wood pile where George's impressive wood piles always stand; and the apple tree by the house is where the Swing Tree, as Jinnee called it, grew and still stands today, though without its swings. This tree was a delightful motif in both her books and her block prints, and when she designed the Horn Book Calendar for 1965, she used the Swing Tree as the theme.

Beyond the barn is the brook and tiny pond, where for many years there was a marble figure of a young boy, curled up on a rock. Today not only George's sculpture appears about the lawns and terraces, but also some of Aris' work, for he has become a fine sculptor and shows an inventive combination of three-dimensional form plus design. Off to the right of the illustration, there would be a path up the hill to George's small stone winter studio.

Jinnee also added more people to the scene than were in her own family, although for many years, the house was rarely deserted. In 1950 the Demetrioi were host family to an American Field Service exchange student from Germany, Hans Petersen. Friends, students, and visitors were continually around. Whoever was there was pressed into whatever activity was going on, from folk singing to haymaking. I will never forget two lady magazine-editors from New York discarding their high-heeled shoes and rushing to help on a Sunday afternoon as a thunderstorm threatened loudly, and George ordered all hands out to save the hay crop. Jinnee often put a sign on the barn door, sternly indicating that she was busy, and inside the barn, though usually camouflaged by a straw beach hat hanging on the wall, was a cartoon she did of herself sticking out her tongue, probably painted after one visitor too many.

It was only in recent years, when time and the need for privacy became more precious, that she lettered a small sign and posted her working hours on the barn door, with a polite request not to interrupt. It is part of Cape

Ann's special ambience for creative people that such a plea is honored, and so over the years Jinnee was able to produce the eight books she wrote and illustrated herself, the few she illustrated for other writers at the beginning of her career, and the about thirty intricately carved linoleum blocks for her textiles, the subjects of which ranged from her friends dancing in a vigorous "Finn Hop" to her last design, "George's Garden."

My personal introduction to the world of Virginia Lee Burton and her husband, George Demetrios, came after the publication of *The Little House*. Grace Hogarth, who planned to leave Houghton Mifflin to return to her husband in wartime London, took me on to learn about editing and producing children's books. She sent me to Folly Cove for two weeks of Life Drawing classes with George, not in the hope that I could ever become an artist, but to train my eye enough to work intelligently with artists and illustrators.

While there, I met a soldier home on leave: my future husband, Robert Natti. He lived nearby, and with two of his brothers had joined the first class in design which Jinnee gave in her barn-studio. Most of her students at that time were neighbors, and the earliest application of their lessons was in designing block-printed table linen, curtains, and wallpaper to be used in their own homes. The idea of selling to the public came later.

Although Jinnee's designs were always popular and she was kept busy for over twenty-five years printing them on the flat-bed proof-press in her barn, her most famous ones were "The Gossips" and "Zaidee and Her Kittens." For many years her living-room curtains bore a "Swing Tree" print: Children in a joyous arc of motion swing from the branches of the well-known apple tree. The couch was covered with "A Rose is a Rose is a Rose," showing the familiar wild rose found by the rocks and beaches of Cape Ann. During the last few years, when she had not been able to settle down to a new book, she painted the woodwork of a small hallway with the rose motif and took great delight in decorating high chairs and toy boxes for her grandchildren. She spent several years on a three-paneled reversible screen, which shows in loving detail the brook she knew so well in different seasons of the year. This screen is of museum-piece interest and quality, as are the two colorful panels of her surroundings in Fiesole as she saw them the summer she spent in Italy with George. Her studio also contained some of her wood carving: a large panel of swirling figures in high relief and a beautiful box she made to house her much-used record player.

While I was an editor at Houghton Mifflin, she was working on *Katy and the Big Snow* (1943). Snowblowers were news then, and I remember her making a rush trip from Gloucester in a snowstorm to sketch from the office windows and then to follow a snowblower around the streets of Boston, even though the new machine never appeared in her book. She had merely convinced herself that Katy, with her shiny, shapely V-plow, made a much better heroine than a fussy, sputtering snowblower ever could.

After Grace Hogarth and I left, the juvenile editors at Houghton Mifflin changed several times, but Jinnee always found comfort and steady encouragement from Lovell Thompson and Hardwick Moseley, and more recently, from Austin Olney and Mary K. Harmon. Houghton Mifflin has published all of her books, and to the best of my knowledge, she never even considered going to another publisher, although she was continually sought after.

The book on which I worked with her closely was *Song of Robin Hood,* published in 1947 after three years of study and drawing on Jinnee's part. Grace Hogarth had accepted Anne Malcolmson's edited selection of the Robin Hood ballads and had asked Grace Castagnetta to arrange piano accompaniments for the melodies. Before she returned to England, Grace had persuaded Jinnee that Robin Hood was a subject she would thoroughly enjoy, one which craved the bold liveliness of her illustration. The format emerged slowly, although the full-page illustrations announcing each ballad were part of the scheme from the beginning. Also there was usually space at the end of each ballad for another drawing. But what bothered everyone was the stiffness and awkward spacing of the short four-lined stanzas sharply bisecting each page. Jinnee had been studying the old manuscripts illumined by the monks, and her study inspired her to illustrate every single verse, a method which would not only balance the area of text on each page with pictures, but would bring out the action in the ballads. Even though Jinnee set herself an appalling schedule of arising at dawn (which came very early on those cold winter mornings of "doubled" daylight saving during the war) and working till evening when windows near the coastline had to be blacked out for security, this infinitely detailed illustration of over four hundred verses added a whole year to the preparation of the book.

I can still see her huddled at her drawing board in the barn that winter, wearing fur-lined officers' boots to keep her feet warm, a mug of coffee always in reach on top of a small coal stove. The only interruptions to her work came in summer with the burgeoning of George's gorgeous vegetable garden, for with his Greek tradition of home-grown food, plus wartime rationing, the garden took precedence even over deadlines. Beans, tomatoes, and corn ripened profusely, and I soon found that learning how to can them was a very real editorial chore. But since the basketfuls of beans were sliced on a handsome polished granite table outdoors in the green shade by the brook, and the jars brought to a boil in a copper boiler over an outdoor fireplace, it was no hardship. Canning in a kitchen never held the same charm.

In her introduction to *Illustrators of Children's Books: 1946–1956,* Bertha Mahony Miller wrote about *Song of Robin Hood,* as she felt it was not only one of the most distinctive books produced in that period but that it would keep a special place in children's literature for years to come. In this same volume, Virginia Lee Burton told in her biographical notes of some of the problems and delights of creating the book: "With the whole family taking up archery, Folly Cove became Sherwood Forest and I could draw my subjects from life."

Jinnee also wrote her own introduction about the illustrations in *Song of Robin Hood,* because she wanted to call attention to her use of specific flowers and plants in decorating the different ballads. And since the author, Anne Malcolmson, had the privilege of dedicating the book to her husband, Jinnee worked a tiny secret dedication "To Aris and Mike from Mummy" into the scrolled border of the introduction.

To pick one full-page drawing from *Robin Hood* to accompany this article is difficult, for they are all intriguing. But "Robin Hood and the Ranger" is a particularly good example of how she made her design theories work for her:

> *When Phoebus had melted the sickles of ice*
> *And likewise the mountains of snow,*
> *Bold Robin Hood he would ramble to see,*
> *To frolic abroad with his bow.*
>
> *He left all his merry men waiting behind,*
> *As through the green valleys he passed.*
> *There did he behold a forester bold,*
> *Who cried out, "Friend, whither so fast?"*

Robin, arms outstretched in open defiance, argues his right to shoot a deer to feed his merry men. The forester gestures his protection of the deer, for they are the King's. The deer are already in flight. In many illustrations the gestures of the men and the running of the deer would be the extent of the action. But this whole illustration is full of movement, and the design helps to bring this about. The wood violets are springing up all over the forest; it is Jinnee's careful control of the size of the flowers and the density with which they grow which keeps this area of the picture from being simply background, underpinnings, or useless decoration. Although only a few trees are used, their swirling arrangement creates the feeling of deep forest. Birds, rushing out of the trees, add to the disturbing sense of confrontation; changes in their size emphasize the sense of flying up and away. The sun, again one of Jinnee's most-used symbols, is indeed the Phoebus of the ballad, with his rays not just decorative effect, but seeming to shoot the spring sunshine into the forest.

Many of the Folly Cove Design exercises were based on how to turn a "black" to a "white" through a "dark gray"; a "medium gray" (half-and-half) to a "light gray." To achieve this thoroughly in doing the homework took time, infinite patience, a steady hand, and a learning eye. It has been necessary here to reduce the illustration from "Robin Hood and the Ranger" to about half its original size, so without a magnifying glass the subtle effect of gradations of tone may be difficult to discern. But using this one illustration as an example of the possibilities, consider the leaves on the tree at the very center of the picture. This is more white than black; thus, a light gray tone. The trees in the middle of each side are a medium tone; the trees at the edge, where black dominates through the white leaves, are the dark gray. Thus the texture and tones of the forest have not stood still to the eye. On the forest floor, the same range of tone is carried out in the wood violets, starting at the left with a black tone and going through medium gray at the left of Robin's foot, to the dark gray behind him, with a highlight of very light gray between the feet of the two men.

Another example of the richness of texture and tone through careful control of the grays is found in her block print, "Low, Low Tide," which dramatically carries the ebb and flow of tidal movement. Starting at the left, the tones in the horizontal lines move from dark gray into light gray to white; then medium gray into black; medium gray, light gray, white and black again. The fish, lobsters, crabs, and kelp which make up the subject matter of the design are in this case almost subordinate to the movement of it. A more complicated design pattern is "Winter Boarders," where the differentiation in gray tones and use of emphatic white space becomes very clear. These textile blocks, 11″ by 17″ in the original size, were each designed so the print would be complete in itself when used singly as a table mat; yet the repetition of the block for tablecloths or yard goods would bring out even more aspects of the design.

Jinnee had incredible patience when it came to technique. She enjoyed using scratchboard because it was the perfect medium to prove quickly that her design theories worked. But carving a linoleum block gave her even more pleasure, and she tried to create her new designs during the winter months, so she could ink them on the block and have them ready to carve as she sat in the spring sunshine on the terrace. The most famous of her blocks was "Zaidee and Her Kittens," based on the family relationships of her Siamese cat, the cat's un-Siamese lover, and the Mendelian characteristics of their offspring. Since Jinnee always presented a set of table mats printed with this designed pedigree to anyone who took one of the kittens, she never had trouble finding homes for them. In newspaper printing, shades of gray change according to the density of the black dots in an area, and commercial "Benday" screens are used by many artists to give these effects quickly. On her Zaidee block, Jinnee carved her tonal effects with hundreds of dots. It is easy to cut a white dot into a black area with the twirl of a sharp knife blade. But cutting the white (unprinted) area away from a small black dot is entirely another matter. The original linoleum block of Zaidee is an incredible piece of carving.

Virginia Lee Burton planned and worked for many years on a book, *Design—and How!,* which presented her Folly Cove Design principles and also gave instruction for hours of homework exercises by which the principles could be practised. She actually made a complete dummy of the book, and using the symbol of a question mark as her subject, showed how to do thousands of the homework exercises. But she herself finally decided it was too overwhelming and would discourage the average student. Design lessons, when she gave the course, were usually spread over a whole winter, and the student never saw all the homework ahead of him at one time. Although she did not change the basic principles about sizes and tones and how to achieve them, she later eliminated many exercises, which, although helpful, were repetitive. But unfortunately she always felt the design book could somehow be improved and never was ready to hand it to the publisher. Teaching the course at intervals perhaps took away some of the urgency to publish it, as did the absorbing business of creating and printing new designs. A large wall hanging called "A Folly Cove Designer" hung for many years by the door of the shop; it was not for sale to the public, but any designer who took the course, had a design passed by the jury, carved it, printed it, and sold it as a member of the group, received one of these hangings printed by Jinnee herself as a diploma. Done with her usual verve and dash, it not only shows the tools used to paint and cut a design, as well as the early method of printing (by jumping on the block), but it also depicts the tremendous relief to the artist of catching an idea with which to begin.

With *The Emperor's New Clothes* (1949), Jinnee turned again to color. The story was one she had liked as a child when her father read it aloud, and the theme of parade, panoply, and elegance was fun to treat with design and embellishment. She retold the story in her own words, so she could control the length of the text and make the type area on each page an integral part of the whole design.

In 1952, *Maybelle the Cable Car* brought her tribute to San Francisco and expressed her delight in the cable cars. The book was credited with helping to preserve the famous cars, and at a ceremony on the 19th of December, 1967, she made a gift of her illustrations to the San Francisco Public Library. This gift includes not only the originals used in the book, but a rather complete collection of preliminary sketches, and some of the discarded versions which she did not use. Seen in its entirety, the collection should be of particular interest to students. The originals and some of the sketches for *Life Story* are in the Free Library of Philadelphia. In November of 1966 the original illustrations for *Song of Robin Hood* were presented to the Boston Public Library. An exquisite example of her intricate linoleum carving is her block, "Grand Right and Left," on exhibit with the collection of Folly Cove fabrics at the Cape Ann Historical Association in Gloucester, Massachusetts.

The study for *Life Story* and the painstaking painting of the full-color originals absorbed eight years of Virginia Lee Burton's life and was exhausting to her, physically and creatively. She talked later about other books she wanted to do, especially one with a Japanese background— after her trip to Japan in the spring of 1964. But she was not in the best of health during her last five years. This bothered her, since she was a great believer in mind over matter and felt that any kind of illness was a sign of weakness. She had a strong New England conscience. What else could have driven her to the years of early rising and the extremely long days of work on her books? But like any disciplined artist, she accepted the necessity of boring routine and infinite detail to make what she did perfect, and she had little patience with anyone's work that she felt too quick, too unfinished, or imitative.

She enjoyed walking through the woods near her home, usually bringing back budded twigs and branches of leaves, flowers, and grasses to study and draw. She was a fine swimmer, and summers found her on what was known as "Jinnee's rock," tipped just at the right angle to catch the sun at Folly Cove. A few years ago she bought a piece of land with a tiny studio on it at the end of Folly Point, where she could retreat and be alone and enjoy the sea. In earlier years for recreation she had played the recorder, and Saturday evenings were often music evenings, as a group of friends joined her with other recorders, violin, and spinet.

As she could not do another book, it is appropriate that *Life Story* was her final, all-encompassing creation. And knowing her deep appreciation for life and all living, growing things, I like to think of her taking a walk through the woods by her little house, and returning to paint her feelings and describe her observations, as she did in her last book: "Yesterday was a day to remember—one of those beautiful warm spring days when one could almost see the plants growing. Lowly little lichens clinging to the rocks brightened, liverworts and velvety mosses carpeted the damp ground, ferns pushed up and unfurled their delicate fronds, new bright green needles tipped the evergreens, buds opened and tiny little leaves unfolded, and the apple trees burst into blossom. In the meadow the sheep grazed happily on the tender new shoots of grass. The miracle of spring was here."

EDITORS' NOTE

Miss Virginia Lee Burton has won the following book awards: In 1943, the Randolph J. Caldecott Medal for *The Little House* (Houghton); in 1948, the Caldecott Medal for her illustrations for the *Song of Robin Hood*, edited by Anne Malcolmson (Houghton); and in 1959, the Lewis Carroll Shelf Award (given annually since 1958 by the University of Wisconsin to the book title worthy of sitting on the shelf with *Alice in Wonderland*) for *The Little House*.

Family Unity
in Natalie Savage Carlson's
Books for Children *

"MAMA, I'VE BEEN so far away. I've seen lots of those places I read about in the *Book of Knowledge*. I've become a writer, too, like I always wanted to be. I've written long stories — too long for the children's page in the *Baltimore Sun*. They're printed in real books with pictures and everything— But I've come back, Mama."

I could imagine my mother opening the door, her black hair parted in the middle and a song fresh on her lips. Then I knew what she would say. "You went too far away, little Natalie. You can't come back. You never can come back here again."

"Oh, but I can go back, Mama. I go back every time that I write a story for children because I put myself into my own childhood while I am writing it."

The foregoing statements are excerpts from a speech given by Natalie Savage Carlson to a group of librarians. Her words are suggestive of a happy childhood cast in a background of strong family attachments. They give some insight as to why family unity is a dominant and recurring theme in her books for children. The author explains that the subtle repetition of the theme in her writing is directly traceable to her own lineage and youth. "My mother is French-Canadian and family unity is one of the outstanding characteristics of this ethnic group. As for myself, I can count on my fingers the times that I came home during childhood and

* By Julie Carlson. From *Elementary English* 45 (February 1968), 214–217. Reprinted with the permission of the National Council of Teachers of English and Julie Carlson.

didn't find my mother there. Although my three oldest sisters were step-children, she knit us together so tightly that when I fill out any biographical questionnaire, I state that I have six sisters — not three sisters and three *half* sisters."

STRONG FAMILY SPIRIT

To people familiar with contemporary children's literature, the name of Natalie Carlson is associated with juvenile stories which are characterized by colorful settings, natural dialogue, Gallic wit, and swift, sure characterization. For me the name is synonymous with "mother" — a warm, loving mother who has always put family before her profession. Since my father is a naval officer, my sister and I grew up without having strong roots in one location; we moved and changed houses, schools, and friends constantly. The family cohesion which our parents inspired gave us the stability to meet and even to anticipate the constant changes which always lay ahead of us. Family togetherness is one of the greatest gifts which my parents gave to me, and my mother offers it to other children in her writing.

Advertisements and reviews constantly cite her dialogue, characterization, and humor as the essence of her style; they occasionally mention family spirit. I do not want what I consider to be one of her greatest gifts to her young readers — strong themes like family unity — to be overshadowed by the former. As Charlotte Huck, Professor of Education at Ohio State University, has stated: "Good books have sturdy plots. Great stories contain more than plot. They have worthy themes which make them memorable and capable of changing the thoughts and lives of their readers."

I mentioned to one of my University advisors who is a children's literature specialist that I had written a research paper on the topic of family unity as a dominant and recurring theme in my mother's books. He suggested that I read books by Eleanor Estes, Elizabeth Enright, Beverly Cleary, and Laura Wilder in whose works he felt the spirit of family togetherness was more obvious. While Laura Wilder's *Little House on the Prairie* and Eleanor Estes's *The Moffats* portray family unity — although not in stronger tones than those of Natalie Carlson — I had the feeling that their families were cast in a social context quite different from that of the present. Elizabeth Enright's Melendy family of *The Four-Story Mistake* is delightful, but idyllic. The closeknit family in Beverly Cleary's *Sister of the Bride* rings true as atypical — if statisticians are to be believed that there is a *typical* — middle class family whose members exhibit mutual concern and cooperation cast in a mid-twentieth century setting.

APPEAL OF FAMILY THEME

Librarians have indicated that the family theme is a perennial favorite of children, but the change in social patterns necessitates a recasting of the family unit in a modern social context. Older juvenile books featuring the family present a stable core which is the social center of life for the family members. For the present generation, the mobile family whose unity is under stress from external social influences is the realistic genus. A book which presents a family realistically must show that mutual concern, give and take, and understanding among members survive in the midst of an era of upheaval and change. A nostalgic backward glance to the home of the "good old days" can present to the young reader an idealistic family divorced from his real world. I believe that Natalie Carlson escapes this trap with sensitive insight. She remembers the happiness of her own childhood and its strong homey ties, and tempers her memories with the realities of present-day society and the adult view of seeing both the pleasures and problems in the rearing of her own children.

In an age in which one can be sure of only one thing—change—the family circle gives the child an anchor of stability and security in the midst of spacial geographic bounds, technological innovations, and social upheavals. It is important that some children's literature emphasize family unity since a child usually is neither consciously aware of, nor appreciative of, the feeling of togetherness in his own family. If the young reader unfortunately is not a member of a closeknit family in his own environment, it might motivate him to value and desire strong family interrelationship when he, in his turn, is an adult and has children of his own.

EMPHASIS ON FAMILY COHESION

Examination of the nineteen books for children by Natalie Carlson which have been published and three manuscripts which have not been published at this writing reveals a preponderance of examples, both explicit and implied, of family cohesion. In the introduction to *The Talking Cat*, which is her first published book, the author presents a homey French-Canadian setting for the stories in the book. It seems almost prophetic that the first pages of her first book set the warm family tone for the majority of the work destined to flow from her mind and imagination. The family unity theme is present time and time again in her books which feature people, rather than animals, as main characters. The introduction to *Sashes Red and Blue* places her French-Canadian tales in the context of stories which might be told at a big family reunion much like the LeBlanc clan is enjoying. The little Nichet cycle of stories included in this collection of stories shows a very real little boy functioning in a large, closeknit family.

In the *orpheline* series, one sees that even orphans in a happy orphanage can enjoy a brand of family unity. The *orphelines* often declare that they belong to one big family, and Madame Flattot thinks of them as being her own children. The "we are one large family" attitude helps them survive the crises of Brigitte's near adoption in *The Happy Orphelines,* the acquisition of a "brother" in *A Brother for the Orphelines,* the choosing of a pet in *A Pet for the Orphelines,* and the expansion of the "family" to include many "brothers" in *The Orphelines in the Enchanted Castle.*

The opening paragraph of *The Tomahawk Family* sets the mood for the struggle between two cultures in Frankie, a Sioux boy who resists American ways. "They lived in a log cabin with corners like clasped fingers—as if they were holding the family tightly together. But logs were not strong enough to hold the Tomahawks together because they were a divided family." This psychologically-split family resolves its cultural conflict and the book closes with a variation of the opening. "Its logs clasped the Tomahawks like fingers holding them tightly together."

Even the stereotyped image of the improvident gypsy in the person of Tito in *The Song of the Lop-Eared Mule* shows a father's fondness and concern for his children's welfare. In striking contrast, readers meet industrious carnival people in *Carnival in Paris.* The son and daughter of traveling performers miss their family very much when they must stay with their aunt and uncle in order to attend school. A happy turn of events physically unites the family for all the days in the year.

Orphaned Belle of *School Bell in the Valley* has a loving family in her Uncle Ned, Aunt Ivy, and their baby daughter. It is obvious that Belle enjoys a tighter family life than Tom Caigle. The Caigle family is influenced by Belle and her family to take more pride in themselves and interest in each other. Tom is persuaded by Belle to leave the hoboes and return to his family which needs him.

Jean-Claude of *Jean-Claude's Island* brings about a reconciliation between his parents and his grandparents while dispelling his own doubts as to whether he is temperamentally in the right family. Another French-Canadian family is met in *The Letter on the Tree.* The youthful hero is viewed in the setting of family life in its many moods of day-to-day living, special holidays, trials, and joys.

The family unity theme in *The Empty Schoolhouse* is powerful, for it portrays the dependence of the children on each other, mother as the quiet figure of strength, and the family meeting real life situations—both big and small. Its full impact is felt when the Negro girl can face a fearful situation outside of the home, because she draws courage from the family members supporting her at home.

Sailor's Choice finds a new home for Jamie and a permanent one for the dog, Sailor. Jamie, whose mother has remarried and left him, had been taken in by the populous Critch family. He stows away on Captain Wight's sealing ship and captures the captain's heart in spite of the boy's aversion to killing baby seals. Arrangements are made with the Critches for Jamie to be raised by Captain Wight and his wife only because Mr. Critch sees the settlement as an opportunity for Jamie.

Armand, the carefree tramp of *The Family under the Bridge,* has his heart stolen by a family of "starlings" and their mother who is trying desperately to keep her family united. He is willing to give up his hobo existence and accept the responsibility . . . and love . . . of his adopted family.

THEMES IN THE MAKING

The theme is present in three manuscripts which are in various phases of preparation for publication. "Chalou" is the story of a dog who ends up with a homey French-Canadian family. "Luigi of the Streets" is about an Italian boy who is very close to his mother and sister. "Ann Aurelia and Dorothy" concerns a girl who has been deserted by her mother and has been shuttled from foster home to foster home. She overcomes her bitterness toward her mother's desertion of her and finally chooses to live with her real mother when the latter returns for her. She is assisted in making her final decision by a Negro girl who has a warm family life.

The theme takes many forms. The family may not be a family in the strict sense of the word as the *orphelines'* family or Captain Wight's family. It may not always be ideal when measured by middle class values as Tito's lazy gypsy family or the slovenly Caigles. The family may be physically united, but psychologically divided as the Tomahawks, or vice versa as in the carnival family. The author seems to show that strong family relationships are important and exist in the midst of varying personalities and problems. At no time does she impose an idyllic family upon her reader and hint that this is what every family should be. She simply shows that family unity is important to the very real children in her books. As she has stated: "Family unity is an important theme for books for children because it gives the readers a feeling of security as well as appreciation and respect for members of their own families. If family togetherness is presented as being desirable, no other moral is needed in a juvenile book."

EDITORS' NOTE

Natalie Savage Carlson's first story was published on the children's page of the *Baltimore Sunday Sun*—"by Natalie Savage, Age 8." At the time she lived on a farm on the Potomac River in western Maryland. Her family lived in Maryland until Natalie was eleven. At that time, they moved to Long Beach, California.

Natalie worked as a newspaper reporter in Long Beach for three years, then married Daniel Carlson, a Naval officer. She and her husband have lived in many states, and traveled extensively. They lived in France for three years, and it provides the setting for many of Mrs. Carlson's books, including *Luigi of the Streets, The Family under the Bridge,* and the popular *Orphelines* books. In fact, Mrs. Carlson inherited a natural love for "things French" from her French-Canadian mother. The first version of *Wings Against the Wind* was written as "homework" for a French class. One of Mrs. Carlson's hobbies is collecting old French books and "trying to translate them."

In 1966, Mrs. Carlson was the United States nominee for the Hans Christian Andersen International Children's Book Award. [This award is given biennially by the International Board on Books for Young People, in recognition of an author or illustrator's entire body of works.]

At present, Mrs. Carlson and her husband live on their estate "Periwinkle" in Newport, Rhode Island.

Ann Nolan Clark:
1953 Newbery Award Winner *

WHO'S WHO IN NEW MEXICO, in 1937, identified Ann Nolan Clark
simply as "teacher and writer." In few people have these two professions
united more propitiously and completely to produce a distinguished and
colorful career.

Ann Nolan Clark's teaching career began with an unpleasant experience, one so unpleasant that she tried out factory work and journalism
before returning to teaching again. Her return was to the children and
people she knew best—the Indians of the Southwest. There, with the
help of a sympathetic principal, she found her place as a teacher. She
never left these people, though she expanded the range of her influence,
geographically from New Mexico to Canada, Central and South America,
and professionally from a teacher of children to a teacher of teachers.
For, in recognition of her wide and rich teaching experience, the Inter-
American Education Foundation sent her to travel and live for five years
in Mexico, Guatemala, Costa Rica, Ecuador, Peru, and Brazil in order
to train native teachers to work with their own people. Out of these experiences came Magic Money, Looking-for-Something, and Secret of the
Andes.

Mrs. Clark's writing for children grew naturally out of her work as a
teacher. As do so many teachers, she found her materials unsuitable for
the children she was teaching, and so proceeded to prepare her own.

* By Evelyn Wenzel. From Elementary English 30 (October 1953), 327–332. Reprinted
with the permission of the National Council of Teachers of English and Miss Evelyn Wenzel.

Again her sphere of influence widened as she joined forces with the U.S. Office of Indian Affairs and undertook to prepare materials for the government's new program for facilitating written communication with and among the Indians in their own, as well as in the English language. Such a program first involved procuring the services of linguistics experts to translate the spoken language of the various tribes into a written language. Mrs. Clark went to live among the tribes to gather material. This experience along with her years of teaching these children qualified her uniquely to write the English texts which were translated into Sioux, Navajo, and Spanish. English and Indian texts were printed in parallel columns. Thus were produced the Indian Reader Series and thus was inspired *In My Mother's House.*

But such distinguished professional advancement that flowered in the presentation last July of the Newbery Award has its roots deep in the living and learning of childhood. In her acceptance speech, Mrs. Clark gives full recognition to the influences of her early life in Las Vegas, the town of her birth:

> It was the days of early Las Vegas that set the pattern for my thinking. It set the pattern for my acceptance of people and folkways and traditions. It set the pattern which the years have deepened.[1]

She identifies four culture patterns which New Mexico gave her people, that of the Indians, the Colonial Spanish, the French Trappers, and that of "the States." She recognizes in her own family background the influence of the European tradition, for the Nolans "were also above all, Irish because grandfather said so."[2] She attributes the success of her books to this influence: "If children like what I write, that's a gift to me from my grandfather's fairies in Ireland."[3]

Her own talents, combined with these cultural influences, provide a unique background for her work.

> . . . all of this gave us understanding, a tolerance and acceptance and appreciation and ease with different people who have other ways of thinking and other ways of living.[4]

It is understandable, then, that Ann Nolan Clark should reveal in her life and writings a strong preoccupation with intercultural relations. Few teachers or writers have seen their responsibility more clearly and devoted themselves more sincerely and wholeheartedly to bringing about better understanding between cultures:

> All children need understanding, but children of segregated racial groups need even more. All children need someone to make a bridge from their world to the world of the adults who surround them. Indian children need this; they have the child problems of growing up, but also they have racial problems, the problems of conflicting interracial patterns between groups, and the conflicts of changing racial patterns within the group. Anyway you look at it, it's rugged to be a child. Often I think more of us did not survive the experiences than meets the eye.[5]

Ann Nolan Clark's books for children fall into two classifications: the bilingual ones written for Indian children primarily as textbooks and published by the U.S. Office of Indian Affairs; and those regularly published for all children. The textbooks came first, the others later, but there is surprisingly little difference in quality between the two types.

The Indian Reader Series definitely presage the later books and constitute far better literary fare than many readers regularly used in public schools across the country. These are truly delightful stories telling of familiar details of the everyday living of the Navajo, Sioux, and Pueblo children; revealing humor and sensitive understanding of these people as individual personalities as well as a minority culture with its problems; and written in simple, often poetic language which has an Indian "flavor" even in English. The readers conform in some degree to the conventional reader format—manuscript printing, short sentences, repetitive words and phrases, many illustrations, and a somewhat controlled vocabulary—but they have a literary quality superior to many of their counterparts in English.

These books contain much that is simple informative material. In the chapter called "Branding," in *Singing Sioux Cowboy,* children are told

> *Cowboys cut the calves from their mothers*
> *They drive the calves into my uncle's corral*
> *Mother calves bawl*
> *Baby calves bawl*
> *Cowboys work fast*
> *Cowboys yell "Yi-peee"*

The "Little Herder" series describes the work of a Navajo girl in each of the four seasons. In autumn she is busy sorting the wool:

I am helping my mother sort the wool
This pile we will keep
> *to spin into yarn for weaving*
> *because its strands*
> *are long and unbroken*

Much of this material was later incorporated into the longer story of *Little Navajo Bluebird. Young Hunter of Picuris* tells a story of life in a Pueblo town:

> *Up, up, up*
> > *to Picuris*
> > *a red-brown town*
> > *a mud walled town*
> > *that hides in a pocket*
> > *of the purple mountains*
> > *above the red brown hills.*

But many of the readers have a stronger thread of story and open with a "come-hither" note no reader could resist. *Who Wants to Be a Prairie Dog?* is "for little Navajos who have not learned to hurry" and begins by addressing the reader

> *This little boy is Mr. Many-Goat's son.*
> *If you do not believe his story it is because*
> *You are not short,*
> *Nor fat*
> *Nor slow*
> *And never, never have*
> > *you been down a*
> > *prairie dog hole.*

A series of four stories are introduced in this intriguing fashion:

> *These are stories*
> > *told just for fun.*
> *They are not true.*
> *They never were.*
> *They could never be.*
> *But what does it matter*
> *in just-for-fun stories?*

Could there be a beginning better calculated to relax the young reader and make him eager to read about the Pine Ridge Porcupine who lived at the Agency, or about Mister Raccoon in the watermelon patch?

Then there are the stories with more serious overtones, meant to present some of the problems of the people of whom they are written. Here Ann Nolan Clark's artistry is at its best, for only a teacher who knows and loves children and a person who has lived and felt with these people could deal with such problems so simply and effectively. *Little Boy with Three Names* tells about a Pueblo boy's summer at home after his first year at Boarding School and shows him confronted with the puzzle of his school name (Little-Joe), his home name (Tso'u), and his church name (Jose la Cruz). Here is a truly artistic handling on a child's level of the problems of conflicting cultures.

The Indian Reader Series cannot be discussed without mention of the illustrations that add so effectively to the stories. Most of them are done by Indian illustrators. Those of Andrew Standing Soldier are especially remarkable.

Ann Nolan Clark's name appears on two textbooks written for all children: *A Child's Story of New Mexico,* written with a co-author, and *Buffalo Caller,* one of the Row, Peterson Basic Social Education Series. The first is rather a traditionally organized geography text; the second, primarily an information book containing the thread of a story.

Much better known than these textbooks are Ann Nolan Clark's commercially published books for children. With the exception of *In My Mother's House* these books were published somewhat later than the textbooks. *In My Mother's House,* originally written for Indian schools in and around Sante Fe, was published as a trade book and immediately became popular and loved by teachers and children alike. It is a book difficult to classify, for, like any piece of art, it becomes for the reader what he wants at the moment. Is it geography, history, poetry, philosophy, or religion? It is none of these, yet it is all of them, and scaled so perfectly "to size" for young children that it almost seems to have been written by them under the guidance of an artist teacher. And perhaps, indeed, it was.

> *Lakes*
> *Are the holding-places*
> *For water,*
> *As the fireplace*
> *Is the holding-place*
> *For fire,*
> *As the plaza*
> *Is the holding place*
> *For people.*
> *I know a lake in the mountains*

My Grandfather told me about it,
My Father told me.
My mother's Brother told me,
But *My heart is the holding place,*
My heart is the keeping place
For the things I know
About the lake in the mountains.

Always will I keep
In my heart
The things that belong there,
As lakes
Keep water
For the people.

After *In My Mother's House,* Ann Nolan Clark becomes the story-teller again, now on a reading level for older children. The addition of the story, however, in no way lessens their value as information books or detracts from their appeal as poetry. The story does enable her to do something for which she feels a strong responsibility: to help Indian children understand their own problems of growing-up and to interpret to children of other cultures these people she knows and loves so well. She says in her "Newbery Award Acceptance":

I do not like morals in stories—at least, if they show. But often I think that groups of children have messages for other groups of children and for grown-ups, too. . . . Each group and each child has some message, some story to tell. (p. 254)

And so she proceeds to tell the stories of the children she has known: of Doli, in *Little Navajo Bluebird,* who must decide whether she will leave her beloved home in the hogan and go away to School; of Tony in *Magic Money,* who has a "secret want," and of his sister Rosita who wants shoes before she goes into the city to work; and, last of all, of Cusi, who finds for himself the "secret of the Andes" and faces and solves his own problem. *Magic Money* and *Little Navajo Bluebird* are beautiful family stories. Tony and Doli, though faced with problems, enjoy the security of love and understanding that all children need. Cusi must discover for himself how this need is being filled for him, for he thinks he wants above all else a family of parents and brothers and sisters. *Looking-for-Something* is the story of Gray Burro, who has the typical human problem of being bored with things as they are and who "follows his ears" into new and strange places until he finds what he is looking for.

It is appropriate that *Secret of the Andes* should have received the Newbery Award, for it seems above all the other books to have a message in it. Mrs. Clark, herself, says that "It had been a gradual piling up of all that I had learned, and of all that I believed." Cusi is not, at first glance, an ordinary boy, but he shares in common with many boys a need for a "family" of his own and he faces a serious vocational choice — whether to remain in the valley and carry on Chuto's work or to go out into the world. The real message of this book is in the way he makes this choice. The Indian belief in an inner directing force which must be respected and fostered with great patience and understanding is one which our culture could well ponder upon and study. For Cusi, coming into manhood meant learning "to read his own heart." He had been restless and full of questions about the mystery of his past but Chuto would not answer, for "the time is not now to know." When the time for knowing did come, Cusi realized that in his heart he must have known all along. Chuto in his wisdom had known, but had been willing to wait: "Of course you knew, but you had to find out that you knew." This is indeed a message for teachers who, with all of their specialized training and access to scientific knowledge, have scarcely begun to know how to wait for youth to "read its own heart."

Few teachers have given themselves so singlemindedly to understanding a people as has Ann Nolan Clark in her long years of work among the Indians; and few writers have been able to effect communication between cultures so sensitively and artistically. Let us hope that this year's Newbery Award marks a milestone rather than the climax in her distinguished career. May Ann Nolan Clark continue to be productive for many years to come.

REFERENCES

1. Ann Nolan Clark, "Newbery Award Acceptance," *The Horn Book,* 29:251, Aug. 1953.
2. *Ibid.,* p. 251.
3. *Ibid.,* p. 257.
4. *Ibid.,* p. 252.
5. *Ibid.,* p. 253.

EDITORS' NOTE

Since the publication of this article, Mrs. Clark has published the following books: *Blue Canyon Horse* (1954 — Viking), *Santiago* (1955 — Viking), *Little Indian Pottery Maker* (1955 — Melmont), *Little Indian*

Basket Maker (1957 – Melmont), *World Song* (1960 – Viking), *Desert People* (1962 – Viking), *Paco's Miracles* (1962 – Farrar), *Medicine Man's Daughter* (1963 – Farrar), *Tia Maria's Garden* (1963 – Viking), *Father Kino, Priest to the Primas* (1963 – Farrar), *Bear Cub* (1965 – Viking), *This for That* (1965 – Golden Gate), *Brother Andre of Montreal* (1967 – Farrar), *Summer is for Growing* (1968 – Farrar), *Along Sunday Trails* (1969 – Viking), and *Journey to the People* (1969 – Viking). As anyone can see, Mrs. Clark has not been idle.

Mrs. Clark's very first book, *In My Mother's House,* won the Book World Children's Spring Book Festival Award in 1941 and was a runner-up for the Caldecott Medal in 1942. It was written as a geography book for nine-year-old Tesuque children. After teaching these Indian children English, she found the material for reading instruction unattractive and boring – boring because the children could not relate to anything in the stories. Even when Indian stories were available, explanations were made throughout for the white readers who knew nothing about the Indian culture. Interestingly, the white children now await every new book with the same enthusiasm as their Indian counterparts.

Mrs. Clark also won the 1952 Book World Children's Spring Book Festival Award for *Looking for Something* (Viking); the 1953 John Newbery Medal for *Secret of the Andes* (Viking); and the 1963 Regina Medal (given annually since 1959 by the Catholic Library Association for continued distinguished contributions to children's literature).

Beverly Cleary:
A Favorite Author of Children *

ONE DAY IN THE LATE 1930s an average-type American boy went to a public library in Yakima, Washington. When the children's librarian suggested that he might enjoy reading about King Arthur, the boy replied, "Aw, I don't want to read about kings. I want to read about human beings." [1] Miss Bunn, the librarian, reacted to the boy's request by remembering that "There were many requests for funny stories and like the librarian of my own childhood, I found these requests difficult to fill. Someday, I told myself, when I found the time, I was going to write a book." [2] Fortunately for children and for children's literature, the librarian found the time to write the story and several more. As Mrs. Clarence T. Cleary, Beverly Bunn Cleary has been a writer since 1950 when her first book, *Henry Huggins,* was published by William Morrow.

In *Emily's Runaway Imagination,* Beverly Cleary sets the story in the rural Oregon of the 1920s, where she spent her own early childhood. Born in 1916, Beverly Bunn Cleary lived as an only child on a small farm near the town of Yamhill, Oregon. As Emily's runaway imagination, combined with some of her mother's practical common sense to help start a library in the small Oregon town of the story, so Beverly Cleary's mother established a town library in ". . . a lodge room upstairs over a bank with a book collection from the State Library in Eugene." [3] Once a week Mrs. Bunn acted as the librarian and brought her daughter Beverly along to the library. As Mrs. Cleary remembers, "It was in this dingy room

* By Margaret Novinger. Reprinted by permission from the *Southeastern Librarian* 18 (Fall 1968), 194–202.

filled with shabby leather-covered chairs and smelling of stale cigar smoke that I made that most magic of discoveries. There were books for children!" [4] Jacobs' *English Fairy Tales* became such a favorite that she insisted on taking it, rather than her teddy bear, to bed each night.

When the family moved to Portland, Beverly Cleary started school and became acquainted through the children's room of the Portland Library Association with the larger world of children's books. By fourth grade Mrs. Cleary described herself as an "omnivorous" reader, but she was also a reader with a problem. She wanted to read stories about ordinary American children who lived as she did and acted like the children she knew—sometimes naughty and only sometimes well behaved. "Book children lived in foreign countries, frequently they were orphans, they solved mysteries, or they had adventures that could never happen to any child I knew. Most of these children were uninterestingly well-behaved, and, if they were not, in the course of the story they learned to be better boys and girls. This was no fun at all." [5] Above all she wanted stories to be funny and stories that could really happen. Her inability to find stories of this type led her to read *Dandelion Cottage* by Carroll Watson Rankin (the story of four girls in a small town in Michigan, sometimes naughty, who were allowed to use a small house for a playhouse if they would dig all the dandelions out of the yard). She said, "I read it over and over, always secure in the knowledge that here was a good book that I was sure I was going to enjoy." [6]

Beverly Cleary began her writing career by reviewing *The Story of Dr. Dolittle* for the Journal Juniors, a club sponsored by the *Portland Journal* newspaper. As a reward she received a copy of the book itself—which was much treasured and enjoyed. An essay about wild animals won a $2.00 award in a contest offered by the local school store in Portland. As a school project Mrs. Cleary wrote a number of essays about her favorite characters from books—Peter Pan, Heidi, Downright Dencey, Joe March—and later wove them into a story, *A Journey Through Bookland*. The teacher for whom she wrote the essays told her that when she grew up she should write stories for children. "I made up my mind that this was exactly what I would do. Someday I would write books—the kind of books I wanted to read." [7]

The "someday" had to wait for Mrs. Cleary to graduate from the U.S. Grant High School in Portland, to receive a bachelor's degree from the University of California at Berkeley, and then a second bachelor's degree from the School of Librarianship at the University of Washington. With her interest in writing children's books Mrs. Cleary felt it was quite natural that she should also want to be a children's librarian. After graduation from the University of Washington she worked as a children's librarian at the Yakima (Washington) Public Library. In 1940 with her marriage to Clarence T. Cleary she moved to Oakland, California, and for the duration of World War II served as post librarian at the Oakland Army Hospital.

Writing about her experiences, Mrs. Cleary said:

> After the war, my husband and I bought a house in the Berkeley hills, and in the linen closet I found several reams of typing paper. "Now I'll have to write a book," I remarked to my husband.
> "Why don't you?" he asked.
> "Because we never have any sharp pencils," I answered.
> The next day he brought home a pencil sharpener and I realized that if I was ever going to write a book, this was the time to do it. I sat down at a table in our spare bedroom and began a story based on an incident that once amused me about two children who had to take their dog home on a streetcar during a heavy rain. This turned into a story about a boy who would be allowed to keep a stray dog if he could manage to take him home on a bus. When I finished that chapter I found I had ideas for another chapter and at the end of two months I had a whole book about Henry Huggins and his dog Ribsy.[8]

HENRY AND EILEEN—THE BOOKS FOR THE MIDDLE YEARS (AGES 8–12)

Someone has said that every good writer creates his world, peopled by his characters in the time and place in which he sets them. The world has not existed before the writer's creation and yet once created we cannot imagine a time when the author's world did not exist, though undiscovered.

In her Henry Huggins' stories Beverly Cleary has created a world within the field of children's literature. It is not, to be sure, a large and majestic world; neither is it a slight nor insignificant one. The world is bounded by childhood and humor and welcomes all children, usually in what we term the middle-years group, to enter and enjoy.

When the stories began in 1950 Henry was an eight-year-old boy, a third grader who lived with his most understanding parents in a house on Klickitat Street in an average small city in Oregon. (It must quickly be added that in the very first episode of *Henry Huggins* a most unusual dog, Ribsy, is added to the family household.) The time on the clock was probably set at "now." Through the years Henry and his friends—Beezus (who is both an understanding friend to Henry, and an older sister), Ramona (the four-year-old younger sister to Beezus (most exasperating, but a sister!), Scooter McCarthy (older boy in the neighborhood with a bicycle and a paper route of his own), and Byron Murphy (who was often busy building his robot)—have grown but at a slower chronological pace so that they are still within the 8- to 12-year-old-age group, of course, with the exception of Ribsy who seems always about the same. In this town, too, lives Ellen Tebbits, another eight-year-old, on Tillamook Street. But she and her friends—Austine Allen (her very best friend) and Otis Spofford (who really isn't a friend but a tease)—have not gotten around yet to meeting Henry and his friends, but maybe they will one day. Henry might be described as the typical American boy next door, but, of course, he is not average. Beverly Cleary has portrayed Henry as living, growing and experiencing the problems and pleasures of contemporary childhood. Adults, too, as parents, relatives, neighbors, teachers and bystanders, live in this world. Mrs. Cleary has presented a very human picture of the relationships between adults and children, often sympathetic and understanding, yet at times troubling and confusing. But on the whole, the children seem to be understanding and on occasions make use of one-upmanship. But above all this is a world of childhood—its language, its humor, its happenings, and its normal ups and downs.

As a librarian I learned at first hand the enthusiasm of children when they make the acquaintance of Henry and his friends. Henry is almost a catalyst. Give one book to a youngster and he will be back to finish the series. There are so many funny episodes to enjoy in the stories that one could start a list and keep right on going. My favorites have been: Henry's attempt to bring Ribsy home on a bus at the rush hour from *Henry Huggins;* Ribsy's bubble bath when he got lost—and found—in *Ribsy;* Ellen Tebbits' secret that she shared with Austine Allen, that they both wore woolen underwear, in *Ellen Tebbits;* Otis Spofford's nutritional help with the class's experimental rat in *Otis Spofford;* and Henry's come-uppance with Ramona when he got her favorite television fellow, Sheriff Bud, to announce on his TV program that he hoped a little girl called Ramona would stop pestering a boy called Henry Huggins in *Henry and the Clubhouse.*

All the episodes are funny, normal and believable. Almost any child in the age group of the stories could identify with the children in the situations.

While the stories together form a series, each book can stand upon its own merit. The characters and the setting tie them together. Beverly

Cleary maintains their individuality as books because of her ability as a writer. To each book she brings humor and an unusual ability to understand children. Her stories are told in everyday dialogue about everyday life as most children in the United States know it.

Louis Darling has done the illustrations for the Henry Huggins' and Ellen Tebbits' books. He is a fine illustrator who has caught the essence of Beverly Cleary's world and because of this his illustrations add greatly to the stories.

Beverly Cleary recalls that after *Henry Huggins* had been accepted for publication by William Morrow, she was rather concerned because at the time she had no children of her own and rather wondered what she had done. She wrote, "I went straight to the library and read up on small boys in Gesell and was enormously relieved to find that Henry Huggins was psychologically sound, and that I really did know quite a bit about boys." [9]

STORIES FOR TEENAGE GIRLS (AGES 11–16)

Jane Purdy of *Fifteen,* Barbara MacLane of *Sister of the Bride,* Jean Jarrett of *Jean and Johnny,* and Shelley Latham of *The Luckiest Girl* have much in common. They are all between the ages of 15 and 16, in junior high school, confronted with both the normal problems of growing up into womanhood, and meeting and adjusting to the special problems of contemporary society. Beverly Cleary's stories for this teen group are intended for girls. From my experience as a librarian I would think it is an unusual boy who would be attracted to any of these stories, due to the connotation of the titles or the pictures of girls on the book jackets. But for her intended reading audience Mrs. Cleary has brought to bear her craft of writing, her unusually sensitive ear for language, and her understanding and humor.

The heroines of the stories have problems — boy-girl relationships, family relationships, search for values, school problems, relationships with friends, and simply the problem of growing up. The problems seem of the kind that must be widely shared by many average American girls, yet this does not mean that because the problems are common to the group they are not perplexing and individualized for each teenager who shares them. The value of the books would seem related to the opportunity they provide for identification and the comforting knowledge that problems are shared and that others have been able to adjust and grow as a result of the similar experiences.

The backgrounds of the stories again follow the pattern of the familiar and known as in the stories Mrs. Cleary has written for children in the middle years. Oregon and California are the regional settings and yet there is no feeling of provincialism in any of Mrs. Cleary's stories, because they could just as well have happened to children in Florida or North Dakota.

Thinking back to my own time as a teenager, in the 1940s, I remembered how few books there were for this age group, or, of the ones available, how few were written with the honesty and style of these teenage books by Mrs. Cleary. The one book I can remember is Maureen Daly's *Seventeenth Summer*. I felt such a sense of identification with the book that I read and re-read it. Mrs. Cleary has brought to her stories this quality of interest in and about junior girls. In this group *Jean and Johnny* was selected for inclusion on the Notable List of Children's Books 1959, by the Children's Services Division of the American Library Association. *The Luckiest Girl,* I felt, was the best developed of Beverly Cleary's stories for this age group. The period of one school year for Shelley Latham, an only child, when she leaves her home in Oregon, her parents, her friends and her school to spend her junior year in southern California with a classmate of her mother's college days who has a large family, presents a realistic picture of the problems of adjustment to the large family of the Michies, especially of her relationship with Kate, the 13-year-old, at a difficult time of life. The problems of boy-girl relationships are presented in a normal way. And yet the ability of Shelley to recognize the difference between infatuation and love and to distinguish between love that is lasting and love that will pass, is movingly portrayed as a sense of growth for the heroine. The relationship between Shelley and her mother is very honestly presented. The story ends with the implication that it may be Shelley who will end the period of separation by coming to understand the reasons for her mother wanting her daughter to be happier, more popular and attractive than she was as a girl.

Beverly Cleary has dealt often with the only child—Henry Huggins, Ellen Tebbits, Shelley Latham, Otis Spofford—in a more consistent number of stories than I can, at the moment, remember being attempted by any other author. Speaking from my own background as an only child, I think she has treated the only child in a very natural way. She has pointed out, as in *The Luckiest Girl,* the problems of adjusting to other children and learning the give and take of relationships in the family. And yet being the only child, as with twin-ness in her pre-school stories, is a natural condition for many children and often their childhoods are normal and filled with many of the same frustrations, and happiness of children with brothers and sisters. The bond of childhood seems for Mrs. Cleary to unify children together in a way that children are not always unified with their parents who happen also to be adults.

Sister of the Bride has many of the qualities of Mrs. Cleary's books in the teenage group, yet it deals with a most contemporary happening, early marriage. However, Mrs. Cleary treats the problem in such a normal and common-sense way that it seems to be just another aspect of contemporary society that young people have adjusted to and accepted and that the problem is now one for adults and parents to accept and live with. In particular the difference in outlook of Rosemary, the nineteen-year-old college freshman and bride-to-be, as she planned her marriage was delightfully handled in the specific question of stainless steel vs. silver flatware for the table. In my own experience this seems to be a point of separation between generations—the rather simple, everyday things and how our point of view toward them reflects a fundamental attitude toward life and how it is to be lived. The compromise on the flatware reflected the coming together of modern Rosemary, her rather starry-eyed sister, Barbara, and her mother's generation. While the story is about Barbara MacLane and her problem of always being two years behind her sister Rosemary, the wedding itself seems to bring together adults, teenagers and young adults into much more of a relationship than any of the other stories in the group.

While the stories in this age group are well written, humorous and contemporary, they do not seem to have the distinction of the Henry and Ellen stories. Other books written by other authors in this field might be compared with Mrs. Cleary's books and the former found to be more significant. But the degree of significance may be more a judgment of the adult than the teenager for whom the stories were written.

Possibly because adolescence is not always the most pleasant time of growing up, in memory we tend to look back more frequently to childhood as a time of joy (though it might well have not been), the stories intended for this age group are difficult to evaluate. Contemporary problems blend with the maturing process to present each generation with new challenges and a new environment for adolescence. Therefore, it is often very difficult to identify with the contemporary adolescent. Because of uniqueness of this period of life for each generation which must face it, reading interests of the teenage group are often hardest to know, and when known the most difficult to meet with appropriate and meaningful (to the teenager himself) books. Beverly Cleary seems to have an ability to understand the teenage girl in junior high and to write in such a way about this period of life that her books are marked with honesty as well as style and readability. If the adolescent can identify with the characters in the stories then possibly this is the meaningful measure of "significance" as applied by the readers of the books.

STORIES FOR THE PRESCHOOL GROUP

My first acquaintance with the four-year-old twins Janet and Jimmy of Beverly Cleary's preschool picture book stories came through a request of a library patron. The woman was the mother of twins herself. When she asked me about "the hole book" my first thought was of Ruth Krauss' *A Hole Is To Dig*. But then the mother remembered that the book was written by Beverly Cleary.

A good picture book is usually the result of a balanced combination of story and illustration. Mary Stevens' lively and humorous illustrations match the sincerity and simplicity of Beverly Cleary's two stories in this picture book group, *The Real Hole*, and *Two Dog Biscuits*. Looking again at Mrs. Cleary's background it is interesting to note that she herself is the mother of twins. Twins are rather an interesting combination in the stories because they are simply used as characters without the stories being tied to the quality of twin-ness. In the stories Janet tends to be the pretender and Jimmy, the realist. In *The Real Hole* Jimmy starts out to dig the biggest hole in the world but then can't quite decide what to do with it. Janet has many pretend solutions but Father comes along with the real grown-up solution for the real grown-up hole: to plant a spruce tree in the hole so that the family at Christmas can have an indoor and out-door tree! *Two Dog Biscuits* presents the twins with another problem when they set out in search of *the* dog worthy of their two dog biscuits. The surprise ending provides a solution more likely to be thought about by a child rather than an adult, cats eat dog biscuits, too!

While Beverly Cleary has written only two books for this age group and in both the plots are rather slight, yet the humor in the stories, the ability of the author to catch the conversation of the children, and Mary Stevens' illustrations result in two delightful picture books.

AND A BOOK FOR THE YOUNGEST

Hullabaloo ABC is the only Cleary book not published by William Morrow. The press is Parnassus, in Berkeley, California. As the title implies, the book is about the ABCs, with appropriate farm yard noises for each letter in the alphabet—"Aha" for the letter "A"; "Cock-a-doodle doo" for "C"; and "Whoa" for "W." Earl Thollander illustrated the book with big pictures that children easily identify with the farm noises.

Again, Mrs. Cleary has set her book in the background of the familiar. This book might be useful for a Head Start group since it gives a realistic picture of one aspect of American life—the farm, and provides an opportunity for the children to participate in making the appropriate "noises."

STORIES IN OTHER DIRECTIONS

Two books written since 1960 seem to stand apart from the mainstream of Beverly Cleary's earlier books. Both books would be enjoyed by children in the 8 to 12 age group, but possibly one would be more enjoyed by girls than boys.

Emily's Runaway Imagination must surely be autobiographical fiction since the story is laid in a small town in rural Oregon during the 1920s, which corresponds to Beverly Cleary's time and place of childhood. Yet the period of the book lends color without distracting from the plot or the characters. Emily Bartlett is a character in her own right and not simply a reflection of Beverly Cleary. As in all the earlier books, Beverly Cleary tells about the adventures of Emily in a humorous and honest way. Many aspects of life are touched upon but the major episode of the story is getting a town library started. With the aid of Emily's imagination, Mother's common sense, the state library in Eugene, donations and a silver tea, and the generosity of the town's only Chinese, Mr. Fong Quock, Pitchfork, Oregon, gets a library—and Emily gets to read *Black Beauty*.

This is one of the most delightful of Beverly Cleary's stories both because of the charm of the story and the author's ability to convey the importance of books and reading as felt by Emily herself.

The Mouse and the Motorcycle is the most recent, published in 1965, of Beverly Cleary's books. It has been described as modern fantasy. The story is quite straightforward and might have happened to any average American boy. Of course, like Keith of the story he would have to have a family that decided to take a car trip across the country and then stop at the Mountain View Inn, be booked into room 215, and happen to have a liking for miniature toys, especially a motorcycle, since the pretend sound (Pb-pb-b-b-b) of the cycle spoke to Ralph of ". . . the highways and speed of distance and dangers and whiskers blown back by the wind." [18] This had to be true since Ralph was the mouse on the motorcycle. Ralph and Keith meet and neither was ". . . surprised that each could understand the other. Two creatures who share a love for a motorcycle naturally spoke the same language." [11] The motorcycle came to life for Ralph because Keith told him that ". . . cars don't go unless you make a noise like Pb-pb-b-b-b." [12] The adventures of Keith and Ralph with the mice and human boarders at the Mountain View Inn are told in the usual artful, humorous and understanding style of Beverly Cleary.

To look at some of the reviews:

Charlotte Jackson in *Atlantic Monthly*

Every page of this modern fantasy is filled with the sort of humorous episode that boys and girls enjoy, making it one of those books that is swapped back and forth until it is worn out.[13]

Ethel L. Heins in *Horn Book Magazine*

Amusing, realistic details worked into an ingenious pattern lend conviction to Beverly Cleary's first work of fantasy. . . . An honest unpretentious book, briskly matter-of-fact in style but imaginative in plot.[14]

Polly Burroughs in *New York Times Book Review*

Logical put inside a frame of the illogical is a prerequisite of fantasy. Unfortunately Beverly Cleary . . . fails to establish the difference in her new book . . . too clever for credibility.[15]

Zena Bailey Sutherland in *Bulletin of the Center for Children's Books*

. . . On second thought why be surprised that Beverly Cleary has done a delightful fanciful story? What other kind of fantasy would she write? Illustrations are like the story — combination of prim detail and an incongruous or wildly imaginative situation. . . . Human-to-human dialogue is good, too.[16]

The final evaluation of the book, of course, will come as with other Beverly Cleary books, from the children themselves. Unfortunately there aren't too many library mice of Ralph's caliber around to sink their teeth into this story — but possibly they would be of the strain that would rather ride the motorcycle than read about it!

It is evident that Beverly Cleary has been more read than written about. An effort to locate material about Mrs. Cleary and her books turns up only short factual biographical sketches, two acceptance letters written when Mrs. Cleary accepted the Young Readers' Choice Award of the Pacific Northwest Library Association, and brief paragraphs in books dealing with the general subject of children's literature.

Since 1950 when *Henry Huggins* was published by William Morrow, Mrs. Cleary has written at least one book a year, adding up to a total of 18, all listed in the current year of *Books in Print*. In the *Children's Catalog*, 1961 edition and current supplements, one finds all but three titles (*The Real Hole, Hullabaloo ABC*, and *Two Dog Biscuits*) listed. In addition all four of Mrs. Cleary's teenage stories are listed both in *Standard Catalog for High School Libraries*, 1962 edition and current supplements, and *Junior High School Library Catalog,* 1965. The Center for Children's Books at the University of Chicago has recommended all but two of Mrs. Cleary's books (*Henry and Beezus, Beezus and Ramona*).[17] Yet in looking at the annual awards given for excellence in the field of children's literature few, if any, of Beverly Cleary's books have been honored. None of her books has won a Newbery Medal nor made the list of runner-ups. Only one of her books has been included on the annual list of Notable Children's Books of the Children's Services Division of the American Library Association, *Jean and Johnny,* 1959.

It is interesting to note, too, that the awards Mrs. Cleary has won for her books have come upon the vote of children themselves. In 1958 Mrs. Cleary won the Dorothy Canfield Fisher Children's Book Award for *Fifteen.* The award is sponsored by the Vermont Congress of Parents and Teachers and the Free Library Commission of Vermont. From a list of 30 books by American authors, Vermont school children in grades 4–8 vote for their favorite book.[18] In 1957 Mrs. Cleary was awarded the Young Readers' Choice Award of the Pacific Northwest Library Association for *Henry and Ribsy;* and again in 1960, for *Henry and the Paper-route.* From a list of 15–20 titles published three years earlier school children in grades 4–8 from Washington, Oregon, Montana, Idaho and British Columbia vote upon their favorite book.[19] Mrs. Cleary ended her acceptance speech for the 1957 PNLA Award by noting:

> The nicest letters that I receive from children are those that include some small incident of such great importance that the child wants to share it. . . . These letters, so charming to read, are always reassuring to me because they reveal that children feel that I understand. Until now they have been one of the most satisfying rewards of writing. Now the Young Readers' Choice Award which comes directly from the vote of children themselves is the best reward of all.[20]

I must say that I have given considerable thought on the one hand, to the lack of interest in the craft of Beverly Cleary as reflected in printed evaluations, summaries or criticisms, and on the other, to the lack of recognition of her works by significant awards in the field of children's books.

From personal experience in working with children in a public library, I know that the Henry Huggins and Ellen Tebbits stories are contemporary favorites of children in the middle-year group. The physical quality and constant need for replacement told an eloquent story of usage without reference to circulation records. Thinking back on it, the children that most often requested the Cleary books resembled Henry, Ellen, Otis and Beezus of the stories themselves. The children came wanting the books because friends or classmates had told them about the "funny" stories.

In my judgment the Henry Huggins books represent Beverly Cleary's unique contribution to the world of children's literature. Beverly Cleary is a versatile and creative writer at all age levels she has attempted: stories for boys and girls in the age group 8–12; stories for teenage girls; picture books for preschool children; and probably many adults at the age level from parent to grandparent. She has also been successful in various forms of writing: contemporary humor, picture books, autobiographical fiction, and modern fantasy.

As librarians we use standards of quality to judge books of value for the collection. While it is not possible for any one writer to constantly reach all standards with each book yet there is a consistent effort evident in Beverly Cleary's work. The following evidence can be cited: (1) she is an author who always writes with integrity and respect for her readers, (2) her characters and plots are believable and lively — though sometimes the plots seem slight in holding together a series of episodes or happenings, (3) she has accuracy and authenticity of background or setting, (4) she has a special style of writing — and it might be added she has an ear for the natural vocabulary of her reader, and (5) she attempts to give the reader something to wonder and think about — as well as a good story to enjoy and laugh about.

Simplicity of style and manner is almost deceptive in Beverly Cleary's stories. She seems to be a natural storyteller with an ear for the language of the contemporary child and an intuitive understanding of the unique personality of the child and his world. While Mrs. Cleary must have called upon many places, people and incidents from her own experience, her stories are not remembrances of things past. Beverly Cleary's stories are about the contemporary, average American child or teenager and most often the time of the story is today. The adults — parents, neighbors, teachers — seem average too. The joys and sadness, the successes and failures, the frustrations, the problems in relationships seem to be the ones that are expected in childhood and adolescence. But there is a need in children's literature for all sides of childhood to be presented. Mrs. Cleary may be called the Boswell of the average child.

REFERENCES

1. Beverly Cleary, "Writing Books About Henry Huggins," *Top of the News*, Vol. 24, December 1957, p. 9.
2. *Ibid.*, p. 9.

3. *Ibid.*, p. 7.
4. *Ibid.*, p. 7.
5. *Ibid.*, p. 8.
6. *Ibid.*, p. 9.
7. *Ibid.*, p. 9.
8. *Ibid.*, p. 10.
9. *Ibid.*, p. 10.
10. Beverly Cleary, *The Mouse and the Motorcycle*, Morrow, 1965, p. 21.
11. *Ibid.*, pp. 38–39.
12. *Ibid.*, p. 44.
13. *Atlantic Monthly*, Vol. 216, December 1965, p. 156.
14. *Horn Book Magazine*, Vol. 41, December 1965, p. 628.
15. *New York Times Book Review*, December 26, 1965, p. 18.
16. *Bulletin of the Center for Children's Books*, University of Chicago, Vol. 19, December 1965, p. 60.
17. *Good Books For Children*, Editor, Mary K. Eakin. 2nd edition, 1962, University of Chicago Press, and Annual lists of recommended books contained in the December issues (1962–1965) of the *Bulletin of the Center for Children's Books*, University of Chicago.
18. *Children's Books, Awards and Prizes*, 1965–1966. The Children's Book Council, New York, p. 3.
19. *Ibid.*, p. 9.
20. Beverly Cleary, "Writing Books About Henry Huggins," *Top of the News*, Vol. 24, December 1957, p. 11.

BIBLIOGRAPHY

CLEARY, BEVERLY, "The 1960 Readers' Choice Award," *PNLA Quarterly*, Vol. 25, April 1961, pp. 175–176.
——. "Writing Books About Henry Huggins," *Top of the News*, Vol. 24, December 1957, pp. 7–11.
GELLER, EVELYN, "WLB: Beverly Cleary," *Wilson Library Bulletin*, Vol. 36, October 1961, p. 179.
More Junior Authors. H. W. Wilson, New York, 1963.

EDITORS' NOTE

Beverly Cleary's latest book, *Ramona the Pest* (Morrow, Junior Books), is a very funny story in which adult-child relationships are handled humorously and perceptively. Four different awards have been presented to the author for this book, attesting to its wide appeal: the 1970 Georgia Children's Book Award (established in 1969—the winner is chosen annually by Georgia school children, voting for their favorite title from a list of twenty books written by authors-in-residence in the United States and published during the five years preceding the award year); the 1971 Nene Award (given annually since 1964 to a fiction title for grades 4–8, nominated and voted upon by children of Hawaii), an award which Mrs. Cleary also received in 1969 for *The Mouse and the Motorcycle* (Morrow,

Junior Books); the 1971 Sequoyah Children's Book Award (given annually since 1959 by the Oklahoma Library Association, Oklahoma Congress of Parents and Teachers—children in grades 4–9 vote for the best book from a master list); and the 1971 Pacific Northwest Library Association Young Readers' Choice Award (given annually since 1940 by the Pacific Northwest Library Association; selection is from a list of 15 titles published three years earlier and voted upon by children of Washington, Oregon, Montana, Idaho and British Columbia, in grades 4–8). Mrs. Cleary received this award on two previous occasions: in 1957, for *Henry and Ribsy,* and in 1960, for *Henry and the Paper Route.*

In 1968, *The Mouse and the Motorcycle* was awarded the William Allen White Children's Book Award (given annually since 1953 by the William Allen White Memorial Library at Kansas State Teachers College, it is chosen from a list of books compiled by specialists and submitted to Kansas school children in grades 4–8).

Elizabeth Coatsworth: Perceptive Impressionist *

POET AND STORYTELLER, Elizabeth Coatsworth is one of the major writers of American literature for children. In her perceptive descriptions of life in early America and life in other countries she has presented realistic characters who exhibit integrity, courage, independence, and compassion. Elizabeth Coatsworth has also won international recognition. Winner of the 1931 Newbery Medal for *The Cat Who Went to Heaven,* she was the American candidate for the Hans Christian Andersen Medal in 1968, and was one of the runner-ups for this award. *The Cat Who Went to Heaven* is listed by *Horn Book* as one of the thirty children's books every adult should know. Her list of books recommended in the *Children's Catalog* is probably longer than that of any other writer. Several of her books have been translated into other languages. For over forty years, Elizabeth Coatsworth has been writing exciting and imaginative stories and poems. She has written that, "Any book should in some way sharpen the reader's appetite for living, whether the reader be seven or seventy." [1] A seeing eye, keen memory, a pen skilled in the art of writing, and an understanding heart have combined to create a body of literature for children that does indeed increase the appetite for living.

To know an author and his works we can read what others have said and what he has written about his work and life. If we are fortunate we can talk with the author; we may see a film or listen to a tape. Most im-

* By Doris Young Kuhn. From *Elementary English* 46 (December 1969), 991–1007. Copyright © 1969 by the National Council of Teachers of English. Reprinted by permission of the publisher and Doris Young Kuhn. This article was based on an interview with Miss Coatsworth by Dr. Kuhn during the summer of 1968.

portant, we can read his works, re-read and compare them, placing his prose and poetry in the total body of literature. In this article, I would like to describe a meeting with Elizabeth Coatsworth at Chimney Farm in Maine before discussing her work.[2]

MEETING THE AUTHOR

A stately figure stood near an arching, gnarled apple tree by the red farmhouse set on a rolling meadow. The graceful black muumuu was edged with white, just as the gingerbread trim on the red house was lacy white. A rhythmic sweep of green grass led the eye to the curve of Damariscotta Lake. The central figure in this *rouge et noir* composition was Elizabeth Coatsworth, extending both hands in welcome to Chimney Farm. Wearing the Hawaiian tutu (grandmother) muumuu at a farm in Maine symbolized her closeness to the wider world she had travelled before the comfortable time of jets, Hilton hotels, and American Express cards. Like events around her, the apple tree twisted and turned, but she stood firm, resolute, belonging to the soil, the winds, the seasons. The friendly handclasp expressed the openness of one who moves toward new people and new experience with zest and curiosity. Although her feet no longer roam the world, her memory for sharp images enables her to analyze and interpret rich experiences of past and present.

While she prepared tea, I recalled lines of her poetry:

> *Strong is the wind,*
> *it wrestles with the dwelling,*
> *it pushes and pants*
> *but the house stands,*
> *the house still stands.*[3]

> *Stones have a dull peace of their own,*
> *I sometimes wish I were a stone,*
> *What helps to make them look secure*
> *is being rounded, to be sure.*
> *Young stones have edges like a thorn,*
> *but old stones are serene and worn.*[4]

The setting seemed to symbolize Miss Coatsworth's prose and poetry. The farm is on a narrow neck of land—reaching out, just as such books as *Jon the Unlucky, The Princess and the Lion,* and *The Place* take the reader to other lands. "I like to live near the edge," she said. However, Chimney Farm is rooted to the past, just as her historical fiction of

Maine, Virginia, and Oklahoma makes life in the past real for modern children. Straight line plots rise like the spruce tree from a sturdy base of reality. In her poetry is the delicacy of the branches, the peace of the water. The lake at last flows to the sea, just as Coatsworth's works express unity through such universal qualities as strength and joy in life and nature.

As a chipmunk scuttled by, Miss Coatsworth remarked, "They vacuum food all day." The humor in her books, like the chipmunk, darts in and out; the reader has to have sharp eyes to catch it.

Love of animals was evident as she talked of feeding raccoons, squirrels, and birds. She no longer has cats but remarked, "Cats seem to fit so many scenes." Cats have certainly played an important part in her prose and poetry. *The Cat and the Captain,* her first book, published in 1927, is the most humorous. The cat who dominated the captain and won the housekeeper's acceptance by cleverly outwitting a robber, is precisely drawn as a sly trickster with human joy, affection, and pride. Loyalty of a cat is evident in the Newbery Award story, *The Cat Who Went to Heaven.* This traditional tale based on the life of the Buddha portrays a courage *to be* that has meaning for today as well as 1930 when it was written. One of her finest poems is "On a Night of Snow," a sonnet about a cat, symbol of mystery. On one level, a dialogue between a mistress who wants the cat to stay by the fire and a cat who wants out, this poem offers other meanings to explore. The questing spirit goes forth despite the image of discomfort.

When our conversation turned to writing, Miss Coatsworth's responses revealed the directness and honesty one senses in all her work. She said she finds more pleasure in writing poetry than in writing prose. "Poems form, or jell; they are quickly over. I enjoy the moment." We paused, and I sensed the joy in the surge of creativity. An indication of this feeling was presented in *The Hand of Apollo* when she wrote of the emotion experienced by a Greek boy as he composed a song:

> He had been standing in the ecstasy of poetic creation, but as he finished his chant, already the vision of what he had meant to say was fading, leaving only his actual words, dull as beach pebbles when the tide goes out. . . . Now, at last, the great act of creation had made him whole, knowing joy as well as sorrow, and a kinship to the living as well as to the dead.[5]

Following the comment that it seemed she used distinctive metaphor in poetry, yet little in her prose, Miss Coatsworth explained, "I try to write prose simply, to keep a clean storyline and to move ahead without much description. I've always been interested in the simple plot line. In writing *Boy With a Parrot,* for example, I tried to include too much history and too many legends. Now that I'm older I write more simply. I'm an impressionist. One has a choice of simplifying or going deeper; I chose to simplify."

In response to a question about the authenticity and detail of her historical fiction and the books about many parts of the world, Miss Coatsworth said she did not keep a journal as she travelled; it was all in the memory. Her own capacity for memory is revealed in *Alice-All-by-Herself.* When questioned about being lost, Alice said she didn't notice much about it:

> But if Alice forgot some things that didn't interest her, she remembered the things that did harder than most people ever remember anything, and that was perhaps what gave her a certain look in her eyes that made strangers look at her twice. And after that, Alice never went out into falling snow without thinking of the sheep and hearing a faint bleating on the wind.[6]

In writing *Bess and the Sphinx,* she recalled incidents from her first trip to Egypt when she was very young. "These memories are more vivid than those of my trip when I was in my twenties." She reads widely, but does not take notes. Historical details were gathered as she and her husband, Henry Beston, visited antique shops, talked with people, and lived in an 18th century house in Hingham, Massachusetts. "I paint a picture, recalling details from many sources. What I don't know, I leave out. Long spaces may be left because I don't try to guess. There was much I didn't know in *Door to the North.* I visited Denmark and became excited when I learned that the first Dane to return to Greenland began to search for the people who once lived there. He, and others, believed that a habitable section might exist within the ice cap. There was emotion left over that I couldn't get into *Door to the North,* so *Jon (Jon the Unlucky)* was written."

When questioned about her techniques for keeping in touch with children, Mrs. Beston replied, "I have eight grandchildren, but you can't write for particular children. I write to please myself. I have to enjoy the story first. It must excite me. Subjects are like sauce pans; you have to find the handle to use one. Characters emerge. I no longer write descriptions of the characters, where born and so forth. Once you create a character, once he stands on his own two feet he takes over and directs the story. . . . I have the grandchildren, but a writer is an amalgam of all ages. I recall vividly what it is to be twenty-five or five. You know because you were."

Asked about letters from children, she replied, with brown eyes snapping, "Pooh! I can see the blackboard behind them. I can see the teacher directing. The same pattern comes from Mississippi and Oklahoma. (How old were you when you started to write? How old are you now? How do you get your ideas?) It is not the child writing. When he says, 'I was assigned to write to you,' or when twelve write the same letter, it is an exercise. I enjoy *genuine* comments, especially about a book the teacher was reading aloud to the class. It takes so much time to answer; when the letters are mere exercises I dislike giving the time. But I do enjoy a correspondence with a girl in Honolulu and a remarkable group of children in a one-room school in Kansas."

The visit concluded with a tour of the house, a comfortable blending of the old, a hearth in the kitchen, a wood stove in the parlor, and the new, central heating. Miss Coatsworth writes in her four poster bed. A large Buddha and a Kashmir wall hanging remind one of her travels in Asia. Letters to be answered were on the mantel, but only a few were there; she meticulously writes many each day. Mementoes of friends and places were in all the rooms — memorabilia of a rich life.

When her husband returned from a drive there was a different aura. Despite his exasperation with illness, he brought a sense of the sea and fields, the winging of birds and joy in all of nature. His own writings are classics. The room brightened with love borne of sharing and respect for the talent of each. Late afternoon light rested on a bowl of flowers of brilliant orange, pink, and purple. "A Spanish arrangement," she said, and I remembered the lines:

> *The quiet and domestic hour,*
> *Sun shining on a flower-filled vase,*
> *the household stir, the moving pen,*
> *such things I praise.*[7]

Work had its place, but she was always wife, neighbor, mother of two daughters. In "Advice to Daughters," she had written that they "Should learn soon to hear the sea / That sounds in the sea shell. . . . Learn soon to see the sky / In any puddle's glass." The poet continues, however, by advising her daughters:

> *Learn to take true content*
> *In talk and flower and seasons,*
> *In following a swift thought,*
> *Or disentangling reasons.*

But never think shell, sea.
Nor call the puddle, sky.
And know content is little
To measure rapture by.[8]

As she walked with me to the car she continued to talk of her work. "This is where I watched the fox and dog. I wrote *The Fox Friend* in half an hour, just as it happened — fox chased dog, dog chased fox." Swallows swooped past the barn toward the bell on top of the house, stirring ripples of golden light. Tall she stood — straight as the pole supporting the Martin house. Here, one was acutely aware of the contrasts she portrays in her writing, the light and darkness, past and present. "Swift Things Are Beautiful" is probably her best known poem, and expresses well these contrasts. Joyously engaged in life, this vigorous woman is keenly aware of the depth of its darkness.

To the Contrasting Dark

Since any grave's too steep, too steep
For any foot to climb,
An absolute like space itself,
An ultimate like time,
And universal as the womb,
Immediate as a touch
I think the wise man will rejoice
And not grieve overmuch.

For grief must go as flows the wind
Or rivers to the sea,
They pass forever across life
Into eternity,
But joy by nature is a flower,
A quick, a burning spark
Owing its moment's gaiety
To the contrasting dark.[9]

On a hillside a few stones marked the graves of those who once lived on this land. In April, 1968, Henry Beston died and was buried in this graveyard at the top of the fields. Elizabeth Coatsworth Beston wrote this news, but her letter did not include a line of sorrow or self-pity. Quickly she moved on to describe the busy summer with her family. Despite personal concerns or world changes, this artist with words continues to create scenes that evoke all the senses. Her stories about warm, human characters convey the joy of nature against the contrasting dark.

READING ABOUT THE AUTHOR

From biographies about Elizabeth Coatsworth we can learn that she was born in Buffalo in 1893. By the age of twelve she had travelled with the family to California, Europe, and Egypt. Upon completion of the Bachelor's degree at Vassar and a Master of Arts at Columbia University in 1916, she and her sister travelled in the Orient. These are but the dry factual bones of an exciting life. Her autobiography of a part of childhood, *Bess and the Sphinx,* gives a vivid picture of a little girl who was already recording impressions of people and places that would be recalled years later.

The first publications were volumes of adult poetry, *Fox Footprints, Atlas and Beyond,* and *Compass Rose.* Stories appeared in *Dial* and *Atlantic Monthly.* In 1927, her first book for children, *The Cat and the Captain,* was written as a result of a challenge from Louise Seaman Bechtel. The second book for children, *The Cat Who Went to Heaven,* received the Newbery Medal in 1931. Since that time, Miss Coatsworth has written over ninety books. Settings include Canada, Egypt, Guatemala, Japan, France, Greenland and the West Indies, as well as many regions of the United States.

In *Bess and the Sphinx,* a picture clear as an Ektachrome transparency is created; the reader senses the inner excitement of a child moving into new experience. Miss Coatsworth's ability to convey movement and breathless action is illustrated in the account of the donkey ride:

Before she knew it, Bess was near the lead, with only Bob ahead. And her donkey was bigger than Bob's, and Bess was smaller than Bob, for after all she was younger. And her donkey boy was running like the wind and shouting, and Bess's donkey was galloping wildly, and Bob was looking over his shoulder and kicking his heels into his donkey to make it go faster. But it was no use. Ali really *had* saved the best donkey for Bess. And with all the grownups pounding along behind, still laughing and shouting, Bess overtook Bob and rode past him. She was the head of the whole procession, and she was wearing her new scarlet jacket with the patent leather belt, her pride and joy. Her heart was beating fast and her cheeks were red with excitement as she galloped right into Egypt. It was bright green with a red road, and it had a woman in black chasing two goats out

of Bess's way and laughing too. There was a distant temple in it
and a blue sky, heavy and bright, and it was all hers.[10]

After the prose, the poem—the episode ends with an ignominious
fall, but the poem reiterates the joy:

To Ride into Egypt

> *To ride into Egypt*
> *On a donkey,*
> *To ride into magic,*
> *To ride into another world,*
> *To the music of little galloping hoofs*
> *While the blue beads shine,*
> *And the flowers loosen from the bridle,*
> *And the donkey boy's running feet send up*
> *Butterflies of dust from the road—*
> *Oh, to ride into Egypt*
> *In a scarlet jacket*
> *Is to ride straight into happiness*
> *And to be a part of it forever.*[11]

The contrasts and similarities of these passages reveal her characteristic
style of prose and poetry. In the poetry we find metaphor and deeper
emotion. Miss Coatsworth notes that with this journey it seemed her
inner life began. Stories, travel, and dreams were woven into her prose
and poetry.

Comments by the Critics

The critics in children's literature have consistently praised the work
of Elizabeth Coatsworth. A reviewer called *The Cat Who Went to
Heaven* "a coherent and beautiful story of the life and legends of Buddha,
done in a manner the child of Western culture can feel and understand.
Her story adds richness to his mental background, bright food for his
imagination, stuff for his dreams." [12] This critic further noted that the
books by Coatsworth were written for fun. "They strike a note of grace,
delicacy, restraint, humor. A book written for fun has a good chance of
being read for fun, too." [13] There is no published record of the acceptance
speech for the award, but Louise Seaman Bechtel wrote about the work
of this author:

Elizabeth Coatsworth's special contribution to children's books
of our times lies in the never-failing, superior intelligence of her

style, and next in her ever-present sense of the poetry of the situation in hand, whether it is expressed in verse or prose, and finally in her choice of interesting subject matter, a worthy challenge to the imaginative reader, young or old.[14]

When *The Enchanted, An Incredible Tale,* was published in 1951, Anne Carroll Moore wrote, "There is an ineradicable magic that defies criticism and analysis and it is this rare quality that gives to *The Enchanted* an atmosphere of pure joy in living at sixteen or at five times sixteen."[15]

Cornelia Meigs' analysis of *Alice-All-By-Herself* emphasized the unity of place and atmosphere and the "moments of that discerning revelation of the small truths of observation which made us catch our breath in wonder that eyes and words can work together to convey so much."[16] Meigs considered the book as one of the few that "do not merely set a scene before us, but which plunge us, our very selves, within the scene so that we are a part of it, actively living it as it goes from page to page."[17]

Reviews in the *Bulletin of the Center for Children's Books* have given praise and identified some flaws. Writing of *Ronnie and the Chief's Son,* the reviewer said, "The author writes beautifully, creating imagery and moods, but the story has little pace despite the drama of the situation."[18] Referring to *Jon the Unlucky,* the critic reported that it was "An interesting story, tightly constructed and gracefully written; the ending seems anticlimactic, since the dramatic unveiling of a sort of Shangrila is vitiated by a dying fall in the tempo of the book."[19] In this journal, *The Sparrow Bush* was considered "A charming book of poetry. . . . The writing is lucid, springy, gay, and affectionate."[20] *The Place* was praised for several qualities of good writing: "The story is constructed deftly, a natural series of incidents leading to the denouement with a gradual heightening of tension. The children are believable and the relationships among them sympathetic; the setting is presented as interesting rather than quaint."[21]

The distinctive qualities of Coatsworth's poetry were noted by the critic for the *New York Herald Tribune* when *Country Poems* was published:

Miss Coatsworth sings of many things, but the essentials of her poetry are that it does sing, and that it manages to sustain throughout its song, without monotony, this note of wonder and delight in the common things of earth and the common experience of human kind.[22]

The analysis of *Troll Weather* sums up the opinions of reviewers over the years:

> Only a few writers are able to tell a story in a style that is warm and beautiful and at the same time simple enough for children who have just learned to read for themselves. Elizabeth Coatsworth is one of the most skillful. Perhaps the writing of many books for all ages has taught her to write always clearly, using the best words for each situation. But I think her genius is as much instinct as skill: she feels each book as a whole; each has its own integrity. This new book has both reality and flavor.[23]

Comments by the Author

Elizabeth Coatsworth has written little about her own work. In the essay, "Upon Writing for Children," she described her approach to writing by telling how the book *Here I Stay* was developed. This story for older readers began with an account she had read of the emigration from Maine to the rich lands of Ohio. The settlers had auctioned off the sick and the old before they left. This dramatic incident was the beginning of the book. Miss Coatsworth said:

> The writer has come upon something in life which has amused or delighted or surprised him. "Look!" he exclaims; and, if he is lucky, the children look. . . .
> Thus out of the farm lands, out of my husband's interests, out of the people and things about us, out of the accounts I read and the things that I imagine, I put the mosaic together, creating a character whom I respected. I saw her world with whatever tenderness and poetry I had at my command, catching a little of life for the time being into a book, as one fills for a moment the palms of one's hands with water from the stream which endlessly flows onward and out of sight.[24]

When she wrote about the development of *The Cat Who Went to Heaven*, Coatsworth said she recalled carvings at a temple in Java. Other memories and incidents contributed:

> I was to read translations of the rebirths and string them together on the thread of a Japanese legend which we had been told in a Kyoto temple one day in the enchanted October of 1916. Later, Tom Handforth sent me a print, which, like the temple scroll,

showed a cat coming to mourn the death of Buddha. It was unusual to see a cat among the other animals. These things lay, with a thousand other impressions, long in my mind, and happened to be the ones I could use.[25]

Miss Coatsworth identified a major criterion for children's books:

Vulgarity and cruelty are the only two things of which I can think that are unsuitable in books for children. I don't mean that stories should always be happy or that they should avoid poverty, sickness, and death, if these are necessary for the carrying on of the plot, but they should avoid sadism or lingering over the details. They should avoid the suggestion of dark things left to stir uneasily in the imagination.[26]

The key to her success may lie in the belief that, "an author should write for children about the things which are of sharpest interest to his own imagination."[27]

Although she did not keep a journal on her many travels, Miss Coatsworth did keep notebooks with anecdotes, descriptions, clippings and poems. Lined tablets and spiral bound theme books kept from 1941 to 1944 are in the library at the University of Maine. Often the note begins as though another person is speaking: "Yes that boathouse at Gladys Fen — and the rapids. Johnny Oye they're called after an Indian who was drowned there." Quotations and stories reflect language patterns and express superstitions. She quotes Annie, speaking of a dull blade, "A witch could ride that knife to London and never cut herself." Descriptions of weather, as "sunshine, turning paler and paler and more ghostly, a corpse day, cold, clammy, lifeless, the Camdens seemed dead heaps on the horizon." Mosquitoes "seem pale debutantes — we see few if any of those black-browed matrons, persistent and heavy with blood, of other years." A moment is transcribed, "Once we passed a roadside stand with a woman in apron and dust cap and sweater waiting on a motorist by the Rembrandtesque light of an oil lamp. I felt the liberation of night and motion and the moon. . . ." There are few poems in the note-books, occasionally we can see the poet at work as she struggles with ideas and feelings and ponderings about a boulder being changed by a river or a kettle reposing on a stove. The notebooks do not describe the tragedies of world events in those years; they are more like files or pages of exercises. In 1963 she wrote that she had forgotten the University had these notebooks; for she had "a filing system like a bluejay's." But impressions, keen observations of people, language, and nature were and are being filed in that amazing mind, to be brought to the page in the creative process.

READING AND STUDYING THE LITERATURE

Reading about an author and his works can only serve to illuminate the reading and understanding of the prose and poetry he has created. Elizabeth Coatsworth's books include historical fiction and stories of other lands. Few deal with the modern city or suburban life although *The Noble Doll* is set in a city in Mexico. Action and suspense are strong elements in most of her books, yet there are quiet stories with only a slight thread of mystery. Others are episodes given continuity through the observations of a child character. One book, *The Children Come Running,* was based upon rhymes and stories from dozens of UNICEF Christmas cards, and sold over 100,000 copies for UNICEF. A reading text, *Runaway Home,* gave children a continuous story instead of the short stories and excerpts found in the typical basal reader.

The Sally stories are perhaps the best known of Miss Coatsworth's historical fiction. *Away Goes Sally* tells about the moving of a Massachusetts house to Maine by pulling it on sled runners. In *Five Bushel Farm,* Sally's friendship with the Indians makes it possible to prevent them from seizing the farm land in return for a promise of hunting rights and five bushels of corn meal each year. Next, the intrepid Sally aids in saving a French boy whose father was killed in the French Revolution. The story of the cruise of *The Fair American* provides excitement as well as accurate knowledge of this period. The ship takes Sally and her family on another adventure in the next book, *The White Horse.* What could be more exciting than to be captured by Barbary pirates, chased by a crowd in an African city, and sold as a slave who becomes involved in the tensions between two wives of a sultan? But Sally remains calm when the Sultan threatens to kill her uncle and displays courage when she saves the pet lion of the Black Lallah who was the enemy of her own mistress.

Miss Coatsworth has written other historical fiction for children. Many of her fine books are overlooked in the rush of current publications. Unfortunately, the illustrations in many of her books do not complement the writing. If some of these well written books could be re-issued, a new audience may find rich treasure. Now, these older books rest in dark covers, but the worn pages give evidence of many readers. *Door to the North,* for example, was published in 1950 as part of a series. The format of the book may discourage modern readers. This is a saga of fourteenth century America, a story of explorers who followed the trail of a lost colony in Greenland. Runes on a stone found in Minnesota set scholars on a mystery trail, and Coatsworth utilized theory and fact to create an exciting story. How did a stone marked 1362 get to Minnesota? Why were Norwegians and Swedes sharing an expedition? How did the Mandan Indians originate? Older readers will enjoy Coatsworth's explanation through the fictional account of the boy who joined the group to vindicate his father's courage. *Sword of the Wilderness* opens with a scene in a cabin where the settlers of 1689 live in fear of unfriendly Indians. The boy, Seth, is taken captive, runs the gauntlet, faces starvation, and learns of Indian ways and values. In a dramatic scene he races to the priest who is able to save another colonist from being burned at the stake. Conflicting cultural values are presented, so that children will become aware of the Indians as humans caught in a struggle for land.

Mystery surrounds *Thief Island* where the Littles settle after being dispossessed of their Maine village home. Was there a ghost on the island? How could the children survive a terrible storm? Even greater suspense is developed in *The House of the Swan,* a story set in a French village where a mysterious white apparition comes to a cavehouse occupied by two children. Explorations of secret tunnels and sinister characters provide breathtaking moments. Occasionally, as here, Coatsworth tends to tell too much after the climax of the story.

Fortunately, *The Golden Horseshoe* has been re-issued. This is the story of eleven-year-old Tamar, daughter of the owner of a Virginia plantation and his Indian wife, and her older half brother who cherishes the memory of his English mother who died. Tamar disguises herself as an Indian boy in order to go with the expedition into the mountains. She foils a plot to prevent her brother Roger's horse from winning a race and wins the wager that she would be among the first to see the land beyond the mountains. Tamar displays even greater courage in renouncing her victory. Plantation life is authentically portrayed in this book for middle graders.

Many of Coatsworth's stories are quiet, rather than exciting. Modern children may find the pace of *The Littlest House* too slow, but little girls will still delight in the discovery of a real house and the fun of fixing it for a fine party and days of play. *The Place* provides a continuing quiet wonder about a place that means so much to the Mexican children who become friends of the daughter of an archeologist. When it is finally revealed as a cave where men have worshipped for centuries in a setting of prehistoric paintings and stalagmites, the climax focuses upon the decision of the American girl. Shall she reveal the *place* to her scientist father and win a reward for herself so she could have the horse she desires? Or shall she protect the secret entrusted to her? *First Adventure* may promise more action than develops in this story of a seven-year-old who followed his dog into the woods outside Plymouth colony. He is lost for three days, and friendly Indians care for him until Miles Standish appears. The author's account is based upon an actual event. A picture book beautifully interpreted by Politi, *The Noble Doll,* is another quiet story with some wonderment about the mysterious Rosita and much worry about the poverty of a once rich lady. A continued tension is drawn through the story of *Ronnie and the Chief's Son.* When the chief's eldest son is accidentally killed, Ronnie hears, "Your father has taken my son, I shall take his." Hidden among the herd of bullocks, Ronnie is taken across the African veldt. In the village, the chief's younger son helps the white boy escape from being ritually sacrificed by helping him merge with a herd of migrating antelopes. The dangers are passed, Ronnie is safe, yet the author does not create a sense of exhilaration or happiness with homecoming. "Now he was rejoiced to be home once more." The joy we might expect is restrained, almost too quiet. The closing sentences make us feel tired and express the nostalgia of the boy for a "dangerous but beautiful wayfaring."

STYLE

It is difficult to characterize the style of a writer who is both storyteller and lyricist. Miss Coatsworth's prose and poetry are outstanding for their incisive, detailed description and vivid sensory impressions. In *Sword of the Wilderness,* the reader shares Seth's sensory experiences of a peaceful morning:

> He could still hear his father speaking to his mother, behind him the sea gulls were crying and the tide made its unceasing lisp against the rocks along the shore; to his left lay the harbor where he so often went swimming, and the fishing sloops at their anchorage faced into the rising tide near the Barbican. The cold dew that beaded the cobwebs spilled across his bare feet, delicious and fresh.[28]

Recent books seem to include more metaphor. Miriam, the princess who ventured forth to warn her brother he had been chosen king and should not flee from the mountain prison where all royal sons were kept, is aware of the beauty of Abyssinia as she walks to the mountain:

The soft light of afternoon made a long shadow for the mountain to stand upon. In the cooler air, the birds flew up above her head, and above the Crest of Wachni the brown kites hung, revolving in a slow spiral like some airy whirlwind which had caught up not sand, but living things.[29]

The action in *Jock's Island* is heightened by the comparison of Jock, the dog, to a matador. When a volcanic eruption forces villagers to leave an island, the animals panic, but the courageous dog tries to protect his master's house from the encroaching bull:

In and out he dances, snapping at Savage's legs, front and back, and always leading the furious creature toward the gate. Red bull and black sky bellowed together; lightning and dog's teeth flashed; and the rain fell like a wall, blinding the bull, while the dog was cool and determined. Charge by charge, Jock led the beast out of Old Tom's garden. Charge by charge, nip by nip, he baited him down the road. He was skillful and as daring as any matador, and he, too had his audience, an audience of sheep and cows staring from the shelter of bushes or from the doors of houses and sheds, and a more fastidious audience of cats, looking out through windows.[30]

A unique aspect of Coatworth's style is the inclusion of poetry in works of fiction. In the interview, she said she followed Kipling in separating chapters with poems. She recalled her childhood, reading Kipling's stories first, then returning to enjoy the poems. Miss Coatsworth's poems inserted in the prose establish mood, enrich the setting, provide clues for plot or character, present images, or raise questions. In *The Fair American,* for example, a poem described a beggar in the African city. Eventually, the reader will realize that the poem foretold the disguise of Uncle Patterson and his means of escape. The poem evokes the city:

> *The city lies like a pale enchantment*
> *Below its hills; and with the sunset*
> *The herons fly to the gardens by the river,*
> *Filling the branches with the white blossoms of their*
>   *bodies;*
> *And when the night comes the stars hover about the*
>   *minarets*
> *Like silver bees hovering about tall lilies,*
> *And the beggars who sit against the white walls in the dust*
>   *of the lanes*
> *Chant the praises of Allah, awake while the city sleeps.*[31]

The songs of the housekeeper in *The Cat Who Went to Heaven* continue the story and express the deep mystery of life, as in the eighth song,

> *This is too great a mystery*
> *for me to comprehend*
> *The mercy of the Buddha*
> *Has no end.*
> *This is too beautiful a thing*
> *To understand—*
> *His garments touch the furthest*
> *Grain of sand.*[32]

In *Away Goes Sally*, poems tie the chapters together. It is in this volume that one of the finest poems appears, "Swift Things Are Beautiful." Some of the books include poems that probably will not be fully understood by the younger readers of the book. Following one chapter of *The Littlest House* we find:

> *There are some men who much prefer*
> *Loneliness for a housekeeper*
> *To any woman. They feel free*
> *To stop the clock (if clock there be!)*
> *So they may wander by the moon*
> *And take their casual rest at noon,*
> *Read their books backwards, eat with knives,*
> *Pass, as they please, unnoticed lives,*
> *With broken pane and swinging door,*
> *And some old cat for counselor.*[33]

In this same story, the reader encounters a poetic description of the mill following the chapter in which Jean rescues the miller's cat:

> *In the mill the spider webs are whitened*
> *And the dark walls and beams are lightened*
> *With the dust of flour; in the mill*
> *The cat walks on white feet, alert and still*
> *And the miller sits in silence with old memories,*
> *And the tide comes whispering inland from the seas*
> *And runs out with a shimmer, faint and green,*
> *Glimpsed through old boards that have long cracks*
> * between,*
> *And the world seems far, far off and of no concern,*
> *And bent Time stops to listen where the great stones*
> * thunder and turn.*[34]

Many of her poems capture a moment of joy, as in "The Rabbit's Song Outside the Tavern."

Coatsworth's poems frequently depend upon contrast for their effectiveness. The rabbits in the above poem look into the tavern at the domestic animals. "They laugh and eat and are warm, / Their food is ready at hand, While hungry out in the cold / We little rabbits stand. / But they never dance as we dance!" In another poem, "Cold winter now is in the wood, / The moon wades deep in snow" contrasts the outdoors with the indoor scene, "Now shall the housewife bake her pies / And keep her kitchen gay." Frequently, Miss Coatsworth speaks for the animals as "The Mouse" in the moonlight hoping for a crumb or the mare who tells the bored colt in "The Barn" of the Christmas stable. Many of the poems depict a conversation between an animal and a human. When warned of the dangers where she hunts, the "Country Cat" says there is no alternative, for her children are hungry. Poems also describe childhood experiences, as "I Took a Little Stick" which tells how a child helped Spring. The strange feeling that comes in observing Mother "Asleep" with a "forgetting face" is poignant loneliness. A bare lilac bush becomes alive and gay when birds fill the branches to create "The Sparrow Bush."

Miss Coatsworth uses a wide variety of rhyme patterns. Some of her poems jingle with rhythm; many express a stately cadence. Frequently, the lines are long and varied in length. The flowing movement reflects the rhythm of the low hills, and river flowing to the sea. Calm and peace emanate from these lines, evoking life on the farm, in the meadow, or on the sea. In the preface to *The Sparrow Bush* the author writes of poems as expressions of racial emotion and rhymes as "poetry in petticoats." It would seem she describes her own poems as she writes, "One doesn't look for beauty in rhymes, though sometimes one may find a little. One may even find a sudden shaft of strangeness. But mostly what one will find are playfulness and good humor." Many of her poems, however, express a deeper emotion.

Miss Coatsworth's restrained style describes the situation, but the reader is expected to sense the emotions of the characters. When young Johnny in *First Adventure* realizes he may never get home, there is no "lump in the throat," no "tear sliding over a cheek." The writer expresses Johnny's thoughts:

But these weren't his people. This village wasn't his village. What was Frances doing? He wanted to tell his father of his adventures.

And have his mother lean over the trundle bed to kiss him good night. But he supposed he'd never see any of them again.[35]

When Sally is sailing away from Africa in *The White Horse* she seems almost too calm for a girl who had been held captive and whose uncle was apparently left behind. Miss Coatsworth leaves the reader to imagine the emotion of the characters. Since children have limited experience and read mainly for action, they may remain unaware of the emotional qualities of a story unless there is some discussion of the possible responses to the situations so clearly delineated in the text.

Frequently, Miss Coatsworth pauses to add an anecdote or explanation, just as would a storyteller in telling his tale. In *Alice-All-By-Herself,* for example, the reader hurries with Alice past a graveyard, but in a breathless paragraph the narrator pauses, with Alice, to note the grave of the wife of a sea captain. Alice recalls how the lady navigated the ship while the captain lay in a fever. Alice stops to place a branch on the grave, and hastens on toward danger.

A comparison of *The Boy With the Parrot,* written in 1939, with *The Place,* published in 1965, illustrates a change in style. In the earlier book, Sebastian ventures from his Guatemalan village to the wider world to earn money as a peddler. Each chapter is an episode in his journey. Miss Coatsworth digresses to tell the history of the conquerors through the device of a tale told by a priest. Many proverbs and religious beliefs are worked into the story. "The little flea will jump far" or "A cock knows only the affairs of his own barnyard" add authentic flavor. In *The Place,* religious beliefs are included with only brief comments, as in the children's talk beside an ancient terrace. Myth is part of the fabric of *The Hand of Apollo,* but in this recent book the author does not pause to relate an entire story.

In many of her books, Coatsworth also stops to present a moral or some wisdom. When she does this, the dialogue may become stiff and unchildlike. Compassionate Sally sees the renegade in *The White Horse* as a man reacting to terrible circumstances, as a "dog that has been badly treated. He doesn't know whether to wag his tail or bite. . . . How unhappy the poor man is!" Sally's story concludes in *The Wonderful Day.* A wild ride, wrong turns, and dangerous storm add to the suspense as she tries to save her uncle's land. All the characters of the previous books enter into this day, and a weaving woman is added, apparently to teach a lesson, "Make something all the time and you'll be doing God's work." In *The Cave,* Fernando realizes he had misjudged the Indian boy. The author feels that it is necessary to point up the following lesson:

"To think that I was angry because you came with me," he said. "How little one knows what is good and what is bad!" [36]

When Princess Miriam sees people herded off to be sold as slaves, she expresses shock in an adult tone:

"Alas!," thought Miriam. "This is a slave dealer and these poor children, no older than I am, are slaves, destined for Madagascar. He has been buying them from the wild tribes. If only I might help them!" [37]

Miss Coatsworth is very skilled in including authentic information unobtrusively, however. In *Dancing Tom,* store boats and theatre boats are described as aspects of pioneer life. Suspense rises throughout this story of a dancing pig that saved a baby's life. *Down Tumbledown Mountain* utilizes the repetition of a folk song, *The Swapping Song,* and the pattern of the accumulative tale in a story that describes early mountain life. In *The Sod House* the Traubels settle in Kansas with the specific purpose of voting for Kansas as a free state. Through the story of their precarious life on the plain, Miss Coatsworth presents issues of pre-Civil war times.

Not only does Miss Coatsworth's sharp eye and piercing memory record details of a scene; her ear is tuned to the language of the time and setting. Maine and New England speech patterns are evident in the Sally stories. When Sally and her relatives are ready to move, they ask, "How soon do we flit?"

As might be expected of such a prolific writer, the quality has been uneven. Most of her work is very well written; a few books, such as *The Giant Golden Book of Cat Stories,* are slight and do not have the fine quality or substance of *Ronnie and the Chief's Son, Sword of the Wilderness,* or *Door to the North.*

Characters in Miss Coatsworth's books are drawn clearly, as though outlined in crayon. There are few details of motivation, and characters seldom change as they interact with events. Action, rather than inner thought or decision, usually takes precedence. The writer places the character in a situation; we see his strengths, and occasional weaknesses, through his action. Sally is unusually resourceful and courageous; although she is impulsive, her cleverness results in triumph over problems.

THEMES

The themes in Coatsworth's books reflect her own strength, pioneer courage, and closeness to nature and domestic life. Many of the stories express the theme of individual courage. Jock, the collie left alone on *Jock's Island,* displays self-discipline and courage. Miriam endangers her own life by confronting the desert, the slave traders, and by breaking a racial taboo to save her brother in *The Princess and the Lion.* The Navajo boy overcomes fear and superstition to save the sheep by leading them to *The Cave. Jon the Unlucky* is one of the best of Coatsworth's books. Orphaned after his ne'er-do-well, boasting father came to Greenland, Jon is accepted by a lost colony of Danes who prefer to remain hidden from the outer world. Jon's ability to read the ancient scrolls makes him a valuable member of the group and thus saves his life. Inner tension mounts when he discovers outsiders and he must decide whether to remain or betray his new friends. Jon's decision reflects the loyalty needed by all men.

Two books for mature readers present unforgettable characters who gained courage. *Silky, An Incredible Tale,* presents Cephas Hawes, a defeated man who is preoccupied with death. The farm is in ruins; his wife has given up attempts to create a family spirit or to keep house. Cephas finds sadistic pleasure in killing a falcon and butchering a hog, as though he could overcome death by causing it. A mysterious, beautiful girl appears to taunt Cephas. After saving his wife in childbirth, Silky disappears — leaving a question about the open gate to the graveyard. But the fantasy ends with new hope for Cephas. *The White Room* is a burrow in the snow where Laura is entombed during a severe blizzard. During the day and night under the snow, this young wife sees clearly the effects of the domination of her sister-in-law. The fine characterizations in this book are drawn tautly to reveal the contrast of an open, joyous person with one of a closed mind and spirit. Miss Coatsworth paints no easy life, but she quietly insists there is a meaning and hope in existence.

Another theme expressed in Miss Coatsworth's work is that of man pitted against Nature. Children face storms with courage in *Thief Island.* As the Virginians in *The Golden Horseshoe* explore a new land, the author makes the reader aware that:

Here man was on sufferance. It was the wilderness that laid down the terms under which he might be allowed to live, a small mean creature at its fringes.[38]

The Secret portrays Nature reclaiming the land when man is not actually controlling it. Through the story of several generations who lived on a farm, she shows the change from wilderness to farm and the gradual return of forest and wild animals as the younger generation moves to the city and the farmhouse becomes a summer residence. The child of the family, lost in the woods, comes upon Indians who have followed the animals to their old haunts. He decides to keep his discovery a secret. Unfortunately, the artist portrays the boy as a dreamer instead of a vigorous observer. The author was concerned that the buildings seemed to be dilapidated. They would have received care from the owners; it was the land that was no longer tamed.

Miss Coatsworth's optimism is reflected in her books and poems. Like the Widow Paulssen in *Troll Weather,* many people only see danger in nature; Miss Coatsworth expresses her belief in friendly trolls who live in golden houses. *Troll Weather* is another quiet story with a thread of mystery; it is truly an affirmation of joy in a beautiful world.

More recent books have raised the question of man's destiny, whether it is determined by him or another force. In *The Hand of Apollo* a young Corinthian is given a chance to live because he spoke courageously to the Macedonian general who put down the Corinthian rebellion. A trader smuggles Dion out of the country. Dion finds refuge on an island where the Temple of Loneliness is tended by an old woman and young girl. He learns that the God of Loneliness works with Asclepius, the Healer, "But like all gods, he can be cruel." Torn between becoming a poet or a warrior, Dion stands on a ship bound for the safety of Alexandria as a shaft of light suddenly pierces the clouds. Like Apollo's hand, it seemed to choose him to be a poet. The God had spoken. Coatsworth's approach to writing seems to express the idea that behavior is foreordained. By taking an incident, a place, a bit of a journal, a newspaper account, an anecdote, a memory, the author creates a story by asking, "Who might be here? What might happen? Why?" She has noted that once created, the characters take over the story. Having created the characters with their strengths and weaknesses and placed them in a time and setting where political events and powers of Nature swirled around them, their behavior was decreed. "Perhaps we follow the god who chooses us and have ourselves no choice in the matter."

Whether the gods chose Elizabeth Coatsworth to write for children or whether she decided to write stories and poems for them, the world is richer for a lifetime of creative effort. From Chimney Farm has come a shelf of books that will continue to enrich the lives of all who encounter the questing spirit of this highly imaginative writer.

REFERENCES

1. Quoted in a summary of Miss Coatsworth's work prepared by editors of The Macmillan Company.
2. The quotations are not exact transcriptions, but notes of the interview were used to recall her statements. Miss Coatsworth read the first draft of this article and graciously edited it.
3. "Strong Is the Wind," *Poems*. Decorations by Vee Guthrie. New York: The Macmillan Company, 1957, p. 49.
4. "Old Stones," *Summer Green*. New York: The Macmillan Company, 1948.
5. *The Hand of Apollo*. Illustrated by Robin Jacques. New York: The Viking Press, 1965, p. 51.
6. *Alice-All-By-Herself*. Illustrated by Marguerite De Angeli. New York: The Macmillan Company, 1937, p. 121.
7. "Such Things I Praise," *Poems, op. cit.*, p. 108.
8. "Advice to Daughters," *Country Poems*. New York: The Macmillan Company, 1942, p. 57.
9. "To the Contrasting Dark," *Ibid.*, p. 71.
10. *Bess and the Sphinx*. Illustrated by Bernice Loewenstein. New York: The Macmillan Company, 1967, p. 30.
11. *Ibid.*, p. 35.
12. Barbara Abbott, "To Timbuctoo and Back," *The Horn Book Magazine*, 6:283–89, November, 1930.
13. *Ibid.*, p. 289.
14. Louise Seaman Bechtel, "Biography" in *Newbery Medal Books: 1922–1955*, edited by Bertha M. Miller and Elinor W. Field. Boston: The Horn Book, Inc., 1955, p. 98.
15. Anne Carroll Moore, "The Three Owls' Notebook," *The Hornbook Magazine*, 27: 316–19, September, 1951, p. 316.
16. Cornelia Meigs, "Alice-All-By-Herself," *The Horn Book Magazine*, 14:77–80, March, 1938, p. 78.
17. *Ibid.*, p. 80.
18. Graduate Library School, University of Chicago, *Bulletin of the Center of Children's Books*, 16:93.
19. *Ibid.*, 18:115.
20. *Ibid.*, 20:96.
21. *Ibid.*, 20:86.
22. New York Herald Tribune Books, November 8, 1942.
23. *The Hornbook Magazine*, 43:198, April, 1967.
24. Elizabeth Coatsworth, "Upon Writing For Children," *The Horn Book Magazine*, 24: 389–95, September, 1948, pp. 389, 395.
25. *Newbery Medal Books: 1922–1955, op. cit.*, pp. 94–95.
26. Coatsworth, *op. cit.*, p. 392.
27. Coatsworth, *op. cit.*, p. 392.
28. *Sword of the Wilderness*. Illustrated by Harve' Stein. New York: The Macmillan Company, 1936, p. 5.
29. *The Princess and the Lion*. Illustrated by Evaline Ness. New York: Pantheon, 1963, p. 70.
30. *Jock's Island*. Illustrated by Lilian Obligado. New York: The Viking Press, 1963, p. 30.
31. *The Fair American*. Illustrated by Helen Sewell. New York: The Macmillan Company, 1940, p. 131.
32. *The Cat Who Went to Heaven*. Illustrated by Lynd Ward. New York: The Macmillan Company, 1930, unpaged.

33. *The Littlest House*. Illustrated by Marguerite Davis. New York: The Macmillan Company, 1940, p. 107.
34. *Ibid.*, p. 43.
35. *First Adventure*. Illustrated by Ralph Ray. New York: The Macmillan Company, 1950, p. 49.
36. *The Cave*. Illustrated by Allan Hauser. New York: The Viking Press, 1958, p. 63.
37. *The Princess and the Lion, op. cit.*, p. 41.
38. *The Golden Horseshoe*. Illustrated by Robert Lawson. New York: The Macmillan Company, 1935, p. 109.

BIBLIOGRAPHY

ABBOTT, BARBARA. "To Timbuctoo and Back," *The Horn Book*, 6:283–89, September, 1930.
BECHTEL, LOUISE SEAMEN. "Elizabeth Coatsworth: Poet and Writer," *The Horn Book*, 12:27–31, January, 1936.
————. "From Java to Maine with Elizabeth Coatsworth," in *Newbery Medal Books: 1922–1955*, edited by Bertha Mahony Miller and Elinor Whitney Field. Boston: The Horn Book, Inc., 1955, pp. 94–98.
COATSWORTH, ELIZABETH. "Autobiographical Sketch," in Kunitz, Stanley J. and Howard Haycraft. *The Junior Book of Authors*, Second edition, New York: The H. W. Wilson Company, 1951, pp. 71–73.
————. "Upon Writing for Children," *The Horn Book*, 24:389–395, September, 1948.
JACOBS, LELAND. "Elizabeth Coatsworth," *Instructor*, 72:100+ November, 1962.
MEIGS, CORNELIA. "Alice-All-By-Herself." *The Horn Book*, 14:77–80, March, 1938.
RICE, MABEL. "The Poetic Prose of Elizabeth Coatsworth," *Elementary English*, 31:3–10, January, 1954.

EDITORS' NOTE

Miss Coatsworth's most recent books are: *Indian Mound Farm* (1969 — Macmillan), *Jock's Island* (1969 — Seafarer), *Grandmother Cat and the Hermit* (1970 — Macmillan), and *Daniel Webster's Horses* (1971 — Garrard). This last book promises to be of great interest to children from grades 3–5. As one of the "Reading Shelf Books," it gives a logical and interesting explanation of a New England legend based on Daniel Webster and his phantom horses. The present story developed from an earlier poem by Elizabeth Coatsworth, "Daniel Webster's Horses." Although the story is about a young boy who is befriended by Daniel Webster, the latter becomes the central figure of the tale. A forthcoming book by Elizabeth Coatsworth is *Good Night,* to be published in April 1972, by Macmillan.

Since her college years, Elizabeth Coatsworth has published more than eighty books. When children ask about her hobbies she says travel is what she likes best, next to writing. She and her husband loved collecting old china and ornaments for the farm and the handicrafts of the Eastern Forest Indians. Although at present she has no pets of her own on her Maine farm, there is a beagle-type dog named Perky, owned by her housekeeper. This animal, with beautiful eyes and a bottomless appetite, is the heroine of *The Fox Friend*. Such animals of the woods as the raccoons, skunks, deer, and foxes still give Miss Coatsworth a great deal of pleasure, as they make their homes near the house or wander on the fringe of the forest.

In addition to the John Newbery Medal, Elizabeth Coatsworth has won the American Institute of Graphic Arts Children's Book Show Award for 1969–70 (given biennially since 1941 by the American Institute of Graphic Arts for books of typographic and artistic merit), for *They Walk in the Night* (Norton), illustrated by Stefan Martin.

Marguerite L. de Angeli: Faith in the Human Spirit *

"AS FAR BACK AS MY MEMORY GOES," writes Marguerite de Angeli, "there was always an itch to draw, the longing to put things down in words." "Putting things down in words" in an artistic way has long been her trademark, and as stated on a citation from the Graduate School of Library Science, Drexel Institute of Technology, she does it with "an inherent sense of sound human values which permeates all her words and reflects an abiding faith in the human spirit."

Marguerite Lofft de Angeli was born in Lapeer, Michigan. She was educated in the public schools of Lapeer and Philadelphia, where the family moved when she was thirteen years old. She was encouraged by a teacher to develop her talents as a singer. She was a contralto in a church choir until 1910 when she married John de Angeli and became a busy wife and mother of five children—John, Arthur, Nina, H. Edward, and Maurice. While the children were very small she began to study drawing and soon was beginning a career as an illustrator. By 1934 she was writing and illustrating her own stories.

Her books seem to fall in definite categories—family related, the Philadelphia area, historical, and minority groups. Her *Mother Goose* is a special within itself.

Mrs. de Angeli has always utilized her personal experiences as a basis for writing. Her first book, *Ted and Nina Go to the Grocery Store,* the jolly story of an everyday adventure (1935, out of print) and two later

* By Paul C. Burns and Ruth Hines. From *Elementary English* 44 (December 1967), 833–839. Reprinted with the permission of the National Council of Teachers of English and Dr. Paul C. Burns and Ruth Hines.

stories, *A Summer Day with Ted and Nina*—a tea party, strawberries, and a lemonade stand are part of summer fun—(1940, out of print) and *Ted and Nina Have a Happy Rainy Day* (1936, out of print) are based on the activities of two of her five children.

Copper-Toed Boots (Doubleday, 1938) is a story based on her father's boyhood in a warm and friendly family in the small northern town, Lapeer, where Marguerite was born. Marguerite loved her father's descriptions of the red leather-topped copper-toed boots he prized when he was a small boy. She treasured also his tales of "tradin" at the store and with his schoolmates, of the episode of a calf in the schoolhouse belfry, of carrying water for the elephants on circus days, of picnicking during blackberry times—and felt that *Copper-Toed Boots* just had to be written so the boys and girls of today could share all the friendly, folk happenings of a little American town in the 1870's.

Her first grandchild entered her books with *Just Like David* (Doubleday, 1951) where six-year-old Jeffery longs to be just like his older brother, an incident that really happened to one of her grandsons. The enduring values of a happy family relationship are certainly reflected in both Mrs. de Angeli's own life and in her books that have become known and loved the world over.

The history of Philadelphia and the colorful customs of the surrounding countryside are used as background material for several of her books. Through the years she has become deeply acquainted with Amish, Quaker, and Pennsylvania Dutch children and their traditions, resulting in such books as *Henner's Lydia* (Doubleday, 1936) which deals with a Pennsylvania Dutch family; *Skippack School* (Doubleday, 1939); *Thee, Hannah!* (Doubleday, 1940); and *Yonie Wondernose* (Doubleday, 1944), about a Pennsylvania Dutch boy who takes care of the farm while his father is away, but whose curiosity is never satisfied.

In each of the forementioned books, the illustrations are warm and lovely; the details of outdoor scenes or interiors are authentic and beautifully composed. In becoming acquainted with the Amish children in *Henner's Lydia*, readers become appreciative of interesting expressions as "It makes nice today," referring to the weather; "supper we must make"; "he's a shussle" (careless); "make the chicken house door fast"; and "apples is ready to snitz for making snitz and nep" (snitz means dried apples and snitz and nep is made by putting cut apples and dumplings in with boiling ham). Appreciation and respect for such differences in dialect are becoming more and more recognized by educators and, of course, the colloquial speech as represented by these expressions add to the authenticity of the book.

Thee, Hannah! is a story of a spirited little Quaker girl who learns to love her plain scoop bonnet. Mrs. de Angeli tells how the book came about.

> There just had to be a Quaker book. I wondered how a child would react to Quaker discipline. . . . My question was answered when I heard a librarian tell of her aunt's aversion to her Quaker bonnet and her kicking it down the stairs when she was a child. . . . I begged to meet Aunt Hannah, and when I heard she was ninety-two, I wanted to meet her right away. Aunt Hannah said I might use her name.[1]

One day Hannah was to go to the bonnet maker's to be fitted. She thought ". . . and there will be flowers on Cecily's new bonnet, too, but mine will just be the same old *hot scoop* . . ." Hannah couldn't understand why Father insisted on making his children wear the bonnets. "Why can't we have bonnets and dresses like Cecily wears?" Father tried to explain, "But thee's a Friend. It would be out of place for thee to wear the frills and furbelows that some people wear. Let thy spirit shine through. Then thee's as handsome as anybody." The episode of how the bonnet became meaningful to Hannah is a touching one. The setting is the time of the Civil War. A run-away slave woman and her small child appealed to Hannah for help. When help had been afforded by Hannah's mother and father and the fugitive family reunited, the woman turned to Hannah, "Li'l Missy," she said, "it's you dat helped me first. I knowed I could trust *you*. I knowed you was a *Friend* 'cause of yo Quaker bonnet." Hannah's bonnet felt light and beautiful—something to be proud of. The "inner light" shone through her eyes and she no more complained about her plain, ugly little bonnet. This story has humor, warm family relationships, and also provides an authentic picture of life just prior to the Civil War.

Another story popular with children of ages seven through ten is *Skippack School*, based upon the real character of Christopher Dock who has come down from the 1700's in the history of Skippack and Germantown as a beloved schoolmaster. This story tells of Eli Shrawder and his family who came by wagon over the road through Philadelphia and the German Town to settle in a new home in Penn's Woods. The Shrawders had come from across the sea to make a home in the Mennonite settlement on the Skippack. The first days there with the neighbors gathered to help build their house were exciting for Eli. But like most real boys he preferred to chase squirrels, go fishing, or work on the wooden bench he

was carving for his mother like the one she had in Germany. Soon, however, with such a schoolmaster as Christopher Dock, he found himself
wanting to learn "his letters." Finally, Eli planned a surprise for his
schoolmates and won a prize from the schoolmaster. There is no doubt of
the author's warm and affectionate appreciation of the people about whom
she writes.

The heritage of history is another quality reflected in the de Angeli life
and books. Her first work of historical fiction was *The Door in the Wall*
(Doubleday, 1949), a John Newbery Medal Winner for the most distinguished contribution to American literature for children in 1950. Here,
in heartwarming language, de Angeli tells the story of Robin de Bureford,
a boy of 14th century England whose personal courage in saving the
castle won the recognition of his King. Central in the story is the vivid
character study of Robin, the crippled son of a great lord, who must learn
to accept his infirmity and find his useful place in life. Brother Luke is
speaking to crippled Robin:

Fret not, my son, none of us is perfect. It is better to have crooked
legs than a crooked spirit. We can only do the best we can with what
we have. That, after all, is the measure of success: what we do with
what we have.[2]

Whether thou'lt walk soon I know not. This I know. We must teach
thy hands to be skillful in many ways and we must teach the mind
to go about whether thy legs will carry thee or no. For reading is
another door in the wall, dost understand, my son?[3]

This story of Robin is based on the childhood experience of a lame,
beautifully charactered friend of the de Angeli's who for several years
was a neighbor, and the title came from a statement often used by Mrs. de
Angeli to her children: "When you come to a stone wall, if you look far
enough, you will find a door in it."

Superbly illustrated by drawings crowded with authentic detail, *Door
in the Wall* is alive with the pageantry of medieval Britain. As Huck and
Young write:

Her many black and white pictures realistically portray the castle,
churches, and the people of the period. These illustrations are as rich
in color and detail as an original illuminated manuscript. The design
of the title and dedication pages remind the reader that fine books
can be works of artistic as well as literary merit.[4]

Mrs. de Angeli visited England and saw many of the churches, castles, and inns which she has portrayed in the background of illustrations for this book. In 1961 this book was selected by the Lewis Carroll Shelf Award Committee of the University of Wisconsin as "worthy to sit on a shelf with *Alice in Wonderland."*

Another historical book, *Black Fox of Lorne* (Doubleday, 1956), came from material gathered on a trip to Scotland. It tells of two young Norsemen, twin brothers, who are shipwrecked on the coast of Scotland. Through study and personal experience, de Angeli has the ability to make history come alive for her readers.

The Old Testament (Doubleday, 1960) again reflects the importance of history to de Angeli and reveals some of her research methods in preparation of a book. The Old Testament stories had long been a part of de Angeli's life and pictures of places and people had been long in mind before it became a book. But she felt a need for further personal experience. As she tells in the foreword to *The Old Testament* ". . . My daughter, Nina, and I went to the Middle East to get the feeling of time and place; to see the palm and olive trees, to feel the burning sun and the coolness of the heights; to appreciate the value of water and what it must have meant to a traveler to have his dusty feet washed as a gesture of hospitality . . . Our sojourn in the Biblical lands left us with a sense of the continuity of life and of the reality of the events and characters of the Bible. We walked where they had walked, felt the dust of the road and the heat of the day." *The Old Testament* is beautifully illustrated in full color and black and white.

Mrs. de Angeli's writing reflects her abiding belief in the importance of understanding among all peoples of all times. The most notable example that can be cited here is *Bright April* (Doubleday, 1946), a story of a little Negro girl's first meeting with predjudice at the age of ten when a young white girl refuses to sit next to her at a Brownie party. This book is so sensitively written that it was named an "Honor Book" in the New York *Herald Tribune's* Book Awards. In this book, the eternal question is asked by the heroine April, "Why must we be different? . . . I don't *feel* different."

Mrs. de Angeli has always had an interest in the foreign born and in minorities. Among other books that fit this category are *Elin's Amerika* (Doubleday, 1941), the story of a little girl who came to the United States with the first Swedish people in 1643; *Up the Hill* (Doubleday, 1942), which tells of a Polish boy in a Pennsylvania mining town who wants to become an artist; *Jared's Island* (Doubleday, 1947), in which a Scottish boy, wrecked off New Jersey in 1760, is rescued by a young

Quaker and later runs off to live with Indians. Mrs. de Angeli's interests in human relations are not restricted to books; she is very active in her home city of Philadelphia. In 1963 she received the Lit Brothers' Good Neighbor Community Service Award ". . . in recognition of continuous outstanding contributions to the education and general betterment of the greater Philadelphia community."

Marguerite de Angeli's *The Book of Nursery and Mother Goose Rhymes* is one of the most beautiful editions of Mother Goose available on the market today. It is a large book, ideal for children and adults to enjoy together. It contains more than 300 rhymes and jingles and almost as many lovely pictures. Some of the illustrations are full page – done in soft clear pastels. Mrs. de Angeli's children are always beautiful and graceful, but lively; the babies are truly enchanting. Detailed backgrounds and numerous decorative touches on many pages make this book an artistic experience. As Arbuthnot [5] says, ". . . for the artist [the illustrations] must have been a labor of love."

> Children and animals dance and prance across the pages. Little flowery bouquets and birds adorn the corners, and plump, pretty babies tumble here and there. The artist tells us that the faces of the family of "God Bless the Master of This House" were drawn from the laughing faces of her own family and many of the other pictures seem to be sketches of real people. [6]

Marguerite de Angeli has gone the full circle – from the little *Ted and Nina* books to the newest *The Ted and Nina Storybook* (Doubleday, 1965). This ever-developing author is still modest about her success. One son tells of his mother's reaction to each of her new works: "How could it be so wonderful? It's only me that did it." Surely there are many more stories chasing round in her head that children await with great anticipation.

REFERENCES

1. Bertha Miller and Elinor Field, eds., *Newbery Medal Books: 1922–1955*. Boston: Horn Book, Inc., 1955, pp. 345–346.
2. Marguerite de Angeli, *The Door in the Wall*. New York: Doubleday, 1949, p. 71.
3. *Ibid.*, p. 28.
4. Charlotte Huck and Doris Young, *Childrens' Literature in the Elementary School*. New York: Holt, Rinehart and Winston, 1961, p. 21.
5. May Hill Arbuthnot, *Children and Books*, 3rd Edition. Chicago: Scott, Foresman and Co., 1964, p. 87.
6. *Ibid.*

EDITORS' NOTE

More than twenty books by Marguerite de Angeli have delighted children everywhere, and now we have the rare treat of reading her most recent work—*Butter at the Old Price, the Autobiography of Marguerite de Angeli,* published by Doubleday in the spring of 1971.

For a lifetime of devotion to literature for children, Mrs. de Angeli was honored, in 1968, by the Catholic Library Association, which awarded her their Regina Medal.

She presently lives in Philadelphia with her husband. This city, as well as the state of Pennsylvania, has honored her time and again with awards and citations which would make up a list much too long to include here, since it would fill a book of its own.

Meindert De Jong *

IN AN AUTOBIOGRAPHICAL SKETCH that was written for the readers of *More Junior Authors,* Meindert De Jong said that writing is "the one thing that gives things life and spice and interest and meaning." [1] And his books have indeed enhanced and vitalized the lives of many young readers. The characters and events that Meindert De Jong created for his junior novels are valued because they stimulate the faculties of children. The situations that each character faces are real, and his characters are truly alive. With matchless insight, forthrightness, sensitivity, and tenderness De Jong portrays his characters' every thought and emotion as though he were actually inside the characters. The characters, each with a real but unique personality, are drawn with understanding. In many of his stories, De Jong writes out of his own childhood. He does not merely depend upon his memory to present a view of childhood, for memory tends to distort, exaggerate, and muddy. As De Jong himself says, he goes down in-deep in-down through himself until he becomes a child again. He goes by way of the subconscious, plummeting deep into the dark subconscious well of childhood, reliving the small event once again. He becomes the child he was.[2]

LIFE AND LORE OF THE NETHERLANDS

Born in Wierum, Friesland in Holland, on March 4, 1906, De Jong lived in this little Netherlands village bordering on the North Sea for the

* By Patricia Jean Cianciolo. From *Elementary English* 45 (October 1968), 725–730. Reprinted with the permission of the National Council of Teachers of English and Patricia Jean Cianciolo.

first eight years of his life. Several of his stories were stimulated by childhood experiences in Wierum. *Dirk's Dog Bello* shows the precarious living that the Dutch fisherman wrest from the sea. It is also an unusual dog story, in which a boy's desperate struggle to maintain his pet, a Great Dane, is depicted. Dirk rescued the dog from the sea, and his efforts to keep him fed and cared for are both amusing and pathetic. De Jong has used the present tense to tell his story.

In the junior novel entitled *Far Out the Long Canal,* De Jong tells of nine-year-old Moonta's desire to skate. With unusual perception and humor the author portrays the boy's intense feelings of embarrassment and his longing to skate like practically everyone else in the Dutch village of Wierum. As Moonta learns to skate and takes his first journey "far out the long canal," the readers experience joy, fright and loneliness.

The folklore of the Netherlands can be learned by reading at least two of De Jong's stories. A North Sea legend about the cat and cradle on a weathervane of a tower by the sea is retold beautifully in *Tower by the Sea.* With the evils of spreading gossip and superstition made apparent, this story of a witch hunt told with mounting drama and momentary terror creates high suspense. Yet the story is brought to a masterful conclusion, and the readers are convinced that each of the characters is filled with an inner peace, understanding, and good will. The readers of *Wheel on the School* are in for a story that is also written with perceptive characterization and gentle humor. Again, with mounting suspense and dramatic action De Jong presents this tale of how the storks came to nest on the rooftop of the schoolhouse in the Dutch fishing village of Shora. Maurice Sendak's effective wash drawings give the story added appeal for children.

When De Jong's family migrated to America, they settled in Grand Rapids, Michigan. In Wierum the father had been a successful architect but such was not his lot in the United States. The De Jongs were quite impoverished financially, and all of the boys, young as they were, worked diligently in whatever ways they could to supplement the family income.

STRONG RELIGIOUS INFLUENCE

Both parents were strict Calvinists. Meindert De Jong attended the elementary schools and the high school conducted by the Dutch Calvinists. He also attended the John Calvin College where he majored in English. At Calvin College he contributed to the *Young Calvinist,* a young people's periodical started by the Christian Reform Group. He studied briefly at the University of Chicago but returned to Calvin College and graduated from that school during the Depression (1929–1930). The influence of this religious education in his home and school is evidenced in his writing. The characters and the themes in most of his stories exemplify the teachings of his church and the moral fiber of its members. In one of his books he has imaginatively reconstructed some of the events as told in the Bible. This unusual compilation of stories is entitled *The Mighty Ones; Great Men and Women of Early Bible Days.* Taking as his focal idea the eleventh chapter of Hebrews, De Jong tells the stories of the men and women of the Old Testament whom Paul cited as witnesses of the faith. In graphic prose he gives a sense of immediacy to the events which involved Noah, Sarah, Abraham, Moses, Gideon, Samson, David, and others. Each story is preceded by an excerpt from the Bible. Harvey Schmidt's illustrations are superb and contributed much to the value of this publication.

POIGNANT ANIMAL STORIES

Since there were no jobs to be had when De Jong was graduated from college, he supported himself at such various and sundry kinds of manual labor as tinning and grave digging. He taught at a college in Iowa for a short time but found that teaching was not to his liking. He then became a farmer. He was not a farmer very many years but several of his stories reveal the groundwork that was laid during his life as a farmer. His books reflect his fondness for all animals and many of them tell the young readers fascinating facts about farm animals and pets. Life on a poultry farm is viewed in *The Big Goose and The Little White Duck.* This is an amusing tale of how a goose makes itself so useful that it is allowed to remain on the farm as a pet. Thus, it is saved from the awful fate of becoming the entree for Grandfather's eighty-eighth birthday celebration dinner. This story is particularly good when read aloud. Originally published in 1938, it was reissued in 1963 with the very attractive illustrations by Nany Ekholm Burkett.

An enchanting story about a little red hen that has lost its toes and a big homeless dog that is steadfast in its determination to protect the hen and provide a home for himself is *Along Came a Dog.* The relationship between the dog and the hen and the way in which the dog wins a place on the farm make for a truly remarkable story. It is a moving and suspenseful story that is told with the tenderness and exquisite narrative skill that are really quite characteristic of De Jong's animal stories.

Another poignant story with a farm setting is *The Last Little Cat.* Born in an old chicken nest in a kennel barn, the last and smallest of a litter of kittens finds warmth and contentment when it falls into the cage of an old blind dog. The old dog and cat live happily together until one night the cat is locked out of the barn. His fears and his attempt to find a "perfect home" are described with sensitive perception.

Mr. De Jong conveys an understanding and a tremendously high sensitivity to the needs and plights of such animals as turtles, skunks, pigs, rabbits, dogs, and cows. He emphasizes a surprising dignity within each animal. A skunk and a tramp become friends in *Smoke Above the Lane,* a story that is written in gentle rhythmic prose. The skunk and tramp become friends during a miserable journey in a boxcar and are temporarily separated hundreds of miles from home. Before the skunk finds his friend again, he manages to throw a whole town into a panic and holds up the Labor Day parade. This is an unusual and amusing story that probably is better appreciated when read aloud.

Hurry Home Candy is a starkly realistic, compassionate story of the long wanderings of a little lost dog that becomes a stray. De Jong's creativeness and artistry are clearly apparent in this novel. The aloneness, the hunger, and the fear experienced by Candy during his odyssey and the mounting suspense as security and companionship appear impending make this an emotionally-filled story. In *Hurry Home Candy* as in his other stories, De Jong has balanced the proportion between the emotion displayed and the cause of the emotion. He encourages true thought, real emotion, wholesome sympathy. Thus he aptly avoids the pitfall of sentimentality. A writer not so competent as De Jong could easily submit to the artificial quality of sentimentality if he chose to have his characters (human or animal) face the same situations as did De Jong.

PORTRAYALS OF OTHER EXPERIENCES

During World War II Meindert De Jong was sent to China and was honored with citations and medals. He spent three years in the general Chungking area, at a little village named Peishiyi. He was a sergeant functioning as official historian for the Chinese-American Composite Wing of the Fourteenth Air Force. This experience provided the fare for one more noteworthy junior novel, *The House of Sixty Fathers.* This is a deeply-felt story, the scene of which is China during the Japanese occupation. The main character is Tien Pao, a small Chinese boy separated from his family when their sampan breaks loose from its moorings and carries him back into the enemy territory from which his family had just escaped. Tien Pao has only his pig, Glory-of-the-Republic, for company as he heads back to the far distant Hengyang. The boy and his pet pig have harrowing experiences as they encounter Chinese guerrillas, Japanese invaders, and American airmen. Throughout all of this Tien Pao is consistently hopeful that he will be reunited with his family. This is indeed a forthright, detailed, and grim portrayal of the personal horrors of war. It is a story that children will readily recognize as excellent writing, for its plot is well constructed; it contains suspense, action, a fast climax, and a satisfying ending. Tien Pao is a flesh and blood person with whom few readers would fail to identify or understand, whose cause they would champion.

Another story in which De Jong portrays a child's personal horror is *Billy and the Unhappy Bull.* Through this intensely exciting story, one experiences what it is like to be isolated in the country during a raging blizzard. In both *The House of Sixty Fathers* and *Billy and the Unhappy Bull,* De Jong reveals again his rare understanding of the important place a favorite pet has in a child's life.

It was stated earlier in this article that De Jong writes as though he were actually inside the book characters experiencing their every emotion and feeling. This talent is especially apparent in the two stories just described but it is also characteristic of three other stories. *Shadrach* is the story of a small boy and his devotion to his little black rabbit. *Singing Hill* is about a small boy new to country living and left to his own devices while his brother and sister are in school. He is lonely, bored, and sometimes afraid. He discovers a hungry old horse in a hilltop pasture; without anyone's knowledge he visits it daily, feeds it, rides it, and shelters it during a storm. In a more recently published story entitled *Puppy Summer,* two children spend the summer at their grandparents' farm raising three puppies, fishing and hunting for Indian arrowheads. In all three stories the children think and feel as children really do think and feel, and family life is portrayed as being filled with wholesome love and understanding. Never are the children idle in thought, feeling and action.

RECOGNITION AS DISTINGUISHED WRITER

De Jong returned to the States after World War II, but for a period of time he felt too disrupted to do any writing. He worked at assorted manual jobs during this period. Eventually he "pieced writing soul and body together again." [3] Currently De Jong resides in Grand Rapids with his wife Hattie. In recent years he has traveled to the Netherlands and to Mexico. Much of his time is still spent in writing fine books for children.

It is readily apparent why Meindert De Jong has gained recognition as a significant author of children's literature. His stories are filled with warm affection, anxiety, and adventure. He obviously loves and respects animals and humanity. Since Meindert De Jong offers so many masterful variations on the theme of peace and good will towards others, it is obvious this is important and meaningful to him. He artfully leads his reading audience toward acceptance of the same wholesome attitudes, thoughts, and conclusions. Examination of his book characters reveals his sensitive perception of childhood as well as of human behavior in general. He has the ability to impress his readers with a certain kinship in the important aspects of living in the Dutch rural culture as well as in rural China and America. He deserves praise for his skillful portraits of all kinds of animals. His style is uncluttered, informal and realistic. He obviously writes about things for which he has considerable respect and which he knows well. His plots are suspenseful, fast moving, and simple. The settings, incidents, and characters are portrayed in great depth. He has an adequate balance among description, dialogue and action. The result of all this is a wealth of dramatic reading for today's children.

Most of the De Jong books have been published in the United States as well as in England. Most of them have appeared, or will appear, in one or more foreign languages including German, Swedish, Dutch, Italian, Hebrew, Japanese, Danish, Finnish, Friesian, Afrikaans, and Polish. De Jong has won several significant awards issued by literary critics and organizations; thus he has been recognized as a creative artist in the field of children's literature. In 1962 Meindert De Jong was awarded the Hans Christian Andersen International Children's Book Medal. With this award he became the first American to be given international recognition as a living author who has made a lasting contribution to children's literature. The award is given every two years by the International Board on Books for Young People. Each country submits the name of its candidate, usually through its Library Association. Mr. De Jong's name was submitted for the award by the Book Evaluation Committee of the Children's Services Division of the American Library Association. His complete works were considered.

De Jong has been the recipient of other major awards. At various times his books have been included in the American Library Association's Notable Children's Books and Distinguished Children's Books. In the lists of "Notable Children's Books" over the years were *Smoke Above the Lane* (1940–1954), *Hurry Home Candy* (1940–1954), *Along Came a Dog* (1958), *The Last Little Cat* (1961), *Nobody Plays with a Cabbage* (1962), *The Singing Hill* (1962), and *Far Out the Long Canal* (1964). Included in the lists of "Distinguished Children's Books" were *The Tower by the Sea* (1950), *Shadrach* (1953) and *Hurry Home Candy* (1953). He was honored with the 1955 Newbery Award Medal for his story *Wheel on the School*. Named as runners up for the Newbery Award were *The House of Sixty Fathers* (1957) and *Along Came a Dog* (1959).

REFERENCES

1. De Jong, Meindert, "Autobiographical Sketch of Meindert De Jong." *More Junior Authors*. Muriel Fuller, editor. New York: The H. W. Wilson Company, 1963, p. 63.
2. De Jong, Meindert, "Acceptance Paper," *Newbery Medal Books: 1922–1955*. Bertha Mahony Miller and Elinor Whitney Field (editors). Boston: The Horn Book, Inc., 1955, pp. 434–439.
3. De Jong, David Cornel. "My Brother Meindert" *Newbery Medal Books: 1922–1955*. (vol. 1). Bertha Mahony Miller and Elinor Whitney Field (editors). Boston: The Horn Book, Inc., 1955, p. 433.

EDITORS' NOTE

One of Meindert De Jong's recent books, *Journey From Peppermint Street* (Harper, 1968), won the first National Book Award for Children's Literature in 1969. This award, contributed by the Children's Book Council and administered by the National Book Committee, is presented annually to a juvenile title that a panel of judges considers the most distinguished by an American citizen published in the U.S. in the preceding year. In March 1969, a prize in the category of children's books was awarded for the first time in its twenty-year history.

After living in Mexico for a number of years, Mr. De Jong now lives in Chapel Hill, North Carolina. His books have been translated into Dutch, German, Swedish, Danish, Italian, Finnish, Japanese, Polish, Portuguese, Spanish, Czech, Slovak, Serbo-Croat, and Afrikaans.

Elizabeth Borton de Treviño *

WHEN ELIZABETH TREVIÑO BEGAN her novel about Juan de Pareja, the slave and assistant of the painter Velázquez, she wrote us, "It has seemed to me that now is the moment to write this story, presenting the nobility and devotion of the slave, and the nobility and affection of the master, in a light that would inspire the young people of each race to look for and appreciate the best in each other."

In Juan de Pareja she found a subject which combines several of her lifelong interests: Spain and the Spanish way of life ("The whole subject of Spain in that epoch enchants me"), the work of the Spanish masters (her novel about El Greco, *The Greek of Toledo,* was published by Crowell in 1959), and the relationships between persons of differing cultures. It was the warmth which she found in the association between Juan and Velázquez which so appealed to Mrs. Treviño's own outgoing nature. She first learned of Juan in Spain, and when she had seen the Velázquez portrait of his slave she determined to write of the two men. "That painting inspired me," she said, "in its dignity and nobility."

Born Elizabeth Borton in Bakersfield, California, Mrs. Treviño graduated from Stanford University with a degree in Latin American history. She studied violin at the Boston Conservatory of Music and later took a job with the Boston *Herald* as a reviewer of the performing arts. Her newspaper assignments began to take her to various parts of the country and eventually she won the assignment she had been hoping for: to write a series of articles about Mexico and the Mexicans.

* By Clare Costello. Reprinted by permission from *Library Journal,* March 15, 1966, pp. 1592–1593.

In Laredo, Texas, she was to be met by a representative of the Monterrey Chamber of Commerce who would escort her across the border and act as her interpreter during her stay. The escort was young, handsome Luis Treviño. The American writer soon found herself being courted. She was taken to see Señor Treviño's favorite places in Monterrey and to meet his family and friends, including his beloved Mamacita—all of which she interpreted as no more than cordial Mexican hospitality. Actually, she went back to Bakersfield an engaged woman, having been heartily approved of by Mamacita and served the vermouth and specially shaped cookies which any Mexican would recognize as engagement cakes; a year later she was married in Bakersfield.

They returned to Monterrey to begin the married life which Elizabeth Treviño describes so charmingly in her autobiography *My Heart Lies South* (Crowell, 1953). Her Mexican roots go deep, though she remains a United States citizen. "Living in another country," she wrote in her autobiography, "with people of another upbringing, under new sets of traditions, speaking another language, at what moment does one suddenly feel that he has fallen into place and is no longer alien? It happens imperceptibly. . . . There is a moment when suddenly all that was outlandish, quaint, and exotic, is restored to strangeness only by the amazed comments of visitors from afar."

The Treviños lived in Monterrey for several years, surrounded by Luis' large family to whom his wife became devoted. They had two sons—Luis, now an artist whose work has recently been exhibited in Mexico, and Enrique, who has just been admitted to the Bar. They later lived in San Angel, a suburb of Mexico City, and are at present in Cuernavaca. Mrs. Treviño continued to write—copy designed to entice American tourists to Mexico, fiction for American magazines, and books for children. Her best known early juvenile books are *About Bellamy* (Harper, 1940) and *A Carpet of Flowers* (Crowell, 1955). An adult novel, *Even as You Love,* was published in 1957 by Crowell. In 1963 she continued the story of her life in Mexico with *Where the Heart Is* (Doubleday). Her most recent novel for adults, *The Fourth Gift* has just appeared in January from Doubleday.

In later years Elizabeth Treviño has taken much interest in a semiprofessional women's string orchestra, the Vivaldi, in which she plays the violin. The Vivaldi has toured Mexico several times. She is fond of gardening and enjoys showing her adopted country to visitors from north of the border.

One of Mrs. Treviño's most captivating gifts as a writer is her ability to see dramatic possibilities in some event barely noted by historians of the period in which it occurred. Several years ago, in a scholarly history of the Spanish galleons, she found a reference to a ruby-eyed white deer sent from the Philippines to Mexico as a gift to the king of Spain. Here was the beginning of a story. That brief reference led to *Nacar, the White Deer* (Farrar, 1963), just as the portrait of Juan de Pareja led her to seek out the story of Velázquez's slave. She is now at work on a novel of Moorish Spain which, like *I, Juan de Pareja* and *Nacar, the White Deer*, has its basis in fact.

The Newbery Medal comes to Elizabeth Borton de Treviño as a magnificent and particularly fitting recognition of a book about which she herself feels strongly. She "cherished the idea for years," she said, and there is no doubt that she has written it with fervor. She has brought to life for American children another land and another century, and within that time and place she has illuminated the human bonds which can and did overcome all external differences — of race, of circumstances, of origin. Significantly, Elizabeth Treviño's own life proves that the heart knows no barriers.

EDITORS' NOTE

Many of Mrs. de Treviño's very early books are sometimes not listed, but she feels they were not truly her creations since they were commissioned. The "Pollyanna" series is one such set of early works.

The books which this fine author has published since the above article was written are: *Casilda of the Rising Moon* (1967 — Farrar), *Turi's Poppa* (1968 — Farrar), *House of Bitterness Street* (1970 — Doubleday), and *Here Is Mexico* (1970 — Farrar).

Roger Duvoisin — Distinguished Contributor to the World of Children's Literature *

IT WAS ONE OF THOSE truly delightful autumn days which north-western New Jersey knows so well — crisp, sunny, yet with a tang in the air. Red and gold were running riot over the rolling hills of northern Somerset when the writer saw, off Route #206, a small white sign, which had been put there expressly so she would not miss her turn. With simply the name Duvoisin on it, the sign told her she had at last arrived at her destination. Then a short drive down a curving wooded lane, and there it was — a Swiss-modernistic house, uniquely and artistically different from the typical early American farm houses with which the area abounds.

Perched on the side of a gentle slope, it looked out on two magnificent mountains meeting in a sharply outlined gap in the distance. And there, directly below the patio from which one obtained this breathtaking view was a large pond in which at any moment the writer expected to see those lovable animals, Petunia, the goose, and Charlie, the gander, gayly pad-dling about with their fluffy offspring!

It was at that moment that the writer met the creator of these animals, her host, Roger Duvoisin, one of America's most distinguished contribu-tors to the field of children's literature, and his charming wife, Louise Fatio Duvoisin, equally famous for her children's books including the *Happy Lion* and the *Happy Lion in Africa*.

My host and hostess led me into the large living room where the touch

* By Ruth E. Kane. From *Elementary English* 33 (November 1956), 411–419. Copyright © 1956 by the National Council of Teachers of English. Reprinted by permission of the pub-lisher and Ruth E. Kane.

of the artist—not the decorator—was to be seen. Indeed, most of the furniture had been made by the artist himself. Although his own paintings are highly sought after collectors' items, none were in evidence on the walls which displayed those of Dufy, Matisse, and Biala.

Duvoisin designed and started to build his home, set in the midst of 15 acres of woodland, in 1940, doing most of the work with his own hands during the war years when building help in this rural area was practically non-existent or very poor. The Duvoisins are not just week-end residents of rural Gladstone, New Jersey; they are practically natives. There is no dilettantism at country living in their life. This is *really* country: barking foxes can be heard at twilight, and weasels regularly visit the Duvoisin chicken coops only to meet their waterloo at the end of Roger Duvoisin's shotgun!

The writer, still hoping for a glimpse of Petunia, learned that the domestic animal population was non-existent because the Duvoisins had just returned from a six months' tour of France, Germany, and Holland, including a trip down the Rhine. Consequently, the animals had been "boarded 'round" at nearby farms and had not as yet returned.

But the Duvoisin menage is usually a sanctuary for at least two dogs and cats, not to mention a plethora of other animals of assorted shapes and sizes. The Duvoisins' younger son, Jacques, when a child, always had several pet ducks following him about. (Probably this explains how *Two Lonely Ducks* was written.) All of the family's former pets, including one exotically beautiful gold and black bantam hen, lived to a hearty old age and were buried in the animal cemetery reserved for these beloved pets, as well as for the uninvited marauders of the fox and weasel clan.

Roger Duvoisin and his wife have never lost their love of animals, and that is one of the reasons why their books are so successful. The whimsical approach, the gentle humor, and the real knowledge of animal reactions displayed in their books come only to those who truly know and love animals.

Although Duvoisin's 16 other books are completely captivating, the writer feels that his warm cheerfulness, his imagination, and love of animals are, perhaps, best expressed in his four Petunia books.

In *Petunia,* the heroine, a very silly goose, indeed, found a book and began to think herself most wise. She became so proud and haughty that her neck stretched right off the page! Although this barnyard busybody couldn't read, she took it upon herself to advise all her friends: King, the rooster; Ida, the hen; Noisy, the dog; Straw, the horse; and Cotton, the kitten. Of course, all her advice, especially when she interpreted "Danger! Firecrackers!" on a mysterious box to mean "Candies," was terribly wrong. With the inevitable explosion away went Petunia's pride! A humbled Petunia, having discovered pages in her book, decided to learn to read before "helping" her friends in the future.

Petunia's Christmas features a series of thrilling adventures wherein our heroine rescued Charlie, a handsome gander, just before he became someone's Christmas dinner. Naturally, Charlie and Petunia were wed, and we can be sure they, with their goslings, came to live happily ever after in the Duvoisins' pond.

Another of Petunia's adventures, recorded in *Petunia and the Song*, included her capture of an apple thief for her owner, a farmer, who then permitted her to sit in the living room to listen to her song on the phonograph.

Poor Petunia, as a result of domestic bliss, had lost her gosling-like figure and was too heavy to fly. However, she wanted to visit the city, but in order to fly a fat goose must reduce. Then she undertook a reducing campaign worthy of a Slenderella Salon with magnificent results — Petunia, slim and sylph-like, at last could fly. So, off she went to the city where she had many exciting adventures in *Petunia Takes a Trip*.

Another enchanting and whimsical tale is that of *The Christmas Whale*. With Christmas but one week away, all of Santa's reindeer came down with the "flu." All of the animals wanted to help, but they just weren't big or strong enough. At last a cod fish suggested the Kindly Whale, who graciously obliged. All the other animals from white polar bears to walruses helped load the presents on her back. In record time the Kindly Whale and Santa Claus delivered all the gifts to New York, South America, Africa, Europe, and Australia. Then, very weary but happy, the Kindly Whale and Santa returned to the North Pole.

The Duvoisins are two humanly pleasant people, truly happy and relaxed. Of average height and large of frame, Roger Duvoisin with a shock of jet black hair and wearing a bright plaid shirt is far from the average layman's conception of the artist, nor are his hands the frail thin ones the same layman associates with the artist; rather they are the hands of one who seemingly has tilled the earth. There is a power of strength and bold line in them which is transmitted to his drawings. Duvoisin is a kindly person — a trait which children and animals unmistakably fathom upon first coming into his presence.

Mrs. Duvoisin is small, slight, cheerful, and gay. Her features are delicately chiseled, and her flashing smile of hospitality puts one at ease in a moment. A native of Lausanne, Switzerland, she met her husband in Geneva; and theirs has been one of those very successful husband and wife writing and illustrating teams. Although highly successful in her own right, attractive, silver-haired Louise Fatio Duvoisin finds praise and self-importance thoroughly alien to her being. She shares her husband's life and work completely and considers her own output of little importance in comparison with his. But he, in turn, is eager to draw attention to her newest achievement.

Then there was Anne, who was visiting her grandparents on the day of the interview. The daughter of the Duvoisins' elder son, now a doctor associated with the new Hunterdon County Medical Center, she was a perfectly delightful child of three and a half, who, during the interview, sat with the writer on the sofa and happily pointed out the specific illustrations in the books to which her grandfather alluded. Incidentally, an experienced child model, Anne, who is dainty and petite with huge brown eyes, simply delights in being told stories.

In fact, her grandfather attributes much of his success in obtaining the child's point of view to years of observing children. This was obtained while telling them stories. Anne has now joined a long line of children — her father, her uncle, and children of neighbors, relatives, and friends — to whom Roger Duvoisin, through the years, has told children's stories.

As a result of all this experience in story telling, he has observed, "In writing children's stories we must strive to give simplicity, satisfaction, and pleasure; for ultimately, it is the child who must be pleased. Children can take more fantasy than adults realize."

To Anne, the best picture in *Petunia's Christmas* — emphasizing that children crave action more than anything else in their illustrations — was Petunia and Charlie's Christmas wedding party at which all the animals and people were dancing merrily together.

Her grandfather felt Anne's choice a good one, noting that children unerringly select that which is most meaningful to them and that which meets their needs.

A second method Duvoisin uses to obtain the child's point of view is memory — that of putting oneself back into one's childhood.

He feels parents must revive and relive their childhood interest in any story they tell. They must really love the story, and they, themselves, must feel and enjoy it. If a parent really puts himself into the story, he will be successful in the telling of it. He can determine his success by the gleam that comes into the child's eye.

Duvoisin does his illustrations first and then has the story follow. He tries to change from one book to another to bring infinite variety to his works. He simply delights in drawing animals. As a boy in Geneva, he felt handicapped because there were only deer in the city zoo. Consequently, he had to wait for the circus to come to town before he could draw his magnificent lions, elephants, and tigers.

Today, he can observe cats, ducks, guinea hens, horses, dogs, cows, and geese as well as the predators and woodland animals from his Somerset County home. However, he observes and sketches his lions, tigers, penguins, polar bears, and animals of this type at both the Bronx and Central Park Zoos in New York City. Since he likes to work with tempera and line drawings, he consequently thinks of animals which can be treated in line drawings.

Smiling gently, he said that it was simply amazing to an artist what a critic can see in, or read into, a book. In his future works he plans to try to get bolder and bolder in line composition and color. He plans further to work for more freshness. Duvoisin says that he thinks continuously of stories which will bring these things to fruition. Sometimes it is an old theme done over freshly which effects the desired objective. However, he ruefully admitted, ideas won't come when you want them to but appear when you least expect them.

Duvoisin has attained his present status as an artist for many reasons: One of these is his tremendous variety which can be demonstrated by *And There Was America* in contrast with *Petunia*. His work is bold and free — not at all stereotyped. There is nothing prissy, sissy-like, or cute about anything he draws. He makes use of direct, bright, bold colors. His art has a sense of humor and an enviable visual freshness. His too, is a certain delightful spontaneity of craftsmanship, design, and color.

Duvoisin's has the same directness and simplicity as the Japanese manner of art. His is the direct line — sure, definite, and economical. There is no superfluity to be found in his illustrations.

His art may be likened to the playing of the piano: first, one learns the exercises; next, one goes through the effort to gain skill; and finally, the expert, playing, just lets the music flow out. So with his art, it starts, swells, flows, and then comes back. His angles are seen from an inventive way, and the body is seen likewise. Perhaps the essence of his books lies in every page's being a deliberate surprise.

Duvoisin is a perfectionist; rarely is he satisfied with his illustrations. In the interview he candidly spoke of which of his drawings he disliked. Sometimes in search of this perfection, he draws from models, but then his drawing loses that certain delightful creativity so typically Duvoisin. He is at his best when drawing from imagination.

His quest for the perfect is seen further in his making a dummy of every page of a book which he is creating. The dummy includes not only the pasted in type and sketches of his illustrations but specific directions concerning the binding, spacing, margins, exact position of the drawings, etc.

Because Duvoisin is an author as well as an artist, "he understands the part illustration should play, and out of this perception and his intelligence he gives freely, unjealously, and as if in each case he were author as well as artist. . . ." [1]

An artist's artist, Duvoisin not only evokes gratitude from authors who feel that he has "finished" their work by so well illustrating their books but also arouses from them:

> unanimity of response and warmth of expression when his best works are referred to. . . . He exemplifies for other artists the possibility of fulfillment in themselves. He indicates how what they are striving for, beyond bare technique and draftsmanship, can be reached. His work is heartening to them. And the fact that he has been received by American publishing as he has disproves the often-made claim that good stuff is not wanted and has no market; and this is invigorating too. [2]

Roger Duvoisin's honors are many. In 1948 he received the coveted Caldecott Medal for illustrating the year's most distinguished picture book, *White Snow, Bright Snow,* written by Alvin Tresselt. It was also selected by the American Institute of Graphic Arts as ranking among the Fifty Best Children's Books for the year.

In 1950, *Hi, Mr. Robin,* also written by Tresselt, was listed among the fifty best books of the year honored by the American Institute of Graphic Arts. In 1952 two of the books Duvoisin illustrated were honored by the *New York Tribune* at its Children's Spring Book Festival, held from May 10–17; *The Talking Cat and Other Stories of French Canada,* written by Natalie Carlson, was given the award for being the best book in the eight to twelve age group, and *Busby and Company* by Herbert Leonard Coggins was awarded honor book status in the same age group.

Mrs. Duvoisin's book *The Happy Lion,* which was illustrated by her husband, was chosen by the *New York Times* as "One of the Ten Best Illustrated Books of 1954." The American Institute of Graphic Arts gave it a place among the fifty best books of 1954, and the American Library Association listed it in its "Distinguished Children's Books of 1954." It has been translated into French and German.

This year (1956) his enchanting and colorful *The House of Four Seasons* also won an Honor Book Award at the Children's Spring Book Festival sponsored by the *New York Herald Tribune* in New York.

The recipient of all these honors, Roger Duvoisin, was born of French-Swiss ancestry in Geneva, Switzerland, in 1904. His father, an architect, although he was kept very busy building houses, always found time to encourage his young son who began to draw almost as soon as he could hold a pencil. The boy was such an omnivorous reader that his parents literally had to shoo him out into the brilliant Swiss countryside, where he then would join his brothers and sisters bicycling.

His drawings of the magnificent yet quizzical lion in *The Happy Lion* and in *The Happy Lion in Africa* were come by naturally when one considers he literally steeped himself, as a child, in tales of the jungle and of the great wilderness that was the American West. His love of animals came early, and it is only to be expected that his childhood reading fare included among his favorites: La Fontaine's tales, *Peter Rabbit*, and Kipling's animal stories. In addition, he read Grimms' and Andersen's fairy tales, *Mother Goose*, *Uncle Tom's Cabin*, *Alice in Wonderland*, *Little Women*, *Moby Dick*, *A Thousand and One Nights*, and books by Jules Verne, Cooper, Mark Twain, Stevenson, and other authors of English and American classics. All these books were read in French; the only English he had was that which he learned as a school boy in Geneva.

Dorothy Waugh tells us (and this should comfort parents worried about their children's obsession with comic books):

He also read all the lurid current trash which he could obtain for small coins. He enjoyed this with the same extravagant appreciation he gave to the other books. He believes in letting a child read anything; in choosing books as in choosing friends the taste, he says, will develop, until, in the end the matured judgment comes to distinguish between qualities which will wear and those which will not. . . .

When Duvoisin thinks now of those books he read as a child, he recalls the vastness, the wonder, the richness, and color which his child mind created; and in illustrating those or other stories he tries once again to live in the large lush land of imagination's childhood.[3]

Duvoisin, the child-artist, delighted in drawing horses, especially galloping ones! But it seems the hoofs presented quite a problem, usually turning out to represent oversized shoes. However, his uncle who had a special talent for drawing horses, elegantly poised on prancing hoofs, came to his rescue.

He despaired of his trees also, as the leaves always seemed to bear an unfortunate resemblance to Christmas tree balls. However, from this despair there was an attempted rescue by his godmother, a well-known painter of enamels, who possessed a special faculty for dealing with leaves and trees.

But apparently she labored in vain, for Duvoisin tells us in an autobiographical note written for Alfred A. Knopf, one of his major publishers: "After that my trees were really bad. Thus I scribbled so many strange things and used up so much white paper that my godmother declared she could see my future very clearly. I would be a painter of enamels. My mother concurred. But my father shook his head. He thought that I would make a better chemist. He was alone against two — so he compromised. I would be an artist but not a painter and a stage designer. That was closer to his own profession. So, when I became of age, I entered an art school."

Roger Duvoisin did not suddenly attain his present prominent position in the front rank of American illustrators. A variety of different types of experiences lay before him after graduation from art school. To begin with, he painted murals, posters, illustrations, and stage scenery, including scenery for the Geneva Opera Company. Thus he received experience to enhance his excellent basic training in design and drawing — two absolute indispensables in the making of a true artist.

Fortunately for us, Duvoisin has always had a third motivating factor in his life in addition to his love of animals and the country. It is a love of travel. So, naturally, when his uncle offered to send him to Paris with a letter of introduction to a friend, the manager of the largest motion picture company in France, who was just then in need of scenery designers, he was delighted. However after only a few days in Paris he became so weary of the city and unhappy in the world of celluloid that he left abruptly without seeing the studio executive — "for fear," he said, "he would hire me."

The next position, that of manager of a century old ceramics factory, founded by Voltaire and located in the charming French farming country, was more to his liking. However, his textile designs were also highly sought after, and he soon found himself working in this medium in Lyons and later in Paris. It was during the Lyons and Paris years that he developed and enhanced his natural flair and talent for creative expression in strikingly gay colors and compositions. So much so, in fact, that his work came to the attention of the New York manager of Maillinson's Silk Company, who was in Paris in search of new talent.

Duvoisin was invited to America with all expenses paid to work for this firm, the only provision being that he agree to work for the concern for four years. Newly married to Louise Fatio Duvoisin, who shared his love of travel, Duvoisin readily agreed to the offer.

Coming to the United States, they felt, would be a thrilling experience and so they anticipated many interesting adventures and

... moreover, one of his friends was already in New York and installed at Maillinson's. The offer could not have been more perfectly timed. He sailed the next week and stayed with Maillinson's for three years, the only period in his life that he has been tied down to regular hours and a routine job. But it was surprisingly tolerable, particularly after his friend from the Ecole Arts et Metiers, joined him. "They were very nice to us," he recalls, and very considerate. They would say how much they would appreciate it if we could take an hour and a half instead of three for lunch, and that it would be a great favor if we should come to work at 9:30 instead of 11." [4]

Roger and Louise Duvoisin engaged an apartment in Brooklyn where he improved his school boy English by reading Jack London's *Call of the Wild* with the help of a French-English dictionary. Life was very pleasant and secure for the young Swiss couple, who liked the United States so much that they decided to become American citizens. (Their final papers came through in 1938.)

However, they had been hardly three years in this country when the depression struck with brutal force, causing Maillinson's Silk Company to fail. Duvoisin found himself jobless. But this catastrophe turned out to be a blessing in disguise and gave Duvoisin to all young people everywhere who like to read or have stories read to them.

He had written two stories for his young son Roger, Jr., now a physician, and he decided to try his luck at having them published. Scribner's accepted *A Little Boy Was Drawing* in 1932, and the Whitman Publishing Company in Chicago brought out his *Donkey-Donkey* in 1933. The die was cast, and Duvoisin has been writing and illustrating children's books ever since. To date, he has written and illustrated twenty books of his own and has illustrated sixty-one books by other authors.

Writing for children, although it seems to be his all consuming love, has not caused him to abandon the many other strings to his bow. He still manages to find time to execute magazine covers, murals, and display advertisements which are so unique that they bring outstanding sales results.

REFERENCES

1. Louis Ansbacher, "The Caldecott Medal is Awarded to Roger Duvoisin." *Publishers' Weekly,* 153:2539, June 19, 1948.
2. *Ibid.,* p. 2540.
3. Dorothy Waugh, "Roger Duvoisin As Illustrator for Children." *The Hornbook Magazine,* 24:19–20, January–February, 1948.
4. Beatrice Creighton, "Duvoisin Gets the Caldecott." *Library Journal,* 73:916, June 15, 1948.

BIBLIOGRAPHY

ANSBACHER, LOUIS. "The Caldecott Medal Is Awarded to Roger Duvoisin." *Publishers' Weekly,* 153:2538–2541, June 19, 1948.

CREIGHTON, BEATRICE. "Duvoisin Gets the Caldecott." *Library Journal*, 73:915–917, June 15, 1948.

WAUGH, DOROTHY. "Roger Duvoisin As Illustrator for Children." *The Hornbook Magazine*, 24:11–22, January–February, 1948.

EDITORS' NOTE

Since 1956, Mr. Duvoisin has written and illustrated the following books: *Day and Night* (1959 – Knopf), *Happy Hunter* (1961 – Hale), *Lonely Veronica* (1963 – Knopf), *Missing Milkman* (1966 – Knopf), *Our Veronica Goes to Petunia's Farm* (1962 – Knopf), *Petunia, Beware* (1958 – Knopf), *Petunia, I Love You* (1965 – Knopf), *Spring Snow* (1963 – Knopf), *Veronica* (1961 – Knopf), *Veronica's Smile* (1964 – Knopf), and *What is Right for Tulip* (1969 – Knopf). In addition, he has been joint author of: *Happy Lion and the Bear* (1964) – with Louise F. Fatio; *Nubber Bear* (1966) – with William Lipkind; and *The Old Bullfrog* (1968) – with Bernice Freschet.

Roger Duvoisin has received innumerable awards as an author-illustrator, as well as illustrator of books by others. In addition to those mentioned previously, a few more recent awards deserve particular mention. In Germany, the first prize for children's books, awarded by the West German government, was given to *The Happy Lion* in 1955. Mrs. Duvoisin conceived the idea for this story from a real event in a small French town. A well-fed lion escaped from the zoo and went peacefully on his way through the community – so much more peacefully than the people who encountered him. Children have so delighted in this story, beautifully illustrated by Roger Duvoisin, that we thought they might enjoy knowing that there really was a real, live "happy lion."

In 1965, the illustrations by Roger Duvoisin in *Hide and Seek Fog* by Alvin Tresselt made the book a Caldecott Medal runner-up. In 1966, along with John Ciardi, Mr. Duvoisin was honored as the first winner of the Rutgers Award for distinguished work in the field of Children's Literature. In 1961, *The Happy Hunter* was the *New York Times* choice for Best Illustrated Children's Books of the Year (chosen by a panel of three judges).

Since 1969, the University of Southern Mississippi has awarded a medal at the spring book festival to a writer or illustrator who has made an outstanding contribution to the field of children's literature. Roger Duvoisin was selected for this honor in 1971.

Mr. Duvoisin still lives with his wife on their fifteen-acre farm in Gladstone, New Jersey. They have two adult sons.

The Meteoric Career
of Ed Emberley *

TWO OF ED EMBERLEY'S outstanding assets as an illustrator of children's books are a strong sense of design and a prolific imagination. He is developing both at a rapid pace.

His sense of design shows most noticeably in his thoroughly stylized illustrations, especially those in bold patterns of flat color, always emphasizing simplified form. His 1966 *Rosebud,* for instance, shows strikingly how he can reduce an object to its simplest and most significant essentials, omitting whatever is not expressive for the purposes of the moment.

Again, his design sense is exemplified in the layout of pages as he effectively adjusts a variety of arrangements of type and illustration on successive page spreads. This is noticeable in *Colonial Life in America,* where interesting movement is sufficiently curtailed by satisfactory balance and proper centripetal control.

As for imagination, this shows in Ed Emberley's exuberant building up of themes with copious commentary. We see it, in *The American West,* in mountains, cabins, spruce trees, spades, sluices, and saucy squirrels; and in *The Parade Book,* where bystanders watching the drum major pass with pronounced verve include every conceivable type of human being in a multiplicity of delightfully expressive attitudes, with balloons, flags, cameras, opera glasses, pipes, dogs, and cats.

Ed's imagination is strongly colored by an active sense of humor. This

* By Dorothy Waugh. Reprinted by permission from *American Artist* 30 (November 1966), 54–61.

may express itself in mountain climbers exerting prodigious effort, or in a dancing child who flings one hand high in abandonment, while with the other she catches a back-kicking ankle as seen in *The Wing on a Flea.*

Exaggeration is, of course, a basic ingredient in humor. We find it in this same "Flea" book (a playful commentary on simple forms, such as the triangle of a flea's wing or a boat's sail, and so on) when we view two drawings of a paunchy pirate leveling first a telescope, then a pistol, peering shrewdly along either from under the very edge of a floppy hat brim. We find it in *Punch & Judy* in the large, innocent goggle-eyes of a toothy saddle horse decoratively caparisoned, contrasted with the glowering squint eyes of a magenta devil wielding a villainous pitchfork and quirking a malevolent tail.

In *Yankee Doodle,* exaggeration draws its laugh, for instance, by the followers of a military parade, including boys with wooden hobby horses and guns, a girl clutching a cat at the most comfortable angle for the girl and the most uncomfortable for the cat, and in an over-weight hen jauntily bringing up the procession's rear.

Thus we have imagination humorously employed by means of exaggeration of *form,* giving us the pirate's or the hen's exalted characterization; and we have humor achieved by imaginative extension of subject matter— or has Ed Emberley actually *seen,* outside his imagination, an obese hen striding with dashing aplomb in the wake of a parade, theatrically keeping in step with the drums?

Imagination emphasized by humor and a strong sense of design is, then, an outstanding characteristic of Ed Emberley's work. What, I asked him, of his tools, methods, and techniques?

When he wants to use pen outlining or patterning, he said, he reaches for a crow quill. He owns many other pens, but always turns instinctively to this, because it produces an accurately clear line. For filling in or for building up solid areas, he uses a felt-tipped pen. These he buys by the dozen, with various-size tips, filled with many colors of ink.

As for paper, he told me that a one-ply kid-finish bristol is overwhelmingly his favorite for drawing, either with a crow quill or a felt pen.

With his flat color patterns Ed often combines areas of mottled color, produced by rendering them with crosshatching. *Punch & Judy* gives us our best examples of this. Line drawings often supplement the flat and mottled color areas in integrated combination with them. Ed's line is usually free and easy, though never merely careless. When necessary it is strictly controlled.

For his flat color work, Ed explained, he sometimes uses a frosted acetate film that is double-layered. The upper layer is a very thin sheet of dark orange plastic held lightly by adhesive to a stiff, translucent lower layer. In response to a request from me, he offered a step-by-step account of his use of this film.

First, he says, he prepares an accurate measured skeleton diagram to show his major forms and the margins within which he must keep. This diagram he tapes on his light table. Over it he tapes a sheet of film for his first color plate—let us say, the red. With a razor-sharp blade he cuts lightly around each form he wants to have print in red. The cutting penetrates the orange layer of the film only. The portion of orange film that is not to print, he peels away and discards. The remaining orange forms will photograph black in the plate-making.

Leaving this completed sheet of film in place over his diagram on the light table, he superimposes another sheet and produces a drawing for the blue plate, in the same fashion. All previous patterns show through as the work progresses.

On the translucent lower layer of the film, lettering or other patterning may be added with pen, grease crayon, or other tool. This gives a complete "drawing" for the key plate.

The woodcut is another favorite medium of expression with Ed Emberley. He uses ordinary pine plank obtained from a local lumber yard. He pulls his proofs of the completed blocks in black printers' ink on domestic rice paper. For the proving he uses three small hand presses of different sizes. Often he locks up lines of type with the woodblocks. Thus the layout for a book page or jacket can be made complete, with type in place with the illustration, ready for the engraver.

Ed owns six fonts of Caslon type, several fonts of bold and decorative wood type, and a miscellaneous collection of display faces procured at various times for specific jobs. Occasionally he has had special lines of old-fashioned type set by the printing office of the New York Public Library on Fifth Avenue at Forty-second Street, where complete and incomplete fonts of a hundred nostalgic faces are available.

Though he does not consider himself a professional letterer, at times Ed has lettered a few words when a bold or fluid line was needed to conform pleasingly with his overall design. When formal lettering is required he places the job with a professional, or asks his publisher to do so.

Ed emphasizes that it is very important for the book illustrator to know the requirements for both offset and letterpress printing, and how to prepare art for reproduction. For this reason he owns a small offset press as well as his three small letterpresses. By using these to produce Christmas cards, mailing pieces to remind editors of his work, and other incidental graphics, he is patently familiar with the limitations and advantages of each printing method.

Ed himself learned the complex ins and outs of printing by working for two years for a direct-mail advertising firm in Boston. There his drawing table was next to the darkroom, where art work was photographed for plate-making; beyond that was the print shop; and nearby, the binding equipment, including the folding machines. In close touch with all these basic operations, Ed says he learned much that is fundamental.

When he opened his own studio, Ed found that he had to show a completed book to obtain professional work. Unpublished sample drawings were not enough. Publishers would not give a contract to an illustrator who could not prove that he was able to carry a book's whole design from beginning to end.

So Ed (who says he can't remember the time when he didn't know he was going to be an illustrator) created a picture book, with text and finished drawings, accompanied by a detailed dummy. This was the individual and now famous *The Wing on a Flea,* published in 1961, and immediately awarded two honors—being listed by the American Library Association among Notable Children's Books of 1961, and by *The New York Times* among the Ten Best Illustrated Books of the Year. Since then, the *Times* has included his *Punch & Judy* among the Eight Best Illustrated Books of 1965, and his *Yankee Doodle* has been named among the American Library Association's selection of Notable Books of 1965.

When his first book came from the press, Ed sent copies to thirty publishers of children's books, enclosing a mailing piece from his private press soliciting work. Three publishers responded at once with assignments!

As of this past summer, Ed has illustrated, since his 1961 debut, twenty children's books for trade publishers, and many text books. At the moment, among other things he is completing illustrations for a series of four text books on the "new math" for children.

Ed recommends to publishers' manufacturing departments the kinds of paper, type, and binding cloth he feels would be effective for his illustrations. Unless a cost differential is involved, the publishers are usually glad to comply.

Texts for a number of Ed's books have been either his own or by his wife, Barbara, who has a sensitive skill with words, as delightfully evidenced in *The Story of Paul Bunyan.* Barbara was actually trained as a fashion artist. The two young people met when both were students at the Massachusetts College of Art in Boston, where Ed specialized in painting, illustration, and design. After four years there, they both took their degrees before Ed did his two-year stint in the Army. In the service he was assigned to a parade division at Governor's Island, wore a two-tone blue uniform and, carrying flag and rifle, marched in endless parades. Out of this, eventually, grew *The Parade Book,* in which he pictures parades galore: military, circus, Mardi Gras, Macy's Thanksgiving, and so on.

In the midst of his Army service, Ed and Barbara were married. They now have two children and live on the North Shore above Boston, in sight of the sea. Boats are a major love. Each summer a long vacation finds the four Emberleys cruising. The remainder of the year Ed works ten hours a day, six days a week—not with a nose-to-the-grindstone feeling, but because his work is such fun he can't leave it. "It's like going into the ocean to swim," he said, laughing, when I commented that this sounded like a stiff pace. "It's hard to get in, but once you're there, hard to leave."

Edward Randolph Emberley was born in Malden, Massachusetts, on October 19, 1931. His childhood and school days were spent in Cambridge. There he washed dishes at Harvard for a year before entering art school.

As far as he knows, he has made no effort to use his son Michael and his daughter Rebecca for professional purposes—as models, critics, or in any other way; yet, being around his own children has made him more conscious of their interests, points of view, and levels of understanding. Both children like to imitate his activities. He and Barbara make sure that the children have plenty of paper, crayons, chalk, and plenty of room, then let it go at that: no instruction, but ample chance to develop freely and to express themselves without restraint.

Six-year-old Michael takes after his father, as from his even earlier childhood he has known what he wants to do for a living when he grows up. Though he has not told his family, he has told all the neighbors that he is going to be an artist.

"Illustrating is a wonderful field," Ed Emberley said enthusiastically as I got up to leave after a pleasant interview. "You deal with nice people. You have challenging work."

Perhaps Barbara, standing by and definitely helping, with full knowledge of art ideals and techniques, has a good deal to do with Ed's happiness in his work. And Michael and Rebecca, two bubblingly healthy children, may be contributing more than they realize, too.

EDITORS' NOTE

Ed Emberley's most recent publication is *Ed Emberley's Drawing Book of Animals,* which shows children how to create creatures from simple shapes. His upcoming book, *Ed Emberley's Drawing Book: Make a World,* will be available in Spring 1972. It elaborates on this highly successful approach, thus promising to be at least as successful as its predecessor. Both drawing books are published by Little, Brown.

Ed Emberley has also written and illustrated *London Bridge is Falling Down* (1967 — Little, Brown), and *Green Says Go* (1968 — Little, Brown). Over twenty books have been illustrated by Emberley for other authors. Notable among these are the books written by Mrs. Emberley and illustrated by her husband: *Night's Nice* (1963 — Doubleday), *Story of Paul Bunyan* (1963 — Prentice-Hall), and *Simon's Song* (1969 — Prentice-Hall). Two other Emberley collaborations were award winners. *Drummer Hoff* (1967 — Prentice-Hall) was the winner of the 1968 Caldecott Medal and *One Wide River to Cross* (1966 — Prentice-Hall), was a runner-up for the 1966 Caldecott Medal.

The Emberleys live in an old house, circa 1690, in Massachusetts. Anything "Early Americana" interests them, as is evidenced by many of their books and the contents of their interesting home. New England, the sea, and things related continue to fascinate Ed Emberley. Music is often an important ingredient to the right working climate when he is busy in his studio; symphonies usually supply the right atmosphere.

Marie Hall Ets —
Her Picture Storybooks *

MARIE HALL ETS' BOOKS are the reflection of a many-faceted life. She was born in Wisconsin, one of six children of a doctor who later became a minister. Her childhood love for animals, wild and tame, finds continued expression in the skill and feeling with which she depicts all kinds of animals in text and drawing. Art student, interior decorator, social worker (always with, or for children), the wife of a doctor — from this potpourri emerges an author-artist of remarkable talent, who for the past twenty years has been enriching the field of books for young children. She is a "born storyteller" in tune with the interests and feelings of the very young. She is a delightful artist and knows how to use illustration to complement and enhance her stories. That she has only produced ten books in twenty years is suggestive of the care and thought which have gone into her work.

In any one of her storybooks the reader will find a simple but absorbing plot which is developed to a logical and satisfying conclusion, involving a situation and characters with natural appeal to children. A happy blend of rhythmic prose, action, humor, pathos, charm, and fantasy is characteristic of her work.

Her illustrations are distinguished by their artistry, composition, pleasant informality, and appropriateness to each story. She captures the subtility of emotional reaction as well as direct action in her drawings.

* By Ruth R. Irvine. From *Elementary English* 33 (May 1956), 259–265. Copyright © 1956 by the National Council of Teachers of English. Reprinted by permission of the publisher.

141

She is meticulous (but never dull) in the reproduction of detail in the text. She is a master of the medium of black and white and uses it with such strength, richness, and variety that one never wishes for a more colorful palette.

Mr. Penny (Viking Press, 1935) has a timeless appeal which belies its early publication date. It is the story of a poor, kindly old man and his large family of mischievous animals. The animals are the familiar farm animals dear to the hearts of children. They are conceived with humor and affection. Their frailties and vanities are human and yet related to their species. The family consists of an old horse named Limpy "who used to limp on his right foreleg because he liked to have it rubbed with liniment and tied up in a bandage like a racehorse," Mooloo the cow "who had beautiful eyes, but who never chewed her cud as other cows do because she was too lazy," Splop the goat, Pugwug a pig, Mimkin the lamb, Chukluk a fat hen, and Doody a rooster, "who arched his tail and strutted when he walked."

Mr. Penny is a good father to his family, up before dawn, cleaning the shed and preparing food for them. When he leaves for his daily work in the factory of the Friend-in-Need Safety Pins in the town of Wuddle, he says goodbye to each animal and tells them to be good while he is gone. He asks Doody "to try to be good!" How like any parent leaving his brood for the day! And just as any group of seven children left to their own devices would get into mischief, the animals led on by Doody have a field day in the neighbor's garden. Retribution comes swiftly. The animals are chased away ignominiously by the angry farmer and his bulldog, Doody loses his beautiful tail to the dog, the animals are sick from over-eating, and disaster threatens when the irate farmer delivers his ultimatum, that Mr. Penny must either pay for the damage, repair it, or lose his animals. The animals come to the rescue and, working secretly at night, restore the garden and plow the fields. Mooloo chews her cud and gives quarts of milk. Chukluk eats the nasty hen's tonic-and-grit and lays beautiful eggs. Doody follows the plow pulled by Limpy and weighted down by Pugwug, and picks up worms for Mr. Penny to sell. Mimkin clips the grass, and Splop clears the fields of stones. The animals learn that it is more fun to work than to be lazy. With their help Mr. Penny soon has the most beautiful garden in Wuddle, he is able to retire from his hated job in the factory, and they all live happily and prosperously together.

The illustrations in *Mr. Penny* are vigorous, humorous, expressive, and faithful to the action and mood of the story. In *Mr. Penny* the author demonstrates her gift for devising singularly appropriate and original names for her characters. The names are as distinctive as portraits.

The Story of a Baby (Viking Press, 1939) is an extraordinary piece of work and in a class quite by itself. In a large size picture storybook the growth of a baby is described from its beginning as "a life too small to be seen at all," through the many stages of embryonic development, to birth and the baby's first smile. It is a book for parents and children to enjoy together, and it is a particularly beautiful way in which to satisfy a child's curiosity about the origin of babies. Text and illustration are sensitive and scientifically accurate, yet rendered in a manner meaningful to a young child. The changing size of the embryo is given reality to the child by continual comparisons with things the child knows—from the size of the tail of a comma (,), to a kernel of rice, to a pussy-willow bud, to a grandmother's thimble. The chorionic sac is first described as "a house with no windows or doors—a house smaller than a grain of salt from the shaker, or a grain of sand from the beach. But this was a house that could grow, and a house that was going to have roots." In a similar vein and with stately cadence the story of new life unfolds in all its wonder.

This book has to be seen and read to be fully appreciated. Its enthusiastic endorsement by the *Journal of the American Medical Association* is a tribute to its quality.

A happy return to fiction is effected with *In The Forest* (Viking Press, 1944). This is a story of more subtle fantasy than *Mr. Penny*. Here the author shows great skill in capturing the blend of fancy and matter-of-factness which is found in children's imaginative play. A little boy with a paper hat and a new horn goes for a walk in the forest. There he meets, by ones and twos, wild animals which children all know from storybooks, hearsay, and visits to the zoo. This is the child's happily egocentric, anthropomorphic world. The animals stop whatever they are doing and go along with the boy, but first, each in his way has to get ready, just as a child would for a trip. The lion must comb his hair; the baby elephants stop their bath, dry themselves, and get partially dressed as a very young child would do; the bears stop counting their peanuts and eating jam; "the monkeys get their best suits from a hole in a tree"; the mother and father kangaroos interrupt the lesson in hopping they were giving their baby; the stork says nothing, but comes too; and the timid rabbit joins the parade on the child's invitation.

Each encounter with a new animal is beautifully developed, with three full-page illustrations and a line or two of text on each page, and tied into the theme of the story by the repetition of the phrase "when I went for a walk in the forest." The animals are good old friends by the time they are seen in a double-page illustration of all eleven of them and the child on their walk. A picnic, with ice cream and cake, and games, is perfectly natural in this make-believe story. The transition back to reality is delightfully handled. Children will appreciate the father who respects his child's fantasy, but takes him safely home to the real world.

My Dog Rinty (Viking Press, 1946) was written in collaboration with Ellen Tarry. The story takes place in Harlem and is one of the few better children's books dealing with a minority group. Young readers will enjoy the mischievous dog, Rinty. They will sympathize with the anguish of his young master, David, when the boy's father insists that the dog be sold because of the trouble he causes—following David to school, chewing holes in carpets, and causing inadvertent damage in shops. Children will share David's joy when a reformed Rinty is returned to him and when they learn that Rinty's mischief was really due to his being a born mouser. A warmly satisfying conclusion is reached when David and Rinty win fame and fortune as the Pied Pipers of Harlem.

What could have been a sprightly, entertaining story is weighted down with a brief plea for slum clearance, a subject of little interest to young children. The book is illustrated with unimaginative photographs in an unsuccessful attempt to add reality to the story. There is much emphasis in the text on the poverty of David's family; yet in each picture the family appear well dressed and groomed, and they seem to be living in quite comfortable quarters. Even street scenes in Harlem do not convey the reality of poverty. They are just dull and drab, and could be any city anywhere. There is not one photograph in this book which suggests poverty as well as Marie Hall Ets' drawings do in *Mr. Penny*.

My Dog Rinty doubtless reflects Mrs. Ets' interest in social work, but one cannot help feeling that it would have been more successful had she done it independently and with her own art work. In all probability the social work flavor would then have evaporated and an engaging story would have resulted.

It is a pleasure to find Marie Hall Ets her own true self again in the delightful story, *Oley, The Sea Monster* (Viking Press, 1947). This is the saga of an appealing seal pup who loses his mother and has many adventures before he finds her again. Children will respond to Oley's grief and longing for his mother and the harbor by the sea where he was born. The sadness of this separation is relieved by Oley's success as the chief attraction at the museum in the big city far from the sea, and by the humor of the confusion and turmoil he creates when he is mistaken for a terrifying sea monster after he is set free in Lake Michigan. His safe return after a long trip through the Great Lakes, down the St. Lawrence River, and along the coast of Maine to his own harbor by the sea and to his mother brings the story to a satisfying conclusion.

This book is animated with one hundred and forty drawings, one for each line of text, a feature which will delight children. Variety in the size of the illustrations adds to their appeal. Each simple drawing is filled with action and feeling. Only a very skillful artist could produce on this scale and maintain such a high level of performance throughout. The double-page picture map of Oley's long trip home adds reality to his journey, and incidentally is an irresistible lesson in geography!

Little Old Automobile (Viking Press, 1948) is the tale of a naughty little car whose response to every request is "No, I don't want to! I don't want to and I won't!" Children will recognize some of their own negativism in the auto's reactions and for a while may wish they could get away with as much as the car does. They will enjoy his run down the hilly road and the discomfort he causes everyone in his way, — a frog, two rabbits, a duck and two hens, a gentle cow, and a farmer's wife with a pig and basket of eggs in her arms. But children know instinctively that such irresponsible behavior cannot continue unchecked without calamity. It is almost a relief when Little Old Automobile meets his come-uppance in a crash with the big, black train. Little Old Automobile goes up in the air, just the way his own victims did earlier in the story, "but Little Old Automobile never came down again. Just pieces came down." There is a quality of poetic justice in the tranquil peace with which his former victims enjoy the salvaged parts of Little Old Automobile.

The illustrations are particularly noteworthy. They successfully define in simple black and white lines the characters, the action, mood, and setting of the tale. Every one of them speaks affectionately of the bucolic charm of rolling, hilly farm country.

Mr. T. W. Anthony Woo (Viking Press, 1951) is well qualified to become one of the classics of young children's books. This is the story of a cat, a dog, and a mouse who live with a kind old man, the Cobbler of Shooska. The cat and dog fight continually, all but demolish the cobbler's shop in the course of their battles, and terrify the little mouse, Mr. T. W. Anthony Woo. An intolerable situation arises when the cobbler's sister, who hates animals, moves in to keep house for him. However, because of Miss Dora's fear of mice, timid little Mr. Woo becomes the reluctant hero of the tale and frightens her away. The dog and cat learn that fighting does not pay, and thereafter the three animals and the cobbler live together in harmony and peace.

Mr. T. W. Anthony Woo is reminiscent of *Mr. Penny* (1935), involving as the earlier book does a kind old man with a family of mischievous animals. However, *Mr. T. W. Anthony Woo* is an even more convincing and satisfying story because the cat, dog, and mouse are more realistically conceived than the farm animals and because the plot development is more soundly based on the facts of animal life. Children also will particularly enjoy a laugh at adult's expense when they laugh at Miss Dora's terror of Mr. Woo.

The illustrations are distinguished by their humor, action, and expression. They clarify the folksy quality of the story and add reality to the details of the text. Mrs. Ets' unfailing skill as an artist is a continual pleasure.

Beasts and Nonsense (Viking Press, 1952) is a venture in nonsense verse, for the most part zoo-inspired. Each verse is accompanied by one of Marie Hall Ets' inimitable drawings. The humor of the verses, however, is rather sophisticated and adult, and of doubtful appeal to young children. Youngsters find zoo animals completely fascinating as they are and will not, I think, particularly enjoy the fun Mrs. Ets pokes at them.

Another Day (Viking Press, 1953) is a sequel to *In the Forest* (1943). Here we meet the same boy, with his paper hat and horn, again in the forest where he joins a confab of the animals. "Each one will show what he can do. Then we'll decide which thing is the best," Old Elephant explains to the child. Each animal performs and shows off one of his natural talents. The child stands on his head and laughs as he tries to pick up peanuts with his nose the way Young Elephant did. His laugh is declared to be the best thing of all. Again, the fantasy ends with Dad calling the child.

This is a charming story, and children will enjoy the sociable animals and their stunts. The illustrations are delightful, full of humor, expression, and action and up to Marie Hall Ets' high standards of draftsmanship and composition. However, the story does not seem as successful as *In the Forest*. In *Another Day* the animals are introduced as a group. The reader never gets to know them as well as the ones in the earlier story. Also, featuring the child's laugh as the most wonderful thing in the world is surely an adult concept and does not reflect a child's feeling. A young child is no more conscious of the beauty of his laugh than he is of his appearance or the sound of his voice.

Play with Me (Viking Press, 1955) is happy proof that Marie Hall Ets continues to grow as an author-artist. This story of a little girl's experience in making friends with meadow and woodland animals is related with a disarming simplicity of great subtlety. There is deep understanding here of a child's yearning to play with all creatures, the frustration which comes when the feeling is not reciprocated, and the exquisite joy felt when a wild creature loses its fear and responds, no matter how tentatively, to the child. This is the most real of all of Mrs. Ets' stories. The animals do not talk, think, or act as people do. They remain unchanged throughout. It is the child who changes, profiting from past experience, so that the animals lose their natural fear of her and "play" with her in their own quiet way.

The pastel illustrations (Mrs. Ets' first use of color in her drawings) are exquisite. The more they are studied, the more one appreciates their subtlety, superb drawing, expression, and appropriateness to a gentle tale. A surprising amount of variety is achieved with a minimum of change in scene and situation. Each gesture of the child is meaningful, even the direction of her eyes. Slight changes in the position of the animals reflect the development of the story. The very restrained use of color somehow manages to illuminate each drawing. Most admirable of all is the way each picture captures a bit of the essence of beauty found in young children and wild creatures.

It is to be hoped that Marie Hall Ets will continue to bring her many talents to the field of literature for young children. First and foremost she is a born storyteller. Her plots are simple and straightforward, involving characters and situations of interest to youngsters. There are no extraneous details, subplots, or incidental characters to confuse young readers. Each character and incident is important to the development of the story, just as each word is essential in the text. A poetic quality in her prose adds to its charm and appeal. Fantasy is never abused with exaggeration. The imagination and humor characteristic of her work have their roots in reality.

The high qualities and skills which Marie Hall Ets brings to storytelling are equally matched by the artistry, good taste, simplicity, directness, and sensitivity of her illustrations. This fortuitous combination of talents makes her one of the outstanding figures in the field of children's picture storybooks. That adults, as well as children, can enjoy her books is an added tribute to her work.

EDITORS' NOTE

At a very early age, Marie Hall Ets displayed an aptitude for drawing which was encouraged by her parents and teachers. From childhood on she also loved all animals and used to go off by herself to observe them in the North Woods of Wisconsin, where her family spent their summers. These early years provided the background for her vivid animal stories. Her travels brought her into contact with children in varying settings and with diversified heritages. As a volunteer worker at a settlement house in Chicago she enjoyed the street games of children. Later she traveled for the United Charities to the mountains of West Virginia, making a cost-of-living survey. The Red Cross sent her to Czechoslovakia to help that government set up a permanent child-health program.

After the death of Mr. Ets in 1943, Mrs. Ets made her permanent home in New York City. She still loves to travel, however, particularly to Wisconsin where, in the summer of 1959, she followed the circuses. Alabama and Mexico are also favorite places to revisit.

Nine Days to Christmas (Viking), which was written in collaboration with a Mexican friend, Aurora Labastida, was awarded the Caldecott Medal in 1960. This story departs from the usual depiction of Mexican children as villagers wearing ponchos and following burros. The authors felt natives of Mexico resented this stereotyping, particularly since 70 percent live in cities. Many Mexicans who served as models recognize themselves with delight in this beautiful book.

Gilberto and the Wind (1963 — Viking) also has a real child as a model — a little boy from La Jolla, California, who has appeared in other books.

Mister Penny's Race Horse (1956 — Viking) was a runner-up in 1957 for the Randolph J. Caldecott Award. *Talking Without Words* (1968 — Viking) won the New York Times Choice of Best Illustrated Children's Books Award for 1969 (an annual selection by three judges made since 1952).

Marie Hall Ets has also written: *Cow's Party* (1958 — Viking), *Mister Penny's Circus* (1961 — Viking), *Automobiles for Mice* (1964 — Viking), *Bad Boy, Good Boy* (1967 — Crowell), and *Beasts and Nonsense* (1968 — Viking).

Exploring History
with Genevieve Foster[*]

ANNIVERSARIES ARE OCCASIONS for thinking of history, whether it be only one year of history, or, as in the case of *Elementary English* this month, a span of thirty years. Almost invariably, when we think of a period of history in our own time, we recreate the course of events in terms of personal experiences. Finding ourselves engaged in this process of thinking, we cannot help calling to mind the author who has used, so successfully, this device for recreating history that it has real meaning for young people.

Genevieve Foster, according to one of the social studies teachers at The Laboratory School, is a creative craftsman in the materials of history. She has created a second dimension in the interpretation of history for young people, creating it, as she has said, out of her own need to understand history. Children, for the most part, have studied history as a vertical column of events, in one country or region, year by year, marking off segments to be learned in one year. Thus, most of us studied the history of our own nation, first, from the discovery to the end of the Revolutionary War, then, to the end of the Civil War, and then, if there were ever time, from the Reconstruction period to the present. Newer curricula have brought some changes in organization and correlation of the subject matter of history, but it is still largely considered in a vertical plane.

To acquire a concept of the relative time of history is not easy. Most

[*] By Sara Innis Fenwick. From *Elementary English* 31 (October 1954), 315–321. Reprinted with the permission of the National Council of Teachers of English and Sara Innis Fenwick.

149

of us adults have very fuzzy ideas of the time occupied by epochs in world history. For example, the Roman Empire beginning in 27 B.C. with the reign of Augustus Caesar, to most people characterized by a few benevolent and more wicked rulers, was soon over-run by Gothic invaders, and declined. The fact that the Romans occupied one area, Britain, for 400 years, which is a period of time as long as Europeans have been on the North American continent, is, usually, a surprising fact. If a time sense is not easy for adults to exercise, how much more difficult it is for children! This fact is underscored for us, daily, when we realize that the *War* we speak of as adults is already ancient history to children, and that when they say the *War* they are referring to the Korean fighting.

Young people today have had contemporary history made alive to them in a most exciting way through the developments in news reporting by radio and television. A horizontal view of history in the making in today's current events is a part of every day's experience for children. They know what is going on in Indo-China, in Germany, in Africa, in the world of science, the world of sport, of drama, music, and art, as well as in those less desirable portions of the current scene in police court and underworld. Children still need, however, as desperately as any generation has ever needed, a similarly broad view of what has happened in the past in order to develop the perspective which will help them to form value judgments. Genevieve Foster, in her "World" books, has provided materials upon which such understandings can be nourished.

George Washington's World, Abraham Lincoln's World, Augustus Caesar's World were not planned as merely supplementary materials for an area of social studies. To use them thus is to limit their usefulness. Mrs. Foster designed them each as an introduction to a period of history, as basic to an understanding that lives of outstanding men who punctuate all history were not lived in isolation, but, while they were exerting qualities of leadership in one country, other men and women were at various stages of their careers in other national scenes. Thus, we read in *George Washington's World* while George Washington was growing up on Ferry Farm in Virginia, Catherine the Great went to Russia, James Watt was busy in his father's shop, Marie Theresa became Queen of Austria, Chien Sung had begun his reign as Emperor of China, George III was growing up in the Court of England, Daniel Boone was learning to hunt. None of these people were without influence on the life of the future leader of our country.

A graphic illustration of the vitality of a program of study based on this approach to a period of history was presented at The Laboratory School,

University of Chicago, during the Summer School, 1954, where the reading activities of the upper-age group, which included children at four grade levels from fifth to ninth, were based upon the book, *George Washington's World*. The objectives of the program included that of developing skill in informational reading, a greater interest in reading of biography, and an appreciation of the history of our nation and its place in world history.

Interest was aroused by discussions of the meaning of the term *contemporary*, and what its significance was to each of the group, in terms of recent world events. *George Washington's World* was introduced, and first enthusiasm was aroused by the double-page illustrations of people and events which were contemporary with the various phases of Washington's life. During the summer session, each one in the group read the book at his own pace. In addition, each child read more material about any one or more persons contemporary with Washington, and shared his reading with the group in various ways: through story, biography, oral report, drawing, and painting. One thirteen-year-old girl, who had never been an enthusiastic reader, became so interested in the patriots of the War of Independence and in their wives, that during the five week summer session she read a biography of Patrick Henry, one of Alexander Hamilton's wife, two of Thomas Jefferson, and one book about Jefferson's daughter. A twelve-year-old boy read Ludwig's *Napoleon* to satisfy his curiosity about the career of the "Little Corporal." Some excellent creative writing was produced, including a sketch about Mozart, written as though by a contemporary. As an outcome of the unit, the group produced in their dramatics class a series of dramatizations of the time of Washington, solving several unusual stage production problems in their efforts to have a series of three or four scenes taking place at the same time. Background scenery was painted in the art class periods. The result was a rich sampling of George Washington's world, each participant choosing his own particular person and scene of interest, and his channel of expression.

It is the wealth of material to appeal to so many varied interests of young people, while exploring history, that is the source of one of the great values of Mrs. Foster's writings. Materials from the fields of science, music, painting, archeology, are all included, and open up many new fields of interest.

As further evidence that the "World" books offer riches for all readers, Mrs. Foster has described the use of the books as a background for the development of a program called *In My Father's World,* in a school where the majority of pupils came from homes in which were first- or second-generation Americans, and which represented many rich national cultures. With their parents' help they put together a broad picture of what life was like, and what history was taking place in the many countries represented by their family's experiences.

Genevieve Foster states that the writing of the "World" books grew out of her own desire to develop an understanding of history. She had always found the subject matter of history to be a vast, unnavigable sea of people, dates, wars, and nations. But, standing above the sea most clearly were the people, always, and it seemed to Mrs. Foster that these must be the most recognizable landmarks to all readers. She felt that it ought to be possible to relate the course of events over the world to the things that happened to one personality whose career touched many of the significant happenings. For, after all, as Mrs. Foster pointed out, this is the way we look back over the contemporary history which has touched our own lives. She remembers the launch that came across the lake to the boat dock on which she sat, dangling her feet in the water, bringing the news that war had broken out in Europe in 1914. In like manner, most adults undoubtedly remember exactly what they were doing on the Sunday afternoon of December 7th, 1941, when the broadcast concert of the Philharmonic Orchestra was interrupted to announce that Pearl Harbor had been bombed.

Mrs. Foster's inspiration to develop this technique in writing history was strengthened by noting the enthusiasm with which her daughter, Joanna, discovered a comparison between the costumes worn in the movie, *Catherine the Great,* and those in the history she was at the time reading about George Washington. Joanna tugged at her mother's sleeve with the question, "Did this Queen live at the same time as George Washington?" and Mrs. Foster was not certain herself, until they had returned home to do some reference work. But she had found her clue to a method for making history more meaningful.

Abraham Lincoln's World was the most difficult to write, Mrs. Foster acknowledged, even as it is the most difficult for children to read. This is understandable when one considers the many upheavals in nationalistic spirit and economics and social change that were breaking the surface of the stream of world history in the period marked by the life of Abraham Lincoln.

Possessing the profound respect for order and accuracy which is a prime requisite for a historian, Genevieve Foster laid the groundwork for each of the three "World" books in a series of chronological charts, wonderfully fascinating and exciting outlines of what was happening around the world, and how, where, and why each event touched the life of the character from whose point of view this particular segment of time is being considered. Having this great wealth of interesting material spread and organized, the author recreated the life of her main character, pulling in the strands of contemporary lives and events in Europe, Asia, South America, Africa, and weaving them precisely, with a style reflecting her originality and vision. Thus she produced a panoramic tapestry of the worlds of George Washington, Abraham Lincoln, and Augustus Caesar. There is excitement, humor, and great fascination in Genevieve Foster's writing.

It is the good fortune of younger readers than the eleven to fifteen-year-old group who form the best audience for the "World" books, that Mrs. Foster's publishers persuaded her to use her research and skill to fill one of the great gaps in children's literature—the well-written, simple biography. The series has been called the Initial biographies.

Mrs. Foster has written the four Initial biographies as introductions to the characters and careers of the four men whose life spans encompassed most our country's history: George Washington, leader in the struggle for Independence and in the first years of the existence of the nation; Andrew Jackson, a part of the great movements of expansion; Abraham Lincoln, who was born only 9 years after Washington's death and piloted the nation through its great test of disunion; and Theodore Roosevelt, who saw Lincoln's funeral train as a boy, and was a leader of the new era and the new century of "growing up" of the United States. The task of writing a brief, introductory biography of George Washington, which was the first of this series, intrigued the author with the demand for extracting from the mass of material which she had collected in the three years' task of writing *George Washington's World*—the essence, so to speak, of the hero's life. She says she was encouraged as she thought of the challenge faced by Mme. Marie Curie as she reduced the carload of pitchblende before she extracted a tiny bit of precious radium. Mrs. Foster achieved a compactly written, interesting, and historically sound biography of Washington, which, while it is simplified, is never "written down"; and she has kept up that high standard in the three following biographies: *Abraham Lincoln* (1950), *Andrew Jackson* (1951), and *Theodore Roosevelt* (1954).

Since the text of each brief biography had to be so distilled to the essential facts, it seemed important that every facet of the presentation should add something to the reader's conception of the character and his life story. The style of writing, sentence length, dialogue, and vocabulary all were viewed as tools by the author, to be used in the telling of the story. Thus, she chose to write of George Washington in a quiet style, with little dialogue, because he was a quiet man. The style of *Abraham Lincoln* mirrors something of the slow tempo of the period, and of the deliberate quality of its hero. *Andrew Jackson* is written in a staccato style, characteristic of the explosive character of "Old Hickory." This example is from the opening pages of *Andrew Jackson:*

Wahoo! Bangity Bang! With a whoop and a holler, Andy Jackson burst out of the door one yellow autumn morning. He snatched up a stick for a gun and went popping and banging down the slope toward the South Carolina post road.

In setting the style for *Theodore Roosevelt,* Mrs. Foster had in mind the tremendous drive and vigor of the man.

With guidance, children reading these biographies can be made aware of qualities of style in writing, and can be helped to appreciate the different ways of writing description and telling a story. Use of these volumes proved valuable in the biography reading experience of a fourth grade group at The Laboratory School. Each child chose a person to read about, read a biography suitable to his level of ability, compared information he had found with other sources, and then wrote a biography of his own, embodying what he thought was important and interesting in the material he had read. Much attention was given to style of writing, and the children learned quickly to react to interesting, picturesque description. Boyhood experiences of chosen characters are emphasized. The two following selected paragraphs give word pictures which the children enjoyed.

Abraham Lincoln—page 12: One summer morning, Abe was asleep on his sacks of cornhusks on the cabin floor. A thin streak of sunlight, slanting in through the logs, fell upon his tight closed eyelids. He blinked, rolled over, and sat up. At that a scrubby little hound jumped up, all a-wriggle, here and there, to cover him with kisses.

George Washington—page 11: The minute he opened his eyes, one April morning, George was out of bed. It was earlier than usual, but he hurried into his shirt, jumped into his brown trousers and tied the shirt string in the back, as fast as possible. He didn't want to waste a minute.

Theodore Roosevelt—page 1–2: What a wonderful day! It was October 27, 1865. And he, Theodore Roosevelt, Jr., who lived at

28 East 20th Street, New York City, was now seven years old. This was his birthday!

The small pale boy sat up long after he had gone to bed, his arms about his knees, thinking it all over. Soft night air gently moved the curtains in the tall nursery window, at his side. In the quiet hall below he heard the clock strike half past eleven.

Some nights, he heard it strike every single hour, nights when he was sick with asthma and could hardly breathe.

A third factor which is a carrier of information in these brief biographies is that of illustration. Mrs. Foster has made the pictures always supplementary to the textual descriptions. Her aim has been to produce pictures which would give an idea of the life of the subject to a child looking at the book, even if he could not read a word. Teachers and librarians will always be grateful to Mrs. Foster for the double-page illustration in *George Washington* which shows a cross-section of the home at Mt. Vernon, giving the arrangement of rooms in the great plantation home.

The illustrations and the design of the books of Genevieve Foster are never an after-thought to the text, because Mrs. Foster is artist as well as writer. She sees each page in its completeness of text, illustration, and design. The illustrations and the page layout are conceived as the text is growing, and Mrs. Foster produces the entire design for each of her volumes, doing the color separation for each illustration herself.

International recognition has been awarded Mrs. Foster for the important contribution she has made to literature for children in the fields of biography and history, and for the interpretation of American history in its relation to world history. *Abraham Lincoln's World* was chosen to go into the CARE packages of books to be sent to schools and libraries abroad. Translations of the "World" books and of the Initial biographies have been made into many foreign languages. Recently, Mrs. Foster has had copies of editions which have been made in French, Greek, Urdu, Bengali, and Arabic languages, and has received word that translations are being made into Turkish and Hebrew. In a world beset with misunderstandings between nations, it is encouraging to know that new generations will have these excellent writings about America, produced by a craftsman with sincerity and integrity, to interpret our country.

To meet Genevieve Foster, personally, is a delightful and heart-warming experience. A lovely and gracious woman, she generously shares her interest and exhilaration in her work. A most charming introduction to her was written by her daughter, Joanna Foster, now with Harcourt Brace & Co., and published in the *Horn Book* magazine, June, 1952.

An anniversary tribute for the contribution she has made to literature for children has been truly merited by Genevieve Foster.

EDITORS' NOTE

Genevieve Foster graduated from the University of Wisconsin and studied for a year at the Chicago Academy of Art. At the time of her marriage she was a commercial artist, and for some years illustrated books and articles for *Child Life* and other magazines. Her own writing did not begin until her daughter, Joanna, was ten years old. From then on, Joanna and her brother served as models for their mother in their large, white house near Lake Michigan in Evanston, Illinois.

As Genevieve Foster became more deeply involved in working toward a unified picture of historical events and people, she found it necessary to travel widely throughout the United States, Canada, Mexico, and Europe. Her travels led finally to a trip around the world, including such places as India, Pakistan, Israel, Egypt, Turkey, Japan, Greece, Indonesia, Cambodia, and Hawaii.

She now resides in New York City and is interested in the theatre, opera, and ballet. Game shows and interviews on television also fascinate her, and she enjoys playing scrabble.

She was a three-time runner-up for the John Newbery Award: in 1945 and again in 1950 for *George Washington's World* (Scribner), and in 1953 for *Birthdays of Freedom,* Vol. I (Scribner).

Mrs. Foster's books now number fifteen, and have been translated into more than twelve languages. Some of these not mentioned in the preceding article are: *World of Captain John Smith* (1959 — Scribner), *World of Columbus and Sons* (1965 — Scribner), *Year of Columbus, 1492* (1969 — Scribner), *Year of the Pilgrims, 1620* (1969 — Scribner), *Year of Independence, 1776* (1970 — Scribner), and *Year of Lincoln, 1861* (1970 — Scribner).

The Work of Doris Gates *

AS THIS ARTICLE GOES TO PRESS, our author-of-the-month, Doris Gates, will be receiving the William Allen White Award at the Kansas Association of School Librarians, in Hutchinson, Kansas, for her latest book, *Little Vic*.

The choice for this Award is made by children in grades three to nine in the State of Kansas. This year's book is the overwhelming choice of 6,000 more children than voted for the first Award, and polled more than twice the ballots cast for any other title.

This shows not only that Doris Gates' stories are important contributions to children's literature as recognized by librarians, teachers, and parents, but that children read them and enjoy them!

The William Allen White Award is one outward indication of the unerring good taste of children who are guided in the direction of good books.

Doris Gates first attained prominence in the field of writing for children in 1940, when she published *Blue Willow*. This book was described as a "modern realistic story of migratory workers." But *Blue Willow* is far more than that, as May Hill Arbuthnot says in her excellent text *Children and Books* (Scott-Foresman), "*Blue Willow* has distinction of style, unusual beauty of theme, and an unforgettable heroine, little Janey Larkin."

* By Charlemae Rollins. From *Elementary English* 31 (December 1954), 459–465. Reprinted with the permission of the National Council of Teachers of English and Charlemae Rollins.

The book has had far-reaching influence in the writing and publishing field. It ushered in a whole new era of children's books facing realistic problems in America. It encouraged other writers and publishers to produce more books dealing with contemporary life. It is often referred to as the "juvenile *Grapes of Wrath*," and has had many imitators.

Julia L. Sauer, distinguished librarian and writer of Rochester, New York, wrote a stirring article in the *Library Journal* (January 15, 1941), titled "Making the World Safe for the Janey Larkins," in which she says in part, "But certainly the greatest need of today of the child 8 to 14, is for books that will make him see, make him think, and help him to relate facts . . . Can impassioned books that depict social conditions be written? Two months ago we should have said, 'We hope so.' Now, we can say, 'Yes,' because it has been done. Doris Gates has written a story of our migratory population. Janey Larkin is an American child with longing in her heart to stay somewhere, to settle so her roots may go down deep in our American soil and draw from it strength and nourishment. She is as real American as Tom Sawyer or Jo March . . . We need many more books about the Janey Larkins in our literature for children . . . and when we get them, we will need courage to give them to our children."

Courageous authors and publishers recognized this need in the 1940's and began to give us realistic stories purposefully slanted toward many of the problems faced by today's children.

Bess Porter Adams, in her recent publication, *About Books and Children* (Henry Holt & Co. 1954), published fourteen years later, says, "In *Blue Willow*, Doris Gates has created a sensitive perceptive character, Janey Larkin, who clings through adversity to the beauty of her treasured blue willow plate. Set against her background of poverty and the insecurity known to migrant workers, Janey is a child to remember long after the book has been laid aside."

Miss Gates in speaking of the book said, "*Blue Willow* shows a child clinging to a symbol of beauty to satisfy the craving for security which the adults around her had failed to provide her with."

In all her stories, Doris Gates recognizes the fact that children live in an adult world and they must fit their dreams and expectations to it. The world of Janey Larkin is a world where things are happening to children — things that are far more important to them than things in history books. When a sixth grader asks for a book about "right now," it is important that the book he reads be one which makes him think and helps him to grow in understanding of the "right now" world.

Before writing *Blue Willow*, Doris Gates wrote *Sarah's Idea*, the story of a little girl whose life on a prune ranch in California parallels her own life. Sarah longed for a burro all her own. She knew she couldn't have a burro simply by asking for it. Her parents had told her so. She had to do something about it. She had great faith in things going *right* instead of wrong. This faith gave her the courage to persevere — to work hard for what she wanted.

This is a book written out of the author's own life experiences, for like Sarah's family, the Gates family lived on a prune ranch in the Santa Clara Valley of California, and Doris had a little gray burro named Jinny. Miss Gates' father was a physician who practiced medicine in a small town. When Doris was Sarah's age, he decided that his two little girls should have the experience of growing up on a ranch. After seventeen years of making his rounds in the rural areas to patients in a side-winding Olds-mobile, he moved his family to the prune ranch that had been his family home. They lived there until Doris and her sister started to high school.

It was here on the beautiful ranch close to horses, dogs, chickens, rabbits, and other animals that her love for all creatures developed. She got to know the neighboring fruit farmers as well as the migrant fruit pickers. Her first hand knowledge of the problems of these people makes her stories vivid and alive with warmth and understanding. It is because she knows and loves the world and the creatures she writes about that her stories find such enthusiastic response from the children.

It is hard indeed to find a little girl who does not immediately identify herself with Kate, who says in *Sensible Kate,* "I'm not cute and I'm not pretty. I'm just sensible." When her new-found friend the young artist questioned this, Kate answered, "Because if you're just sensible, you always have to do what's expected of you, and if you're pretty people don't seem to care." "Why not do the unexpected some day just for fun?" he asked. "No," she said, "I'd better stick to being just sensible. After all, a person has to have something and I'd better make the most of what I've got. Being sensible is better than not being anything at all."

To quote just this to a reluctant girl reader, preferably one who is ob-viously not pretty or cute (and the majority are in this group), is sufficient introduction to this book. When the book is returned the librarian knows by the radiant smile on the reader's face that she is one with Kate, who says at the end of the book, "I'd rather be Sensible Kate than anyone in the world. Even a Movie Actress!"

Many teachers and mothers, too, have unconsciously blessed the author for such a satisfying story and one that girls find completely believable. There are, of course, other factors in the book — the adopted child and the universal appeal of the orphan. Kate is an orphan, but her story is no tear-jerker in the maudlin sense. It does touch the heart, but in a straight-forward happy fashion. If there are tears in it they are tears of two kinds—happiness as well as sadness. Many little girls want and need books that make them cry a little. Nearly every librarian knows a little girl who asks for "a sad book."

Sensible Kate is not a sad book in that sense. It shows a child meeting every phase of living: birth, death, loneliness, antagonism, friendship, and adjusting to these things with dignity.

My Brother Mike also deals with the child without a permanent family, the very real problem of the foster-child. This is perhaps the least understood of all the Gates books, and yet is one of the most needed books in many libraries today. It touches the problem of the returned convict. (It is the only children's book to this writer's knowledge that deals with this important theme.) It took four years to write this story.

Doris Gates said, "I wrote the book after a visit to San Quentin penitentiary where I talked to many of the men at a meeting of a club formed of convicts. Some of the men spoke of their children and it suddenly occurred to me that some of these men would have to return to their children. How would they feel about it? Above all, how would the children feel?"

"This is a deeply perceptive book," says Josette Frank in *Your Child's Reading Today* (Doubleday, 1954).

Indeed, Doris Gates is a "deeply perceptive" person, and a courageous writer—one who is not afraid to write about a child who comes to grips with reality as Billy, the foster-child, does.

Here is a story about a lonely little boy living in a foster home where there is no love, understanding, or warmth. He longs for a hero. Fundamentally, it is a longing for his own father. It matters little that his imaginary hero rides in a new Cadillac instead of on a "prancing steed in shining armour." This longing is just as real and just as satisfying when it is realized. The realization comes in the form of a tramp whom he meets accidentally on the edge of town. Complete understanding and companionship come from Billy's friendship with the tramp, who tells him about a fabulous character, "My Brother Mike."

Doris Gates said, "This book evoked two of the most significant letters that I have ever received from readers. In each case the writer insisted that the book had changed his life. One writer was a boy and one a young girl."

North Fork is another story which was the subject of much controversy when it was published in 1945. Critics of the book resented what they called "a negative approach to the racial question."

It concerns Drew Saunders, a spoiled heir to the lumber mills in North Fork. After the death of his parents, his aunt, fearing he would grow up into a snob, sent him to North Fork to spend a year in a school where he was the only white boy in the 8th grade class. All the others were American Indians. It was there, high in the Sierras, that he learned to value each individual for his own worth. But this truth was learned the hard way. A plane crash in the snow-covered mountains brought crowds of airline officials to the little settlement of North Fork. Monty, the Indian boy who had gradually grown to be his friend, showed him what it meant to believe in one's fellow man. Piney, an old Indian who lived all alone in the mountains, had heard the plane crash but no one believed him — no one but Monty, the Indian boy. And Drew Saunders knew why they didn't believe him. Simply because he was an Indian! But the old man was right and the others were wrong. After Monty found the wrecked plane and was rewarded with a scholarship, Drew thought, "Never again," he vowed, "as long as he lived would his reactions to any man's statements be conditioned by his color. Piney had known and the white man hadn't. Monty had trusted that knowledge and trusting, had achieved what no man up to that moment had been able to achieve."

Drew's ambitions grew and matured. He would become not just a wealthy mill owner, but a lumberman who loved the pine trees and wanted to conserve the great forests.

The U.S. Bureau of Forestry commended Doris Gates for her contribution to the Conservation Program and congratulated her on the fact that all the information in the book is absolutely correct.

Far more important is the fact that the Indian children of North Fork loved the story and proudly presented it as a play in their school. Over the years they have considered it "our book."

Another important concept that *North Fork* brings to the attention of young people is death. This is rarely found in current children's books, but Josette Frank says, "Some concept of death is necessary to everyone, and this includes children."

The understanding teacher in the story helped Drew, whose own parents had been killed in an airplane crash, to understand and accept death in this way: "When you get to studying history, really studying it, you'll discover that a lot of progress has come out of tragedy. It's as if the dead spurred the living on. The only real tragedy comes when people die in vain . . . The living owe the dead an obligation. They have a debt to all the suffering that has been endured in the past. Your father was a good man, a good lumberman, and a good forester. He had dreams and plans, all right. Now it's your job to make those dreams come true for him, and to add to them even better dreams of your own. I suspect that that's about all that living really is, Drew."

Julia Sauer's article continues to throw light on books that come to grips with everyday problems. She says, "Books on such subjects should not attempt to solve these problems; they cannot solve them . . . but it can at least present them so that children may be turning them over in their minds and hearts as they grow in understanding with these pictures before them. Answers and solutions may come. Prejudice in all its forms and establishments — class, racial, religious — could be combated in children's books. It is not enough to turn down books that show prejudice. We need a positive approach and no child is too young to need it."

Few cowboy stories for younger boys and girls are as full of fun and authentic ranch activities as *Trouble for Jerry*. Jerry's trouble was in the form of "dudes" — and girl dudes at that — two girls whose plans included a visit that would last the whole summer. Jerry's troubles caused him to forget his obligation as a host, but the dudes, particularly Sarah and her burro, helped Jerry to understand that girls can be good sports and helpful companions.

River Ranch is a book which Doris Gates explains was written with a purpose. She set out to write an "easy book for older children." She heard that a writer who objected to the dialect planned to "clean up" the grammar in Will James' *Smoky,* and re-write it. She says, "I had no thought that I might forestall the re-writing of *Smoky*. I simply felt as one who loved children's literature, and as an author of children's books it was my duty to recognize the need for these special books in a special field and to supply at least one in an effort to save the great books for children."

River Ranch does serve a worthy purpose. Any librarian or teacher faced with the problem of finding an exciting story for a teen-ager in high school whose reading ability is below 6th grade, is grateful for this book. Boys are especially attracted because the story is a fast-paced account of cattle rustlers, mystery, and exciting adventure on a ranch. Here, as in all her books, Miss Gates writes of California, where she lives. Here also is a book growing out of a need that Doris Gates as a librarian knew first hand. She has been a Children's Librarian and she is aware of the problems faced by librarians. She has been a teacher, and therefore is aware of the difficulties that arise with slow readers who are too mature for "easy readers."

At a meeting of librarians, Doris Gates told an unforgettable story about a little migrant farm girl who longed for a tree at Christmas. Her family couldn't afford to buy a tree, so she found a perfectly symmetrical tumbleweed which represented for her the spirit of Christmas. Hesitating to share its beauty for fear adults would not understand, she hid her "tree." But she was rewarded when a keenly discerning social worker saw it and understood that a makeshift Christmas tree—a tumbleweed— could mean more to a little girl than all the tinsel balls to be found in the dime store.

After hearing the story, two Negro librarians timidly approached her and suggested that she write a story about Negroes for children. Doris Gates was instantly interested, but skeptical and with deep sincerity asked, "But do you think I can? I'd love to try."

Her deep understanding and enjoyment of all kinds of people makes her the perfect choice of a writer for a story such as *Little Vic*. She says of it, "I have always had clear images of what each one of the children in my books looked like. I could pick them out of a crowd. And Pony Rivers happened to be a Negro. I had wanted all children to identify with Pony without knowing the color of his skin. I wanted them to feel with him, to suffer with him and then find out after he had, that the color of his skin made no difference at all between his feelings and theirs."

Little Vic is often listed as a horse story, and indeed it is, but more than that it is the story of a homeless orphan's devotion to an ideal. Without home or parents to love, it is easy to understand how a boy like Pony could lavish all his devotion on a beautiful colt—a colt which everyone, even his owners, agreed would never amount to anything. He followed the horse whenever he was sold, working without pay, just to be allowed to care for him. In spite of all outward appearances, he never wavered in his faith and confidence that Little Vic would some day win a great race.

Doris Gates' stories are often classified as "Stories of Family Life," and they are well placed in that category. Five of her eight books have to do with children in broken homes and three are about children in happy well-adjusted homes. One is an outstanding example of a devoted and understanding step-mother.

Whether she is writing about children in well-adjusted homes where there is love and security, or whether she points up the lack of these fundamental values in other stories, her emphasis is on the importance of family life. She writes about children with a sharpened perception of their deeper needs.

In an article in the *Horn Book* (July 1941) entitled, "Pasture Enough," she makes a moving plea for more getting together for reading by families:

"Reading is by no means the only interest which we as families can share with our children, but it is a good one with which to begin since all interests may radiate from it."

Doris Gates is married. Her husband is a famous Los Angeles lawyer. At present she is living in beautiful Carmel (by the sea) California, where she devotes all her time to her writing and her lovely home.

She says, "I don't like cities except as places to visit and I am passionately fond of the outdoors. I love animals and can't imagine living without a dog. I think it goes without saying, I enjoy people. The only ones I find dull are those who are complacent."

EDITORS' NOTE

Since publication of the foregoing article, Doris Gates has written *Cat and Mrs. Cary* (1962 – Viking) and *Elderberry Bush* (1967 – Viking). The latter is another story based on her own childhood on a prune ranch outside San Jose, California. The father depicted in this book was taken from real life, and there really was an elderberry bush.

The popularity of *Blue Willow* and *Sensible Kate* are evidenced in new editions by Seafarer Viking – the former in 1969 and the latter in 1970. *Blue Willow* was the runner-up in 1941 for the John Newbery Medal. In 1942, it received the Commonwealth Club of California Literature Award (given annually since 1939 to the finest juvenile work on any subject by a Californian). In 1961, it was honored by the Lewis Carroll Shelf Award (given annually since 1958 by the University of Wisconsin for titles considered worthy of sitting on a shelf with *Alice in Wonderland*).

Little Vic received the William Allen White Children's Book Award in 1954 (an annual award given by the William Allen White Memorial Library at Kansas State Teachers College, and voted on by Kansas school children in grades 4–8 choosing from a list chosen by specialists).

In writing about Doris Gates, Charlemae Rollins quotes her as saying she cannot imagine living without a dog. Children might be interested in knowing that her present housemates are a Doberman pinscher named Tor and a cat named Topey.

"Who Thunk You Up, Dr. Seuss?" *

LA JOLLA, CALIF.

WITH HIS EQUINE NOSE, crinkly-soft eyes and loping mooselike walk, he looks for all the world as though he had sprung full-blown from his own drawing board. All that is missing when you see Theodor S. Geisel plain is the signature below, two words warmly familiar to millions of children and their grateful parents—Dr. Seuss. They are, of course, one and the same: Ted Geisel of La Jolla, Calif., and Dr. Seuss, the pseudonym he has used for three decades while writing and illustrating, slowly and painfully, 30-odd children's books. Year after year, his books are all best sellers and all are still in print. His latest, *I Can Lick 30 Tigers Today and Other Stories* and *My Book About Me,* are due in the stalls this autumn.

"Counting Lewis Carroll and allowing for A. A. Milne," a reviewer once noted, "Dr. Seuss has become the most important name ever pressed on a children's book jacket." Bennett Cerf, Seuss's publisher at Random House since the late '30's, adds to that estimate with: "I've published any number of great writers, from Faulkner to O'Hara, but there's only one genius on my authors list. His name is Ted Geisel." Geisel shrugs off the compliment. "If I'm such a genius," he wants to know, "why is it that I have to work so hard? I know my stuff looks like it was done in 23 seconds but every word is a struggle and every sentence is like the pangs of birth."

Seuss's juvenile readers, unconcerned about his genius standing,

* By Donald Freeman. From *San Jose Mercury News,* June 15, 1969, sec. Parade, pp. 12–13. © 1969 by *San Jose Mercury News.* Reprinted by permission.

respond with their own kind of brightly turned words of praise. "This is the funniest book I ever read in nine years," a 9-year-old wrote to Seuss. Another: "Dr. Seuss, you have an imagination with a long tail!" ("Now there," says Seuss, "is a kid who's going places!") Yet another wrote about a Seuss book: "All would like it from age 6 to 44 – that's how old my mother is." An 8-year-old wrote: "Dear Dr. Seuss, you sure thunk up a lot of funny books. You sure thunk up a million funny animals . . . Who thunk you up, Dr. Seuss?"

AN ALMOST-DOCTOR

Geisel admits that he thunk up Dr. Seuss with ease – Seuss is his mother's maiden name and his own middle name. The "Dr." he lightly assumed in view of his post-graduate pursuit of a doctorate in literature at Oxford, which he never obtained. The world of Seussiana, however, he thunk up only by that inexplicable but immensely fruitful creative process from which, over the years, has flowed such wildly fanciful creatures as the Drum-Tummied Snumm "who can drum any tune that you might care to hum" and the sneetches and nerkles and nutches "who live in small caves, known as nitches, for hutches" and Thidwick the Big-Hearted Moose and Yertle the Turtle and the Bippo-no-Bungus from Hippo-no-Hungus, not to mention the Tufted Mazurka from the Isle of Yerka and the Scrooge of a beast known as a Grinch who very nearly stole Christmas. Where does he get his ideas? "I get them," Geisel confides, "in a little town near Zybliknov where I spend an occasional weekend."

Usually the Seuss stories sum up a moral, always easy to take. But Geisel winces at the comment of one critic who saw him as "the greatest moralist since Elsie Dinsmore." Running a hand fiercely through his unkempt silver-gray hair, Geisel insists: "It's impossible to write anything without making a statement in some way." In *The Sneetches,* for instance, Seuss rings the bell for equality and against snobbery. The story dwells on the Star-Belly Sneetches with stars on their bellies and they're snooty to the Plain-Belly Sneetches who realize, in the end, that they're just as good, anyway. In *How the Grinch Stole Christmas,* the evil Grinch makes off with all the presents in Who-ville, but the Whos, those resourceful miniature creatures, celebrate without presents, saying: "Maybe Christmas doesn't come from a store. Maybe Christmas . . . means a little bit more."

Aside from his *Yertle the Turtle,* a parable on Hitler, Geisel set out only once to moralize. Soon after producing a film documentary on Japan – it won him one of his three Academy Awards (the others were for *Hitler Lives,* a documentary short, and the animated cartoon, *Gerald McBoing-Boing)* — Geisel wrote *Horton Hears a Who.* Here the tiny Whos symbolize the Japanese people, defeated in war and seeking their own form of democracy. Probably the message of Dr. Seuss to the world of both children and grownups may be summed up in one line from that book. The line goes: "A person is a person no matter how small." Ted Geisel nods as he contemplates this simple moral. "It's true, you know," he says. "No matter how small, a person *is* a person."

To augment the subtle messages, the works of Dr. Seuss are splashed with creatures that come in improbable colors and shapes and verse rhythms. Consider the following from his *Green Eggs and Ham:*

> *Do you like*
> *Green eggs and ham?*
> *I do not like them*
> *Sam-I-am*
> *I do not like*
> *Green eggs and ham . . .*
> *I do not like them*
> *here or there*
> *I do not like them*
> *anywhere . . .*

Seuss has also churned out gloriously inspired squelches. In "You're a Mean One, Mr. Grinch," one of his lyrics for the award-winning TV production of his *How the Grinch Stole Christmas,* he has a chorus lash out with:

"You're a bad banana with a greasy black peel. Your brain is full of spiders; you've garlic in your soul. Your heart is full of unwashed socks; your soul is full of gunk." And then the malevolent topper: "You're a three-decker sauerkraut and toadstool sandwich with arsenic sauce!"

HOME IN A TOWER

The style of the words, as with most writers, reflects the man himself and inside Ted Geisel there resides a full complement of smiling, restlessly impish demons. He views the world, in short, from a special, charmingly eccentric tilt.

With his wife, Audrey, who has a smile that would bedazzle a snerkle or a grinch, Geisel lives and works in a converted watchtower, now a showplace of a home that overlooks the Pacific waters with a breath-stopping view from the highest hill in La Jolla. A small printed sign on the door warns: "Beware of the Cat." The Geisels have no cats unless one counts the 400 or so feline specimens in his various paintings. One also contains about 200 faces of cats in a cluster; it's called, appropriately, "A Plethora of Cats." In contrast to another distinguished American author-illustrator, the late James Thurber who drew wistful dogs, Geisel leans to cats, an animal for which he professes no particular affection. "The truth of the matter," says Ted, "is that I like dogs much better than cats but I never draw them."

It was a cat drawing, in fact, that led Geisel to first cranking out books for 6-year-olds. This happy accident occurred in the mid-1950's when educators and parents were concernedly asking themselves: Why Can't Johnny Read? His publisher suggested that Geisel enter the void with a book including no more than 348 words of one syllable but wouldn't have, as Geisel says, "any of the old dull stuff like Dick has a ball. Dick likes the ball. The ball is red, red, red." For months, Geisel grappled helplessly with the assignment. One night, he was rummaging through his discarded sketches when he spotted one of a rakish-looking cat he had drawn wearing a stovepipe hat at a cavalier angle. Since both "cat" and "hat" were on the word list, Geisel parlayed them into *The Cat in the Hat,* a comic gem now a supplementary text for first-graders. The book's success led Random House to inaugurate Beginner Books, of which he is president. Lately, Seuss has launched Bright and Early Books appealing to pre-schoolers.

For these books he sometimes uses the name of Theo. LeSieg—Geisel spelled backwards. "I keep writing behind pseudonyms but I don't really know why," Geisel says. "Is it shyness? Am I hiding? I used to tell myself I used 'Dr. Seuss' to save my real name for when I write The Great American Novel. But what most people don't know, and I rarely remind them, is that I already wrote my Great American Novel, unpublished and deservedly so. This was over 40 years ago and I can't even remember what it was about. First I wrote it in two volumes. Then I trimmed it to one volume, then I cut it to a long short story, then a paragraph. Finally I sold it as a two-line caption for a cartoon."

Since then, with one exception, Geisel has written his fiction strictly for children—"adults are merely obsolete children and nuts to them," he says. In 1939, he wrote a humor book for grownups called *The Seven Lady Godivas.* In wacky word and drawing, Geisel relates that there really were seven Lady Godivas and the legendary *voyeur* who peeked as she rode by on the horse undraped wasn't a Peeping Tom but a local chap called Tom Peeping—Peeping being his surname. "I tried to draw my

Godivas as very sexy babes," Geisel recalls, bemusedly thumbing through the book. "But look at them—they're neuter and sexless and have no shape at all." They don't, either. But then, Geisel never did study art.

Geisel's predilection for animals is probably traceable to his boyhood in Springfield, Mass., where he was born on March 4, 1904. Since his father's duties as supervisor of public parks included the overseeing of the city's zoo, young Ted and his sister often romped with the animals. One incident in his boyhood left Geisel with a dread of audiences. He turns down all invitations to give speeches and over him lingers a reputation, more myth than fact, for shyness. When Geisel was 14, Theodore Roosevelt came to town to address a World War I bond rally and to give medals to Boy Scouts with the best bond-selling records. Along with the other boys, Geisel sat nervously as their names were called out to receive the medals. Sadly, Geisel's name had been inadvertently omitted from the list. Finally, there was Roosevelt and Ted Geisel sitting alone on the platform. "I can still hear it now," Geisel says. "Teddy Roosevelt looking around and asking, 'What is this little boy doing here?' And all those eyes from the audience staring right through me, the people whispering, 'Ted Geisel tried to get a medal and he didn't deserve it.' I can hear them saying, 'What's he *doing* there?' Even today, I find myself asking, 'What *am* I doing here?' "

YANKS AT OXFORD

Later, Geisel attended Dartmouth, where he nurtured hopes of becoming a professor of literature. For graduate work he went to Oxford where he met a fellow American, a literature student named Helen Palmer who was intrigued by the winged horses he was forever doodling in his notebooks. She sensed that Geisel's true bent was toward art and wisely steered him along that path. She also became his wife. A talented writer and editor herself, Helen Palmer Geisel was the author of several children's books and editor in chief of Beginner Books until her death in 1967.

It was in 1927 that Geisel's cartoons landed in the magazines of the day such as *Judge, Vanity Fair* and the old *Life*. During his tenure in advertising, he conceived the Seuss Navy, a popular pre-World War II promotional antic, along with the catchphrase, "Quick Henry, the Flit!" Geisel's first children's book, *And to Think That I Saw It on Mulberry Street,* was very nearly his last. After getting rejection slips from 27 publishers, Geisel was ready to quit when, one day, he met an old Dartmouth friend who had just been tapped as children's book editor at Vanguard Press. He promptly snapped it up. *Mulberry* has gone through over 20 editions and still sells 15,000 copies a year.

Geisel sees himself essentially as a writer who draws. "The drawing is fun," he says. "The writing is murder." For one 60-page Seuss book, both story and illustrations, the usual gestation period is a full year or more. And for every 50 pages of manuscript he finds acceptable, he hurls 500 pages on the floor, the receptacle as well for at least 95 percent of his drawings. When the words won't come, Geisel will stare glumly out at the Pacific or, if the creative well turns completely dry, he may topple his lean, six-foot frame on the nearest couch, thrash the air and groan in misery. The efforts he used to throw away he now dispatches by mail, at the university's request, to the UCLA library, which also houses the original drawings and manuscripts of all the Seuss books.

"TIME AND SWEAT"

"The 'creative process,'" Geisel says, mocking the words, "consists for me of two things—time and sweat. Too many writers have only contempt and condescension for children, which is why they give them such degrading corn about bunnies. But the kids often have no choice. Mama doesn't know any better and she buys the gooky treacle they call children's books in supermarkets. When you write for kids, you can't lose them for one second. If you don't take the child forward with each turn of the page, you're cooked." Geisel ponders the notion that he is a perfectionist. "A perfectionist," he says, finally, "is a guy who works toward something he knows he's not going to get. There is no perfection. If there's one secret to my writing, it's simply this—eliminate the unnecessary."

As a relief from the delicious drudgery of authorship, Geisel paints with fairly serious intent, allowing his flair for the absurd to erupt with wacky titles.

Meanwhile, Geisel weighs the imponderables of his fame. "Dr. Seuss," he murmured. "It's not easy being him, knowing that every time at bat you have to deliver. And whenever kids see me, they're inevitably disappointed. They expect Dr. Seuss to have a red nose and baggy pants and a beard and a horn. I say I'm Dr. Seuss and they don't believe me." Geisel nonetheless holds a mystic affinity with children although he has never fathered any of his own. "You make 'em," he says, "and I'll amuse 'em." And that he does, better than anyone else this side of Who-ville, which is not far from the wilds of Hippo-no-Hungus.

EDITORS' NOTE

Theodor Seuss Geisel (Dr. Seuss) has delighted young children with his many imaginative and humorous books. Three of his books, *Horton Hears a Who* (1954 – Random House), *How the Grinch Stole Christmas* (1957 – Random House), and *The Cat in the Hat* (1957 – Beginner Books), have been made into animated specials and shown on television. He uses his skill in presenting and creating reading material for the youngest readers in his position as president of Beginner Books, a division of Random House.

Some of the most recent Dr. Seuss books are: *The Lorax* (1971 – Random House), *I Can Draw It Myself* (1970 – Beginner Books), *My Book About Me* (1971 – Beginner Books), *I Can Write* (1971 – Beginner Books), and *Mr. Brown Can Moo! Can You?* (1970 – Bright and Early Books).

Dr. Seuss books are published in Great Britain, Japan, and Israel. The original drawings and manuscripts of all Dr. Seuss books are in the Special Collections Division of the Library at the University of California at Los Angeles.

Little Toot — Hero *

TWO LITTLE BOYS were coming away from the city library. Proceeding at a very slow pace, they were looking at the beginning pages of their books. Then one of the children began peering at the book of his friend. The page was turned and the next was examined closely. Heads together, the two boys finally stood still and read, as heavy traffic on an exceedingly busy street rushed past them. What was the book which was holding these youngsters spellbound? As the boy lifted it to turn a page, the title on the cover flashed into view. It was *Little Toot*.

Just twenty-one years ago *Little Toot* was published, and this account of a gay little tugboat has maintained, and perhaps even increased, its popularity through the years. Many a teacher of young children has seen Little Toot dart from the pages of this newer classic and into the lives of boys and girls with a swiftness and smoothness rivalling a modern jet. This is an action story of tremendous appeal to all and to boys especially, a story not only written but also illustrated by one of America's outstanding artists, Hardie Gramatky. The pictures are as exciting as the words.

Hardie Gramatky has had an action-filled life himself. Born in Dallas, Texas, he was reared in Los Angeles, California. While he attended Stanford University and an art school, he often would go on sketching tours for many days, driving wherever the notion led him and painting numerous pictures. He had many types of jobs: in a bank, in a logging camp, and on a freighter and a lumber schooner. He was the ghost-writer of a well-

* By Helen W. Painter. From *Elementary English* 37 (October 1960), 363–367. Reprinted with the permission of the National Council of Teachers of English and Helen W. Painter.

known comic strip. Later he was an animator for Walt Disney for six years.

Going East, he got an assignment with *Fortune* Magazine as a pictorial reporter. He tells that he stood hip-deep in water to paint the Mississippi flood, did sketches at 30° below zero in Hudson Bay, and made water colors of the lovely Bahamas. Mr. Gramatky has since worked as artist-reporter for most of the leading magazines and publications today and handled national advertising accounts for outstanding agencies.

Between trips he had a studio in a building off Wall Street, from which he could see the boats on the East River. He once reported that, when his eyes tired from work, he liked to look at the boats. He found the tugs fascinating, some "gay and aimless" and others "grim and purposeful." As he watched them he thought they were much like people. He made countless sketches and he found that one boat seemed to assume a personality of its own. That boat became Little Toot in a book of the same name. After being turned down by several publishers with the explanation "children weren't thinking that way," *Little Toot* was published in 1939 and was an immediate success. From several Hollywood offers the movie rights were sold to Walt Disney. The book has appeared on radio and television, been part of the CARE-UNESCO book program, been the subject of a float in the Pasadena Tournament of Roses, been made into a film strip and into recordings, and has the distinction of being rated by the Library of Congress as one of the all-time great books in children's literature. All bookmobiles serving the Los Angeles Public Library are called Little Toots. Leading books dealing with children's literature refer to Mr. Gramatky and this book of his especially.

What is the story? It concerns Little Toot, who lived at the foot of an old wharf, "the silliest little tugboat you ever saw." (In the first sentence his characteristics are made clear.) Because the only sound that he could make was a gay, small toot, he was called Little Toot. He could, however, send up big, round smoke balls.

Little Toot's family was extremely important, for Big Toot was the biggest and fastest tug on the river and Grandfather Toot was "an old sea dog who breathes smoke." But Little Toot hated work and did not see why he should pull ships bigger than he was to the ocean. Besides, he liked to play.

When he was ridiculed by the other tugs for his frivolity, Little Toot, angry and ashamed, fled from them to sulk and mope by himself. Drifting aimlessly with the current, he did not see a big storm approaching until he heard the great waves of the ocean pounding the rocks. Then against the blackness of the sky arched a great rocket from an ocean liner, caught between two of the enormous rocks. Wildly excited, Little Toot began puffing smoke balls to signal for help. Up river all the tugs saw the s.o.s. and rushed to the rescue.

> Out from many wharves steamed a
> great fleet — big boats,
>   little boats,
>   fat ones,
>   and skinny ones . . .
> . . . With Big Toot himself right in
> the lead, like an admiral at the
> head of his fleet . . .

The fleet, however, could not make any headway in the rough seas.

Suddenly above the storm rose the gay toot of Little Toot as he rode the waves. The crew of the huge liner threw a line to the little tugboat who, when the waves hit the ship, pulled the vessel free. (Surely it must have been a wonderful thing to see!)

The people on board began to cheer. . . .

And the whole tugboat fleet insisted upon Little Toot's escorting the great boat back into the harbor.

Little Toot was a hero! And Grandfather Toot blasted the news all over the river. Well, after that Little Toot became quite a different fellow. He even changed his tune . . .

And it is said that he can haul as big a load as his father can . . . that is, when Big Toot hasn't a very big load to haul . . .

What a clever ending for any reader.

What has made *Little Toot* so famous? Annis Duff thinks it achieved its success in her home through "sheer force of personality." She writes in *Bequest of Wings:*[1]

> *Little Toot* . . . is a person, and this is the most perfect example of transference of human characteristics to an inanimate object. . . . There is such gusto in the pictures and such forthrightness in the manner of telling the story that the reader, especially if he is a small boy, is captivated at once . . . events move at a breathless pace, and before you have quite finished reading the last page the little listener flips the book over and says, "Now, read it again."

Surely in our modern worlds machines are tremendously important. Mr. Gramatky knows children and their interest in the realistic aspects of their environment. "Children, as well as their elders, are fascinated by trains, boats, trucks, tractors, and other mechanical contrivances." [2] Commenting on Hardie Gramatky and another writer who published in the same year stories of personified machinery, May Hill Arbuthnot' writes that they "have taken full advantage of the fact that to this generation a machine is something alive and individual" and they have "proved beyond doubt not only that machines are one of the modern child's liveliest and most continuous interests but that they can be a thrilling center of a good story." [3] To personify machinery, Mr. Gramatky has added appealing individuality to saucy Little Toot. Mr. Gramatky believes that a page comes alive through animation, that it seems to move and take off into space. Children delight in these personifications. The book provides wonderful entertainment not only for small boys but for the entire family to read aloud.

Mr. Gramatky's pictures entrance his reader-viewers, for with fresh, vigorous, bold strokes he throws bright, deep colors on paper. To have pictures done by such an outstanding artist would in itself give the book a special claim to fame. As Miriam Huber states: [4]

A significant aspect of children's book illustration in the United States today is the number of famous artists who bring to the making of pictures for children the same seriousness and responsibility of approach that they give to making fine paintings.

Mr. Gramatky's record does, indeed, confirm his status as a "water colorist of distinction." [5] He has won more than thirty top water color awards, including the Chicago International and the National Academy prizes. His paintings have been exhibited in all the large museums and galleries in North and South America and in Europe, and some are now in traveling exhibition in the Far East. Many are in permanent public and private collections.

Pictures must harmonize with the text, however, if they are to be the most forceful. The perfect blending of story and picture can perhaps be achieved only when one individual does both the writing and illustrating. Not long ago Hardie Gramatky pointed out that pictures tell much that words cannot and that balance between the writing and pictures must be achieved. Saying that he never could see how a person could illustrate another's story, he added: "I feel I get on so well with my illustrator!"

Truly in a Gramatky book the pictures are "part and parcel" of the story, "physically and psychologically, from the very beginning." [6] When Little Toot cuts a figure 8 so big there is hardly room for it between the two shores of the river, the picture beside the brief text shows a mischievous Toot at such play, with the 8 hitting each bank and with little smoke balls trailing behind him. When the boats become so annoyed with him and he is so lonesome that his spirits droop, the sketch shows even his smokestack, flag, and whistle bent sadly downward. No child has trouble reading the pictures and thus understanding the story, so graphically does each sketch give all the details. The colors match, too, the feelings denoted by the words, as the deep blues and blacks of the storm or the lavish color of the city dock scenes. Truly the pictures interpret the story.

But what of the story itself? The book has a well developed plot. Pointing out that many people today are doing mood books (pictures to portray a mood but with inaction in the text) Johnson, Sickels, and Sayers say that children respond with enthusiasm to a book that has a story to tell.[7] Surely *Little Toot* has a story with a satisfying theme. A captivating character, often as playful and mischievous as any child (and therefore so understandable to children), is unhappy over the situation in which he finds himself, though it may be of his own making. However, as the climax is reached—and the children grow still and breathless at the suspense—the personified machine earns his right to be a hero. From sympathy at the humanized plot, the child relaxes happily at an ending that is deeply satisfying and rewarding.

Perhaps we should examine also the accuracy of the story materials, for children are interested in and most observant of details. Factual material should be handled skillfully, and it should be presented with truth and a respect for the intelligence of the child. A sincere artist-illustrator will go to great lengths to insure for even the young reader accuracy in a story that is not basically an informational one. The boats themselves in *Little Toot*, as was mentioned earlier, are drawn directly from those on New York's East River. The duties of the tugboat are explained simply and clearly at the level of the young child.

"You see the world through the child's eyes," Mr. Gramatky says. "Then you must play back that world but not make it sound too sweet or not talk down to the child. It must be an honest effort, delivered as a person-to-person talk."

Just as important as the content of the book is the manner or style in which it is written. Here, too, is revealed the skill of the writer to make a book readable. There is a gay, masculine touch to Mr. Gramatky's words and pictures that makes them breeze through the pages. The story is not awkward or stilted but flows evenly and smoothly. The plot is lively and the characters well drawn. And the prose is good—it reads well. However hard it is to define style, we recognize whether it is there or not. Surely the reader senses it in this book. Much of the charm is due in large part to the picturesque words used, as "candystick smokestack," "skinny boats," and "spit the salt water out of his smokestack." Undoubtedly it is expressive writing.

Little Toot was the first of a popular series by Hardie Gramatky and is still probably the special favorite. The other books, however, are deserving of mention here. The next to appear was *Hercules,* which has been made into a movie and a television presentation. The U.S. State Department chose this story to represent American children's entertainment at the Brussels' World's Fair and sent the original drawings to countries in the Far East. Hercules is an old-fashioned fire engine drawn by horses. Though outmoded, he comes into his own when the new trucks break down on their way to a fire, and he earns the right to be placed in a museum. The action is tremendous and the pictures are magnificent in strong, virile colors.

Loopy is the story of a plane used to train student pilots. When a show-off runs him into a storm and bails out, Loopy realizes his dream of teaching the birds to fly and becoming a sky writer. Incidentally, has there ever been a child who, when the show-off takes Loopy under a bridge, hasn't yelled with delight: "Look, there's Little Toot." Sure enough, Toot is there in the river.

Creeper's Jeep was the first Gramatky book in a Connecticut setting close to the author's home. Creeper is a typical boy who never gets anything done until one day he wins a wonderful new red jeep. The jeep must be put up for sale, however, until he saves the animals from a barn fire.

Sparky resulted from a tour in search of true Americana. Sparky is a lively little trolley car who runs into trouble with the mayor. The car has been sentenced to become a diner and is on his last run when he saves some children from the path of the mayor's run-away automobile.

Homer and the Circus Train completes the list to now.[8] Representing the work of five years and re-done at least twenty-five times, the book shows that a good book is not so easy even for an experienced author-illustrator to do. Homer is a personable caboose who sees everything in reverse, much to the amusement of the other railroad cars. When a coupling gives way and the train shoots back over a hazardous mountain track, Homer brings the animal cargo through safely. Again, the pictures are wonderfully vivid indeed.

What is the secret of the charm of *Little Toot* and the other Gramatky books? Maybe it is the childlike, irrepressible character who ceases to be a machine but becomes a human personality which delights us all. Whatever the secret, there is no doubt that the appeal is there for children and adults alike. For those of us who are privileged to know Mr. Gramatky there may be evident another reason. To quote from Annis Duff: [9]

It is not so much the books written expressly for children so much as it is the books written out of the minds that have not lost their childhood that will form the body of literature which shall be classic for the young.

The great product in children's literature is created, someone has said, by the person who keeps the core of childhood within him while others grow old through and through. It could be, therefore, that the secret lies in the modest but captivating Mr. Gramatky himself.

REFERENCES

1. Annis Duff, *Bequest of Wings*, p. 48. New York: The Viking Press, 1950.
2. Bess P. Adams, *About Books and Children*, p. 132. New York: Henry Holt, 1953.
3. May Hill Arbuthnot, *Children and Books*, p. 309. New York: Scott, Foresman and Co., 1947.
4. Miriam B. Huber, *Story and Verse for Children*, p. 33. Rev. Ed. New York: The Macmillan Co., 1955.
5. May Hill Arbuthnot, *Children and Books*, p. 341. Rev. Ed. New York: Scott, Foresman and Co., 1957.
6. Lynd Ward, "The Book Artist and the Twenty-Five Years." *Horn-Book* 25 (December, 1949), 373–381.
7. Edna Johnson, Evelyn Sickels, and Frances Sayers, *Anthology of Children's Literature*, p. 71. Boston: Houghton Mifflin Co., 1959.
8. Each of the books has been published by G. P. Putnam's Sons, N.Y.
9. Duff, *op. cit.*, p. 20.

EDITORS' NOTE

In May 1965, there was a 25th anniversary party on a tug at Battery Park in Manhattan for *Little Toot,* and for the publication of *Little Toot on the Thames.* The little tugboat has been honored in innumerable ways, such as using its name on bookmobiles in California, headlining the end of a tugboat strike with "Little Toot Gets Back to Work," as well as calling Gramatky's own assignment to Vietnam "Little Toot Goes to Viet Nam." Walt Disney made it into a movie, Capitol records recorded the story, and Weston Woods Studios made a filmstrip. In addition to many other awards, this popular book received the Lewis Carroll Shelf Award in 1969 (awarded annually to the book worthy of sitting on a shelf with *Alice in Wonderland*). Most recently it was selected for the bibliography of "Sesame Street."

Mr. Gramatky co-authored the "Ellsworth Elephant" series appearing in *Family Circle* magazine from 1959 to 1962. His *Hercules* was chosen by the United States State Department to represent children's entertainment at the Brussels World's Fair.

Museums here and abroad and private collections boast permanent acquisition of much of Mr. Gramatky's art work. In the watercolor field, he has been honored more than thirty times with awards.

Presently, he lives with Mrs. Gramatky in Westport, Connecticut, where he is working on a children's book set in Italy.

Mr. Gramatky's most recent books are: *Bolivar* (1961 — Putnam), *Nikos and the Sea God* (1963 — Putnam), *Little Toot on the Thames* (1964 — Putnam), *Little Toot on the Grand Canal* (1968 — Putnam), and *Happy's Christmas* (1970 — Putnam).

Berta and Elmer Hader [*]

"WE WERE MARRIED IN 1919 and have lived happily ever since." With these words spoken in an interview a few years ago, Berta Hader summarized the wonderful partnership that has resulted in many books for children, books that take their place among the best of present day writing and illustration.

From early childhood both Berta and Elmer Hader were interested in drawing and painting. Berta Hoerner was born in Mexico of American parents during the temporary residence that her father's business required. She remembers that her mother spent much time making watercolor sketches of the picturesque Mexicans and their colorful houses. It seemed only natural that the small daughter should find a deep interest in this form of expression.

Elmer, a native Californian, found a sympathetic and understanding teacher in the third grade in San Francisco. Her encouragement helped develop his natural aptitude for drawing. While a student in high school, the great earthquake and fire of 1906 interrupted his education. Although very young he was a bugler with the Coast Artillery of the National Guard and helped with rescue work and clearing away rubble. Following that period he spent a few months as a surveyor in the American River region and had a turn at firing a locomotive when he was seventeen.

The rebuilding of the Art School which had been destroyed in the great disaster drew him there to study and he had three years on scholarships

* By Mabel F. Altstetter. From *Elementary English* 32 (December 1955), 501–506. Reprinted with the permission of the National Council of Teachers of English.

which his talent made possible for him to secure. He was eager to go to France to study but he needed money to do so. For three years he toured the United States on a vaudeville circuit in a feature called "A Picture a Minute." He saved enough money to go to Paris for almost three years and had the recognition of the invitation to exhibit a picture in an important show.

Intending to make a career as a landscape artist, Elmer Hader returned to San Francisco just before the outbreak of the first World War. He enlisted as a camoufleur with the United States Engineers and returned at the close of the war to New York where he opened a studio.

Berta Hoerner went with her parents from Mexico to Texas and then to New York where she received most of her schooling. After high school the family moved to Seattle and there she entered the University of Washington to major in journalism. After a year and a half she decided to give all of her time to drawing and left Seattle for San Francisco where she studied for a time at the California School of Design. There followed a period of activity as a newspaper artist, a fashion designer, and a miniature painter.

Berta and Elmer Hader had met in San Francisco and when Berta went to New York to specialize in children's feature pages for magazines they decided to be married and together they illustrated a number of juveniles for Macmillan called the Happy Hour series. They also illustrated books written by Alice Dalgliesh, Cornelia Meigs, Melicent Lee, Hamilton Williamson, and others. While their first work for children had a certain charm there was really nothing distinctive that set their work above average.

With the publication of the *Mother Goose Picture Book* in 1930 they found their real place in children's books and have devoted themselves exclusively to this area since that time. There have been occasional pieces of work that do not measure up to their current high standards; *Whiffy McMann, The Farmer in the Dell, Stop, Look and Listen* seem to have come into being as "pot-boilers" and there is nothing about them of the warmth and liveliness that characterize the books that have come from their studio in the last two decades.

Perhaps their seasoning came from the rich life that stemmed from building their own home and growing into it so that it became a part of them as the house and land took on the stamp of their personality.

They had hunted a long time for just the right spot and one day they came upon it near Nyack, New York and each recognized the rightness of the place at once. It was a steep highside so overgrown with scrub and briars that their friends thought they were insane to think of building there. It is at the second widest place in the Hudson river which the Dutch had called Tappan Zee just twenty-five miles from New York City. The Haders found an old quarry where sandstone for building some of New York's "brownstone fronts" had come from. There was a pile of rock by the quarry and they started with that as a base for their house. After the foundation was laid and the cement floor poured the artists had to work awhile to get money for the next step. They had no blue prints and the house just grew from one stage to another. The large living room is built around a fireplace nine feet across. Red sandstone and yellow and gray cobbles with peaked green roof make the house look as if it had always been there as it snuggles against the hillside one hundred feet above the river. There are odd-shaped terraces all about the house for the Haders and their friends eat out of doors whenever possible and having a number of terraces to choose from one can always be found that is just right for sun or shade or shelter from the wind. Birds have houses built into the walls of the terraces and the houses have real doors with real hinges. Flowers grow everywhere. Best of all, there is a spring on the steep hill that makes a stream and a waterfall that tumbles and splashes over mossy rocks to a pool at the foot of great willows. The trees give the house its name of Willow Hill.

One of the very important reasons for having the house is that the Haders have friends about them constantly. They can provide sleeping room for fourteen guests and on weekends most of the space is taken. One friend reports that it is a rare thing for them to sit down to a Sunday morning breakfast with fewer than eight people. One coffee pot holds twenty cups and a number of smaller ones are pressed into use when needed. Berta is an artist with food as well as with pencil and brush, as her lucky friends will testify. Thanksgiving and Christmas dinners are something to remember always.

The house is constantly being added to or remodeled; the roof has been changed at least three times. Most of the work is done with their own hands and with their own materials. They tell the story of the fun and work of this building in *The Little Stone House*. Children who live nearby are always welcome and like to come to the studio and the house. The studio stands apart from the main house and has a fireplace and great wide windows overlooking the Hudson Valley.

Animals and birds are welcome and make themselves at home. Deer come to the pool to drink and meadow mice, skunks, squirrels, chipmunks, groundhogs, rabbits, and raccoons are a part of everyday living. They may even come inside the house and a friend says that on one of her visits a chipmunk sat in the center of a warm blueberry pie. Owls call all night long and other birds sing and nest around the hospitable terraces.

That the Haders love and understand animals and birds can be readily understood from looking at their books. Their illustrations catch the wonder and curiosity of wild animals and the patience and contentment of the domesticated ones. They are never guilty of cuteness or coyness in their drawings. The grace and flow of movement that all animals have are caught and held on the page. They are able to show animal emotion too, and one can only chuckle at the astonished look on the cow's face when she finds herself suspended in a sling in *Rainbow's End* or watch with sadness the pony's head droop with fatigue in the mine in *Spunky*. The joy in swift running as *Midget and Bridget* gallop across the end papers of that book gives a sense of freedom to the reader that makes the hardships and happiness of the two animals almost a personal thing.

The happy partnership of the Haders shows itself in their way of working. One may begin a drawing and the other finish it. They plan their stories together and go over the plots suggesting and examining points of the story, and the writing is shared. Their stories always have a great deal of action which children love. The action may be simple as in *Little White Foot* whose adventures come in making a home in the attic among the Christmas tree ornaments and in an old doll's house to complicated shipwreck in *Rainbow's End* or mystery and storm in *Tommy Thatcher Goes to Sea*. The Haders are artists at telling a story whether it be about banana country (in *Green and Gold*), life in New York (in *Big City*), Mexico (in *Midget and Bridget*), the sea and the Maine coast (in *Rainbow's End*), or the simple things that catch the ebb and flow of country life (in *Under the Pig Nut Tree, Squirrely of Willow Hill* and *Little White Foot*). The words of *The Big Snow* are particularly appropriate; the slow beginning of the storm, the deepening fall of flakes and the silence, like no other silence, that comes after a heavy snow are all caught for the reader as the lines run across the pages among exquisite drawings:

> *A beautiful snow flake fell*
> *through the air*
> *Then two flakes floated safely*
> *to earth*
> *followed by three,*
> *then four.*
> *The snow flakes fell faster and*
> *faster and faster,*
> *Millions of snowflakes fell from*
> *the sky.*

It snowed all that night and all
the next day. Thick
snow covered the branches
of all the trees.
A blanket of snow covered the
meadows, the hills and
the valleys.
The snow was heavy on the roofs
of the houses and
barns.

The snow stopped falling on the evening of the second day. Once again the big silvery moon rose in the sky. The owls winged noiselessly from the sycamore to the pine woods. Nothing stirred in the silent snow-covered land.

There are wholesome adult-child relationships in the books also and while there is no attempt to preach or point a moral the reader cannot escape the sense of values that emerges in all situations. An excellent example is that found in *Jamaica Johnny* when Johnny discovers the importance of school and of knowing how to read. Kindness to animals is never talked about but it permeates every page and drawing.

The Haders' Caldecott award book (1949) is *The Big Snow*. They were puzzling over the choice of a subject for a new book when the big snow of 1947 paralyzed New York City and most of that area. The Haders' grounds were so filled with snow that they had much labor to shovel paths to feed the helpless wild things. Out of that experience came a beautiful book with snowflakes on blue for end papers and appealing pictures of hungry birds and animals who were dependent on human beings for help. The picture of the wistful groundhog alone would have won a prize. The format of the book, the type and paper all add up to a distinguished book. The artist-writers are fortunate in their publisher.

During the best period of their creating the Haders have found an amusing and charming way of signing their books with a small cartoon of themselves on the back of the title page. In *Spunky* they are in a small pony cart; in *Tommy Thatcher* they are in a boat, in *Jamaica Johnny* they are standing with sketching pad and camera close to a burro ridden by a native woman. In their newest release *Home on the Range* they are each astride a cow pony and Elmer is seen with a banjo and Berta with a songbook.

Children like the Haders' books. Elmer said once, perhaps with his tongue in his cheek, that "the complete ignorance of the psychological impact on the young mind leaves us free to draw and to write as we

please." He added that they never try out their material on children because their criticism and comments can be downright discouraging. This
"take it or leave it" attitude makes the books stand on their own merit
with children. That they like and read them is attested by the fact that
usually the books after a period of use must be rebound, a high tribute to
any writer.

The Haders have given us great warmth from their own rich and satisfying lives. Their love of life and their happiness with each other over-
flow into everything they draw or write. We have a Newbery Medal and
a Caldecott Medal. We ought to have a Newbery-Caldecott Medal, too!

EDITORS' NOTE

Berta and Elmer Hader's most recent books are: *Reindeer Trail*
(1959 — Macmillan), *Mister Billy's Gun* (1960 — Macmillan), *Quack
Quack* (1961 — Macmillan), *Little Antelope: An Indian for a Day* (1962 —
Macmillan), *Snow in the City* (1963 — Macmillan), and *Two is Company,
Three's a Crowd* (1965 — Macmillan).

Although Berta and Elmer Hader have no children of their own, they
welcome the villagers to their woods. Here the children love to build
dams and try to catch the fish which are always too quick for them.

The preservation of the natural beauty of not only their own woods
but those throughout our country concerns the Haders very much. They
feel that the conservation of wild life is very important to the joy of living,
and they are hopeful that their books make children acutely aware of the
charm to be found around them in the outdoors.

VIRGINIA HAMILTON

Portrait of the Author
as a Working Writer *

NOW THE PORTRAIT OF AN AUTHOR has always been awesome,
although the gilt fleur-de-lis motif which framed past portraits is replaced
these days by the institutional sleekness of polished chrome. Picture, if
you wish, the author posed with profile prominent, with eyes seeming to
look inward and backward at the same time, and seated in her Meis chair
in the manner of a modern-day Whistler's mother. She appears superbly
matter-of-fact. Still young, the calm expression of her face bespeaks the
functional competence of the suburban matron.

A portrait is only as good as the artist who created it. For an accurate
portrait, the artist must have experienced something of life and must
translate his own experience into the interpretation of the author.

A close look at the portrait reveals what we were unable to see from
a distance; from afar, the chrome frame had bewitched and beguiled us.
Up close, we see that the author has lines of stress and strain on the fore-
head, around the mouth and under the eyes. Her hands, which had seemed
to rest delicately in her lap, actually claw at the fabric of her culotte.

The author is tired. The author drinks too much coffee, gets too little
sleep and is overweight. No longer a delicate mystery shrouded in possibilities, students open doors for her and old gentlemen tip their hats.
Such is the coming of Over Thirty for a born lady writer. The portrait is
disappointing to the author when she stands in front of it, but it is un-

* By Virginia Hamilton. From *Elementary English* 48 (April 1971), 237–240+. Copyright
© 1971 by the National Council of Teachers of English. Reprinted by permission of the
publisher and Virginia Hamilton.

deniably true. Still, she wishes that somehow the portrait might show all the years of living and partly living that went into it; that the portrait could say more than its simplistic statement of time's passage. There is more of it, she feels—oh, much more—and so she decides to write it out. That's always her way, to write it down. Thus she holds on to time and makes it solid. She gives time quality and thereby denies its quantity.

Time is of quality: I do not have the time, I tell you. A grand time was had by all. Remember the time?

I remember the time I stood uncertain on the backward edge of the Beat Generation wondering what foward motion I should attempt. The generations of Pepsi people, of hippies, of peace and freedom and of black and beautiful were out of range beyond me and others like me who, although a bit lost, anticipated what was to come by our urge to be on the move.

Maybe that's why I felt compelled to strike out on my own for the Big Apple of Manhattan, that institution for reformed wastrels. I knew a few things even then. I knew that I would be a writer, I knew that I had to learn my craft away from all the kind people who wanted to help and did help but maybe hadn't realized there came a time when help was not what was needed. I knew a poem by Langston Hughes: "my soul grows deep like the rivers" the poem sings. Deep. Yes, that's what I was looking for.

When I lived in the East Village of New York City, it was known as the Lower East Side. There were no life styles such as Puerto Rican, hippy and head. There were the teachers from the newly defunct Black Mountain College; resident Poles, Yugoslavs and Czechs; a Shakespearean theater group and eastern European Jews in black greatcoats and wide-brim hats. There existed little communication between the groups or between the groups and myself. No police cars cruised through the streets at ten-minute intervals. No plainclothesmen searched for runaway teenyboppers and no troubled fathers exhausted the known crash pads hunting for lost sons.

We of the Lower East Side isolated ourselves from one another and insulated ourselves for that which we thought was worth the loneliness: independence, self-knowledge and self-expression and safety from intrusion of a chaotic world. If there was a time at all when we came closer together, it was on that day of the week when we publicly acknowledged our debt to the rivers. On Sunday, we all made it over to the river, either the East, which was never my favorite, or the Hudson, the kind of river I especially took to heart.

People in cities always go down to their rivers. They pay tribute in a way that at first was inexplicable to me. But as time passed, I began to comprehend the tribute and the need. I moved across town to Greenwich Village and closer to my favorite river. I could spend days writing and get nowhere. But if I went down to the river to sit awhile, I could come back home feeling as though I had partaken of a healing potion.

Eventually, my writing grew better as the experience of myself alone and cut off from all things familiar deepened inside me. Soon I could spend a day writing and, by evening, rather than incoherency I had created a kind of unity of thought. I hadn't learned to write a whole story yet, but there were themes that continued throughout. I knew enough to take hold of those themes and separate them from the rest by cutting the rest away. Then, rewriting those themes, I concentrated on sentences. And if a sentence did not follow what had gone before, it too was cut away.

Eventually, also, I knew the writing of Carson McCullers pretty well. I learned from her what a good sentence was. "In the town there were two mutes and they were always together," she had written. For a working writer, such a sentence is profoundly exciting. It stays in the mind for years.

Having learned in the Village that my writing had progressed thematically, I no longer needed to stop the process of time and my own experience. I had lived a rather solitary existence. I often went for days without talking to anyone. Working half days as a cost accountant in order to eat occasionally, I hid myself within columns of figures and made no friends.

However, it was time now to step into the flow of the city and to wet my feet in the stream of city people. I moved out of the Village and uptown, closer to my people and still near the Hudson River. My river changes uptown. It has Riverside Park along its steep banks and the park is beautiful, full of children and dogs. All sorts of people rest, lounge, read their papers, sunbathe and sing. They all needed the river in some way as I did.

My writing grew better as I grew older inside. I came to understand that the river's flow was the flow of freedom inside us all. We wonder about it in this way: What do you suppose is beyond the bridge there—a town, another park? What sort of place is Bear Mountain—are there really brown bears? I think I'll walk awhile and see what's beyond that bend in the river.

So it is that the river is the mind of people, ever flowing to some other where. Whenever any of us grow deep like the rivers it is because we have learned to allow our minds to flow free as rivers flow. And so the reason rivers figure so largely in my writing and ever will. But it was years before

I realized that the Hudson River was not the river which had nourished me. From the time I discovered my need to move, it must have been another river that had caused the need. I am talking about the Ohio River, sixty miles from the place I was born and the river so necessary, so symbolic for my people.

The Ohio River needs no orchestration to explain it. It needs no fury of words nor purple narrative for an image of it. It is simply grand the way an Ohio sky is grand for those of us who are related to it through the quality of time and memory. Wherever we go, we carry the quality — that piece of sky, that particular reach of land and that river — with us.

Having lived ten and more years in New York, I discovered that my mind had never left Ohio. And so I returned to the river and the country. I could write. I had done it. I had pulled past and present, memory and experience together and grown deep like the river. Time now for the author to become a working writer and, indeed, I have. Whatever else I do — buy groceries, raise my children, take care of my husband, plant crocuses — I write each morning and every night. I think, I dream writing, and writing is who I am. How much time I spend at it, who I write for, why I wrote and what next I will write, fall in the realm of propaganda. The fact is that I must write and writing is work, hard and exacting. The best job I've ever had.

The portrait of the Author is complete. Know that I don't mind if it reveals the lines of stress and time. It is my own picture as I created it. I am the artist, the author and the working writer, and we are doing what we set out to do.

I write of the black experience. You've heard the phrase often enough, perhaps understood it, wondered about it or even dismissed it as a kind of subversive nationalism. You may not have thought of children's books using that term or of my books in particular. But the black experience is the fact of my writing from my first book. *Zeely,* through the third, *The Time-Ago Tales of Jahdu.*

I attempt in each book to take hold of one single theme of the black experience and present it as clearly as I can. I don't mean to make the writing of fiction sound cold or calculating — it isn't at all. In the beginning, an idea takes hold of the writer in a special way which demands the getting it down on paper. From there, using whatever skill or craft he has learned, the writer develops the idea into a theme which becomes the basis of the plot.

A professor at Antioch College once gave me some advice. He told me I would go far if I would concentrate on using conventional forms of structure and simple language in my writing. "Your stories are wild enough without your inventing a new novel form." I took his advice. More and more I reach for the unconventional theme while depending on the solid base of tried and true structure and easy language.

The black experience in America is deep like the rivers of this country. At times through our history it became submerged only to emerge again and again. Each time it emerges, it seems strong, more explicit and insistent.

There are themes in my writing that are strains through the whole of black history. The strain of the wanderer, like the theme of Jahdu; the strain of the fleeing slave or the persecuted moving and searching for a better place becomes the theme of the Night Traveller in *Zeely*. And the black man hiding his true self, ever acting so that those who betray him will never touch him. Thus we have such a man in the actor son of Mr. Pluto in *The House of Dies Drear:*

"We wear the mask that grins and lies" he says, speaking from the Dunbar Poem.

The books I have written can be seen as a reflection of my past experience. I have brought myself up to the present and into the eye of the future. What will be the themes of my future writings? There are two books which I am working on and they are as different from one another as from the three already written. They do not attempt to cover the whole of the black experience; rather, they each take a theme out of it, as did my other three books. Perhaps some day when I've written my last book, there will stand the whole of the black experience in white America as I see it. Actually, I never write thinking in these terms. It's only when working out a book that I realize how hugely logical is the writer's unconscious life.

Examining the first of the two themes I'm working on, we have the failure of a black, quite obese junior high school youth to develop any area of successful contact with the white world that determines the limitations of his life. By the time we first meet the boy, who is called Junior Brown, his unique intelligence and his mental isolation are already apparent. He spends his anguished days trying to cope with the monstrous fantasy that has come to live in the home of his deranged piano teacher, Miss Peebs. The youth, Junior Brown, tries desperately to save the sanity of Miss Peebs by entering her fantasy and dealing with the apparition who lives there. Junior Brown and Miss Peebs both live in the same isolation caused by the same conditions and Junior instinctively knows that by saving her he may save himself.

The second book concerns the boy, M. C. Higgins, whose country of hills and mountains along the Ohio River is being destroyed by strip mining. As the earth is poisoned by the mindless force invisible behind the invading mining machines, so too are the hill people annihilated. I am speaking mainly of a spiritual annihilation. These people do not prevail over the condition of their lives, which causes an atrophy of the spirit. They endure—the emptiness, the oppression, the dull sameness. They endure it. That is, all save M. C. who lives by means of his courage, and his strength and daring. There are boys like M. C. who when they become men are legends, and there are legends—pure fictional men—who have become real to us. We know Wild Bill Hickok and Billy the Kid, Nat Turner and Crispus Attucks, all who once lived. We have C. C. Rider, Long John and Staggalee, whose lives are far more fiction than fact. Finally, we have the extraordinary legend of John Henry, not the song, but the legend which states that when John Henry was born, he spat in the fire and asked his mother why everyone including the dog had been fed and not he. Not waiting for a reply, he ordered his mother to prepare him an enormous, sumptuous meal. His mother prepared the food but John Henry did not eat it. He rose from his pallet. He turned his back on his mother and stalked out of the house never to return.

Nothing erases the legend of the man-made man, the natural man from our memory. Such men hold an essential life style in common. They do not need to prevail as we do. I suppose that is why I created my own M. C. Higgins. He, the same as the others of his kind, will not prevail or endure either. He is content to survive when he understands that the aim of his life is to live it in terms that only he can define. And so he lives it up and if he is like Nat Turner, may destroy himself in the process. If he is a John Henry he will burst his heart proving he is a man. In any event he will live not just some life he was born into but his own life, never loving it and never hating it either.

What sort of world is it I create, where the people seem imbued with an isolation of the spirit? Old Mr. Pluto, alone for years in his cave. Zeely, separated by her very height; and little Jahdu, a lone traveler born of no woman but in an oven. You might well ask, what is it I'm getting at. Not actually knowing, I sense that finding out is the reason I persist. I sense also that finding out is far less important than the quest and the pleasure of writing along the way.

I've attempted here to make the writer and writing more understandable. Those of us who write have a deep love of language and a need to make reading an extraordinary experience for children. In my own young days, I knew the excitement of coming across a book which touched and changed me. Now I experience while writing the shock of finding out that I might have a good story working. It hits me as though I had been asleep and awoke with a start. Always when that happens, I am reminded of my childhood when, skimming a book with only mild interest, I would start suddenly alert and begin reading in earnest.

For children, reading is the discovery of new worlds of color and texture. For me, writing for children is the creation of worlds of darkness and light. There is an essential line between us, a line of thought and ultimately of communication. Each book must speak: "This is what I have to say," in the hope that each reader will answer: "That is what I wanted to know."

Thank you.

EDITORS' NOTE

In three successive years, Virginia Hamilton has received recognition and been honored with the following awards: In 1967, the Nancy Block Memorial Award for *Zeely* (Macmillan) (given annually by the Downtown Community School in New York for the outstanding children's book of the year on inter-group relations); in 1968, the Edgar Allen Poe Award for *The House of Dies Drear* (Macmillan) (since 1961, this award is given by the Mystery Writers of America for the best juvenile mystery of the previous year); and in 1969, the Ohioana Book Award for *The House of Dies Drear* (Macmillan) (awarded annually to an Ohioan, either born there or living in the state for a minimum of five years, who has written an outstanding book in the preceding year).

Carolyn Haywood *

THE PUBLICATION OF CAROLYN HAYWOOD'S *B is for Betsy* in 1939 was a significant event in the children's book world. The heroine is the kind of little girl one might find in any first grade class in the United States. The things that happen to her might happen to any child, but Miss Haywood makes the everyday activities of Betsy and her friends both exciting and funny. This was a new idea in literature for children. Since that time Miss Haywood has continued to write realistic stories about children at home and school that are entertaining and easy to read.

Carolyn Haywood was born in Philadelphia and educated in the public schools there. As a young girl she enjoyed drawing and painting. At that time she thought that it would be wonderful to illustrate a story book someday, but that it would be even more wonderful to pose for a magazine cover.

Miss Haywood graduated from Philadelphia Normal School and studied drawing and painting at the Pennsylvania Academy of Fine Arts. Here she won a Cresson European Scholarship. She also studied with Elizabeth Shippen Green Elliott, Jesse Willcox Smith, and Violet Oakley. Since all of these artists had been pupils of the distinguished American illustrator, Howard Pyle, Miss Haywood calls herself a "grand-pupil" of Pyle.

Miss Haywood began her career as a portrait painter, specializing in

* By Paul C. Burns and Ruth Hines. From *Elementary English* 47 (February 1970), 172–175. Reprinted with the permission of the National Council of Teachers of English and Paul C. Burns and Ruth Hines.

work with children. From the pupils of Howard Pyle she had learned much about writing and illustrating children's books, and after a time, decided to try it herself. She planned a picture book with little text, but she met an editor who suggested that she write about American boys and girls and the things they like to do. From this suggestion came *B is for Betsy* and all the other delightful stories that have followed since 1939.

B is for Betsy (Harcourt, 1939) describes Betsy's experiences during her first year of school and her vacation on her grandfather's farm. Dora V. Smith [1] comments on one episode in this book:

> The children's circus performance is a masterpiece. Two little boys playing elephant under a big gray covering get their legs entangled, and the elephant collapses on the floor. Only a person who has played circus in the first grade could have described the scene so realistically.

Betsy and Billy (Harcourt, 1941) continues the adventures of Betsy and her friends in the second grade. Billy finds it difficult to stay out of trouble. *Back to School with Betsy* (Harcourt, 1943) and *Betsy and the Boys* (Harcourt, 1945) take the same characters through the third and fourth grades. Several other books by Haywood deal with other interesting and amusing incidents in the lives of Betsy and her friends.

The Betsy stories find an enthusiastic audience among young readers because they are close to their own experiences and interests. Children are interested in the events described and problems presented. The characters are not, however, as clearly defined as in the author's "Eddie" stories.

In *Little Eddie* (Morrow, 1947) Carolyn Haywood has created a real boy whose delightful personality endears him to children and adults alike. Eddie Wilson, seven years old, is a collector of all kinds of things — signs, stray cats, and telegraph poles. His family labels his collection "junk," but Eddie calls it "valuable property." Sometimes Eddie's junk turns out to be more valuable than it seems. Miss Haywood is often asked if the children in her books are real. Most of them are not, but just after she finished the story *Little Eddie* she met a small boy who was actually called Little Eddie and who might have been the Eddie of the story. Miss Haywood and this Little Eddie spent three days together while he posed for the illustrations for the book. After this, Eddie Wilson was a little something more than make-believe.

In *Eddie and the Fire Engine* (Morrow, 1949) Eddie is a year older and still the avid collector of "valuable property." This time Eddie's hilarious activities center around an old fire engine and a goat appropriately named Gardenia.

The next "Eddie" book, *Eddie and Gardenia* (Morrow, 1951), finds Gardenia causing trouble in the Wilson household. When Gardenia chews up the top of Mr. Wilson's new Buick convertible, even Eddie realizes that she has to go. Eddie goes along when Gardenia is sent to his uncle's ranch in Texas. Here Eddie spends several months and becomes a real cowboy.

In *Eddie's Pay Dirt* (Morrow, 1953), Eddie returns from Texas resplendent in a Mexican costume and brings along the strangest collection of "valuable property" yet. Eddie must make an important moral decision when his "pay dirt," given to him by his friend Manuel, turns out to be truly valuable. Eddie knows Manuel did not realize the value of his gift. Should he give it back or keep it to buy the horse he has always wanted? Eddie's parents offer guidance but leave the decision to Eddie.

Louella the parrot, another piece of valuable property brought from Texas, is featured in *Eddie and Louella* (Morrow, 1959). *Eddie and His Big Deals* (Morrow, 1955) is one of the best of the Eddie series. Eddie finds himself in competition with another collector who turns out to be, of all things, a girl! Eddie engages in a complicated series of exchanges — big deals — in order to obtain a printing press from his rival. Eddie's experiences with the school orchestra and a gardening project are the subjects of other books by Miss Haywood.

In addition to her "Betsy" and "Eddie" books, Carolyn Haywood has written several books about adopted children, Penny and Peter. These books can help children to understand the relationships of parents to adopted children. She has also written a number of other books not related to any of the series, but full of humorous situations in which children become involved — on the farm, twin "mixups," and riding the school bus. On one occasion when asked about her writing, Miss Haywood said, "Of all the delightful features about make-believe children, the most convenient one is that their author can control not only their growing up but their growing down. The world of books is indeed an 'Alice in Wonderland' world where there are bottles marked 'Drink me' and cakes marked 'Eat me' with the inevitable Alice results."

Carolyn Haywood ranks high among the favorite authors of children between the ages of seven and ten. Her stories are good for reading aloud to young children for, in many cases, each chapter is a complete story, though related to other chapters of the book. Good readers in the second grade and most third graders can read the books for themselves. They satisfy the need of beginning readers for a "fat" book — one that looks like a "grown-up" book instead of a picture book. The "Eddie" stories are enjoyed by older children and are especially appreciated by the slower or more reluctant reader in the middle or upper grades.

Children find more than entertainment in Miss Haywood's books. Her characters have their problems as well as their fun. They receive their share of scoldings from adults, have their disappointments, and some of their good ideas don't turn out well at all. However, they learn to accept their failures and begin new projects and explore new fields. Their relationships with parents and other adults are warm and friendly. Books such as these help children to grow in understanding of themselves and others. They help them to see that some frustration is a natural part of growing up and give them subtle encouragement in their own endeavors.

Carolyn Haywood has been able to attain both of her childhood goals. She not only has illustrated books, but also has posed for a magazine cover. She was the model for the mother in some of Jessie Willcox Smith's covers for *Good Housekeeping*. All this in addition to receiving such critical acclaim by reviewers for her contribution to children's literature as "stories are always wholesome and gay"; "knows small children inside out"; and "gets better with every book"!

REFERENCES

1. Smith, Dora V., *Fifty Years of Children's Books*, Champaign, Illinois: National Council of Teachers of English, 1963, pp. 39–40.

EDITORS' NOTE

The editors consider the above article on Carolyn Haywood to be complete and up-to-date, and have no additional biographic or publishing information to add.

In Marguerite Henry —
The Thread That Runs So True *

SAMUEL RIDDLE, owner of Man O'War, used to say that "thoroughbreds have an extra quality greater than speed." He called it heart. "Thoroughbreds don't cry," he would say.

Is it because Marguerite Henry is a thoroughbred, is it because she has that extra quality called "heart" that she is able to make us laugh a little and cry a little, and satisfy us wholeheartedly when she tells a story?

While she may have loved animals all her life, she has not known them intimately all her life. Born in the city of Milwaukee, without ever really knowing Bonnie, the family horse, whose character belied her name, Mrs. Henry herself says she learned about horses as an adult. Today many of us believe her to be the best author of children's horse stories in this era, perhaps of all time.

Whence come her insight into the minds and hearts of people and animals? Can it be from the warmth of her own family living, her happy childhood? Whence comes this sensitivity to the fundamental needs of all creatures, human and four-footed, for love, for independence, for security, for achievement, for companionship, for solving problems, for growing up? Can the phenomenal amount of research which she has done for each book account for the depth of understanding she evidences in her writing? What are the qualities, the characteristics, the aspirations of this creator or interpreter of Little Bub, of Reddy, Misty, Rosalind, and

* By Miriam E. Wilt. From *Elementary English* 31 (November 1954), 387–395. Reprinted with the permission of the National Council of Teachers of English and Miriam E. Wilt.

Grimalkin and Little or Nothing? But the animal characters are not the only heroes. Grandma and Grandpa Beebe, Joel and Agba, Gibson and Benjamin White, and scores of other humans share the "Queen's Plate" as youths, four-footed and two, stretch toward maturity. For each animal one or more human friends, for each youth the wisdom and guidance of age. While all of the writing is not equally powerful, it is within the stories themselves that one must look for "the thread that runs so true," the thread that reveals Marguerite Henry in the truest light.

The gay, sparkling, charming Mrs. Henry with the merry laughing eyes was born Marguerite Breithaupt, in Milwaukee, in 1902. In those peaceful golden years of the beginning of the twentieth century she, the youngest of five children, while not pampered and petted, grew up surrounded by love, security, and warm family happiness.

When Marguerite was eleven years old after having, in her words, gotten "printer's ink in her blood" as a child in her father's Milwaukee print shop, a magical place with colored pads and pencils that made a big black swath on the paper, she wrote a story which was accepted by the old *Delineator* Magazine. During high school in Milwaukee and study for a degree at the State Teachers College, she wrote prolifically. When she married soon after graduation, the Henrys moved to Chicago. Here she wrote articles for *The Nation's Business, The Saturday Evening Post,* about Steel Production for *System* and Occupational Therapy for the *World Book Encyclopedia.*

In 1939 she and her husband moved to Mole Meadows, where under the spell of country living and the wonders of nature, she wrote *Auno and Tauno.* In her words, "I knew that this was it. This was the kind of writing I liked best." The story of *Auno and Tauno* grew out of the reminiscences of Beda and Effendi, a Finnish couple, whose fingers braided and rolled ropes of dough or whittled while their tongues spun tales of Finland. It is a simple little story of family life in Finland during peace times.

In 1941, she published *Dilly, Dally and Sally,* a story in which Mrs. Henry's sister says is reflected the childhood of Marguerite herself; in 1942, *Geraldine Belinda*; in 1943, *Birds at Home*; and in 1944, *A Boy and a Dog.* These four books are hard to locate in our libraries today, but the Geography series, eight about Latin America and eight about neighboring countries, published in 1941, and those written in 1945 and 1946 are still much read as collateral reading and are found in many school and public libraries.

Mrs. Henry has had several illustrators. A few of her early books were illustrated by Gladys Rourke Blackwood, Diane Thore, and Ottilie Fox; Kurt Weise illustrated the geography books; Lawrence Dresser, *Robert Fulton.* The illustrations of Blackwood, of Thorne, and Fox were childlike and gay; those of Kurt Weise sharp, clear, colorful, and informative; Dresser's ink drawings, while few in number, picked up the mood of the narrative; but it was the professional wedding of Wesley Dennis and Marguerite Henry as artist and story teller that has most intrigued the readers. Wesley Dennis knows, loves, and can paint animals, especially horses. Many readers agree that this author-illustrator team has produced some of the most beautiful and worthwhile books ever published for children. Although written for children, people of all ages thrill to the beauty of language; richness of illustration; homely philosophy; authentic information spiced with imagination and phantasy; the portrayal of characters, four-footed and two, rich in human values; and the awareness of the fundamental needs of all God's creatures.

In 1945 came the first of the horse books, books destined to bring Marguerite Henry fame. In *A Critical History of Children's Literature,* the authors state, "Marguerite Henry has written many books, but it is for her horse stories that she is known. She has told several stories based on the fascinating story of famous lives of horses."[1]

At the "postage stamp" farm, Mole Hill, lives Friday, one of the Morgan Horses. It is the story of his ancestor, the sire of the famous breed of Morgan horses, that is told in *Justin Morgan Had a Horse.* Justin Morgan, a poor teacher and singing master, traveling with Joel, one of his pupils, to collect a debt, took in payment two colts. The one was a big and brawny beast and was quickly sold, the other was a runt whom the horse trader dubbed worthless. Joel, impressed by the quick intelligence and loveable qualities of the odd little colt, persuaded Justin to keep him. Joel loved Bub and gentled him. The schoolmaster rented Little Bub to a lumber man, who soon discovered his strength of pull and entered him in competition. Not only was Bub strong, but he was fleet; and after he proved his ability to pay his own way, Justin no longer had to rent him out. Races won paid the schoolmaster's debts and because of his strength and speed the horse was coveted by many men. When Justin Morgan later became sick, he took Little Bub to his sister's home, where after a long illness Justin died. Joel lost track of Little Bub after Justin's death. Joel went on to finish his apprenticeship and start a mill of his own. Years later, one night on the way to a meeting he heard what sounded to him like a "familiar whinny in the night." In front of Chase's Inn, hitched with a team of six horses, he found Bub, broken by hard work and ill treatment.

There was not a proud head nor a beautiful arched neck among them. Suddenly the neighing began again. Now Joel was close enough to see which horse moved.

His heart seemed to stop altogether, then began beating wildly.

"So help me!" he breathed. " 'Tis the littlest horse in the team. 'Tis Justin Morgan! That's who 'tis—Justin Morgan!"

In a flash he was holding the horse's face in his hands and combing the matted forelock with his fingers. He tried to thaw the tiny icicles that clung to the horse's whiskers. "My poor Little Bub!" he whispered softly. "My poor, shivering, frightened Little Bub, with his ribs a-sticking out like barrel staves!"

The little horse was trembling—not from cold but from joy.

By borrowing twenty dollars from the man to whom he had been apprenticed, Joel was able, at last, to buy Little Bub. He fed and doctored and loved him, and brought him back to health to sire many fine colts who became famous for their smallness, prodigious strength, swiftness, and indomitable spirit.

". . . and likely nobody will ever know who was the little colt's mother and who was his father. He was just a little work horse that cleared the fields and helped Vermont grow up." Then suddenly Joel's face lit up as if he had just thought of something for the first time. "Why, come to think of it, he's like us. He's American, that's what he is. American." [p. 84]

The likeness did not stop with looks. It went deeper. Justin Morgan's grandchildren inherited an inner something. Men gave it various names. Courage. Power. Intelligence. The heart to go on forever. Some called it a high free spirit and let it go at that. [p. 85]

This is the kind of book that makes you proud and sometimes brings a lump to your throat. It was runner-up for the Newbery Medal, received the Friends of Literature Award and the Junior Scholastic Gold Seal Award. But this was only the forerunner of better books to come in which all of the original values were enriched and deepened.

Following *Justin Morgan* came *Robert Fulton, Boy Craftsman*. This is believed by many to be best of the series of "The Childhood of Famous Americans." In *Robert Fulton,* the same rich human values are present. It isn't fiction, yet it reads like a novel. In it a real boy comes alive. Days of the past flash with color and hum with activity.

The writing in this story does not have the quality of later books nor of *Justin Morgan*. The sentences are short and choppy, the vocabulary limited, but to serve the purpose for which it was written, this probably had to be. It is the story of a boy whose mother understood the needs of her children for love and understanding, for security despite economic limitations, who encouraged children to discover and experiment and meet life situations, one who loved wholeheartedly and one who was loved. It is a satisfying book and helps to make history live for young insecure readers.

The Little Fellow was also published in 1945. The illustrations by Diana Thorne, while excellent, lack to some extent the life-like quality of Dennis' horses. The story lacks the gripping poignancy of books written for older children. This story for young children, however, spells out for them two very real and personal problems, present in the four-footed animal society as well as in the two-footed human one, the task of growing up and that of adjusting to the other and younger children. Chip was the youngest and the "onliest" one and he gloried in his world until Chocolate, his mother, disciplined him and the appearance of a younger colt made life seem hard and unkind.

Chip's lesson was not an easy one to learn. He suffered as only children can who seem to feel their security threatened, but Chip came through and so will they, perhaps helped along by a story like *The Little Fellow*.

In 1945 and 1946 the second eight geography books were published. These were about Australia, New Zealand, the Bahama Islands, Bermuda, the British Honduras, Hawaii, and the Virgin Islands. These, like the former, are good, informational books illustrated by Kurt Weise.

Benjamin West and His Cat, Grimalkin was published in 1947. This suspenseful tale of a boy who grew up to be an artist and his cat, Grimalkin, is one of the most unusual and best of the biographies for children. Life in the Quaker home was not always quiet and sedate. Benjamin had many adventures, from the arrival of Grimalkin clear through to his trip to Philadelphia to become a painter. He bounced through his days, using his ingenuity to circumvent lack of materials and his great love of painting to win his parents' permission to study art. Benjamin was not always the studious, hard-working boy his father would have him be, but strangely in many ways Ben's father gave the boy help and encouragement, even though Mr. West believed this activity to be worldly.

Shamrock Queen! Irish setter, best bird dog up and down the river, but just Reddy to her master. *Always Reddy* was published in 1947. *Always Reddy* is a calm little tale of a man and his dog, perhaps inspired by Mr. Henry's love of his pet dog. It is a good story, but it does not tug at the heart strings as do some of the others. A bird dog growing too old to hunt, her puppy growing up to take her place, childhood, youth, and old age, the eternal struggle for a place in the sun, and a conclusion that satisfies everyone. While the plot is a substantial one, some of the incidents and settings seem less natural and lifelike than those in most of the books. It doesn't seem to be that it's dogs rather than horses, for Benjamin West has those "horse story qualities." In some unexplainable way, something seems to be lacking. Perhaps it's just the reader missing the rich drama, the suspense, or the laughter of children.

For those of us who first met Marguerite Henry in *Misty of Chincoteague,* probably none of her books will ever take its place in our hearts. Honors have and will be awarded to others, circulation may be higher for many, but for us there will never be another Misty. For Misty is just Misty, and our introduction to a magical land of fact, phantasy, and legend woven into stories that entwine around our heart strings like ivy clinging to the wall.

Misty. A phantom foaled her, but she came out of the mist, and she adopted the human race as her own.

Misty speaks for herself. It is one of the finest horse stories ever written. Chincoteague is a way of life. The salt air of the Atlantic is in it. The fine sense of values, the feeling of drama, the deft characterization all blend together to give us Misty.

Sea Star, Orphan of Chincoteague, a sequel to *Misty,* did not follow immediately. *King of the Wind* was the next book to be published, but for the sake of continuity *Sea Star* will be discussed next.

When there was no money to pay Uncle Clarence Lee's tuition fees, Paul and Maureen were faced with a decision. Paul and Maureen loved Misty as folks can love only creatures whose lives they saved, whom they have gentled, petted, loved and cared for, but—

> Then white-faced, they nodded to each other. "Grandma," Paul spoke very quickly, as if he were afraid he might change his mind, "two movie men were here today. They came to buy Misty."
>
> "For two hundred and fifty dollars," added Maureen. . . .
>
> "You didn't sell her!" she exclaimed aghast. . . .
>
> "You see, Grandma," Maureen explained very carefully as if she were talking to a little girl, "Misty really doesn't belong just to us any more. She's grown bigger than our island. She's in a book, Grandma. Now she belongs to boys and girls everywhere." . . .
>
> "Clarence, did you *let* the children sell Misty?" Grandpa took a long time folding his handkerchief and getting it back into his pocket. He cleared his throat. At last he said, "What else could I do, Ida? Misty is their'n. Besides, them men was dead right!" . . .

And in work, hard work, there was solace for their heavy hearts. Pony Penning again and the wild excitement of roundup, races, and auction,

Paul and Maureen escaped to the beach to gather oysters for Grandma and to try to forget:

> And there not a hundred yards away, standing quiet, was a spindle-legged foal. It had a crooked star on its forehead. And as it stood with its legs all splayed out, it looked like a tiny wooden carving against a cardboard sea. . . .
> "Don't go after him, Maureen. He's afeared. Stand quiet. Might be he'll come to us." Cautiously, as a child who has lighted a firecracker comes back to see if it will explode, so the foal came a step toward them. Then another out of wild curiousness, and another. When Paul and Maureen still did not move, he grew bold, dancing closer and closer, asking questions with his pricked ears and repeating them with his small question mark of a tail. . . . [pp. 106–107]
> Maureen stood dripping wet, watching. "Don't call him Lonesome," she said. "That's too sad of a name. Let's call him Sea Star."
> Paul seemed to be talking to himself. "Why that name's exactly right. An hour ago we didn't want to look at a pony. Now this orphan has wound himself around us just the way sea stars wind themselves around oysters."

Sea Star was lonesome for his mother, homesick for Assateague, and frightened. Everything they tried to do seemed to fail. Sea Star refused to eat no matter how tempting Grandpa Beebe, Grandma Beebe, Maureen, or Paul made the mash or grass. He got thinner and thinner until they were sure he would die. The scent of myrtle leaves and some human help brought about a union between a dull spiritless mare who had lost her colt, and Sea Star, the orphan.

> Grandpa dropped his voice to fit the quiet. "Me and yer Grandma have had a good many head of children," he mused to himself, "but when each one went off to work or to war, we always got a little dread inside of us. Lasted for days. But then . . ."
> "Then what?" asked Maureen.
> "Always somebody was left behind to stay a spell with us. Even when all our children was growed up and didn't need us, then you two come along and the empty feelin' was gone." [p. 171]

In 1948, Marguerite Henry takes us briefly to Arabia for the beginnings of *King of the Wind,* a story of Sham, the Godolphin Arabian, the ancestor of Man O'War. Here in a story true to all known facts, spiced with the inspiring legends of the past, Agba, a Moroccan mute, Grimalkin, a cat, and Sham move through starvation, maltreatment, and loneliness from the Sultan's stable of prize Arabian horses to France and finally to England to sire a race of horses famous around the world. In the words of one reviewer, it makes you laugh a little, cry a little, and satisfies.

And then there was *Little or Nothing from Nottingham.* One wonders whether a book of this nature isn't a necessity for both the author and the reader after the highly charged emotional experience of stories like *King of the Wind* or *Sea Star. Little or Nothing* is a gentle book, a laughing book, a circus book. And what more can be said? A trick dog in a circus, a dog that buries bones and naturally takes a foreleg stand, Little or Nothing clowns through his days wearing rabbits' ears; rides on his friend Elf the elephant's head; buries huge bones underneath the wagon and searches for them each morning, eventually even suspecting his friends of stealing his bones, until he finally discovered that he lives in "The Wonder City that Moves by Night." It's a joyous book that delights circus fans young and old, as well as thousands of children to whom a dog is a second self and the circus is the epitome of romance and glory. In the opinion of this writer, this is the best of Henry's books for *younger* readers, but it seems to have no age limit.

In *Born to Trot,* published in 1950, we might ask which is more important—Rosalind, a trotter's road to the championship, or Gibson White's road to health? Rosalind's story is simply:

Rosalind wanted to win. She meant to win. [p. 209]

Success followed upon success in Rosalind's life, but for Gib, through boyhood and youth, it was an uphill fight all the way. He grew up, however, to drive Rosalind's colts to their records. Without his father, Rosalind's trainer and rider, Gib probably would never have made it, for somehow Benjamin knew—

"Yes, I'm sure the boy needs a strong dose of horse medicine." [p. 52]

The book is fun to read, but in addition, it is packed with information about, enthusiasm for, and the excitement of harness racing.

In Gib's words—

"I'm the luckiest fellow in the world. I not only have a great filly. I've got a great dad."

There is majesty, splendor, grandeur in *Album of Horses* published in 1950. As one pores over the fascinating legends and facts of all breeds of horses, one can hardly fail to realize the painstaking research that has gone into the book. Ponies, mules, Arabians parade through the pages. It's as exciting as a novel, as dramatic as a play, and as informative as an encyclopedia, but it's more than that. In it one senses the glories of the past, the hopes for the future. To those who have not known the horse world, it swings wide the gates, and to those already initiated there is romance and glamor and color and "heart."

Here one thrills to:

Always the desert warrior preferred to ride a mare to battle. Banat er Rih, he called her, which in Arabic means "Daughter of the Wind." She was his own tentfolk, eating what they ate, dozing when they dozed, children sometimes slept between her feet, their heads pillowed on her belly. [p. 12]

A man needs someone to believe in him, a horse has this need, too. [p. 14]

The thoroughbred is a creature of bone and blood and bottom. By bottom, he means stamina and the wind of a fox. [p. 14]

Thoroughbreds don't cry.

And then in 1953 came *Brighty of the Grand Canyon,* wild, free, lovable. A story of adventure, mystery, beauty, and human-animal companionship. A bond stronger than ropes, chains, or distance that existed between a man and a burro.

Brighty gave up freedom voluntarily, but no one, *no one* could take it away from him except temporarily. His need of humans when he was ill, when he was hurt, when he was hungry, or when he was lonely brought him back again and again to human dangers, but always he was a bright free spirit. With Jack Irons, the mountain lion, the jacks, the blizzard on the other side of the river, he lost to win again. Always Uncle Jim brought to him sympathy and healing brews, always Brighty brought to Uncle Jim loyalty, love, and faith and a willingness to serve. But because Brighty gave of his free will to Uncle Jim, he was ever free to go and:

"Feller," he said, shaking his head, "I'm mighty obliged for the help, but don't get too domesticated on me." . . . [p. 12]

But halfway in, he hesitated. He raised his head skyward as if pondering some great decision. Then quite suddenly he backed out of the gate, his muzzle grazing Uncle Jim's shoulder. With a flirt of his heels he bounded away toward his trail, a winking, grey fleck in the dusk. . . .

He stood looking until he could see Brighty no more. Then he smiled his slow, understanding smile as he trudged home alone. . . . [p. 109]

"Maybe," he grinned to the riders behind him, "maybe it's Bright Angel."

Of course, everyone knows that Brighty has long since left this earth. But some animals, like some men leave a trail of glory behind them. They give their spirit to the place where they have lived, and remain forever a part of the rocks and streams and the wind and sky. [p. 222]

Extensive, painstaking, thorough research has gone into each book. Moreover, the illustrator, sensing the mood of the story, supplies such an abundance of fine detail that even in a one-inch picture depicting the rigging of a schooner a small boy is shown in the crow's nest.

Here are no preachy, moralistic goody-goody characters. Here are creatures good, bad, and indifferent parading through the pages of the books. Here are pictures painted with words, people characterized by their behavior. Here is an honest forthright author who has never failed or fooled her readers. For each book she spends months and months on research, writes thousands of letters, and talks to anybody that might know. Every detail must be accurate, every statement true.

But, furthermore, she seems to have the ability "to be inside the skin of the story's protagonist." * It is this ability, we suspect, that explains the secret of her success in presenting characters as they really are. Solutions to problems are not the pat "happy ever after" endings, but a realistic meeting of conflict carried through to a logical conclusion. King of the Wind never raced, but his colts did; Misty was sold, but Sea Star came to fill the gap; Gibson White did not ride Rosalind in the Hambletonian, although he was later to ride her foals; Reddy did not hunt again, but he found another responsibility. All creatures must grow up to face life as it is and always there is the wisdom of age to gentle, to help, and to push a little. There's no saccharine sweet moral to her stories, but a salty common sense, laced with humor, a few tears, and a "heart."

"Horses are honest always," says Mrs. Henry, "sometimes people are not." But she has complete faith in animals and in children and it is returned full measure. And because children and animals *know,* we be-

---

* Semrod—*Publisher's Weekly.*

lieve Mrs. Henry is a *"thoroughbred"* with that something extra called "heart." We hope that Marguerite Henry will always have "a tablet for her thoughts" as she did when she was a little child in her father's print shop.

REFERENCES

1. Cornelia Meigs, Anne Eaton, Elizabeth Nesbitt, Ruth Hill Viguers, *A Critical History of Children's Literature,* New York, The Macmillan Co., p. 559.

EDITORS' NOTE

Rand McNally and Company, publishers of many of Marguerite Henry's books, let us in on the scoop that this author is currently working on a new, major children's novel — her first since *Mustang* — which is scheduled for publication in the fall of 1972.

In addition to *Mustang: Wild Spirit of the West* (Random House), other recent books by Marguerite Henry are: *Cinnabar, the One O'Clock Fox* (1956 — Random House), *Muley-Ears, Nobody's Dog* (1959 — Random House-Hale), *Marguerite Henry's All About Horses* (1962 — Random House), *Dear Marguerite Henry* (1969 — Random House), *Dear Readers and Riders* (1969 — Random House), *Christine* (1970 — Belline), *Ginger's Place* (1970 — Belline), and *Album of Dogs* (1970 — Rand McNally). Nine of the most popular of the horse stories are now available in paperback editions.

Just completed (July 1971) is the filming of *Justin Morgan Had a Horse* by the Walt Disney studio, to be released either as a two-part television showing on the "Wonderful World of Disney," or as a full-length motion picture in theatres, or both. In addition, King International will soon begin filming the motion picture version of *King of the Wind.*

By haunting libraries and travelling across country and oceans, Marguerite Henry has been able to bring authenticity to her stories. Before writing *King of the Wind,* she dug into old books and yellowed manuscripts on Morocco, France, and England, tracing the life story of the Godolphin Arabian. For *Misty of Chincoteague,* she visited Chincoteague Island many times, absorbing the quaint speech patterns peculiar to that area. For *Brighty,* she rode up and down the perilous trails of the Grand Canyon. Three trips to Italy gave her first-hand knowledge of the customs of the people and the habits of the animals for *Gaudenzia.*

She lives with her husband in Rancho Santa Fe, California, where there are more horses than people. They have no children of their own, but many nieces, nephews, and friends give helpful suggestions while Marguerite is writing a book.

Few writers have been honored as many times as Marguerite Henry. Books which have received awards, in some cases more than once, are: *Misty*—The 1961 Lewis Carroll Shelf Award (given since 1951 by the University of Wisconsin for the title worthy of sitting on the shelf with *Alice in Wonderland*) and the 1949 John Newbery award; *Sea Star*—The 1952 Pacific Northwest Library Association Young Readers' Choice (given annually for a title published three years earlier; school children vote from a list submitted to them); *Brighty of the Grand Canyon*—The 1956 William Allen White Children's Book award (voted upon annually since 1953 by Kansas school children); *Justin Morgan Had a Horse*— Runner-up for the 1946 John Newbery award; *Black Gold*—The 1960 Sequoyah Children's Book Award (given annually since 1959 by the Oklahoma Library Association; children vote for the best book from a submitted master list); and *Mustang*—The 1970 Sequoyah Award as well as the 1966 Western Heritage Juvenile Award (given annually since 1960 by the National Cowboy Hall of Fame and the Western Heritage Center to the juvenile that best portrays the authentic American West).

In 1961, Marguerite Henry was given the Children's Reading Round Table Award (presented annually since 1953 to a mid-westerner for outstanding achievement in the field of children's literature). In that same year, *Gaudenzia* was presented the Clara Ingram Judson Award (given annually since then for the best in children's literature written by a mid-westerner).

Holling C. Holling: Author and Illustrator *

IT HAS BEEN SAID that an author or an artist who turns his talents toward literature for children doesn't have to know much. Holling C. Holling as an author-illustrator has certainly produced some writings and illustrations that refute such a statement. He has provided children with books that are filled with beauty — beauty that is natural and real, beauty that is rich in understandings of the past and the present, beauty that points youngsters toward the future, and that holds enjoyment and pleasure for the young reader. In other words, Holling C. Holling has the ability to portray the deep-down beauty of a river, a lake, a freighter, or a lonely tree on the Great Plains in such a way that he leads his reader to enjoy, appreciate, and understand them beyond mere factual understanding.

Mr. Holling's books are not hastily prepared or stereotyped. Only through much research, thought, and observation could he have written his books. In the Foreword to *The Book of Indians* Mr. Holling makes it clear to his readers that he is concerned with authenticity and that children need authentic materials to read. He states:

> As a boy, I wanted to know all about Indians. How did they really live? Did they always have horses? Did they always wear war-bonnets? How did they make those arrowpoints that Grandfather

* By Irvin L. Ramsey. From *Elementary English* 31 (February 1954), 67–71. Copyright © 1954 by the National Council of Teachers of English. Reprinted by permission of the publisher.

found in the fields? There were thousands of questions in my mind, and very few answers in the books I had.

In later years I began to look for the answers in many places. I am still asking questions. In all parts of the country scientists are digging in the earth, writing about what they have found, and the things they find and the books they write are being stored in museums and libraries. Mrs. Holling and I have visited these museums and libraries and have talked with the scientists themselves. Besides that we have lived with Indians. In the northern forests we paddled their birchbark canoes, and slept in their wicki-ups. We rode our horses beside theirs across the great plains and camped in their teepees in the mountains. In the desert they made us feel at home in their pueblos. We have fished with them in the surf of the Pacific Ocean. This book is the result of some of that hunting, riding, camping and research.

In his acknowledgment in *Minn of the Mississippi,* Mr. Holling further indicates the intent with which he writes:

This is a book about a river, and a turtle in it. I thought that I knew the river well; but long residence in southern California tends to drain the memory of sustained wetness such as is found in rivers. As for turtles—hadn't I caught bushels of them in Grandfather's woodlot pond? Yet that was long ago. How long I didn't realize until, on a visit to Michigan, this book was begun. Much had been forgotten, and much I really had never known. Once again I must begin a brooding activity—"research." Once more I must go to school to rivers—and to turtles . . .

The 1951 edition of *The Junior Book of Authors* provides further information concerning the interests and experiences which Mr. Holling utilizes in his writings. It states:

. . . Holling Clancy Holling graduated from . . . the Art Institute of Chicago . . .

Mr. Holling's occupations and activities, past and present, include work on a Michigan farm and carpentry. He has also served as grocery clerk, factory worker, and for two seasons as a sailor on Great Lakes ore boats. Three years were spent in the taxidermy department of the Field Museum and several years as idea man, artist, and copy writer in a national advertising firm.

Much of the material in Mr. Holling's *Paddle-to-the-Sea, Tree in the Trail,* and *Seabird* is known to him at first hand, for his amusements and hobbies include the use of primitive arti-facts, implements, weapons, and "lost art" processes, the study of wild animal behavior, music (with emphasis on primitive and ancient instruments and scores), canoeing, archery, hunting, fishing, field trips by foot, horse and canoe. He has traveled a great deal in the wilderness. In addition, he does much historical research.

Such experiences as these are the backgrounds from which he has significantly created in words and pictures *The Book of Indians, The Book of Cowboys, Paddle-to-the-Sea, Tree in the Trail, Seabird,* and *Minn of the Mississippi.* These books are all close to life — American life that boys and girls can and want to comprehend.

It is difficult to classify Mr. Holling's books. This seems due to the fact that he has combined the techniques of fiction with many areas of information into single books that portray a total pattern of life. Perhaps this is the most distinguishing characteristic of Mr. Holling's writings. This combination indicates that this author has not based his works solely on child interests but has also concerned himself with writing for children in terms of how they learn and develop.

Mr. Holling is an author who trusts children with big ideas. He has recognized child curiosities and child interests. He has attempted to satisfy these curiosities and interests in a meaningful way. Sometimes he achieves this effect through descriptions of natural phenomena; sometimes through historical description; sometimes through industrial explanations. For example, he tells in *Seabird* about glaciers and the beginning of an iceberg in this way:

> The flying Gull crosses frozen rivers of glaciers — gigantic icicles laid along the valleys. Moving inch by inch to the sea, they ended in ice walls towering up from the water . . .
> . . . An ice-chunk big as a hill split off from the walls and dropped into the sea. It sank and heaved upward again, a white mountain gushing foam. Thunders of its falling rolled for miles. Mad waves lashed the cliffs, rushed to sea tossing ice cakes, and lost themselves in the gray veil of a summer snowstorm. Yet even this birth of a floating iceberg . . .

In *Tree in the Trail* he gives the historical picture of the caravan at the end of the journey:

The huge wagons, high as haystacks, rocked past corrals of sheep, goats and burros. Ducks and pigs scrambled out of irrigation ditches and fled noisily. It was a great day for the men, eight hundred miles from Independence. It was a great day for the happy people of Santa Fe. Guns boomed, church bells rang. Spanish welcomes were shouted from doorways and flat rooftops. The train rumbled through crooked streets walled by whitewashed adobe houses. Starbright and Bugle stepped proudly, leading the caravan. And the yoke's bells jingled merrily to the open plaza, at the very center of town.

In *Paddle-to-the-Sea* Mr. Holling describes a sawmill:

The mill, a mass of red buildings on stilts above the river bank, opened its wide mouth in the main building. From the mouth ran the log chute, a giant tongue, licking into the water. A heavy chain of spikes moved up the center of the chute, turned over a wheel and repushed the logs onto the spikes which carried them up the chute into the open mouth. A buzzing noise which sometimes became a shriek came from inside the mill. The great saws were at work.

If one were inclined to present children with isolated geographical, scientific, historical, and social facts, he would find it difficult to defend his position against children who have traveled with Minn, Paddle, Seabird, Peter and Barbara Ann, and Buffalo-Calf. Children who are familiar with these books and have lived with the characters in them would see no value in rigorous drills and memory exercises devoted to learning such dull unrelated statements as: the source of the river is the place where the river begins; the mouth of a river is the place where the river empties into a larger body of water; upstream is toward the source of the river; an iceberg is a floating piece of ice that has broken off from a glacier; Jamestown was settled in 1607; the Santa Fe trail started at St. Louis, Missouri and ended at Santa Fe, New Mexico; a turtle is a reptile that is cold-blooded and has a toothless beak and a bony shell which protects the body, the head, and the limbs. With Holling, his young readers have come to know that information achieves life qualities not because they are facts which make a difference in daily life.

This author has consistently concerned himself with the concept of change and its influence upon our way of life; he has presented backgrounds for the development of social and moral values. Yet, it would be unfair criticism to say that he has been dogmatic in his presentations; he has dealt with problems in settings that are real and genuinely reflective of locales. Unfortunately, many children need the good counsel offered to Peter and Barbara Ann by Idaho Ike in *The Book of Cowboys:*

"People in the East think sometimes that all a cowboy does is ride around on buckin' broncs, shootin' all over the place with sixguns and rifles!" said Idaho Ike . . . "But nowadays there's no need for guns out here most of the time. Of course, when you're in rattle-snake country, a revolver comes in handy and sometimes a coyote or wolf that's been killin' stock needs attendin' to. But today a cow-puncher could ride most all the time and never need any kind of a gun. . . ."

In *The Book of Indians,* Mr. Holling points out that children who lived long before Peter and Barbara Ann experienced similar problems, too:

. . . Dust-Cloud kept watch over the stranger who had fever and tossed about in the feather robes they gave him and mumbled words. Corn-Flower had never heard such strange words. They rippled on and on like water over stones, not like the soft gutteral words of her people.

"He is a human being," smiled Dust-Cloud, "and he is like us. . . ."

The captives were sorrowful at first and grumbled. But this new village was really much better than their own. Besides, there were other captives, from their tribe, in neighboring houses, and when they had forgotten the noise of that awful battle, they settled down to enjoy themselves as best they could. . . .

Raven liked the boy and the girl his father had brought. . . .

Though the boy sulked and the girl cried at first, they soon became fast friends with Raven. It was not at all like two slaves and a master.

Such problems are not exclusive to understandings about Cowboys and Indians; the boy of the bayou also has his problems:

"Ah hate tuttles—" muttered the boy softly. Then he shrieked "TUTTLES! . . . AH HATE TUTTLES! AH HATE! AH HATE! AH HATE! . . ."

Minn sank quickly, but now came a torrent of blows. . . .

Then it was over. The pole jerked upward, the bayou settled to shadowy calm, but the voice snarled on—"Ah hate everything! . . . Call me pore white trash. Call *me* white trash! Whut if Pappy hain't got no money! He got cricks in th' back. Cain't do nothin' but sleep—an' whup me. . . . But *they* ain't got no right. *They* ain't got th' say of *me*. Jes' wait. Jes' wait till Ah git a MILLION DOLLARS! . . .

"Hey you, ole crow up thar—think you is safe, huh? Jes' wait. With a million dollahs—know whut Ah'd do? Buy me 'at shiny gun Ah seen—an' blow you, Crow, to feathahs so fine they'd sift down like soot! Buy a cannon an' blow up th' bayous an' all th' folks! . . . But no—that ain't so smart. . . . Buy me a yacht. An' all th' things Ah seen, up to New Orleans. Then they'd butter up! They'd say 'please' to me! . . . An' ah'd go political. They'd vote fer me, if'n Ah was growed. Ah'd run th' State—maybe git to be *Prezzy-dunt!*" With sudden energy he pushed the johnboat from the tree. "WHY, AH COULD BOSS TH' WORLD . . . If'n Ah had me a measly li'l ole million dollahs! . . ."

Mr. Holling has been imaginative as he has selected and developed plots that have simplicity, child-likeness, and a strong sense of reality. Would it be difficult to find a boy with a turtle; or a boy with a carving; or a boy with a favorite tree; or a boy with a bow and arrow; or a boy with a cowboy suit?

Though there is a similarity in the plots of his books, Mr. Holling has not been repetitious or monotonous. He has developed plots in such a way that his characters meet life situations related to and consistent with the locales in which they find themselves. His plots have adventure, sincerity, authenticity, and appeal. In all his stories his characters grow and live through struggle for security, they endure hardships, they sense pleasure, and they interpret life. Mr. Holling has maintained a balance among these basic needs and has woven them into true pictures that provide children with literature commensurate with their interests, needs, and capabilities.

Mr. Holling's books are beautifully illustrated, especially *Seabird, Paddle-to-the-Sea, Tree in the Trail,* and *Minn of the Mississippi.* Mrs. Holling is also an artist and has contributed much to the illustrations. In his acknowledgment in *Tree in the Trail,* Mr. Holling gives recognition to Mrs. Holling's contributions:

I wish to thank my wife, Lucille Webster Holling, for her help in completing the illustrations in this book; her many hours of research on the trail of obscure data have contributed greatly to authoritative detail, and she designed the color map.

In their illustrations, the Hollings have effectively used deep dark colors that illustrate so well the moods of their stories. The formats of all their books are large and their illustrations are large full-page illustrations that in *Paddle-to-the-Sea, Seabird,* and *Tree in the Trail* illustrate one single page of writing; in *Minn of the Mississippi* there is a full-page illustration for every two or three pages of writing.

In the illustrations one finds the same fullness and completeness, as well as exactness, that is so manifest in the writings. They are not just pictures that specifically illustrate a point; they have depth and meaning that go beyond mere usefulness or immediacy. When one looks at Holling's pictures, he sees more than just a turtle in a river or a whaling boat at sea; he sees life that is complex, both dependent and independent, and he sees life that is ongoing. These illustrations have more than color, more than design, and more than specific interpretations. Mr. Holling knows that his illustrations must be true to the content and he also knows that an illustration should be good art.

Mr. Holling has employed the technique of further providing the reader with scientific and historical technicalities through the use of black-and-white diagrams and illustrations in the wide margins. This technique may be questionable; for some readers the books may appear to be cluttered with so much detail that they seem to be text-bookish. It does seem plausible though that here is a provision for the more advanced reader who is interested in greater detail than that given in the story. Too, it is a provision for adults, and there are adults who could profit from and enjoy these books.

Mr. Holling realizes that children no longer need to be crammed with namby-pamby stories. He realizes that they are capable of developing deep understandings of the realities of their natural-social world. He has provided them with literature rich in those things which lead to appreciation and interpretation of life.

EDITORS' NOTE

Since the publication of the foregoing article, Holling C. Holling and his wife, Lucille Webster Holling, have researched, written about, and illustrated the life habits of the Hermit Crab with their usual thoroughness. The resulting book, *Pagoo* (1957—Houghton and Hale), was subsequently used as the basis for a film, "Story of a Book," which was distributed by Churchill Films in 1962. Mr. and Mrs. Holling demonstrated in the film how they gathered information for the story. They take the viewer through all the steps necessary to the publishing of a book. *Paddle to the Sea* (Houghton), was also made into a film in 1967 by the Nature Film Board of Canada, and is distributed by McGraw-Hill. Both films are now available through Syracuse University.

Paddle to the Sea was a runner-up for the John Newbery Award and also received the Lewis Carroll Shelf Award (given annually to the title worthy of sitting on a shelf with *Alice in Wonderland*). *Seabird* (Houghton) won the Commonwealth Club of California Literature Award in 1948 (given annually for the finest juvenile on any subject by a Californian) and was also a runner-up for the John Newbery Award in 1949. *Minn of the Mississippi* (Houghton) was a runner-up for the John Newbery Award in 1952.

As a resident of Southern California, Mr. Holling was entitled to be considered for the Southern California Children's Literature Award, which he received in 1960. This award is given to the author who has made the most comprehensive contribution of lasting value in the field of children's literature.

Kristin Hunter—
Profile of an Author *

DID ANY OF YOUR childhood reading leave a permanent mark?
Yes, probably all of it, and I was a voracious reader. I remember best *The Water Babies* (Kingsley), Halliburton's *Occident* and *Orient* (made me want to travel), Isadora Duncan's *My Life* (made me want to be an artist) and *Don Quixote* from the Harvard Classics (most of which I'd read before age 12).

What did you read during your teenage years?
Sad to say, better and more difficult stuff than I read now. Philosophy (Berkeley, Langer, Kant, Schopenhauer), many poets and playwrights, anybody like Henry Miller who was avant-garde enough to be published by New Directions, opaque novelists like Henry Green and Virginia Woolf, etc. Today I'm too lazy or too opinionated to tackle such demanding stuff.

How did you get your first break?
Through the good offices of a columnist aunt, I was invited to write a youth column for a weekly Negro newspaper at age 14. The column continued for six years and soon allowed me to sound off on any subject I wished, not just the social activities of local youth.

Why do you write for older children?
To avoid succumbing to the temptation to write down and be overly cute or condescending, therefore false. Older children can be addressed

* From *Top of the News* 26 (January 1970), 148–151. Reprinted with the permission of the American Library Association.

217

on an adult or near-adult level. I can literally "level" with them without watering down or falsifying my style or my content.

Can a writer be too realistic?

Yes, if he emphasizes "facts" at the expense of the deeper truths of felt life and the creative imagination. I deplore both the adult non-novels which are really compendiums of facts on airports, advertising, drugs, etc. — and the new children's books which emphasize rockets and computers instead of fantasy or people. Dull, dull, dull!

Did you ever meet Sister Lou?

No, except in my imagination, where large chunks of me and smaller chunks of all the other people I've known reside and occasionally combine in a mysterious way to generate fictional characters with a life of their own.

Who are your favorite novelists?

Nelson Algren, Bruce Jay Friedman, Chester Himes, Henry James, J. P. Donleavy, Ralph Ellison, Edward Louis Wallant, Colette, Balzac, and whoever I'm reading at the moment (Doris Lessing and Stephen Becker).

Contrast what you read as a child with books about black children today.

There were no black children in the books I read as a child, though I remember a racist incident in one of the *Bobbsey Twins* books (involving their servants) that enraged me for months. I haven't seen any of today's books about black children except my own, but I hope they're peopled with three-dimensional characters, not just blackfaced Dicks and Janes.

What advice have you for future writers?

Read all you can till you're 20, live all you can till you're 30, and write all you can after that. And fight all your life against regimentation, automation, and standardization — all the forms of the Machine which want to make you obsolete.

What bothers you about librarians and libraries?

Locally, they all know me too well and treat me as a celebrity instead of letting me relax and browse and be anonymous. I hate being made a fuss over anywhere, but especially in libraries and bookstores. Generally, I wish librarians cared more about people than books, I wish fines could be abolished or at least dropped after a written or telephoned notice that the reader needs to keep the book longer, and I wish libraries were more homelike and less institutional. In other words, I wish they were places where you could kick your shoes off. Maybe that's because my feet hurt a lot, and libraries are seldom within comfortable walking distance. For an example of what I mean, consider the Phillips Gallery in Washington, D.C., the only comfortable place I've ever seen that dispenses culture. But I think it would be best of all if libraries were to go to the people and books could be borrowed in every tavern, barber shop, and drug-store.

EDITORS' NOTE

Kristin Hunter's books include *Landlord* (1964 – Avon), *Soul Brothers and Sister Lou* (1968 – Scribner; 1969 – Avon), *God Bless the Child* (1970 – Bantam), and *Boss Cat* (1971 – Scribner). This latest book is the story of Pharaoh, the cat, who takes over the Tanner family's apartment much to Mom's chagrin. It is a humorous and delightful story.

Soul Brothers and Sister Lou won the 1968 Council on Interracial Books for Children Award. Miss Hunter was the first to receive this award for the 12–16-year-old category, as the creator of the most un-biased portrait of the life of a minority group. Black, American Indian, Chicano, or Puerto Rican writers, who have never published a book for children, are eligible for this Award.

In another area, Kristin Hunter won recognition by being awarded first prize by the Fund for the Republic for a television script on school segregation. Entitled "A Minority of One," it appeared in revised and abbreviated form on a C.B.S. series entitled "A Light Unto My Feet," in 1956.

In 1965, she received the Athanaeum of Philadelphia Literary Award; in 1959 – the John Hay Whitney Fellowship for minority group writing.

Born in Philadelphia, the daughter of two school-teachers, Kristin Hunter also prepared for the teaching profession at the University of Pennsylvania. Finding classroom discipline too difficult for her, she turned to her second vocation – writing – and has had unquestionable success.

In private life, she makes her home with her husband in Philadelphia. She plans to continue in her efforts to help minority children build positive images of themselves, and to help all children grow in their awareness of the world as it really is.

Clara Ingram Judson:
Interpreter of America *

CLARA INGRAM JUDSON'S PHILOSOPHY of life is reflected in all her writings. There one will find her deep love for home and family, her abiding faith in all kinds of people and her belief that these are the foundations of the past and the promise of a greater America tomorrow.

Before she began her "They Came From" series she had already written more than forty books. But it was this series of seven famous titles which first made her known as an outstanding writer for children. Before she wrote these books, however, she had a colorful career; yet everything she did only enriched her life and broadened her background for all her later writings.

Growing up in the Mid-west with three brothers, she learned very early from her parents the importance of cooperation and responsibility in the home. Later, when she married, her own family concern with two daughters strengthened her deep conviction that love of home and loyalty to one's country are the profound basis of the good life.

Ideas for writing came as she convalesced from a long illness. First she told little stories to please her own small daughters at bedtime. Her children enjoyed them so much that Clara Judson sent them to a local newspaper, which accepted and published them. The home town boys and girls read them avidly and the editor urged her to write more stories for a daily column, later syndicated as a national newspaper feature.

* By Charlemae Rollins. From *Elementary English* 30 (December 1953), 477–484. Reprinted with the permission of the National Council of Teachers of English and Charlemae Rollins.

In 1915 her first book, *Flower Fairies,* was published. It was one of the very earliest "modern" fairy tales, a fore-runner of the stories now known as realistic stories that ended the too-long era of sentimentalism in children's books.

Today, *Flower Fairies* would be considered quite sentimental, but in 1915 it must have been a real answer to a desperate need for simple little stories for very young children.

Her first great success in the juvenile book field came with the nineteen volumes in the "Mary Jane" series, written to stress the simple ways of getting along with others in the home, in school, and in the community, Children bought and read the books with such pleasure that both author and publisher recognized the need for more books that are fun to read and yet convey some worthwhile message.

Then came *Play Days,* a photographic picture book of stories and poetry. This showed Mrs. Judson's versatility and also her pioneering spirit. Experimenting with photographs in children's books was then a revolutionary idea. Rand McNally published her *Child Life Cook Book* — which was followed by two other illustrated cook books for children. This pioneering venture, pictures of the finished products — a luscious cake or pie or even biscuits — opened a whole new field of illustrated cook books, not only for children, but for adults as well.

During the first World War, the Treasury Department sent her to many of the large high schools in Illinois to speak in the educational campaign for War Bonds. This work led Clara Judson into the field of lecturing to women's clubs, Farm and Home Bureaus, State extension meetings, and Adult Education courses in colleges and universities all over the country. With the coming of radio, she began broadcasting on such subjects as child training and the business side of home making. Later, she wrote and published several books on economics for adults. This interesting work brought her in touch with a great variety of people and increased her knowledge of America.

In the back of her mind persisted the idea of the importance of the family unit as the contributing factor to the making of a good life in America. Her desire to share the knowledge that she had gained was the impetus which drove her relentlessly on to write more about the importance of people, both adults and children, getting to know each other and cooperating.

When her grandchildren asked about the milkman, the postman, and the deliveryman, she realized that children want to know about the people who work. Then came the first important contributions: *People Who Come to Our House* (Rand McNally, 1940), an attractive factual story book about the postman, painter, plumber, milkman, and other workers who come to our houses; *People Who Work near Our House* (Rand McNally, 1942), told about the barber, busdriver, street-sweeper, filling station attendant, and other workers near our houses; and *People Who Work in The Country and in the City* (Rand McNally, 1943), told of those farther away—the farmer, dairyman, market-gardener, cheese-maker, poultry-raiser, and the rural postman. Material of this kind was needed not only by parents but teachers. It is good to know that these three excellent books are still available through the Cadmus Press. In 1948; the Broadman Press published another similar book, *Summer Time,* which also stresses what children can do together in the home.

Mrs. Judson has always known that children are people. She does not approve of "books written for children" as such. She feels that the young readers are quicker and more sensitive than adults to detect factual errors and books written down to them. It takes little time for them to sense the "And now dear children, would you like to hear what the bad, bad fox did to the little children?" type of story. In a lecture at the University of Chicago she said:

> As a matter of fact our use of the word "children" is odd. We speak it as carelessly as the word "love." We love a fragrance, a scene, a symphony, the person we marry, or an ideal. Yet the emotions involved are quite diverse. Equally varied is the use of the word children. I call my grandchildren children—one is in the Navy, the others in college. I call their parents my children; yet certainly they are adults. Pupils in the nursery school are spoken of as children— the same word—with such a variety of meanings. It would seem that we who work with words might evolve something more accurate. When our books are read by young readers we are fortunate. The best an author can hope to do with an adult is to instigate some slight alterations. If one can reach a young mind there is hope of helping to make a blueprint for the future. I care so deeply about the ideals which motivate my work that I confess I crave readers who are in the growing, expanding phase of thinking. I well know that only the highest standards will interest them.

With these ideals as her goal, it is not surprising that Clara Judson was able to write during the same period a group of books for older boys and girls as well as the books already mentioned. In 1938 she wrote *Pioneer Girl,* a life of Frances E. Willard, which gave an excellent picture of the life in America a century ago. This was followed by *Boat Builder: Story of Robert Fulton* (Scribners, 1940); *Railway Engineer: Story of George Stephenson* (Scribners, 1941); *Soldier Doctor: Story of William Gorgas* (Scribners, 1942); and *Donald McKay: Designer of Clipper Ships* (Scribners, 1943). These were fictionized biographies presenting an exciting picture of shipbuilding, railroads, clipper ships, steamboating, and medicine in the 19th century. Although they were fiction, careful research was the keynote, and each book shows her skill and superior craftsmanship.

As she was writing these biographies she seems to have absorbed many of the characteristics of her heroes and heroines, particularly the craftsman, Donald McKay. She was also becoming more aware of the deeper needs of her readers.

An exciting thought took hold of her one night in a Pullman berth after an exhausting day of lectures in Lincoln, Nebraska. She had been unable to get hotel accommodations and was invited to spend the night in a private home. Her hostess, a Swedish woman, wanted very much to hear her lecture, but the week's ironing stood in her way. Mrs. Judson offered to help with the work in the morning and when she began to iron the exquisitely embroidered linens, she was amazed to find such priceless treasures in the modest home.

When asked if she had made them, the woman answered casually, "Oh, those; we brought them when we came from Sweden." This phrase was the magic that kept Mrs. Judson awake in her berth. It was indeed that which gave her the famous "Tapestry Idea." She had always disagreed with those who thought of America as a "melting pot." The people she met, instead of being melted down, were definitely being gradually woven into the vast tapestry of our national life — a tapestry in which beauty comes from the variety and the un-likeness of the many threads and strength created by the wealth of skills and culture. "What holds these threads together?" she asked herself. "What, but a common dream of freedom and opportunity for a better life, the differences on the surface being differences of skills and manners and habits."

That night she resolved to write books for young people that would show the richness brought to our land and the strength and idealism that were here ready to be used if only we had the understanding to make them available. She set out to study the history and manners, customs, and beliefs of the people who had come to live in America. She was thrilled to learn from cold facts that "our differences, though interesting, are relatively trivial and our likenesses are profound." Here was an opportunity to put into living stories all her concepts of democracy, all her knowledge of family life, and beliefs in the importance of cooperation.

None of the publishers she approached were interested in the idea until her faith finally sent her to Houghton-Mifflin. The far-seeing editor in this pioneering publishing company agreed to publish a series of books on seven different nationality groups. Strangely enough, the first one he selected was about the Swedish emigrants, although he hadn't heard the story about the linens.

Her research, experience, and knowledge made her acutely aware of the economic problems of the minorities she was to write about. She knew there would be other problems too, but she also knew there would be answers to these problems, and she set out to find them as each of "her families" found and solved their problems.

She felt that if these books were to win wide appeal, they must be good in every way. They must be true to the life presented, interesting, and well-written. The characters must be living people, not wooden automatons upon which to hang a plot. There must be facts, not "lumps that the author has not taken the trouble to absorb," and each book must "flame with true inspiration."

They Came from Sweden is the story of the Larssons, a Swedish family who migrated to New York in 1856. It is readable and interesting, describing their skills, character, background, and aims. She wanted to show in this book as well as the others a real picture of the region in which they settled, how their neighbors reacted to them and how they in turn learned to accept the American customs. It is a good story because it is an honest portrayal of the life of that period, and full of the little homey family details that children enjoy. Their first lonely Christmas in the new land appeals to old and young alike, and their hardy acceptance and enjoyment of new customs and people is the final fulfillment of their dreams. This first book is indeed an excellent introduction to the other titles that follow.

They Came from France (1942) tells about the Remy family that settled in New Orleans with the desire to make a fortune and then return to their beloved home in Paris. How they learned to love the new land and new people is simply but graphically told.

They Came from Scotland (1944) began a new and exciting idea in the series. In addition to the contributions made by the nationality group, there was a slight mystery and some adventure in the story. Children were enjoying the stories about new people and they were being used in schools to help teach understanding, and as pioneer stories also.

It was decided to drop the series title, "They Came From," in favor of a straight title, and use the series idea as a subtitle to designate the nationality group. So the fourth book is *Petar's Treasure: They Came from Dalmatia* (1945). It also introduced a mystery element and told about a penniless family that came steerage from their native home in Dalmatia to settle in a fishing and canning community in Biloxi, Mississippi. There they learn to share the life of a poor but thrifty, hard-working people. An entirely new concept came into this story when a Negro boy was introduced as Petar's friend and companion. He is presented without condescension or stereotyping. He is completely accepted as an equal by Petar's family and even in the church one is surprised to find him and his family worshipping.

Mrs. Judson's careful research brought out the fact that in 1906, in the Catholic church of this region, all kinds of people worshipped together. This is characteristic of the type of research done for all her work. She reads old newspapers, legal documents, personal letters and diaries, as well as countless interviews with living persons. Her main characters are fiction only in the sense that the actual happenings are a composite of what happened to many families. Her secondary characters in all the stories are real people and are called by their real names and do what each actually did in that year and place. The incident in the book of Steve Sekul at Ellis Island actually happened. He allowed Mrs. Judson to use his own experiences in the book.

Michael's Victory: They Came from Ireland (1946) is the story of the O'Haras, an Irish family (then called Shanty Irish) driven from Ireland because of the potato famine. Here they, along with hundreds of other courageous Irish, helped to build the railroads of America. They, more than any of the other groups, found hostility. This was because of the economic rivalry between the railroad workers and the canal-boat operators who found the railroads a serious threat to their security. The building of the railroad furnishes thrilling material in addition to the colorful speech and the humor of the Irish. This is one of the most popular titles in the series.

The second most popular story of the series is *The Lost Violin: They Came from Bohemia* (1947). The Bohemians who came to Chicago just before the World's Fair were skilled workers and artisans. They brought their talents to the new world because they wanted political and religious freedom. No famine caused them to leave their homes, where many were well-to-do people who often had to take serious economic set-backs while they learned the new language and ways of Americans. The mystery of the violin holds the interest of both boys and girls, although the main character of this book is a heroine. There are several famous personages in this story, such as Jane Addams, Anton Dvorak and others.

Mrs. Judson says that it is her last book in the series, *The Green Gin-*

ger Jar: Story of the Chinese in Chicago (1949) that taught her more than all the others about the "tapestry that is America." Most of the people in this story did not "come from" other countries at all, but were born in America. For the first time she found herself on the other side of the fence. The Chinese showed her she was "different." She was a person with a "label." She was referred to as a "Westerner." When she dug deep into the matter to find the reason, since she was neither a cowboy nor a movie star, she found that it was because centuries ago the first white man came to the Western Wall of China, knocked and was admitted to do business; because he had come West he was a "Sai-Yan," a West-man, and from that day until this his kind were "Westerners." So are labels made:

> she said. Suddenly uncomfortable, I looked at my hands—such a funny color, neither yellow nor brown; certainly not the white I had called them, and so lacking the grace of every Chinese hand. I thought of my hair, a mousey grey, not a rich black; my eyes, pale blue, not a melting brown. I thought of our odd way of eating, spreading food all over the plate where it cools instead of putting it into a bowl. I looked at our odd dress, lacking in grace and comfort, and of our social crudeness, without question, our slang and our lack of expressed gratitude. How odd we Westerners were, indeed. Yet the Chinese are patient with us. But on further thought I took comfort, for I saw that underneath our differences were likenesses and much more important than food and dress and manners. We both love our families; we try to be honest and industrious and we cherish our freedom. Even with picturesque differences we are more alike than unlike. We are brothers in spite of vestiges of the past and better forgotten.

The last book in the series is a story of contemporary life in Chicago. It combines the old and the new. The historical part of Old China was represented by the grandmother, and the modern young Chinese-Americans who are trying to bring the past and present together as well as East and West. *The Green Ginger Jar* very fittingly ends the series.

Dozens of children's books are written each year pleading for understanding, brotherhood, tolerance, even democracy, but none are more forthright and sound than these books which tell a good story about real people, showing how they live, work, play, suffer, and survive. Richly basic in all these stories are their accuracy of historic detail and the understanding characterization. To obtain this accuracy, Mrs. Judson spares neither time nor trouble. She spends hours of research in libraries, reading old newspapers, poring over dusty immigration laws, and as many economic journals as are available.

Another important mark of her careful craftsmanship is her keen insight into the characteristics of her families. In none of her characters does one find the stereotypes so often used by slipshod writers as an easy means of portraying minorities. Her conversation in the stories as well as in her biographies is based on actual conversations taken from diaries and journals of the period.

This interest in America and her government opened an entirely new area of interest for Mrs. Judson—a desire to write about the distinguished men in the government, notably our great presidents. Although many biographies have already been written, she felt that there needed to be newer interpretations because children were forming many misconceptions and erroneous ideas about them. A new biography should bring new light and a fresh point of view for the young people of this age. This must, of course, come from new research, more intensive reading of letters, journals, newspapers, and magazines published during their lifetime, more study of the history and economic background of their times. If a book is fiction, readers deserve to find in it essential truth. If the work is biography or history, the content must be factually accurate and truthfully interpreted.

Nothing gives an author more insight into a man's life than the reading of his letters. Any writer who undertakes the job of re-creating a great man's life in a book must necessarily bring something of himself to that task. It is this one thing more than anything else which marks the work of Mrs. Judson; more of her deeper self seems to shine through the biographies than in the fiction. She puts into them all the love she has for her own immediate family as well as the compassion she feels for all mankind.

When she undertook the task of writing *Abraham Lincoln, Friend of the People* (Wilcox & Follett, 1950), she journeyed to the little cabin on Knob Creek in Kentucky. There the new idea came in a flash as she looked at the home of the Lincolns. His poverty had always been overstressed, but they were not poor when judged by the standards of the times. True, the family did not have "things," but no one around them had things, either. Lincoln's father was a good farmer and hunter; there was plenty of wholesome food to eat. His mother was a skillful sewer, so the family had warm, comfortable clothing. And they had something that many strive for today—security. More than that, Mrs. Judson makes one feel the love that the Lincolns had for each other.

A new slant on George Washington's life came to light in the Library of

Congress while she was reading the diary of a private soldier who served with him at Valley Forge. His words, "The General came by and pitched. The General is a good pitcher," showed a different side of Washington. How many people would ever think of General Washington as a good baseball pitcher? So Mrs. Judson portrayed him not as an aristocrat, but as a friendly person—a farmer with countless friends, a man who cared about his family and his fellow men. The *University of Chicago Bulletin* comments, "A fitting companion volume to the outstanding *Abraham Lincoln, George Washington* is a dramatized biography in Mrs. Judson's distinguished style and presents material never before used in a story for young people."

Mrs. Judson says that *Thomas Jefferson, Champion of the People,* was the hardest of all the biographies to write because Jefferson's life was not as full of exciting incidents as the other two—"his excitements were mental and of the spirit." He was working for the same freedoms as the other two, but in a different way. Jefferson is generally thought of as the writer of the Declaration of Independence. This document was written when he was 33 years of age, but he lived to be 83. During those later years he was working to show people what freedom, equality, and liberty really meant.

A reviewer in the *Horn Book* says of Mrs. Judson's *Thomas Jefferson,* "Jefferson emerges as a real person; the dreamer and builder of government designed to give new freedoms and equal opportunity to all; the scholar who found joy in music, architecture, farming, inventing, and educating; the family man delighting in his daughters and his many grandchildren.

In *Theodore Roosevelt* (Wilcox & Follett, 1953) she shows how his courage overcame early and serious ill health; how it took him through years of minor political jobs with more frustrations than successes, tragic losses by sudden death of wife and mother, war service and the better known service to his country as President, as well as his work for human betterment and conservation. Mrs. Judson is now working on a life of Andrew Jackson, another great President.

In all the books one finds the mothers preparing the foods characteristic of each country, the fathers honest, skillful workers in many fields.

In all the homes one finds family love and a feeling of security—not the security of a check on the first of every month—but an assurance of love and faith in each other and in those around them.

In all her heroes and heroines, whether true or fictional characters, the young readers feel their inherent honesty and their love for one another.

Deep in every title is found her philosophy: "Peace, real lasting peace, is a growth from the hearthside, spreading then to the neighborhood, the community, the town, the country, and some day, to the world — and our hope lies in our children. I feel deeply that as we help children to understand their neighbors we help in the understanding of world problems."

EDITORS' NOTE

Clara Ingram Judson's books have won numerous awards and honors. Among these are the Children's Reading Round Table Award (given to a mid-westerner for outstanding achievements in children's literature); the 1959 Indiana Authors' Day Award (given annually to the most distinguished books by Hoosier writers) for *St. Lawrence Seaway;* runner-up for the Newbery Medal for *Abraham Lincoln, Friend of the People* in 1951, *Theodore Roosevelt, Fighting Patriot* in 1954, and *Mr. Justice Holmes* in 1957; and the Laura Ingalls Wilder Award (given every five years to an author or illustrator whose books, published in the United States, have made a lasting contribution to literature for children) in 1960.

Three of Mrs. Judson's biographies, written for young people, were rewritten by her for the primary grades. The primary editions are entitled *Christopher Columbus, George Washington,* and *Abraham Lincoln.* Her books have been translated into many languages, among which are Japanese, Burmese, Urdu and Tamil.

Mrs. Judson died in 1960 at the age of eighty-one. In 1961, the Clara Ingram Judson Award was established in her memory. The Award, a prize of $500, is given annually by the Society of Midland Authors to the most outstanding book written for children by a native or resident of Mid-America.

Ezra Jack Keats
Author and Illustrator *

IN OCTOBER, 1967 Ezra Jack Keats received an invitation from Her Imperial Majesty Farah Pahlevi, Empress of Iran, to be a delegate of the United States and a guest of honor at the Second Teheran International Festival of Films for Children. Entries from many countries would be shown, including the film version of his book *Whistle for Willie*, produced by Weston Woods Studio.

This was the latest recognition of Ezra Jack Keats' colorful, imaginative, and tender books for children. *The Snowy Day (Viking,* 1962) won for its author-illustrator the Caldecott Award in 1963. Made into a film by Weston Woods Studio, it won the prize for the best children's film at the Venice Film Festival.

The Snowy Day and others of his books have been included in several lists of the best books of the year.

Reviewers, parents, teachers, and librarians have praised his books and children have delighted in them.

In the past seven years ten books have come from Ezra Keats' drawing board. Most of them are for children: *My Dog Is Lost!; Mi Perro Se Ha Perdido* (written with Pat Cherr, *Crowell,* 1960); *The Snowy Day (Viking,* 1962); *Whistle for Willie (Viking,* 1963); *Zoo, Where Are You?* (story by Ann McGovern, *Harper,* 1964); *John Henry: An American Legend (Pantheon,* 1965); *Jennie's Hat (Harper & Row,* 1966); and *Peter's Chair (Harper & Row,* 1967).

* By Florence B. Freedman. From *Elementary English* 46 (January 1969), 55–65. Reprinted with the permission of the National Council of Teachers of English and Florence B. Freedman.

For older children and adults he has illustrated *The Naughty Boy,* a light poem written by the famous John Keats in his youth (*Viking,* 1965); *In a Spring Garden,* a book of haiku edited by Richard Lewis (*Dial,* 1965); and *God Is in the Mountain,* Keats' own selection of beautiful and profound statements from many religions (*Holt,* 1966).

When I visited Ezra Keats to interview him for this article, I remembered back through our years of friendship to our first meeting, when he and forty other students entered my fifth term English class at Thomas Jefferson High School in the East New York section of Brooklyn.

I saw him then, but I noticed him first during a discussion of *Silas Marner.*

A student had just made the conventional statement that Silas Marner was a miser. The tall, skinny, quiet boy in the last row, last seat, rose as if propelled to his feet. "Silas Marner was *not* a miser," he said. "He loved beauty, and those gold coins were the only beauty he knew!"

Several students disputed his statement. Ezra remonstrated, "If Silas Marner was a miser, so am I!" Then with impassioned and unexpected eloquence he said that he hoarded tubes of oil paint just as Silas Marner did his coins. He had saved up for them and bought them one by one, but he had never used them, because he did not think he was a good enough artist. But when he came home from school he would unscrew their caps, gloat over the dabs of brilliant color that were revealed, then put the caps back on; he would hold the tubes which seemed to vibrate with hidden power, count them, and put them away again, unused. "So if Silas Marner is a miser," he concluded, "I am, too."

(Since then I have often heard teachers who complain about antiquated curricula say contemptuously, "Are they *still* teaching *Silas Marner?*" Unlike them, I treasure *Silas Marner* because it revealed to me and the class that there was an artist in our midst, and set a pattern for the students of relating events and characters of this tale of nineteenth century England to the life and people they knew.)

The students in that English class became friendly with each other and with me. Ezra said his mother would like to meet me, and invited me to his home, which was on the third floor of a walkup apartment building near the school. I soon began to visit almost every Friday afternoon. I remember the kitchen, which served as "family room." Gleaming white with touches of Delft blue in oilcloth, dish towels, and utensils, it was like a Dutch interior. His mother, soft-spoken and gentle, made this a haven for troubled neighbors, family, and friends. We would have cake and coffee, often with a neighbor or cousin or friend, and talk until her husband's return from work indicated that I had, as usual, stayed longer than I had intended.

It seems to me as though that kitchen was a small center of deep concern for others—family, friends, neighbors, and troubled people everywhere. Now I see this feeling at the center of Ezra Keats' books for children.

In his childhood Ezra had few books. When, at the age of five or six he had to be hospitalized, he took all his well-worn books with him, but found that they had to be taken home. He asked his mother to bring him more books. On the following visitors' day, she brought a neatly wrapped package. What was his disappointment to find that they were the same books he had originally brought from home!

Luxuries such as books were hard to come by, for his father had to struggle to make a living. Ezra's parents had immigrated to the United States from Poland when they were in their teens, seeking to escape the persecution of Jews in Poland. They met and married in this country, and settled in Brooklyn. They had three children, of whom Ezra was the youngest.

Like most children, Ezra liked to draw. His first intimation that his drawings were valued came from his mother. One day when he was nine or ten he suddenly discovered a perfect surface for drawing—the enameled top of the kitchen table, and soon covered it with pictures of cottages with smoke curling from their chimneys, and people of all kinds, including a Chinese with pigtails and an American Indian. He expected a scolding from his mother. Instead she said that the drawings were so nice, it was a shame to wash them off. "So she got out the tablecloth which we used only on Friday nights and she covered the whole little mural and every time a neighbor would come in, she'd unveil it to show what I had done. They'd all say, 'Mmm, isn't that nice.' They couldn't say anything else, Mother was so proud." [1]

Her enthusiasm was not shared by Ezra's father. As the son showed his increasing devotion to art, the father increased his opposition. He was a waiter in Greenwich Village where he saw artists who were eccentric or starving—often both. This was not the future he wanted for his son.

Now painting became a conspiracy between mother and son. The interval between school and the father's arrival from work was a busy one. As soon as footsteps were heard mounting the stairs, there was a quick dismantling and putting away. (The hiding place was under the oilcloth cover of the sewing machine.)

Yet there must have been a deep struggle within the father between his dream of conventional success for his son and his pride in his son's talent. Occasionally he brought home a tube of paint, saying that a starving artist had traded it for a bowl of soup, thus reinforcing the association of starvation and art, while helping his son.

The father continued to bring home tubes of paint (while Ezra considered himself lucky because so many artists needed bowls of soup).

One day, however, the father's lack of sophistication ended Ezra's belief in his story. He brought home a package of brushes, obviously a child's set from the 5 & 10, which no professional artist would have used. Ezra then knew that his father had been buying supplies from his meager earnings.

Throughout his childhood Ezra longed for a real "paint set," which the family could never afford to get him. His older brother suggested that he write Clara Bow and "Peaches" Browning, two glamorous Brooklyn girls who obviously could afford to become patrons of the arts. He wrote his letters laboriously on lined paper. All he received in return was a publicity photograph from the "It" girl.

It was not until his graduation from high school that Ezra received his first sketch box as a gift from a teacher; he used it for many years, refilling its contents, and tying it together with string when its hinges broke. It became a talisman.

Although he continued to seem antagonistic to his son's devotion to art, Ezra's father took him to the Metropolitan Museum of Art where he showed him what he thought to be the greatest paintings—the Gilbert Stuart portrait of George Washington, and also portraits of other Presidents and statesmen. Ezra found this dull. Then—

"Suddenly I looked down the length of the corridor and at the other end was an arched doorway which opened to another gallery, completely bathed in sunlight. Framed in that arch was Daumier's 'Third Class Carriage.' I had never heard of Daumier and I knew nothing about his painting . . . I felt a pounding in my heart and I just turned toward it and walked toward it as though hypnotized. As I got closer to it, it glowed more magnificently. . . ."[2]

This marvelous discovery led to continued interest in Daumier's work. Several years later when he received a book about Daumier from one of his high school teachers, he set himself the task of learning Daumier's technique by painstakingly making copies in oil paint of the illustrations.

Ezra's father's pride in his son's work, never expressed to him, was finally poignantly revealed. Just before Ezra's graduation from high school, his father suffered a fatal heart attack while away from home. Ezra went to identify him.

"As part of the procedure the police asked me to look through his wallet. I found myself staring deep into his secret feelings. There in his wallet were worn and tattered newspaper clippings of the notices of the awards I had won. My silent admirer and supplier—torn between dread of my leading a life of hardship and real pride in my work."[3]

Some years later, the artistic sense that Ezra's mother showed in her appreciation and encouragement of her son's work, finally flowered on canvas. Several years after Ezra was graduated from high school, his mother became ill and was ordered to rest as much as possible. Knowing that she would not sit idle, Ezra gave her canvas and paints and suggested that she try her hand at painting.

She demurred. She was no artist, and besides she had her work to do. Ezra had to find a good reason for her to spend her time at painting. (At that time, I had taken a maternity leave from teaching but our friendship continued.) Since she had been talking of sending a gift to my new baby son, he suggested that she do some paintings for his nursery. Afraid to venture into original work, she found some pictures to copy, but was soon dissatisfied with them.

One day Ezra came home to find that his mother had painted a picture of two children on a park bench with quite remarkable rendition of grass. In response to his amazed question, she said, "I didn't know how to paint grass, so I looked through your art books. That Van Gogh—he does the best grass, so I copied him." This and the other paintings that Ezra's mother did for my son's nursery, now hang in my grandsons' room. Their unusual quality makes one wish she had not started to paint so late in life.

Ezra's sister, Mae, also possesses talent in art, expressed in her youth only in sewing and embroidery. In her mature years, she began to study art, and hesitantly entered a few of her works in an exhibit of art by members of New York City's Civil Service. To her surprise, she won awards in three categories—painting, sculpture, and ceramics.

Ezra's own paintings during his high school years were far different from his work today. When he finally gained enough confidence to use the precious paints he had spoken of in English class, he created oil paintings which expressed the reactions of a sensitive, talented adolescent to the world of the Depression. In somber and subtle tones he depicted the view from his window, of tenements revealing only a wedge of empty lot below and gray sky above. In other paintings the only warmth was the dim glow of the stove of the vendor of sweet potatoes, and the scant fire around which homeless men huddled in a vacant lot, their despair revealed in their angular bent bodies—the temper of the times in the streaked and stormy sky above. The latter painting won for him first prize in the National Scholastic contest, which led in turn to a scholarship to the Art Students' League.

After his graduation from high school, however, Ezra could not avail himself of the scholarship, but had to find any work he could. For a time he was a muralist under W.P.A. Then he got a job in the production of comic books. The young artist, distressed at having to paint comics, was amazed at the seriousness with which the editors, artists, and publishers approached their production. The sequences, plotted and designed by the author-illustrator, were discussed in lengthy editorial conferences, then assigned as piecework to the lesser illustrators.

At first Ezra was allowed to draw only the backgrounds; later, he was trusted with the task of drawing Captain Marvel's body; he had just been promoted to being permitted to draw Captain Marvel's head, when he was called to serve in the U.S. Army.

Keats served for three years, working on training manuals and on camouflage. When World War II ended, he was able to spend a year in Europe, mostly in Paris. There the somber, dark style of his earlier oils gave way to light, lyric watercolors, many of which were used by *The New York Times Book Review* to illustrate its "Letter from Paris." A painting of St. Michel was selected by the National Academy of Design for exhibit.

Upon his return from abroad, Keats did illustrations of stories for magazines, among them the then popular *Collier's*, covers for the *Reader's Digest*, and book jackets.

It was Elizabeth Riley, art director at Crowell, who, according to Keats, "turned the whole direction of my work." Impressed by a book jacket Keats had done for a novel by V. Sackville-West, she asked him to do a jacket for a junior novel by Phyllis Whitney. Moved by the warm, human quality of the work, Keats did twelve sketches instead of the usual three or four. Miss Riley then suggested that he illustrate E. H. Lansing's children's book, *Jubilant for Sure* (*Crowell*, 1954).

The book was set in Kentucky, a part of the country which the artist had never visited. Desiring accuracy he set out on a trip South.

One day, from an ice truck on which he had gotten a hitch, he saw a typical shack, with an old porch and a rocker. He asked the driver to stop, stood at the roadside, and began to sketch the shack, including in his drawing a golden-haired four year old girl who was watching him intently from the porch. While he was showing his drawing to the child, who had never seen anyone draw before, her mother came out and asked him to stay to have lunch with the family. At their insistence he remained for a week, noting and sketching material for *Jubilant for Sure*. This book was later selected as one of the fifty best illustrated books of the year.

This assignment led to others. There is a sizable shelf of children's books by various authors illustrated by Ezra Jack Keats. Among them he particularly enjoyed illustrating *Nihal of Ceylon* (*Crowell*, 1960), about a twelve-year-old who wanted to be an artist. Its author, Eleanor A.

Murphey, had spent some time in Ceylon where she and her husband worked for the Friends Service Committee.

After a time, however, Keats found illustrating books written by others too limiting. His first venture into writing his own book was in collaboration with Pat Cherr. Entitled *My Dog Is Lost!; ¡Mi Perro Se Ha Perdido* (*Crowell,* 1960) it tells of eight-year-old Juanito, who on his second day in New York, loses his dog. Not knowing any English he sets out alone to find him, trying to make his plight understood to people on the way: the friendly teller in the bank which bears the sign, "Aqui se habla Español," children in various parts of the city, and a helpful policeman. With gesture and sign language Juanito succeeds in describing his red, shaggy dog, who is finally returned barking happily in Spanish—"jau-jau." The book was of interest to all children, but especially so to the Puerto Rican children who understood the Spanish words and were pleased to see them in a story book. Some of them wondered whether he was Spanish.

One class committee wrote: "We are the other committee. We like when someone finds what he is looking for. So we liked *My Dog Is Lost* or *Mi Perro Se Ha Perdido.* That was fun, the name in Spanish on the back.

"The policeman was good. In your book, he helped. In my neighborhood, I don't know if the policeman would have helped. The children wold (would) have laughed at me.

"We would like to like to know about you. Are you Spanish? Do you have children? Do you make your own paint? My house paint is not such a real color. I would like the recipe for your paint.

"Your friendly friends . . ."

Gaining confidence from the success of the book in which he had collaborated, Ezra Keats set out to write his own books, beginning with *The Snowy Day* (*Viking,* 1962).

For him this was a new experience in illustration. The drawings needed no longer be illustrations of a text. Now text and drawings could reinforce each other to provide an integrated experience for ear and eye.

The Snowy Day is a gentle tale of a young child, Peter, who goes out to have fun in the snow, brings home a snowball in his pocket, is later disappointed to find it has melted, but is happy to find the next morning that he has awakened to another snowy day. The illustrations, in paint and collage, with simple forms, delicate patterns, and a variety of textures, are not merely visual representations of the text; they are another way of telling about Peter's day. For example, from the pictures, but not from the text, we see that Peter is a Negro child. But there is no feeling that this is a book with a purpose or a message. Its direct and lyrical quality leads the adult reader to recognize that Keats was not trying to do an "ethnic" book. It is just that children come in different colors, and Peter is brown. To children this is a book about a child.

The Snowy Day won the Caldecott Medal for "the most distinguished American picture book for children" in 1963. In his acceptance speech, Ezra Jack Keats told how the book came to be:

> I would like to tell you how *The Snowy Day* was done, and how I arrived at the technique used in it. However, it would be more accurate to say that I found myself participating in the evolvement of the book.
>
> First let me tell you about its beginnings. Years ago, long before I ever thought of doing children's books, while looking through a magazine I came upon four candid photos of a little boy about three or four years old. His expressive face, his body attitudes, the very way he wore his clothes, totally captivated me. I clipped the strip of photos and stuck it on my studio wall, where it stayed for quite a while, and then it was put away.
>
> As the years went by, these pictures would find their way back to my walls, offering me fresh pleasure at each encounter.
>
> In more recent years, while illustrating children's books, the desire to do my own story about this little boy began to germinate. Up he went again—this time above my drawing table. He was my model and inspiration. Finally I began work on *The Snowy Day*. When the book was finished and on the presses, I told Annis Duff, whose guidance and empathy have been immeasurable, about my long association with this little boy. How many years was it? I went over to *Life* magazine and had it checked. To my astonishment they informed me that I had found him twenty-two years ago!
>
> Now for the technique—I had no idea as to how the book would be illustrated, except that I wanted to add a few bits of patterned paper to supplement the painting.
>
> As work progressed, one swatch of material suggested another, and before I realized it, each page was being handled in a style I had never worked in before. A rather strange sequence of events came into play. I worked—and waited. Then quite unexpectedly I would come across just the appropriate material for the page I was working on.
>
> . . . The creative efforts of people from many lands contributed to the materials in the book. Some of the papers used for the collage came from Japan, some from Italy, some from Sweden, many from our own country.
>
> The mother's dress is made of the kind of oilcloth used for lining

cupboards. I made a big sheet of snow-texture by rolling white paint over wet inks on paper and achieved the effect of snow flakes by cutting patterns out of gum erasers, dipping them into paint, and then stamping them onto the pages. The gray background for the pages where Peter goes to sleep was made by spattering India ink with a toothbrush.

Friends would enthusiastically discuss the things they did as children in the snow, others would suggest nuances of plot, or change of a word. All of us wanted so much to see little Peter march through these pages, experiencing, in the purity and innocence of childhood, the joys of a first snow.

I can honestly say that Peter came into being because we wanted him; and I hope that, as the Scriptures say, "a little child shall lead them," and that he will show in his own way the wisdom of a pure heart.[4]

Keats continued to use collage, the technique of *The Snowy Day,* in subsequent books, because it seemed especially appropriate for illustrating books for children. He explained:

My use of collage in *The Snowy Day* occurred so naturally I hardly realized it at the time. I had planned to use just a bit of patterned paper here or there as I worked on the book. But then one thing called for another. New relationships of colors and patterns were formed, each expressing something in a very special way. When the book was finished, I was somewhat startled to discover that my way of working had been transformed. I had wanted this book to be special. And in turn, I was rewarded with a technique which I feel has great potential.

Collage evokes an immediate sensory response. Because of this quality it has special appeal for children, who experience the world in this immediate way. Since *The Snowy Day* my mail from children often includes collage material for me or collage pictures of their own, showing such creativity as to turn an adult wistful and envious. . . .[5]

The Snowy Day has done considerable traveling. It has been translated into several languages, including Swedish, Norwegian, and Danish. In a way the British edition is also a translation: for example, *sidewalk* had to be changed to *pavement.*

The State Department sent *The Snowy Day* and the original painting of the bathtub scene to several international exhibits of children's books including one in Prague. At the Frankfurt Book Fair it represented the United States in an exhibit of the hundred most beautiful children's books.

The film of *The Snowy Day* (made by Weston Woods Studio) won the prize at the Venice Film Festival. Its successor, *Whistle for Willie,* was shown at the Second Teheran International Festival, where its author was a guest of honor.

In *Whistle for Willie* the small hero of *The Snowy Day* has acquired a dachshund named Willie. The story is a simple one of effort and satisfaction.

This is how a fourth grader retold it in a letter to the author: "I enjoyed reading *Whistle for Willie.* It was a very interesting book. I like the book because the little boy named Peter tried to whistle, but he couldn't. He believed he could, so he kept on trying to whistle. One day he showed his family that he could whistle. He was happy and everyone was too. I am glad that the story had a happy ending."

Another child, addressing his letter, "Dear Mr. Keats, You joyful book writer," said of *Whistle for Willie:* "We liked the colorful pictures. Every page had colorful pictures not just sometimes." A classmate added, "We laughed when we saw the Mother. She looks like a bear. Louis said she looks like she likes fun because she looks jolly. I like fat Mothers."

And they signed the letter, "Your Bookworms."

His next book gave Keats the opportunity to use collage in bold heroic form and brilliant color. In *John Henry: An American Legend* (*Pantheon,* 1965) Keats retold the legend of the powerful Negro rail worker — how he grew from a strong baby (almost bursting from the page with a hammer in his hand) to a great steel-driving man who struck a blow for humanity by beating the steam drill.

The double-page collage illustrations enhance the dramatic tale. Children respond to the direct, convincing tale with its strong illustrations.

A little girl from Brooklyn wrote: "I think your book John Henry is a beautiful book. I especially liked the part when John Henry was a little fat baby. The most exciting part was when there was a race and John Henry beat the steam drill. I felt sad, very sad, when John Henry died. Did he really die? Was John Henry really colored? Where did you find out the story of John Henry? Was John Henry married? What was his wife's name? Write to me, please."

Keats, who always answers children's letters, responded,

". . . I would like to answer your questions as best I can.

"Yes, John Henry was a Negro. He was married and his wife's name was Polly Ann. I don't think he had any children, but I'm not sure.

"He was born about 100 years ago. He was so big and strong, and also kind, that those who met him told their friends and children all about him. As the years went by, people wrote it down and sang songs about brave John Henry, and how he beat the machine, even at the cost of his life. He showed that there is nothing greater on earth than people.

"They still tell the stories and sing songs about him, and they always will, forever and ever.

Your friend,
Ezra Jack Keats"

Keats returned to the style and manner of *The Snowy Day* in a story about a little girl.

In *Jennie's Hat (Harper & Row,* 1966) Jennie's heart is set on having a lavish new bonnet, but the one she receives is a plain white straw. She looks with envy at the bonnets she sees in church. On her way home, birds fly down with bits of lace and leaves to beautify her hat, crowning it with their chief treasure, a nest of baby birds. She proudly wears the magnificent hat home. Just before she enters the door the birds swoop down to remove the nest of baby birds, but leave the hat adorned with the rest of their gifts. Jennie's mother packs it away in all its magnificence.

There is no attempt to explain the event as a dream or a wish—it is as real as the joy of the children who hear the story and look at the pictures.

The author explains the genesis of the story as a remembered image. He writes, "A picture of an old lady and man with a flock of birds circling around their heads stayed in my mind many years. Those birds seemed to be bringing this couple something. And so emerged the image of Jennie's bird friends, bringing her a shower of gifts to fulfill her heart's desire. . . . In addition to the painting, dried leaves, strips of fabrics, old valentines, postcards, lithographs and other memorabilia, cutout paper flowers, paper fans, bits of old wallpaper, and cutouts of background materials from my own books all became part of *Jennie's Hat.*" [6]

In 1966, when *Jennie's Hat* was published, Ezra Keats contributed five designs for UNICEF holiday cards, representing joys of sharing around the world.

He also compiled a book for adults as well as for children—*God Is in the Mountain (Holt,* 1966). The book consists of ideas quoted from the great books of many religions, the words relating to the illustrations as melody and counterpoint. He says of the illustrations, which were only in two colors, ". . . Because I did not wish to intrude upon the religious experiences selected, I kept the elements simple to create an appropriate mood and background." [7]

Since 1960, when he began writing and illustrating his own books,

Ezra Keats has illustrated only three books by other writers: one is Ann McGovern's *Zoo, Where Are You?* (*Harper & Row*, 1964). (The publishers issued the illustrations in a separated album.) Another was Richard Lewis's collection of haiku, entitled *In a Spring Garden* (*Dial*, 1965) for which the artist evoked the changing seasons in delicate illustrations using paint and collage. The third is an odd and lovely little book — an illustrated presentation of a poem written by John Keats in his youth, *The Naughty Boy* (*Viking*, 1965; British edition, 1966). Here Ezra Keats used collage and paint in red and white to match the delicate mischief of the poem.

In his latest book, Keats returned to Peter — *Peter's Chair* (*Harper & Row*, 1967). A bit older now, Peter is dismayed to find that his bassinet and high chair have been painted pink to accommodate a baby sister (who appears in the book as a froth of lace with only one tiny brown hand showing).

Peter's own blue chair has so far escaped the transformation. Taking his chair, a picture of himself as a baby, and his dog Willie, Peter leaves home, camping on the street under his window. He resists his mother's invitation to return. Then comes "the moment of truth." He decides to sit down and finds that the chair is too small for him! His return home is not a surrender, however. He tricks his mother by placing a pair of his sneakers under the draperies and then emerging from another part of the room.

Peter's Chair ends with Peter sitting in a full-size chair at the table, then helping his father paint the chair pink. Willie's pink pawprints trail off the last page.

Hopefully the paws are pattering toward new books in which Peter will grow older and meet new problems and adventures — for these books are important as well as engaging.

As a mother who had read *The Snowy Day* to her four-year-old son wrote to Ezra Keats: ". . . It is important for Negro children to see books about themselves and it is important for non-Negro children to see the universal experiences of childhood through the eyes of some one other than a blue-eyed blond."

But whether the books to come are about Peter, Jennie, Juanito, a child of Iran, or other children, whether they consist of legends, poems, or stories, we know that they will enchant the eye and engage the heart.

REFERENCES

1. Ezra Jack Keats in interview with Esther Hautzig. *The Horn Book Magazine* (August 1963), 366.
2. *Ibid.*, p. 368.

3. Ezra Jack Keats, "A Coveted Prize Reaped from Seeds Sown in Brooklyn," *Magazine of Books* (Chicago Tribune), May 12, 1963. 3A.
4. Given at the meeting of the American Library Association in Chicago, July 15, 1963. Published in *The Horn Book Magazine* (August 1963), 361+.
5. Ezra Jack Keats, "Ezra Jack Keats on Collage as an Illustrative Medium," *Publishers' Weekly* (April 4, 1966), 94–95.
6. *Ibid.*, p. 95.
7. *Ibid.*

EDITORS' NOTE

Since publication of this article, Mr. Keats has written and illustrated several other books about Peter and his adventures—*A Letter to Amy* (1968), *Goggles* (1969), *Hi, Cat!* (1970), and a new book, *Pet Show*, to be published in 1972. Another recent book, also for the young child, is *Apt. 3* (1971).

Ezra Jack Keats was the winner of the 1963 Caldecott Medal for *The Snowy Day*, and a runner-up for the same Medal in 1970 for *Goggles*. *Hi, Cat!* was selected by the American Institute of Graphic Arts Children's Book Show (biennial selection for typographic and artistic merit) for 1969–1970, and it also received the 1970 Boston Globe–Horn Book Award for outstanding illustrations.

Mr. Keats has been asked to donate his literary estate—correspondence, manuscripts, illustrations—to Harvard University. He is the first children's book author-illustrator to receive this honor.

Elaine L. Konigsburg[*]

JENNIFER, HECATE, MACBETH, William McKinley, and Me, Elizabeth, Elaine Konigsburg's first book, arrived at Atheneum unheralded. It simply came in one day with the afternoon mail. The letter with it said, "Enclosed is a manuscript entitled *Jennifer, Hecate, Macbeth, William McKinley, and Me, Elizabeth,* which I would like you to consider for publication. I have also enclosed several sample illustrations, which I hope you will like. Thank you. Sincerely, Elaine L. Konigsburg."

I'd like to be able to report that the manuscript was read and accepted within a few days. But such is not the way with unannounced material, or almost any material for that matter. In the welter of details that demand attention, the things that editors most want to do are most often the things that are continually pushed aside. So it was several months before Elaine Konigsburg climbed the four flights of stairs to the children's department, in the house that was then Atheneum, to discuss her book.

She was relatively short, had dark hair, and dark eyes that glinted with an awareness of the foolishness and fun in the world. Her conversation was as pungent and as full of rich humor as her book. But there was a dignity and a sense of solidity about her that gave her wit and humor depth and dimension, and made it apparent that this was not a one-book author.

We had lunch, and she described her method of working. Her three children were all in school. Before the school swallowed them up for

* By Jean Karl. Reprinted by permission from *Library Journal,* March 15, 1968, pp. 1285–1286.

portions of every day, there had been no time to write. But once they were all gone, there were mornings. With everyone, including her husband, David, out the door, and if one overlooked unmade beds and dishes in the sink, there were several hours for the typewriter and a book. It was an old ambition, but one that had had to wait. Mrs. Konigsburg wrote mornings, then read what she had written to the children when they came home for lunch. Their reaction determined what happened next: "They laugh or they don't," she said, "which means I revise or I don't." But whatever came next waited for the next morning. Afternoons were for dirty dishes, unmade beds and the chores a lively household entails.

At the time we talked, she mentioned that there had been no pause in her schedule since the completion of *Jennifer.* . . . She was working on another book, and, in fact, would soon have at least a first draft finished. She only hinted at the subject.

Later, when we began to plan the publication of *Jennifer,* we realized it had come too late to be a 1966 book. It would have to be issued in spring 1967. This was April 1966; and as we talked, a few more details about the second book made me hope it would soon be ready, though I knew that the pictures for *Jennifer, Hecate, Macbeth, William McKinley, and Me, Elizabeth,* which she would do herself, would take time and would keep her from writing for a while.

From the Mixed-Up Files of Mrs. Basil E. Frankweiler arrived in the afternoon mail on July 1, 1966. It was not unheralded. The accompanying letter read: "Suburban children are still very much on my mind; I submit Exhibit B: my manuscript, *From the Mixed-Up Files of Mrs. Basil E. Frankweiler.* I am enclosing only one sample drawing—one of the bed in which the children slept. I hope you will like Claudia and Jamie Kincaid and Mrs. Frankweiler, too. Sincerely, Elaine L. Konigsburg." It was read almost immediately and with such delight that it seemed imperative to publish it as soon as possible. It was too good to keep from children (and adults) for any longer than absolutely necessary. It was scheduled for fall 1967.

Because the pictures for the second book required more research than those for the first, and because some facts had to be checked out at the museum—or scouted out when the museum was reluctant to divulge information about cleaning schedules etc., because of security—Mrs. Konigsburg spent most of her free time in fall 1966 posing her own children at appropriate spots in the museum, under the eyes of suspicious guards, and carefully observing the routines. The results produced a book that comes as close to possibility and accuracy as the museum's understandable bent towards secrecy will allow. In fact, the book even includes the museum's own map made from the original art prepared for a visitor's guide to the museum, and used with the museum's permission.

And so, there were two books published in 1967 by Elaine Konigsburg: *Jennifer* and *From the Mixed-Up Files.* . . . That there were two in some ways is not so surprising as the fact that there were any at all. For Elaine Konigsburg, like almost everyone else in the world, did not begin life determined to write a great children's book.

She was born in New York City and grew up in Pennsylvania. After graduating with top academic honors from high school in the small mill town of Farrell, she worked for a year as a bookkeeper at a wholesale meat plant, met David Konigsburg, whom she later married, and entered the Carnegie Institute of Technology. There, in addition to studying chemistry and biology, she was (at different times) manager of the dormitory laundry and dry cleaning concession, playground instructor, waitress, library page, etc. She received her B.S. in chemistry in 1952. Then, "determined to push back the frontier of science," she says, "I continued studying organic chemistry at the University of Pittsburgh Graduate School. After two years there I found that the only thing I had succeeded in pushing back was my hairline; I twice blew up the laboratory sink, losing my eyebrows and bangs in the flash." While she studied, she worked first as a research assistant in the university's Tissue Culture Laboratory, and then as a graduate teaching assistant.

In 1954 her husband received his doctorate in psychology and they moved to Jacksonville, Florida. There Mrs. Konigsburg taught science and biology at a private school until her oldest son, Paul, was born. Laurie and Ross followed one year and three years after. It was after Laurie's birth that Mrs. Konigsburg became interested in painting. The first exhibition in which she showed her work brought her a first prize.

After the family moved North again, settling first in Saddle Brook, New Jersey, then in Port Chester, New York, she studied at the Art Students League in New York City and found time to begin her first book. Writing was something she had long wanted to try, having conquered science and art; and children's books seemed somehow the thing she most wanted to write. There was, she felt, so much about life that children needed to see in a book, and there were so many of their own observations that they needed to find confirmed in books. When the family moved back to Jacksonville, Florida, last summer, and an opportunity came to teach science again, she refused in favor of those free mornings for writing. Not that writing came at once. It was October 1967 before she wrote: "My muse has finally moved to Florida. There is time now to write something besides lists for the grocery and hardware stores."

But before that new book, started long before in Port Chester, was quite finished, there came Saturday, January 13, 1968. Early that morning the phone rang just as a moving van was pulling up to the front of the apartment building where the Konigsburgs lived. They were moving from the apartment to their new home. That phone call told Elaine Konigsburg she had won the Newbery Award for *From the Mixed-Up Files of Mrs. Basil E. Frankweiler,* and that her first book was a runner-up for the award. "Did you know that joy can move book cartons," she asks in a subsequent letter, "and dishes and even major appliances — if not mountains? I have never known such unmitigated out-loud joy."

The Konigsburg family has moved to a new city and a new house since the two prize-winning books were written, but all indications are that Elaine Konigsburg has remained herself through it all. Her third book will soon be complete, after a few more morning sessions, and she feels there will always be something more to be said in books "that combine humor with insight, books peculiarly sensitive to our times, and to children's needs today."

EDITORS' NOTE

In addition to winning the 1968 Newbery Medal for *From the Mixed-Up Files of Mrs. Basil E. Frankweiler,* Elaine Konigsburg has also won the Lewis Carroll Shelf Award (given to a book worthy of sharing the shelf with *Alice in Wonderland*), and the 1970 William Allen White Children's Book Award (best book selected annually by Kansas school children in grades 4–8 from a list chosen by specialists) for this book. *Jennifer, Hecate, Macbeth, William McKinley and Me, Elizabeth,* was a runner-up for the 1968 Newbery Medal.

Mrs. Konigsburg's third book, *About the B'nai Bagels,* was published by Atheneum in 1969, as was her latest book, *Altogether One at a Time,* published in 1971. The latter is an anthology of four short stories "concerned with the good and bad in life."

The Konigsburg family now lives in Jacksonville, Florida, where Mrs. Konigsburg is planning to write more books inspired by her children and other children she knows.

Ruth Krauss:
A Very Special Author *

WITH THE REMOVAL of fairy tales from the nursery, and the advent of the realistic "here and now" type of story, there has been some lament that there is no longer any "imagination" in books for young children. Many adults have felt that the pre-school child is being brought up almost exclusively on a literary diet of steam shovels, trains, tugboats, tractors, and the like, which might serve to limit his outlook on life to its narrowly technological and mechanical aspects. Perhaps in reaction to this tendency, or perhaps merely accidentally, there has recently developed a new kind of imaginative picture book literature, not dependent on the stylized conventions of the fairy tale, which draws its inspiration from children's own fantasies, desires, word play, and sense of humor.

One of the pioneers in this development was Margaret Wise Brown whose seemingly rambling, pointless, and "silly" stories made many parents shake their heads in wonder at the odd tastes of their young children who were enchanted with these books. At present, other authors are striking out into new writing patterns of their own on the picture book level. One of these is Beatrice Schenk de Regniers, whose highly individualized style has evoked a great deal of interest and discussion. Perhaps the most controversial (among adults, at least) is Ruth Krauss who has probably gone further than any other author in experimenting with the form and content of picture books.

After reading through Miss Krauss' books, one may first be impressed

* By Anne Martin. From *Elementary English* 32 (November 1955), 427–434. Reprinted with the permission of the National Council of Teachers of English and Anne Martin.

by the wide range of mood and purpose. There is the quiet determination in *The Carrot Seed,* the whimsical word play in *Bears,* the warm tenderness in *The Bundle Book,* the boisterous fun in *A Very Special House,* the practical (and impractical) advice to bored youngsters in *How to Make An Earthquake.* In spite of this variety, there seem to be certain underlying assumptions about children which have shaped the style and content of all of Miss Krauss' books. While such assumptions are only implicit and are never formulated into a doctrine, they might be stated somewhat along these lines:

That children are neither cute darlings to be patronized, nor miniature adults to be civilized, but rather lively, well-organized people with codes, ideas, and ambitions of their own which often need a chance to be worked out.

That children are fascinated by language—the trying out of nonsense syllables, the defining of familiar terms, the groping for expression of feelings, the striving to communicate ideas.

That children, like older people, have special dreams and desires which can only be gratified by fantasy, and that they love to indulge in these day dreams.

That children have an exuberance and joy in daily living, and an irrepressible sense of the ridiculous which may differ radically from an adult's idea of what is funny.

That these assumptions are so clearly conveyed in her picture books, indicates that Miss Krauss has made good use of some special abilities and advantages. It is clear from her material that Miss Krauss has had close contact with young children which permitted her to observe carefully their patterns of speech, make-believe games, and ways of telling stories or narrating events. She has an ear for the kind of word play and nonsense talk that brings immediate response from children, and an unusual insight into some of the complicated emotions and relationships beneath children's verbal expressions. Along with the craftsmanship to organize her material effectively so that it becomes meaningful and enjoyable to the child reader, Miss Krauss has added one extra dimension —the experimental attitude. When her material demanded it, she has permitted herself to depart from the conventional form of children's books in an attempt to create new, more suitable forms. Since pictorial representation is of primary importance in books for young children, Miss Krauss has been fortunate in the collaboration of good artists whose illustrations serve to represent, clarify, and even interpret the action and mood of the texts. Probably the best way to illustrate all the foregoing assertions is to examine rather closely the content and style of the books themselves.

Three of the earlier books seem to be definitely related in theme and execution. These are *The Carrot Seed, The Growing Story,* and *The Backward Day.* All are written in a casual but concise style (*The Carrot Seed* almost abruptly in terse, single sentences on each page) and all tell an uninterrupted story without digressions or explanations. All have an atmosphere of calm but single-minded drive towards a climax. In each book, an unnamed "little boy" is obsessed with a particular idea or plan which he follows through purposefully and successfully to the end. In *The Growing Story,* the little boy is determined to find out whether he himself is growing like the animals and plants around him, and, after a summer of discouraging doubts, he triumphantly shouts out his proof when he tries on his winter clothes, "Hey! . . . My pants are too little and my coat is too little. I'm growing too." In *The Backward Day,* "A little boy woke up one morning and got out of bed. He said to himself, 'Today is backward day.'" This gives him the opportunity of doing such wonderfully peculiar things as walking downstairs backwards, wearing his underwear over his coat, and saying "goodnight" at breakfast time. In both these books, the boys' families are amazingly patient and cooperative. In *The Carrot Seed,* however, the little boy has to pursue his project of planting and caring for a carrot seed against the scorn and disbelief of his whole family until, in a highly effective understatement, comes the emphatic climax, "And then, one day, a carrot came up just as the little boy had known it would" (dramatized by a humorous illustration of a giant carrot on a wheelbarrow).

These may seem like trivial plots to adults, and hardly worth writing about, but to a young child it is tremendously exciting to know that he is part of a growing world, or that sometimes he may be right and his elders mistaken, or that by his own actions he may, at least temporarily, change the established habits of daily life. These ideas open up a whole realm of speculations to the child about his own place as an autonomous individual, no longer completely dependent on adults, capable of initiating and completing projects of his own. At the same time, there is the humorous acceptance of limitations. In *The Backward Day,* after a maximum exploitation of his lovely idea, the little boy realizes its impractibility (and perhaps also its gradual monotony) and is permitted to make a dignified withdrawal of the whole cumbersome business by merely starting the day all over again, this time frontwards.

With the possible exception of *The Growing Story* which lacks the light touch of the other two, these books can also be enjoyed purely at the story level without any deeper implications. The appealing, wide-eyed stoic in *The Carrot Seed* (incidentally, this, like many of the other books, is illustrated by Crockett Johnson, the author's husband and well-known creator of Barnaby) is lovable just for himself, and the blandly described details of what is involved in doing things "backward oh backward oh backward oh backward oh backward" are completely satisfactory in their own right. Whatever other implications there may be, they are injected subtly enough so that the reader may be aware of them or not, according to his own capabilities or desires.

In just the same way, *The Bundle Book,* where a pleasant young mother spends a long time guessing just what the "strange bundle" on her bed might be, can be enjoyed merely as a guessing game (and what young child doesn't love to play at hiding and "fooling" his parents) and for Helen Stone's soft, accurate illustrations of the squirming bundle. But beyond the fast-moving story line there emerges a strong and almost inescapable feeling of a real and unsentimental love relationship between this mother and her child, a feeling with which the young reader can easily identify because this love relationship, or lack of it, with his own parents is one of the most important things in his life.

In contrast to these books, *The Happy Day* and *Bears* make their appeal purely on the fun and nonsense level. The text of *The Happy Day* is perhaps somewhat disappointing. In rhythmically relating the story of several species of hibernating animals which discover a miraculous flower growing in the snow, the text becomes almost monotonously repetitious with its constant refrain of "They sniff. They run. They run. They sniff." Fortunately, the suspense is sustained and the climax heightened by Marc Simont's admirable black and white illustrations of warm, sleepy, furry animals suddenly galvanized into swiftly graceful action. The contrasts of warmth and cold, sleep and rapid motion, search and discovery, come through in spite of a rather artificial plot.

The ingenious, tongue-tickling text of *Bears,* however, is quite equal to Phyllis Rowand's masterful illustrations of ridiculous, lovable bears of all sizes and amazing capabilities. These "bears everywheres" are a special species, closer to teddies than to zoo bears, as they slide down bannisters "on the stairs," are lost in suds while "washing hairs," and do practically anything as long as it rhymes. The only possible false note may be the inclusion of "millionaires" whose top hats and cigars are quite meaningless to two- and three-year-old readers, but that's an insignificant objection. *Bears* is the kind of book that young children can look at repeatedly, finding previously undiscovered details in the pictures, "reading" and giggling at the text, even inventing more rhymes in the same vein.

All the previously discussed books are written in a straight-forward, economical style, the writer being an objective author telling a story.

I Can Fly, Miss Krauss' contribution to the Little Golden Book series, might be considered a transition piece. It marks a shift away from the style of the earlier books toward the experiments with a first person narrative in a child's own idiom of speech and thought carried out in *A Hole Is to Dig*, *A Very Special House*, and *I'll Be You and You Be Me*. Very close in spirit to *Bears*, *I Can Fly* is an invitation to make-believe and mimicry full of delightfully silly rhymes ("Who can walk like a bug? Me! Ug ug.") very much like the ones children improvise all the time. The ending is an inspired burst of "Gubble gubble gubble, I'm a mubble in a pubble. I can play I'm anything that's anything. . . ." Illustrated in Mary Blair's witty, colorful pictures, this book is probably one of the most successfully executed of the very inexpensive picture books. Where *I Can Fly* tentatively approaches a child's way of talking and playing, there is a real evolution in the other three books from a reflection of a child's world in *A Hole Is to Dig* to an increasingly abstract representation of children's desires and feelings in *A Very Special House* and *I'll Be You and You Be Me*. All three are illustrated in Maurice Sendak's expressive black and white drawings which are sensitively responsive to the changing form of the texts.

A Hole Is to Dig contains a group of unrelated definitions of familiar objects and concepts in a child's world, expressed in the way children would, and in most cases probably really did, explain these terms. For older children and adults, this book is a funny and even touching experience because the definitions are such a curious combination of incredible narrowness of understanding and a vastly profound vision of what is true and important. Thus we can smile at "a face is so you can make faces," but we can only hold our breaths at "a dream is to look at the night and see things." In our harried life of household worries about orderliness and sanitation, it is well to be reminded that "dogs are to kiss people," or that "mud is to jump in and slide in and yell doodleedoodleedoo." There are also bits of that pre-school age humor which can be so exasperating to adults, such as "a tablespoon is to eat a table with," followed by an appropriate pantomime, probably at great length. Perhaps this book has almost more to say to older people than to young children. For the child who lives within these concepts, the book is enjoyable because it is a true picture of his world. For the adult who has pigeonholed familiar objects too easily and thoughtlessly, it is a glimpse into a kaleidoscopic range of meanings.

A Very Special House depicts another aspect of the child's life—his dream world, as opposed to the real world in *A Hole Is to Dig*. This lively fantasy embodies all the exciting things a particular little boy would like to do in a house of his own, and they are also the things that are usually most disapproved by parents and teachers. Walls are to draw on, chairs are to climb on, doors to swing on, beds to jump on. The house is filled with rioting, scurrying animals (and a giant) with which to share secrets, play wild games, and shout delicious nonsense words like "ooie ooie ooie." The climax is a mad confusion of shouting and mischief where "nobody ever says stop stop stop." Yet all the time the little boy knows that this special house is "right in the middle—oh it's ret in the meedle—oh it's root in the moodle of my head head head." He is content just to think about it, and, to show that he was just fooling anyway, he punctuates his stream of imagination with a crazy jump in the air which lands him "bung" down on his bottom, at which he exits with a happy, shamefaced smile. Obviously, the child reader can also gain a harmless release of his disapproved desires on the verbal, imaginative level. The humor in text and pictures is of the slapstick variety, though there are also several nasty digs at the social conventions of the adult world.

It is an amazing feat that Miss Krauss has successfully depicted a world of riot, chaos, and confusion by employing a strictly disciplined, rhythmical, almost lyrical style in symmetrical form. The text begins and ends on the note of clowning to the sound of "dee dee dee oh," and the real narrative begins and ends with the chant of "I know a house—it's not a squirrel house, it's not a donkey house . . ." The build-up from a rather calm description of the house, through an increasingly excited portrayal of activity, until the noisy climax, is achieved through the skillful change from long complete sentences, to interrupted thoughts, to irregular short phrases, and finally to the large print repetition of a single word. The deceptively easy, natural flow of the monologue is actually accomplished only by means of an extremely controlled style, carefully worked out to the last nonsense syllable.

In connection with *A Very Special House* it is interesting to mention an earlier book by Ruth Krauss which, though very different in purpose and style, somewhat foreshadows her later books. *The Big World and the Little House* is a self-conscious, almost moralistic attempt to describe the relationship between the world and the individual. The style is uneven, and there is an awkward juxtaposition of varying ideas and moods. But there is also something of the poetic, rhythmical quality of *A Very Special House* in many passages such as:

Inside the house there were no beds, no tables, no chairs. No rugs were on its floors, no pictures on its walls. No smoke was in its chimney. At night it was part of the dark.

A more startling resemblance lies in some of the ideas which were later developed more fully in *A Very Special House,* though of course in a different context. In the little house "you could put your feet on the chairs and it didn't hurt them," and grandma painted the walls "with one wall special for drawing pictures on. It was also special for washing them off." Perhaps the "special house" had its genesis in the "little house," four years before its actual creation.

Turning from *A Very Special House* to *I'll Be You and You Be Me* is somewhat akin to turning from *Portrait of the Artist as a Young Man* to *Ulysses.* In both cases there is the tremendous step from a challenging but easily understandable plot line to a fragmentary, constantly shifting point of view and emphasis. It would certainly be ridiculous to make a real comparison between Ruth Krauss and James Joyce, but there is no doubt that this book is an experiment with a completely new art form for children.

The general themes of the book may be vaguely described as feeling tones — loving, liking, dreaming, wishing, wanting, happiness, and probably a few others. In order to express these, Miss Krauss uses a variety of literary forms, including stories, poems, monologues, a play, a parody, a near-parable, and even "a mystery." Within this large variety of forms there are basically two kinds of writing: first, the same child-like material with which Miss Krauss proved herself to be so proficient in *A Hole Is to Dig* and *A Very Special House,* and, secondly, an adult expression of what the child may be feeling, an apparent attempt to express for the child some things that he feels deeply but doesn't, or perhaps can't, often discuss.

The first type of writing, which makes up the bulk of the selections in this book, is represented by such items as the monologue by an older child about a baby:

> he can't talk yet
> but I can understand him —
> even when he's over at his house and he
> yells and nobody knows what he means —
> I know. I could tell other people for
> him . . .

The second type of writing can be most clearly exemplified by such fragments as "A horse that's lost could be dreaming of the girl that's going to find him." In this passage there is again an echo of *The Big World and the Little House* in the intensity of feeling that doesn't quite come across. Perhaps that is because an adult, using adult symbolism, is speaking not as an adult writing for children, but as a child representing supposedly childish feelings. The result can not be genuine expression for either child or adult.

Because the themes of this book are so large and generalized, there seems to be a lack of focus and unity, although most of the individual pieces are significant and self-contained. It would have been a shame to exclude such gems as "I think I'll grow up to be a bunny before I grow up to be a lady," and its inclusion could probably be justified in terms of the theme of friendliness and intimacy, but there is no one feeling or direction strong enough to pull all these little pieces into a comprehensive whole. Thus this experiment comes dangerously close to being an ordinary collection, not because the form itself is necessarily unwieldy, but because the internal structure has not been sufficiently integrated. Yet there is a degree of freedom in the development of theme and mood in both text and illustration (at one point the artist draws a complete dream sequence which is not described in the text at all) which is almost impossible in the more traditional books for children. While this book is not altogether equal to its conception or to the excellence of some of its individual parts, it certainly points the way to new creative art forms in the field of writing for children.

Miss Krauss' latest book to date, *Is This You?*, is less impressive than her other work. Similar in purpose to her earlier *How to Make an Earthquake*, this book is of the how-to-amuse-yourself variety in that it gives instructions for producing an original book. But while *How to Make an Earthquake* contains a number of ingenious ideas, some of them undoubtedly originated by children and explained in the familiar pattern of children's make-believe ("one person has to be the World. And then somebody has to be the sun . . ."), *Is This You?* is built on the single pattern of ludicrous possibilities. Thus to the question "Is this how you take a bath?" one illustration depicts a little boy in a bird bath, and another in a hippopotamus pool. Some breakfast eating suggestions include a piano leg and an earthworm. While some of the combinations are genuinely funny, the rigid pattern produces an effect of rather forced humor, and the kind of book the child is instructed to make comes close to the dull, standardized composition topics of "My Family," "My Home," "My Friends," etc. In spite of the book's cleverness and amusing illustrations, it forces the reader into specific and stereotyped responses. In *How to Make an Earthquake*, on the contrary, there is much scope for imaginative play. Many of the ideas may have a very familiar ring to parents and teachers. Few children can resist the delight of playing parent and subjecting their adult "child" to an ordeal of this sort:

> Then you take the child by the hand and say, "You *have* to.
> Come on. Let's go."
> And the child says, "No no no." And the child cries.
> But you make the child go to the party anyway . . .

The detailed descriptions of such common childhood amusements as making "mish-mosh" out of odd bits of food, elevate these to the status of important projects and real games. Even a quite young child can get much satisfaction out of following step by step directions, especially when they are written in language close enough to his own so that he can understand them easily.

Since *Is This You?* is not a story book and is somewhat out of line with most of Miss Krauss' writing, it gives little indication of the direction she intends to follow. It remains to be seen whether she will revert to some of her earlier styles, or continue to work along the lines of *I'll Be You and You Be Me,* or perhaps strike out into completely new areas of experimentation. Whatever path Miss Krauss will take, it is almost certain that young readers will leave analysis, criticism, puzzlement, and amazement to the adults. For them a Ruth Krauss book "is to look at" over and over again, to quote from and laugh at and talk about, and even (going along with Sendak's illustrations) to hug lovingly and to drop off to sleep with.

EDITORS' NOTE

Ruth Krauss was born in Baltimore, Maryland. She studied art and music at Peabody Conservatory and is a graduate of the Parsons School of Fine and Applied Art in New York City. In 1941, she married Crockett Johnson, an author-illustrator of numerous children's books. At present they live in Rowayton, Connecticut.

Miss Krauss has written over twenty-five books for children and her work is widely known and esteemed. A library has been dedicated to her in Grenville, Delaware. Her most recent books are *This Thumbprint,* published in 1967 and illustrated by the author, and *I Write It,* 1970.

Robert Lawson:
Author and Illustrator*

PEGASUS BEING SHOD in the midst of a deep forest by a group of elves, an etching entitled *We Fix Flats*—such is the jolly humor of the man who was awarded the Caldecott Medal in 1941 for *They Were Strong and Good* and the Newbery Medal in 1945 for *Rabbit Hill.*

Up to the present time, Robert Lawson is the only person who, as author and illustrator of children's books, has won both of these coveted awards. The warm personality, boundless imagination, robust philosophy, and extraordinary humor of this gentle man are evident in some twenty books of his own, over thirty etchings, innumerable magazine illustrations, and the forty or more books which he illustrated for other authors.

By the time he had written and illustrated *They Were Strong and Good,* Mr. Lawson had formulated a clear philosophy and definite values for his work. They are set forth in his acceptance speech when he received the Caldecott Medal (8).

He felt that the terms "children's author" or "children's illustrator" seemed slightly condescending to children. He had never seen in the work of any illustrator whom children had loved for generations the slightest indication that they were catering to limited tastes or limited understanding. Children, he felt, were less limited than adults, because they had no stupid second-hand notions of what they ought to like, or how they ought to think. "They do not know that they ought to admire

* By Annette H. Weston. From *Elementary English* 47 (January 1970), 74–84. Reprinted with permission of the National Council of Teachers of English and Annette H. Weston.

certain art because it is 'naive' or 'spontaneous' or because it has been drawn with a kitchen spoon on a discarded shirt front. They are, for a pitifully few short years, honest and sincere, clear-eyed and open-minded. To give them anything less than the utmost that we possess of frankness, honesty and sincerity is, to my mind, the lowest possible crime."

Mr. Lawson never missed an opportunity to treat with gentle satire and piercing, but kindly, humor any "scientific" edicts about what children should read. A speech, recorded in *The Horn Book* (6), deals with that subject at great length. He discussed the reasons children turn so frequently to the comic books, and the sort of help parents and teachers and librarians could give them, and the responsibilities of authors and illustrators and editors. "No one," he said, "can possibly tell what tiny detail of a drawing or what seemingly trivial phrase in a story will be the spark that sets off a great flash in the mind of some child, a flash that will leave a glow there until the day he dies.

"I have had many letters from children about books and drawings I have done and it is amazing to see what different things have given different children their greatest thrill. Nothing that you could possibly count on, nothing that could possibly be planned, a tiny detail in the corner of some drawing, a particular word or phrase, has opened a window for some child; it has given him a glimpse of something that will remain forever."

BIOGRAPHICAL SKETCH

Contrary to the general trend of artistic migration to New York City, Robert Lawson was one of the rare few who was born in New York City and chose to emigrate. He was born on October 4, 1892 in New York City, but shortly after his birth his family moved to Montclair, New Jersey, where he grew up and where he attended high school (4). In an autobiographical sketch prepared in 1956 for publicity purposes, he claimed that he was an omnivorous reader and a devoted admirer of the fine illustrators who flourished when he was a boy, but that he had no particular ambition either to write or to draw and that he showed no great aptitude in either field. Perhaps he was exercising undue modesty in this sketch because many years earlier he mentioned in a speech that he had earned his first artistic reward when he had won first place in a poster contest in high school. The reward was one dollar in cash.

The following quotation from a biographical sketch in the *Magazine of the Junior Heritage Club* seems to be the only material which contains some detailed discussion of his boyhood.

"My mother taught me to like good books. She never forbade my reading trashy books or the funny papers, she didn't care what I read, as long as I was reading something. But she always gave me the finest books that could be had, with the most beautiful illustrations. She always spoke of trashy reading as 'sculch.' The books she read herself, both English and French, were always good books and she talked about them so interestingly and so lovingly that I just naturally got to like good books better than 'sculch.' . . . She drew and painted too; and about once a year we would go in to New York to spend a day at the Metropolitan Museum. She never told me what I should like or shouldn't like, we just looked at everything and had a grand time. We always had lunch in the restaurant there, which was down next to the room where the Egyptian mummies were kept. We usually had chicken croquettes and Mother always said they were made for the mummies.

"My father was not a great reader, but he loved *Uncle Remus* and used to read it to us by the hour. When I tried to read it myself, I never could understand the dialect very well, but Father came from Alabama — and when he read it, it sounded fine. He told me stories about the Civil War, too. He had been a soldier in that when he was just fifteen years old.

"When I was in High School, I was told that I would have to decide what I was going to do in the world. I wanted to be an engineer and build bridges and railroads in Afghanistan or Peru, like the men I was always reading about in Richard Harding Davis' stories. But, since I had always avoided mathematics of every sort, and mathematics seemed to be quite necessary, that wasn't possible.

"For some time we had lived in George Innes' old house, and my brother and I had his studio for our bedroom. I didn't know much about George Innes then, except that he had been a famous artist, but it was a very pleasant room and I thought it would be nice to be an artist and work in a big, airy room like that.

"And then there was a chap who used to play baseball up at the Club, whom I admired tremendously. He had a long nose and jolly eyes and whenever he threw a ball, he took the most graceful poses. He wasn't much of a ball player, but he was always laughing and pleasant to us kids. I learned that his name was George Bellows and that he was an artist, too. So I decided that I'd like to be an artist and be pleasant and laughing like George Bellows and work in a big roomy studio like George

Innes'. My father did not think much of the idea; he wanted me to go into the dry goods business (13)."

However, he claims that it was chiefly due to his mother's urging that he entered the New York School of Fine and Applied Arts (later called Parsons School) in 1911, where he studied for three years under Rae Sloan Bredin and Howard Giles (17). While there, he received scholarships in life drawing and illustration.

In June of 1914 he "stepped proudly forth from Art School, prepared to set the world on fire as an illustrator. Unfortunately someone in Europe beat me to it and in August of that year started a conflagration that sent mine into a temporary eclipse. The world became so excited over the novelty of its first World War that it did little note nor long remember the appearance of my first published drawing in *Harper's Weekly* that September, although to me it seemed an event of colossal importance." This first published drawing was a full page decoration for a poem on the invasion of Belgium.

In 1922 he married Marie Abrams, also an artist and illustrator, and in 1923 they settled in Westport, Conn. There are several references in Mr. Lawson's papers to "the period when my wife and I did nothing but Christmas cards (3)." They had agreed that each of them would produce one design a day until the house was paid for and they did just that for almost three years. "We said Merry Christmas and Happy Easter and Please Get Well Soon in several thousand different ways and forms, and were once spoken of as 'the Rembrandts of the Greeting Card Trade (13).'" After 1929 all this work ceased with the depression so that in 1930 he took up etching and in the three years that he worked in that medium he produced thirty-one plates and had two one-man shows in New York, but made very little money. These were the lean years during which they sold the house in Westport and went to live in New York for some three years, looking for new work and making new connections. In 1930 he illustrated his first book, *The Wee Men of Ballywooden* by Arthur Mason. From then on his book illustrating commissions gradually increased and it was in 1937 that he became famous as the illustrator of Munro Leaf's *Story of Ferdinand*.

In 1936 the Lawsons returned to the country and built Rabbit Hill on Weston Road in Westport, where they lived and worked together until their deaths, Marie in 1956 and less than a year later, Robert (14). They loved this home, particularly the garden where Mr. Lawson surrounded himself with models of many of the animals through whom he chose to speak of his outlook on life and the world. We know also that he collected antique firearms and it is interesting to note that they crop up in his illustrations, for example, in *Ben and Me* and in *Captain Kidd's Cat.*

FROM FERDINAND TO AMOS

The story of *The Story of Ferdinand,* which catapulted Robert Lawson to fame as an illustrator, is in itself an amusing story. Munro Leaf, then editor at F. A. Stokes, had for some time wanted to write a book especially for his friend, Robert Lawson, to illustrate. He wanted it to be a book that would give free rein to Lawson's talent, a book in which the text and drawings would be of equal importance, complementing each other to the extent that together they would form a single unit. It was decided that the text would be about the creatures of fantasy, which Lawson drew so well. Some time later Leaf appeared at Lawson's studio with a text that he had produced "in forty minutes one rainy Sunday afternoon" on two wrinkled sheets of yellow paper. Lawson wrote in a manuscript for a speech ". . . But it was about a BULL . . . as far as I can remember I had never drawn a bull in my life, and the problems of drawing a bull with expressions and emotions at various ages seemed impossible." Nothing was done with the text for two or three months, but Lawson went through clippings and reference books, studied Spanish landscapes and architecture, bull anatomy, bullfighting, and the costumes of picadors, matadors, banderilleros and their horses, trappings, and attendants. By the time the pencil sketches were finished both Leaf and Lawson became really enthusiastic about the humor in the work and jokingly prophesied that it would eventually sell as many as 20,000 copies. They had created a genuinely funny situation: peaceful Ferdinand cast in the role of man-eating terror! To the philosophic, Ferdinand's plight may suggest amusing human parallels. The youngsters take it literally (1). In a little more than two years after publication date, *Ferdinand* had sold more than 250,000 copies.

In 1938 Robert Lawson illustrated three books. *Mr. Popper's Penguins* by Florence and Richard Atwater is a delightful story because of its matter-of-fact handling of the absurd, almost convincing the reader that it would be quite simple to bring up a family of penguins in a refrigerator and travel about the country exhibiting them (2). Eleanor Farjeon's *One Foot in Fairyland* is a collection of sixteen stories ranging from pure fairy tales to stories of reality that offer full scope to Mr. Lawson's imagination and creativity. The third was another collaboration with Munro Leaf which was entitled *Wee Gillis.* The feeling of Scotland is as sure and true as the feeling of Spain was in *The Story of Ferdinand* and evidently entailed as much research into details. This delightful picture book is about a small boy who had difficulty in deciding whether to live in the Highlands or Lowlands of Scotland. Mr. Lawson's drawings, touched with a robust humor, reproduce the atmosphere of the actual country (2).

The year of 1939 saw the production of only two books, but these two may well be considered among the most important of Mr. Lawson's career. The first was a new edition of Bunyan's *Pilgrim's Progress,* which Mr. Lawson considered his favorite work, and the second was *Ben and Me,* which he wrote and illustrated himself, thus launching on a career as author.

His own first book, *Ben and Me,* published in 1939, initiated a pattern, used in many of his works, of chronicling history through the pets of great men. His versions of history were often witty spoofs of heroes which were equally amusing to children and adults.

Mr. Lawson told a Sales Conference at Little, Brown & Co. in 1941 that when it had been suggested that a book about some historical character and his pet might be a good idea, he "made a list of famous people and clawed it over and then I stewed over it for several weeks and then settled more or less on Ben Franklin. He'd always struck me as a pretty pompous, self-satisfied old scoundrel, but the pet seemed to be the stumbling block. So I thought that over for several weeks and then one day as I was looking at that portrait of Franklin in his fur cap and that dirty looking old fur-collared dressing gown and thinking about how he must have smelled, he didn't believe much in bathing, you know, except in summer, and my wife just happened to say, 'That fur cap certainly is an awful looking rat's nest.'

"Well, that was just what we needed. If it was a rat's nest, why not a mouse's? So Amos suddenly took form. The origin of the name is simple. Amos — A mouse. Then we decided that I'd better write it myself because we couldn't find any author who could write such a cockeyed story. Usually I can illustrate other people's stories with no trouble. In this case the illustrator had a great deal of fault to find with the story and vice versa. By the time we finished we were both very mixed up and hardly on speaking terms."

Ben and Me was done with brush and black tempera (17) and has been called "a nonsense story for all ages," (2) and "a touching history with sheer nonsense told in a way that would doubtless have delighted the genial Mr. Franklin himself." (12) It is excellent for starting young readers on biography, and it is even funnier after they piece together the main events of Franklin's life (1). Mr. Lawson has sustained a mood of gentle irony throughout the book. An amusing anecdote about *Ben and Me* is told by a school librarian who had to defend his having the book on his shelves against a charge of its having Communistic leanings. In a description of the battle of the mice in the French court, the Russian mice were described as being the fiercest fighters. The librarian had to explain before a School Board meeting that in Ben Franklin's times these would have to have been Czarist mice, after which explanation the book was allowed to remain on his shelves. The success of *Ben and Me* led Mr. Lawson to write and illustrate several other books following its pattern of biography told by pets.

THE CALDECOTT MEDAL

They Were Strong and Good, it must be remembered, was written the year before the United States became involved in World War II. The book was distinctly serious, patriotic and very much of the flag-waving type. Many critics have felt that it could not compare artistically with *Rabbit Hill,* which Lawson did five years later. It certainly should have warmed the hearts of those who complained about *The Story of Ferdinand* and *Ben and Me.* Still, compared with the crop of picture books published in 1940, it was outstanding and did have considerable merit. The pictures range from North to South, from the sea to a farm, from gay to tragic, and while the text is almost laconic, the pictures are rich in detail (11). In a speech in Cleveland in October 1940, Mr. Lawson described the book and told what he felt about it:

"It hasn't much story, just a simple account, mostly in pictures, of my mother and my father and their mothers and 'fathers, my grandparents. But it is pretty much the story of *your* parents and grandparents too. None of them were great and famous. It doesn't matter whether they were sea-captains or preachers or cowboys or farmers or hardware merchants or just good mothers. They were simple, ordinary people of the generation before us – who worked hard and were strong and good, and who, each in his own small way, helped to build up this great country out of a wilderness. They have turned this all over to us and it is up to us to keep it a great nation. I have hoped that just presenting a simple picture of some of these people would give to the young people of this time, and perhaps to their parents, a feeling of pride in their country and their forbears and a feeling of great responsibility. Right now our country could do with a lot of both.

"I hope that this book will cause some of the young people of today to look back and think about what they did, these parents and grand-parents and great-grandparents of ours, and to think about what we haven't done and to feel, as I do, a little ashamed of ourselves and to decide to do something about it, to be a little more worthy of them.

"They hadn't any cars or school buses to carry them to school, often there were no schools to carry them to. My father went to war when he was fourteen and worked hard at business all the rest of his life. I don't know how or when he found time to study, yet he knew more of Latin and Greek than I ever did, he was better at mathematics than I can ever hope to be, and when he was seventy years old his handwriting was one of the most beautiful I have ever seen, and at eighty-four, when he died, he had more and better teeth, more hair, more strength and more sense than most people I know now who are half his age.

"My mother, who was brought up among Indians and lumberjacks in Minnesota, spoke several languages, knew more about music and books than most people that I know now, she painted very well and could skate, shoot a pistol, ride a bicycle, or drive a horse as well as anyone, and had plenty of time to raise a family of six children.

"How did they manage to do all these things? I don't know except that they worked hard and were strong and good. I do not want to be gloomy and I certainly do not pretend to be any prophet, but most people feel that the immediate future of children all over the world is a very uncertain one. No one knows what they will have to face.

"But one thing I do feel very sure and very cheerful about. That this is a great country and that we are a great and tough people. No one has ever gotten us down yet. And I know that the people who come out on top are those people who work hard and are strong and good. If you are not, then we might as well change our song from 'God bless America' to 'God help America.'

"So think about your forefathers and think about your country and get to work — hard. Get to work hard at everything you do. Get so that you can say 'I'm as good a man as my father or my grandfather or my great-grandfather and I could lick the pants off any of them at anything, at any time.' When you get to that point our country will remain great and be safe — against anybody, or anything."

Arbuthnot felt the book was not too successful as biography or fiction, but that it was useful in rousing children's interest in their own ancestors (1). Smith thought it contained some of the most moving pages in all our picture books (15). The picture of a ragged boy, limping down the war-desolated road, is one of the memorable pages in all picture book litera-ture. In these pages there is strength, tenderness, and beauty of line (16).

A review in the *Herald Tribune* Book Section on September 29, 1940 felt that the book was an expression of that ideal of individual human values on which the destiny of the world depends. The *Westport Town Crier* on January 15, 1953 quoted from Elizabeth Gray Vining in her best seller *Windows for the Crown Prince* that a book of Lawson's called *They Were Strong and Good* contributed to the democratization of the son of the Japanese Emperor. It is interesting to note that a Chinese edition was printed in Taiwan by World Book in 1953, with the original, but badly reproduced, illustrations.

THE NEWBERY MEDAL

The publication in 1944 of *Country Colic* by Little, Brown & Co. and of *Rabbit Hill* by Viking is the subject of yet another of the amusing anecdotes about his work that Mr. Lawson relished so much. It seems that he had been commissioned by Little, Brown & Co. to write a book about the trials and tribulations of country life (7). In a speech for the BBC Children's Hour delivered on May 4, 1956, he said, "I was going to tell how the rabbits and the woodchucks ate up everything you planted and how the deer trampled down the garden and the skunks upset the garbage pail and foxes killed all the chickens, of how the roof leaked and the cellar was always flooded.

"But when I started to write I got quite fond of Little Georgie (who is the young rabbit hero of the book) and of his mother and father and even of his crabby old Uncle Analdas. Soon I became much more interested in them and in old Porkey (the woodchuck) and Phewie (the skunk) than I was in gardens, or leaking roofs, or flooded cellars.

"The first thing I knew the little animals had taken over the book entirely and apparently were writing their own story. I don't know just who did write it, but I don't remember having much to do with it. It just sort of went along by itself." Approximately one-quarter of a million copies of *Rabbit Hill* have been sold since its publication on October 4, 1944, the birthday of Robert Lawson and of St. Francis of Assisi. It has been published in French, Spanish, German, Dutch, Hebrew, and Norwegian.

Who could have foretold that this simple, charming story of the small animals living at Rabbit Hill would have become a modern classic? Talking beast stories in which we see ourselves in fur are an ancient form, yet from suspicious Uncle Analdas to worrying Mother Rabbit, the animals are delightfully individualized. Arbuthnot writes that this story and its illustrations should do more than any lecture to develop in young children a feeling of tenderness and regard for small animals (1). Meigs comments that "Mr. Lawson realized the full capacity of his genius in a simple tale, *Rabbit Hill,* a book beautiful both in illustration and style, and so refreshing, spontaneous and natural as to seem to have reached the printed page without anyone's effort. Here are animals each of whom remains his very special animal self no matter how much he speaks with man's tongue. Mr. Lawson knows and loves the small animals of the countryside and he can write fantasy that is original and heart-warming (12)." At no time does one feel that Mr. Lawson is being didactic yet we see how parental indulgence was fatal to some rabbits. The entire theme of the book is one of hope. There are always New Folks and New Times coming and there is always kindness and generosity to be found. The New Folks erected a statue of St. Francis of Assisi with a pool, where small animals could drink and a ledge around it where food was set out each night. The inscription on the ledge read, "There is enough for all."

EVALUATION

If one feels, as many critics do, that Robert Lawson had reached the apogee of his talent, both artistically and literarily, with the creation of *Rabbit Hill,* it must be immediately stated that there was no diminution, no sliding down-hill, of that talent in the remaining twelve years of his life after the publication of *Rabbit Hill.* They were full and satisfying years in which his humor deepened and mellowed and was reflected in his work as well as in the speeches he delivered and the articles he wrote from time to time. They were productive years also. They saw the publication of seventeen new works plus innumerable foreign language editions of earlier works. Mr. Lawson enjoyed a firmly established reputation in the field of children's literature. His stories ranged from the "talking beast" stories of the *Rabbit Hill* type through the broad humor of *Mr. Twigg's Mistake* and the satiric humor of *McWinney's Jaunt.*

The Indian philosopher Tagore speaks of "sounds and movements and lines and colors" as "man's other languages." Mr. Lawson's works demonstrate the fortuitous combination of the use of the language of words and the language of lines and colors to complement each other. The fluidity and unity of text and illustrations in his books would be difficult to achieve if the author and illustrator were not the same person.

Yet he also seemed to possess the sensitivity and ability to project another's thoughts because some of his finest work has been done illustrating for another author. Nor was his style set and monotonous. It possessed a wide range of expression.

As Mr. Coleman, Viking's Art Editor, said when questioned about Lawson's using the ancient form of speaking through animals. "The king's fool can say what the king's knight dare not." In the traditional manner of satirists he used animal society as an analogue with which to poke fun at human society. Mr. Lawson's comments were often satirical, but the satire is the warmly loving, affectionately chiding satire of Horace, never the vituperative, shrilly hating satire of Juvenal. In the tradition of Horace one remembers the great eighteenth century caricaturist Daumier. While there is no artistic analogy between Daumier's corpulent bourgeoisie and Lawson's delicately-drawn animals, both are illuminated by a love for life, and for all living things, that takes the barb out of satire.

In the historical series, he has succeeded admirably in making the famous hero of the story more human. Most peoples, and especially Americans, tend to place their heroes on pedestals, lift them above the trivia of hum-drum everyday life so that they no longer seem "even as you or I." To mention George Washington's dentures seems sacrilegious, but they bring him back to the realm of human beings with problems and discomforts who, despite them, could perform great deeds. Amos, the mouse, makes Benjamin Franklin a fallible, lovable human being and removes from him the austerity with which our national myths have surrounded him. Through McDermot, the cat, we see Captain Kidd not as a murderous pirate and scoundrel of history, but as the "fall guy" for powerful interests.

Bertha Mahoney probably described Robert Lawson best in two short sentences. "He is witty as well as wise in two of the arts of expression. He has a rare philosophy—he never takes himself too seriously, and he never takes his art too lightly (10)." Marie Lawson wrote in an article for *The Horn Book* that "his world is our own real world, but he has a deeper perception, a wider horizon; he believes in these things himself. He has the peculiar art of mingling fact with fantasy and making people believe it, which is completely beyond analysis (5)."

At the time of Mr. Lawson's death, *The Horn Book* published an editorial signed J. D. L., Jennie D. Lindquist, eulogizing Mr. Lawson and his work. It mentioned the newly published *The Great Wheel* and remarked that it was very different from *Ben and Me* and the "historical tales. It is gay, refreshing, and distinguished by humor, breeziness, and good writing." The tribute ended with "New Folks coming, Robert Lawson, New Folks coming every year to love the books you left as a rich gift to American literature and art (9)."

REFERENCES

1. Arbuthnot, May Hill. *Children and Books.* Rev. ed. Chicago: Scott, Foresman, 1957.
2. Eaton, Anne Thaxter. *Treasure for the Taking.* Rev. ed. New York: Viking, 1957.
3. Henderson, Rose. "Robert Lawson, Master of Fantasy," *New York Herald Tribune* Sunday Magazine Section, (November 30, 1930) 14–15.
4. Kunitz, Stanley J. and Haycraft, Howard, eds. *Junior Book of Authors.* 2nd ed. New York: H. W. Wilson, 1951.
5. Lawson, Marie A. "Master of Rabbit Hill: Robert Lawson," *The Horn Book,* (July–August, 1945) 239–242.
6. Lawson, Robert. "Make Me a Child Again," *The Horn Book,* (Christmas, 1940) 447–456.
7. Lawson, Robert. "The Newbery Medal Acceptance Speech," *The Horn Book,* (July–August, 1945) 233–238.
8. Lawson, Robert. "On Children and Books," *Childhood Education,* (February, 1942) 268–273.
9. Lindquist, J. L. "The Master of Rabbit Hill," *The Horn Book,* (August, 1957) 273.
10. Mahoney, Bertha E., and others. *Illustrators of Children's Books, 1744–1945.* Boston: Horn Book, 1946.
11. Massee, May. "Robert Lawson, 1940 Caldecott Winner," *The Library Journal,* (July, 1941) 591–592.
12. Meigs, Cornelia, and others. *A Critical History of Children's Literature.* New York: Macmillan, 1953.
13. *Monthly Magazine of the Junior Heritage Club,* n. d.
14. "Robert Lawson, Illustrator, Dies." *New York Times,* May 28, 1957, 33.
15. Smith, Irene. *A History of the Newbery and Caldecott Medals.* New York: Viking, 1957.
16. Smith, Irene. "Newbery and Caldecott Award Winners," *American Library Assn. Bulletin,* (July, 1941) 422–429.
17. Watson, Ernest W. *Forty Illustrators and How They Work.* New York: Watson, 195–.

EDITORS' NOTE

Awards and honors won by Robert Lawson include a runner-up for the 1938 Caldecott Medal for *Four and Twenty Blackbirds,* written by Helen Dean Fish and illustrated by Lawson; the 1941 Caldecott Medal for *They Were Strong and Good;* the 1961 and 1963 Lewis Carroll Shelf Awards (worthy to sit on the shelf with *Alice in Wonderland*) for *Ben and Me* and *Rabbit Hill,* respectively; the Newbery Medal for *Rabbit Hill* in 1945; and a runner-up for the Newbery in 1958 for *The Great Wheel.*

Lois Lenski:
Children's Interpreter *

NO OTHER AUTHOR of children's literature has so richly interpreted childhood and the American scene as has Lois Lenski. Her books reflect a perceptive understanding of children of all ages while they realistically present the diversity of background and culture which forms the strength and pattern of the American kaleidoscope.

Lois Lenski's "Davy" books are written for the pre-school child. These little books are deceptively simple in both text and illustrations as they portray the daily experiences of one child. It is this very simplicity which eludes most authors of books for the youngest. Miss Lenski understands what is important to the two- and three-year-old and she presents it in a direct manner without any tone of condescension or "cuteness." She can convey excitement in the commonplace as she identifies the satisfaction derived by a pre-schooler in learning to dress himself, or the anticipation of a birthday party. The young child's world is circumscribed by the sphere of his own activities. These simple events frequently appear insignificant and unimportant when they are compared to the busy concerns of adults. Lois Lenski's "Davy" books restore them to their proper place of magnitude in the child's small world.

Besides his own activities, the young child is always interested in the weather, the seasons and their effect upon his world. Lenski has provided four books, *Spring Is Here, Now It's Fall, I Like Winter,* and *On a*

* By Charlotte S. Huck. From *Catholic Library World* 40 (1969), 346–350. Reprinted by special permission from *The Lois Lenski Collection in the University of Oklahoma Library,* 1963, published by the University of Oklahoma Library and the School of Library Science, Norman, Oklahoma.

Summer Day, which satisfy this interest. In cheerful rhymed text, she captures the spirit of each season and emphasizes its particular play opportunities. An added feature of each of these stories is the inclusion of music for the words of the text. These little books are the same size and format as the "Davy" books—just right for small hands to hold. *Animals for Me* is another popular book of similar size which capitalizes on young children's universal love of animals.

Books need to do more than reflect children's daily experiences, they should also extend them. Boys and girls of five, six and seven are naturally curious about their world and appreciate Lenski's straight-forward presentation of information in her stories of the activities of that eternal small boy in adult clothing, Mr. Small. In *Little Farm,* Mr. Small cares for his farm and uses his machinery in the cheerful, matter-of-fact way that characterizes his actions in *The Little Auto, The Little Sail Boat, The Little Fire Engine, The Little Train,* and *The Little Airplane.* In all these books, Miss Lenski presents a simple yet accurate explanation of the operation of each of these vehicles. Usually, in at least one illustration, the salient feature of the machine or equipment is clearly labeled. In *Cowboy Small* and *Policeman Small* all the tools of their occupation are pictured while the text emphasizes their vocational responsibilities. The technical terminology and detailed information in these books are frequently reflected in children's conversation and dramatic play. Young children do want answers to their questions but not complex ones. Lois Lenski's "Mr. Small" books satisfy the primary age child without overwhelming him.

Much as the "Davy" and "Mr. Small" books are beloved by children, Lois Lenski's regional stories are thoroughly enjoyed by children in the middle grades. And it is these stories of children from under-privileged families in various parts of our country which probably represent Lois Lenski's greatest contribution to the field of juvenile literature.

Her regional stories are written for two age groups, the Round-about America Series which are easy-reading books for children in the third and fourth grades and her Regional Series which are for somewhat more mature readers. Her foreword to the Round-about America Series describes her purpose in writing these stories:

Come, let us look at the ways of life in our country. Let us go into out-of-the-way
    corners, up on the hills and down in the valleys, into city streets and village homes.

Let us see and get to know the people. Here and there, round
about America, are
friends worth knowing.[1]

Through the writings of Lois Lenski, hundreds of American children
have come to know intimately the hardships, the joys, the disappointments, the hopes of other American boys and girls whom they would
never have met or even knew existed. The horizons of children from sheltered homes are widened as they read of other American children who
are too poor to own shoes or to go to a movie. Different ways of living
are described in these books but none are judged better than others.
Lois Lenski never judges but she helps the reader understand the reasons which necessitate a particular way of life.

The settings of her Round-about America stories are vividly portrayed
as evidenced by this description of a crowded tenement in *We Live in the
City:*

Children were playing. Babies in buggies were crying. Hanging
street signs flapped in the wind. Trains on the Grove Street El
roared by overhead. A radio in the fish store played loud music.
Women leaned out of windows above. They called to children in
the streets.[2]

The plots of most of the Round-about America Series are episodic but
this is appropriate to the author's desire to show the everyday life of the
children in a particular region or minority group. Four of the books,
*We Live in the South, We Live by the River, We Live in the City, We
Live in the Country* are collections of short stories which show the varying influence of a particular geographical location on the lives of people.
The effect of an emergency government housing project on the lives of
children is portrayed in *Project Boy* while the dominance of a particular
crop is stressed in *Peanuts for Billy Ben* and *Berries in the Scoop.* Another of the series, *Little Sioux Girl,* describes Indian reservation life of
1950. The mingling of the old and new, the need for better schools and
more adequate medical care is made clear in this story of an Indian girl
who faced prejudice, yet found pride in her heritage.

Lois Lenski's finest regional stories have been written for older
children from nine to fourteen. There are some fourteen books in this
Regional Series which depict the lives of American children in many

different, often unheard of, places. Miss Lenski explains her purpose in writing these books in the foreword of *Strawberry Girl.*

> In this series of regional books for American children, I am trying to present vivid, sympathetic pictures of the real life of different localities. We need to know our country better; to know and understand people different from ourselves; so that we can say: "This then is the way these people live. Because I understand it, I admire and love them." [3]

These books are authentic in every detail, for Miss Lenski gathers all the information for her stories through first hand experience with the section of the country about which she is currently writing. She lives among the people, sketching, talking and listening to their problems and concerns. This meticulous research is revealed in the accuracy with which she describes their homes, the food they eat, their work and their play. In *Cotton in My Sack,* her descriptions of the heat of the sun in the fields, the weight of a full cotton sack and the resulting weariness of body are based upon actual experiences in the cotton fields.

The ring of authenticity is heard clearly in the natural speech patterns of her characters. She has preserved the rhythm of speech which is typical of the region while making judicious use of slang and colloquialisms. In *Strawberry Girl,* for example, children in the middle grades have an opportunity to hear the color and flavor of such idiomatic phrases as used by the Florida "Crackers" as "gettin biggity," "totin water," "right purty," and "plumb good." They can discuss the meanings and origins of such idioms and hopefully they will learn to appreciate the richness of our regional variations of language patterns.

This same respect for realism is revealed in Lenski's character descriptions. Her characters speak and act in accordance with their age, culture and educational backgrounds. She courageously portrays drunken fathers, improvident parents and objectionable neighbors as these are a part of the real life drama of the children in her stories. Her books are not without hope, however. They do more than mirror the despondent life of underprivileged families. There is warmth and family solidarity, there is love and joy along with despair and sadness. Frequently, the children in her books exhibit greater wisdom than their parents. In *Judy's Journey,* it is Judy's persistent dream and desire for a permanent home which finally convinces her father to give up their migratory life. Birdie Boyer wanted an education and an organ and her strawberry crop provided both in *Strawberry Girl.* In her foreword to *Cotton in My Sack,* Miss Lenski expresses her admiration for the courage, stoicism and fortitude of the cotton children in these words:

> They had seen sorrow and so they were compassionate. They had seen meanness, and so they valued goodness. They had endured hardships, and so theirs was an attitude not of escape but acceptance. They were ready for whatever life might bring. And because sorrow, meanness and hardship were a part of their lives, they had a better understanding of the joy of living, which comes by a full sharing in human adventure.[4]

While Miss Lenski is best known for her regional stories, her earliest writing was historical fiction for older children. Again her concern for accuracy and authenticity is clearly reflected in these fine historical novels. Even in these stories of the past the discerning reader can see the author's incipient interest in the problems of human relations. In her book *A-Going to the Westward,* she tellingly writes of the adjustments which Yankees from Connecticut, Pennsylvania Dutchmen and Kentucky southerners faced as they learned to live together in the wilderness of the Ohio country in the early 1800's. The theme of the exciting book, *Indian Captive: The Story of Mary Jemison,* is the basic conflict between the Indians' and early settlers' way of life. Based upon the actual accounts of the capture of a twelve-year-old girl by the Seneca Indians, the plot revolves around Mary's determination not to accept the Indian ways despite their kind treatment of her. Almost without her realizing it, when she begins to understand the Indians, she finds that she loves them. When the time comes for her to decide whether she will remain with them or go with the English, she elects to stay. Whether Lois Lenski writes of the hardships faced in the past or the present, she writes with compassion, understanding and respect for mankind.

Miss Lenski has illustrated all of her own books in a style which is uniquely her own and readily identifiable. Her knowledge of children extends to their preferences and appreciation for art. In her "Davy" books, for example, she has taken into consideration the very young child's inability to see perspective and has included little or no background in her illustrations. Her "Mr. Small" books reflect the same careful attention to essential detail as represented in the text. Her drawings for both these series are done in two colors in a simple almost childlike manner. She frequently includes the sun in her pictures, a characteristic feature of young children's drawings. Her figures are done in a soft crayon wash and have a rounded look. Mr. Small has the size and proportion of a four-year-old even though he is dressed as an adult. This helps the young child to identify with Mr. Small.

The illustrations for the Round-about America Series are realistic black and white sketches. Her Regional Series show even more accurate detail in the soft pencil drawings of the interiors of homes and schools. Her pictures of people express more emotion than do those in her books for younger children. Realism is portrayed in the disheveled appearance of the children and their shabby homes. Interesting and detailed end papers summarize events of the story as in *Judy's Journey,* or portray the locale as in *San Francisco Boy,* or an important environmental aspect such as the company store in *Coal Camp Girl.* Lenski's art work is sketched on the spot and is as authentic as the incidences in her stories.

It is only as one views the writings and illustrations of Lois Lenski's in their entirety that one can comprehend her vast contribution to children's literature. She is a prolific writer producing many books of various types and for different age groups. She has never sacrificed quality for quantity and each of her books makes a distinctive contribution to the type of literature it represents. The essence of her greatness is in the versatility of her writing, for her work encompasses all of childhood. No author has interpreted American children more accurately or perceptively; no author has given more abundantly to children than has Lois Lenski.

REFERENCES

1. Lois Lenski, *Little Sioux Girl.* Philadelphia: J. B. Lippincott Company, 1954. Foreword.
2. Lois Lenski, *We Live in the City.* Philadelphia: J. B. Lippincott Company, 1954. p. 99.
3. Lois Lenski, *Strawberry Girl.* Philadelphia: J. B. Lippincott Company, 1954. Foreword, p. xi.
4. Lois Lenski, *Cotton in My Sack.* Philadelphia: J. B. Lippincott Company, 1949. Foreword, p. xi.

EDITORS' NOTE

Lois Lenski was born in Springfield, Ohio, on October 14, 1893. She was the fourth of five children. Her childhood and early youth were spent in a small Ohio farming town of about two hundred people, where her father was a Lutheran minister. Later the family moved to Columbus and Lois attended Ohio State University, where she took courses in education and majored in art.

Although Miss Lenski received a B.S. in Education from Ohio State in 1915, she never taught school. She enrolled at the Art Students League in New York City where she studied part-time for four years, meanwhile taking odd jobs to pay her expenses. She also spent a year in London studying at the Westminster School of Art.

In 1921, Miss Lenski married Arthur Covey, a well-known mural painter, who died in 1960. They had one son, Stephen, around whom many of her picture books developed. The Coveys lived, for most of their married life, in a farmhouse built in 1790, in Torrington, Connecticut. Because of Miss Lenski's poor health they spent many of their winters in the South, where the ideas for her regional books developed.

Lois Lenski's two main hobbies are her children's painting classes and gardening. In her painting classes she has worked with children of various social backgrounds and her studios are decorated with paintings and murals made by school children not only from her own classes, but from different sections of the country. She enjoys working with plants and flowers and built her own rock garden at her Connecticut home. Partly because of her interest in gardening, she recently moved from Connecticut to Florida, where she can garden all year.

Miss Lenski is a prolific writer. In addition to writing and illustrating approximately one hundred of her own books, she has illustrated fifty-seven children's books by other authors. Her honors and awards include the 1944 Ohioana Medal (for outstanding books written by Ohio authors) for *Bayou Suzette;* runner-up for the Newbery Medal in 1942 for *Indian Captive: The Story of Mary Jemison;* the 1946 Newbery Medal for *Strawberry Girl;* the 1947 Child Study Association of America, Children's Book Award (for best book dealing realistically with some problem in the contemporary world) for *Judy's Journey;* and The Catholic Library Association's Regina Medal in 1969 (for continued distinguished contributions to children's literature).

Miss Lenski has also received honorary degrees from Wartburg College, the University of North Carolina, Capitol University and Southwestern College. Her latest books are *City Poems* and *Debbie and Her Pets,* both published by Walck in 1971.

Julius Lester:
Newbery Runner-up *

"I HAVE A STRONG Salinger streak in me," he commented over an Irish bacon and eggs lunch at the Blarney Stone. A small, comfortable bar with robust man's food, it was his choice of a place where we could meet without his having to put on a tie and jacket, which he refuses to wear anywhere. He was dressed in hooded jacket, sweatshirt, and faded slacks. His face is leaner than the publicity photos convey, the slight beard more straggly, the eyes reflecting wariness faded into indifference, the mouth, sensitive and pursed in perpetual reflectiveness, recalling some old, vanquished vulnerability.

The first black writer to make the Newbery-Caldecott list of winners or runners-up with *To Be a Slave* (Dial), Julius Lester combines writing with a round of activities that include photography, songwriting, recording albums, journalism, teaching, and running a radio show. Born in St. Louis, he relishes New York for the pace it allows him; he lived in San Francisco for a short time, loved it, gave it up as too Utopian. "I couldn't do any work."

Lester was born in 1929 in St. Louis, but raised in Nashville and Kansas City, Kansas. He attended Fisk University and went to New York a year after his 1960 graduation, working as a bookstore clerk, welfare investigator, and guitar teacher before he turned to writing. His articles now appear in the *Village Voice, New York Free Press, Sing Out* and *Broadside;* he does a column of political analysis for *The Guardian* and

* By Evelyn Geller. Reprinted by permission from *Library Journal*, May 15, 1969, pp. 2070–2071.

275

The Movement; has co-authored, with Pete Seeger, *The Twelve-String Guitar as Played by Leadbelly;* and written poems in *American Dialogue* which will appear in three anthologies: *New Jazz Poets, Negro Poetry for High School Students,* and *Poems Against the Way the World Is.* Vanguard has issued two albums in which he sings original and Afro-American traditional songs to his own guitar accompaniment.

In 1966 Lester joined the Student Nonviolent Coordinating Committee as head of the photo department and is now a field secretary with SNCC. In spring 1966 he spent a month in North Vietnam photographing U.S. bombing of civilian targets, attended the first session of Bertrand Russell War Crimes Tribunal in Stockholm, and went to Cuba with Stokely Carmichael to attend the Organization of Latin American Solidarity Conference. In the past year he has taught "The History of Black Resistance" at the New School and conducted a radio show, *The Great Proletarian Cultural Revolution,* on WBAI-FM, the New York listener-supported radio station.

Lester is married to the former Joan Steinau and is the father of two children, who figure in his reasons for writing children's books. He came to the attention of Dial's children's book editor, Phyllis Fogleman, through an adult book he had just written for the company—*Look Out, Whitey, Black Power's Gon' Get Your Mama* (1968), a mordant survey of white America and the Black Power movement dating back to the 19th Century. Dial was the second publisher to which that book had been submitted, the first having wanted to work over the content and change the title, which Lester insisted on ("No black man would pass by a book with that name").

At the time, Lester had a large assemblage of manuscripts culled from research at the Library of Congress in 1963. He had been drawn there through his reading of B. A. Botkin's *Lay My Burden Down* (University of Chicago, 1945), which was based on the LC collections. "It didn't give me a good feeling about my history." Nor did the Federal Writers Project's *The Negro in Virginia,* recounting the testimony of former slaves. "The whites came from the same area in which they were interviewing," Lester says. "They never got a straight answer."

His father, a minister closely related to old people in the community, was his link with the past. His grandmother had been a slave but never spoke about it. His own dissatisfaction was tied, somehow, to this silence. "I never knew how to refute that feeling—that their having been slaves meant being bad." So he went down to the Library of Congress to see what had been left out of the published works. "I xeroxed everything that struck me and compared it."

His work at the Library of Congress brought out masses of material, most unpublished. Ironically, the same sources produced a picture of slavery that differed sharply from its earlier reflections in published works.

By 1968, partly because publishers were "ready" for this kind of material, partly because he was aware of how few books he could give his own children to read, the children's book venture appealed to him. Pulling the most relevant material out of the mass of sources and documents at his disposal was the immediate problem, and it was approached by way of emotion, rather than pure scholarship. "I just took what hit me in the gut," he says. Avoiding the more sensational descriptions of cruelty and rebellion, Lester was still uncompromising in choosing narrations of the raids on African tribes, the squalid passage to America, the horrors of the auction block, the beginnings of resistance, the period of "emancipation."

The result is a superb editorial job, combining original slave accounts and reports of immediate observers with author's comments (set off in an italic type) that provide continuity and insight in a carefully matched style. In its muted account, the book has the allusiveness of poetry. Like *Black Rage* (which despite its sloppy methodology conveys the psychic imprint of slavery) it quietly lays bare the shame of American history while making slavery, suffering, and resistance part of his black child's heritage. Its manner of revealing dignity in humiliation, expressing the haunting, ever-present sense of the slave experience in the racial memory, is reminiscent of the Jews' ritual celebration of their history of persecution.

Lester is now engaged in two other works for young people, a teen novel of an interracial romance, and a compilation of African folk tales for the younger child. He is still concerned that so few books on blacks exist for the very young child, apart from works like Ezra Keats' picture books and the recent *Harriet and the Promised Land* by Jacob Lawrence, which left him wildly enthusiastic. We commented on the controversy that *Harriet* has raised among black librarians who feel the sophistication of the art work eludes the black child, and confirms his own sense of inferiority through its distortions and the anonymity it conveys. Lester disagreed strongly.

"You must be doing something as a parent, then, that librarians are not doing with the book."

"Well, man, you have to explain it. My child," he said in his slurred, not quite drawling voice, "wanted to know about all kinds of things, like what chariots were. She wanted to know why Harriet's hand was so big. So I asked her, 'Did you ever walk so long that your feet felt they were as big as your body? That's how Harriet felt when she was scrubbing floors.' " (His daughter Jody would readily understand this explanation; she recently described an alligator, Lester says, as an animal whose smile goes down to its tail.)

At the time of our meeting, Lester had been embroiled in a controversy that hinged on the reading, over his WBAI program, of a pathological anti-Semitic poem by a 15-year-old black junior high school student. Having been interrogated to death on this issue, he threatened to call off the interview if he was questioned on it. But we were pretty sensitive about being censored for an interview, and besides felt this issue (the entire question of verbal aggression, reverse prejudice, projection) was important for what it said about the feelings of black children, and what the implications were for freedom of expression in writing, in line with the current curricular vogue in schools and the present encouragement of teen writing in public libraries. We asked him for his thoughts.

In answering, Lester went back to a course he had taught in the South some years ago to black teenagers. "There was a girl in my class whose brother was the first black child to integrate a high school. And what did she decide to write about in her composition? Her first dance! I had to *push* those kids to write about their own experiences and their own feelings. And once they got these out, the results were unbelievable. They have to learn that whatever they feel, whatever they write, is going to be acceptable. And if they say to themselves, 'I feel hate,' they have to express this, too."

We observed that the literary quality of *To Be a Slave* hinged on its tone of hushed horror and a restraint which was more eloquent, in the end, than sentimentality or vituperation. He dismissed this indifferently.

"You have to understand the tone that comes from my horn as well as the notes that I'm blowing. In *To Be a Slave,* I wanted that material to speak for itself. I was Virgil, leading you through Hell. I was writing the history of the anonymous, and had to give *them* a voice. The material had to speak for itself."

"But, I adapt my tools to my message," Lester added, "I veer between my rapier and my club." He chuckled. "Read *Whitey.*"

EDITORS' NOTE

In addition to being a runner-up for the 1969 Newbery Medal, Mr. Lester's book, *To Be a Slave,* also received the 1968 Nancy Bloch Memorial Award (given annually to an outstanding children's book on intergroup relations) and the 1970 Lewis Carroll Shelf Award (given to a book worthy to sit on the shelf with *Alice in Wonderland*).

Julius Lester's other children's books are *Black Folktales* (Dial, 1969), and a new book—his first for young children—*The Knee-High Man and Other Black Folktales,* to be published by Dial in the spring of 1972.

Mr. Lester feels that only blacks should write about blacks. In an April 10, 1970, letter to the *New York Times* Children's Book Editor, he states: "We no longer (and never did) need whites to interpret our lives or our culture. Whites can only give a white interpretation of blacks, which tells us a lot about whites, but nothing about blacks."

The Chronicles of Narnia and the Adolescent Reader *

IN 1956, the Carnegie Medal, awarded annually for the best children's book published in the British Empire, was bestowed by the Library Association on Professor Clive Staples Lewis for his volume entitled *The Last Battle*. This book was the seventh and last of a unified series of works on the mythical land of Narnia—a series begun by Professor Lewis in 1950 with the *The Lion, the Witch and the Wardrobe,* and continued, at yearly intervais, by *Prince Caspian* (1951), *The Voyage of the "Dawn Treader"* (1952), *The Silver Chair* (1953), *The Horse and His Boy* (1954), and *The Magician's Nephew* (1955). The dearth of high-quality modern publications suitable for adolescents, together with a general lack of acquaintance with the Narnia Chronicles in this country, provides sufficient justification for a detailed examination of these works. In this article an attempt will be made to study both the literary quality of the Chronicles and the religious values which can accrue to the adolescent who reads them. It is sincerely hoped that the magic as well as the remarkable character of these volumes will become evident to the perusers of this study.

THE AUTHOR OF THE CHRONICLES

If the axiomatic truth is conceded that a book reflects the personality of its author, then there is good reason at the outset of this paper to become familiar with the basic facts of C. S. Lewis' life. *Who's Who,*

* By John W. Montgomery. Reprinted from the September–October 1959 issue of *Religious Education* 54 (September 1959), 418–428, by permission of the publisher, The Religious Education Association, New York City.

1958, informs us that Dr. Lewis was born November 29, 1898, the son of a Belfast Solicitor. His education at Oxford was interrupted by military service during the First World War, but was completed with honors. From 1924 until 1954, he was associated with Oxford in a teaching capacity (Fellow and Tutor of Magdalen College, 1925–1954). In 1954, he became Professor of Medieval and Renaissance English at Cambridge, which position he currently holds. He was married in 1956. His scholarly honors include a D.D. from St. Andrews, a D. ès Lettres from Laval University (Quebec), and election as a Fellow of the Royal Society of Literature and Fellow of the British Academy. His most famous scholarly publication is *The Allegory of Love* (1936; reprinted with corrections, 1938), a study of the medieval courtly love tradition with special emphasis upon its allegorical manifestations in literature.

But it is not as a professor or even as a medieval scholar that C. S. Lewis has attained his chief renown; it is rather as an apologist for the Christian faith. In his recent spiritual autobiography (*Surprised by Joy,* 1955), he informs us that his desertion of the Church of Ireland as a youth, and his acceptance of an atheistic philosophy of life, were followed by a quest for lasting satisfaction, or "joy" — and that this search finally led him, via the writings of George Macdonald, to an adult acceptance of Christian doctrine and membership in the Church of Ireland.[1] One result of his spiritual pilgrimage has been the production of some of the most penetrating theological works of our time, all of them characterized by high literary quality. The most familiar of his writings is undoubtedly *The Screwtape Letters* (1942), the supposed correspondence of a senior devil in hell who instructs a minor demon on earth in the fine art of temptation. Lewis' work entitled *Miracles* (1947) is one of the most trenchant refutations ever written of Hume's argument against the miraculous. His BBC broadcast talks have been published as *The Case for Christianity* (1943) and *Christian Behaviour* (1943). Professor Lewis has also authored a trilogy of adult science fiction novels (*Out of the Silent Planet,* 1938; *Perelandra,* 1943; *That Hideous Strength,* 1945), through which various facets of the Christian gospel are presented allegorically. Allegory was extensively used with the same end in view in his *The Pilgrim's Regress* (1933) and *The Great Divorce* (1946).

The works here mentioned, together with Dr. Lewis' numerous other writings, have led to such evaluations of the man and his literary labors as the following:

Classical Christianity — with or without mysticism — is one of the strongest contenders in the desperate race to replace that discredited secularism now visibly going to pieces. Of all the writers advocating Classical Christianity, none combines versatility, literary skill, and psychological insight so richly as C. S. Lewis. He is peculiarly capable of reaching and influencing the people who will influence the masses day after tomorrow.[2]

When . . . we turn away from reading that is largely vocational— lawyers from legal tomes, doctors from their specialties, clerics from eschatology, educators from standardized tests, scientists from their individual deities of precision—if we no longer read history and biography avidly and if we no longer keep up the pretense that poetry is part of the natural reading of men interested in literature, let us permit C. S. Lewis and others with like gifts to remind us that men still write using a style and discussing a subject matter that is clear and clean; that the modern novelist or dramatist, for example, who frequently disturbs the muddy bottom of the pool and then invites us either to drink of dirty water or to swim in it is not the only type of person from whom we may receive invitations to refresh ourselves.[3]

Experience shows, however, that neither scholarly ability, nor skill as a novelist for adults, nor even good intentions, is any guarantee of success in the field of children's literature. We therefore turn our attention to Professor Lewis' seven Narnia Chronicles themselves.

THE CHRONICLES AS LITERATURE

Plots and Characters

Aristotle, in his *Poetics,* correctly asserted that the two central elements in a dramatic production were its characters and its plot—the latter being of greater consequence than the former. Each of the Narnia books will now be described in terms of these two essential characteristics.

The Lion, the Witch and the Wardrobe introduces the reader, via the adventures of four English children, to the magical realm of Narnia— which is not "another planet, you know; they're part of our world and you could get to them if you went far enough—but a really other world— another Nature—another universe—somewhere you would never reach even if you travelled through the space of this universe for ever and ever." [4] The four children are Peter (a courageous youth on the borderline of adulthood), Susan (his slightly younger sister, rather timid, more interested in becoming an adult than in enjoying her present age), Edmund (their younger brother, of mean disposition at the outset), and Lucy (the youngest of the four, bright, cheerful, spiritually discerning). These Pevensie children were sent to the country mansion of one Professor Digory Kirke in order to be safe from the London air-raids of the Second World War. While exploring and playing Hide-and-Seek in the fascinating old house, the children—first Lucy and then the others—enter Narnia through an old Wardrobe. Narnia time is not like Earth time, so whenever the children return to our world, they discover that no time at all has passed here. The children find Narnia a land of perpetual winter (but without Christmas ever coming), because the country is under the control of a White Witch from the North, who turns into statues all those inhabitants of the country who would oppose her. Edmund, principally out of jealousy toward Peter, sides with the White Witch, and is eventually made thoroughly miserable through his allegiance to her. The Witch's desire is to capture the four children, in order to thwart an old prophecy which says that "When Adam's flesh and Adam's bone / Sits at Cair Paravel [Narnia's capital] in throne, / The evil time will be over and done." The citizens of Narnia (Talking Beasts, Fawns, and like creatures) feel sure that the coming of the children heralds a new age—and that the Great Lion named Aslan will soon destroy the White Witch's power. This is just what happens: the forces of the Witch are conquered in battle; Aslan himself gives his life so that Edmund's treachery will not receive its rightful consequences at the hands of the Witch (but Aslan is then miraculously restored); those turned to stone by the Witch become normal again when Aslan breathes on them; spring comes to Narnia; and the children are crowned Kings and Queens of Narnia, with Peter as High King.

In *Prince Caspian,* the Pevensies return to Narnia. One year has passed according to our time, but several hundred years have gone by in Narnia. The children were in a railway station ready to enter on another school year when—suddenly—they found themselves in Narnia again. Cair Paravel is in ruins. The land has for many generations been under the rule of the Telmarines, who, like the children, are "sons of Adam and daughters of Eve," but who conquered Narnia by an invasion from a neighboring country. Under Telmarine rule, no Talking Beasts or other mythical creatures dare live in the open, and the present (usurper) King has told his nephew, Prince Caspian, that all the old legends are "all nonsense, for babies." Caspian runs away, however, and the inhabitants of "Old Narnia" rally around him and a War of Liberation takes place. Caspian's forces are sorely pressed, and he blows a magic horn which had been given to Susan during her previous adventure in Narnia, and which had been found by the old tutor of the Prince. It was the blowing of this horn that brought the Pevensies into Narnia again. By Aslan's guidance they are led to the place where Caspian's Uncle is defeated. Aslan then gives the Telmarines the choice of remaining in Narnia under Caspian's rule or returning to our world (from which they, as pirates, had originally come—through "one of the chinks or chasms between that world and this"). Some of the Telmarines choose Narnia, but most of the older men refuse to live in a land they cannot rule, and return to the Earth. The Pevensies find that their time to leave Narnia has come; and Aslan tells Peter and Susan that they are "getting too old" to visit Narnia again.

The Voyage of the "Dawn Treader" chronicles Edmund and Lucy's last adventure in Narnia—an adventure in which they are accompanied by their cousin, Eustace Clarence Scrubb. Before his visit to Narnia, Eustace was not the most likable chap in the world.

> He didn't call his Father and Mother "Father" and "Mother," but Harold and Alberta. They were very up-to-date and advanced people. They were vegetarians, non-smokers and teetotallers and wore a special kind of underclothes. . . . Eustace Clarence liked animals, especially beetles, if they were dead and pinned on a card. He liked books if they were books of information and had pictures of grain elevators or of fat foreign children doing exercises in model schools. Eustace Clarence disliked his cousins the four Pevensies. . . . But he was quite glad when he heard that Edmund and Lucy were coming to stay. For deep down inside him he liked bossing and bullying; and . . . he knew that there are dozens of ways to give people a bad time if you are in your own home and they are only visitors.

While gazing at a sea picture in the Scrubb home, Edmund, Lucy, and Eustace find themselves actually drawn into it, and they join King Caspian on a sea expedition. A year of Earth time has passed since Edmund and Lucy's last visit, and three years of Narnian time have gone by. Caspian has set out from Narnia to find seven nobles whom his Uncle, many years before, had gotten rid of by sending to explore "the unknown Eastern Seas beyond the Lone Islands." In the King's service is the mouse-knight Reepicheep, whose valor and singleminded allegiance to Aslan surpasses that of any other character in the Narnia Chronicles; Reepicheep does not wish merely to find the seven lords—he wants to find the country of Aslan himself, which is supposed to lie beyond the world's end. Numerous Odyssey-like adventures occur on this voyage, such as Eustace's transformation into a dragon because of his greed and his restoration by the personal intervention of Aslan after he becomes humble and realizes how selfish he has been. The seven lords never reached the East, it is discovered; one married, settled for security, and ceased his Eastern journey; two died because of the fascination treasure and wealth held for them; one became enmeshed in his own dream-life; and three, at the very "beginning of the end of the world," never quite reached Aslan's country because of spiritual presumption and lack of love. When Caspian's ship, "The Dawn Treader," reaches the border-line between the Narnian world and Aslan's land, only Reepicheep crosses over. Caspian himself cannot go with him because of the respon-sibilities he has as King and because he was unkind to the others near the end of the journey; and Edmund, Lucy, and a transformed Eustace must return to their own world.

In *The Silver Chair,* Eustace and a school friend, Jill Pole, find them-selves in Narnia at the very end of Caspian's reign. Ten years before, the Queen had been killed by a poisonous serpent while she was on a holiday in the northern part of Narnia. Her son, Prince Rilian, sought the serpent to kill it, but instead met a beautiful woman in green and was not seen again. Now Aslan has called Eustace and his friend into Narnia to find the Prince, for Caspian is close to death and has no other heir. Aslan gives them specific instructions, and they discover that when these are not precisely followed difficulties result on every side. They are accom-panied on their journey to the Wild Lands of the North by Puddleglum, a cross between a man and a frog, who though of humorously pessimistic temperament ("what with enemies, and mountains, and rivers to cross, and losing our way, and next to nothing to eat, and sore feet, we'll hardly notice the weather"), is a stalwart servant of Aslan. They discover that the snake and the green lady are one in the same, and that for ten years she has kept Rilian entranced in her underground kingdom of almost total darkness — on the promise that as soon as she has undermined Narnia, she will give him his own land to rule (jointly with her, of course). With the aid of Eustace and Jill, Rilian destroys the Silver Chair which has caused his enchantment, and kills the green lady (the Queen of Under-land), just in time to prevent the conquest of Narnia.

The Horse and His Boy "stands apart from the main cycle."[5] During the reign of High King Peter we are taken south from Narnia into the land of Calormen, whose government is similar to that of a medieval, oriental despotism on Earth. There we meet Shasta, an orphan boy who has been brought up by a harsh fisherman. One day Shasta meets a Narnian Talking Horse who was stolen from Narnia as a foal, and the two determine to escape to Narnia — or at least to Archenland, a kingdom allied to Narnia and directly south of it. The Talking Horse (named "Breehy-hinny-brinny-hoohy-hah," or "Bree" for short!) is a little too vain and proud, and quite critical of others, but is a nominal believer in Aslan, for, as he says, "All Narnians swear by *him*." On their journey, they meet two other émigrés: Aravis, the daughter of a Calormen lord who wished to marry her to an unpleasant old noble, and her Narnian Talking Horse named Hwin. In the Calormen city of Tashbaan, Shasta unexpectedly meets visiting Prince Corin of Archenland (who is almost his double). The two become friends, and express the hope of meeting again if Shasta makes good his escape. Aravis meanwhile overhears the treacherous plot of Rabadash, son of the Calormen King (or "Tisroc"), to capture Archenland without official declaration of war. With Aslan's guidance, Shasta, Aravis, and the Horses reach Archenland in time to save the country; defiant Rabadash is temporarily turned into a donkey by Aslan; Bree discovers what a vital, personal relationship with Aslan can be like; and Shasta finds that he is the long-lost brother of Prince Corin, and the next heir to the Archenland throne.

The Magician's Nephew provides the cosmological setting for all the Chronicles. Here we encounter Professor Digory Kirke again—but this time as a boy, back when "Mr. Sherlock Holmes was still living in Baker Street." Digory and his nextdoor neighbor, Polly Plummer, discover that Digory's Uncle is a magician of the evil, but rather simple-minded, variety. Through his magic they enter "the Wood between the Worlds," a place of connection among the numerous "worlds" (of which ours is only one) in the universe. First they visit a dying world—one which was destroyed by a Queen who, when she saw that she could not rule that world, determined to ruin it by uttering a "Deplorable Word" that she had discovered. Digory's selfish curiosity results in the awakening of that evil Queen, and she follows the children back into our world for a brief time, and then (together with Digory's Uncle and a kind of London cabby) into a third world—Narnia—at the time of its creation. Here they witness Aslan as he builds a world ("when you listened to his song you heard the things he was making up: when you looked round you, you saw them"). Because Digory, a son of Adam, has brought evil (in the person of the Queen—or, as she would later be called, the White Witch) into Aslan's new world, Aslan commissions him to travel to a wonderful Garden in the Western Wild and there to pick an apple from a tree of life. This apple is to be planted in Narnia so that Narnia will have protection against the Witch for many years. Digory accomplishes his mission, and Aslan gives him a similar apple to revive his dying mother at home. The cabby remained in Narnia as her first King. After giving the apple to his mother, Digory buried the core in his backyard, and in later years built a wardrobe out of the tree that grew up from it—the same wardrobe, of course, through which the Pevensies would first enter Narnia.

The Last Battle records the final events in the history of Narnia. Several generations have passed since the reign of Caspian. An evil ape persuades a simple donkey that he should wear a lion's skin and pretend to be Aslan—thereby insuring that the Narnians will follow every order that the ape, as "Aslan's" mediator, gives them. The ape then enters into a compact with Calormenes, and soon many of the Narnians are engaged in slave labor activities by sanction of the pseudo-Aslan. The present King of Narnia, Tirian by name, can hardly believe that the true Aslan would allow his people to fall into slavery, and calls for help out of the past. Eustace and Jill arrive, but they are unable to stop the conquest of Narnia by the Calormenes, for by now many Narnians have come to believe that Aslan and the cruel god of Calormen (called "Tash") are really one ("Tashlan"), and others have become so disillusioned that they believe in the existence of neither. In the final battle, the children and Tirian suddenly find themselves in a Stable on the battlefield—a Stable which had housed the pseudo-Aslan and for a time had actually contained Tash. But "the Stable seen from within and the Stable seen from without are two different places"; indeed, "its inside is bigger than its outside." Inside, they find the previous Kings and Queens of Narnia, and those from our world who had been in Narnia before—the Pevensies, Professor Kirke, etc.—and all of them have become wondrously youthful and yet truly mature. Susan, however, is not among them; she "is no longer a friend of Narnia . . . Whenever you've tried to get her to come and talk about Narnia or do anything about Narnia, she says, 'What wonderful memories you have! Fancy your still thinking about all those funny games we used to play when we were children.' . . . I wish she *would* grow up. She wasted all her school time wanting to be the age she is now, and she'll waste all the rest of her life trying to stay that age." The inside of the Stable is a beautiful land—more beautiful than any they have ever seen. Aslan is there, and he brings about the end of Narnia on the outside of the Stable. Through the Stable door come creatures without number—including all the old animal and mythical friends of past adventures. Each looks into Aslan's face as he passes the doorway, and some go to the left and disappear, while others go to the right into the beautiful countryside. Aslan bounds away to the right—to the West—and all the creatures on his right follow him "farther up and farther in." They discover that they are in a new Narnia—more "real" than the former one.

As one creature puts it, "I have come home at last! This is my real country! I belong here. This is the land I have been looking for all my life, though I never knew it till now. The reason why we loved the old Narnia is that it sometimes looked a little like this." When they arrive at the Garden in the Western Wild, it is Reepicheep who welcomes them; and the Garden turns out to be yet another Narnia—"like an onion: except that as you go in and in, each circle is larger than the last." This Narnia is a spur "jutting out from the great mountains of Aslan," and *real* England is seen as one of the many other spurs. Across the mountains the Pevensies see their own mother and father, and even Professor Kirke's old house—for in the *real* countries "no good thing is destroyed." Aslan then tells them that (as they vaguely suspected) the friends of Narnia were precipitated into the Stable from a fatal railway accident. "Your father and mother and all of you are—as you used to call it in the Shadowlands—dead. The term is over: the holidays have begun. The dream is ended: this is the morning."

"And as He spoke He no longer looked to them like a lion; but the things that began to happen after that were so great and beautiful that I cannot write them. And for us this is the end of all the stories, and we can most truly say that they all lived happily ever after. But for them it was only the beginning of the real story. All their life in this world and all their adventures in Narnia had only been the cover and the title page: now at last they were beginning Chapter One of the Great Story which no one on earth has read: which goes on forever: in which every chapter is better than the one before."

The Allegory

The brief biographical sketch of C. S. Lewis given at the beginning of this paper indicated his strong interest both in Christian apologetics and in allegory. As the reader has already recognized from the plot summaries just presented, the Narnia Chronicles contain powerful and deep Christian allegory woven into their very fiber. It is this allegorical thread, more than any other factor, which makes of the Chronicles "an integrated single conception."[6] The theme is that basic of all themes, Redemption through Christ. In *The Voyage of the "Dawn Treader"* Lucy reads a wonderful story in a Magician's Book, and then tries to remember it. "'How can I have forgotten?,'" she asks. "'It was about a cup and a sword and a tree and a green hill, I know that much. But I can't remember and what *shall* I do?' And she never could remember; ever since that day what Lucy means by a good story is a story which reminds her of the forgotten story in the Magician's Book." [7] And, needless to say, this is also what Professor Lewis means by a good story—one which will remind the reader of the One who was nailed to a tree on his behalf, and who now guides the believer, expects great things of him through faith, and waits to receive him into his everlasting kingdom when his work on earth is done.

Aslan is the Divine Christ—God revealed to creatures in a form in which they can at least partially understand him and love him.[8] In *The Lion, the Witch and the Wardrobe*, Aslan is not ultimately defeated when the Witch (*i.e.*, the Devil) demands, on the basis of "deep magic from the dawn of time" (*i.e.*, God's justice) that Edmund must pay with his life for his volitional allegiance to her. Aslan dies in Edmund's stead, and is resurrected through "deeper magic from *before* the dawn of time" (*i.e.*, God's love). In *Prince Caspian*, Narnia is redeemed from a different evil—from human beings who would force themselves upon and assert control over those whom Christ has put under his own authority and under the authority of the ministers (the Kings of Narnia) whom *he* has chosen. *The Voyage of the "Dawn Treader"* indicates the perils which a man encounters in seeking Christ's kingdom; Reepicheep is a glorious example of the person who "seeks first the Kingdom of God and His righteousness." *The Silver Chair* gives further insight into the strategy of the Demonic, which would plunge us into a world of spiritual darkness by pretending to give us the things to which God has *already* entitled us by His grace.[9] In *The Horse and His Boy* we see Christ's guiding hand over a person's life; at one point Aslan says to Shasta: "I was the lion who forced you to join with Aravis. I was the cat who comforted you among the houses of the dead. I was the lion who drove the jackals from you while you slept . . . , and I was the lion you do not remember who pushed the boat in which you lay, a child near death, so that it came to shore where a man sat, wakeful at midnight, to receive you." [10] *The Magician's Nephew* draws back the curtain on Creation,[11] and on the entrance of sin into a world through pride and presumption; and it shows us how easily a world can be destroyed through the ravages of such sin. In referring to the dying world which she visited, Polly asks, " 'But we're not quite as bad as that world, are we Aslan?' 'Not yet, Daughter of Eve,' he said. 'Not yet. But you are growing more like it. It is not certain that some wicked one of your race will not find out a secret evil as the Deplorable Word and use it to destroy all living things.' " [12] A timely warning on our age of atomic weapons! In *The Last Battle* the Biblical story of the end of human history is graphically portrayed: the Antichrist, the battle of Armageddon, death (represented by the Stable which is larger on the inside than on the outside), the General Resurrection, and the consummation of the Plan of Redemption in a New Heaven and a New Earth.

And Narnia—what does Narnia itself symbolize? Narnia is a world, a state of mind, in which spiritual issues assume clarity, reality, and a place of paramount importance. The Pevensies are forbidden to return to Narnia when they reach adulthood not because Narnia is a mythical land only for children (as is the case in *Peter Pan*), but because they were brought to Narnia originally to learn the most basic lesson in life: that of seeking *first* God's Kingdom. Once learned, this lesson is to be applied in their own world. When the "Dawn Treader" had reached "the very end of the (Narnian) world,"

between them and the foot of the sky there was something so white on the green grass that even with their eagles' eyes they could hardly look at it. They came on and saw that it was a Lamb.

"Come and have breakfast," said the Lamb in its sweet milky voice.

Then they noticed for the first time that there was a fire lit on the grass and fish roasting on it.[13] They sat down and ate the fish, hungry now for the first time for many days. And it was the most delicious food they had ever tasted.

"Please, Lamb," said Lucy, "is this the way to Aslan's country?"

"Not for you," said the Lamb. "For you the door into Aslan's country is from your own world."

"What!" said Edmund. "Is there a way into Aslan's country from our world too?"

"There is a way into my country from all the worlds," said the Lamb; but as he spoke his snowy white flushed into tawny gold and his size changed and he was Aslan himself, towering above them and scattering light from his mane.

"Oh, Aslan," said Lucy. "Will you tell us how to get into your country from our world?"

"I shall be telling you all the time," said Aslan. "But I will not tell you how long or short the way will be; only that it lies across a river [i.e., the river of Death]. But do not fear that, for I am the great Bridge Builder. And now come; I will open the door in the sky and send you to your own land."

"Please, Aslan," said Lucy. "Before we do, will you tell us when we can come back to Narnia again? Please. And Oh, do, do, do make it soon."

"Dearest," said Aslan very gently, "you and your brother will never come back to Narnia."

"Oh, *Aslan*!!" said Edmund and Lucy both together in despairing voices.

"You are too old, children," said Aslan, "and you must begin to come close to your own world now."

"It isn't Narnia, you know," sobbed Lucy. "It's *you*. We shan't meet *you* there. And how can we live, never meeting you?"

"But you shall meet me, dear one," said Aslan.

"Are—are you there too, Sir?" said Edmund.

"I am." said Aslan. "But there I have another name. You must learn to know me by that name. This was the very reason why you were brought to Narnia, that by knowing me here for a little, you may know me better there." [14]

THE CHRONICLES AND THE ADOLESCENT

Appeal

In determining the appropriateness of a book for a given age-group, two fundamental questions must be answered: Will the book appeal to readers of that age? and Does the book have definite value for readers of that age? We begin with the first of these questions, since, as Paul Hazard has pointed out in his *Books, Children, and Men*, adults have frequently done great harm to children by foisting upon them so-called "good" books which in reality have had little appeal for the children themselves.

The Chronicles of Narnia fall into that class of literature known as the "modern imaginative story" or "literary fairy tale," of which the most distinguished exemplar is undoubtedly *Alice in Wonderland*. The critics, in fact, have not been slow to class Professor Lewis' books with the latter. *The Manchester Guardian* wrote of *The Voyage of the "Dawn Treader,"* "C. S. Lewis keeps up his power to enter other worlds in the same dream-like and certain way as Hans Andersen or Lewis Carroll"; and *Books of Today* stated in its review of *The Lion, the Witch and the Wardrobe,* "This fairy tale is as good as any children's book written in the last twenty years and not unworthy to share a shelf with *Alice in Wonderland*."

The problem, of course, is to discover at what age such imaginative stories exercise their appeal to readers. It is true that "the reading of fantasy really knows no age limits"; [15] and it is also true that "some children heartily dislike fantasy." [16] But the question still remains: For those who like fantasy, at what age do books of the *Alice in Wonderland* variety have the deepest and most comprehensive appeal? Arbuthnot's decision with regard to *Alice* seems directly applicable to the Narnia Chronicles:

> When college students are asked what books they remember enjoying as children there is more disagreement over *Alice* than over any other book. Some disliked it heartily or were bored by it; some say *Alice* was one of their favorite books, not as children but at the high-school age. This is perhaps where it really belongs. Most of those who liked *Alice* as children, ten or under had heard it read aloud by adults who enjoyed it.[17]

The greatest pleasure will undoubtedly be derived from the Narnia Chronicles when they can be appreciated both on the fantasy-adventure and on the allegorical level.[18] Until one reaches early adolescence, the allegory will almost certainly escape him; but if he waits until adulthood to read the tales, the adventure element may not exercise the breathless hold on him which it could at a younger age. In discussing "literature for young adolescents" (ages 13–14, grades 7–8), Bess Porter Adams includes in the constellation of reading interests eight items, of which five ("from atoms to planets," "pleasure with animals," "historical and adventure stories," "legendary hero tales," "books for laughter") are directly applicable to the Narnia Chronicles;[19] and she asserts: "Active as the adolescent is, he still finds time for day dream. . . . Books may help satisfy the longings which lead to daydreaming. The best of the adventure and imaginative stories stimulate and satisfy the reader's desire for romantic adventure while leaving him eager for personal action."[20] If this is granted, then there should be little doubt concerning the appeal of the Narnia books for the sensitive, imaginative young adolescent of junior high school age.

Value

But by no means all of the printed material which appeals to the adolescent is worth the time required to read it. In the discussion which followed his talk on children's literature at the Bournemouth Conference of the Library Association, Professor Lewis was questioned on the practical value of his fantasy tales; his answer is very illuminating.

> Mr. L. M. Bickerton (Worthing) considered that Dr. Lewis's paper had raised points that we as librarians must consider—our policy had been to provide more and more of the practical type of book

written by authors like Ransome and De Selincourt that taught children how to handle boats, etc., but he wondered what practical use fantasy, such as Dr. Lewis advocated, could have for the child. Dr. Lewis agreed that practical things were first class, but that although fantasy might not help a boy to build a boat, it would help him immensely should he ever find himself on a sinking boat.[21]

Here the basic issue is raised as to the value of the Narnia Chronicles: Does the child face significant problems of a deeper nature than material ones—problems which the Narnia books can aid in solving? Professor Lewis says Yes, and refers to such a basic religio-philosophical problem as death.

Robert J. Havighurst confirms Dr. Lewis' judgement when he presents as one of the ten specific "developmental tasks" of adolescence the problem of "acquiring a set of values and an ethical system as a guide to behavior,"[22] and states that "the crowning accomplishment of adolescence is the achieving of a mature set of values and a set of ethical controls that characterize a good man and a good citizen."[23] As the Christian Church has recognized through its age-old rite of Confirmation (normally entered upon during early adolescence), the adolescent years are crucial for decision-making in the matter of a personal *Weltanschauung* or world-view.[24] If this is the case, we are led to ask: Can the Narnia Chronicles in fact aid in providing the adolescent with a meaningful life-orientation?

In his lecture "On Three Ways of Writing for Children," Professor Lewis says, "The two theories [of the fairy tale] which are most often in my mind are those of Tolkien and of Jung," and expresses the opinion that Tolkien's essay "is perhaps the most important contribution to the subject that anyone has yet made."[25] Jung's view (widely accepted both among psychoanalysts and among folklore scholars today) is that the fairy tale presents concepts and images which correspond to the basic universal symbols (or "Archetypes") in man's unconscious mind.[26] Lewis agrees with this, but feels that Jung does not go far enough. "The mystery of primordial images is deeper, their origin more remote, their cave more hid, their fountain less accessible than those suspect who have yet dug deepest, sounded with the longest cord, or journeyed farthest in the wilderness."[27] J. R. R. Tolkien, Dr. Lewis believes, has succeeded in explaining the central significance of the fairy tale and its importance for life-orientation. Tolkien summarizes his position as follows:

The Gospels contain . . . a story of a larger kind which embraces all the essence of fairy-stories. They contain many marvels — peculiarly artistic, beautiful, and moving; "mythical" in their perfect, self-contained significance; and at the same time powerfully symbolic and allegorical; and among the marvels is the greatest and most complete conceivable eucatastrophe. The Birth of Christ is the eucatastrophe of Man's history. The Resurrection is the eucatastrophe of the story of the Incarnation. This story begins and ends in joy. It has pre-eminently the "inner consistency of reality." There is no tale ever told that men would rather find was true, and none which so many sceptical men have accepted as true on its own merits. For the Art of it has the supremely convincing tone of Primary Art, that is, of Creation. To reject it leads either to sadness or to wrath.

It is not difficult to imagine the peculiar excitement and joy that one would feel, if any specially beautiful fairy-story were found to be "primarily" true, its narrative to be history, without thereby necessarily losing the mythical or allegorical significance that it had possessed. . . . The joy would have exactly the same quality, if not the same degree, as the joy which the "turn" in a fairy-story gives: such has the very taste of primary truth. (Otherwise its name would not be joy.[28]) It looks forward (or backward: the direction in this regard is unimportant) to the Great Eucatastrophe. The Christian joy, the *Gloria,* is of the same kind; but it is pre-eminently (infinitely, if our capacity were not finite) high and joyous. Because this story is supreme; and it is true. Art has been verified. God is the Lord, of angels, and of men — and of elves. Legend and History have met and fused.[29]

To Tolkien and to Lewis, tales such as the Narnia Chronicles can, by their very nature, serve as pointers to the great theme of Christian Redemption. Moreover, they will establish in the hearts of the sensitive reader an appreciation of, and a longing for, the Christian Story. If one believes that ethics cannot survive without proper inner motivation; that religion provides the only really effective ethical impetus which men have ever experienced; that Jesus made no mistake when he said, "I am the Way, the Truth, and the Life: no man cometh unto the Father, but by me"[30] (*i.e.,* that Aslan and Tash can never be fused into a Tashlan); and that adolescents in our culture need personal fellowship with the Lord Jesus more than they need anything else — if we believe these things, then we will unquestionably find the Chronicles of Narnia of lasting value to the adolescents whom we seek to win for Christ.

REFERENCES

1. Lewis acknowledged his debt to Macdonald by editing *George Macdonald: An Anthology* in 1946.
2. Chad Walsh, *C. S. Lewis: Apostle to the Skeptics* (New York, Macmillan, 1949), p. 171. The Bibliography at the end of Walsh's book gives a complete description of Lewis' publications through 1949. David Daiches, one of my former professors at Cornell University and now a professor at Cambridge University, writes of Lewis: "Such religious revival as there has been in post-war Britain appears to have been confined to the better educated. Its symbol is not Billy Graham, the American evangelist whose carefully staged campaigns caused considerable temporary excitement in 1954 and 1955, but, say, C. S. Lewis, a literary scholar and critic of considerable brilliance and at the same time a highly sophisticated Christian apologist," (*The Present Age in British Literature* [Bloomington, Indiana University Press, 1958], p. 13).
3. George F. Cassell, *Clive Staples Lewis* (Chicago, Chicago Literary Club, 1950), pp. 25–26.
4. Lewis, *The Magician's Nephew* (New York, Macmillan, 1955), pp. 18–19. The Narnia Chronicles can be most cheaply obtained in their British editions (write: The Children's Bookshop, 22 Broad Street, Oxford).
5. M. S. Crouch, "Chronicles of Narnia," *Junior Bookshelf*, XX (Nov., 1956), 249.
6. Frank M. Gardner, "The Carnegie Medal Award for 1956," *Library Association Record*, LIX; 4th series, XXIV (May, 1957), 168.
7. Lewis, *The Voyage of the "Dawn Treader"* (London, Bles, 1952), p. 144. Cf. Lewis, "On Stories," *Essays Presented to Charles Williams* (London, Oxford University Press, 1947), pp. 90–105.
8. Aslan is not simply "God," as Crouch asserts (*op. cit.,* p. 252), for he is referred to on several occasions as "the son of the Emperor over Sea" (*e.g.* in *The Voyage of the "Dawn Treader,"* p. 104).
9. Cf. Satan's appeal to Jesus in the wilderness: "The devil, taking him up into an high mountain, shewed unto him all the kingdoms of the world in a moment of time. And the devil said unto him, All this power will I give thee, and the glory of them: for that is delivered unto me; and to whomsoever I will I give it. If thou therefore wilt worship me, all shall be thine" (Luke 4:5–7).
10. Lewis, *The Horse and His Boy* (London, Bles, 1954), p. 147.
11. Dr. Lewis is theologically correct in viewing Aslan (Christ) as Creator. According to John: "the word" (Christ) "was God. The same was at the beginning with God. All things were made by him; and without him was not any thing made that was made" (vs. 1–3).
12. *The Magician's Nephew,* pp. 159–60.
13. Cf. Christ's post-Resurrection appearance to his disciples as recorded in John 21.
14. *The Voyage of the "Dawn Treader,"* pp. 221–22.
15. Josette Frank, *Your Child's Reading Today* (Garden City, Doubleday, 1954), p. 127. Cf. Lillian H. Smith, *The Unreluctant Years* (Chicago, American Library Association, 1953), chap. 10 ("Fantasy"), pp. 149–62.
16. May Hill Arbuthnot, *Children and Books* (Chicago, Scott, Foresman, 1947), p. 292.
17. *Ibid.*
18. The following statement by Gardner concerning the Narnia Chronicles is, in my opinion, woefully inadequate: "There is the same underlying theme of Christian mysticism as there is in Dr. Lewis' 'Perelandra' trilogy of adult novels, but that need not trouble the young reader. To him or her these are stories of an almost real but marvellous world, visited from time to time by young human beings, who have to prove their honour and worthiness to be in Narnia [!]" (*loc. cit.*).
19. Bess Porter Adams, *About Books and Children; Historical Survey of Children's Literature* (New York, Holt, 1953), chap. 9, pp. 253–57.
20. *Ibid.,* p. 256. Note in this connection the excellent essay by Padraic Colum entitled "Imagination and Children's Literature" and included in Phyllis Fenner, *The Proof of the Pudding: What Children Read* (New York, John Day, 1957), pp. 222–25.

21. Lewis, "On Three Ways of Writing for Children," *Library Association. Proceedings, Papers and Summaries of Discussions at the Bournemouth Conference 29th April to 2nd May 1952* (London Library Association, 1952), p. 28 ("Discussion").

22. Robert J. Havighurst, *Developmental Tasks and Education,* 2d ed. (New York, Longman's Green, 1952), pp. 62–71. Havighurst gives empirical data in support of this adolescent task in his *Human Development and Education* (New York, Longmans, Green, 1953), pp. 311–17.

23. *Ibid.,* p. 142.

24. Note that Amelia H. Munson astutely includes as one of five "dominant characteristics" of adolescence "audacity of belief" (*An Ample Field* [Chicago, American Library Association, 1950], p. 8).

25. Lewis, "On Three Ways of Writing for Children," p. 24.

26. See, *e.g.,* C. G. Jung and K. Kerényi, *Einführung in das Wesen der Mythologie,* 4th ed. (Zürich, Rhein-Verlag, 1951).

27. Lewis, "Psycho-analysis and Literary Criticism," *Essays and Studies by Members of the English Association,* XXVII (1941), 21.

28. Cf. the title of C. S. Lewis' autobiography, referred to above: *Surprised by Joy.*

29. J. R. R. Tolkien, "On Fairy-Stories," *Essays Presented to Charles Williams,* pp. 83–84.

30. John 14:6.

EDITORS' NOTE

Clive Staples Lewis was born in Belfast, Ireland, in 1898 and died in Oxford, England, in 1963. He was the younger of two sons in a motherless home. Since his father was working and his brother was at boarding school, he spent a great deal of time alone in a house full of books. This may have accounted for his literary bent.

It was not until 1950 that he published the first volume of *The Chronicles of Narnia—The Lion, the Witch and the Wardrobe—*which he dedicated to his goddaughter. The seven books which comprise *The Chronicles* are his only stories for children. Lewis felt that the world of imagination is a place where adults and children can meet as equals. His *Chronicles,* as he hoped they would be, are tales for readers of all ages.

His awards include the 1956 Carnegie Medal (given annually for a children's book of outstanding merit written by a British subject and published in the United Kingdom) for *The Last Battle,* and the 1962 Lewis Carroll Shelf Award (given by the University of Wisconsin to a book worthy of sitting on the shelf with *Alice in Wonderland*) for *The Lion, the Witch and the Wardrobe.*

Astrid Lindgren, the Swedish Writer of Children's Books *

IN 1944, fairly late in life, Astrid Lindgren published her first book which was entitled *Britt-Mari lättar sitt hjärta* (*Britt-Mari Opens Her Heart*). With its acute understanding of a child's mind and the breezy freshness of its style this book gave promise of a future attractive writer of children's books.

This promise was amply fulfilled in her second book entitled *Pippi Langstrump* (*Pippi Longstocking*) which, it is interesting to note, was the first attempt made by the author to write a book for children. The moderate success of *Britt-Mari lättar sitt hjärta* persuaded her publisher to produce *Pippi Longstocking* which, some time before the publication of *Britt-Mari,* had been rejected by another publisher.

It would be unfair to judge the quality of Astrid Lindgren's writing by the fantastic and often nonsensical actions performed by Pippi, who is the central figure in three of the writer's most popular books. The success of this trilogy demonstrates how much children appreciate nonsense and, by the reactions of adults towards Pippi's every day antics and bravado, how little many grown up people appreciate the unreality and immaturity of the child's world.

In Sweden some parents and teachers have criticised Pippi's unconventional behaviour and language. Here opinion stands against opinion and it would be hard for one side to convince the other regarding what is right and wrong about child behaviour. There can be few adults, however,

* By Sten Hagliden. Reprinted by permission from *The Junior Bookshelf* 23 (July 1959), 113–121.

who would deny the uncommonly fresh humour, the wealth of bright ideas and genuine hearty character of Pippi Longstocking.

Pippi, a little girl with red pigtails, does all manner of strange, impossible and unconventional things. She sleeps on her bed with her feet where her head should be. She is so strong that she can lift her horse on to the veranda of her house, and as a "turn up stuffer" — a characteristic that can only be understood by reading her adventures — she is perfectly ruthless and yet so tender and careful of a small wounded bird. Clearly, therefore, Pippi leads a fantastic yet real and free life in her house, Villa Villekulla, and also in the South Seas where her later adventures are laid.

In the South Seas Pippi reveals her giant strength. When Tommy, her native play-mate, falls into the sea where a shark rushes to get a fine morsel, Pippi without hesitation jumps into the water. She takes the bloodthirsty beast by both hands and keeps him above water.

"'Aren't you ashamed of yourself?' she cries. The shark looked around, surprised and very ill at ease by bad conscience and lack of water for his lungs. 'Promise never to do such a cruel thing again and I will let you go.' Then with all her strength she throws the shark far into the sea." Such unusual and vivacious actions ensure the character of Pippi Longstocking a place amongst the classic figures in Swedish children's books.

If funny incidents bubble up in the three books about Pippi, Astrid Lindgren's humour is more subdued in the stories about the Bullerby children. The quality of her humour is, however, none the worse for that, rather the opposite. The question is whether Astrid Lindgren in the Bullerby books does not reach furthest as an entertaining story teller, since she shows in these three volumes what a fine and deep child psychologist she is. Listen, for instance, to Lisa at Bullerby, telling about her beloved grandpa. "In summertime he usually sits underneath the big elm tree that grows on the lawn just outside the North Farm. There he sits and lets the sun shine on him and then suddenly he says: 'Well, well, well!' We asked him why he says 'Well, well, well!' and then Grandpa told us that he speaks like that because he thinks of his youth. But imagine that there is such a nice Grandpa as ours! I like him so much. I would much rather have him than a dog."

Comic incidents — so common in *Pippi Longstocking* — appear here too. They flower also in *Kajsa Kavat* (*Kate Courageous*) — read, for instance, the story *Hoppa Högst* (*To Jump Highest*) — a collection of short stories for children, often characterized by vivid realism.

That Astrid Lindgren understands and also can write about adolescent youth with its unrest, its sudden movements between sentimental affection and aggressive opposition, and its longing for love, is well demonstrated in such books as *Kerstin och jag* (*Kerstin and I*) and in the Kati books—*Kati i Amerika, Kati vid Kaptensgatan* and *Kati i Paris* (*Kati in America, Kati at Captain Street* and *Kati in Paris*). Here the author also shows at frequent intervals her sparkling wittiness.

She has also written picture books of undoubted value for small children. Another type of book is the *Bill Bergson* series. What fine powers of descriptive writing the author shows in the three books about this remarkable detective. It is not only her invention of the story and the concentration of suspense that fascinates the reader. The whole gallery of characters and the summer atmosphere of the small town are given with unusual clarity. Sometimes the summer atmosphere assumes a dark, threatening almost frightening aspect, as when Eva-Lotta during a thunder storm meets the old man Gren's murderer and flees in wild panic. This episode in *Mästerdetektiven Blomkvist lever farligt* (*Bill Bergson Lives Dangerously*) has an etched realism, worthy of any great artist.

Astrid Lindgren has let the events of the Bill Bergson books take place at Vimmerby, her native town on the Swedish East coast, which to some extent she has romanticized. If these books are read aloud to children they listen with fascinated attention.

It is not easy to judge how Astrid Lindgren's work would stand the test of time if she had not written *Nils Karlsson Pyssling* (*Niels, The Midget*) and *Mio, Min Mio* (*Mio, My Son*). These two books which have much in common, have in a way crowned all her books. The former includes the story *Allra käraste syster* (*Most Dear Sister*), the most gentle and the tenderest semi-fairy tale written in the Swedish language. These tales confirm that Astrid Lindgren is not only an entertaining writer but that in her nature she also possesses a deeper quality, an affinity with and tenderness towards the unhappy and downtrodden. This is especially revealed in *Mio, My Son,* where in a finely woven web of symbolic writing she shows her sensitive and optimistic attitude to life.

Rasmus på Luffen (*Rasmus and The Vagabond*) is a most lively book. The story is about Rasmus, the orphan boy, who lived at the beginning of the twentieth century. Rasmus leaves the orphanage and walks out on to the highways and byways. There he encounters Oskar, the tramp, who is so warmhearted and quiet. Oskar has a home, but in summer time his urge compels him to leave hearth and home for the open road. Oskar and Rasmus certainly have a number of varying experiences, both humdrum and mysterious. The latter culminate when Oskar and Rasmus meet Lif and Liander, two suspect characters, who are capable of the most unworthy deeds. By Rasmus' ingenuity and with Oskar's help the two criminals are handed over to the police. In the end Rasmus finds a home with

Oskar and his wife, Martina. "He stopped on the porch and waited for Oskar. There was his kitten lying, asleep in the sunshine. Yes, it was a miraculous day. He had a lake, a cat, a father, and a mother. He had a home!"

With a singularly strong intuition Astrid Lindgren interprets a lonely, unwanted child with personal troubles, shyness and need of care and love. The story is enriched by realistic pictures of the beautiful Swedish "roadside summer" and of the unlimited freedom enjoyed by tramps on highroads now so rapidly being superseded by the tarred motor roads of our time. Although *Rasmus and The Vagabond* is written for children, the present writer feels that the young man of twenty and the old lady of eighty could read the story with the same interest and enthusiasm.

It should be noted that the Rasmus who appears in the author's next work, *Rasmus, Pontus och Toker* (*Rasmus, Pontus and Toker*), is not the same as the character in her previous book. The surname of this Rasmus is Persson and he is the son of a kindhearted policeman who, like many of his kind, is shrewd and quick. Pontus is one of Rasmus' school-fellows and "Toker" is the faithful dog. Through the temptations of a circus the trio fall in with Alfredo, a man who in spite of his bulk is both wily and smart. Ernst, his assistant, is no better. They both covet a nobleman's treasure of silver which they succeed in stealing. That is, however, not the worst that happens; they steal and capture "Toker," the best and finest dog of all centuries. Children's strong feeling for animals is the new element in this book.

Finally, a few words about Astrid Lindgren's latest book *Barnen på Bråkmakaregatan* (1958) (*The Children in Trouble Maker Street*), which is related to the "Bullerby" books. Jonas and his two sisters, Maria and Lotta at Pottery Street lead a life just as pleasant and nice as that of the Bullerby children. Lotta enjoys herself and is the most enjoyable of the three characters. Once when Lotta had a cold in her head she walked into a shop, she sniffled and sniffled and finally there was a lady in the shop who said to her: "I say, haven't you got a hanky?" — "Certainly, but I don't lend it to people I don't know."

Astrid Lindgren has won a great deal of recognition for her work. The first time that the Swedish Nils Holgersson Plaque was awarded — it is the finest mark of distinction for any writer of books for children and young people — it went to Astrid Lindgren. She has been given several other awards, and in the summer of 1958 she received — at the Fifth Conference of the International Board on Books for Young People in Florence — the Hans Christian Andersen Medal.

It can be said without exaggeration that in Sweden she is looked upon as ranking amongst the finest contemporary writers of children's books.

In expressing her thanks at Florence she said amongst other things: "Sometimes people ask me: 'Couldn't you write a book for adults?' as if they meant that now I have written so many children's books it is about time I did something better. The truth is I do not want to write for adults! I want to write for readers who can create miracles, and you know children do this when they read."

Allow me to conclude this article by quoting a few words from the same speech: "Children in our day view films, listen in, look at T.V., read comics — it may be interesting but it has not very much to do with imagination. A child alone with its books creates in the secret room of its mind its own pictures which surpass everything else. Such pictures are necessary for all mankind. The day when children's imagination no longer can create those pictures, will be a day of loss to our race."

EDITORS' NOTE

Astrid Lindgren was born on a farm in Sweden. After completing her schooling she worked in a newspaper office. She is married and has a son and daughter. Presently she is an editor in a Swedish publishing house.

Although Miss Lindgren did a great deal of creative writing during her school days, as an adult she did not have enough confidence in her writing ability to continue her creative endeavors. In 1944, however, while walking in Stockholm, she slipped in the snow and broke her ankle. She was forced to stay in bed, and this confinement resulted in *Pippi Longstockings,* her first book for children.

Miss Lindgren has written over twenty-five books and has made several children's films. She also worked on a television series about Pippi. Her most recent books are *Karlsson-on-the-Roof* (Viking, 1971), and *Emil's Pranks* (Follett, 1971).

Among Astrid Lindgren's awards and honors is the coveted Hans Christian Andersen Award (given biennially by the International Board on Books for Young People in recognition of the individual's entire body of work), which she received in 1958. Her book, *Sia Lives on Kilimanjaro,* received a *New York Herald Tribune* Children's Spring Festival Award in 1959, and *The Tomten* received a 1970 Lewis Carroll Shelf Award (given annually to books worthy of sitting on the shelf with *Alice in Wonderland*).

Miss Lindgren spends her winters in an apartment in Stockholm and her summers in a house by the Baltic Sea, about fifty-six miles from Stockholm. She says she writes most of her books on the little balcony of her summer house, where she can keep one eye on her writing and the other on the water and the ships passing by.

My Books for Children*

AMONG THE MANY varied things I have done in my life few have given me more and greater satisfactions than my children's books. For an artist, to work for others means compromises which, however reasonable they may be, often leave the initial idea marred, transformed, devitalized.

That is why I have chosen, for my children's books, to collaborate with no one, but rather to invent, write and illustrate my own stories. I know that there are better writers and better illustrators, but I hope to achieve a coherence between form and content which even the closest, most intimate co-operation between different people cannot reach.

When a story takes shape in my imagination, it does so in sentences and images. Sometimes the words trail the pictures and often it is the other way around, but the give and take between the two happens almost simultaneously in the privacy of my own mind. And so the form expresses the content in a direct, convincing manner.

In the last six years I have done five books: four fables and a picture book of a very special kind. They are for children from three to six years old. I did not make that decision—my publisher did. People who buy a book for a particular child find the indication of an age bracket helpful. But I have had many letters from children who are older than six telling me that they like my books. Besides, I am fifty-four years old and I too like them.

* By Leo Lionni. This article is reprinted by permission from the October 1964 issue of the *Wilson Library Bulletin;* pp. 142–145. Copyright © 1964 by the H. W. Wilson Company.

When I have a story in mind I am not conscious of the average age of my potential readers. I believe, in fact, that a good children's book should appeal to all people who have not completely lost their original joy and wonder in life. When I am asked the embarrassing question of what do I know about children, their psychology, and their needs, I must confess my total ignorance. I know no more about children than the average parent or grandparent. I like to watch them, and when they are exceptionally sweet I like to hold them on my knee. But often I have not much patience for them. This is childish of me, perhaps, since children have very little patience with other children. The fact is that I really don't make books for children at all. I make them for that part of us, of myself and of my friends, which has never changed, which is still child.

The wonder I feel when I lie in the grass watching a small world of giants, in which blades of grass are sequoia trees and a beetle a charging rhinoceros, has not changed since I was a little boy. I can still walk the beach for hours looking for a perfectly round or heart-shaped pebble. And my daydreams are still very much the same. In the comfortable covers of my bed I still challenge dragons and despite the love for my wife to whom I have been happily married for more than 30 years, I still save blond maidens from the claws of monsters on barren mountaintops.

A criticism that has often been made of my books and of my work in general is the absence of a consistent personal style. Most illustrators evolve a manner, which identifies them instantly, even if their signature is absent from their work. This technique, this comfortable form, is used no matter what the content is and no matter how it changes from story to story.

This preoccupation with style often derives from the artist's desire to have a personality which differentiates him from his colleagues. Often it is simply laziness. But sometimes it is an overwhelming urge to forge things into a personal mold. Many of my colleagues are neither artificially constructed personalities, nor lazy exploiters of a few easy mannerisms. They sincerely and almost unknowingly repeat the same attitudes and gestures. They see all colors through their particular prism and use the lines and shapes that are congenial to them over and over again.

It just happens that I do not aspire to that sort of style. I find greater joy and satisfaction in developing a form for each idea. Style, the way I see it, is deeper, more subtle and therefore more difficult to detect. Style is more than a technical mannerism, more than a consistent way to apply colors or to wiggle a line. It is a method of going directly to the heart of each situation and seeing and depicting it in its own specific term; it is participating in each particular mood and finding the proper technique for expressing it; it is presenting clearly, without detours and unnecessary frills, what is talked about; it is understanding and feeling about characters and environments the way we feel about ourselves and our world. A formal, independent style does not allow such complete identification; it does not permit each story, each character to live its own life. It dresses the actors with the same costumes, over and over again, no matter what their play is and no matter what their roles are.

You may have asked yourselves, when you saw my books: birds, worms, fish, flowers, pebbles . . . what about people? Of course my books, like all fables, are about people. Worms don't measure, torn paper doesn't go to school, little fish don't organize, birds don't engage in philanthropy, and pebbles don't make words. My characters are humans in disguise and their little problems and situations are human problems, human situations. The game of identifying, of finding ourselves in the things around us is as old as history. We understand things only in terms of ourselves and in reference to ourselves.

The child must be able to identify with the characters in my books, otherwise my stories will remain outside of him, to be looked at, at the most, as a thing not needed. Our capacity to identify, to feel pain and joy that is not our own, is our greatest gift. When it fails us, we become cruel and dangerous to others and to ourselves. It is important that children be encouraged to identify, to find themselves in others.

And then there is another aspect of the allegory as a storytelling technique. It is easier to isolate situations, to bring them to a clean, uncluttered, symbolic pitch *outside* of ourselves. What a ponderous, complex story *Swimmy* would have been if some cruel dictator had slaughtered a whole village and only a little boy had been able to escape. One would have had to describe a plausible historical background and justify the characters in all the intricacies of human terms. Of course one can write such stories. Tolstoy could, Hemingway could. But I am not a novelist. To tell and illustrate such an epic in 30 pages for small children would be an absurd task.

The protagonist of my books is often an individual who is, because of special circumstances, an outcast, a rebel, a victim, or a hero. His story ends happily because of his intelligence (the inchworm), his vitality and resourcefulness (Swimmy), his goodness (Tico), or simply because his will and patience turn the law of averages to his advantage. Often he has to learn through suffering (Little Blue, Swimmy, Tico), but it is always his own vitality, his discovery that life is a positive, exciting fact, that makes him come out on top.

I have no programs for my books, no conscious direction which I force myself to follow. The world which excites me, like Swimmy's world, is too vast and too varied for that. I must confess that the moment a story is formed in my mind, I always have a moment of panic in which I ask myself: is there another story just as good? Will this be the last one?

But this insecurity which so often accompanies the termination of works of fiction is irrational. The world in which we move is an ever-changing spectacle, revealing around each corner new adventures, new beauty and, of course, new problems. This infinite stream of experiences will never run dry. It is in the realities around me, in fact, that I find the assurance that my work will continue, for it is there that I will always find the stuff for my stories.

I like to write about birds because I have birds at home: parrots, pigeons, chickens, and finches. I like to write about fish because I used to have an aquarium and I cannot pass a bridge without stopping to search the stream for its mysterious inhabitants. I like to draw plants because at home we have an olive grove and a vineyard and in the spring the soil bursts with wild flowers that no one planted or planned. And I like to draw pebbles because there are really many pebbles on my beach. I am always looking for a perfectly round one, although I know that I can only find one on a billiard table.

I want my stories to have a beginning, a development, and an end. No matter how modest they are, they must have the ingredients of the classical drama: suspense and resolution. They should also have a moral. In some of my stories, the moral is quite simple and obvious; in others it may be more difficult to articulate. Their intent is not always a warning that could be summed up in a few words. More often my stories are meant to stimulate the mind, to create an awareness, to destroy a prejudice. In that sense, they may not have a moral, but in their intentions, at least, they *are* moral.

I have often been asked about hidden meanings. Is *Little Blue and Little Yellow* a book about racial segregation? Does *Swimmy* have Marxist implications? Does *Inch by Inch* deal with space and time? Is *Tico* (about to be published) a Freudian fable of love and hate?

To all these questions I must, of course, answer, No. I do not set out with such programmatic notions in mind. Yet all works of art, no matter how simple in scope, must have more than one level of meaning. Children's books are no exception. Meanings that are veiled and implied often take a more permanent place in one's heart and mind than the ones that are too explicitly hammered into one's consciousness. Children, especially, tend to resist overt pressure of authority by forgetting. To help them search and discover for themselves a value system that will be personally and socially useful is, I believe, a more promising endeavor.

The kind of care that is taken in printing books is, I believe, very important. Children must grow up with a sense of quality, of excellence. To have little respect for our materials and for the things we make means to have little respect for the people for whom these things are meant. Shoddy workmanship makes for a shoddy environment for Man. There are perhaps more dramatic roles for the artist in our industrial society, but I feel that one of our major responsibilities is to measure the standards of the mass-produced objects we design with the same exacting yardstick we use for our own artifacts. Children, especially, will have to learn, through our example, the satisfactions of quality.

I remember that when I was a child I admired the way my uncle drew. He was an architect but he drew portraits of all of us. I was fascinated by his cross-hatching, by the way he patiently built up the shadows in his drawings. Those memories disappeared in the turmoil of my adult life only to come back in a more tangible form: the quest for quality which I want to transmit in turn to the children who read my books.

EDITORS' NOTE

Leo Lionni was born in Amsterdam in 1910. He spent his childhood in Holland and Belgium and received a Ph.D. in Economics from the University of Genoa, Italy. As an artist and designer he is self-taught.

In 1939 he came to the United States, where he was Art Director for N. W. Ayer and Son, a Philadelphia advertising agency. Later he served as Art Director of Fortune Magazine, Design Director for Olivetti Corporation, head of the Graphic Design Department at the Parsons School of Design, and co-editor of *Print*.

Mr. Lionni has won many national and international awards for his work as an art director and illustrator. In 1955, the National Society of Art Directors named him "Art Director of the Year," and in 1956, he received the Architectural League Gold Medal for Architecture.

One-man exhibitions of his paintings have been held in numerous museums and art galleries both here and abroad. In 1967, Lionni was appointed "George Miller" lecturer at the University of Illinois, and received a grant from the Graham Foundation for Advanced Studies in Fine Arts. He is a former President of the American Institute of Graphic Arts and a member of the Alliance Graphique Internationale.

Leo Lionni has also won both national and international awards for his children's books. These include the German Government Illustrated Book Award, the "Golden Apple," at the First International Biennial of Book Illustration in Bratislava, Czechoslovakia; the 1962 Lewis Carroll Shelf Award (worthy to sit on the shelf with *Alice in Wonderland*) for *Inch by Inch; The New York Times* list of best illustrated books of the year for *Little Blue and Little Yellow* in 1959, *Inch by Inch* in 1960, *Swimmy* in 1963, and *Frederick* in 1967; runner-up for the Caldecott Medal for *Inch by Inch* in 1961, *Swimmy* in 1964, *Frederick* in 1968, and *Alexander and the Wind-Up Mouse* in 1970. Two of his books have also won prizes for excellence in design and artistic merit from the American Institute of Graphic Arts Children's Book Show—*Frederick,* in 1968, and *Alexander and the Wind-Up Mouse,* in 1970.

Mr. Lionni's most recent books are *Fish Is Fish* (1970) and *Theodore and the Talking Mushroom* (1971). Presently, he lives in Lavagna, Italy, where he is busy with painting, writing and film-making.

Robert McCloskey:
Master of Humorous Realism *

THERE IS A STORY about a little boy who had spent hours of satisfaction with *Blueberries for Sal*. One day he approached the librarian at
the children's division and asked hopefully: "Do you have any more
books about little kids picking things?" His delight in the story, his re-
assurance through its theme, and his enchantment with the pictures led
the boy to call for more.

For many years children and adults have been calling for more from
Robert McCloskey, one of the great figures in literature for children
today. The fact that he has twice won the Caldecott Award for distinguished illustrations—the first person to win the honor a second time—
attests to his artistic skill, which in workmanship and quality is extensive.
But in both pictures and writing McCloskey has brought a gentle humor,
what Ruth Sawyer calls "a simmering of fun in the everyday run of
things." [1] This quality, plus the ability to portray facets of ordinary but
real living which are familiar to all of us, creates a kind of magnet that
draws us together, like "little kids picking things." Perhaps seldom has an
individual in his representation of reality verging on the comic made
greater use of his own background and personal characteristics in his
work than has Robert McCloskey.

McCloskey is an author, artist, inventor, humorist, musician, genial
satirist, and portrayer of authentic Americana. He is a shy, modest, re-
tiring person whose eyes look through dark-rimmed glasses in his own

* By Helen W. Painter. From *Elementary English* 45 (February 1968), 145–158. Reprinted
with the permission of the National Council of Teachers of English and Helen W. Painter.

special way of seeing the world and whose quiet voice retains a boyish quality that causes Lentil and Homer suddenly to flash into mind. However, just what has been his life? And what ideas and personal philosophy has he given to children and to the world? Let us look closely.

John Robert McCloskey was born in Hamilton, Ohio, on September 15, 1914. Those people who have watched *The Lively Art of Picture Books* will recall the big, white house where he was born and also the peak of the house in the rear which was the home where he grew up and from which the "funny old washbasin made of marble" was transplanted into *Lentil*. McCloskey writes of attending public school in Hamilton,

> . . . and from the time my fingers were long enough to play the scale I took piano lessons. I started next to play the harmonica, the drums, and then the oboe. The musician's life was the life for me — that is, until I became interested in things electrical and mechanical. I collected old electric motors and bits of wire, old clocks and Meccano sets. I built trains and cranes with remote controls, my family's Christmas trees revolved, lights flashed and buzzers buzzed, fuses blew and sparks flew! The inventor's life was the life for me — that is, until I started making drawings for the high-school paper and the high-school annual.[2]

His talent for inventing mechanical contraptions must have led to many an interesting situation. Marc Simont (later a Caldecott winner for *A Tree Is Nice*) believes that it was very hard on the mother, for there seemed always to be something new to devise and try. Once, Simont tells, McCloskey came up with a machine for whipping cream. Being a generous boy, he didn't spare the juice; so when this whirling monster came in contact with the cream, it splattered a milky-way pattern around all four kitchen walls.[3]

He had an after-school job teaching hobbies at the YMCA. He taught "other boys how to play the harmonica, and shepherded them to concerts at churches, grange meetings, lodge meetings and such." He also helped boys make model airplanes and taught another group "to do soap carving. They met in the shower room once a week and the chips fell unhindered."[4] During his senior year (1932) he won a national Scholastics Award, a scholarship to the Vesper George School of Art in Boston, where he went to study though his parents wanted him to go to college. Two years later his first important commission was obtained, executing the bas-reliefs for Hamilton's municipal building.

After studying three winters in Boston and counseling in a boys' camp near Hamilton for three summers, he moved to New York in 1935. With samples of his work, he called upon May Massee, editor of Junior Books, Viking Press. "She told him to go back for more training and really learn to draw." [5] In his Acceptance Paper for his first Caldecott Award, McCloskey spoke of that meeting as he talked of his viewpoint toward art then.[6]

> I was studying to be an artist, and I was hell-bent on creating *art*.
> My mind in those days was filled with odd bits of Greek mythology,
> with accent on Pegasus, Spanish galleons, Oriental dragons, and all
> the stuff that really and truly great art is made of. . . . It never would
> have occurred to me to *draw* those things [ducks] or to *paint* them.
> . . . That gives you a vague idea of the way things stood. But I don't
> regard the time and thought as wasted. I certainly got rid of a lot of
> ham ideas at an early age.
>   . . . I went to call on an editor of children's books. I came into
> her office with my folio under my arm and sat on the edge of my
> chair. She looked at the examples of the great art I had brought along
> (they were woodcuts, fraught with black drama). I don't remember
> *just* the words she used to tell me to get wise to myself and shelve
> the dragons, Pegasus, limpid pool business, and learn how and what
> to "art" with. I think we talked mostly of Ohio.

For the next two years he studied at the National Academy of Design in New York City. Here he won the President's Award and began exhibiting his work at the Academy, at the Tiffany Foundation, and at the Society of Independent Artists in Boston. During the summers he studied painting and worked under Jerry Farnsworth in Provincetown on Cape Cod.[7] He says, in referring to those days,[8]

> I never sold an oil painting, only a few water colors at most modest
> prices — and financially my career was a bust. Rather than go on
> PWA or WPA, I took a bread and butter job doing a form of com-
> mercial art I had little interest in.

Before long he returned to Ohio and there began drawing everyday life. Shortly afterward, he took a portfolio of new paintings back to New York City. These helped him get a job in Cambridge assisting Francis Scott Bradford in making huge murals for the Lever Brothers building. The murals included famous people of Beacon Hill, and we are told that he had as much fun getting the socialites to pose as he got from actually painting.[9] In 1939 he won the Prix de Rome, but the war prevented his acceptance. He did call again on Miss Massee, however, and she published his story and drawings for *Lentil,* his first book, in 1940.

In 1940 McCloskey married Margaret Durand. A former New York children's librarian, Peggy Durand was the daughter of Ruth Sawyer, famous storyteller and writer. In 1941 *Make Way for Ducklings* appeared, winning the Caldecott Award the next year as the most distinguished picture book for children. In 1943 *Homer Price* was published, a book McCloskey wanted to finish before he went into the army. During World War II McCloskey was a sergeant, stationed for three years at Fort McClellan, Alabama, where he made visual aids for the infantry. His comment on his experiences there was thus: "My greatest contribution to the war effort was inventing a machine to enable short lieutenants to flip over large training charts in a high breeze." [10]

In 1945 his first child, Sally, was born; in 1948, Jane. Shortly afterward, the McCloskeys sailed for Italy for a year. In Rome, McCloskey had a studio as a fellow of the American Academy. While he did little painting, he learned mosaic techniques in glass and in marble. In the winter of 1955 he returned to Mexico for two months of painting. Generally, however, Maine has been the inspiration for most of his work, with the appearance of *Blueberries for Sal, Centerburg Tales, One Morning in Maine, Time of Wonder,* and *Burt Dow* over the last many years. While the family lives in Croton Falls, New York, in winter, summers for the past twenty years have been spent on an island in Penobscot Bay, near Cape Rosier, Maine. McCloskey says there are two small islands which he calls home, Scott Islands.[11] His studio is a tall barn, where on cool or foggy mornings a few sticks of wood in a stove warm things up.

To turn from his life [12] to his work is to read from the same page, for rarely has a person so mirrored his experiences as has McCloskey in his books. Surely the lesson on art which May Massee taught him long ago has never been forgotten in its emphasis upon his portraying what he knows best. Whether it is a boy, an invention, a musical instrument, the loss of a child's tooth, or an island, McCloskey writes from his own life with the authenticity, humor, and exaggeration that form his days and his zest for living.

His first book, *Lentil* (1940), was a picture-story book about a young harmonica player. Lentil lived in Alto, Ohio, and his only unhappiness was that he could not sing or even whistle because he could not pucker his lips. But since he wanted to make music, he bought a harmonica and practiced, especially in the bathtub where the tone was best. One day Colonel Carter, the town's favorite son and benefactor, came for a visit.

Everybody had prepared a welcome except Old Sneep. When the train pulled in, Old Sneep's sucking on a lemon got the mouths of the musicians so puckered up that they could not play. Lentil and his harmonica came to the rescue. "So you never can tell what will happen when you learn to play the harmonica." [13]

There is no doubt that *Lentil* is partly autobiographical. As a boy McCloskey was a master of the mouth organ, and the Harmonica Club of which he was a member is still recalled for its orchestral sounding music.[14] In fact, McCloskey "once offered his services to Major Bowes and was promptly offered two engagements in a vaudeville circuit, which, however, he declined." [15] When the book was published, he traveled from schoolhouse to library in the midwest and eastern states, playing for the children "as though he were remembering his own childhood." [16] Like Lentil, he carried the harmonica in his pocket and filled the room with the music of "Comin' Round the Mountain." [17]

McCloskey himself says that the end page of *Lentil* depicts the Ohio countryside of forty years ago, that the bathroom with its washbasin is the bathroom upstairs in the house where he grew up. Hamilton's Soldiers and Sailors Monument is the one in the book, only he "whittled it down in size and scaled it down to fit a smaller town." [18]

Critics hailed *Lentil* as a boy classic, as a piece of authentic Americana, and as a book of appeal for all ages. Arbuthnot called it a "juvenile Main Street." [19] Readers seem to agree. Large-scale pictures look exactly right, with girls jumping rope, boys playing marbles, dogs slinking away from Lentil's squawks, birds laughing at his sounds, and a train crossing the bridge into town. All details, even to the wrinkled rug in the bathroom, are homespun and natural. Humor shines from the pages.

The next book, *Make Way for Ducklings* (1941), has a fascinating story to tell and as fascinating a story behind it. Mr. and Mrs. Mallard searched for a safe place to hatch ducklings and found it on an island in the Charles River, not far from the Public Gardens in Boston. Here the eggs were laid and eight ducklings hatched. While Mrs. Mallard cared for the children, Mr. Mallard went exploring the river, promising to meet the family in the Public Garden. ("Just like a man!" a college student once quipped.) When the time came for the trip to the park, Mrs. Mallard had to have the policeman, Mike, help her and her family through Boston traffic, but they made it safely and found Mr. Mallard waiting.

The picture book, this time for young children, is done in the same rich sepia toning as *Lentil*, with the drawings bleeding off the pages "in order to obtain a maximum of pictorial effect." [20] There are no small pictures. Each of the thirty-one is a large double-spread. To the person who knows, here *is* Boston: the State House, Louisburg Square, Beacon Hill, the Public Gardens' entrance, statues, the bridge over the pond, swanboats, the island—all present in authentic detail. The magnificent pictures of ducks and ducklings portray characterization and feathers to an exact degree. Even the uncritical observer would recognize the excellence of illustrations which made this work a true Caldecott winner and a story "among the indispensable classics of childhood." [21]

Probably many of us have seen newspaper photographs showing traffic being stopped to permit the crossing of a mother duck and her family in safety. Surely such pictures lend credence to the book's story and realism. McCloskey has pointed out that, while living on Beacon Hill, he walked each day through the Public Gardens on his way to art school. He liked the ducks but had no thought then of drawing them. Four years later on his return to Boston he noticed the ducks' traffic problem and heard some stories about them, and the book "just sort of developed from there."

When he started making the final sketches, he realized that he really knew little about the habits and anatomy of mallard ducks. First, therefore, he went to the American Museum of Natural History in New York and make careful sketches of the two stuffed mallards and the skins and nests brought carefully from the cases for him. At the Museum Library he

> ... found a top view of a duck's cranium, with minute measurements and a rough estimate of how many years ago ducks were fish. But hidden somewhere I found valuable information on the molting and mating habits of mallards.[22]

At the Public Gardens he fed peanuts and popcorn to ducks to note "the bob of their heads and the tilt of their tails." An ornithologist at Cornell, Dr. George M. Sutton, helped him study markings on skins and make notes about wings. After watching McCloskey in the laboratory spend hours handling duck wings, studying bills and feet, and feeling the texture of feathers, Dr. Sutton said: [23]

> I wish all illustrators had that same sense of honesty in what they undertake to draw. We ornithologists like to see the birds which go into children's books drawn right. . . . And if it is going to be a mallard it should look like a mallard and not a pintail or a puddle-duck.

Realizing that he needed models, McCloskey went to the old Washington Market one cold morning and asked a poultry dealer for some mallards. As the ducks were pointed out, the dealer made a grab and brought out a squawking bird by the neck. Although two were mistakes, all four were bought.

> I tried to get ducks that looked as much like mallards as possible. But those in the market were largely puddle-duck. My drawings show the same kind of mix-up, I guess. Children don't care, but ornithologists turn a feather when they see them.
>
> Anyway, I came home by subway with the ducklings in a carton. That was fine until they started quacking. But we made it.[24]

McCloskey was then sharing an upstairs apartment with Marc Simont in an old residence on West 21st Street in Greenwich Village. Mr. Simont did not "bat an eye" at the new roommates but he was "distinctly not interested." The noise, especially in the early morning, led to many complaints from neighbors. McCloskey found that, in the make-shift pen in the corner, the ducks huddled together. Therefore, they had to be turned loose in the daytime. The next few weeks the artist crawled on hands and knees after them with his sketch pad and a box of cleansing tissues. In sketching a little one preening feathers on his breast, McCloskey found that the others wandered off rapidly. He recalls,[25]

> I had to slow those ducks down somehow so I could make the sketches. The only thing that worked was red wine. They loved it and went into slow motion right away.

In the bathtub the ducks splashed "all over the place," and the lady downstairs complained of leaks in the ceiling.

From his experiences McCloskey has said fervently: [26]

> If you ever see an artist draw a horse, or a lion, or a duck, the lines flowing from his brush or crayon in just the right place so that all the horse's feet touch the ground, the lion couldn't be mistaken for a pin cushion, and the duck *is* a duck, and you think "My, how easily and quickly he does that, it must be a talent he was born with," well, think it if you must but don't *say* it! Little do you realize what might be going into that drawing—day after day of following horses in a meadow with hot sun, prickles, and flies, or coming home from the Zoo exhausted at night with the people in the car looking about and trying to place that distinctive smell, or what splashing and housemaid's knee is behind each nonchalant stroke of that duck's wing!

Back to Boston he went to make background sketches. Then again in New York he purchased six ducklings and filled more sketch books with happy, sad, inquisitive, and bored ducks, and "running, walking, standing, sitting, stretching, swimming, scratching, sleeping ducklings."

Ducks grow quickly from fluffiness to pin feathers, he found, and his drawings reflected this fact in the last part of the book. The ordinary names as Jane and Jim were discarded for names in duck language. In fact, McCloskey has commented: [27]

You more or less have to think like a duck, too, and it helps you. You think of being just as small as you can, and just thinking back to your own childhood can help you with that.

With bulging sketchbooks, McCloskey made a final dummy. Lithographic reproduction was planned. He used

. . . grained zinc plates on which he made drawings with a grease, or litho, crayon. Drawings were made the same size as those in the finished book. Each to be exact because changes could not be made on the plates.[28]

The plates were used "to make proofs in black ink," which, in turn, were used to make "large press-sized plates" treated to be receptive to ink for final printing.

In 1943 the third book was published. *Homer Price,* the "hilarious story of a small town boy and the predicaments he creates," was received with enthusiasm by boys and girls alike. Homer is one of the best known of present-day book children who are earnest youngsters caught in ludicrous situations, who have "schemes that collapse," but who survive and soon launch "even grander projects." [29] Perhaps one key to the popularity is that boys can identify well with friendly, ingenious Homer, who, like Lentil, in physical reality looks much like his creator. Centerburg, Homer's home town, is McCloskey's home town. McCloskey tells that in *Homer Price, Centerburg Tales,* and *Lentil* the Ohio countryside of forty years ago is shown in "remembered pictures — no actual places, people, or things." [30] However, as Leone Garvey writes: [31]

All I know about Centerburg is that it is situated where Highway 56 joins Highway 56a, but Homer Price . . . is essentially the Middle West. On second thought it is any small American town and most American boys can meet there and recognize themselves and one another.

Perhaps children can meet themselves in each of the six tales, which afford some gay satire and some exaggeration. The writing is easy and flowing, from Homer's capture of the robbers with the help of Aroma, his skunk; the spoof of the comics in Superman's catastrophe; through the "rollicking good fun" [32] of the automatic doughnut machine that would not stop; the ball-of-string contest, which pokes a finger at anyone's pet economies; the musical mousetrap story, the Pied Piper in modern style; and the mass-produced housing allotment, where people could not find their own homes. It is a book for older children, for teachers to read aloud or, even better, to tell. Just be sure to keep the inimitable McCloskey wording, especially as Uncle Ulysses says, [33]

> The rings of batter kept right on dropping into the hot fat, and the automatic gadget kept right on turning them over, and the other gadget kept right on giving them a little push, and the doughnuts kept right on rolling down the little chute just as regular as a clock can tick — they just kept right on a-comin', an' a-comin', an' a-comin', an' a-comin'.

McCloskey has pictured Homer as the modern child with varied interests and absorption in many things. Arbuthnot states [34] that "the tales and the pictures are caustically amusing. Some of these yarns are a shade too extravagant and too incredible, but they have an astringent humor." They have been recommended as "rib-ticklers to count on" in days of insecurity and tension. [35]

James Daugherty, calling Homer a real boy, welcomed him to Tom Sawyer's gang. An artist-writer himself, Daugherty looked closely at the characters and found "humorous reality" even in the objects in each scene, with drawings to be gone over "again and again with renewed delight in all their details." He comments: [36]

> The satire is warm and genial and tolerant so that you feel these pictures are the autobiography of a generous mind as well as a shrewd and witty recording of familiar scenes. It is the true comedy of democracy in the great American tradition. . . .
> It is America laughing at itself with a broad and genial humanity, without bitterness or sourness or sophistication.

It would be impossible to leave a discussion of *Homer Price* without referring to an explanation of McCloskey about the "number of robbers that are in that bed," when Homer and Aroma make their sensational capture.

I get letters and more questions about that because I put in this Homer story five robbers in the bed when I had only four in the story. Well, it's all a matter of miscounting. I was doing this story right when I was being inducted into the army. I don't know whether you know but in every book every square inch of space is counted. . . . I don't know who goofed . . . but suddenly they had this blank space right in the center of this story, and they wanted a picture in there so it didn't look empty. So here I was with the army breathing down my neck and they said, "Please make this picture," which I proceeded to do. That's how five men got in there instead of the four. It's a simple matter of bad arithmetic, starting with the design of the book.

When McCloskey wrote further adventures of Homer in *Centerburg Tales* (1951), laughter again poured forth, as in the gravitty-bitties episode (a spoof on cereal-box prizes) and in the story of the school-teacher and the automatic juke box. Grampa Hercules adds some intriguing tall tales. There is a tug at the heart, though, in the kindness of the children who go to great lengths to make everything right, after the townspeople have ridiculed the old storyteller who got carried away with his yarn.

Except for *Centerburg Tales*, McCloskey's next three publications depicted his family and their summers in Maine and on the island which he "has made so imperishably his own in the picture books he has created there." [37] The first such book was *Blueberries for Sal* in 1948. Little Sal and her mother one day go to Blueberry Hill to pick blueberries. On the other side of the hill Little Bear and his mother come to eat blueberries. The youngsters go slowly and before long they are all mixed up with different mothers. The writing and the pictures give no hint of danger except to say that "she was old enough to be shy" when telling of Little Bear's mother and of Little Sal's mother. Young children adore the story and read the large pictures easily. The excellent line drawings and even the print are done in the deep color of blueberries.

We are told that, while the bear is imagined, the rest of the story

> . . . is completely real. Sal is Bob's own daughter, and the mother is his wife, Peggy. The kitchen in the endpapers is their own kitchen, with the exception of the fascinating old stove—he "borrowed" that from his mother-in-law's house in Hancock, Maine.[38]

An outstanding book, *Blueberries for Sal* was a runner-up for the Caldecott Award. As a family story, it must have brought "the fragrance of childhood" back to Peggy McCloskey, who had similar memories.[39]

In *One Morning in Maine* (1952) McCloskey adds two-year-old Jane and himself to a warm family story which also is full of homey details and affection. There are pictures of Sal squeezing toothpaste on Jane's brush, Sal patting the dog as mother explains that a loose tooth means that she has become a big girl, Jane peering from her high chair at the cat drinking spilled milk, Sal telling animals and birds about her tooth and then getting her father to help look for it in the mud where they had dug clams, McCloskey rowing to the store because the outboard motor would not start, and the storekeeper giving a vanilla ice cream cone to Jane "so the drips won't spot." Beautiful dark blue double-page spreads give a reader a feeling of the island, the water, and the coast in a most impressionable way. The family, of course, is real, as are the English setter, Penny, and the black cat, Mozzarella. The village is the actual one to which the McCloskeys go for supplies.

When *Time of Wonder* appeared in 1957, the island and the family were shown in water colors, painted and re-painted over a three-year period while the artist worked to get what he wanted, a completely different book. It was his first book in full color. While the slight but rhythmic story tells of the beauty of the island during changes of season and tide, and of the coming of the storm, this superb book may well serve a deeper purpose. May Massee writes that the children who read and look at it

> . . . will be very subtly taught to love and wonder at the world they live in and to appreciate the privilege of living in it. This, surely, is the best that we can give to children, and Robert McCloskey has well earned the Caldecott medal for the second time. . . .[40]

A safe, familiar world meets the hurricane but with the security of close family relationships. Children can see beauty in the paintings. The forest quiet with the sound of growing ferns, the soft greens of slowly unfurling fiddleheads, the spreading rain-rings on water, the ghostly gray and yellow fog, the bright stars and their reflections, the lighted window as the dark winds of the hurricane close in on house and forest — all are effective representations to show nature. Here a child reads about real things and "reaches beyond his immediate environment to the outer world." [41]

Sal and Jane are a little older and thus the book is for the older child, but the splendid pictures and poetic prose are for children of all ages. Serene at the beginning and at the end, the book reads thus: [42]

Out of islands that poke their rocky shores above the waters of Penobscot Bay, you can watch the time of the world go by, from minute to minute, hour to hour, from day to day, season to season.

> *Take a farewell look*
> *at the waves and sky.*
> *Take a farewell sniff*
> *of the salty sea.*
> *A little bit sad*
> *about the place your are leaving,*
> *a little bit glad*
> *about the place you are going.*
> *It is a time of quiet wonder—*
> *for wondering, for instance:*
> *Where do the hummingbirds go*
> *in a hurricane?*

In 1963 *Burt Dow: Deep-Water Man* was published. It is a tall tale in bold and lavish color. Burt Dow pulls a Jonah-act when a whale gives him refuge in a storm, because the old fisherman had done the whale a favor by putting a peppermint-striped band-aid over the hole in its tail where a cod hook had snagged it. The typical McCloskey humor shows in many places besides the unrealistic plot, as in the name of the dory, the *Tidley-Idley;* the giggling gull, those tittering and teetering are extremely expressive; in the paint on the boat planks, identifiable as the leftover pink from Ginny Poor's pantry or the tan trim from Capt'n Haskell's house; and in the old-fashioned pitcher pump in the boat for bailing out the water. Similarly humor appears in the text as, when the whale said, "Ah-H-H!" in the classic tradition, Burt set the throttle and guided the *Tidley-Idley* into the whale's mouth and "navigated the length of the gullet and into the whale's tummy, without so much as touching a tonsil on the way down!"[43] In fact, the frontispiece truly establishes the tone of exaggerated nonsense for the whole book, for it shows the giggling gull mischievously making webbed tracks through pink paint spilling from an overturned bucket.

The story is a Maine tale. McCloskey has explained that Burt is a real person, a retired deep-water man or one who has sailed vessels all over the world. The book was planned almost entirely before pencil was put to paper and, while the first drawing was changed, the "text read almost exactly as it did in my first draft." Photographs for the plates were made in Holland with the printing done in this country.

These, then, are the eight books both written and illustrated by Robert McCloskey.[44] They give, together with his life story, a look at this man, which would be interesting in itself. It is incomplete, however, for only as we search further through a man's thoughts can we really touch his philosophy. Let us look, finally, at some of his own comments about his work.

What is McCloskey's own thought about doing work in children's books? Years ago he made his viewpoint very clear. In his first Acceptance Paper in 1942 he stated emphatically: [45]

. . . I'm not an authority on children's literature, or on graphic arts, or on children's illustrations. In fact, I'm not a children's illustrator. I'm just an artist who, among other things, does children's books.

I didn't start life training with any burning desire to create little gems for the young or give my all for good old children's books. But like a musician who likes to have his music listened to, the architect who likes to build houses that are homes, I like to have my pictures looked at and enjoyed. I grew a bit tired of turning out water colors by the ream and having only one in four hundred ever find a useful spot on a wall, the others stored in portfolios in some gallery or with canvases in a dusty studio corner. Yes, I'm working on children's illustration, I'm proud of that. But I'm still for hire — to paint, sculp, whittle, or blast if it's on some job that will bring pleasure and be used, whether it be in a bank, post office, or chicken coop.

This was Robert McCloskey at age twenty-seven.[46] More than twenty years later, however, he was still proclaiming: [47]

What I'm interested in is communicating with people. I like to know my work is being looked at and enjoyed. When you paint a mural in a bank or post office, you never know whether your work is being seen or not. People who frequent banks and post offices are usually busy cashing checks and licking stamps. They don't notice murals, and if they do, they seldom write and tell you so. Thirty years ago I did the sculpture for a public building, and during all those years I received perhaps six letters from people who have noticed. On the other hand everyday brings me more letters than that from children, from parents, from teachers and librarians who've read my books.

McCloskey's imagination, industry, and integrity have been the subject of many critical comments. McCloskey himself says that "no effort is too great to find out as much as possible about the things you know you are drawing. It's a good feeling to be able to put down a line and know that it is right." [48]

Perhaps it is this feeling which somehow is communicated to children that satisfies their desire for things to be true. Perhaps, too, it is this careful workmanship which has made him a thorough but rather slow producer. He has stated:

> I'm not prolific — I have to wait until it bubbles out. It may take two years but I live with it. . . . I can't go at the drop of a hat. It took two years to do *Homer* and three years for the next.

Though people in television and other media have approached him, he cannot "write to order." He mentions that he had a letter asking him to rewrite *Homer Price* with a limited vocabulary, with Uncle Ulysses being made Uncle Jim, for example. "I don't approve of writing or drawing down to children. Leave *Homer* as it is." [49]

Exactly how does he work, anyway? All of his books start as pictures, he says, and with an idea inside his head.

> I think in pictures. All of my training has been as an artist. I don't know anything about children's literature or I've never taken any courses in writing. I fill in between pictures with words. My first book I wrote in order to have something to illustrate. [50]

Cutting, adding, pasting, he comes up with a "bundle of scraps" of words and sketches, but, while the preliminary material may not look like much, he "has captured an idea." Then he works on pictures and writing.

> I used up some four boxes of pencils just making preliminary roughs for *Burt Dow*. There are sometimes as many as twenty or thirty drawings before I turn out the one you see in the book — not completed drawings, of course, but just finding out and exploring the best possible way of presenting this particular picture.

Usually it takes about two years from the time he first starts writing the story until it ends as a finished book. (It took a year just to write and rewrite many times the 1152 words of *Make Way for Ducklings*. [51]) The story must be able "to stand by itself" before he turns to the final art work.

In emphasizing the importance of drawing and its relationship to his work, McCloskey speaks clearly in *The Lively Art of Picture Books:*

Speaking of drawing, people will say, "Oh, he's so clever with his hands. He can draw so well." And, true, hands do play a part in drawing but it's an automatic part like shuffling cards or knitting. Drawing is most of all a way of seeing and thinking. Let me explain. Drawing a tree you must think of the relationship and proportion of twigs to branches, to trunk, even to the roots that you do not see; and you must feel the balance and thrust of this growing thing and its relationship to other trees, a rock, the ocean.

Your hand is trained, of course, . . . but your mind is ticking away like mad. It's racing and comparing and thinking a thousand things that no one will ever see in the picture, but the picture will be different for your having thought of them. In drawing your mind can project. For instance, I can look at one doughnut and think of a light snack. I can look at 15,000 doughnuts and come up with a story. After years of drawing, with me this way of thinking has become a habit. I can't turn it off at the end of an eight-hour day. It goes right on ticking, whether or not I have a brush in my hand.[52]

He continues:

Most of my friends and neighbors just don't seem to see as I do, even looking at simple things like a ball of string, a mousetrap, or an abstract expressionist painting. Sometimes they're amused, sometimes they yawn, and sometimes they're annoyed; and it gets pretty lonely up here on Cloud Nine, or up here on the roof like Old Sneep, and they're all down there, looking up at me like I'm some kind of nut. But I'm not a nut, really, as anybody can see. I have one foot resting on reality and the other foot planted firmly on a banana peel.

Finally, though he speaks with the splendid and unconscious humor that pervades his living and his work, McCloskey feels very serious about the place of drawing and design in the education of children. In his second Acceptance Speech for the Caldecott Award, he pleaded for the teaching of design so that children can come to appreciate art in a land "fast acquiring an environment of machines, by machines, for machines."[53] He wanted children to be helped "really to see and evaluate" their surroundings. He spoke of such elements as repetition, rhythm, color, texture, form, and space relationships affecting our lives and urged that we put design to work in creating beauty.

While in other writing and pictures, McCloskey has shown "Progress" and machines, perhaps he has expressed himself no more splendidly about them than in the modern housing episode in *Homer Price*. However, he does not leave us discouraged; the satire becomes almost kind. As James Daugherty has written, there is a comforting feeling that

> . . . although Centerburg can and does take the machine age in its stride, the salt and character, the humanities and the individualism of Our Town remain triumphant and that democracy will keep her rendezvous with destiny, musical mousetraps, and all.[54]

So here we have an added dimension to Robert McCloskey, a gifted man with spirited, unforgettable pictures; with control of line ranging from soft, quiet beauty to genial exaggeration; with rare ability for humor and the interpretation through realistic details, of which children never tire; and with the "feel" of America permeating all his production. Ruth Sawyer once wished that he would

> . . . not lose the shy gentleness that runs as strong and as compelling in him as his integrity. It looses a quality, a sort of depth charge to all he does, that brings to the surface the best that he can do.[55]

Truly she prophesied well.

REFERENCES

1. Ruth Sawyer, "Robert McCloskey: Good Craftsman and Fine Artist," *Publishers' Weekly*, 141 (June 27, 1942) 2348–50.
2. *Robert McCloskey*. New York: Viking, n.d. 4 pp.
3. Marc Simont, "Bob McCloskey, Inventor," in Lee Kingman, ed., *Newbery and Caldecott Medal Books: 1956–1965*. Boston: The Horn Book, 1965, pp. 196–7.
4. Margaret McCloskey, "Robert McCloskey — Biographical Note," in Lee Kingman, ed., *Newbery and Caldecott Medal Books: 1956–1965*. Boston: The Horn Book, 1965, pp. 194–5.
5. *Loc. cit.*
6. Robert McCloskey, "Ducklings at Home and Abroad," in Bertha M. Miller and Elinor W. Field, eds., *Caldecott Medal Books: 1938–1957*. Boston: The Horn Book, 1957, pp. 79–84.
7. Ruth Hill Viguers, Marcia Dalphin, and Bertha M. Miller, *Illustrators of Children's Books, 1946–1956*. Boston: The Horn Book, 1958, p. 151.

8. "McCloskey, Robert," in Maxine Block, ed., *Current Biography*. New York: The H. W. Wilson Co., 1942, p. 544.

9. Ruth Sawyer, *op. cit.*

10. Margaret McCloskey, *op. cit.*

11. *The Lively Art of Picture Books*. Weston, Connecticut: Weston Woods Studio, 1964.

12. During his early writing years especially, McCloskey often traveled to book fairs. For a typical day at a Cleveland Book Fair, involving Marguerite Henry and Louis Slobodkin, the reader must read his hilarious account in "Peeping," in J. Allen Figurel, ed., *Vistas in Reading*, Proceedings of the IRA, 1966, Vol. 11, Part 1. Newark, Delaware: IRA, 1967, pp. 21–4.

13. Robert McCloskey, *Lentil*. New York: Viking, 1940.

14. Mary Harbage, "Robert McCloskey, He Doesn't Forget," *Elementary English*, 31 (May, 1954) 251–9.

15. *Robert McCloskey, op. cit.*

16. Ruth Sawyer, *op. cit.*

17. Meribah K. Bowen, "Springfield Children Know Their Authors," *Wilson Library Bulletin*, 17 (May, 1943) 710–11.

18. *The Lively Art of Picture Books, op. cit.*

19. May Hill Arbuthnot, *Children and Books*. Third Edition. Chicago: Scott, Foresman and Company, 1964, p. 441.

20. Esther Averill, "What Is a Picture Book?" in Bertha M. Miller and Elinor W. Field, eds., *Caldecott Medal Books: 1938–1957*. Boston: The Horn Book, 1957, pp. 307–14.

21. Dora V. Smith, *Fifty Years of Children's Books*. Champaign, Illinois: NCTE, 1963, p. 56.

22. Robert McCloskey, "Ducklings at Home and Abroad," *op. cit.*

23. Ruth Sawyer, *op. cit.*

24. Nancy Larrick, "Robert McCloskey's *Make Way for Ducklings*," *Elementary English*, 37 (March, 1960) 143–8.

25. *Loc. cit.*

26. Robert McCloskey, "Ducklings at Home and Abroad," *op. cit.*

27. Speech by Mr. McCloskey at The University of Akron, April 28, 1962.

28. Nancy Larrick, *op. cit.*

29. Nancy Larrick, *A Teacher's Guide to Children's Books*. Columbus, Ohio: Charles Merrill Co., 1960, p. 237.

30. *The Lively Art of Picture Books, op. cit.*

31. Leone Garvey, "Regional Stories," *Horn Book Magazine*, 27 (March–April, 1951) 123–30.

32. Edna Johnson, Evelyn Sickels, and Frances C. Sayers, *Anthology of Children's Literature*. Third Edition. Boston: Houghton Mifflin Co., 1959, p. 938.

33. Robert McCloskey, *Homer Price*. New York: Viking, 1943, p. 68.

34. Arbuthnot, *op. cit.*, p. 441.

35. "Hunter's Fare," *Horn Book Magazine*, 27 (March–April, 1951) 135.

36. James Daugherty, "Homer Price," *Horn Book Magazine*, 19 (November, 1943) 425–6.

37. Anne Carroll Moore, "The Three Owls' Notebook," *Horn Book Magazine*, 30 (December, 1954) 411–4.

38. *Robert McCloskey, op. cit.*

39. Margaret Durand McCloskey, "Our Fair Lady!" *Horn Book Magazine*, 41 (October, 1965) 481–6.

40. May Massee, "Robert McCloskey—Wins Second Caldecott Medal," *Library Journal*, 83 (April 15, 1958) 1243–4, 1248.

41. James S. Smith, *A Critical Approach to Children's Literature*. New York: McGraw-Hill, 1967, p. 134.

42. Robert McCloskey, *Time of Wonder.* New York: Viking, 1957.
43. Robert McCloskey, *Burt Dow: Deep-Water Man.* New York: Viking, 1963.
44. McCloskey has illustrated some books for other writers and, as usual, critics have hailed his excellent pictures. Probably the book which should be cited here is Ruth Sawyer's *Journey Cake, Ho!* (New York: Viking, 1953), a runner-up for the Caldecott Award in 1954. Anne Carroll Moore in "The Three Owls' Notebook" (*Horn Book Magazine,* 29 (October, 1953) 344–6) terms his drawings for this story as some of his "freest and most expressive," with effective use of red-browns and blue-grays to create the mountain background.
45. Robert McCloskey, "Ducklings at Home and Abroad," *op. cit.*
46. Miriam Huber (*Story and Verse for Children.* Third Edition. New York: Macmillan, 1965, p. 831) points out that this observation of being primarily an artist applies to most of our distinguished illustrators of children's books. She says that they also do adult illustration, with "no difference in their seriousness and responsibility of approach toward children's books. In our best books, then, there is no 'talking down' to children, either in pictures or in text."
47. *The Lively Art of Picture Books, op. cit.*
48. Robert McCloskey, "Ducklings at Home and Abroad," *op. cit.*
49. Speech by Mr. McCloskey at the IRA Convention, Dallas, Texas, May 7, 1966.
50. *The Lively Art of Picture Books, op. cit.*
51. Nancy Larrick, "Robert McCloskey's *Make Way for Ducklings," op. cit.*
52. Once McCloskey gave an effective demonstration of this thinking by making a sketch of Homer carrying a tray of doughnuts. Instead of stacking doughnuts from the bottom up, he said that it was much easier to start at the top of the stack and just go down until he got to the bottom of the stack! He proceeded to draw in just that way.
53. Robert McCloskey, "Caldecott Award Acceptance." In Lee Kingman, ed., *Newbery and Caldecott Medal Books: 1956–1965.* Boston: The Horn Book, 1965, pp. 188–93.
54. James Daugherty, *op. cit.*
55. Ruth Sawyer, *op. cit.*

EDITORS' NOTE

In addition to the eight books which he has both written and illustrated, Robert McCloskey has illustrated seven others. The most recent of these have been two volumes of the Henry Reed series by Keith Robertson, all of which McCloskey has illustrated. The titles of the two latest volumes are *Henry Reed's Baby-Sitting Service* (1966), and *Henry Reed's Big Show* (1970).

Robert McCloskey has not written any children's books since *Burt Dow: Deep-Water Man,* in 1963. He has been involved in constructing puppets and in working out new techniques both in their design and their use.

Mr. McCloskey has won numerous awards and honors. In addition to being one of the two people to be awarded the Caldecott Medal twice, once for *Make Way for Ducklings* in 1942, and again for *Time of Wonder* in 1958, he has been a runner-up for this award on three occasions — *Blueberries for Sal,* in 1949, *One Morning in Maine,* in 1953, and *Jour-*

ney Cake, Ho!, in 1954. The latter book was written by his mother-in-law, Ruth Sawyer.

Among his other honors are The Ohioana Book Award (given to Ohio authors who have written outstanding books) for *Blueberries for Sal* in 1949, and for *Time of Wonder* in 1958, and The Pacific Northwest Library Association Young Readers' Choice Award for *Homer Price* in 1947. In 1964, McCloskey was awarded an honorary Doctor of Literature by Miami University (Oxford, Ohio).

Enjoying Festivals
with Katherine Milhous *

GREAT WET FLAKES of snow fall from leaden skies upon a city sprawled across rolling hills and along the banks of the Lehigh River. As dusk falls, a great star—the many-pointed star of Bethlehem—can be seen dimly, shining over the town to the west. A feeling of festivity is in the air. Windows are lighted with candles, and the beautifully symmetrical community tree stands in a blaze of color on the bridge. Bethlehem, Pennsylvania, the "Christmas City of America," is ready to celebrate its two-hundred-sixteenth Christmas Eve.

This night the Moravians will celebrate, as they have for more than two hundred years, the Children's Love Feast held in the massive grey stone church situated in the heart of the old town. Here children of all ages will come to worship in a service filled with magnificent music, where the sound of singing swells and rolls like organ music in a cathedral. During one portion of the service, the air of a party will settle over the congregation as men and women pass down the aisles of the church carrying trays of goodies for the children—trays heaped with sugar buns and filled with mugs of steaming black coffee. Later, the darkened church will be filled with a blaze of light as the trays come down the aisle once more, filled with fragrant beeswax candles. As each child receives his tiny candle which has a colored paper frill at the base (red for girls, green for boys) to keep the hot wax from burning tender fingers, the party air will vanish because the children understand that this is the night on which the Christ Child was born.

* By Elaine Templin. From *Elementary English* 34 (November 1957), 435–443. Reprinted with the permission of the National Council of Teachers of English and Elaine Templin.

327

It is natural that Katherine Milhous, always a lover of festivals, should have chosen this locale, this season, and these people for the setting of her first American Christmas story, *Snow Over Bethlehem*, for here, perhaps more than in any other section of our country, Christmas has always been a festival devoted especially to children.

In *Snow Over Bethlehem*, published in 1945, Miss Milhous tells an exciting, authentic story of how the children of the Moravian settlement at Nazareth, Pennsylvania, were sent in rumbling, canvass-covered ox carts to Bethlehem at Christmas time for protection from the Indians. There, in the crowded quarters of the barricaded Nursery Building, the children of Nazareth spent the weeks remaining to Christmas happily unaware of the danger which was threatening all of them.

Both through her story and her illustrations, Miss Milhous indicates the loving care with which the children were treated. She tells how they were shielded from fear by Sister Gertrand, the children's story-teller; by Sister Magdalena who played gay little carols on the harpsichord for the children to sing; by Anna Johanna, the kind-hearted girl who made her promise of a Christmas surprise come true; and by enormous Brother Polycarp, the jovial night watchman, who called the hours in rhyme:

> *'Tis seven o'clock, and I must homeward hurry*
> *Ere my poor wife does die of fret and worry.*

Strangely enough, it was the music, which is a heritage of the Moravians, that kept the Indians from attacking the settlement as they had planned to do. The high, sweet, piercing sound made by the trombones playing traditional Christmas music from the Bell Tower at four o'clock on that Christmas morning of 1755 had frightened them away, and thus the colony was saved to tell and retell the story each year "when the snow again falls over Bethlehem and the children gather about the Christmas Crib."

Katherine Milhous, the artist-writer who brought this story to the children of America, is a native Philadelphian of Irish-Quaker ancestry. Her father was an old-time label printer who made his own wood-cuts. Her mother was a fine seamstress with artistic appreciation.

As was the custom in Philadelphia, the family lived above the father's shop. Much of Katherine's early life, therefore, was spent in the print shop where, it is said, she sat dangerously near the thundering presses and drew pictures on scraps of paper; for, even as a child, Katherine wanted passionately to become an artist.

While she was still quite young, Katherine moved with her family to nearby Pitman Grove, New Jersey, the home of her maternal grandmother, where she and her younger sister, Dorothy, attended school. Pitman Grove, a small town situated in a fertile region sometimes known as the "Truck Patch of the East," was an old Methodist camp-meeting town—a bustling, exciting place in summer, a dull and dreary place in winter when most of the tiny frame cottages were vacant. It was a country town with few children and one small school—a town with no library or any other cultural facility. Such a town had little to offer a curious and imaginative child but, as Miss Milhous says, "artist children have a way of thriving on rocky soil. They need few roots and draw their sustenance from other sources." [1]

Katherine's family owned a small library, consisting mostly of English classics and fairy tales, built up by means of bargain sets of books purchased by her mother on rare trips to Philadelphia. These books were read and reread by Katherine, for they revealed to her a fascinating new world of foreign places and people. A special favorite was *Bimbi* by Ouida—a book filled with exciting, imaginative tales which were more adult than child-like. However, this book is credited by Miss Milhous as having been the source of the courage necessary for her to become an artist. A favorite author in those days was Willa Cather whose quiet, serious books were quite the opposite of *Bimbi*.

From her childhood experiences and avid reading Katherine gained a variety of creative ideas. One of these, the desire to take a caravan trip, was realized many years later when she and two artist friends spent a memorable September jogging along the country roads of Pennsylvania in a Dearborn wagon pulled by a plough horse. This was a leisurely trip taken in the days when the Model T's were still a popular mode of transportation. The artists traveled without a specific itinerary, stopping whenever and wherever they saw something they wished to sketch or paint. Throughout their journey their horse ambled along at a "goose pace" and refused to be hurried—a fact that no doubt endeared him to his drivers.

Much of Katherine's experience as a member of this caravan was woven later into a book titled *Herodia: the Lovely Puppet*. Published in 1942, *Herodia* tells the story of a little girl who joins a traveling puppet show and travels the Pennsylvania highways and byways with Professor Blair in much the same manner that Katherine and her friends had traveled them.

In this book we see many evidences of another interest developed by Miss Milhous in her younger days—an interest in the countryside and an awareness of nature. She learned, for example, about astronomy when she spent long hours on crisp wintery nights standing on a flat, snow-covered New Jersey field while she studied the sky by means of a sky map with only a bicycle lamp for illumination. She learned about weather from studying the skies during all the seasons of the year and she modestly admits that she still can do a pretty fair job of predicting the weather.

In *Herodia,* both her keen sensitivity to nature and that sense of childish wonder which she still possesses are revealed in the word pictures which she paints:

> Early the next morning the sun broke through the mists that hung over a woods on the outskirts of the village. Casting a yellow spotlight, now here, now there, it finally came to rest on the banks of a small stream . . . the yellow spotlight darted about, seeking out the pebbles in the brook and the patches of wild flowers under the trees.

During her childhood Miss Milhous developed still a third interest — that of making small things with her hands — for she learned while quite young that her own rather bare home could be made bright and gay with greens from the woods, with painted Easter eggs and paper valentines. Miss Milhous has drawn on this childhood interest to make an important contribution to the realm of children's literature in an era that is tending more and more to be dominated by automation and mechanization, for she has created three books designed to provide young readers with an opportunity to experience the joy that comes from creating small objects with their hands.

The first of these books, *The Egg Tree,* is perhaps the most widely known of the three. It was selected by the Children's Committee of the American Institute of Graphic Arts as one of the best designed books subsequent to 1945, and was awarded the Caldecott Medal in 1951.

The Egg Tree is a charming Easter story about a Pennsylvania Dutch family who painted eggs and hung them on a tree for all of their friends and neighbors to enjoy. It was such a beautiful tree that, as Grandmom said, "It makes a body feel as if Spring has come right into the house."

> Hundreds of eggs hung from its branches. When the sun streamed in the tree looked like a piece of the rainbow.

Beautifully illustrated with authentic Pennsylvania Dutch designs done in muted tones of pink, yellow, greyed blues, and red, *The Egg Tree* is indeed a picture book of distinction. Egg designs were used in a traditional manner throughout the book. The best known of these is probably The Horn-blowing Rooster who was immortalized this past autumn when he appeared as an eight-foot mural on the wall of the stair-well leading down to the children's room of the Rittenhouse Square Library in Philadelphia.

Scarcely was this book off the presses, however, when Miss Milhous was deluged with letters asking if the making of an Easter egg tree was a traditional Pennsylvania Dutch custom. After much searching and questioning the artist-writer was able to verify the fact that the decorating of such a tree has actually been a tradition in various counties of Pennsylvania for more than a century. In fact, Colonel Henry W. Shoemaker, State Archivist of Pennsylvania, "asserts that in some localities the Easter egg tree is even more cherished than the Christmas tree." [2]

Miss Milhous accounts for the perpetuation of such traditions in Pennsylvania when she says, "Of all peoples on earth . . . the Germans are the most holiday-loving and certainly the most tenacious in holding to their traditions. In the Pennsylvania Dutch country no old-world symbolism ever quite dies out; the scholar keeps it alive by conscious devotion to cultural heritage — the farmer, unconsciously, through his very isolation." [3]

Two huge scrapbooks, compiled by Miss Milhous, contain thousands of snapshots, clippings, and letters sent to her from all sections of our country telling about Easter egg trees made by children, librarians, and teachers subsequent to the reading of her book, *The Egg Tree*. These scrapbooks provide evidence that a custom, once exclusively Pennsylvania Dutch, is now being adopted by Americans everywhere.

Appolonia's Valentine, the second of her books designed to encourage the creativity of young readers, was published in 1954. It is the story of two Amish children, Appolonia and Dan, who attend a little red schoolhouse in Bucks County, Pennsylvania. It is February and we hear the teacher say:

A valentine is a thought that you put down on paper in beautiful shapes and colors. Our Pennsylvania Dutch grandfathers and grandmothers made lovely valentines. They knew that the best valentines are those you make yourselves. Perhaps we can make some like theirs. Let me show you how they made them.

Subsequently the artist-writer gives explicit directions for folding a square of paper to cut a lacework design, and includes a page of lovely illustrations to give readers a number of ideas that they can use in making their own "tokens of love and friendship."

But *Appolonia's Valentine* is more than a book of instructions. It is the gentle story of a shy, sensitive, artistic little girl who is afraid the valentine she makes will be less attractive than those completed by her classmates. However, with the encouragement given her by her brother, Dan, she works to earn money for a paintbox and a set of brushes so she can paint her valentine "because she couldn't ever cut anything that wasn't crooked and ugly."

The completed valentine, sent to Jean-Jacques, a French pen pal, was a truly beautiful one "made of all the things she loved so well . . . decorated with colored tulips and birds, leaves and berries, with angels carrying a wreath—and with a little house with a bird on the chimney."

Jean-Jacques' assurance that Appolonia was a fine artist, together with the admiration shown her work by her classmates, brought happiness to the shy little girl who decides at that moment to become a real artist. One senses that Miss Milhous reaffirms her own feeling for the life of an artist through Appolonia who reasons that such a life "would be hard work . . . But it would be happy work."

Soon after she completed high school, Katherine's ambition to become an artist was furthered by her mother who somehow secured enough money to enroll her in classes at The Philadelphia Museum's School of Art. For three of the four years she spent in attending art classes, Miss Milhous commuted daily from her home to Philadelphia—a distance of seventeen miles. At night she did newspaper drawings to cover expenses. Later she worked for and won an art scholarship.

Much of her early work was done in black and white for newspapers and magazines; but she continued to study all aspects of graphic arts, to work on murals and other decorative forms of art. At one time she did caricatures speedily and deftly. At one time she also painted watercolors for exhibition purposes, but her work in recent years as an artist-writer has kept her too busy to pursue many of these earlier forms of art expression.

During the depression, when there was little or no work to be had as an artist, Katherine, in order to provide the bare essentials of food and lodging, began studying sculpture at The Pennsylvania Academy of the Fine Arts. And, although sculpture poses many problems new to a painter, she succeeded in winning a Cresson Traveling Scholarship in 1934. All that summer she traveled alone in Italy and France, studying the world's sculptural masterpieces. When she returned to the United States, she became a supervisor on the Federal Art Project. A series of Pennsylvania Dutch posters that she designed while connected with the Project attracted the attention of Alice Dalgliesh, juvenile editor for Charles Scribner's Sons, and launched her on her career as a children's book illustrator. Later, through the encouragement of Miss Dalgliesh, she became an artist-writer of children's books.

Her first work for Charles Scribner's Sons was the illustrating of two books of folk and fairy tales selected for publication by Miss Dalgliesh. The first of these, *Once On a Time,* was published in 1938. To this book of folk tales Miss Milhous brought a striking posterlike type of illustration, a skillful use of bright strong colors, and a fine understanding of the folk art of the countries from which the stories come. The second book, *Happily Ever After,* was published a year later. Its illustrations, executed in pale pinks and blues, have a delicate porcelain-like quality that serve to enhance this collection of beloved fairy tales.

The first book to be written and illustrated by Miss Milhous was *Lovina.* Published in 1940, it is a simply written, boldly illustrated story of the plain people—the Amish who cultivate the farm country around Lancaster, Pennsylvania—people who continue to live in much the same quiet, uncomplicated manner as did the family depicted in this story set in 1861.

> The plain people lived plainly. They believed that God had given them all the good and beautiful things that they needed—trees and flowers, fruit and grain, horses and cows, work and rest. But, in order to work, Pop needed wagons and plows and a big barn. Mom needed a house and brooms, baskets and dishes. They all needed dishes, even Katzi.

Throughout the early portion of this book, interest is centered on the dishes owned by the family—"seven pretty dishes all covered with birds and flowers, people and animals which were bought by great-great grandpop Troyer."

One by one the pretty dishes become broken, but Mom reflected the family's apparent unconcern over the losses:

> "Ach!" said Mom as the plate went on the stones. "It makes no never mind. It was a worldly plate after all."

As a grandmom, however, Lovina shows a more worldly interest in her own plate and arranges for it to be placed in a museum to assure its continued safety.

Miss Milhous introduces a concept in this first book that is rarely found in picture books—a concept considered too difficult for the very young to grasp. She pictures the heroine, Lovina, as a young girl in the beginning of the story and as a grandmother at the story's end. In spite of this, however, *Lovina* is more appealing than most "first books"; for its illustrations are gay and colorful, bold and uncluttered, and typical of the native art of the Pennsylvania Dutch. Moreover, her characters are pictured as plain, comfortable-looking, friendly people and one has the feeling from the beginning that they would be nice folks to know.

In the same year Miss Milhous completed *Lovina* she illustrated *A Book for Jennifer*, by Alice Dalgliesh. This is a beautifully designed and exquisitely illustrated book. Katherine's visits to England and her knowledge of the styles of various periods helped her to give the pictures a real, eighteenth century flavor. It presents charming, winsome children, elegant ladies and gentlemen, and a thoroughly captivating cat. The illustrations have much the same flavor as those done for her own book, *Herodia: The Lovely Puppet*.

Corporal Keeperupper, published in 1943, was a book with a purpose, for, through this story of a tiny wooden soldier who claims to have served under General Washington, Miss Milhous attempted to help children understand that no matter how small they were, they could do something "on the Home Front . . . to help the soldiers on the Fighting Front." While the purpose was worthy enough, it seems unlikely that this slim book could have become a favorite of many young readers; for the story is wordy, loosely plotted, and lacking in excitement. Even the illustrations lack much of the warm and friendly quality so apparent in all of her other work.

Katherine's fourth book, *The First Christmas Crib*, was published in 1944. It had been inspired by a visit to the St. Francis country when Miss Milhous was touring England, Belgium, France, and Italy with an artist friend. It tells how St. Francis of Assisi made the first *creche* in the church of the little village of Greccio, Italy, in 1223.

While less appealing than either of her later American Christmas stories, *The First Christmas Crib* presents little known facts concerning the people and the customs of that long ago era. The illustrations for this book are dainty miniatures done in soft pinks, yellows and browns. They are gentle and spiritual in quality and add much to the text.

Between 1945 and 1947 — those war years when printers were difficult to procure — Miss Milhous worked for Charles Scribner's Sons as a designer of other people's books. For a time, therefore, she lived in Tudor City and worked in lower Manhattan, judging the color printing on the great offset presses. It was natural that she should have been asked to do this work since she has a basic knowledge of the printing process through her early experiences in her father's print shop, and since she has always designed and dummied her own books in addition to writing and illustrating them.

Her most recent publication, *With Bells On,* is the second of her American Christmas stories. A Junior Literary Guild selection when it was published in 1955, this book pictures old Pennsylvania in Conestoga wagon days at a time when a wagoner returned "with bells on" only if he had not been stuck in the bad roads. For it was customary in those early days for a wagoner to give his bells as a reward to his rescuer.

With Bells On tells of the making of a "putz," or Christmas manger scene in preparation for Jonathan's homecoming, and suggests that the young reader make his own Christmas "putz" after reading the book. Through the festive preparations made by Chrissly and Becky in this story, one senses that Miss Milhous is affirming her own feeling for Christmas and her own delight in making things with her hands in preparation for the "Great Day."

The making of a "putz" is a charming old-world custom brought to America by the Moravians more than two hundred years ago—a custom maintained to this day by the Moravians of Bethlehem, Pennsylvania. The center of every "putz" is a *creche* with the stable and the Holy Family, the shepherds herding flocks of woolly white sheep, the Wise Men riding camel-back across desert sands, and a host of tiny pink wax angels, blowing trumpets, hung by threads from the ceiling over the stable. But from this point forward each "putz" varies from every other, for the imagination of the maker is allowed complete freedom during the making. The availability of space and materials seem to be the sole deterrent factors. Thus a "putz" may consist of a few figures resting on a bed of moss on a table, or it may fill an entire room.

The central figures of a "putz" are usually of wood and are hand-carved. A few, brought from the old world, have remained with families for many generations. Others were carved by the ancestors of the present-day "putz" makers. Some few have been purchased in stores in this country. The most treasured ones, however, such as the little shepherd in *Snow Over Bethlehem,* were brought from Moravia more than two hundred years ago. These little figures, six to eight inches in height, are handled with loving care and are stored in spacious attics from one season to the next. However, when the child of a Moravian family marries, it is customary to give him or her one or more of the cherished little figures to help in establishing the new family "putz." Thus, this beautiful tradition has been perpetuated from generation to generation.

Each "putz" has a theme and no two themes are alike. One maker may endeavor to introduce animals of the world in their native habitat; another may develop an Alpine scene that presents miniature people coming from every direction to worship the Wonder Child. But, whatever the theme, each "putz" is a work of exquisite beauty — a miniature scene developed with painstaking care and executed with true artistry.

It is customary for the door of the room to be kept locked until Christmas morning when the children are allowed to view the "putz" for the first time. Kneeling before such a scene, lighted either by strategically placed electric lights or by the traditional Moravian beeswax candles, a child could not help feeling the deep meaning of Christmas — the humility and wonder mingled with a sense of deep, abiding love.

In her book, *With Bells On,* Katherine Milhous presents the story of a reverent, closely-knit pioneer family who lived simply, loved one another deeply, and worked together to accomplish an objective. They knew the true meaning of Christmas giving, for, as Mother said, "We, like the Wise Men, can give only of what we have."

And so:

Jonathan had whittled the ox and the donkey and brought presents from the city.

Grandpa had carved the Holy family and kept the farm.

Chrissly had built the stable and the tiny village.

Becky had made the star and the angels, and helped gather the greens.

Mother had baked the bread and cookies and made the little people for the putz.

Katze (the cat) had given cheerful company and warmed them in bed.

They had *all* made Christmas. So, too, had Mr. Greensleeves, with his window full of toys, and the peddler who drove his sleigh through the snow. So, too, had Gus, the ox, and Hossasock, the horse. And the cows who gave the milk, and the hens who laid the eggs, and the bees who made the honey. So, too, had the evergreens in the woods and the Christmas rose blooming in the snow.

They had all given of what they had — and together they had made this wonderful Christmas.

The illustrations for this book are large and bold, strong and colorful. Indeed, they differ in quality from any work previously published by Miss Milhous, for they give the appearance of wood cuts although the originals were watercolors. While Miss Milhous credits the unusual quality of the illustrations to the color-separation process used in their production, it is obvious that more than a technical process has produced the artistry and strength of this work.

These illustrations have a simple, uncluttered appearance, but it is impossible for a reader to grasp all the facets of each illustration with a cursory glance. For example, the first illustration depicts Jonathan, Chrissly, and Becky setting "out on their walk through the woods" to meet Uncle Ned with whom Jonathan is to make the trip to Philadelphia. A second appraisal of this illustration, however, reveals the startling fact that there are mice, squirrels, rabbits, and chipmunks in their snug homes beneath the ground over which the children are walking. However, this secondary theme in no way distracts the reader from the major purpose of the illustration—the introduction of the central characters of the story—and what a delight it is to discover that they are here as a part of what first appears to be no more than a graceful design.

Patrick and the Golden Slippers is the only Milhous book with a Philadelphia setting. Published in 1951, it pictures the colorful New Year's Day Mummer's parade, a tradition that became an annual city-wide celebration at the close of the nineteenth century.

The history of Mummery in this country dates back more than two hundred seventy-five years and is believed to be the oldest folk custom in America—a custom begun by the Germans who settled outside Philadelphia long before William Penn arrived from England. In those early days, masqueraders "used to sing and dance before the houses and people would give them cakes and pennies." Many of them carried pistols for protection along with their bells and sundry noisemakers. Those who shot in the New Year became New Year's Shooters—men who eventually established the Mummer's or Shooter's clubs throughout the city, where members prepare for each year's parade. These "clubs" are often busy places, for as Pop told Patrick, "A good Mummer always plans for the next parade as soon as one parade is over."

Since the prizes for the best dressed, best playing, and best marching bands are large, there is keen rivalry among the various "clubs." Therefore, strangers rarely are allowed inside them, for it is feared that such persons would give away precious costume secrets. Miss Milhous was an exception to this rule, however; so, through Patrick, we catch a glimpse of the inside of such a workshop:

> Inside the workshop all was bright and glittering as a Christmas tree. Silver stars and golden crowns hung from the chandeliers.

At long tables sat the sewing women. Some were embroidering capes with lovely designs of hearts and flowers. Others were trimming costumes with tinsel and spangles and with sequins in every color of the rainbow.

The Mummer's costumes are truly magnificent. They generally consist of a huge feathered headdress, a beautifully embroidered and sequin or tinsel-trimmed satin cape that matches the color of the headdress, and a satin suit trimmed in the same manner as the cape. One such elaborate costume is described by Miss Milhous:

The Snow King's headdress was in the shape of a giant snowflake. His train was nearly the length of a city block and it was carried by many page boys dressed as Snow Men.

Patrick and the Golden Slippers is a rollicking story in which the artist-writer has managed to catch and to hold the feeling of excitement generated by parades everywhere. It pictures a small boy, Patrick, who applies for and receives the job of shoeshine boy to gild the shoes of all the members of the "Brotherly Love String Band" — the same band in which his father plays the violin. In return for his work Patrick is promised a Mascot's suit so he can march in the parade. And march he did! He "strutted and shuffled to the music" in such an audacious manner that he led the band to victory. This book has high reader interest, and its illustrations are soft-toned and charming throughout.

Katherine Milhous holds herself to the standard that good art must have an intangible, indefinable force that is felt rather than seen; and this quality pervades all of her work.

In addition, her work has the sturdy quality of pioneer living. It tells of people who know the joy of creating gifts with their hands, of people who appreciate the wonders and beauties of nature, of people who live simple lives and have close and loving family ties that are made closer through the celebration of holidays and festivals, of people devoted to all things beautiful and to the creators of such beauty.

Such a person has much to offer the children of America. It is reassuring, therefore, to know that the coming year will bring young readers another book from Katherine Milhous — a book that will present another aspect of her beloved Philadelphia to young people everywhere.

REFERENCES

1. Milhous, Katherine, "The Egg Tree and How it Grew," *The Horn Book*. July–August, 1951. p. 226.

2. *Ibid.*, p. 224.
3. *Ibid.*, p. 223.

EDITORS' NOTE

Miss Milhous currently resides in Philadelphia. She loves to travel and has traveled widely. Her awards include the 1951 Caldecott Medal for *The Egg Tree,* and a 1967 citation from the Drexel Institute of Technology in Philadelphia.

WLB Biography:
Mary Norton*

AGAIN AND AGAIN, in appraising the work of Mary Norton, critics have been impelled to draw comparisons with classics of the imagination. Her fantasies for children have brought to mind *Water Babies, Wind in the Willows,* and *Alice in Wonderland.* Her characters have been enjoyed for their Dickensian flavor. Her miniature creatures have been welcomed as little people in the tradition that antedates even Swift and Grimm.

A creator of magic and whimsy for young readers, Mary Norton has led an active life in the very real world. The daughter of a physician, Reginald Spenser Pearson (a descendant of the poet Edmund Spenser), and Mary Savile Hughes Pearson, she was born in London December 10, 1903. At eight she was sent to a school kept by two Anglican nuns, the family nurse having been able to cope with her four brothers, but not with the "naughty Miss Mary." For the next seven years she attended a more orthodox convent school. A sojourn in France followed and then she returned to London. (Her father, who had taken over a large practice in Lambeth, later became mayor of that borough.) A family friend, hearing of her longing to act, obtained an audition for her with the Old Vic Shakespeare Theatre and she began a brief stage career in *The Merchant of Venice.*

The following year—1927—she married Robert Charles Norton and went to live in Portugal, where her husband's ship-owning family had been established since the end of the Napoleonic wars. Despite the grad-

---

* By Ruth Ulman. This article is reprinted by permission from the May 1962 issue of the *Wilson Library Bulletin,* p. 767. Copyright © 1962 by the H. W. Wilson Company.

ual deterioration of their business enterprises during the depression, the Nortons and their children (two sons and two daughters) remained in Portugal until the outbreak of World War II. During the war Mrs. Norton worked first in England with the War Office and then for two years in New York with the British Purchasing Commission. She returned to London during the flying-bomb period and resumed a part-time acting career. At the end of the war her eyes were blasted by a V-2 bomb and she did not see the victory celebrations, but fortunately an operation restored her vision.

It was in the United States that she started to write, as she puts it, "in grim earnest" to help support the children and the house she had rented in Connecticut. (Her husband, left behind in Portugal, joined the staff of the British Embassy there and subsequently enlisted as a gunner in the British navy.) Her first efforts were short stories, articles, translations from the Portuguese. Later she wrote down some of the stories she told her children, and, with the encouragement of American editors, began to feel less of an amateur. Back in London, she continued to write.

Her first book, *The Magic Bed-Knob; or, How to Become a Witch in Ten Easy Lessons* (Putnam, 1944), was the story of three children, a demure spinster learning to become a witch, and a flying bed. The book was lauded for its unique charm and humor and with its 1947 sequel, *Bonfires and Broomsticks,* gained further popularity in dramatized form over the BBC. The work, which the poet John Betjeman called "quite the best modern fairy story I have read," was reissued under the title *Bed-knob and Broomstick* (Harcourt, 1957).

The fantasies that have enchanted adults as well as imaginative children are the four books about the Borrowers, a family of six-inch people hiding in out-of-the-way corners and maintaining their microcosmic existence by "borrowing" from humans who lose them all sorts of useful things — matchboxes, pins, bottle stoppers, postage stamps. The first of the series (all published by Harcourt) was *The Borrowers,* which won the Library Association Carnegie Medal in England as the outstanding children's book of 1952 and captivated critics when published in the United States the following year. "This . . . rare and delicious addition to children's literature," wrote the *Louisville Courier-Journal* reviewer, "deserves to take its place on the shelf of undying classics with Mary Poppins, Christoper Robin, and the other monuments." The three sequels — *The Borrowers Afield* (1955), *The Borrowers Afloat* (1959), and *The Borrowers Aloft* (published in 1961 and, according to Mrs. Norton, the last in the series) — were equally well received and prompted, for all their originality, still more comparisons with Swift, Dickens, Carroll,

E. Nesbit, and Grahame. The adventures of Pod and Homily and their daughter Arrietty—living quietly under the floor of a Victorian country house, braving the dangers of the open fields, being swept away in a leaky teakettle on a riverbank, or escaping from an attic prison by means of a toy balloon—continued to delight readers. Most reviews, except for one or two minor reservations about plot elements somewhat sinister for eight-year-olds or the depiction of such "disagreeables" as old eggshells and hairpins, echoed Ellen Lewis Buell's summation of Mary Norton's art: "Like the great makers of fantasy, Mrs. Norton writes on two levels. Even while we are fascinated by the details of this miniature life and by the borrowers' ingenuity, we are amused by their frailties or deeply moved by their courage."

Mary Norton now lives in a cottage in Essex. She reports that she is a member of the P.E.N. club and that her own list of favorite authors is endless. Her religious affiliation is Church of England and her political affiliation Liberal. For recreation she enjoys swimming, riding, and non-necessary travel.

EDITORS' NOTE

Mary Norton's first book, *The Magic Bed-knob; or How to Become a Witch in Ten Easy Lessons*, was published in 1944 and reissued in 1957 as *Bed-knob and Broomstick*. It is now a Walt Disney film. Miss Norton has written a new book about the Borrowers—*Poor Stainless*, published in 1971. This book, like the others of the series, is illustrated by Beth and Joe Krush and published by Harcourt.

Miss Norton received for *The Borrowers* both the 1952 Carnegie Medal (given annually for a children's book of outstanding merit written by a British subject and published in the United Kingdom) and the 1960 Lewis Carroll Shelf Award (for a book worthy of sitting on the shelf with *Alice in Wonderland*).

Scott O'Dell *

LOS ANGELES WAS a frontier town when I was born there around the turn of the century. It had more horses than automobiles, more jack rabbits than people. The very first sound I remember was a wildcat scratching on the roof as I lay in bed.

My father was a railroad man so we moved a lot, but never far. Wherever we went, it was into frontier country like Los Angeles. There was San Pedro, which is a part of Los Angeles. And Rattlesnake Island, across the bay from San Pedro, where we lived in a house on stilts and the waves came up and washed under us every day. And sailing ships went by.

That is why, I suppose, the feel of the frontier and the sound of the sea are in my books.

Island of the Blue Dolphins, my first story for children, came directly from the memory of the years I lived at Rattlesnake Island and San Pedro. From the days when with other boys of my age I voyaged out on summer mornings in search of the world.

We left the landlocked world and went to sea, each of us on separate logs. The logs had been towed into the harbor in great rafts bound together from the forests of Oregon. They were twelve feet long or longer, rough with splinters and covered with tar. But to each of us young Magellans they were proud canoes, dugouts fashioned by ax and fire, graceful, fierce-prowed, the equal of any storm.

We freed them from the deep-water slips where they waited for the

* By Scott O'Dell. Reprinted by permission from Houghton Mifflin, Boston, Massachusetts.

sawmill. Paddling with our hands, we set to sea, to the breakwater and even to Portuguese Bend. We returned hours later, the watery world encompassed.

Other mornings, in sun or rain, we went to Dead Man's Island, a rocky islet near the entrance to San Pedro Harbor. There we pried abalones from the crevices and searched for devilfish in the sea-washed caves.

The memory of these times also went into the writing of *Island of the Blue Dolphins*.

One of those summers my mother and I traveled across the country to visit an aunt and uncle who lived in a small coal-mining town in West Virginia. The miners with lamps on their caps, the blind mules that shoved the carts back and forth in the mine, the electric dolly that hauled the coal out of the mine and the small steam engine that pulled it away to the railroad tipple — all these things fascinated me. Remembering them and that long-ago summer, I wrote *Journey to Jericho*.

Grammar and high school fascinated me, too. But not college, not Occidental nor Stanford nor the University of Wisconsin. By this time I had my heart set upon writing. However, most of the courses I was forced to take to graduate had little to do with learning to write. So I forgot graduation and took only the courses I wanted — psychology, philosophy, history and English.

I therefore have a sense of comradeship with the students of today. I agree with those who say that they feel like prisoners marching in lockstep toward some unknown goal. I agree that classes are often too large, for I remember a Stanford class in Shakespeare which numbered seventy-six, seventy-five of whom were girls. What can you learn about Shakespeare in such surroundings, even if you're a girl?

After college I was a cameraman on the second company of the original motion picture of *Ben Hur,* carrying the first Technicolor camera, made by hand at M.I.T., around the Roman countryside. I spent a year with the Air Force in Texas during World War II, several years as a book editor on a Los Angeles newspaper. The past twenty years I have devoted to writing, ten of those years writing for adults and the last ten for children.

To say that my books were written *for* children is not exactly true. In one sense they were written for myself, out of happy and unhappy memories and a personal need. But all of them lie in the emotional area that children share with adults.

Writing for children is more fun than writing for adults and more rewarding. Children have the ability, which most adults have lost, the knack to be someone else, of living through stories the lives of other people. Six months after the publication of an adult book, there's a big silence.

Or so it is with me. But with a book for children it's just the opposite. If children like your book they respond for a long time, by thousands of letters. It is this response, this concern and act of friendship, that for me makes the task of writing worth the doing.

There are, of course, a few letters that you would never miss. The letter, for example, from the girl in Minnesota who wrote, asking a dozen or more questions. To have answered them all would have taken two hours, which I didn't have. After a week or so, when she failed to hear from me, she wrote again. She said among other things: ". . . if I don't get a reply from you in five days I will send a letter to another author I know. Anyway, I like her books better than yours."

In their letters children ask dozens of questions. Some are personal, like "How much money do you make?" but mostly they want to know how you work, how stories are put together, how long it takes to write a story, and what is the most important thing a writer should have.

Anthony Trollope, the great English storyteller, said that the most important thing was a piece of sealing wax with which to fasten your pants to a chair. And I agree with him.

Writing is hard work. The only part of it I really enjoy is the research, which takes three or four months. The story itself as a rule takes about six months.

I write, when I do write, which is about half my time, from seven in the morning until noon, every day of the week. I use an electric typewriter, because when you turn it on it has a little purr that invites you to start writing instead of looking out the window. I sometimes use a pen and work very slowly. But I can write with anything and anywhere and have—in Spain and Italy, Germany and France and England and Mexico, in Rancho Santa Fe, a beautiful place in Southern California, where I now live.

When I am not writing I like to read and to work in the sun. I like to garden, to plant trees of all kinds, to be on the sea, fishing some, watching the weather, the sea birds, the whales moving north and south with the seasons, the dolphins, and all the life of the changing waters.

These are the books I have written for children, a few facts about them, the years they were published:

1960 *Island of the Blue Dolphins,* based upon the true story of a girl who was left upon an island near the coast of Southern California and lived there for eighteen years, alone.

1966 *The King's Fifth* describes the adventures of a band of young Spaniards who in the sixteenth century searched for the Seven Golden Cities of Cíbola. The search took them across the Sea of Cortez, into country that is now Arizona and New Mexico, to the Grand Canyon, to Death Valley and beyond. To gather material for this book I followed their trail for more than a thousand miles by boat, automobile and on foot.

1967   *The Black Pearl,* drawn from legend, laid in the seaport of La Paz in Baja California, a tale of good and evil, a giant Manta ray and a fabulous pearl.

1968   *The Dark Canoe* was inspired by one of my favorite novels, *Moby Dick.* Reading Melville's book for the sixth or seventh time, I was struck by the words "dark canoe." The words refer to a coffin changed into a life buoy, which saves the life of the man who tells the story. What has become of this canoe, I asked myself. Is it still drifting around the world? Did it drift into Magdalena Bay in Baja California, as some believe? Can fiction, the written word, be as real as things you can touch?

1969   *Journey to Jericho* is a boy's journey from a coal mine in West Virginia to a lumber camp in California, with complications before and after and along the way.

1970   *Sing Down the Moon.* In 1961 I spent part of the summer in Navaho country, where the states of Arizona and New Mexico, Colorado and Utah meet. This story about Bright Morning and her flock of sheep is the result of those days among the Navahos. I think of it as a modest tribute not only to this Indian girl but also to the courage of the human spirit.

The Treasure of Topo-el-Bampo, to be published in the spring of 1972, concerns two small burros, the richest silver mine and the poorest village in Mexico.

Once in the Spring, which I am working on now and hope to finish next year, is the story of a voyage from California to Ketchikan, Alaska. It follows in the wake of the early Spanish and Portuguese explorers, the Manila galleons, the whaling ships and the fast New England clippers.

EDITORS' NOTE

Mr. O'Dell, a relative newcomer to the field of children's books, has won many awards and honors. For his first book, *Island of the Blue Dolphins,* published in 1960, he received the Southern California Notable

Book Award (most distinguished contribution to children's literature by a Southern Californian), the 1961 Lewis Carroll Shelf Award (worthy of sharing the shelf with *Alice in Wonderland*), the 1961 Newbery Medal, and the 1963 William Allen White Award (best book selected annually by Kansas school children in grades 4–8 from a list chosen by specialists). *Island of the Blue Dolphins* was placed on the 1962 Honor List by the International Board on Books for Young People. Books chosen for this biennial list are representative of the best in children's literature from each country and are considered suitable for publication throughout the world, since the objective of IBBY is to encourage world understanding through children's literature.

Island of the Blue Dolphins was also one of the few children's books to become a movie. Mr. O'Dell was somewhat disappointed in the film version, however, as the time the Indian girl spent on the Island was reduced in the film from eighteen years to four. With this drastically reduced time span, he felt that changes taking place in the character of the protagonist could not be fully expressed.

Mr. O'Dell was a Newbery runner-up for two of his books, *The King's Fifth,* in 1967, and *The Black Pearl,* in 1968. He was recently nominated for the Hans Christian Andersen Award, which is given biennially to one author and one illustrator (since 1966), in recognition of his entire body of work. When Scott O'Dell was asked how he felt about the nomination for this award he said, "It is a great honor to be chosen as a representative of the United States. When an author's entire body of work is being recognized for recommendation, that is distinction in itself. It is very rewarding for me to write for children. I have a sincere feeling that I am able to say something to children, that someone is listening. I am not just entertaining them; I hope that somewhere in each of my books there is something they will take away from it that is important to them as a person."

To the Children with Love, from Leo Politi *

WADING THROUGH DUSTY WEEDS atop Bunker Hill, once the show place of old Los Angeles, Leo Politi came to a halt on the spot where a Victorian mansion had stood as recently as yesterday. Thanks to the efficiency of modern wrecking crews, the land was as free of identity as if it had never seen eighty years of gracious living, gradual decline, and decay.

Something caught the artist's eyes—a balustrade from a veranda. Tenderly he gathered it up and gazed down Bunker Hill Avenue, where several derelict houses waited to see which of them would be next in the scheme of urban renewal.

As if in answer to their unasked question, Politi said, "Who knows? Maybe the Judge Brousseau house or the Castle with its ghost."

He did not like to think of it, but the next victim could be Angel's Flight, with its tiny nickel-a-ride cars that struggle to the top of the Hill like windup toys. Via the dust jacket of his new picture book, *Piccolo's Prank,* he had just reassured readers that the cable car under which the tiny monkey had ridden would remain as a landmark of bygone years. A bronze plaque even designated it as such. But suddenly there were fresh rumors that Angel's Flight would be a casualty in this new Battle of Bunker Hill. It might be torn down or taken apart and reassembled at Disneyland or some other amusement park. Historical societies, cultural heritage boards, and just plain citizens with their letters to editors—none have been able to stem the flow of a progress that obliterates the past.

* By Roberta Nichols. Reprinted by permission from *Horn Book* 42 (April 1966), 218–222.

"Even if the houses could not be saved," Politi lamented, "I should have liked to collect stained-glass windows and ornamental gingerbread and given them to schools so that children would have something of the past to treasure."

But he was denied that. Before the wrecking crew moves in with angry, swinging-ball crane, salable items are wrenched from the houses and sold. Stained-glass windows add an air of elegance to the carriage-trade cocktail lounge; a heavy newel post is a conversation piece when wired for a lamp base.

The only other way to preserve the past of Bunker Hill for an increasingly rootless generation of children was to collect it in stories and pictures and give it back to them as part of their heritage. *Piccolo's Prank* was the result.

Mr. Politi decided that part of the action would take place on the Hill itself, with Angel's Flight playing an important role. The cast of characters would include a German organ-grinder who had lived on the Hill. A touch of the brush converted him into the expansive Italian Luigi of the flowing moustache, because organ-grinders are *supposed* to be Italian. A roller-skating monkey became Piccolo.

The story does not take place during the fashionable years of Bunker Hill, but later, after the old mansions had been converted into boarding houses and apartments — when children (at this late date mostly the grandchildren of residents) romped through tangled gardens that were especially beautiful because their owners could not afford gardeners. Elderly people rocked on verandas or observed the life of the city from third-floor balconies.

This was the Bunker Hill that Politi had come to in the 1930s. Although he had grown up in Italy and had attended the Institute of Monza art school on a scholarship, he is a native Californian. "My grandfather had a vineyard near Fresno. He prided himself on his skill as a wine maker," says Politi, who is also a perfectionist.

So Bunker Hill became home, and Olvera Street, on the Plaza below, was his place of business. This was the very birthplace of Los Angeles, where in 1781 the governor of Alta California sent twelve families, composed of Spaniards, Negroes, Indians, Chinese, and a half-breed, to found a new city. Through the efforts of many dedicated people the area has been designated as a historical landmark and is a popular tourist attraction.

Here Politi set up an easel before El Paseo Cafe and waited for business that came only in dribbles, because the country was in the midst of the Great Depression. But at least he had time to observe and sketch the life around him, its intrigues, pleasures, and sorrows. His roots were reaching deep into the soil of old Los Angeles. And as Americans like to believe, talent and perseverance were rewarded. His work came to the attention of a publisher who commissioned him to illustrate books about South America. When asked to illustrate a proposed children's book about Olvera Street, Politi reasoned that no one was better qualified than he to interpret the street. He asked for and got the chance to write as well as illustrate *Pedro, the Angel of Olvera Street,* the story of the Christmas posadas. Later, there was *Juanita,* about the blessing of the animals. Sketchbook and sensitive ear produced the story of the Chinese New Year in Los Angeles' Chinatown. That was *Moy Moy.*

In 1950 *Song of the Swallows* won the Caldecott Award. For this story Politi ventured some fifty miles away to the Mission of San Juan Capistrano, where he recorded the legend of the swallows' annual return on Saint Joseph's day. Although he could not have known at the time, he may have been preserving a vanishing bit of folklore. The swallows have become lax in keeping schedules. Numbers of them have deserted the mission for nearby Leisure World, a senior citizens' retirement community.

Obviously this is not good for tradition or the tourist trade, so biologists have been called in from the University of California at Riverside to study the situation with an eye to preventing a mass exodus. They note that the once sleepy village of San Juan Capistrano has become a bustling city where housing tracts have replaced orange groves and woods. Ponds, marshes, and irrigation ditches, once the source of food and material for nests, have been drained. As remedies the biologists have suggested such things as offering the birds ready-made nests and giving them back a pond or two—a kind of cradle-to-grave security in return for keeping a tradition alive.

If it is not kept alive—if the swallows become casualties to progress and only the mission remains—at least Politi has saved the essence of the past for children in *Song of the Swallows.*

In case nothing of Bunker Hill survives to stand like an indigent relative among skyscrapers and town houses, there will be the sketches and paintings that he has been making almost from the day that he carried his small possessions to a rooming house on the Hill. When word came that the area was doomed, he had a backlog of material. Now began a feverish race against time to set down the final days. In 1964 the collection went into the nostalgic *Bunker Hill, Los Angeles* (Desert-Southwest, Inc.), "reminiscences of bygone days," already in a second printing. Encouraged by the reception of his first adult book, he interspersed work on *Piccolo's Prank* with another adult book that will be published soon, *The Park*. This is a protest against the destruction of natural beauty — ancient trees, lakes, wild life, the contours of the hills — in order to make freeways and quick access to ball parks and shopping centers.

Guest appearances on television and at schools and libraries provide Politi with opportunity for impassioned pleas to save landmarks, to preserve California's rich cultural heritage for future generations. Although he feels that his is a small, unheard voice, there is little doubt that he is a sharp grain of sand in City Hall's oyster. But cities must do the best they can: clear slums and make valuable land carry its share of the tax burden.

Last year the city purchased twenty of the illustrations from *Bunker Hill, Los Angeles* and is housing them, at least for the present, at the Central Library. Because he did not want the collection broken up, Politi donated other sketches and paintings, some of which he used in *Piccolo's Prank*.

If the Castle, a misnomer, because it is actually an ornate Victorian mansion, should be saved, Politi hopes it will become a museum where, behind the glowing stained-glass door that he has painted so many times under so many different lights, the pictures will hang permanently. But even if the Castle is reduced to rubble and Angel's Flight is carted away to some amusement park, still they will survive along with the rest of the colorful past that Leo Politi collects and gives back to the children in pictures and words — with understanding and love. Always with love.

EDITORS' NOTE

Leo Politi was born in 1908 in Fresno, California. When he was seven years old, the family returned to his mother's childhood home in Brani, Italy. He attended school in Italy, and at the age of fifteen was awarded a scholarship to the National Art Institute at Monza, near Milan. Here he studied drawing, sculpture, architecture, and design for six years. Shortly after graduation he returned to the United States and settled in the Mexican section of Los Angeles, which became the setting for several of his books.

In 1938 Leo married Helen Fontes, and he also published his first book, *Pancho*. He and his wife are still residents of Los Angeles. They have a son, a daughter, and several grandchildren. Leo is fond of animals and has four dogs which appear in his latest book, *Emmet* (1971).

Mr. Politi has written and illustrated seventeen books. He has also illustrated over a dozen books for other writers. His most recent books are

Piccolo's Prank, Mieko and *Emmet*. His honors include a runner-up for the Caldecott Medal for *Pedro, The Angel of Olvera Street* in 1947, and for *Juanita* in 1949; the 1950 Caldecott Medal for *Song of the Swallows;* the 1966 Regina Medal given by the Catholic Library Association for "continued distinguished contribution to children's literature"; and the Southern California Children's Literature Award (most distinguished contribution to children's literature by a Southern Californian) for the illustrations in *Moy Moy* in 1960.

MARIANA PRIETO

Mariana Prieto: She Has Something to Say*

LAST SEPTEMBER I ENROLLED in a creative writing class in the Adult Education Program of Miami Senior High School. That was my introduction to Mariana Prieto, ninety-eight pounds of literature-on-the-go.

THE TEACHER

Never will I forget our first class! Our dynamic little teacher said to us, "Now you, as the author, will want to. . . ." Twenty adult students sat straighter at their school desks. Ladies patted their hair and gentlemen adjusted their ties. She had addressed us as *authors!*

We had all felt naked. Our pretentious aspirations to write were exposed when we took our seats. Mrs. Prieto's first act was to cover our nakedness with a cloak of dignity and hope. We have since learned that this deep concern for others is the core of the woman and of her writings.

THE WOMAN

Mariana Prieto was born in Cincinnati, Ohio, but her family moved to Cuba when she was six months old. She spoke Spanish before she learned English. Educated in Cuban schools, she later attended the University of Miami and the University of Florida.

Mrs. Prieto has had a busy life. She has appeared on radio programs in

* By Irene Buckley. From *Elementary English* 44 (January 1967), 7–11. Reprinted with the permission of the National Council of Teachers of English and Irene Buckley.

353

Spanish and English. Her writings have been printed in Spanish, English, Swedish, and Braille. Her articles and short stories have appeared in such major magazines as *Mademoiselle, The Country Gentlemen, The Woman,* and many others. During World War II she taught Spanish to Army Air Corps officers and enlisted men. Before her affiliation with the public school Adult Education Division, she taught creative writing in the Evening Division of the University of Miami.

THE WRITER

Mrs. Prieto has now channeled two major areas of her background— her writing and her knowledge of Latin American peoples—into the writing of dual language children's books. This brings to her a greater reward and sense of fulfillment than anything else she has done. Her books have been recommended by *The Library Journal,* Child Study Association of America, *The Horn Book,* and American Library Association.

She teaches her adult writing students that unless a story has "something to say," it has no excuse for being. This is clearly demonstrated in her children's books. They are full of warmth and understanding. They all have a strong plot structure, pointing out a moral without preaching. They have something to say to a child in any language, particularly in the area of social studies. Her newest book, which will be released this year, deals with the subject of migrant children struggling to cross both the language and the race barriers.

Her stories are set against authentic regional backgrounds. Since she has lived in Latin America, she weaves a beautiful tale of the Mayans, who live in fear and awe of the "little people." The child can close his eyes and see tiny men in tremendous hats hiding behind every tree in the woods.

She has also lived in United States cities with large Spanish-speaking communities and has a poignant understanding of the child who is growing up somewhere between the old world and the new.

THE LANGUAGE ARTS

Mrs. Prieto is fully cognizant of the importance of the language arts in a child's study program. Because she spoke both English and Spanish as a child, she is well aware that the bilingual child has a tremendous handicap in problems of speech and reading. She has therefore dedicated much time and research to the use of dual-language story books.

Mrs. Mary E. Decker (1), elementary librarian in Rhinebeck, New York, discusses the use of books as classroom aids in dealing with the problems of the bilingual child:

The school library should be able to furnish many suitable books for reading aloud. . . . Often the illustrations of children's books provide a starting place for conversation and vocabulary practice. . . . The relevant dual-language dictionary is basic equipment, indispensable for the teacher. . . . It may be fun and informative to vary instruction by using books written in the students' native language. . . . It is comforting to a child to see his first language again, perhaps to read it aloud.

Each of Mrs. Prieto's books is a self-contained unit, providing all the tools suggested by Mrs. Decker. Each illustration is accompanied by both English and Spanish texts, side by side. Each book contains vocabularies in English and Spanish, with phonetic pronunciations. Informational notes concerning words and customs of the Latin American people are included in her books. Not only does the child "see his first language again," but he sees it against his native background. For the Spanish-speaking child lost in a world of typical American storybooks, her books are truly a "touch of home."

This is not to say that the wise little rooster or Itzo, the mouse, will be of interest only to the bilingual child whose first language is Spanish. The format of English and Spanish, side by side for easy comparison, is extremely helpful for English-speaking children whose second language is Spanish, and many elementary schools today are teaching conversational Spanish. Mrs. Prieto's books are written for children from grades two to six.

The English-speaking child also welcomes the change in background as a reading experience. Just as we adults love to read about faraway places which we may never see for ourselves, so children love to "travel" by storybook.

AH UCU AND ITZO

Ah Ucu and Itzo (2) is a touching tale of a little Mayan boy in Yucatan and his pet mouse, Itzo. This story proves to the reader, through the intriguing medium of a completely foreign setting, that even a child can be master of his destiny. Through his own efforts and hard work, Ah Ucu managed to save his pet mouse *and* his parents' corn crop. "Ah Ucu worked day after day for the old man" and "earned six ears of corn."

Special subject teachers and readers will be particularly interested in the explanation of the Mayan folktale of the "little people" (alux) and in the vocabulary of Mayan words. "In the Mayan language, the prefix *ah* was placed before each boy's name: Ah Ucu."

All children respond to tales of fairies and witches. They will understand that the "little people" have to be coaxed and bribed.

Ah Ucu's mother and father built a small house in the cornfield (col) for the little people. "We must put the floorboards close together," his father had said, "so that their long beards will not get caught between." . . . They wanted the corn (ixim) to grow high, and it is the "little people" who can make it grow.

This text is accompanied by a delightful underground illustration of a row of little men standing on the backs of other little men, each one pushing up against a cornstalk to "make it grow." Their sombreros are stacked beside them as they work.

THE WISE ROOSTER

The Wise Rooster (3) is a re-creation of a favorite Latin American legend: The animals in the stable in Bethlehem were given the power of speech the night the Christ-child was born.

And so it was that one night not long before Christmas, Grandmother Mena took little Alicia, her granddaughter, on her lap and told her the story of the night the animals talked. This is the story she told.

The child learns that humility is rewarded, but vanity is punished. The animals rejoiced when they discovered "they all had voices and could talk just like people!" All the good little animals "talked happily together of how each in his separate way would serve the new-born King," but one vain little donkey spoiled it all—for himself and for his companions.

The silly donkey had broken the spell because he wasted precious words praising himself . . . and so it was, none could talk ever again.

A KITE FOR CARLOS

Mrs. Prieto's most recently released book, just off the press, is *A Kite for Carlos* (4). It is set in the Spanish-speaking community of Ybor City, in Tampa, Florida, and deals with the immigrant problem through three generations.

Grandfather believed that a boy's birthday could not be properly honored without the traditional chicken and yellow rice. Carlos wanted "hot dogs, popcorn, and a birthday cake" for his birthday party. Mother served both, to prove that Carlos was indeed a United States citizen, but that it was also important to retain the customs of the old country.

This theme is laced through the main plot, which involves that magic moment of "firstness," and Carlos' wish to have "the most beautiful kite in the world" for his birthday. Carlos lost his beautiful kite through his own foolish disobedience. Though his grandfather promised to make another, Carlos realized that no other kite could ever be quite so magnificent as his birthday kite.

"MY BOOKS ARE CHILD-TESTED"

Mrs. Prieto's black eyes sparkle when she discusses collaborating with her ten-year-old grandson. "He is a tremendous help. I get a child's-eye view of the situation by discussing my work with him."

She reads her stories aloud, listening for melody and cadence.

"I use short sentences and 'happy' words," she says, "but I do not limit myself to standard vocabulary lists. I strive always for clarity and simplicity in expressing the problem and solution. I follow the analyst's method of reading my stories aloud to the neighborhood children, then asking them to draw the pictures the story conjures up for them. From this I evaluate the effectiveness of my writing and know whether or not I have expressed what I wanted to say."

She visits various schools and discusses her books with her readers.

Mrs. Prieto told our writing class recently that her publisher had just accepted her newest book. "I sat down and cried when I read his letter because he understood exactly what I was trying to say in this book."

This, through all the technicalities of vocabulary aids and instructional notes, ancient customs and modern social problems, is Mariana Prieto's reason for writing. She has "something to say" to her children.

REFERENCES

1. Decker, Mary E., "From 'Si' to 'Yes'," *Elementary English,* 42 (January, 1965) 35–37.
2. Prieto, Mariana, *Ah Ucu and Itzo.* New York: The John Day Company, Inc., 1964.
3. Prieto, Mariana, *The Wise Rooster.* New York: The John Day Company, Inc., 1962.
4. Prieto, Mariana, *A Kite for Carlos.* New York: The John Day Company, Inc., 1966.

EDITORS' NOTE

In 1968 and 1969 Mrs. Prieto made research trips to Mexico and Spain to gather material for her books. Her recent books include *When the Monkeys Wore Sombreros* (1969, Harvey House), *Johnny Lost*

(1969, John Day), and *Raimundo, The Unwilling Warrior* (1971, Harvey House). Books to appear in 1972 include *Play It in Spanish* (John Day), *Pablo's Petunias* (Oddo), and *Craft and Hobby Fun* (Standard).

Mrs. Prieto notes in an April, 1968, article in *The Horn Book:* "I endeavor to do books that will appeal equally to the Spanish-speaking child and the English-speaking child. Because I lived in both worlds, I have tried to bring to my stories the advantages of both. I trust that through these books my readers understand each other better and capture something of the magic and cadence of Spanish, and the practicality and charm of English."

Margret and H. A. Rey *

AMONG CHILDREN we seem to be known best as the parents of *Curious George,* the little monkey hero of some of our books. "I thought you were monkeys too," said a little boy who had been eager to meet us, disappointment written all over his face.

Not all our children's books are about George, but they are all about animals. We both love them, and one of the first things we do when we come to a new town is visit the Zoo.

In Hamburg, Germany, where both of us were born, H.A. (which stands for Hans Augusto) lived close to the famous Hagenbeck Zoo and, as a child, spent much of his free time there. That's where he learned to imitate animal voices. He is proudest of his lion roar, and once he roared for 3000 children in the Atlanta Civic Auditorium, thus making the headlines in the *Atlanta Constitution* for the first and last time.

Over the years we have owned an assortment of animals: turtles in Paris; monkeys in Brazil, which unfortunately died on a trip to Europe; alligators, chameleons and newts in New Hampshire, where we live in summer; and dogs, of course. We always have a cocker spaniel and H.A. generally manages to get him into some picture in each of our books.

H.A. also has written and illustrated two books on astronomy. One for children, which is written so simply that even adults can understand it; and one for adults, which today's children, growing up in the space age, often master better than their elders.

* By Margret and H. A. Rey. Reprinted by permission from Houghton Mifflin, Boston, Massachusetts.

The books on astronomy are, in a way, a by-product of the First World War. There's no ill wind. . . . H.A., as an eighteen-year-old G.I. in the German army, carried in his knapsack a pocket book on astronomy, the stars being a handy subject to study in those blacked-out nights. But the book was not much help for the beginning star-gazer, and the way the constellations were presented stumped him. So, many years later, still being dissatisfied with the existing books, he worked out a new way to show the constellations and ended up by doing his own books on astronomy.

In 1900, when he was two years old, H.A. started drawing, mostly horses. At that time one could still see horses all over the city. He went to what in Europe is called a Humanistic Gymnasium, a school that starts Latin in the fourth grade, then Greek, then French, and then English. From this early exposure to five languages—German being the fifth, of course—he developed a lasting interest in linguistics. He speaks four languages fluently and has a smattering of half a dozen others.

After school and the First World War he studied whatever aroused his curiosity: philosophy, medicine, languages; but he never went to an art school. To pay the grocery bills while studying he designed posters for a Circus, then lithographed them directly on stone, an experience that came in handy in later years when he had to do the color separations for his book illustrations.

H.A. still gets nostalgic thinking of those Circus days, when he befriended many an animal—seals, elephants, chimps—and got to know them intimately.

Margret is the one in the family with the formal art education. After school she studied at the Bauhaus in Dessau, the Academy of Art in Duesseldorf, and an art school in Berlin. She even had a one-man show of her watercolors in Berlin in the early twenties. Then, being restless, she switched to writing, did newspaper work for a little while, and later became a copywriter in an advertising agency. At one point she wrote singing commercials in praise of margarine, an experience which left her with undying hate for commercials. (We now have a "blab-off" on our T.V. set and cut off the sound the moment a plug gets obnoxious.)

Being restless again, Margret switched to photography, worked in a photographic studio in London for a short time, and then opened her own studio in Hamburg, Germany, just when Hitler came into power.

But back to H.A. He decided to leave Germany in 1923, when the German postwar inflation had become so catastrophic that the money he would receive for a poster one day would not be enough to buy a lunch a week later. He went to Rio de Janeiro, Brazil, and became a business executive in a relative's firm, where among other things he sold bathtubs up and down the Amazon River. He pursued this rather uncongenial activity until 1935, when Margret showed up in Rio de Janeiro.

We had met in Hamburg just before H.A. went to Brazil. As H.A. tells the story, he met Margret in her father's house at a party for her older sister, and his first glimpse of her was when she came sliding down a banister.

With Hitler in power Margret had decided to leave Germany and work as a photographer in Brazil. The first thing she did when she saw H.A. again was to persuade him to leave business. He did, and we started working together, as a sort of two-man advertising agency, doing a little of everything: wedding photos, posters, newspaper articles (which Margret wrote and H.A. illustrated), and whole advertising campaigns. Four months later we got married. We went to Europe on our honeymoon, roamed around a.bit, and finally came to Paris, where we planned to stay for two weeks. We stayed for four years, in the same hotel in Montmartre where we first took lodging. We might still be there had the Second World War not started.

In Paris we did our first children's book. It came about by accident: H.A. had done a few humorous drawings of a giraffe for a Paris periodical. An editor at Gallimard, the French publishing house, saw them and called us up to ask whether we could not make a children's book out of them. We did and this became our first book, *Cecily G. and the Nine Monkeys,* one of the nine being George, incidentally.

Ever since we have done mostly children's books, and it seems to agree with us. (H.A. is still surprised that he is being paid for what he likes to do best and would do anyhow.)

In June 1940, on a rainy morning before dawn, a few hours before the Nazis entered, we left Paris on bicycles, with nothing but warm coats and our manuscripts (*Curious George* among them) tied to the baggage racks, and started pedaling south. We finally made it to Lisbon, by train, having sold our bicycles to custom officials at the French-Spanish border. After a brief interlude in Rio de Janeiro, our migrations came to an end one clear, crisp October morning in 1940, when we saw the Statue of Liberty rise above the harbor of New York and landed in the U.S.A.

We took a small apartment in Greenwich Village, rolled up our sleeves and were ready to start from scratch. We did not know a single publisher, but before the week was over, we had found a home for *Curious George* at Houghton Mifflin Company.

After twenty-three years in New York's Greenwich Village, we moved to Cambridge in 1963, and are spending the summers in our cottage in

Waterville, N.H., where Margret has developed into an ardent gardener, while H.A. retreats to his studio in the woods and tries hard not to get involved in horticultural activities.

How do we work together and who does what? Basically H.A. illustrates and Margret writes. But that is not the whole story. H.A. also has the ideas for a book which Margret then turns into a story. And Margret sometimes writes her own books, such as *Pretzel* and *Spotty*, and H.A. does the illustrations, at times changing the story a little to fit his pictures. And the astronomy books H.A. does all by himself—no, not quite. Margret sometimes rewrites parts of them to make them easier to understand for the layman. For Margret is a layman in astronomy, and H.A. by now is nearly a professional. So it is confusing and at times it confuses even us.

One thing is clear, though: doing a book is hard work for us. People sometimes think we dash them off. We wish we could. We work very long on each one, frequently over a year. We write and rewrite, we draw and redraw, we fight over the plot, the beginning, the ending, the illustrations—as a matter of fact our work is nearly the only thing we do fight about.

And where do the ideas come from? We wish we knew. Sometimes they don't come. Soaking in a hot bathtub—a news item in the papers—a piece of conversation at a party—it all helps. Once we heard a biochemist tell how, as a boy, he had made a bargain with his mother to give the kitchen floor a thorough scrubbing in order to get money for a chemistry set. So one day, while his parents were out, he sprinkled the contents of a large package of soap flakes on the floor, pulled the garden hose through the window and turned the water on. . . . In *Curious George Gets a Medal* George emulates this experiment with spectacular results.

Our books have been translated into about a dozen different languages, and it is fun for us to leaf through our authors' copies of these foreign editions. It does not matter much that there are some we cannot read, such as Finnish and Japanese—it so happens that we know the story.

EDITORS' NOTE

H.A. Rey teaches astronomy at the Cambridge Center for Adult Education, and he says that his books on astronomy are based on a star identification system which he invented. He is a member of the Amateur

Astronomers Association, the American Association for the Advancement of Science, and the Federation of American Scientists.

Margret and H.A. received the 1966 Child Study Association of America Children's Book Award (given for the best book dealing realistically with some problem in the child's contemporary world) for *Curious George Goes to the Hospital.* H.A. was named in the 1957 *New York Times* List of Best Illustrated Books of the Year for *Curious George Gets a Medal,* and he also received the 1960 Louis Carroll Shelf Award (for a book worthy to sit on the shelf with *Alice in Wonderland*) for *Curious George Takes a Job.* Currently, the Reys are working on several more children's books.

Questions to an Artist
Who Is Also an Author[*]

MAURICE SENDAK BEGAN his career as a professional illustrator while he was still a high school student in Brooklyn, N.Y., adapting "Mutt and Jeff" comic strips for publication in comic books. After completing high school he studied at the Art Students League and worked in the design and construction of window displays. His unusual talents soon came to the attention of Ursula Nordstrom, the children's book editor at Harper's, for whom he illustrated Marcel Aymé's *The Wonderful Farm* (1951). He has since illustrated over 60 books, including 10 which he himself has written. His illustrations for Ruth Krauss' *A Hole Is to Dig* (1952) and Else Minarik's *Little Bear* (1959) drew widespread acclaim. As both writer and illustrator, he has produced a number of children's books which have already become classics, including *Kenny's Window* (1956), *Very Far Away* (1957), *The Sign on Rosie's Door* (1960), *The Nutshell Library* (1962), *Where the Wild Things Are* (1963), *Higglety Pigglety Pop!* (1967), and *In the Night Kitchen* (1970). Mr. Sendak was awarded the American Library Association's Randolph Caldecott Medal in 1964 for *Where the Wild Things Are*. In 1970 he became the first American to receive the coveted Illustrator's Medal of the Hans Christian Andersen Awards.

In a National Children's Book Week program sponsored by the Gertrude Clarke Whittall Poetry and Literature Fund, Mr. Sendak presented some of his ideas about children's literature in an informal question-and-

[*] No copyright claimed for this article. It is reprinted in part from *The Quarterly Journal* of The Library of Congress, October, 1971, pp. 263–280.

answer session at the Library of Congress. The questions were addressed to Mr. Sendak by Miss Virginia Haviland, head of the Library's Children's Book Section. The following article is based on a transcript of the discussion, held in the Coolidge Auditorium on November 16, 1970.

Miss Haviland: As a starter, let's ask: What did a book mean to you as a child? And what kinds of books did you have?

Mr. Sendak: I think I'll start with the kinds of books, because back in the thirties I didn't have any "official" children's books (I refer to the classics). The only thing I can remember is cheap paperbacks, comic books. That's principally where I started. My sister bought me my first book, *The Prince and the Pauper*. A ritual began with that book which I recall very clearly. The first thing was to set it up on the table and stare at it for a long time. Not because I was impressed with Mark Twain; it was just such a beautiful object. Then came the smelling of it. I think the smelling of books began with *The Prince and the Pauper,* because it was printed on particularly fine paper, unlike the Disney books I had gotten previous to that, which were printed on very poor paper and smelled poor. *The Prince and the Paper—Pauper—*smelled good and it also had a shiny cover, a laminated cover. I flipped over that. And it was very solid. I mean, it was bound very tightly. I remember trying to bite into it, which I don't imagine is what my sister intended when she bought the book for me. But the last thing I did with the book was to read it. It was all right. But I think it started then, a passion for books and bookmaking. I wanted to be an illustrator very early in my life; to be involved in books in some way—to make books. And the making of books, and the touching of books—there's so much more to a book than just the reading; there is a sensuousness. I've seen children touch books, fondle books, smell books, and it's all the reason in the world why books should be beautifully produced.

Miss Haviland: Our questions to you, which are questions I think you have often answered for university and other groups, come as questions to you as an author and questions to you as an artist. Let's begin with the group of questions that have to do with you as an author. What part do you think fantasy should play in a child's life?

Mr. Sendak: Well, fantasy is so all-pervasive in a child's life: I believe there's no part of our lives, our adult as well as child life, when we're not fantasizing, but we prefer to relegate fantasy to children, as though it were some tomfoolery only fit for the immature minds of the young. Children do live in fantasy *and* reality; they move back and forth very easily in a way that we no longer remember how to do. And in writing for children you just must assume they have this incredible flexibility, this cool sense of the logic of illogic, and that they can move with you very easily from one sphere to another without any problems. Fantasy is the core of all writing for children, as I think it is for the writing of any book, for any creative act, perhaps for the act of living. Certainly it is crucial to my work. . . . My books don't come about by "ideas" or by thinking of a particular subject and exclaiming "Gee, that's a terrific idea, I'll put it down!" They never quite come to me that way; they well up. In the way a dream comes to us at night, feelings come to me, and then I must rush to put them down. But these fantasies have to be given physical form, so you build a house around them, and the house is what you call a story, and the painting of the house is the bookmaking. But essentially it's a dream, or it's a fantasy.

Miss Haviland: Are you, yourself, remembering daydreams? And a belief in fantasy that came out of your own childhood?

Mr. Sendak: I can't recall my childhood any more than most of us can. There are sequences and scenes I remember much as we all do. But I do seem to have the knack of recalling the emotional quality of childhood, so that in *Wild Things* — I can remember the feeling, when I was a child (I don't remember who the people were, but there were people who had come to our house, relatives perhaps) and I remember they looked extremely ugly to me. . . . It's not the recollection of my own particular childhood that I put down in books, but the feeling—like that particular feeling of fear of adults, who are totally unaware that what they say to children is sometimes taken quite literally. And that when they pinch your cheek out of affection, it hurts; and that, when they suggest they could "hug you to death," you back away—any number of such things.

Miss Haviland: It would be interesting to find out whether you can account for the fact that college students seem to enjoy *Where the Wild Things Are* and *Higglety Pigglety Pop!* as much as children do. The question is: whom do you see as your audience?

Mr. Sendak: Well, I suppose primarily children, but not really. Because I don't write for children specifically. I certainly am not conscious of sitting down and writing a book for children. I think it would be fatal if one did. So I write *books,* and I hope that they are books anybody can read. I mean, there was a time in history when books like *Alice in Wonderland* and the fairy tales of George Macdonald were read by everybody.

They were not segregated for children. So I'd like to think I have a large audience, and if college students like my books, that's fine. . . .

Miss Haviland: Some other college students have asked how you, as a writer in this post-Freudian era, can resolve the problem of not consciously manipulating the unconscious.

Mr. Sendak: [After a pause] Well, that's a problem. The Victorians were very fortunate. *Alice in Wonderland* is full of images and symbols, which are extremely beautiful and sometimes frightening. We know that Carroll had no Freud, and the book came pouring out of his unconscious, as happened with George Macdonald in *Princess and the Goblin*. These authors touched on some very primal images in quite a fascinating way. It is more difficult for us to do because we do know so much, we've read so much. I hope I don't consciously manipulate my material. I do not analyze my work; if something strikes me and I get excited, then I want it to be a book. If it begins to die as I work, then of course it's not a book. But I think I do get away occasionally with walking that fine unconscious line. The things I've written in which there are conscious unconscious things, are very—you can't put your finger on it, certainly children can put their fingers on it, they are *the* most critical audience in the world, they smell a rat instantly. You cannot fool them, you really cannot fool them. They're tough to work for. And if they sense—and they know adults do these books—if they sense for one minute that I was faking this, I would know it. Now, *Wild Things* walked a very fine line in this particular sense. It was accepted by children largely, and that's the only proof I have that I've done it. . . .

Miss Haviland: Some readers have been intrigued by the relationships between your characters Kenny, Martin, Max, and Mickey. Would you say in what way these children may be the same child, or in what ways they are not?

Mr. Sendak: They are the same child, of course. Three of them have the initial "M." I don't think that's an accident, although I thought of that only while I was working on the last book. The first boy was Kenny, and he was named after a specific person. But a thread of meaning connects all the children. I can do a very rough analysis, I suppose. Kenny is a frustrated and introverted child. And Martin is fussy and sulking and not very brave. Max is tremendously brave but in a rage. And Mickey is extremely brave and very happy. I can follow that—I don't know if you can—but in the characters there is a kind of progress from holding back to coming forth which I'd like to think is me, not so much as a child or pretending that I'm a child but as a creative artist who also gets freer and freer with each book and opens up more and more.

Miss Haviland: Many persons right now are asking what inspired you to produce this new book, *In the Night Kitchen?*

Mr. Sendak: Well, that is a difficult question. It comes out of a lot of things, and they are very hard to describe, because they are not so clear to me. There are a few clues. When I was a child there was an advertisement which I remember very clearly. It was for the Sunshine Bakers. And the advertisement read "We Bake While You Sleep!" It seemed to me the most sadistic thing in the world, because all I wanted to do was stay up and watch. And it seemed so absurdly cruel and arbitrary for them to do it while I slept. And also for them to think I would think that was terrific stuff on their part, you know, and would eat their product on top of that. It bothered me a good deal, and I remember I used to save the coupons showing the three fat little Sunshine bakers going off to this magic place, wherever it was, at night to have their fun, while I had to go to bed. This book was a sort of vendetta book to get back at them and to say that I am now old enough to stay up at night and know what is happening in the Night Kitchen! The other clue is a rather odd fantasy of mine when I was a child. I lived in Brooklyn and to travel to Manhattan was a big deal, even though it was so close. I couldn't go by myself, and I counted a good deal on my elder sister. She took us—my brother and myself—to Radio City Music Hall, or the Roxy, or some such place. Now, the point of going to New York was that you *ate* in New York. Now we get back to eating again. Somehow to me New York represented eating. And eating in a very fashionable, elegant, superlatively mysterious place like Longchamps. You got dressed up, and you went uptown, and it was night when you got there, and there were lots of windows blinking, and you went straight to a place to eat. It was one of the most exciting things of my childhood, to do this. Cross the bridge, and see the city approaching, and get there, and have your dinner, and then go to a movie, and come home. So, again, *In the Night Kitchen* is a kind of homage to New York City, the city I loved so much and still love. It had a special quality for me as a child. It also is homage to the things that really affected me esthetically. I did not get to museums, I did not see art books. I was really quite rough in the sense of what was going on artistically. *Fantasia* was perhaps the most esthetic experience of my childhood, and that's a very dubious experience. But mainly there were the comic books and there was Walt Disney, and, more than anything else, there were the movies and radio, especially the movies. The early films, such as the Gold

Digger movies and *King Kong* and other monster films, were the stuff that my books are composed of now. I am surprised, and this is really unconscious—I was looking at *Where the Wild Things Are* not too long ago with a friend, who had found something which amused her a good deal. She is a film collector, and she opened to one page of the book, where one of the wild things is leaning out of the cave. And then she held alongside it a still from *King Kong,* and it was, literally, a copy. But I had not seen the still, of course; I could not have remembered the sequence. Obviously, it had impressed itself on my brain, and there it was: I mean, exactly the proportions of cave to cliff, and proportions of monster coming out of cave. It was really quite extraordinary, the effect the films did have on me.

It was only much later, when I was a practicing illustrator and writer, that I got to know the classic children's books and read them. I did not know them as a child; I did not know pictures or paintings or writing when I was growing up. Brooklyn was a more or less civilized place, let me assure you, but this particular thing didn't get to me until quite late. And I think it's reflected in my work. I am what is commonly referred to as a late bloomer. I am happy for that.

Miss Haviland: That brings us to the question of whom you believe to be some of the great writers for children? You have made some allusions already, but would you enlarge on that?

Mr. Sendak: George Macdonald I think of as probably the greatest of the Victorian writers for children. It's the combination of planes, levels, that he worked on. George Macdonald can tell a conventional fairy tale; it has all the form that a fairy tale must have. At the same time, he manages to inundate the story with a kind of dream-magic, or unconscious power. *The Princess and the Goblin:* Irene's travels through the cave with the goblins are so strange, they can only come out of the deepest dream stuff. The fact that he can weave both of these things together is exactly what I love so much in his work, and what I try to emulate. And he is a model; he is someone I try to copy in many ways. There are other writers, like Charles Dickens, who has precisely this quality of the urgency of childhood. The peculiar charm of being in a room in a Dickens novel, where the furniture is alive, the fire is alive, where saucepans are alive, where chairs move, where every inanimate object has a personality. This is that particularly vivid quality that children have, of endowing everything with life. And Dickens sees and hears as children do. He has a marvelous ear for what's going on socially and politically, and on one level he's telling you a straightforward story. But underneath there is the intensity of the little boy staring out at everything and looking, and examining, and watching, and feeling intensely, and suffering immensely, which is what I think makes Dickens a superb writer. The same is true of George Macdonald. Another favorite writer is Henry James. I first became enthusiastic over Henry James when I read some of the earlier novels about young children. His incredible power of putting himself in the position of young children, viewing the adult world; and his uncanny sense of how difficult and painful it is to be a child. And even harder to be an adolescent. Now, these are people who write from their child sources, their dream sources. They don't forget them. William Blake is my favorite—and, of course, *The Songs of Innocence* and *The Songs of Experience* tell you all about this: what it is to be a child—not childish, but a child inside your adult self—and how much better a person you are for being such. So that my favorite writers are never writers who have written books specifically for children. I don't believe in that kind of writing. I don't believe in people who consciously write for children. The great ones have always just written books. And there are many more, but I can't think of them now.

Miss Haviland: Now let's take a group of questions set to you as an artist. In a photo bulletin issued by our State Department, a comment is made that critics credit—and I'm quoting now—"a hidden little boy, Maurice, between four and eight, with the dreamlike quality of the pictures created by Sendak the man." And further in this piece, the journalist quoted you as saying that your new book, *In the Night Kitchen,* is your idea of what books looked like to you as a four-year-old. Would you elaborate on this quotation?

Mr. Sendak: Well, I think I did that already. I mean, the city as I felt it as a child. It also was an attempt to capture the look of the books that meant so much to me in the thirties and the early forties—they were not glamorous, "artistic" books; they were very cheap, full-color books that, up to a short time ago, I thought were contemptible. But for some odd reason, my old love for them has returned. My taste in English graphics and German fairy tales came much later, and it really is, I think, on my part at least an honest attempt to get back to those things that did mean an awful lot to me as a child. They weren't fancy, they were good, and *In the Night Kitchen* was an attempt to make a beautiful book that at the same time still suggested those early inexpensive books that were read by most children I knew.

Miss Haviland: One librarian recalls hearing you speak in the 1950's, a time between the publishing of your illustrations for *A Hole Is to Dig* and of those for *Little Bear,* when you said that your roots go back to Caldecott. And this past April, when you accepted the Hans Christian Andersen International Medal, you named another string of artists whom you credit with stimulating you. I remember you mentioned William Blake, whom you've already spoken of here, George Cruikshank and Boutet de Monvel, Wilhelm Busch, Heinrich Hoffmann. Could you talk about the specific elements that you think you find there that are particularly relevant to the children's book illustrator?

Mr. Sendak: I hated school and my own particular way was to learn by myself. Many of the artists who influenced me were illustrators I accidentally came upon. I knew the Grimm's *Fairy Tales* illustrated by George Cruikshank, and I just went after everything I could put my hands on that was illustrated by Cruikshank and copied his style. Quite as simply as that. I wanted to crosshatch the way he did. Then I found Wilhelm Busch and I was off again. But happily Wilhelm Busch also crosshatched, so the Cruikshank crosshatching wasn't entirely wasted. And so an artist grows. I leaned very heavily on these people. I developed taste from these illustrators. Boutet de Monvel, the French illustrator, who is still not terribly well known (which is a great surprise to me), illustrated in the twenties, or earlier perhaps—had the most glorious sense of design and refinement of style. His pictures are so beautifully felt and they are supremely elegant as only French illustration can be. They are very clear, very transparent, extremely fine. At the same time, they can be very tragic. There are things in his drawings, which perhaps now would even seem too strong for children—although at one point, they did not. There is a perfect example of his method in one of his illustrations for the *Fables* of La Fontaine—"The Wolf and the Lamb." They are a series of drawings, very much like a comic strip. It's like a ballet. The little lamb moves toward the stream and begins to drink, and the ferocious wolf appears and says: "What are you doing here? This is my water!" Of course, he's rationalizing the whole thing, he's going to eat the lamb up anyway, but he's putting on this big act about it being his water. Now, the lamb knows that there's no chance for escape, and while the wolf is bristling—and in each drawing his chest gets puffier and his fangs get fangier, and his eyes are blazing, and he looks horrendous—now, in proportion to him, growing larger on the page, the lamb dwindles. It has immediately accepted its fate, it can't outrun the wolf, it doesn't even listen to the words of the wolf, this is all beside the point: it is going to die, and it prepares itself for death. And while the wolf goes through this inane harangue, the lamb folds itself in preparation for its death. It leans down, it puts its head to one side, it curls up very gently, and its final gesture is to lay its head down on the ground. And at that moment the wolf pounces and destroys the lamb. It is one of the most beautiful sequences I've ever seen and one of the most honest in a children's book. There's no pretense of the lamb escaping, or of there being a happy ending — this is the way it is, it does happen this way sometimes, that's what de Monvel is saying. And this is what I believe children appreciate. People rage against the Grimm's fairy tales, forgetting that originally the brothers Grimm had — I'm going off the track a little bit — assembled the tales not for children but for historical and philological reasons. They were afraid their past was being lost in all the upheavals of that period, and the tales were put out as a scholarly edition of peasant tales not to be forgotten as part of the heritage of their homeland. Well, lo and behold, children began to read them. And the second edition was called *The Household Tales* because children were devouring the books — not literally — I'm going to be so conscious of that from here on. The whole point I'm making, although I have forgotten the point frankly, is that those illustrators and writers that attracted me were the ones who did not seem at all to be hung up by the fact that their audiences were small people. They were telling the truth, just the way it was. This could be done if it were esthetically beautiful, if it were well written — simply, if it were a work of art, then it was fine. Now *Der Struwwelpeter* was one of the books that I loved very much — graphically, it *is* one of the most beautiful books in the world. One might complain about the cutting off of fingers, and the choking to death, and being burned alive, and might we.l have a case there — but, esthetically, for an artist growing up it was a good book to look at and a lot of my early books were affected strongly by the German illustrators. When I came to picture books, it was Randolph Caldecott who really did put me where I wanted to be. Caldecott is an illustrator, he is a songwriter, he is a choreographer, he is a stage manager, he is a decorator, he is a theater person; he's superb, simply. And he can take four lines of verse that have very little meaning in themselves and stretch them into a book that has tremendous meaning — not overloaded, no sentimentality in it. Everybody meets with a bad ending in *Froggie Went A-Courting*. Froggie gets eaten at the end by a duck, which is very sad, and the story usually ends on that note. But in Caldecott's version, he introduces, oddly enough, a human family. They observe the tragedy much as a Greek chorus might — one can almost hear their comments. In the last picture, we see Froggie's hat going downstream, all that remains of him. And standing on the bank are mother, father, and child — and it's startling for a moment until you realize what he's done: the little girl is clutching the mother's long Victorian skirt. And it's as though she's just been told the story, she's very upset, obviously. There are no words; I'm just inventing what I think this means—Froggie is dead, it alarms her, and for support she's hanging on to her mother's skirt. Her mother has a very quiet, resigned expression on her face. She's very gently pointing with her parasol toward the stream as the hat moves away, and the father is looking very sad. They're both expressing to the child, "Yes, it is very sad, but this does happen—that is the way the story ended, it can't be helped. But you have us. Hold on, everything is all right." And this is impressive in a simple rhyming book for children; it's extremely beautiful. It's full of fun, it's full of beautiful drawings, and it's full of truth. And I think Caldecott did it best, much better than anyone else who ever lived.

Miss Haviland: One critic, at the last Biennale of Illustration at Bratislava, said: "There is no fundamental difference between illustrations for children and those for adults." Would you comment on that?

Mr. Sendak: I don't agree at all, of course. I intensely do not believe in illustrations for adults. For preschool children who cannot read, pictures are extremely valuable. But even children who do read move in a very different world. As for adults, I personally find it offensive to read, I will *not* read, a novel that is illustrated. I always use this example, and many people here who know me have heard me carry on about this particular one, the case of *Anna Karenina:* the audacity of any illustrator who would draw Anna after Tolstoy has described her in the best way possible! Now, everyone who's read the book knows exactly what she looks like, or what he wants her to look like. Tolstoy is superb. And then to get an artist so asinine as to think he's going to draw Anna! Or Melville: it's incredible. People illustrate *Moby-Dick.* It's an insane thing to do, in my estimation. There is every difference in the world between illustrations for adults and illustrations for children. I don't know why there *are* illustrations for adults. They make no sense to me at all.

Miss Haviland: Out of that same Biennale of Illustration, where you represented the United States as our juror, there was considerable disagreement, I recall disagreement in theory, on the importance of kinds of art as illustrations. You were there, could you bring this into the picture?

Mr. Sendak: Well, I'm not sure I know exactly what you mean, but as I recall there was a European point of view as to what illustrations accomplish in a children's book, as opposed to what we believe is the function of illustration. I didn't know such a difference of opinion existed until we were in Czechoslovakia. And it was quite extraordinary. Partly, perhaps, because there is a dearth of original writing, they tend more often to re-illustrate their classic and fairy tales, and the illustrations take on a dominance and importance which I, as an illustrator, do not approve of. The books often become showcases for artists. I mean, you turn pages and there are extremely beautiful illustrations, but so far as I can see they could be taken out of one book and put into another. Whereas here, we are very much involved in making the illustrations work in a very specific way inside a book. Now, a picture is there, not because there should be a picture there; there is a purpose for a picture – we are embellishing, or we are enlarging, or we are involving ourselves in some very deep way with the writer of the book, so that the book (when it is finally illustrated) means more than it did when it was just written. Which is not to say we are making the words more important; we are perhaps opening up the words in a way that children at first did not see was possible. In the United States we work to bring pictures and words together to achieve a wholeness in the book, which I was very surprised to find is not at all important in many European countries. It's not a matter of right or wrong, it's just that it is so different! There it was so much a matter of graphics, of beauty of picture; here graphic acrobatics are less important.

Miss Haviland: One critic has asked why you changed from the "fine engraved style" of *Higglety Pigglety Pop!* back to what this person calls the "fat style" of your earlier work?

Mr. Sendak: Umm, "fat style." Well, I think the only way to answer that is to discuss the business of style. Style, to me, is purely a means to an end, and the more styles you have, the better. One should be able to junk a style very quickly. I think one of the worst things that can happen in some of the training schools for young men and women who are going to be illustrators is the tremendous focusing on "style," on preparation for coming out into the world and meeting the great, horned monsters, book editors. And how to take them on. And style seems to be one of the things. It's a great mistake. To get trapped in a style is to lose all flexibility. And I have worked very hard not to get trapped in that way. Now, I think my work looks like me, generally speaking; over a series of books, you can tell I've done them (much as I may regret many of them). I worked up a very elaborate pen and ink style in *Higglety,* which is very finely cross-hatched. But I can abandon that for a magic marker, as I did in *Night Kitchen,* and just go back to very simple, outlined, broad drawings with flat, or flatter, colors. Each book obviously demands an individual stylistic approach. If you have one style, then you're going to do the same book over and over, which is, of course, pretty dull. Lots of styles permit you to walk in and out of all kinds of books. It is a great bore worrying about style. So, my point is to have a fine style, a fat style, a fairly slim style, and an extremely stout style.

Miss Haviland: This question comes to you as both an artist and an author. Do you think of your books first in words or in pictures?

Mr. Sendak: In words. In fact, I don't think of the pictures at all. It's a very strange, schizophrenic sort of thing; I've thought of that very often. Sometimes after I've written something I find that there are things in my story that I don't draw well. And if it were any other person's book, I'd consider not doing it. But I've written it and I'm stuck with it, which is proof to me that I have not (at least consciously) been seduced by the tale's graphic potential. I don't think in terms of pictures at all; I find it's much more interesting and difficult to write, and illustration now becomes secondary in my life. . . .

Miss Haviland: Some artists feel that creating a work is a very separate experience and vastly more satisfying than what happens when the work goes out into the world. How do you evaluate the private experience as compared with the public experience?

Mr. Sendak: Well, there really is no comparison. The private experience is extraordinary, because it's all yours, nobody knows about it, nobody's going to find out about it, and you have it all to yourself for as long as it takes you to finish the book. *In the Night Kitchen* took two years of concentrated work. *The Wild Things* took about the same length of time, maybe a little less. During that time you are completely absorbed in this dream, this fantasy, whatever it is. The pleasure you get is extraordinary. You live in a very strange world, really quite divorced from this dull, real world. When I'm working on a book, I see very few people, do very few things but think about my book, dream about my book, love it, hate it, pull hairs out of my head; and the only time I speak to people is when I want to complain about it. And then it's over, and then it's finished, and the great shock comes when it is printed! And that's much like giving birth, and always a difficult birth. A book being printed is a major topic in itself; it is a very difficult thing to see through. What was once very dream-like and transparent and what you thought was a magic moment has now become a real thing in a printing press, and it's going through a big machine, and it looks lousy, and it has to be done all over again. And so gradually your particular transparent little dream is becoming more real, and more terrible every moment. And then finally it is a book. And you become extremely depressed, because you realize that what was so superb and different is really just another book! How strange. It looks like all the other things you've done. And then it goes out into the world, and your child, who was so private and who was living with you for two years, now is everybody's child. Some people knock him on the head, some kick him in the rump, and others like him very much. It's a totally different experience. It takes me a long time to shift gears. I am now in the process. It's only a few weeks since the book came out, and I don't know quite yet how to adjust to the fact that people are looking at it, and criticizing it.

Miss Haviland: Looking at the publishing world, we can see a very big question: Do you think that children's book publishing is significantly different today than it was when you began in the early fifties? And, if you do, in what respect do you see this?

Mr. Sendak: Well, yes, of course, it is very different than when I began in the early fifties. For one thing, the world seemed quieter then, and there was more opportunity to do experimental kinds of books. More important, there was time for young people to grow quietly. If you're an artist, you really need the time to grow quietly and not feel competitive or pushed. It was that way in the early fifties. One could develop gradually. Now, of course, it is much more competitive, and we do many more books but, alas, not many more great books. Something is lost. There is a rush, we are flooded with books, books come pouring out of the publishing meat grinder. And, the quality has dropped severely. We may be able to print a book better, but intrinsically the book, perhaps, is not better than it was. We have a backlist of books, superb books, by Margaret Wise Brown, by Ruth Krauss, by lots of people. I'd much rather we just took a year off, a moratorium: no more books. For a year, maybe two—just stop publishing. And get those old books back, let the children see them! Books don't go out of fashion with children; they only go out of fashion with adults. So that kids are deprived of works of art which are no longer around simply because new ones keep coming out. Every Christmas we are inundated with new books, and it's the inundation which I really find quite depressing.

Miss Haviland: Would you generalize in any way on what has been happening in other countries as you have traveled abroad and looked at picture books?

Mr. Sendak: Since I've generalized all this time, I could go a little further. There was a great moment in the middle fifties when, suddenly, the foreign books came to America. Books from Switzerland, the Hans Fischer books and the Carigiet books. We'd never seen them; it was a revolution in American bookmaking. We suddenly began to look very European. It was the best thing that could have happened to us, we *looked* terrific! But, of course, Europeans were then doing the most superb books. England invented the children's book as we know it. And now, in the sixties and seventies, certainly America is leading the world in the manufacture of children's books. It's disappointing, I find, going to Europe (with the exception of England and Switzerland) and finding so few contemporary children's books. I don't know if you found this to be true, but I did. In France there is *Babar* and the great old ones, but there are very few new ones. There *are* new ones, of course, but none that we get to see and none that seemingly even French people or Italians get to see — it seems they have dropped back considerably. I could be wrong. In my travels I've discussed this matter with illustrators and editors — and this is certainly the impression I've gotten.

Miss Haviland: Is there any point that you would like to make, aside from the questions that have been brought up to you before and which you've answered again tonight?

Mr. Sendak: I love my work very much, it means everything to me. I would like to see a time when children's books were not segregated from adult books, a time when people didn't think of children's books as a minor art form, a little Peterpanville, a cutesy-darling place where you could Have Fun, Laugh Your Head Off. I know so many adult writers whom I would happily chop into pieces, who say, "Well, I think I'll take a moment and sit down and knock off a kiddy book! It looks like so much fun, it's obviously easy—." And, of course, they write a lousy book. You hope they will and they do! It would be so much better if everyone felt that children's books are for everybody, that we simply write books, that we are a community of writers and artists, that we are all seriously involved in the business of writing. And if everyone felt that writing for children is a serious business, perhaps even more serious than a lot of other forms of writing, and if, when such books are reviewed and discussed, they were discussed on this serious level, and that we would be taken seriously as artists. I would like to do away with the division into age categories of children over here and adults over there, which is confusing to me and I think probably confusing to children. It's very confusing to many people who don't even know how to buy a children's book. I think if I have any particular hope it is this: that we all should simply be artists and just write books and stop pretending that there is such a thing as being able to sit down and write a book for a child: it is quite impossible. One simply writes books.

EDITORS' NOTE

Mr. Sendak's most recent books are *In the Night Kitchen* (1970), and *In the Night Kitchen Coloring Book* (1971).

Kate Seredy: A Person
Worth Knowing *

LIFE IN HUNGARY

Who is this woman who has shared her heart with us in stories, stories of faith and courage, stories alive with light and beauty, graced with her own wonderful illustrations? Kate Seredy is a daughter of Hungary, a transplanted foster-child to America. Her roots are part of the land. She stands unafraid, facing the time to come when all men shall truly love each other and peace and contentment shall reign over all.

She begins long ago, in Budapest, just before the turn of this century, growing up there during the turbulent years before World War I. As with any person, she is the sum of her experiences, the product of her culture, her environment, and her tradition; and in these she has a very rich inheritance, indeed.

Hungary, then, was like an island in Europe, a land with a natural organic unity. Her history was long and troubled, her language unrelated to those of her neighbors, her social structure still greatly stratified, just emerging from medieval feudalism. The aristocracy and gentry were strongly prejudiced against industry and banking. They thought of themselves as the people of the land, and passionately wanted to remain that. As the leading groups in society, they were, until the war, essentially conservative, and the intellectuals, who centered in rapidly growing Budapest, were ineffective. The story of the peasants was one of misery,

* By Aileen M. Kassen. From *Elementary English* 45 (March 1968), 303–315. Reprinted with the permission of the National Council of Teachers of English and Aileen M. Kassen.

social injustice, and emigration.[1,2] Yet, despite the generally oppressive conditions, the Magyar peasant was proud, deeply religious, and intensely dedicated to freedom.[3,4]

Kate Seredy's father was a well-known teacher. He was not just an ordinary teacher, but one of those especially gifted human beings whose contact with young people seems to deepen their awareness and bring each one a clearer picture of their worth and goal in life.[5] She remembers their simple home in Budapest as filled with books, music, and conversation, all of it the best, because there was no room for things that were not beautiful. Listening to the adult conversation, she absorbed a deep respect for good workmanship and for words.[6] To her father she pays homage as the source of her ideals, not just hers alone, but those of generations of others who grew up under his influence.

As a nine-year-old, a "pale skinny city child and being an only child, very much spoiled," she accompanied her father and an entourage of famous artists and scientists to the countryside where they were to study peasant art and life.[7] Although she paid as little attention to the object of the trip as she could, she came home full of deep unforgettable impressions.

> My mind was like a sensitive moving picture film, recording an incredible number of pictures . . . my impressions were meaningless . . . until passing years and new, conscious observations developed them. . . .[8]

THE YOUNG ARTIST

She started to draw for children as soon as she was old enough to go to school and after high school went to The Academy of Art in Budapest. In the summer vacations she studied art in Italy, France, and Germany.[9] During this time she worked to learn to draw, to conquer the discipline of pure line and form, to know every bone and muscle in the human body, becoming an artist in whose drawings fresh beauty could be seen and old truths reborn. World War I then came crashing down.

For two years during the war she was a nurse in front-line hospitals until she herself became ill and spent months recovering her mind and spirit. These are years she chooses to forget because of her revulsion toward violence. Yet, they too taught her valuable lessons.

> . . . that it doesn't matter how tired you are in mind and body; as long as there is a job to be done, the job comes first. It has got to be done.[10]

When the war was over, she illustrated two children's books. She suspects they were acclaimed because she was her father's daughter, and the glory quite went to her head.

In 1922, Hungary was in political turmoil and economic crisis, not yet recovered from war and internal revolution. Miss Seredy, along with many other Hungarians, decided to come to America. Once in New York, she says that it took her only two weeks to see what "real" artists were doing and to realize how much she had to learn.[11] Her determination to succeed and her father's teachings gave her strength in the difficult times ahead. Alone in a new country, unable to speak the language, she supported herself with any kind of work, painting lampshades, stenciling greeting cards, and finally graduating to illustrating sheet music covers. In all her autobiographical notes, she minimizes what must have been lonely, trying years.

Then, from a chance meeting in 1926 with Willy Pogany, a fellow Hungarian, came a start—a letter of introduction to a publishing house leading to her first job as an illustrator for an educational book.[12] She was launched on her chosen career! Over the next nine years, she illustrated other peoples' books; first, textbooks, some fifteen; then, children's trade books. Of these, *Caddie Woodlawn,* by Carol Ryrie Brink, the Newbery Prize winner for 1935, and *With Harp and Lute,* by B. J. Thompson, have found a permanent place in children's book collections.

Miss Seredy often talked to the editors about her pictures, debating their relationship to the text and their proper role in the completed book. She came to the conclusion that "continuous direct contact with children" would give her answers to these questions.[13] So in 1933, she opened a bookstore known as "The Story Book House" in her home, an old Dutch colonial in Ridgewood, New Jersey. Though the ambitious project lasted but a year and was a financial disaster, she learned much from the children who came to buy and who stayed to discuss their feelings about the books. She became convinced that good pictures could sell *any* book and that children never fail to respond to beauty.[14]

THE TURN TO WRITING

One momentous afternoon she visited Miss May Massee, children's editor of Viking House. Miss Massee's genius as an editor, according to Ruth Sawyer, was that of discovering "what each artist had to give to his work, and, having discovered this, how best he could use it, bring it to fulfillment."[15] To Kate Seredy, who delighted her, she said, "I like the way you tell a story. Go home and write a book about your childhood in Hungary." [16]

Miss Seredy did go home that cold February of 1935 and

... because I had nothing else to do, started to write. I wrote until I was sure I had proven that I couldn't, then sent the crate full of longhand pages to the editor. [17]

By return mail, instead of the manuscript which she was expecting, she received a contract. [18] That manuscript, with only a few grammatical changes, enriched by her own illustrations, became *The Good Master*. It was a success overnight, and her new path was charted.

Home for her at this time was an old barn of a place that practically sat on a river at the foot of a hill in the Ramapo Mountains of New Jersey. The ménage was completed by a collection of animals. Encouraged by the reception of *The Good Master*, Miss Seredy wrote her second book, *Listening*, now out of print. Although busy, life was far from smooth. All kinds of household disasters plagued her, from floods, to grass fires. Blanche Thompson, a good friend, described it as an adventurous saga that would have made a movie serial. [19]

The next year, in 1936, she proudly bought a one hundred acre farm in Hamilton, New York. Hamilton is a small town near the Hudson River not too far from New York City, but far enough though for the peace and solitude she craved. It was beautiful! The charming old house looked out from its knoll to rolling hills and broad meadows, complete with fruit trees and a peaceful river. At first she tried to farm it, but that proved "near-fatal." [20] She settled down to simply live in the house and "let the grass grow wild." [21] The days were never long enough for her. She furnished her home with pieces rescued from auction sales, attics, and cellars, which she then lovingly refinished. She played the piano, cared for her garden, made her own clothes, and did pottery. The heart of her house was her studio and there at her drawing board she worked. She sketched and resketched endlessly until she was satisfied with her finished drawing. There were always animals around her, wild creatures from her own fields, tame ones invited to share her nest, and ones not so tame that came uninvited. [22] Here she lived and worked for twenty years, writing and illustrating six books of her own and illustrating many books by others.

Miss Thompson found Kate Seredy hard to describe, like a changeling. She was delighted with her puckish humor, her blue eyes that somehow seemed black, her hands so long and slender. [23] Miss Seredy was small, her hair black and wavy, and she moved quickly and surely. One of the things she liked best was to chase hunters off her land. She considered them, along with tent caterpillars and authors who talk down to children, her personal enemies.[24]

After twenty years in her old house, she exchanged its atmosphere, charm, and all the innumerable problems big and small that insist upon intruding on the country-dweller, for "the comfort and functionalism of a . . . streamlined 'Pre-fab' " in the town of Hamilton.[25] During the last twelve years she has added four more books to that row bearing her name.

"Out of nowhere" sums up her attitude toward her career as a children's author.[26] She somehow still does not accept the fact that she has put words on paper and indeed "made" a book. It seems too overwhelming, this concept of being a writer. She claims she doesn't know how. The creative process of writing remains alien while that of drawing is as natural as her being. Initially each of her books began as a picture book. With these she feels secure, for she sees her craft as merely an extension of her hand. But all of the books, except for *Gypsy,* became also an extension of her mind. They were stories that had to be told, people that had to talk.[27] Some of them just seemed to pour out of that enormous unseen hidden self, and others had to be brought forward with effort.

ENDURING BOOKS

The Good Master and *The White Stag* are for me her most enduring books. I feel *A Tree for Peter* has special value as a Christmas story; *Gypsy* as a satisfying picture story book focused on growth and birth. Her other seven have many merits to recommend them, but, for one reason or another, they do not achieve quite the same level of significance. Although all the books she has written are warm, attractive and worthy of attention, it is the first two above that most richly deserve the accolade of "classic." Each of these, in its own way, is everlasting.

Of all Miss Seredy's books, *The Good Master* is the most popular, and deservedly so. Children love it! It gives them warm feelings of security and the goodness of life and presents a world they can easily accept. It is the story of spoiled, motherless Cousin Kate from Budapest, who comes to live with her uncle, The Good Master, his wife and son, Jansci, on their farm on the Hungarian plain. It depicts Kate's growth towards a more complete human being. From early spring until deep winter, in the days before the first World War, Kate follows and participates in the cycle of farm life and in the meaningful holidays that punctuate its rhythm. She learns from her experiences and the people around her a new order of values.

Permeating the story and unifying it is the belief that life at its best is simple—its rewards, love, peace, and happiness can be gained by honest work close to the soil—and that man must surely be eternally grateful to God for these blessings. In this belief, the author reflects the basic tenets of the Magyar—absolute faith coupled with a not unemotional attachment to the land and its fruits.

Most frequently, it is the men who passionately enunciate these concerns. Pista, a humble shepherd, affirms,

> The sky gives me sunshine and rain. The ground gives me food. The spring gives me water. The sheep give me shelter and clothes. The beautiful flowers, the animals, the birds, show me what to carve with my knife. Can money and schools give me better things? [28]

And later in the narrative he again contrasts the impotence of money with the richness gained by giving of oneself. The Good Master in his beautiful explanation of Easter as the holiday of joy, love, and giving, of new life and new hope, echoes this eternal triangle of man, soil, and God.[29] As Kate herself assumes more responsibility around the farm, and particularly when she decides to plant and to tend a flower garden, she too comes to understand the miracle of life and to be grateful to God for this gift. Until she has seen her jobs through and learned the importance of her physical contribution, she is unable to appreciate the emotional returns granted to those whose life is devoted to caring and nurturing growing things.

The Good Master offers more than a lesson. It is also real people, skillfully drawn, gentle humor, graphic pictures of a time and place now gone forever, drama and excitement, plus an introduction to Hungarian folklore. Without doubt, Miss Seredy's stunning color portraits of Jansci and Kate that serve as a frontispiece help the reader initially to identify with the children. However, through the judicious use of telling incidents, the two children quickly stand on their own feet. Kate is first described as a delicate city cousin. Her introduction by the railroad guard nicely contrasts with the mental images Jansci has built up. The guard says,

> Here, take this—this imp, this unspeakable little devil—take her and welcome . . . I'd rather travel with a bag of screaming monkeys than her, anytime.[30]

The conflict of the book is set. Will The Good Master be able to tame her? How will he do it?

In the very first chapter, Kate, Jansci, Father (The Good Master), and the Hungarian plain itself are all established, partially through their own actions, and partially through what Miss Seredy as the omniscient narrator says about them. There is no introspection; what exists is open to any observer. Kate is like a chameleon. In these few pages she goes from just any kind of a little girl with plain black hair, a smudgy face, and skinny legs, to a bantam rooster tense and poised; to a miniature whirlwind; to a poor, sweet little kitten; to finally, a hellion, standing alone, bolt upright on the seat of the wagon, reins and whip in hand and grinning from ear to ear.[31] She might be plain but she certainly isn't a sissy. The boy readers accept her and the girls adore her!

In the simple existence on the farm, it is the incongruities of life that make for laughter and Miss Seredy lightens the story with touches of humor. For instance, Jansci, dreaming of rescuing the princess from a dragon, is knocked off his seat and back to reality by his sweet cow, and husky father angrily swings a broom as little Kate on the rafters above artfully and successfully dodges his swipes.

The book is liberally illustrated with graceful watercolor paintings tied perfectly to the text itself. They focus on the people or the horses, and background is rarely suggested. In shades of black and grey, with white used as an important color, it is the posture of the characters that gives them life. As one child said, "They look like they would keep on moving. They don't look frozen."[32] The pictures are simple, basically realistic, though at times they move toward the idealized concept. The lines are mainly curved and rhythmic, conveying roundness of form, and even in the midst of drama, softness. The folds of a dress, the attitude of a hand, or the sweep of a horse's back add movement and emphasis. Total placement of the paintings on the page varies considerably; some are framed in curves, some are round, triangular or square, but they all help the reader visualize the incidents and achieve immediacy.

Stylized designs are used as chapter headings and one-half and one-third page pictures are above them at the end and beginnings of the chapters. All these add richness and give the book much visual appeal. Repeated in the designs are the traditional symbols of peasant art.

Kate Seredy's knowledge and love of nature is highly developed in her style and use of imagery. "The air was drenched with their sweet, heady perfume," horses "glittering hoofs were made of diamonds," "The dark blue sky, cloudless, like an inverted blue bowl," are ways she invites the reader to visualize her scenes.[33,34,35] Most often, the response suggested is a concrete, visual one. One would expect that from a writer who was first an artist. She leaves no setting incomplete; each is filled in and often embroidered. Short sentences stud the paragraphs which present relatively simple structure, and dialogue makes up a very large part of the book. Sometimes the figure of speech is unique, strikingly suggestive, as "fields of ripening wheat which looked like lakes of flowing honey, waving and billowing in the wind"; sometimes it is a common one, such as the ferry boat owner who looked "as white as a sheet." [36,37] Repetition of words and of key phrases is frequent. This establishes patterns which are pleasant.

> The sleigh bells were cheerful; without them there would have been utter silence. The lanterns were comforting; without them there would have been utter darkness.[38]

It is an easy book to read aloud and the total effect is natural.

Both from the pictures and from the words, costumes and countryside take on a life of their own. Give a reader crayons and he could color in Kate's dresses, or draw an interior floor plan of the farmhouse and furnish it with ease. The great Hungarian plain, in all its multitude of moods, and the villages it cradles, are recreated vividly.

Then, too, the relationship of The Good Master and the men who worked for him, the shepherds, and horse herders, the hired harvesters, is made quite clear. It is a relationship of dignity, not one of servitude. They admire each other and find pride in their respective roles. As was pointed out earlier, this was hardly the typical situation in Hungary during those years. The Good Master, like the famous Laura Ingalls Wilder series, sets before its readers a simpler time, when men could leave small patches of wheat uncut in their freshly hand-mowed fields, patches that sheltered a partridge nest.

The drama of the book is largely connected to the incidents built around the horses. This device presages the almost legendary role that horses were to have in several of Miss Seredy's later books. The horse had great historical and mythological importance to the Magyars.[39] In The Good Master, it is the horses that bring excitement and challenge, as in a horse race between Kate and Jansci, in their successful leading of a stampede, and in Jansci's thrilling riding-rescue of drowning Kate.

THE HUNGARIAN BACKGROUND

Woven skillfully through the book are four retellings of old legends, three Hungarian, one Turkish. The Turks besides being related to the Magyars had occupied Hungary for hundreds of years and left their mark upon the indigenous civilization. Although some critics might feel these tales impede the narrative flow, for me they add color and further illuminate the character of Hungarian life.

In recalling that first visit to the Hungarian plains when she was a little girl, Miss Seredy describes the peasants that she met as a people whose feet were firmly planted in the soil and whose hearts and minds were open to all good things in life. In *The Good Master,* all she did, in her own mind, was to give a frame to the picture that had been painted for her many years before, and also, it seems to me, to echo some of her own reactions to situations.[40]

The White Stag, Miss Seredy's third manuscript, received the Newbery Award in 1937 as the most distinguished book for children published that year in America. This heroic legend, her father's favorite story, is an epic account of the travels and travails of the ancient Huns and Magyars as they followed the fabled White Stag from their hunting grounds in Asia to their destiny and future home on the Hungarian Plains.

In her telling, she gives homage to this brave band of men, and from the ringing prose and the powerful illustrations there shines forth a vision of unparalleled determination, pride, and faith.[41] As a retelling of a story that is the basis of a nation's heritage, it is excellent. The words are clear and strong and from the very beginning to the last line there is not an extra phrase. The integration of text and illustrations is remarkable. Almost every picture is sweeping, dramatic, and somehow bigger-than-life. This helps to convey the traditional atmosphere of wonder and excitement. The narrative leaps ahead, from episode to episode, unified by the goal and purpose of the migration.

Some have questioned the glorification of Attila, but Kate Seredy is not worried, nor are the children who read this book.[42] She knows that history takes up the thread of the story and justly condemns him and his later rapacious deeds. The children understand that adventure and glory are mixed with suffering and pain, and they take away an intense picture that emphasizes belief in God and man's enduring values.[43] In a book discussion, a ten-year-old summed it up by saying,

> Well, at the end, I sat down for five minutes and thought about the book. I put it altogether as one thing, and sort of measured out how much good they had and how much bad. I decided that for all the bad, they did have a good amount of good at the end when they came to the promised land. It was a great book.[44]

And the author herself says of it,

I like to dream of the day when the light of faith (The White Stag) —
will again outshine the flaming red light of intolerance . . . In this
spirit I pass on the legend . . . to a new generation of children, not
as a story to glorify war and conquest but as a great story of faith,
courage, and belief in a guiding hand.[45]

This paper started with the question of the author's identity. It must
now consider another question. What has been her contribution to the
field of children's literature? When one looks at a room of Rubens in the
Louvre, or at a gallery in New York City whose every wall is covered
with Rothkos, one comes away with a total impression of a man and an
artist. The same can be said for the experience of reading the eleven
books published by Kate Seredy. The values that are brought out in *The
Good Master* and *The White Stag* reappear in almost every one of her
books. As she restates them, she deepens their meaning and extends their
significance, though never quite as successfully as in her two classics.

THE GOOD MAN AND THE GOOD LIFE

For her, the good man and the good life are inextricably intertwined.
Happiness in life must be earned, and along with the necessity of hard
work, go faith and hope. It is in a sense a double-sided image. As Father
Matthias, the kindly old priest in *Philomena* says, "One must use both
head and heart to make things come out right . . . one must make them
work together like a team of horses." [46] Peter, in *A Tree for Peter,* works
hard to keep his garden and to plant his tree, waiting and hoping for the
miracle to happen.

The miracle, or the dream, however, never is realized in Miss Seredy's
works without cooperation and love; these are the essential ingredients.
Success ultimately depends not on just an individual's heart and mind
balancing each other, but on all the characters in her stories pulling together toward their goal. Love, as Papa, in *A Brand-New Uncle* explains,
is not only important but necessary to everyone, for we all want to feel
needed, and having a friend makes toting troubles easier.[47]

The concept of interdependence is expanded in *The Singing Tree* and
The Chestry Oak to include all the people in the world working together
for peace and brotherhood. Grigori, the capable sweet Russian prisoner
that Jansci brings home to help, declares, "All same, Jansci . . . Li'l'
Russian, li'l' German, li'l' Hungarian," all men were brothers.[48] With
Nana, in *The Chestry Oak,* Miss Seredy seems to affirm that God has

given men the means to conquer evil when they work together with a wall of prayers.[49]

The greatest evil for mankind in Kate Seredy's books, is undoubtedly war, "that stampede . . . the mad whirlwind that sucks in man . . . and spits out crippled wrecks." [50] In her view, the little people of the world do not make war. It is a terror forced on them. Again Grigori communicates this belief by stating that no *good* man can kill and laugh.[51] It is interesting that both Father in *The Singing Tree* and Michael in *The Chestry Oak* are emotionally unable to stand the horror of the slaughter, and both react by completely blacking out their overwhelming experiences. Miss Seredy's nursing experience in the first World War had made her a confirmed pacifist and demonstrated to her the senselessness of war.[52]

Looked at simply, she is an optimist, and her books confirm a positive world view. Gran, the central character in *The Open Gate,* believes that nothing bad ever happens without some good in it some place.[53] Nana, the stalwart nurse in *The Chestry Oak,* teaches Michael, the hero, that nothing fine and noble will ever perish as long as there are hearts to remember.[54] This optimism is tied to Miss Seredy's bond with the land, where there are always signs of renewal and hope. In *A Tree for Peter, The Chestry Oak,* and *The Singing Tree,* trees as objects in nature stand as true symbols of this affirmation of life and growth.

Opposing growth, besides the wickedness of war, is the crowded modern city. In all but one of the books, Miss Seredy sees the city as robbing man of his dignity, his initiative, his sense of values, his very identity. Farm and rural life alone hold a sense of permanency. There is no synthesis here. She does not, except in *The Tenement Tree,* see the vigor, excitement, and challenge of an urban way of life, nor does she see the limitations inherent in the world of the farmer. In *The Singing Tree* and in *The Open Gate,* this belief is so outspoken and romanticized as to raise questions for the modern reader. It is undoubtedly valuable for today's children to understand the wonders and rewards of living close to nature, an experience which is denied to most of them. But it is equally valuable, and it seems to me, very important, for these children also to see the possibilities for achieving selfhood in their mechanized, computerized world. Courage and faith, the two lanterns Miss Seredy gives man to light the way into the future, can be as effective in the city as they are on the farm.

Ideas are not, however, usually what children are looking for in their books, and Miss Seredy is aware of this. "Teach?" she says. "I wasn't trying to. I was only telling stories." [55] Sometimes in *The Singing Tree,*

The Open Gate, and even in *The Chestry Oak,* the teachings get in the way of the story. She seems to have some trouble in controlling her didactic impulse. The lessons are at times too pointed or a bit overdrawn. Their moral and religious overtones hint at preachiness. *A Tree for Peter, A Brand-New Uncle,* and *Philomena* are infused with an almost religious quality that comes precariously close to sentimentality.

LITERARY QUALITIES

Most often the story in Miss Seredy's books carries the reader along. Interest in the plot is achieved by the suspense built into it. The resolution is guessed at but not known; the problem grows naturally. *The Chestry Oak* contains many compelling incidents. It is structurally divided into three: the life of its hero, Michael, in Hungary before World War II; his period of relative amnesia (resulting from emotional trauma); and his refuge and new life in America. Michael's wild ride on the stallion is unforgettable. However, the book is flawed by a lack of clarity in the middle section and its relation and transition to the final section, and also by a contrived ending.

Parading through Miss Seredy's books are memorable characters. Nana, in *The Chestry Oak,* the epitome of peasant womanhood, is amazing. She is immensely wise and loving. Her teaching and understanding symbolize the ideal mother, one who can help her child develop to his fullest potential, who in no way holds too tight to his developing personality, and who is ready to relinquish the bond when the time is ripe. *The Chestry Oak* is as rich in fine characterization as is *The Good Master.* Somehow for me, the family in *The Open Gate* is hard to believe, and the personalities of Mama and Papa in *A Brand-New Uncle* come a bit too close to studied types. Most frequently, though, Miss Seredy is swift and skillful in establishing characters that talk and act like real people and not like puppets. A child reader commented, "Some characters do things in the order of the plot but these seem to really have to think about it and decide." [56]

In reviewing Kate Seredy's style, it seems to me important to remember that English is her adopted language. Some of the greatest English writers have written in other than their native tongues. Joseph Conrad was acclaimed for his mastery, and today Vladimir Nabokov, thought by many to be the finest living author, is working in his third language. To conquer a second or a third language, to make it completely part of one, is without question a tremendous achievement. Hungarian is a Finnish-Ugrian language, not related to Indo-European tongues. It is considered particularly difficult for a Hungarian to make the very basic changes necessary for learning English.[57]

In light of this, it is especially noteworthy that Miss Seredy has developed such skill and such a fine sense of language. Her stories seem to tumble out, the rhythm of their words closely allied with their meaning, and the dialogue and descriptive passages balanced. Children are well aware of her ability.

> I like the way she makes you see the pictures even though there is no illustration on the page: You have the picture in your mind and you know what it's like.[58]

And another,

"Her words are made into pictures even though they are not descriptions."[59] Perhaps this is testimony to Miss Seredy's early training as an artist; certainly it underscores a sure understanding of the power of words.

Kate Seredy seems to be strongest in her handling of stories set against her native background. In *The Chestry Oak,* published in 1948, her stylistic talents are seen in their full maturity, rich and eloquent. For me there are many passages that are immensely impressive. A scene at the beginning, of Nana in the great Chestry Palace, is Seredy fiction at its best, creating a world of the imagination yet a world well understood. As one child added, "I do like the way she puts a feeling on you. It's sort of like a spell!"[60]

Gypsy, a picture story of a cat, for the youngest reader, is the most controlled and reserved of her books. She says that she spent three years whittling down the story to the brief captions that appear, and the honing is clearly evident.[61] *Gypsy* is a quiet book, to be read at quiet times, and its style is well suited to its story. In most of her other books this restraint and moderation is not so obvious or apparent.

CONCLUSION

It seems appropriate to end an appraisal of Miss Seredy with some thoughts on her illustrations. They give to children clear pictures of Hungary, of horses, of small animals, of honest, simple people. Only *Lazy Tinka* is printed in color; all the others are monochromatic.

> Even though they aren't in color, with the words, they fill the black and white sketches in and make them look colored,[62]

was the way one little girl explained her reaction to the illustrations. The pictures always extend and decorate the text and seem well-placed. They contribute so much meaning to the stories that it is hard to consider them separately without doing an injustice to her creative power.[63] The very best of them, in *The White Stag, The Good Master,* and *The Chestry Oak,* are strong and very beautiful; those of the animals in *The Tenement Tree* and *Gypsy* are alive and design perfect. As a whole group, they are of distinguished quality!

May Hill Arbuthnot, one of the deans of children's literature, sends us to find books for boys and girls to balance the speed and confusion of our modern world; books that build strength and steadfastness in the child, develop his faith in the essential decency and nobility of life, and give him feelings for the wonder and goodness of the universe.[64] Kate Seredy's books do just this. She is a person worth knowing!

REFERENCES

1. Emil Lengyel, *1,000 Years of Hungary.* New York: John Day Company, 1958, pp. 1–22, 164–186.
2. Arthur J. May, *The Hapsburg Monarchy 1867–1914.* Harvard University Press, 1951, pp. 343–386, 439–449.
3. Frances H. E. Palmer, *Austro-Hungarian Life in Town and Country.* New York: G. P. Putnam's Sons, 1903, pp. 45–65.
4. Joseph Domjan, *Hungarian Heroes and Legends.* Princeton, New Jersey: D. Van Nostrand, 1963.
5. Kate Seredy, " 'The White Stag,' An Immortal Legend," *Publishers' Weekly,* 133 (June 18, 1938) 2355–2356.
6. Kate Seredy, "Newbery Medal Acceptance," *The Horn Book Magazine,* 14 (July, 1938) 226–229.
7. Kate Seredy, "The Country of 'The Good Master,' " *Elementary English Review,* 13 (May, 1936) 167–168.
8. *Ibid.*
9. Kate Seredy, "Newbery Medal Acceptance."
10. *Ibid.*
11. Kate Seredy, "Newbery Medal Acceptance."
12. Kate Seredy, "A Letter about Her Books and Her Life," *The Horn Book Magazine,* 11 (July–August, 1935) 230–235.
13. Kate Seredy, "The Experiment in Children's Bookselling," *The Publishers' Weekly,* 125 (April 14, 1934) 1435–1437.
14. *Ibid.*
15. Ruth Sawyer, "To May Massee," *The Horn Book Magazine,* 43 (April, 1967) 229–231.
16. Stanley J. Kunitz and Howard Haycraft (eds.), *The Junior Book of Authors.* Second edition, revised. New York: H. W. Wilson Co., 1951, pp. 270–271.
17. Kunitz and Haycraft, *op. cit.*
18. Kate Seredy, *The Horn Book Magazine,* 11.
19. Blanche Jennings Thompson, "On Listening Hill," *Elementary English Review,* 15 (October, 1938) 217–220.
20. Kunitz and Haycraft, *op. cit.*

21. *Ibid.*
22. Thompson, *op. cit.*
23. *Ibid.*
24. Kate Seredy, *The Horn Book Magazine,* 11.
25. Kate Seredy, "Concerning Myself," *Newbery Medal Books: 1922–1955,* edited by Bertha Mahoney Miller and Elinor Whitney Field. Boston: The Horn Book Incorporated, 1955, pp. 161–162.
26. *Ibid.*
27. *Ibid.*
28. Kate Seredy, *The Good Master.* New York: The Viking Press, 1937, pp. 76–77.
29. *Ibid.,* p. 53.
30. *Ibid.,* p. 20.
31. *Ibid.,* pp. 20–25.
32. A taped small group discussion on Kate Seredy, fifth grade, Mrs. Barbara Fox, teacher, Boulevard School, Shaker Heights, Ohio, Spring, 1967.
33. *Ibid.,* p. 92.
34. *Ibid.,* p. 18.
35. *Ibid.,* p. 23.
36. *Ibid.,* p. 145.
37. *Ibid.,* p. 140.
38. *Ibid.,* p. 189.
39. Lois Markey, "Kate Seredy's World," *Elementary English,* 29 (December, 1952) 451–457.
40. Seredy, *The Publishers' Weekly,* 125.
41. Kate Seredy, *The White Stag.* New York: The Viking Press, 1937, p. 8.
42. Seredy, *Publishers' Weekly,* 133.
43. Mary Gould Davis, *"The White Stag,* Winner of the John Newbery Medal for 1937," *Library Journal,* 63 (June 15, 1936) 488–489.
44. A taped small group discussion on Kate Seredy. Shaker Heights, Ohio, Spring, 1967.
45. Seredy, *Publishers' Weekly,* 133.
46. Kate Seredy, *Philomena.* New York: The Viking Press, 1955, p. 29.
47. Kate Seredy, *A Brand-New Uncle.* New York: The Viking Press, 1961, p. 61.
48. Kate Seredy, *The Singing Tree.* New York: The Viking Press, 1939, p. 218.
49. Kate Seredy, *The Chestry Oak.* New York: The Junior Literary Guild and The Viking Press, 1948, p. 15.
50. Seredy, *The Singing Tree,* p. 163.
51. *Ibid.,* p. 203.
52. Seredy, *The Horn Book Magazine,* 11.
53. Kate Seredy, *The Open Gate.* New York: The Viking Press, 1943, p. 13.
54. Seredy, *The Chestry Oak,* p. 64.
55. Seredy, *Publishers' Weekly,* 133.
56. A taped small group discussion on Kate Seredy, Spring, 1967.
57. Lengyel, *op. cit.,* p. 10.
58. A taped small group discussion on Kate Seredy, Spring, 1967.
59. A taped small group discussion on Kate Seredy, Spring, 1967.
60. A taped small group discussion on Kate Seredy, Spring, 1967.
61. Miller and Field, *op. cit.*
62. A taped small group discussion on Kate Seredy, Spring, 1967.
63. Peggy M. Sutor, "Kate Seredy: A Bio-Bibliography," unpublished master's paper, Florida State University, 1955.

64. May Hill Arbuthnot, *Children and Books*. Chicago: Scott, Foresman and Company, as quoted in *The Horn Book Magazine*, 43 (April, 1967) 160.

BIBLIOGRAPHY

The Good Master, 1935. Ages 9–12. The story of the "gentling" of impish Cousin Kate on her uncle's farm in pre-World War I Hungary.

The White Stag, 1936. Ages 9–14. A retelling of the legend of the Huns and the Magyars and their dramatic migration to Hungary. Newbery Prize, 1937.

The Singing Tree, 1939. Ages 9–12. A continuation of *The Good Master,* taking the characters through the difficult years of World War I.

A Tree for Peter, 1941. Ages 8–10. Little lame Peter who lives in Shantytown finds hope and a better life through the help of a mysterious stranger. Appropriate for a Christmas list.

The Open Gate, 1943. Ages 9–12. How a city family takes an old farm and turns it into a successful rewarding venture, all without really meaning to.

The Chestry Oak, 1948. Ages 9–12. Michael, Prince of Chestry, grows up in Hungary during World War II, survives the devastation and finds a new life, complete with his beloved horses and a family in New England, U.S.A.

Gypsy, 1951, Ages 4–7. A picture story book of the birth, life, and motherhood of an ordinary looking cat named Gypsy.

Philomena, 1955. Ages 8–10. Before finding her long-lost aunt, orphaned Philomena has adventures and misadventures in old Budapest.

The Tenement Tree, 1959. Ages 5–8. Descriptions, mainly with pictures, of all the small animals that live in the countryside and of the beauty waiting to be discovered in the city.

A Brand-New Uncle, 1961. Ages 9–12. An older couple, seeking freedom from their multiple family relationships, are unable to resist the temptation of involvement with a lone, unloved boy.

Lazy Tinka, 1962. Ages 5–8. Told in folklore style, the story of a little peasant girl who had to learn to be a responsible member of her family.

EDITORS' NOTE

Kate Seredy's honors and awards include the Newbery Medal in 1938 for *White Stag* and the Caldecott Medal in 1945 for *The Christmas Anna Angel,* by Ruth Sawyer, which Miss Seredy illustrated. She was twice a runner-up for the Newbery Medal—in 1936, for *The Good Master,* and in 1940, for *The Singing Tree.* In 1959, she received the Lewis Carroll Shelf Award (worthy of sharing the shelf with *Alice in Wonderland*) for *White Stag.*

Miss Seredy has not published any books since *Lazy Tinka,* written in 1962. Currently, she is working on a book for young people which she has tentatively titled *The Search for God.*

Kate Seredy lives in an old house called "Listening Hill" in the Hudson Valley Region of New York State. Her house is well supplied with books and with Hungarian designs which she has painted. Her hobbies are gardening, sewing, pottery making, wood carving, antique collecting, and piano playing.

John R. Tunis:
A Commitment to Values *

WHETHER WARS really are lost or won on the playing field is of course debatable. Still, few persons would deny that important lessons sometimes may be learned there. John R. Tunis, now in his seventies, has written about sport as it relates to the larger questions of life in some two thousand articles and a score of books perennially popular with young people. Not surprisingly, sport has provided a contrapuntal theme for Tunis' own life. His recent autobiography, *A Measure of Independence,* movingly describes his youth, first in rural New York state, later in the shadow of Harvard Yard, revealing clearly how the games he played (along with the boys' books he read) profoundly influenced his sense of values. The qualities Tunis prizes – courage, persistence, teamwork, the evaluation of people according to merit instead of race or religion or social class – underlie his books, just as they have marked his life.

Young readers seldom if ever choose a book because it purports to teach a lesson. So, initially at least, Tunis' appeal is to those who want simply to read exciting sports stories. Whatever "message" he imparts comes through vivid incidents and realistic characterizations. Often situations are drawn directly from his own experience. He describes in his autobiography, for example, the night in Boston when, stopping to buy popcorn near Harvard Square, he and his younger brother Robert were attacked by a gang of East Cambridge boys:

* By William Jay Jacobs. Reprinted by permission from *Horn Book* 43 (February 1967), 48–54.

In several minutes it was over, the attackers had fled with my bag of popcorn intact. I can see my brother as I helped him up in the dim light, cut badly about the face and head, bawling from his wounds, yet still clutching his half-torn bag of popcorn.[1]

In Tunis' *Keystone Kids,* Spike Russell recalls a similar moment in the childhood of his younger brother Bob.

> Hey, Ma! Can we have some popcorn, can we?
> About the stand were half a dozen kids from the Richman gang. But the popcorn wasn't ready and the Old Lady had to return. Bob said he'd wait, so she gave him ten cents for two bags.
> All the time Spike had known he shouldn't go off and leave Bob standing there alone with the gang. They reached home and he didn't come and he didn't come. Then he came. He came crying, with blood over his face and arms, and two torn bags with only a fistful of popcorn.[2]

The descriptions in Tunis' books have a remarkable vividness—the product of careful attention to detail, along with an almost intuitive talent for capturing the fleeting instant or the elusive mood. We experience the sinking sensation in an athlete's stomach while the national anthem is being played before a big game; the peculiar pungent odors of the locker room; the clack-clack, clackety-clack of spikes on the stadium runway; the high-pitched feminine shriek of the cheering section; the agony of the long-distance runner, his lungs searing, his legs like leaden rods; the frenzy of the crowd at a high-school basketball game in Indiana; the easy grace of the baseball training camp in Florida. Significantly, when Tunis writes about Indiana basketball or the training camp he has observed it firsthand. The indelible quality of his descriptions is not an accident but the result of painstaking research on the scene—a habit Tunis credits to Harold Ross, his mentor on the *New Yorker* staff.

Nowhere is Tunis' representational skill in greater evidence than in situations of high tension and action, as at the climax of *World Series:*

> With desperation Lanahan slid into second. Then realizing he was beaten, he dug his spikes into Ed's left leg, bowling him over before he could snap the ball to first. It dribbled dangerously along the dirt toward the grass in right field.
> Instantly the situation changed. The Cleveland coaches on the base lines became dancing figures, on their toes yelling. The stands

rose shrieking. The whole diamond was alive with shouts and the figures of racing men, as Lanahan jumped up and dashed for third while McClusky turning first darted for second. This might be the game, the fifty thousand dollar break, the whole thing. The two runners tore for the forward bases as the ball bounded aimlessly.[3]

Yet Tunis is scrupulous in his use of action scenes, never employing them as a substitute for character development. Consequently, he avoids the stereotyped, wooden sports-story character who deals only in black-and-white issues. His personalities are complex and credible. When the usually mild-mannered "Kid from Tomkinsville," Roy Tucker, flares up and hits a sportswriter, it is Dave Leonard, his manager—the one man he most admires—who confronts him with the charge:

> "That's correct, Dave. . . . [He] said I was scared. Called me yellow. I heard him . . . I turned round and heard him say it."
> "So you socked him on the chin."
> "Uhuh. Most anyone would, with any guts."
> "Not ballplayers, Roy."
> "If they don't, they'd oughta . . ."
> There was a moment's pause. "Well, Roy, if that's the way you feel about things, I really don't know that baseball can use you any more."
> The train lurched round a corner. Awkwardly the Kid pulled himself back onto his seat. He was dazed, almost as if he'd been beaned. Dave didn't understand, didn't see his angle at all.[3]

When he is fined and asked to apologize to the sportswriter, Roy is bewildered and upset. In a scene reflecting the influence of Tunis' own father, a minister, and of values more familiar in a nineteenth-century context, the old ballplayer leans over and confides:

> "Roy, it's like this. There's lots of injustices in life and lots in baseball too, because baseball is part of life. We simply have to make the best of them, that's all. This is a tough situation for you and I'm sorry; but you got yourself in it and you'll have to get yourself out."[3]

But there are some injustices in life, Tunis is convinced, that we should not simply "make the best of," especially the injustices of racial and religious prejudice.

Many young readers have never suffered discrimination. They are shocked to hear of religious quotas for entrance to medical schools or, before Jackie Robinson, the color bar in big-league baseball. Others experience prejudice early. Picturing circumstances almost identical to those encountered by Lionel in J. D. Salinger's short story "Down at the Dinghy," Tunis captures in *Keystone Kids* the frustration and disbelief of a young ballplayer upon his first glimpse of the river separating him from other men:

> ". . . I must have been eight or nine years old . . . one day I was playing alone in the street, and another boy from down the road came by and said, 'Hey, are you a kike? Are you a kike?' . . . And I said, 'Am I a kite? Of course I'm not a kite.' 'Ha,' he said, 'I guess you don't know what a kike is.' So I went inside and found my mother. 'Ma,' I said, 'what's a kike, what is it?' My mother, she looked at me a long, long while. Finally she told me. She told me lots. . . ." [2]

What is to be done about bigotry? In Tunis' *All-American* Ronald Perry learns that a Negro player on the high-school football team he captains will not be permitted to accompany the team to a post-season invitational game in the South. He protests, but is told to remember that much money is involved in the game, that the reputation of the town is at stake, and that "We can't change society overnight." Still, Ronny persists and, despite cries of "Bolshevism" from the local press and threats of retaliation against his father from businessmen with a stake in the game, he persuades the team to rescind its acceptance.

> "Mind if I ask you one question?" [demands Ronald] "This is the Abraham Lincoln High. D'you think . . . d'you guess Abraham Lincoln would like this? Would he say ok, leaving a colored boy off our team when we go to Miami?" [4]

In a ceremony at the town depot only a few days before, the Negro player's brother, along with others bound for military service and possible death, had boarded a train while the high-school band played "The Star-Spangled Banner."

The issue of prejudice in sport strikes close at the values Tunis considers important, since the toleration of inequities in our leisure-time activities inevitably calls into question other premises operative in American society. Why, for example, is being a winner so important in the United

States? How valid, as Tunis asks in his autobiography, is General Douglas MacArthur's claim that "There's no substitute for victory?" And a corollary: Why is it that Little League baseball tends so often to degrade the boys and to corrupt their parents?

Especially in *Yea! Wildcats* (Harcourt) and *A City for Lincoln* (Harcourt), stories about high-school basketball in Indiana, Tunis tries to show how the doctrine of "victory at any cost" can make interscholastic sport nothing less than "a training ground for a jungle society." How profoundly, he asks, are human values eroded when a team sees the town's leading citizens pressuring the coach or the principal for tickets to the state tournament, or stealing a key player from a neighboring town by offering his father a better job? What does it mean when only two hundred and fifty of seven hundred and fifty tickets are available to the students? What are the lessons to be learned from the coach who deliberately encourages his players to disable an opponent or who sends in an expendable second stringer to provoke a fist fight with the other team's star, hoping that both will be ejected from the game? Finally, in Tunis' words:

> . . . does . . . interscholastic basketball induce those qualities we like to consider important in a democracy—tolerance, compassion, generosity, kindness, respect for the rights of others, to name only a few? Not as a rule, if one wants to win.[1]

What then are some of the finer qualities presumably encouraged by sport? Two of the most important are persistence and courage. Tunis himself claims to have acquired the habit of persistence through years of tennis, when he learned to concentrate, to take defeat, to "stay with it no matter what the score," to work at something until it is done. He recalls the belief of Sir Wilfred Trotter, the distinguished English surgeon and philosopher, that the real contribution of the English to world culture is "an interest in struggling toward an unpredictable goal. The Englishman's games," wrote Trotter, "have made him infinitely less fatalistic, and as a result of the discipline of sport he will keep struggling when his intellect tells him it is a lost cause." [1] As Tunis points out, it was probably this aspect of the Englishman's temperament that saved us all, during June, 1940, from the nightmare of Nazi enslavement.

Sometimes Tunis portrays persistence in terms of physical stamina and will, as in a crucial race run by Jim Wellington in *Iron Duke:*

> . . . His whole frame ached . . . and foam was on his lips and drooling down to his chin. . . .

"Go on, Duke, go on. Keep it up. You can. . . ." But the Duke didn't feel like going on. His mouth was parched, his legs were iron rods and every step meant pain. No, not pain, agony. He was suffering so much that the cheering and noise from the stands was confused and nebulous. There couldn't be much more, many more laps to go. There surely . . . couldn't be much more left.[5]

Courage is also a hallmark of Tunis' heroes. In *Keystone Kids,* Jocko Klein, the Jewish catcher, must prove to his teammates and to himself that he is not "yellow" before he is accepted as "the catcher of the Dodgers." Don Henderson, the basketball coach in *A City for Lincoln,* triumphs over the selfish business interests of Springfield, Indiana, and the local Republican machine, but more importantly over public apathy and the fear of "becoming involved," both signs of malignancy in our society. In *Son of the Valley* (Hale), young Johnny Heiskell demonstrates to neighbors and his tradition-bound father that modern farming methods and cooperation with the Tennessee Valley Authority will help, not hurt, their prospects. In the course of his struggle against obstinacy Johnny becomes a man.

Tunis suggests other dimensions of courageous behavior: courage in battle, as in *Silence over Dunkerque* (Morrow); courage to stand for a social principle in the face of one's friends and teammates, as in *All-American;* courage to keep trying, even after chance has delivered an apparently unjust blow, as in *The Kid from Tomkinsville* (Harcourt).

With courage often comes growth and transformation: the realization that sometimes the team does not win on the last page, even if it deserves to, and that in life, as Tunis declares,

> you cannot always or even often have your own way, that the manner in which we face up to defeat and disappointment is a test of growth and part of the development of character.[1]

The reader of the Tunis books learns that one really can be a success — possibly more of a success — after failing to make The Circle at Harvard or being cut from the freshman football squad. He learns that there is a world of bigger things than victory in the high-school basketball game; that a substantial outlay of honest, sometimes unpleasant self-examination may be required before one develops a proper sense of proportion; that becoming a man is not an easy process.

Persistence, courage, a sense of proportion. These are values to which Tunis subscribes. They are also indispensible ingredients for the teamwork essential to democracy. The analogy to sport is scarcely novel, yet somehow Tunis presents it in fresh perspective. From his own youth he recalls the time when his headmaster put to a vote of the whole school a point, ostensibly, of sport. The question was whether, in the forthcoming Boston Athletic Association games, Dekkie Thurber, the school's best sprinter, should run in the sprints, in which he would run more or less for himself, or should stay fresh for the relay races, in which he would be competing for the entire school. As Tunis tells it, the headmaster spoke; the coach spoke; Dekkie Thurber spoke; the president of the senior class spoke.

> After considerable talk, a vote was taken. Dekkie was to run the relay races as part of the . . . team, and nothing else. He ran, and . . . we won the interscholastic title. . . . Every boy in that school received a lesson to remember.[1]

Others write about the Dekkie Thurbers and the Mickey Mantles, the team stars. Tunis is perhaps alone in the attention he gives to the unsung workers of the democratic team, like the clubhouse attendant of *Keystone Kids,* Old Chiselbeak:

> Old Chisel, the man no one ever saw, who took your dirty clothes and handed out clean towels and cokes, and packed the trunks and kept the keys to the safe and did the thousand things no one ever saw. Chisel was part of the team, too; and . . . part of America. . . . He was the millions and millions who never have their names in the line-up, who never play before the crowd, who never hit home runs and get the fan's applause; who work all over the United States, underpaid, unknown, unrewarded. The Chiselbeaks are part of the team, too.[2]

John R. Tunis is both idealist and optimist. In his autobiography he declares,

> Faith has always been a part of me, faith in the great land of my birth, faith in Jefferson's dream of a democratic society, but especially faith in the individual, faith that man is free to shape his own destiny.[1]

His books for young people reflect this view. Further, they are written with the conviction that

We do not have to indoctrinate our young people, or claim our system is perfect. We need only to show the system with its drawbacks and defects, and hope our young people of today will do something later to change it.[1]

Is such a belief utopian? Do young people understand a book that says these things? Do they get the point?

Yes, [answers Tunis] because they are not yet corrupted. They still believe in the essential decencies, in fair play, in the slogans and clichés we mouth but do not practice. They read, and they wonder why our ideals are so at variance with real life.[1]

The ideals Tunis presents in his books have not been at variance with his own life. Like his most memorable characters, he has met setbacks and disappointments with determination. Often at great sacrifice, he has maintained his integrity and "a measure of independence." An entire generation of Americans has looked forward to (and learned from) the Tunis books. Superbly realistic and well-written stories, they are above all the imaginative testimony of a man who stands for something, a man with a commitment to values.

REFERENCES

Sources of quotations from books by John R. Tunis:
1. *A Measure of Independence: The Autobiography of John R. Tunis.* Copyright © 1964 by Lucy R. Tunis. Reprinted by permission of Atheneum Publishers.
2. *Keystone Kids* (Harcourt, Brace & World, Inc.).
3. *World Series* (Harcourt, Brace & World, Inc.).
4. *All-American* (Harcourt, Brace & World, Inc.).
5. *Iron Duke* (Harcourt, Brace & World, Inc.).

EDITORS' NOTE

John R. Tunis was born in Boston on December 7, 1889, and was graduated from Harvard in 1911. He served in France during World War I, and in 1920 became a sports writer. He wrote for the *New York Evening Post* and was connected with the National Broadcasting Company. For the latter, he covered major tennis matches in this country and Europe.

He has written numerous articles, generally on the subjects of sports and education, for practically every magazine in the United States. For the young reader, pre-adolescent, and teenager, John Tunis has written many popular sports stories, some of which candidly discuss the problems minority-group youngsters have in winning a place on the team or in the community. Some of his books, such as *Silence over Dunkirque* (1962), and *His Enemy, His Friend* (1967), emphasize the realistic details of wartime and underscore its brutality.

His honors include the 1943 Children's Book Award of the Child Study Association of America (given to the best book which deals realistically with some problem in the young person's contemporary world) for *Keystone Kids,* and the *New York Herald Tribune* Children's Spring Book Festival Award of 1938 for *The Iron Duke.*

May McNeer Ward
and Lynd Ward*

A FEW YEARS AGO we faced a large audience of children assembled
for a Chicago Book Fair and nervously wondered what these youngsters
would think of a writer and artist so completely unaccustomed to public
speaking. And then came the introduction, in which it was announced that
Lynd Ward had been born "back of the yards" in Chicago. Cheers shook
the rafters and brought relieved grins to our faces. Although Lynd was too
young to remember his early years in the stockyard area, his entrance into
the world there has had a special meaning for him. His father was a
Methodist minister whose first charge was the Northwestern University
Settlement House, where he became part of the movement sparked by
Jane Addams and others to better the conditions in that vast "melting
pot." Throughout childhood, with homes in Oak Park and Evanston, Ill.,
and later in Newton Center, Mass., and Englewood, N.J., Lynd's family
was always close to the problems of those who lived "back of the yards."

In that first hot summer in 1905 he was a baby who was never well,
and his parents wondered if they would be able to raise him. The remedy
they took was an unusual one. The previous year his father had journeyed
by train, and then, with a local guide, by canoe into the Canadian wilderness northeast of Sault Ste Marie, where he bought land from which the
Ojibways had just been removed to a Reserve. And so Mr. and Mrs.
H. F. Ward, pioneers in spirit, brought their two children to the newly
built log cabin on Lonely Lake. They made the trip from the railroad by

*By May McNeer Ward and Lynd Ward. Reprinted by permission from Houghton Mifflin,
Boston, Massachusetts.

wagon along a rutted trail, and up the lake to the far shore in a leaky row-boat, and there they remained until snow powdered the red and yellow autumn leaves. When they returned to Chicago in October Lynd was in good health.

It is my belief that these two experiences, engendered in his earliest years, and carried through his growing time, created in Lynd's character and in his work a profound respect for the dignity of the human spirit in all peoples, and a close bond with the strength of the wilderness.

My own background was just a bit different. I was brought up by my mother, a gentle artist with a twinkle in the eye, and her identical twin sister, who was given to picking up and moving suddenly, on impulse, and who, when she moved, took us with her. My "mothers" were widows and, except for certain eccentricities, as much a part of the old south as lineage and pride together could produce. My brother and I acquired a reluctant first-hand knowledge of almost every part of southern geography until whim took us back to Tampa, Florida, our home base. As a result I was never allowed to finish a term in grammar school, and have gaps in my education large enough to compete with the Grand Canyon.

Yet, somehow or other, and mainly by good luck, I did arrive in the Journalism School at Columbia University, and there met Lynd Ward, an art student at Teachers College. We were married in 1926, just after graduation, and went off to Europe to travel a little, then settle in Leipzig, Germany, where Lynd wanted to study the graphic arts. In that cold, gray northern winter, while I learned to cook on a monster of a tile stove, Lynd was studying a German grammar every night, and in the day learning wood engraving, etching, and lithography at the Academy for Graphic Art. In spare time we prowled book stores, and there he discovered a little story told in woodcuts, done by the Belgian artist, Frans Masereal. This engendered a flood of ideas of his own for a woodcut novel. In 1929, when he was twenty-four and back in America, *God's Man* was published. It was a novel without words, the first woodcut story to appear in America. In the 1930's Lynd published five more, two of these in small limited editions.

There is no graphic medium requiring more patience, skill, and hard labor than wood engraving, and yet while he was working on novels in woodcut Lynd was also illustrating books. His first book for adults was a gift edition of Oscar Wilde's *The Ballad of Reading Gaol*, published by Macy-Masius. And our first joint book was a Japanese folk tale called *Prince Bantam*. From then on I have worked on books for children — biography, history, regional, and fiction. Lynd has illustrated many classics for George Macy's Limited Editions Club, and in 1954 he re-

ceived the Limited Editions Silver Medal for twenty-five years of distinguished service in book illustration. He has illustrated a large number
of books for children by different authors, the list including some of his
wife's, his sister's, and his daughter Nanda's, and he has also worked with
his daughter Robin, who is a book designer.

Our summers, quite naturally, are usually spent at Lonely Lake, in the
Canadian bush, and Lynd's feeling for this land has appeared in *The
Biggest Bear*, a winner of the Caldecott Medal for 1953. It was his first
book as author and artist. He has done illustrations for Henry Steele
Commager's *Robert E. Lee*, Esther Forbes's *Paul Revere*, Stewart Holbrook's *Ethan Allen*, and my texts for *Abraham Lincoln* and *Mark Twain*,
all in the Houghton Mifflin America's Series. We worked together, as
well, on *Little Baptiste* and *My Friend Mac*—taking us back to the
Canadian woods once again. Among our books are a number issued by
several different publishing firms, including *The California Gold Rush*,
and others in the Random House Landmark Series, and for Abingdon
Press *Give Me Freedom*, and *Armed With Courage*, winner of the
Thomas A. Edison Award; for Farrar, Straus and Giroux *The Mexican
Story*, *The Canadian Story* and *The American Indian Story*.

The second book for which Lynd did both text and illustrations he
called *Nic of the Woods*, and in it he told the story of Nickle, son of Dime,
and of how a city dog learned of the quiet wonder, and of the dangers of
the forest.

Although he uses lithography, ink, oil painting, and other media in his
illustrations, for prints Lynd usually works in wood engraving. He exhibits with The National Academy, of which he is a member, as well as
in the annual exhibitions of The Society of American Graphic Artists, of
which he was president for six years. His graphic works have been shown
in many parts of the country, as well as abroad, and are in the permanent
collections of The Smithsonian Institute, The Library of Congress, The
Newark Museum, and others.

As for hobbies, Lynd enjoys carpentry and stonework, but has less
enthusiasm for gardening, as he says there is nothing permanent about it
except the weeds. This emotion he embodied (to disregard symbolism)
in a wood engraving showing a man bent over a hoe beneath a thistle
towering about twenty feet above him. Lynd's love for stonework is noto-
rious in every neighborhood we have ever inhabited. Always, both in
Lambs Lane, Cresskill, N.J., and in Canada, we have great piles of
rocks, or slates and rubble for fill. He used to play the accordion by ear,
but has almost given that up as requiring too much energy, and now he
contents himself with constructing walls, walks, and fireplaces beautiful

to view and never known to smoke, but with a starvation hazard attached. He will not come to meals as long as wet mortar holds out, and labors on by moon or lantern light, while somehow or other his recipe for cement mix gets larger and larger.

When our daughters moved out on their own we bought our tiny house and added a studio larger than the original building. In this room I have my typewriter desk in a very small corner, and Lynd occupies the remainder of the studio, where his drawing and painting equipment and research materials more than rival his overflowing mortar trough. Studio work is directed and overseen in person by Mr. Scratch, our Persian-Alley cat, who walks impartially first on my typewriter keys while I am typing, and then in Lynd's wet paint. At present our daughter Robin lives in San Francisco. Nanda, now a photographer and writer, her husband, Bob Haynes, who is an artist as well as a professor, and our seven-year-old grand-daughter, Tamara Lynd, or Tammie, are residents of south Jersey.

Our cherished possessions include a gothic bookcase from my old home in the south, an ancient wooden Indian, and books and books and books. Lynd's weakness is buying all kinds and descriptions of books, and I will admit, if pressed, that more books than stones arrive at our door. I think that probably our most fascinating volume is a copy of *The Biggest Bear,* bound in real bearskin, sent to Lynd one Christmas by his friends at Houghton Mifflin. This is the only book that has aroused the enthusiasm of Mr. Scratch. We continue to hope that the binding was not actually cut from the hide of Johnny Orchard's bear.

EDITORS' NOTE

Awards and honors won by Lynd Ward include a runner-up for the 1950 Caldecott Medal for *America's Ethan Allen,* by Stewart Holbrook, which Ward illustrated, and the 1953 Caldecott Medal for *The Biggest Bear,* which he wrote and illustrated. He also received the 1969 Rutgers University Award, given to New Jersey residents for a distinguished contribution to children's literature.

May McNeer Ward was made an honorary member of the Boys' Clubs of America and she received the Thomas Alva Edison Award (for special excellence in contributing to character development of children) for *Armed with Courage,* 1958. Four of her books have been translated into thirteen languages—including Burmese, Arabic, and Greek. Her most recent book, *Stranger in the Pines* (1971), is illustrated by her husband, Lynd.

The Designs
of E. B. White*

BACK IN 1938, with his tongue in his cheek, E. B. White wrote, "Close physical contact with the field of juvenile literature leads me to the conclusion that it must be a lot of fun to write for children—reasonably easy work, perhaps even important work." He had just been sampling the children's books which flooded his house in those days jostling for a place in his wife's annual New Yorker column, and he had come away "gibbering." Yet even then, as he later admitted, he had tucked away in his desk drawer a dozen episodes in the continuing story of a boy named Stuart, who was only two inches high and looked like a mouse. The character had come to him in a dream back in the 1920's, he said, and had been committed to paper for an audience no larger than any favorite uncle might command.

Finally, in 1945, the chapters were taken out of the desk drawer for good; the mouse went public; *Stuart Little* was published. Seven years later came *Charlotte's Web*. "I am not a fast worker, as you can see," he wrote in an all-purpose letter which his publisher, Harper & Row, sends to the fans who write him. He has just won the 1970 Laura Ingalls Wilder Medal for a lasting contribution to children's literature ("It is deeply satisfying to win a prize in front of a lot of people," he wrote in *Charlotte's Web*,) and has been named a runner-up for the Hans Christian Andersen Medal for authors. His new book, *The Trumpet of the Swan*, is scheduled for publication in June.

* By Gerald Weales. From *The New York Times*, May 24, 1970, sec. 7—pt. 2, p.2+. © 1970 by The New York Times Company. Reprinted by permission.

Although I doubt that writing the books has been particularly easy, surely White's tongue has come out of his cheek as far as the rest of the opening quotation is concerned. Yet, it is not the author's fun nor the books' importance that concern me here. I have been considering how the books are made.

When White revised *The Elements of Style,* the writer's manual by William Strunk, Jr., he introduced a new Rule 8: "Choose a suitable design and hold to it." Taken at face value, without the qualifications that follow, that sounds rather like Stuart Little's method for winning a boat race: "I'll sail the Wasp straight and true, and let the Lillian B. Womrath go yawing all over the pond." But writing a book is a boat race of a very special kind; sometimes, as White says, "the best design is no design," and, in any case, "The writer will in part follow this design, in part deviate from it."

Deviation is the art of *Stuart Little.* The way the story grew is probably partly responsible for this. White's word *episode,* is the key method. The book is really a series of self-contained incidents, designed to be read to a child (or by a child) whenever the occasion arises. Although White is quite capable of using a cliff-hanger when an incident spans two chapters (for the best suspense, close the book on "Stuart's down the mousehole" at the end of Chapter IV) and although many a family has read the book in the traditional chapter-a-night way, a week or two could pass between readings with no disturbing disruption of the story and episodes need not be taken in sequence. Having once heard the story, any child is likely to ask over and over again, "read me about the sailboat race."

Yet *Stuart Little* is not a collection of short stories, as *Winnie-the-Pooh.* When White sat down to write or re-write or redact or whatever one does to a twenty-year accumulation of episodes, he found the perfect genre to encompass his separate passages. White has called the book "my innocent tale of the quest for beauty," and so it is. In quest literature, whether it be picaresque novel or Grail romance, the search is only the string on which the beads of incident hang. In *Stuart Little,* the quest does not begin until the book is more than half finished, and even then it is interrupted by apparently peripheral adventures: Stuart's day as a substitute teacher; his courtship of Harriet Ames, who, being two inches tall, might have been just the right girl for him.

In emphasizing the separate units in *Stuart Little,* I do not intend to deny the design, for the quest requires a continuing hero and it usually resorts to recurring figures and verbal or thematic echoes. Stuart's bravery is established when he goes down the drain to get his mother's ring. His sense of adventure, his resourcefulness, even that touch of dandified pompousness which recalls Lancelot, are all dramatized before beauty — in the person of Margalo, the fugitive bird, flies in and out of his life. There is a nice thematic line from Katharine's souvenir pillow in the schoolroom chapter to the canoe with which Stuart hopes to impress Harriet. The pillow was the gift of a boy Katharine met at summer camp and the canoe, also a souvenir, is labeled "Summer Memories." But the little girl will not let Stuart have the pillow and the canoe is smashed before he can use it — and rightly so. They represent the comfort of settling for less and are not for Stuart; after all, he, like Cuchulain, is a hero. But, despite these thematic lines, the book has no real ending. The quest for beauty is necessarily open-ended; we can always cheerfully pick up our hero at any point on his journey.

The design of *Charlotte's Web* is more intricate, a fact that would surely please Charlotte. In 1948, White wrote "Death of a Pig" which appeared in *Atlantic Monthly,* an oddly affecting account of how he failed to save the life of a sick pig, made ironic by the fact that the pig had been bought to act its part in the "tragedy" of the spring pig fattened for winter butchering. Since literature is not life, White set out in *Charlotte's Web* to save his pig in retrospect, this time not from an unexpected illness but from its presumably fated "tragedy." The main plot, then, is that staple of adventure literature — the rescue of the innocent. The hero, however, is neither Jack Dalton nor a knight disguised as a wandering bard; it is a committee of sorts, consisting of a little girl, a rather wordy spider and a rat named Templeton. Nor is there a villain; Wilbur has to be saved from the inevitable course of events. Fern rescues Wilbur in the first chapter, pleading with her father not to kill him because he is a runt, only to learn that he must grow up to be bacon in any case. Then Charlotte, out of love and friendship, and Templeton, out of greed, join forces and save the pig again. If the natural processes cannot be disrupted now and then, what is fantasy for?

Yet, E. B. White tells the story of Wilbur's escape within a context that embraces the natural world, the process of growth and change. The subplot is Fern's story, her growing up and out of the barn where she feels at one with the animals into the world of men. One of the loveliest things in the book is that White chooses the scene of Wilbur's triumph, the prize-giving that saves his life, when all the formerly indifferent humans dance around him, to let Fern break away, to let her think not of Wilbur and Charlotte but of Henry Fussy and a ride on the Ferris wheel. Allied to the rescue story is the plot implicit in Charlotte's methods, the advertising slogans in her web ("SOME PIG!"), a comment on the gullibility of man, a kind of self-delusion which in this book at least is life-giving. Finally, from the opening threat to Wilbur to Charlotte's lonely death toward the end, the book holds to the idea of death as a fact of life, but the last chapter brings new spiders, new lambs, new goslings, another spring. The book is not about the charmed life of Wilbur, but about real life and all that implies.

Charlotte's Web is probably a better book than *Stuart Little,* a more complicated one, a deeper one. Yet, I confess a fondness for that boy who looks like a mouse. "If *I* had been very small at birth, would you have killed *me?*" cries Fern in *Charlotte's Web.* If E. B. White had followed all the conventionally wise advice that saw his mouse child as a runt that would do his reputation no good, he would have killed Stuart at birth. Thank God, he didn't. As Charlotte would say, SOME MOUSE!

EDITORS' NOTE

Elwyn Brooks White was born in Mt. Vernon, New York, in 1899. His father was a piano manufacturer with a business in New York City. Mr. White attended the public schools of Mt. Vernon and was graduated from Cornell University in 1921. After finishing college, he travelled around for several years working at various kinds of jobs. Finally he joined the staff of the *New Yorker* magazine, which at the time was in its infancy. This was a happy marriage and Mr. White has written many satirical sketches, poems, essays, and editorials for this publication, as well as essays which have appeared in *Harper's Magazine.* In addition, he is the author of eighteen books of prose and poetry.

In 1929, Mr. White married Katherine Angell, who was at the time the literary editor of the *New Yorker.* They have a son and three grandchildren. In 1938, the Whites moved to a farm in Maine. Some of the animals which are raised on the farm have appeared in his stories and books. He says he finds writing difficult and bad for one's disposition, but he keeps at it.

Mr. White has written only three books for children. For the first two, *Stuart Little* and *Charlotte's Web,* he received the 1970 Laura Ingalls Wilder Medal, which is given every five years "to an author or illustrator whose books, published in the United States, have over a period of years made a substantial and lasting contribution to literature for children." He was also a runner-up for the 1970 Hans Christian Andersen Award, given by the International Board on Books for Young People for the entire body of works of an author or illustrator.

Charlotte's Web was a runner-up for the Newbery Medal in 1953. It also won the Lewis Carroll Shelf Award in 1958 (worthy to sit on the shelf with *Alice in Wonderland*), and the George Stone Center for Children's Books Recognition of Merit Award in 1970 (given by the Claremont Reading Conference to the author of a children's book which has the capacity "to arouse in children an awareness of the beauty and complexity of their expanding universe").

The year 1970 marked the 25th anniversary of *Stuart Little* and the publication of Mr. White's third book for children, *The Trumpet of the Swan*. This book was a leading contender for the 1971 National Book Award, Children's Book Category (given to American citizens only for the juvenile title considered most distinguished by a panel of judges). It was chosen also by the International Board on Books for Young People for the 1972 Honor List. This selection indicates that not only is the book considered to be representative of the best in children's literature, but that it is suitable for publication throughout the world.

In 1963, Mr. White was awarded the Presidential Medal of Freedom by President John F. Kennedy. He has also received a Gold Medal for Essays and Criticism from the National Institute of Arts and Letters, as well as honorary degrees from seven colleges and universities.

Antic Disposition *

MR. WILDSMITH, or may I call you Brian?
Of course.

When and where were you born?
1930, Peristone, Yorkshire, England.

And was that a good place to be born?
Well, I didn't have much choice. The Yorkshire people are hardworking, efficient, thrifty and levelheaded: they drink wine, beer, play the finest cricket and football in England, have the loveliest countryside, do the best cooking and produce most of what makes England what it is!!!

I suppose you drew and painted from a very early age?
Yes, I was 16 years old when I started.

Really?
Yes.

Where did you receive your art education?
I won a scholarship to the Slade School of Fine Arts, University College, London.

When you left did you start illustrating books?
No. I had to go into the army and teach.

* By Brian Wildsmith. Reprinted by permission from *Library Journal*, November 15, 1965, pp. 5035–5038.

What? Art?
No. I taught mathematics, you know 2 + 2 = 4, etc.

I suppose you were a very sympathetic and successful teacher, were you not?
Yes. Our unit held the record number of failures for the Army first-class mathematics exam.

Let's leave the army out and get back to art, shall we?
Yes. Let's.

Who gave you your first assignment in black and white book illustration?
Oxford University Press.

Who gave you your first assignment in color and what was it?
Oxford University Press. *Tales from the Arabian Nights.*

And was this well reviewed?
Yes, one review began, "But the descent is steep to Brian Wildsmith's attack on the Arabian Nights. The seemingly aimless scribbles are splashed lavishly and untidily with bright smudges of paint," etc., etc.

You seem to know that quote by heart.
Yes.

Brian, after such reviews who published your second book in color?
Oxford University Press. It was the *ABC.*

Brian, what kind of an artist would you describe yourself as?
Oh, about 160 pounds of solid muscle, 6'2" tall with dark wavy hair, blue eyes. I guess I could be taken for Gregory Peck.

Really Brian, you're pulling my leg. Seriously, why do you illustrate young children's books?
Seriously, I believe in the Jesuit saying "Give me a child under seven years and he is mine forever." How often have we left all that is good and free in our culture to be brought before the child too late, when his taste has already been formed, maltreated, warped and destroyed by the everlasting rubbish that is still thought by many to be good enough for children. I hope my picture books will help alleviate this, and perhaps guide them to finer and greater paths.

But how?
Well, I try to reconcile the beauties of form and color in pure painting with the problems of illustrating a given text. By attracting the child to

the stories in picture form, consciously or subconsciously (it doesn't matter which), the shapes and colors seep into the child's artistic digestive system, and he is aroused and stimulated by them.

Do you really think that young children are aware of and understand form and color?

Of course. Children are fascinated by color and form; whether they understand it or not I couldn't say. I don't think one *understands* the arts: one is moved, provoked, or stimulated, and one enjoys. But understand completely, no! All works of art, whatever the medium of expression, have in them some secret of creation that makes them universal and timeless. You can dissect their physical make-up—composition, form, texture, pattern, but all these are nothing without this elusive quality of creativity—"soul," if you wish.

Brian, you mentioned earlier the problems of illustrating; could you elaborate?

Certainly. You see, working at home has its problems. One is amongst domestic upheavals that occur from time to time, and one is always on tap to look after the baby or help hang out the wash. You know what women are?

No.

Well they are always after you to do something or fix things around the house.

Looking around I don't get the impression that you do very much.

Ah well, I solved that problem.

How?

I left all the lights without shades on them.

What happened?

Oh you know what women are. These shadeless lights became an obsession with my wife and she forgot all about the other things that needed doing.

But I notice that all the lights have shades.

Yes, that scheme lasted for four years. Now I've removed the door handles and you have to use a screwdriver to open the doors.

And is this ruse working?

Yes, but fetching the screwdriver for my wife is driving me insane.

Could we get back to the problems of illustrating.

Sorry, I do tend to ramble. I meant to say that there are, roughly, at a quick count, two ways of illustrating a book. The first is to give, shall we say, a diagrammatic representation of the text; the sole aim is putting the text into picture form. The other way is to enlarge on the text, to create a pictorial form that is at one with the text and yet is a thing unto itself.

Is this second way difficult?

Yes. In the same way that one does not interpret and play Bach like Chopin, one should give a different interpretation to all one's books. Similarly, the book, in some way which even the artist does not understand, should make its own form, carve its own way through the artist's subconscious, until it has become the physical concrete expression of an idea. On the face of it the act of creativity is impossible to achieve; the miracle of art is that it can be achieved at all.

But how can one work subconsciously and yet to a positive end?

Again, it's rather like the musician giving a performance in which he has to immerse himself completely in his music yet listen acutely to his own performance. This is achieved only by a great deal of hard work — getting to know the work, taking it apart note by note and achieving technical mastery, and finally, reconstructing the entire work and letting it flow spontaneously from the musician as though it were a part of him, as indeed it is by now.

Interpreting a book is a similar process. This of course is the ideal, if one were capable of achieving it. Indeed the real problems of art are psychological and not technical; perhaps it would be a good thing if our colleges of art were staffed not by art teachers but by psychologists.

What do you think is the secret that makes for the best children's books?

Most of us, particularly the male, have in our makeup much of the child. The trick is to recapture this state when working. The other trick is to be able to switch it off again.

Do children really appreciate good art in books?

I think children like most things good and bad, providing there is some *special* appeal for them. It is distressing that there is so much bad work with this appeal and not enough fine work to fascinate the child. The child is unbiased; not having been indoctrinated into what is good or bad, he is open to anything that is put before him and appreciates a thing for what it is and not what it ought to be. How often in libraries and bookshops do we see adults choosing books for children, saying (very often of good books) "No, I'm afraid little Fred won't like that," when it is the debased judgment and taste of the adult that doesn't like and can't accept it.

Many of us realize the artistic damage that was inflicted on us in our early years. The fact that some never recover is sad, for some of the deepest and most satisfying moments in our lives come to us through art. The artist illustrating for children has a special responsibility to uncover their sensibility while it is still plastic. In a way we are all artists, but it is the true performer of the arts who crystalizes, expresses and lays bare the feelings we all have.

EDITORS' NOTE

Brian Wildsmith, his wife, and their four children (three girls and one boy), spend their summers in an apartment in Gerona, Spain. The rest of the year they live in Dulwich, London. Despite Brian's obvious fascination with animals, the family has no pets, as he feels a city environment is not a good place to keep one.

Mr. Wildsmith was awarded the 1962 Kate Greenaway Medal (given annually by the British Library Association to the most distinguished illustrated children's book) for *Brian Wildsmith's ABC,* and he was a runner-up for this medal in 1964 for two of his works, *The Lion and the Rat* and *The Oxford Book of Poetry for Children.* His *Brian Wildsmith's Birds* was on the *New York Times* List of Best Illustrated Children's Books in 1967.

His most recent work, entitled *Brian Wildsmith's Puzzles,* was published by Franklin Watts in 1971. The book is a set of puzzles with no definite answers, for primary-grade children. It is illustrated with Wildsmith's exquisite colorful artwork.

MAIA WOJCIECHOWSKA

What Did I Say, Dear?*

MAIA WOJCIECHOWSKA RODMAN, an author who promises to be as colorful as she is quotable, formerly worked in the gilded ("or is it chromed?") world of book publicity. As Maia Rodman, she is the mother of "a 12-year-old reader" and, as Maia Wojciechowska, she has just embarked on a fulltime career of writing books for children. She calls this article "a slightly incoherent credo — why I gave up a secure job for the less stable chain-and-ball of writing."

Wojciechowska is pronounced VOI-che-HOH-vskah, a name to remember. Why not say it aloud a few times?

[In the following dialogue, "Mother Maia" is used when Rodman-the-mother is speaking; "Author Maia" is used when Wojciechowska-the-author is speaking.]

Mother Maia: The reason I decided to interview you rather than a well-known children's book author is that I hope you might have some fresh ideas. A certain complacency, a doctrinaire attitude, I feel, sets in the minute an author has "arrived." Since you're just beginning to write for children, you couldn't have too many set ideas — or do you?

Author Maia: Are you trying to ask me why I decided to write for children?

Mother Maia: No, but you obviously want to tell me. Go ahead; why did you?

* By Maia Wojciechowska. Reprinted by permission from *Library Journal*, March 15, 1964, pp. 1385–1386+.

Author Maia: Because I feel a lack of interesting books for children between the ages of nine and 13. After the picture books, practically uniformly fun to look at, it ceases to be entertaining to read, unless you go right on to the classics or Nancy Drew. Of course there are exceptions.

Mother Maia: You are vague. All I've learned from your answer is that you intend to write for children between the ages of nine and 13.

Author Maia: Correct. That's the age a child suffers most from impositions on his intelligence. He is old enough to think, but few give him the respect due that new achievement. At home he is still being ordered around without the courtesy of an explanation. While his childhood is being denied him by a forced participation in the work, worries and responsibilities of the adult world, that world is shrouded from him.

Mother Maia: Not so loud; my daughter might hear.

Author Maia: I do feel that a child has every right to be amused when he sits down to the inactive pastime of reading. Kids are keenly aware of the world around them; it is their misfortune that nobody talks to them intelligently about anything, much less about the important things. They want to find out, on their own terms (without being bored), what life is all about. That's why they sometimes sit and read instead of running and looking.

Mother Maia: And do you plan to do all that for them through the books you write? Or are you just talking big?

Author Maia: Years ago I wrote a book about Haiti called *Market Day for Ti André*. The title itself suggests the book to be a bore. It was published, I like to think, only because it treated a country not often described in a children's book. My second book, *The Shadow of a Bull*, also treats a subject rarely found among juveniles — bullfighting. I wrote *Shadow* because I wanted to do a book for children about fear. Not the bumpy-ghost fear, but the fear that grips deep and has to be either fought against or surrendered to.

Mother Maia: You have not answered my question.

Author Maia: My next book is a biography of Alvar Núñez Cabeza de Vaca; it will be called *Odyssey of Courage* when it is published. I'm writing it for two reasons: 1) my old reason, that there is no book for children on the subject; and 2) the man himself, an amazingly noble human being at a time (the conquest of the Americas) when human nobility was at its lowest ebb. So the book will be about nobility and courage, twin sisters of character.

Mother Maia: Woof. You *are* talking big.

Author Maia: Another book I have completed, *The Enchanted Stable,* although a story about a horse, is much more than that. It's about old age and death.

Mother Maia: Granted all those are the major themes of life. But how do you expect to sell them to parents and librarians?

Author Maia: I expect to sell them to publishers whose province will be to sell them to parents and librarians. I expect to write the books. Write them well enough to interest the children and to entertain them.

Mother Maia: And you think you can do that?

Author Maia: If I didn't, I'd be at some other job. I want to do other books – about love, and about pride, and about the tight world of selfishness. Those will be the themes underlining the stories. Not one of the books, I hope, will surrender the entertainment value to the theme. For I believe that the key word, as long as you're writing fiction, is entertainment. Entertain, by golly, or don't write fiction!

Mother Maia: Is that your weapon against television?

Author Maia: Who said anything against television? I find it terribly entertaining most of the time. My own 12-year-old is glued to the set from seven at night until 10.

Mother Maia: So is mine, yet she finds time to read at least one, more often two, books a week.

Author Maia: Ah. But what has she been reading?

Mother Maia: At present she is reading by herself into the endless world of Carolyn Keene. But since she was small, everything from picture books to Dickens and Shakespeare have been read to her. She is being still read to occasionally, at the breakfast table, such authors as Conrad and George Eliot.

Author Maia: Your sentences are badly constructed.

Mother Maia: I never claimed to be a writer; that burden's on you. But who is interviewing whom? I have one more question. How come you are so sure that there aren't any of the kinds of books you want to write already on the library shelves?

Author Maia: Well naturally there are some. There is *A Wrinkle in Time,* for instance. But judging from the jackets (and when one is a writer one tends to do that), there are precious few other books of that caliber.

Mother Maia: All I can say to that is good luck with your jacket designer.

EDITORS' NOTE

Maia Wojciechowska was born in Warsaw, Poland, on August 7, 1927. She came to the United States in 1942 and attended the Sacred Heart Academy in Los Angeles, California, from which she was graduated in 1945. She enrolled in Immaculate Heart College in Hollywood, California, but dropped out after a year.

In 1950, she married a writer, Selden Rodman, from whom she was divorced in 1957. They have one daughter, Oriana. At present Maia and her daughter live in Ramapo Park, Oakland, New Jersey.

Before settling down to a full-time career of writing books for children, Maia tried a variety of jobs including waitress, undercover detective, tennis instructor, masseuse, copygirl, assistant editor, and literary agent.

Miss Wojciechowska's honors include the Newbery Medal in 1965 and the *New York Herald Tribune* Children's Spring Festival Award in 1964, both for *Shadow of a Bull.*

At present Maia is working on several books. She recently signed a contract for four children's books to be published by Harcourt, the first of which is scheduled for Spring, 1972. Her most recent books are *Tuned Out* (1968), *Hey, What's Wrong with This One* (1969), both published by Harpers, and *The Rotten Years* (1971), published by Doubleday.

Elizabeth Yates:
Artist with Words *

ELIZABETH YATES ONCE INVENTED the following conversation: "Are you bothered by ideas?" she improvised.

"Oh, yes, I am," might come the reply.

"Then you certainly must be a writer," she concluded. "I'm always being bothered by ideas that will not let me rest."

Ideas rooted in universal truth appear with quiet beauty and power in her books. For example, in *Amos Fortune, Free Man,* she wrote: "The wind of freedom that was passing over the world left nothing untouched." [1] When she speaks of these truths, she puts them into writing that is distinguished. As John and Annah Putnam walked beside the oxen into the Pawnee country, while the Indians came swiftly to circle their wagon, Annah asked: "Will they know we're saying that our hearts are homing?" [2] So often does Elizabeth Yates have the exact phrasing to paint a vivid word picture that her books are like the canvas of an artist. Like a painter with his paints, she is an artist with words.

Who is Elizabeth Yates, who writes so well and with such conviction? Who is this woman with gentle dignity, who speaks with a deliberate, resonant voice and beautiful enunciation? What forces have molded her strong character and forged her beliefs with deep integrity? How has she come to write with a smooth liquid flow that, as in the Indian child's song, is "like creek water slipping over stones?" [3]

* By Helen W. Painter. From *Elementary English* 42 (October 1965), 617–628+. Reprinted with the permission of the National Council of Teachers of English and Helen W. Painter.

Elizabeth Yates was born in Buffalo, New York, the second youngest of seven children. She spent long summer days on her father's farm south of Buffalo, where she performed the duties of a farm child and enjoyed the companionship of many pets. She liked horseback riding and often went on day-long rides. On rainy days she put down in copy books the stories that made up her thoughts. Her secret refuge was the unused pigeon loft to which she climbed by ladder.[4] In the evenings her parents might read aloud or all the family act in plays written by her older sister.

When she was about ten, she was given by this sister a list of books to read in the next eight years. While she had "to reach to understand some," the books set her on the path of reading. "I write to repay my sister for this," Miss Yates said once. "The story has come full circle." Reading was always a pleasure. She tells how she used to crawl under a bed, and, hidden by the valance, read undisturbed for hours,

> . . . vulnerable only to a dust mop or a carpet sweeper. I can re-member the safe but wicked joy I felt when I heard my name being called all over the house, especially if my nose was buried in *Oliver Twist* or *At the Back of the North Wind,* which I had heard my mother say were too old for me.[5]

She attended school in Buffalo. After graduation she spent a year at boarding school and then a summer abroad. In 1926 and for three years she worked in New York. In her free time she did writing of every type. She worked on a magazine and a newspaper, reviewed books, prepared articles and stories, and, as advised by a friend, wrote something every day. In New York she met William McGreal—"I can still remember him coming up the stairs with a big bowl of ice cubes." His business firm sent him to England, from where shortly he sent a cable asking her to marry him. She did so at the age of twenty-three, in the dim light of a November day in London.

The next ten years were centered in London. There was opportunity, however, for trips in the British Isles,[6] several months in Paris, a half year in Switzerland, and two months in Iceland. Mountain climbing was a favorite activity of the McGreals. They loved England but knew that at some far-off time they would return to New England.

That day came much sooner than she ever thought. She knew before her marriage that William McGreal had had an eye injury as a young man, with resulting periodic attacks of great pain. She had known, too, that a time might come when he would lose his sight but their youth and hope precluded this happening. As, however, his vision lessened, an eye doctor suggested that he live a quieter life with fewer pressures, a life which perhaps might conserve his sight enough for him to see for a few more years. Late in the same year they returned to the United States, rented a car in Boston, and set out for a small town which they had known and liked. Their dream had always been of a little house and farm. One winter day they found their future home. It was a small house about a mile from Peterborough, New Hampshire, with a farm of sixty-seven acres, two-thirds wooded. The house, about one hundred fifty years old, yielded some exciting discoveries: home-made bricks and blackened cranes in fireplaces long boarded up, and delicate stenciled designs on plaster walls.[7] The house was modernized but the McGreals left many of the old features intact. Beyond the dining room was a porch from which they could see the field, the small valley and brook, and the wooded hills or mountains rising to the east.

They named their home Shieling, from memories of the Isle of Skye and a shepherd's shieling. The word *shieling* could be traced back to shield, a type of shelter. The name seemed especially significant to them.

As the future loomed before them, the two talked about what they might do. They abandoned hopes of farming the thin, rocky land, of raising musk oxen. They put in a garden, planted flowers, and, as crops matured, filled their cellar with canned fruits, vegetables, and jellies — "a rainbow on the shelf." Life was full of satisfaction.

That winter a Boston eye surgeon suggested an operation to salvage Mr. McGreal's waning sight. The operation was a failure, but all pain was now gone. In her deeply moving book *The Lighted Heart*, Elizabeth Yates wrote of her reaction to the words of the doctor after the surgery: "You will have to build your lives now on the fact that your husband is blind." The full impact of his sentence struck her with force as she was driving home, and with anger at life, she "beat her hands on the steering wheel. . . . Then I thought of Bill and the depths he must have reached during his weeks alone in the hospital."[8]

It is significant of this woman that, after the first shock, never again in her book about themselves does she yield to such open despair. Occasionally wistful and poignant notes interject themselves — going about with eyes closed or blindfolded so as to understand blindness a little, tearing up a letter to him when she suddenly realized that he would never be able to read it, and yearning for eyes to meet or smiles to be exchanged. Her longing for the visual cues was there but generally submerged in her thoughts of him. His blindness could not be forgotten, of course, It was a "grief without end."

> Blindness was the simple fact within which we lived. I would not
> be able to forget it: not once, neither tomorrow, nor ten years from
> tomorrow.[9]

Her strength emanates from pages of the book. She speaks of the deeper meaning of their affection, of their learning to live a new kind of life, of feeling the value of each day as it came, and of treasuring true friendships.[10] She wrote once: "I did not know the world was made of love until Bill lost his sight." [11] She tells of her husband's gallantry and courage, but through them she also bespeaks her own.

Surely the pictures she gives of her husband portray him as fundamentally a man of profound philosophy and character whom it would have been a privilege to know. True, his was not always an even acceptance of his blindness. There was much frustration or, as in learning braille, nervous tension. But he was realistic. He said, "When I knew that I would not see again, I put all thoughts of sight — even as a wish — out of my mind."

He learned to assume many duties at home, helped cut wood, and rented the pastures for sheep. He taught boys in a residential school for the blind. Before the next school year he became Executive Director of the New Hampshire Association for the Blind, a service to which he devoted almost a decade. (He then became its first vice president, a position he held until his death.[12]) He spoke often with humor, as in calling his seven large volumes in braille his Vest Pocket Dictionary. Surely he has given his wife deep affection, expressed in a touching note on their twenty-fifth wedding anniversary. It reads in part: [13]

> And then for me, one day, the mist thickened in the valleys and
> even on the mountaintops. For a long, long time it seemed the view
> was lost.
> Then slowly, feeling your firm hand in mine, through your clear
> eyes, there came to me an inner sense of light and almost an outer
> view. Quietly sitting here, on this our day, I see these things and
> pray that I may never forget in the busyness of life that you have
> stood beside me in love, in laughter, and in strength —

Here in *The Lighted Heart,* a book seasoned and long in coming, Elizabeth Yates has written a true story of deep emotion, great strength, and indomitable courage. In addition, she has set down her own love story. No account of her other writing, much less of her self, would be possible without dwelling upon this book. Mr. McGreal once said of her:

"Her heart is with the simple basic qualities of human life." [14] Truly both William and Elizabeth Yates McGreal were " 'as one whose heart shines like a greate star in his breaste.' " [15]

It is not unusual, then, that one of Miss Yates' books, her most recent one, should treat in specific terms a subject of which she knows so much. *Carolina's Courage* is filled with tenderness, faith, and bravery. It promises to be a story for little girls especially to love. Children will want to know that Miss Yates got from a friend an Indian doll about a hundred years old. A trace of buffalo hair still runs down its back and the doll retains some of its greasy smell. The doll seemed to tell her a story, the theme of which is true in its conviction. "In pioneer days people knew what it was to share," Miss Yates says. "Today is there any truth which we need more than to share what we have and what we are?" So she first told the story to the children who come each Monday for Story Hour, and eventually the finished book came into being.

Carolina Putnam, ten years old, lived on a poor hill farm in New Hampshire in the middle 1800's. When her father decided that the family would go to the Platte in Nebraska, where land was available for the taking, she and her brother were each given the choice of one thing of their very own to take along. For Carolina this was no problem, for her dearest treasure was Lydia-Lou, her beautiful china and sawdust doll. Lyddy represented home, friends, and safety all the long months westward. Not far from their destination the family stopped their covered wagon at an encampment where the pioneering folk had gathered in fear of Indian trouble ahead. In the wait that followed, Carolina took Lyddy upstream. As she played with her doll in a lovely green nook, Carolina suddenly faced an Indian girl. The newcomer had a stiff, greasy doll of "buffalo hide with a bit of the tail for hair," beads for the face, and a feather in the headband. Though deeply frightened, Carolina made gestures of friendship. When the girls parted, the Indian child clung to Lyddy. Remembering her father's insistence that pioneer people must share, Carolina reluctantly gave up her treasure for the Indian doll. That doll became the means of safe conduct through Pawnee territory for the Putnams and their fellow travelers.

As well as the strong convictions, the tenderness and love in the story may well meet the need of some of its readers, for Carolina is a child rich in family affection. The father is mentioned as firm but gentle. During the times of early stopping on the westward trail, he took his little daughter exploring. The mother, after a few days with a farm family, brought a bit of blue cloth for her, a new dress for Lyddy. Carolina whispers about the loss of Lyddy while she is held tightly in her father's arms. The child responds to her family with equal warmth. Early in the book when the father tells her that they will leave almost everything she has ever known, Carolina waits until she is alone to bury her face against the cow's flank and cry.

> Alone with the friendly creatures, Carolina was sure of one thing, and that was that she had not become a pioneer. Perhaps tomorrow she would be, but tonight she was a New Hampshire child, born and bred, crying for the only home she had ever known and soon would never know again.[16]

Later, when the mother must leave behind the clock which has "ticked away all the years," Carolina snuggles close to ask, "Haven't you anything of your own, the way I have Lyddy?"

Strong religious belief underlies the story. The Bible is carried in the best place in the wagon, to be taken out each Sunday for reading during the day of rest. When Carolina looks in farewell at the home village, she thinks it looks sheltered "as if God had cupped it in the palm of His hand." Later in Nebraska she sees a flat land spread wide "on the palm of God's open hand." In the Pawnee country when fear envelops them, the child asks her mother who helps keep her father from being afraid and the mother answers "God."

The book is filled with vivid words and details like colors that cover the background of a canvas. The wagon is described with minuteness. Piece by piece, equipment and supplies are added. As the oxen move the wagon from the dooryard onto the road, the old horse trots across the field and whinnies. Notes tucked into a mound of earth are left on the trail. The wording is very descriptive. On the plains the Putnams see a rocking chair "rocking in the prairie wind as if an invisible person were sitting on it," and a grandfather clock "ticking away time in the emptiness of space." Elizabeth Yates talks of the "wind-threaded silence of the prairies" as the family walks "into the future." This is the kind of language to which we want to tune the ears of our children.

While *Carolina's Courage* is a new publication, some years ago Miss Yates wrote two books which also portrayed family life for children: *Mountain Born* in 1943 [17] and *A Place for Peter* in 1952.[18] In the first book Peter is six, living in the warm atmosphere of parents, Benj (the old hired man), and sheep. A little black cosset becomes Peter's own charge. The story is filled with happiness, the glory of the seasons, and the love of the boy and his pet ewe. In the second book Peter is thirteen, striving for recognition from his father who still sees his son as a young child.

When the mother is called away for some months, Peter assumes the responsibilities of a farm boy. With the help of Benj and the farm animals, Peter lives through a challenging time. He emerges from the winter with a close relationship to his father. While many writers have treated the father-son theme, Miss Yates' account of the mountain country and seasons, together with the raising of sheep, makes her books more than a story of conflict. May Hill Arbuthnot says:

> The succession of seasons and seasonal work, the beauty of woods, meadows, hills, and sky, and, above all, the closeness of these men to their farm animals make this a warm and beautiful story. . . . Such family love and respect can ease the pangs of growing up as nothing else can and in addition can give the child a picture of his own life stretching ahead of him, rich with promise.[19]

Always as a part of her writing, Elizabeth Yates builds a firm background of fact and experience. For *Mountain Born* she once told how she spent hours with a shepherd in New Hampshire, that she might come to know something about sheep and sheep-raising. She believed that the lives of sheep and shepherds are much as they were in David's time, and much the same all over the world. "There is a constancy to them that makes them something of a common denominator to civilization." Too, she was given a sweater made "from wool spun as it was sheared. The feel of it was rough and sturdy; the smell of it was strong and oily. I liked to bury my nose deep in it — and somehow, much of the story came from those moments."[20] (In fact, Peter has such a coat made from his beloved Biddy's wool.)

It was in her own house that Elizabeth Yates first saw stencils, an experience that eventually led in 1943 to the splendid book for young people, *Patterns on the Wall,* which received a *New York Herald Tribune* Spring Festival Award. When the workmen were renovating the one-hundred-fifty year old house after the McGreals had just purchased it, faint designs were visible on plaster. Carefully, seven layers of paper were removed, and there on the plaster's "dove-gray surface, were stencil designs in moss green and terra cotta: flowers, oak leaves, pineapples, and little hearts." While the stencils were being restored, Miss Yates studied about this New England craft which flourished in the early nineteenth century. "The colors were the ones obtained from natural sources; the pineapple was the symbol of hospitality; hearts were used only when the house was being readied for a bride."[21]

The art of stenciling plus true data about the terrible weather of 1816 in New Hampshire formed the facts for *Patterns on the Wall*. Skillfully does Elizabeth Yates manipulate the details of the post-colonial period, the ideas of great men of the day, the food and thoughts of simple folks, and the southern New Hampshire setting as she tells about Jared Austin, an apprentice and then journeyman painter who had beauty in his finger-tips. Near the beginning she has a traveler point out to Jared's unbelieving father that, as always happened, with independence assured in the land and men being free, there was time for expression in the arts. Under Jared's sensitive hands, walls came alive to beauty.

Yet the times did indeed try men's souls. As Jared worked at his craft and helped people with a consideration and accomplishment that drew men to regard him with growing suspicion, the year of "eighteen-hundred-and-froze-to-death" came. Weather unknown before to man gripped the area. There was snow during every month of the year of 1816. The stock died and plantings froze; the land was blighted with near-starvation; and men became half crazed as they struggled to survive. In their doubts they turned to Jared as a scapegoat, saying that he was a devil and had brought the cold. To Jared, with hurt in his heart at the loss of his beloved Jennet to Corban Cristy, came growth. Through pain a man grew up, he came to know, "up — a little nearer the stars, a little closer to God; not that God was distant but that man had to find out how near He was." [22] The beauty created by his own hands warmed him and thus, as Miss Yates quoted Hannah More, "Faith and works together grow."

Combining her research and her own strong faith has led to many other books by Elizabeth Yates. *Pebble in a Pool* [23] is the biography of Dorothy Canfield Fisher, written over a three-year period. The first year was spent in reading the voluminous material of Mrs. Fisher — letters at the University of Vermont library, seven hundred articles, and fifty books. Twice a month she visited and talked with Mrs. Fisher, into whose hands the book was placed a month before death. The reader of the biography will find striking parallels in the philosophy of the art of living between the writer and the one written about.

Though each book has great religious faith permeating it, *Your Prayers and Mine* and *Amos Fortune, Free Man* represent two approaches. While Miss Yates has published other religious stories, as *Children of the Bible* [24] and *The Christmas Story*,[25] *Your Prayers and Mine* forms a fascinating collection of prayers from many countries, people, religions, and centuries. Miss Yates says that she wrote in pencil her first book of prayers as a child, giving it to her oldest brother to take with him to war. A long time later she began to copy prayers which she found in various places and these make up the ones in this small book. They are a compilation that would interest any student. Here are a few: [26]

Oh Lord, Thou knowest how busy I must be this day; if I forget thee, do not Thou forget me.

Sir Jacob Astley, England, 17 c.

Dear God, Be good to me. The sea is so wide and my boat is so small.

Breton fisherman, France

Here needy he stands,
And I am he.

Osage Indian Prayer

From the walls of an old inn in Lancaster, England, came these words:

Give us, Lord, a bit o' sun,
A bit of work and a bit o' fun; . . .
Give us, too, a bit of a song
And a tale, and a book to help us along.
An' give us our share o' sorrow's lesson
That we may prove how grief's a blessin'.
Give us, Lord, a chance to be
Our goodly best, brave, wise, and free,
Our goodly best for ourself, and others,
Till all men learn to live as brothers.

The last line of this prayer signals the hope underlying the book *Amos Fortune, Free Man*. A true story of a man who lived from 1710 to 1801, Amos' life is traced from Africa, where he was a prince; to Boston, where he was sold as a slave; to Jaffrey, New Hampshire, where he plied his trade as a tanner and died free. Amos was a strong but gentle man who purchased his own freedom at the age of sixty and that of others when he could accumulate enough money. While some cruelty is mentioned, perhaps one of the strong points of the book is the portrayal of what well must have been the good fortune of many slaves, their good treatment by kindly masters. A religious man, Amos sought a sign from the Lord, and in his will designated his money to go to the church and the school.

Amos Fortune, Free Man has won many honors: the Newbery Award in 1951, the *Herald Tribune* Spring Festival Award, and the first William Allen White Children's Book Award (1953). It is simply written, with the universal truths which must be part of a distinguished book. In her own words, Miss Yates remarks: "A tanner by trade, he proved through his life that the measure of a man's humanity is the extent and intensity of his love for mankind." [27] At another time she said that "the glory of neighborliness is in the knowledge that we live in a land where a plain man can become significant if his work is well done." Again, she wrote: "The free man, who knows why he is free, knows that freedom is the essence of life." [28]

Elizabeth Yates says that she stands in awe of what the book has done.[29] The idea of Amos Fortune first came to her one summer evening when she went to the little town of Jaffrey Center, some seven miles from Peterborough, to the Amos Fortune Lecture Series. Before the lecture started, she went to the churchyard on top of the hill to see the stone marking Amos Fortune's grave. She has described the summer evening very clearly—the singing of distant thrushes, the late sunset light over Monadnock Mountain, and the warm wind in the tall pines. Toward the far stone wall she saw the high, slender, slate gravestone of Amos Fortune. Beside his was his wife's, Violet, equal to his in height and thus different from wives' stones tapered low at other graves. She read both inscriptions, weathered but still readable in the fine carving of one hundred fifty years ago:

Sacred
to the memory of
AMOS FORTUNE
who was born free
in Africa a slave in America
he purchased liberty
professed Christianity
lived reputably and
died hopefully
Nov. 17, 1801
Aet. 91

Sacred
to the memory of
VIOLET
by sale the slave
of Amos Fortune by
marriage his wife by
her fidelity his friend

and solace she died
his widow
Sept. 13, 1802
Aet. 73

Miss Yates went to the lecture but heard nothing, for her mind was occupied with questions about this man. For a year she did research on his life, read his important papers, particularly the freedom and his will, and studied African slave trading. She saw his home, his lantern, and his compass. The notes in her notebook grew to an inch thick. Then she started writing. going from history into some imagination.[30] Early accounts had mentioned that all types had been made slaves. Amos had a desire for service, implying leadership. From this she concluded that he must have been a leader of his people. Since he read and wrote so soon in America, he must have been taught by a Quaker, as were so many Africans taught by the Quaker women in their kitchens. His regard for women must have gone back to someone dear in his past, perhaps a sister. His love of God and his fellowmen must have come from the fervent presentation of religion made to him by the Quakers.

The intent of the book is expressed thus by its author: [31]

In a world such as ours is today, with much of the best thought devoting itself to means of destruction, it is good to be reminded of a life such as Amos Fortune's. He lived the only force that is greater than any bomb: simple affection, deep-hearted love. Modes change but not values, and all that he stood for in his day is vital to ours: those "inalienable rights" whose achievement is part of the long mountain we all are climbing as we emerge from our various forms of slavery into the fullness of freedom.

Finally, this account of Elizabeth Yates could not be given without special reference to *Someday You'll Write,* a book in which she speaks clearly and inspiringly about her craftsmanship. It is a must for all children, for every child retains the spark of creativity. The book really began with a question from Joyce, a little girl who had come since the age of five to the Monday afternoon Story Hour of Miss Yates and a friend. Joyce, now eleven, wanted to know what book she could get that would tell her how to become a writer. Miss Yates did searching and inquiring. Finding nothing, she told Joyce to bring her a list of points about which she wanted to know and they would do a book together. Joyce appeared with an enormous pad of paper, six pencils, and eight subjects, which later became the chapter headings. Miss Yates' favorite topic was the one, "How to continue — but not too long — and keep your reader interested!"

Despite more than twenty years of writing and of working with writers' conferences in Vermont and Wisconsin, Miss Yates found the book hard to do and she spent most of the winter on it. Preparing primarily for Joyce, she wanted to show that "writing is hard work, it is discipline, and it is a long, long time before anything happens." While she tells that she wanted to be a writer before she knew how to read, it was ten years before she published. Had she published earlier, she questions whether or not her own ideals would have been established, for it "took that long to know what I really stand for and believe in." She thinks that writing must be approached as a craft and developed as a craftsman will, through long and patient work. She gives suggestions about reading, working conditions, and tools. She discusses the spark which a subject for a story must strike in a reader and gives a rule for finding the right length of a story: "Have something to say and stop when you have said it." She speaks about interesting beginnings, rewarding endings, style, the golden thread of a man's life which guides the writing of a biography, and the disciplined exercises that writing demands. She urges reading aloud to test one's work — something she applies to her own writing.

Because she herself uses words so well, let us look at a few suggestions which she makes about them.[32]

> Your inner ear will begin to respond to the sound of words and the way they are used in relation to each other. Their aptness and the way they conveyed beauty and spoke truth are all part of what held you to the book.
> Note particular words, . . . and add them to your own vocabulary. Here, again, are tools, and the sensitive craftsman will care for words as for any valued piece of equipment. Try your newly acquired words in different combinations; experiment with them as an artist does with colors. Words serve their purpose when well employed.

In her address for the William Allen White Award, she speaks of the appeal of words for herself as a small child.[33]

> Written words were wonderful things for they linked her with the world — . . . they even threw out strands frail as a spider's web yet

strong into a possible world of the future. Words were bridges across which memory could travel, fancy would play, and hope might reach. And the written word that speaks in silence still is to her the most wonderful thing in the world.

Above all, Miss Yates urges young writers not to hesitate but to "use the ideas that won't let you rest." She goes on to say:

Let imagination lead you wherever it will but be sure you feed it with all the facts you can gain. Let your story begin in such a way that it not only will capture the interest of your readers but engage their hearts. Have your story end with sufficient satisfaction so that your thoughts have been accounted for, no loose strand has been left, and yet there is, at the closing of the book, a surging forward for the reader. Perhaps the easiest way is to say that the reader has a new conviction of some facet of truth that is tremendously real to the writer.[34]

Once asked if she would ever give up writing for any other job, Miss Yates reviewed her "cloud castles." She had once longed to be an ambassador, to play a Gaelic harp, and to find high adventure among distant mountains. Writing, she realized,

. . . embraced all my early dreams: the thoughts I entertained and the ways I used to convey them to others could serve as ambassadors of understanding; the words I chose and the rhythms followed as sentences grew to paragraphs and paragraphs to pages could, in their way, make music; and always there would be the challenge to explore high places as I searched for new ways to present old truths.[35]

REFERENCES

1. Elizabeth Yates, *Amos Fortune, Free Man*. New York: Aladdin Books, 1950, p. 72.
2. Elizabeth Yates, *Carolina's Courage*. New York: E. P. Dutton and Co., 1964, p. 95.
3. *Ibid.,* p. 80.
4. "About Elizabeth Yates." New York: E. P. Dutton and Co., n.d.
5. Elizabeth Yates, "Climbing Some Mountain in the Mind," *Horn Book Magazine,* 27 (July–August, 1951) 268–78.
6. During a visit to Cornwall in 1939, Miss Yates collected some legends of Enys Tregarthen, published the next year under the title *Piskey Folk*. The book is illustrated by William McGreal.

7. Elizabeth Yates, *The Lighted Heart*. New York: E. P. Dutton and Co., 1961, pp. 14–15.

8. *Ibid.*, pp. 54–5.

9. *Ibid.*, pp. 65–6.

10. One friendship especially cherished has been that of Mary in the book, or Nora S. Unwin. Miss Unwin came from England to visit the McGreals and then decided to live in this country. For five years she lived with them, but her home now is located just a walk through the yard from her friends. "I could not do what I do without her," Miss Yates says. It should also be noted that Miss Unwin has illustrated most of Miss Yates' books.

11. Elizabeth Yates, *The Lighted Heart*, p. 237.

12. William McGreal died December 16, 1963. In an editorial in *The Peterborough Transcript* December 19, 1963, Kate S. Kendall spoke of this man as one "who gave a new concept of courage and compassion and gaiety." (Printed in Louise A. Nickerson's *Widening Rays*. Concord, New Hampshire: New Hampshire Association for the Blind, 1964. p. 42.) Governor King designated September of 1964 as Sight Saving Month in New Hampshire in honor of Mr. McGreal. A scholarship fund, administered by the Association, has been established in his memory.

13. *Ibid.*, pp. 241–2.

14. William McGreal, "Elizabeth Yates," *Horn Book Magazine*, 27 (July–August, 1951) 262–7.

15. Elizabeth Yates, *The Lighted Heart, op. cit.*, p. 229.

16. Elizabeth Yates, *Carolina's Courage, op. cit.*, p. 16.

17. Elizabeth Yates, *Mountain Born*. New York: Coward-McCann, 1943.

18. Elizabeth Yates, *A Place for Peter*. New York: Coward-McCann, 1952.

19. May Hill Arbuthnot, *Children and Books*. 3rd Ed. Chicago: Scott, Foresman and Co., 1964, p. 444.

20. From the book jacket to *Mountain Born*.

21. Elizabeth Yates, *The Lighted Heart, op. cit.*, p. 15.

22. Elizabeth Yates, *Patterns on the Wall*. New York: E. P. Dutton and Co., 1943, p. 146.

23. Elizabeth Yates, *Pebble in a Pool*. New York: E. P. Dutton and Co., 1958.

24. Elizabeth Yates, *Children of the Bible*. New York: E. P. Dutton and Co., 1950.

25. Elizabeth Yates, *The Christmas Story*. New York: E. P. Dutton and Co., 1949.

26. Elizabeth Yates, *Your Prayers and Mine*. Cambridge Mass.: Houghton Mifflin Co., Riverside Press, 1954.

27. Elizabeth Yates, "Everyman's Quest." The First William Allen White Book Award Address. Secured through the courtesy of Miss Irene Hansen, Kansas State Teachers College, Emporia, Kansas.

28. Elizabeth Yates, "Together: Watchword and Challenge." An address for Emporia State College Students. Also secured through the courtesy of Miss Irene Hansen.

29. Elizabeth Yates once asked the opinion of this writer as to why *Amos Fortune* had been so much more popular than *Prudence Crandell*. *Prudence Crandell, Woman of Courage* (New York: E. P. Dutton and Co., 1955), is a very interesting biography of a young Quaker teacher who opened her school to Negro girls in 1833. The townspeople of Canterbury, Conn., threatened and imprisoned her and passed a law against such a school.

30. Elizabeth Yates, "Climbing Some Mountain in the Mind," *op. cit.*

31. *Loc. cit.*

32. Elizabeth Yates, *Someday You'll Write*. New York: E. P. Dutton and Co., 1962, p. 13.

33. Elizabeth Yates, "Everyman's Quest," *op. cit.*

34. Speech by Miss Yates at the University of Akron, April 20, 1963.

35. Elizabeth Yates, "Please Answer This. . . ," *Horn Book Magazine* 39 (April, 1963) 162–4.

EDITORS' NOTE

Mrs. Yates still lives on her farm in Peterborough, New Hampshire, where she is an active member of her community. In 1967, she wrote *New Hampshire,* which was published by Coward and is part of their State of the Nation Series. Her latest book, published by Dutton in 1971, is *Sarah Whitcher's Story.*

Prizes and honors won by Elizabeth Yates include the Jane Addams Book Award (given to the children's book of the year that best combines literary merit and themes of brotherhood) for *Rainbow Round the World* in 1955; the *New York Herald Tribune* Children's Spring Book Festival Award for *Patterns on the Wall* in 1943, and for *Amos Fortune, Free Man* in 1950; a runner-up for the Newbery Medal for *Mountain Born* in 1944; the Newbery Medal for *Amos Fortune, Free Man* in 1951; and the William Allen White Children's Book Award (Kansas children in grades 4–8 vote from a list chosen by specialists) for *Amos Fortune, Free Man* in 1953. The Sarah Josepha Hale Award, given to a "distinguished author whose work and life reflect the literary tradition of New England," was awarded to Mrs. Yates in 1970.

Appendix

The Appendix includes the English-language works of each author and author-illustrator. The list is arranged alphabetically by author or author-illustrator. The books are listed in chronological order. British, Canadian, and Australian editions are included only when they are either the first editions published or are the only ones currently in print.

If an author-illustrator has illustrated the work of another author, these titles are listed separately under "Illustrated Works."

Where a work was originally published by one publisher but is presently published by another, both editions are included unless no date for the former is given in BIP or CBIP, in which case the latter publisher is given instead of the original publisher.

ARDIZZONE, EDWARD
AUTHORED & ILLUSTRATED WORKS
Little Tim and the Brave Sea Captain. New York: Oxford, 1936.
Lucy Brown and Mr. Grimes. New York: Oxford, 1937.
Tim and Lucy Go to Sea. New York: H. Z. Walck, 1938.
Baggage to the Enemy. Forest Hills, N.Y.: Transatlantic Arts, 1941.
Paul, the Hero of the Fire. Boston: Houghton Mifflin, 1949.
Tim to the Rescue. New York: H. Z. Walck, 1949.
Tim and Charlotte. New York: Oxford, 1951.
Tim in Danger. New York: H. Z. Walck, 1953.
Little Tim and the Brave Sea Captain. 2nd ed. New York: H. Z. Walck, 1955.

Tim All Alone. New York: H. Z. Walck, 1956.
Ding Dong Bell. [with Percy Young]. London: William Heinemann, 1957.
Tim and Lucy Go to Sea. New York: H. Z. Walck, 1958.
Nicholas and the Fast Moving Diesel. New York: H. Z. Walck, 1959.
John the Clockmaker. New York: H. Z. Walck, 1960.
Tim's Friend Towser. New York: H. Z. Walck, 1962.
Paul, the Hero of the Fire. New York: H. Z. Walck, 1963.
Diana and Her Rhinoceros. New York: H. Z. Walck, 1964.
Peter the Wanderer. New York: H. Z. Walck, 1964.
Tim and Ginger. New York: H. Z. Walck, 1965.

The Little Girl and the Tiny Doll. [with Aingelda Ardizzone]. London: Constable, 1966.

Sarah and Simon and No Red Paint. New York: Dial Press, 1966.

Tim to the Lighthouse. New York: H. Z. Walck, 1968.

Ding Dong Bell. reprint. [with Percy Young]. New York: Dover, 1969.

Johnny's Bad Day. London: Bodley Head, 1970.

The Wrong Side of the Bed. New York: Doubleday, 1970.

Lucy Brown and Mr. Grimes. New York: H. Z. Walck, 1971.

The Young Ardizzone. New York: Macmillan, 1971.

ILLUSTRATED WORKS

Great Expectations. [Charles Dickens]. New York: Heritage Press, 1939.

Local. [Maurice Gorham]. London: Cassell, 1939.

Mimff. [Hildegarde Kaeser]. New York: Oxford, 1939.

My Uncle Silas. [Herbert Bates]. London: Jonathan Cape, 1939.

Road to Bordeaux. [C. D. Freeman and Douglas Cooper]. New York: Harper, 1941.

Peacock Pie. new ed. [Walter De La Mare]. London: Faber & Faber, 1946.

Hey Nonny Yes. [H. Fordham, comp.]. London: Saturn Press, 1947.

Pilgrim's Progress. [John Bunyan]. London: Faber & Faber, 1947.

Peter Pan. [J. M. Barrie]. New York: Scribner, 1950.

Londoners. [Maurice Gorham]. New York: British Book Centre, 1951.

Back to the Local. [Maurice Gorham]. New York: British Book Centre, 1952.

Blackbird in the Lilac. [James Reeves]. New York: Oxford, 1952.

Warden. [Anthony Trollope]. New York: Oxford, 1952.

Barchester Towers. [Anthony Trollope]. New York: Oxford, 1953.

Peacock Pie. reissue. [Walter De La Mare]. London: Faber & Faber, 1953.

Pilgrim's Progress. new ed. [John Bunyan]. London: Faber & Faber, 1953.

Fantastic Tale of the Plucky Sailor and the Postage Stamp. [Stephen Corrin]. Forest Hills, N.Y.: Transatlantic Arts, 1954.

Mimff Takes Over. [Hildegarde Kaeser]. London: Oxford, 1954.

Little Bookroom. [Eleanor Farjeon]. New York: H. Z. Walck, 1955.

Newcomes. [William Thackeray]. New York: Heritage Press, 1955.

Pictures on the Pavement. [George Stonier]. London: Michael Joseph, 1955.

History of Henry Esmond. [William Thackeray]. New York: Heritage Press, 1956.

Hunting with Mr. Jorrocks, from Handley Cross. [Robert Surtees]. New York: Oxford, 1956.

Pigeons and Princesses. [James Reeves]. London: William Heinemann, 1956.

St. Luke's Life of Christ. [John Phillips, trans.]. London: William Collins, 1956.

School in Our Village. [Joan Goldman]. London: B. T. Batsford, 1957.

Sun Slower, Sun Faster. [Meriol Trevor]. New York: Sheed & Ward, 1957.

Wandering Moon. [James Reeves]. London: William Heinemann, 1957.

Jim at the Corner. [Eleanor Farjeon]. New York: H. Z. Walck, 1958.

Minnow Leads to Treasure. [Phillipa Pearce]. Cleveland: World, 1958.

Pinky Pie. [Eleanor Estes]. New York: Harcourt Brace, 1958.

Story of Joseph. [Walter De La Mare]. London: Faber & Faber, 1958.

Blackbird in the Lilac. [James Reeves]. New York: Dutton, 1959.

Comedies. [William Shakespeare]. New York: Heritage Press, 1959.

Holiday Trench. [Joan Ballantyne]. London: Thomas Nelson, 1959.

Story of Moses. [Walter De La Mare]. London: Faber & Faber, 1959.

Boyhoods of Great Composers. [Catherine Gough]. New York: H. Z. Walck, 1960.

Exploits of Don Quixote. [Miguel de Cervantes Saavedra]. New York: H. Z. Walck, 1960.

Island MacKenzie. [U. M. Williams]. New York: Morrow, 1960.

Story of Samuel and Saul. [Walter De La Mare]. London: Faber & Faber, 1960.

Titus in Trouble. [James Reeves]. New York: H. Z. Walck, 1960.

The Adventures of Huckleberry Finn. [Samuel Clemens]. London: William Heinemann, 1961.

The Adventures of Tom Sawyer. [Samuel Clemens]. London: William Heinemann, 1961.

Peacock Pie. new ed. New York: Alfred A. Knopf, 1961.

The Penny Fiddle. [Robert Graves]. New York: Doubleday, 1961.

Stories from the Bible. [Walter De La Mare]. New York: Alfred A. Knopf, 1961.

The Island of Fish in the Trees. [Eva Wuorio]. Cleveland: World, 1962.

Mrs. Malone. [Eleanor Farjeon]. New York: H. Z. Walck, 1962.

Kaleidoscope. [Eleanor Farjeon]. New York: H. Z. Walck, 1963.

The Singing Cupboard. [Dana Faralla]. Philadelphia: Lippincott, 1963.

Alley. [Eleanor Estes]. New York: Harcourt Brace, 1964.

Hello Elephant. [Jan Wahl]. New York: Holt, Rinehart & Winston, 1964.

The Land of Right Up and Down. [Eva Wuorio]. Cleveland: World, 1964.

Swanhilda-of-the-Swans. [Dana Faralla]. Philadelphia: Lippincott, 1964.

Thirty-Nine Steps. [John Buchan]. New York: Dutton, 1964.

The Old Nurse's Stocking-Basket. [Eleanor Farjeon]. New York: H. Z. Walck, 1965.

The Witch Family. [Eleanor Estes]. New York: Harcourt Brace, 1965.

Book for Eleanor Farjeon. [N. Lewis, ed.]. New York: H. Z. Walck, 1966.

Long Ago When I Was Young. [Edith Bland]. New York: Franklin Watts, 1966.

Muffletumps. [Jan Wahl]. New York: Holt, Rinehart & Winston, 1966.

The Secret Shoemakers. [J. L. K. and W. K. Grimm]. New York: Abelard Schuman, 1966.

Daddy-Long-Legs. [Jean Webster]. New York: Meredith Press, 1967.

Kali and the Golden Mirror. [Eva Wuorio]. Cleveland: World, 1967.

Likely Place. [Paula Fox]. New York: Macmillan, 1967.

Little Girl and the Tiny Doll. [Aingelda Ardizzone]. New York: Delacorte Press, 1967.

The Magic Summer. [Noel Streatfield]. New York: Random House, 1967.

Miranda the Great. [Eleanor Estes]. New York: Harcourt Brace, 1967.

Nurse Matilda Goes to Town. [C. Brand]. New York: Dutton, 1968.

Rhyming Will. [James Reeves]. New York: McGraw-Hill, 1968.

Robinson Crusoe. [Daniel Defoe]. London: Nonesuch Press, 1968.

Truants. [John Walsh]. Chicago: Rand McNally, 1968.

Do You Remember What Happened. [Jean Chapman]. Sydney: Angus & Robertson, 1969.

Otterbury Incident. [Cecil Lewis]. Cleveland: World, 1969.

A Riot of Quiet. [Virginia Sicotte]. New York: Holt, Rinehart & Winston, 1969.

The Angel and the Donkey. [James Reeves]. New York: McGraw-Hill, 1970.

Dick Whittington. [Kathleen Lines]. New York: H. Z. Walck, 1970.

BEMELMANS, LUDWIG

AUTHORED & ILLUSTRATED WORKS

Hansi. New York: Viking Press, 1934.

Castle Number Nine. New York: Viking Press, 1937.

Golden Basket. New York: Viking Press, 1937.

My War With the United States. New York: Viking Press, 1937.

Life Class. New York: Viking Press, 1938.

Quito Express. New York: Viking Press, 1938.

Madeline. New York: Viking Press, 1939.

Small Beer. New York: Putnam, 1939.

Fifi. New York: Simon & Schuster, 1940.

At Your Service. Evanston, Ill.: Row Peterson, 1941.

Donkey Inside. New York: Viking Press, 1941.

Hotel Splendide. New York: Viking Press, 1941.

I Love You, I Love You, I Love You. New York: Viking Press, 1942.

Rosebud. New York: Random House, 1942.

Now I Lay Me Down to Sleep. New York: Viking Press, 1943.

Blue Danube. New York: Viking Press, 1945.

Hotel Bemelmans. New York: Viking Press, 1946.

Dirty Eddie. New York: Viking Press, 1947.

Best of Times. New York: Simon & Schuster, 1948.

Eye of God. New York: Viking Press, 1949.

Sunshine. New York: Simon & Schuster, 1950.

Happy Place. Boston: Little, Brown, 1952.

How to Travel Incognito. Boston: Little, Brown, 1952.

Father, Dear Father. New York: Viking Press, 1953.

Madeline's Rescue. New York: Viking Press, 1953.

High World. New York: Harper & Row, 1954.

Parsley. New York: Harper & Row, 1955.

To the One I Love the Best. New York: Viking Press, 1955.

World of Bemelmans. New York: Viking Press, 1955.

Holiday in France. Boston: Houghton Mifflin, 1957.

Madeline and the Bad Hat. New York: Viking Press, 1957.

Woman of My Life. New York: Viking Press, 1957.

My Life in Art. New York: Harper & Row, 1958.

Madeline and the Gypsies. New York: Viking Press, 1959.

Are You Hungry, Are You Cold. Cleveland: World, 1960.

Welcome Home! New York: Harper & Row, 1960.

Italian Holiday. Boston: Houghton Mifflin, 1961.

Madeline in London. New York: Viking Press, 1961.

Marina. New York: Harper & Row, 1962.

On Board Noah's Ark. New York: Viking Press, 1962.

The Street Where the Heart Lies. Cleveland: World, 1962.

The Donkey Inside. New York: Dutton, 1964.

ILLUSTRATED WORKS

Noodle. [Munro Leaf]. New York: Scholastic Book Service, 1937.

Literary Life and the Hell With It. [Whit Burnett]. New York: Harper & Row, 1939.

Luchow's German Cookbook. [Leonard Mitchell]. New York: Doubleday, 1952.

La Bonne Table. [Donald and Eleanor Friede, eds.]. New York: Simon & Schuster, 1964.

BROWN, MARGARET WISE

Children's Year. New York: Harper & Row, 1937.

When the Wind Blew. New York: Harper & Row, 1937.

Bumble Bugs and Elephants. Reading, Mass.: W. R. Scott, 1938.

Fish with the Deep Sea Smile. New York: Dutton, 1938.

Little Fireman. Reading, Mass.: W. R. Scott, 1938.

Streamlined Pig. New York: Harper & Row, 1938.

City Noisy Book. New York: Harper & Row, 1939.

Little Pig's Picnic and Other Stories. Lexington, Mass.: Heath, 1939.

Noisy Book. Reading, Mass.: W. R. Scott, 1939.

The World is Round or Rose is a Rose. Reading, Mass.: W. R. Scott, 1939.

Comical Tragedy or Tragical Comedy of Punch and Judy. Reading, Mass.: W. R. Scott, 1940.

Country Noisy Book. New York: Harper & Row, 1940.

Fables of Jean de la Fontaine. New York: Harper & Row, 1940.

Baby Animals. New York: Random House, 1941.

Brer Rabbit. New York: Harper & Row, 1941.

Bumble Bugs and Elephants, rev. ed. Reading, Mass.: W. R. Scott, 1941.

Polite Penguin. New York: Harper & Row, 1941.

Poodle and the Sheep. New York: Dutton, 1941.

Seashore Noisy Book. New York: Harper & Row, 1941.

Don't Frighten the Lion. New York: Harper & Row, 1942.

Indoor Noisy Book. New York: Harper & Row, 1942.

Night and Day. New York: Harper & Row, 1942.

Runaway Bunny. New York: Harper & Row, 1942.

Big Dog, Little Dog. New York: Doubleday, 1943.

Child's Good Night Book. Reading, Mass.: W. R. Scott, 1943.

Little Chicken. New York: Harper & Row, 1943.

Little Children. New York: Harper & Row, 1943.

Noisy Bird Book. Reading, Mass.: W. R. Scott, 1943.

SHHhhh. . . . . . Bang. New York: Harper & Row, 1943.

Animals, Plants and Machines. [with Lucy Mitchell]. Lexington, Mass.: Heath, 1944.

Big Fur Secret. New York: Harper & Row, 1944.

Black and White. New York: Harper & Row, 1944.

Farm and City. [with Lucy Mitchell]. Lexington, Mass.: Heath, 1944.

Horses. New York: Harper & Row, 1944.

Red Light, Green Light. New York: Doubleday, 1944.

They All Saw It. New York: Harper & Row, 1944.

Willie's Walk to Grandmama. [with Rockbridge Campbell]. Reading, Mass.: W. R. Scott, 1944.

House of A Hundred Windows. New York: Harper & Row, 1945.

Little Fisherman. Reading, Mass.: W. R. Scott, 1945.

Little Lost Lamb. New York: Doubleday, 1945.

Little Fur Family. New York: Harper & Row, 1946.

The Little Island. New York: Doubleday, 1946.

Man in the Manhole and the Fix-It Men. [with Edith Hurd]. Reading, Mass.: W. R. Scott, 1946.

Bad Little Duckhunter. Reading, Mass.: W. R. Scott, 1947.

First Story. New York: Harper & Row, 1947.

Golden Egg Book. New York: Simon & Schuster, 1947.

Goodnight Moon. New York: Harper & Row, 1947.

Sleepy Little Lion. New York: Harper & Row, 1947.

Winter Noisy Book. New York: Harper & Row, 1947.

Little Cowboy. Reading, Mass.: W. R. Scott, 1948.

Little Farmer. Reading, Mass.: W. R. Scott, 1948.

Wait Till the Moon is Full. New York: Harper & Row, 1948.

Wonderful Story Book. New York: Simon & Schuster, 1948.

Important Book. New York: Harper & Row, 1949.

My World. New York: Harper & Row, 1949.

Pussycat's Christmas. New York: T. Y. Crowell, 1949.

Two Little Trains. Reading, Mass.: Addison-Wesley, 1949.

Dark Wood of the Golden Birds. New York: Harper & Row, 1950.

Dream Book. New York: Random House, 1950.

Peppermint Family. New York: Harper & Row, 1950.

Child's Good Night Book. new ed. Reading, Mass.: Addison-Wesley, 1951.

Fox Eyes. New York: Pantheon, 1951.

Little Fur Family. new ed. New York: Harper & Row, 1951.

Pussy Willow. New York: Simon & Schuster, 1951.

Quiet Noisy Book. New York: Harper & Row, 1951.

Summer Noisy Book. New York: Harper & Row, 1951.

Child's Good Morning. Reading, Mass.: W. R. Scott, 1952.

Christmas in the Barn. New York: T. Y. Crowell, 1952.

The Duck. New York: Harper & Row, 1952.

Little Fireman. rev. ed. Reading, Mass.: Addison-Wesley, 1952.

Noon Balloon. New York: Harper & Row, 1952.

Where Have You Been? New York: T. Y. Crowell, 1952.

Golden Bunny and 17 Other Stories and Poems. New York: Simon & Schuster, 1953.

Hidden House. New York: Holt, Rinehart & Winston, 1953.

Little Frightened Tiger. New York: Doubleday, 1953.

Sleepy ABC. New York: Lothrop, Lee & Shephard, 1953.

Two Lives. [with Lucy Mitchell]. New York: Simon & Schuster, 1953.

Friendly Book. New York: Simon & Schuster, 1954.

Little Fur Tree. New York: T. Y. Crowell, 1954.

Little Indian. New York: Simon & Schuster, 1954.

Wheel on the Chimney. Philadelphia: Lippincott, 1954.

Willie's Adventures. Reading, Mass.: Addison-Wesley, 1954.

Little Brass Band. New York: Harper & Row, 1955.

Man in the Manhole and the Fix-It Men. reissue. [with Edith Hurd]. Reading, Mass.: W. R. Scott, 1955.

Seven Stories About a Cat Named Sneakers. Reading, Mass.: W. R. Scott, 1955.

Young Kangaroo. Reading, Mass.: Addison-Wesley, 1955.

Big Red Barn. Reading, Mass.: Addison-Wesley, 1956.

David's Little Indian. Reading, Mass.: W. R. Scott, 1956.

Home for a Bunny. New York: Simon & Schuster, 1956.

Three Little Animals. New York: Harper & Row, 1956.

Whistle for the Train. New York: Doubleday, 1956.

Color Kittens. New York: Simon & Schuster, 1958.

Dead Bird. Reading, Mass.: Addison-Wesley, 1958.

Train to Timbuctoo. New York: Simon & Schuster, 1958.

Nibble, Nibble. Reading, Mass.: Addison-Wesley, 1959.

Diggers. New York: Harper & Row, 1960.

Wonderful House. rev. ed. New York: Golden Press, 1960.

Four Fur Feet. Reading, Mass.: Addison-Wesley, 1961.

On Christmas Eve. Reading, Mass.: Addison-Wesley, 1961.

The Golden Bunny, and 17 Other Stories and Poems. New York: Golden Press, 1963.

The Golden Egg Book. New York: Western Press, 1963.

Where Have You Been? New York: Hastings House, 1963.

Five Little Firemen. [with Edith Hurd]. New York: Golden Press, 1967.

Margaret Wise Brown's Golden Sleepy Book. new ed. New York: Golden Press, 1971.

BULLA, CLYDE ROBERT

Donkey Cart. New York: T. Y. Crowell, 1946.

Riding the Pony Express. New York: T. Y. Crowell, 1948.

Secret Valley. New York: T. Y. Crowell, 1949.

Surprise for a Cowboy. New York: T. Y. Crowell, 1950.

Ranch for Danny. New York: T. Y. Crowell, 1951.

Johnny Hong of Chinatown. New York: T. Y. Crowell, 1952.

Song of St. Francis. New York: T. Y. Crowell, 1952.

We Are Thy Children. [with Lois Lenski]. New York: T. Y. Crowell, 1952.

Eagle Feather. New York: T. Y. Crowell, 1953.

Star of Wild Horse Canyon. New York: T. Y. Crowell, 1953.

Down the Mississippi. New York: T. Y. Crowell, 1954.

Songs of Mr. Small. [with Lois Lenski]. New York: Oxford, 1954.

Squanto, Friend of the White Man. New York: T. Y. Crowell, 1954.

Dog Named Penny. Boston: Ginn, 1955.

Poppy Seeds. New York: T. Y. Crowell, 1955.

White Sails to China. New York: T. Y. Crowell, 1955.

John Billington. New York: T. Y. Crowell, 1956.

Sword in the Tree. New York: T. Y. Crowell, 1956.

Old Charlie. New York: T. Y. Crowell, 1957.

Ghost Town Treasure. New York: T. Y. Crowell, 1958.

Pirate's Promise. New York: T. Y. Crowell, 1958.

Songs of the City. [with Lois Lenski]. New York: E. B. Marks, 1958.

Stories of Favorite Operas. New York: T. Y. Crowell, 1959.

Valentine Cat. New York: T. Y. Crowell, 1959.

Three Dollar Mule. New York: T. Y. Crowell, 1960.

Tree is a Plant. New York: T. Y. Crowell, 1960.

Benito. New York: T. Y. Crowell, 1961.

The Sugar Pear Tree. New York: T. Y. Crowell, 1961.

The Ring and the Fire. New York: T. Y. Crowell, 1962.

What Makes a Shadow. New York: T. Y. Crowell, 1962.

Indian Hill. New York: T. Y. Crowell, 1963.

Viking Adventure. New York: T. Y. Crowell, 1963.

More Stories of Favorite Operas. New York: T. Y. Crowell, 1965.

St. Valentine's Day. New York: T. Y. Crowell, 1965.

Lincoln's Birthday. New York: T. Y. Crowell, 1966.

White Bird. New York: T. Y. Crowell, 1966.

Flowerpot Gardens. New York: T. Y. Crowell, 1967.

Washington's Birthday. New York: T. Y. Crowell, 1967.

The Ghost of Windy Hill. New York: T. Y. Crowell, 1968.

Mika's Apple Tree. New York: T. Y. Crowell, 1968.

Stories of Gilbert and Sullivan Operas. New York: T. Y. Crowell, 1968.

The Moon Singer. New York: T. Y. Crowell, 1969.

New Boy in Dublin. New York: T. Y. Crowell, 1969.

Jonah and the Great Fish. New York: T. Y. Crowell, 1970.

Joseph the Dreamer. New York: T. Y. Crowell, 1971.

Pocahontas and the Strangers. New York: T. Y. Crowell, 1971.

BURTON, VIRGINIA LEE

AUTHORED & ILLUSTRATED WORKS

Choo Choo. Boston: Houghton Mifflin, 1937.

Mike Mulligan and His Steam Shovel. Boston: Houghton Mifflin, 1939.

Calico, the Wonder Horse. Boston: Houghton Mifflin, 1941.

Choo Choo. new ed. Boston: Houghton Mifflin, 1941.

Little House. Boston: Houghton Mifflin, 1942.

Katy and the Big Snow. Boston: Houghton Mifflin, 1943.

Calico, the Wonder Horse. new ed. Boston: Houghton Mifflin, 1950.

Maybelle, the Cable Car. Boston: Houghton Mifflin, 1952.

Life Story. Boston: Houghton Mifflin, 1962.

ILLUSTRATED WORKS

Fast Sooner Hound. [Arna Bontemps and Jack Conroy]. Boston: Houghton Mifflin, 1942.

Song of Robin Hood. [Anne Malcolmson, ed.]. Boston: Houghton Mifflin, 1947.

The Emperor's New Clothes. [Hans Christian Andersen]. Boston: Houghton Mifflin, 1949.

CARLSON, NATALIE SAVAGE

Talking Cat, and Other Stories of French Canada. New York: Harper & Row, 1952.

Alphonse, That Bearded One. New York: Harcourt Brace, 1954.

Wings Against the Wind. New York: Harper & Row, 1955.

Sashes Red and Blue. New York: Harper & Row, 1956.

Happy Orpheline. New York: Harper & Row, 1957.

Hortense, the Cow for a Queen. New York: Harcourt Brace, 1957.

Family Under the Bridge. New York: Harper & Row, 1958.

A Brother for the Orphelines. New York: Harper & Row, 1959.

Evangeline, Pigeon of Paris. New York: Harcourt Brace, 1960.

Tomahawk Family. New York: Harper & Row, 1960.

The Song of the Lop-Eared Mule. New York: Harper & Row, 1961.

Carnival in Paris. New York: Harper & Row, 1962.

A Pet for the Orphelines. New York: Harper & Row, 1962.

Jean-Claude's Island. New York: Harper & Row, 1963.

School Bell in the Valley. New York: Harcourt Brace, 1963.

The Letter on the Tree. New York: Harper & Row, 1964.

The Orphelines in the Enchanted Castle. New York: Harper & Row, 1964.

The Empty Schoolhouse. New York: Harper & Row, 1965.

Sailor's Choice. New York: Harper & Row, 1966.

Chalou. New York: Harper & Row, 1967.

Luigi of the Streets. New York: Harper & Row, 1967.

Ann Aurelia and Dorothy. New York: Harper & Row, 1968.

Befana's Gift. New York: Harper & Row, 1969.

The Family on the Waterfront. Glasgow: Blackie & Son, 1969.

Marchers for the Dream. New York: Harper & Row, 1969.

Under the Bridge. Glasgow: Blackie & Son, 1969.

A Grandson for the Asking. Glasgow: Blackie & Son, 1970.

The Half Sisters. New York: Harper & Row, 1970.

Luvvy and the Girls. New York: Harper & Row, 1971.

CLARK, ANN NOLAN

Child's Story of New Mexico. [with Frances Carey]. Lincoln, Neb.: University Publishing, 1941.

In My Mother's House. New York: Viking Press, 1941.

Buffalo Caller. Evanston, Ill.: Row, Peterson, 1942.

Little Navajo Bluebird. New York: Viking Press, 1943.

Magic Money. New York: Viking Press, 1950.

Child's Story of New Mexico. 2nd ed. [with Frances Carey]. Lincoln, Neb.: University Publishing, 1952.

Looking-for-Something. New York: Viking Press, 1952.

Secret of the Andes. New York: Viking Press, 1952.

Blue Canyon Horse. New York: Viking Press, 1954.

Little Indian Pottery Maker. Chicago: Melmont, 1955.

Santiago. New York: Viking Press, 1955.

Third Monkey. New York: Viking Press, 1956.

Little Indian Basket Maker. Chicago: Melmont, 1957.

Santo for Pasqualita. New York: Viking Press, 1959.

World Song. New York: Viking Press, 1960.

The Desert People. New York: Viking Press, 1962.

Paco's Miracle. New York: Farrar, Straus & Giroux, 1962.

Father Kino. New York: Farrar, Straus & Giroux, 1963.

Medicine Man's Daughter. New York: Farrar, Straus & Giroux, 1963.

Tia Maria's Garden. New York: Viking Press, 1963.

Bear Cub. New York: Viking Press, 1965.

This for That. San Carlos, Calif.: Golden Gate, 1965.

Brother Andre of Montreal. New York: Farrar, Straus & Giroux, 1967.

Summer is for Growing. New York: Farrar, Straus & Giroux, 1968.

Along Sandy Trails. New York: Viking Press, 1969.

Journey to the People. New York: Viking Press, 1969.

Circle of the Seasons. New York: Farrar, Straus & Giroux, 1970.

CLEARY, BEVERLY

Henry Huggins. New York: Morrow, 1950.

Ellen Tebbits. New York: Morrow, 1951.

Henry and Beezus. New York: Morrow, 1952.

Otis Spofford. New York: Morrow, 1953.

Henry and Ribsy. New York: Morrow, 1954.

Beezus and Ramona. New York: Morrow, 1955.

Fifteen. New York: Morrow, 1956.

Henry and the Paper Route. New York: Morrow, 1957.

Luckiest Girl. New York: Morrow, 1958.

Jean and Johnny. New York: Morrow, 1959.

Hullabaloo ABC. Berkeley, Calif.: Parnassus Press, 1960.

Real Hole. New York: Morrow, 1960.

Emily's Runaway Imagination. New York: Morrow, 1961.

Two Dog Biscuits. New York: Morrow, 1961.

Henry and the Clubhouse. New York: Morrow, 1962.

Sister of the Bride. New York: Morrow, 1963.

Ribsy. New York: Morrow, 1964.

The Mouse and the Motorcycle. New York: Morrow, 1965.

Mitch and Amy. New York: Morrow, 1967.

Ramona and the Pest. New York: Morrow, 1968.

Runaway Ralph. New York: Morrow, 1970.

Here's Beaver. New York: Berkley Publishing, 1971.

COATSWORTH, ELIZABETH

Fox Footprints. New York: Alfred A. Knopf, 1923.

Atlas and Beyond. New York: Harper & Row, 1924.

Cat and the Captain. New York: Macmillan, 1927.

Compass Rose. New York: Coward-McCann, 1929.

Sun's Diary. New York: Macmillan, 1929.

Toutou in Bondage. New York: Macmillan, 1929.

Boy, with a Parrot. New York: Macmillan, 1930.

Cat Who Went to Heaven. New York: Macmillan, 1930.

Knock at the Door. New York: Macmillan, 1931.

The Cricket and the Emperor's Son. New York: Macmillan, 1932.

Away Goes Sally. New York: Macmillan, 1934.

Golden Horseshoe. New York: Macmillan, 1935.

Sword of the Wilderness. New York: Macmillan, 1936.

Alice-All-By-Herself. New York: Macmillan, 1937.

Dancing Tom. New York: Macmillan, 1938.

Here I Stay. New York: Coward-McCann, 1938.

Five Bushel Farm. New York: Macmillan, 1939.

Fair American. New York: Macmillan, 1940.

Littlest House. New York: Macmillan, 1940.

Toast to the King. New York: Coward-McCann, 1940.

Tonio and the Stranger. New York: Grosset, 1941.

Trunk. New York: Macmillan, 1941.

You Shall Have a Carriage. New York: Macmillan, 1941.

Alice and Jerry Books, 6th Reader. [with Mabel O'Donnell]. Evanston, Ill.: Row, Peterson, 1940–42.

Country Poems. New York: Macmillan, 1942.

Forgotten Island. New York: Grosset, 1942.

Houseboat Summer. New York: Macmillan, 1942.

White Horse. New York: Macmillan, 1942.

Thief Island. New York: Macmillan, 1943.

Twelve Months Make a Year. New York: Macmillan, 1943.

Big Green Umbrella. New York: Grosset, 1944.

Country Neighborhood. New York: Macmillan, 1944.

Dancing Tom. reissue. New York: Macmillan, 1944.

Trudy and the Tree House. New York: Macmillan, 1944.

Kitten Stand. New York: Grosset, 1945.

Tales of the Gauchos. New York: Alfred A. Knopf, 1946.

Wonderful Day. New York: Macmillan, 1946.

Maine Ways. New York: Macmillan, 1947.

Plum Daffy Adventure. New York: Macmillan, 1947.

Up Hill and Down. New York: Alfred A. Knopf, 1947.

Cat Who Went to Heaven. reissue. New York: Macmillan, 1948.

House of the Swan. New York: Macmillan, 1948.

South Shore Town. New York: Macmillan, 1948.

Summer Green. New York: Macmillan, 1948.

Creaking Stair. New York: Coward-McCann, 1949.

Little Haymakers. New York: Macmillan, 1949.

Captain's Daughter. New York: Macmillan, 1950.

Door to the North. New York: Holt, Rinehart & Winston, 1950.

First Adventure. New York: Macmillan, 1950.

Night and the Cat. New York: Macmillan, 1950.

Away Goes Sally. reissue. New York: Macmillan, 1951.

Dollar for Luck. New York: Macmillan, 1951.

Enchanted. New York: Pantheon, 1951.

Maine Ways. reissue. New York: Macmillan, 1951.

Wishing Pear. New York: Macmillan, 1951.

Wonderful Day. reissue. New York: Macmillan, 1951.

Boston Bells. New York: Macmillan, 1952.

Last Fort. New York: Holt, Rinehart & Winston, 1952.

Aunt Flora. New York: Macmillan, 1953.

Giant Golden Book of Cat Stories. New York: Simon & Schuster, 1953.

Giant Golden Book of Dog Stories. New York: Simon & Schuster, 1953.

Old Whirlwind. New York: Macmillan, 1953.

Silky. New York: Pantheon, 1953.

Horse Stories. [with Kate Barnes]. New York: Simon & Schuster, 1954.

Mountain Bride. New York: Pantheon, 1954.

Sod House. New York: Macmillan, 1954.

Cherry Ann and the Dragon Horse. New York: Macmillan, 1955.

Mouse Chorus. New York: Pantheon, 1955.

Hide and Seek. New York: Pantheon, 1956.

Peddler's Cart. New York: Macmillan, 1956.

Giant Golden Book of Dogs, Cats and Horses. [with Kate Barnes]. New York: Simon & Schuster, 1957.

Poems. New York: Macmillan, 1957.

Cat Who Went to Heaven. new ed. New York: Macmillan, 1958.

Cave. New York: Viking Press, 1958.

Dog from Nowhere. New York: Harper & Row, 1958.

Down Tumbledown Mountain. Evanston, Ill.: Row, Peterson, 1958.

Peaceable Kingdom and Other Poems. New York: Pantheon, 1958.

White Room. New York: Pantheon, 1958.

You Say You Saw a Camel. Evanston, Ill.: Row, Peterson, 1958.

Pika and the Roses. New York: Pantheon, 1959.

Children Come Running. New York: Golden Press, 1960.

Desert Dan. New York: Viking Press, 1960.

Indian Encounters. New York: Macmillan, 1960.

Lonely Maria. New York: Pantheon, 1960.

The Noble Doll. New York: Viking Press, 1961.

Ronnie and the Chief's Son. New York: Macmillan, 1962.

Jock's Island. New York: Viking Press, 1963.

The Princess and the Lion. New York: Pantheon, 1963.

Jon the Unlucky. New York: Holt, Rinehart & Winston, 1964.

The Hand of Apollo. New York: Viking Press, 1965.

Reading Round Table: Blue Book. New York: American Book, 1965.

Reading Round Table: Green Book. New York: American Book, 1965.

The Secret. New York: Macmillan, 1965.

The Fox Friend. New York: Macmillan, 1966.

The Place. New York: Holt, Rinehart & Winston, 1966.

The Sparrow Bush. New York: W. W. Norton, 1966.

Bess and the Sphinx. New York: Macmillan, 1967.

Chimney Farm Bedtime Stories. New York: Holt, Rinehart & Winston, 1967.

The Ox-Team. London: Hamish Hamilton, 1967.

Troll Weather. New York: Macmillan, 1967.

American Adventures. New York: Macmillan, 1968.

Bob Bodden and the Good Ship Rover. Scarsdale, N.Y.: Garrard, 1968.

Down Half the World. New York: Macmillan, 1968.

Golden Horseshoe. rev. ed. New York: Macmillan, 1968.

Lighthouse Island. New York: W. W. Norton, 1968.

The Lucky Ones. New York: Macmillan, 1968.

Maine Memories. Brattleboro, Vt.: Stephen Greene, 1968.

George and Red. New York: Macmillan, 1969.

Indian Mound Farm. New York: Macmillan, 1969.

Jock's Island. reissue. New York: Viking Press, 1969.

They Walk in the Night. New York: W. W. Norton, 1969.

Bob Bodden and the Seagoing Farm. Scarsdale, N.Y.: Garrard, 1970.

Especially Maine. Brattleboro, Vt.: Stephen Greene, 1970.

Grandmother Cat and the Hermit. New York: Macmillan, 1970.
Daniel Webster's Horses. Scarsdale, N.Y.: Garrard, 1971.
The Snow Parlor and Other Bedtime Stories. New York: Grosset & Dunlap, 1971.
Under the Green Willow. New York: Macmillan, 1971.

DE ANGELI, MARGUERITE L.

AUTHORED & ILLUSTRATED WORKS

Ted and Nina Go to the Grocery Store. New York: Doubleday, 1935.
Henner's Lydia. New York: Doubleday, 1936.
Ted and Nina Have a Happy Rainy Day. New York: Doubleday, 1936.
Petite Suzanne. New York: Doubleday, 1937.
Copper-Toed Boots. New York: Doubleday, 1938.
Skippack School. New York: Doubleday, 1939.
Summer Day with Ted and Nina. New York: Doubleday, 1940.
Thee, Hannah. New York: Doubleday, 1940.
Elin's Amerika. New York: Doubleday, 1941.
Up the Hill. New York: Doubleday, 1942.
Turkey for Christmas. Philadelphia: Westminster, 1944.
Yonie Wondernose. New York: Doubleday, 1944.
Bright April. New York: Doubleday, 1946.
Jared's Island. New York: Doubleday, 1947.
Door in the Wall. New York: Doubleday, 1949.
Just Like David. New York: Doubleday, 1951.
Black Fox of Lorne. New York: Doubleday, 1956.
The Empty Barn. [with Arthur De Angeli]. Philadelphia: Westminster, 1961.
A Pocket Full of Poesies. New York: Doubleday, 1961.
Skippack School. reissue. New York: Doubleday, 1961.
The Door in the Wall. reissue. New York: Doubleday, 1964.
The Ted and Nina Storybook. New York: Doubleday, 1965.
Just Like David. reissue. New York: Doubleday, 1967.
Door in the Wall: A Play. New York: Doubleday, 1969.

ILLUSTRATED WORKS

Covered Bridge. [Cornelia Meigs]. New York: Macmillan, 1936.

Alice-All-By-Herself. [Elizabeth Coatsworth]. New York: Macmillan, 1937.
Red Sky Over Rome. [Anne D. Kyle]. Boston: Houghton Mifflin, 1938.
Princess and the Gypsy. [Jeanne Alcanter de Brahm]. Philadelphia: Lippincott, 1940.
Prayers and Graces for Little Children. [Quail Hawkins, comp.]. New York: Grosset, 1941.
In and Out. [Thomas Robinson]. New York: Viking Press, 1943.
Book of Nursery and Mother Goose Rhymes. New York: Doubleday, 1954.
They Loved to Laugh. [Kathryn Worth]. New York: Doubleday, 1959.
The Old Testament. New York: Doubleday, 1960.
Book of Favorite Hymns. New York: Doubleday, 1963.
The Goose Girl. [J. L. K. and W. K. Grimm]. New York: Doubleday, 1964.
Butter at the Old Price, the Autobiography of Marguerite De Angeli. New York: Doubleday, 1971.

DE JONG, MEINDERT

Big Goose and the Little White Duck. New York: Harper & Row, 1938.
Dirk's Dog, Bello. New York: Harper & Row, 1939.
Bell of the Harbor. New York: Harper & Row, 1941.
Wheels Over the Bridge. New York: Harper & Row, 1941.
Cat That Walked a Week. New York: Harper & Row, 1943.
Little Stray Dog. New York: Harper & Row, 1943.
Billy and the Unhappy Bull. New York: Harper & Row, 1946.
Bible Days. Grand Rapids, Mich.: Fideler, 1948.
Good Luck Duck. New York: Harper & Row, 1950.
Tower By the Sea. New York: Harper & Row, 1950.
Smoke Above the Lane. New York: Harper & Row, 1951.
Hurry Home, Candy. New York: Harper & Row, 1953.
Shadrach. New York: Harper & Row, 1953.
Wheel on the School. New York: Harper & Row, 1954.
Little Cow and the Turtle. New York: Harper & Row, 1955.
House of Sixty Fathers. New York: Harper & Row, 1956.
Along Came a Dog. New York: Harper & Row, 1958.

Mighty Ones. New York: Harper & Row, 1959.
The Last Little Cat. New York: Harper & Row, 1961.
Nobody Plays With a Cabbage. New York: Harper & Row, 1962.
The Singing Hill. New York: Harper & Row, 1962.
Far Out the Long Canal. New York: Harper & Row, 1964.
Puppy Summer. New York: Harper & Row, 1966.
Journey from Peppermint Street. New York: Harper & Row, 1968.
A Horse Came Running. New York: Macmillan, 1970.
The Easter Cat. New York: Macmillan, 1971.

DE TREVIÑO, ELIZABETH BORTON

Pollyanna in Hollywood. New York: A. L. Burt, 1933.
Our Little Aztec Cousin. Boston: L. C. Page, 1934.
Pollyanna's Castle in Mexico. Boston: L. C. Page, 1934.
Our Little Ethiopian Cousin. Boston: L. C. Page, 1935.
Pollyanna's Door to Happiness. Boston: L. C. Page, 1936.
Pollyanna's Golden Horseshoe. Boston: L. C. Page, 1939.
About Bellamy. New York: Harper & Row, 1940.
Pollyanna and the Secret Mission. Boston: L. C. Page, 1951.
My Heart Lies South. New York: T. Y. Crowell, 1953.
Carpet of Flowers. New York: T. Y. Crowell, 1955.
Even As You Love. New York: T. Y. Crowell, 1957.
Greek of Toledo. New York: T. Y. Crowell, 1959.
Where the Heart Is. New York: Doubleday, 1962.
Nacar, the White Deer. New York: Farrar, Straus & Giroux, 1963.
I, Juan de Pareja. New York: Farrar, Straus & Giroux, 1965.
The Fourth Gift. New York: Doubleday, 1966.
Casilda of the Rising Moon. New York: Farrar, Straus & Giroux, 1967.
Turi's Poppa. New York: Farrar, Straus & Giroux, 1968.
Here is Mexico. New York: Farrar, Straus & Giroux, 1970.
The House on Bitterness Street. New York: Doubleday, 1970.

Beyond the Gates of Hercules. New York: Farrar, Straus & Giroux, 1971.

DUVOISIN, ROGER
AUTHORED & ILLUSTRATED WORKS
Little Boy Was Drawing. New York: Scribner, 1932.
Donkey-Donkey. Racine, Wis.: Whitman, 1933.
All Aboard! New York: Grosset, 1935.
And There Was America. New York: Alfred A. Knopf, 1938.
Donkey-Donkey. New York: Grosset, 1940.
Christmas Cake in Search of its Owner. New York: American Artists Group, 1941.
Three Sneezes and Other Swiss Tales. New York: Alfred A. Knopf, 1941.
They Put Out to Sea. New York: Alfred A. Knopf, 1943.
Christmas Whale. New York: Alfred A. Knopf, 1945.
Chanticleer. New York: Grosset, 1947.
Four Corners of the World. New York: Alfred A. Knopf, 1948.
Petunia. New York: Alfred A. Knopf, 1950.
Petunia and the Song. New York: Alfred A. Knopf, 1951.
A for the Ark. New York: Lothrop, Lee & Shephard, 1952.
Petunia's Christmas. New York: Alfred A. Knopf, 1952.
Petunia Takes a Trip. New York: Alfred A. Knopf, 1953.
Easter Treat. New York: Alfred A. Knopf, 1954.
One Thousand Christmas Beards. New York: Alfred A. Knopf, 1955.
Two Lonely Ducks. New York: Alfred A. Knopf, 1955.
House of Four Seasons. New York: Lothrop, Lee & Shephard, 1956.
Petunia Beware. New York: Alfred A. Knopf, 1958.
Day and Night. New York: Alfred A. Knopf, 1960.
The Happy Hunter. Eau Claire, Wis.: Hale, 1961.
Veronica. New York: Alfred A. Knopf, 1961.
Our Veronica Goes to Petunia's Farm. New York: Alfred A. Knopf, 1962.
Lonely Veronica. New York: Alfred A. Knopf, 1963.
Spring Snow. New York: Alfred A. Knopf, 1963.
Veronica's Smile. New York: Alfred A. Knopf, 1964.
Petunia, I Love You. New York: Alfred A. Knopf, 1965.

The Missing Milkman. New York: Alfred A. Knopf, 1967.
Donkey-Donkey. New York: Parents Magazine, 1968.
What is Right for Tulip ... New York: Alfred A. Knopf, 1969.
Veronica and the Birthday Present. New York: Alfred A. Knopf, 1971.

ILLUSTRATED WORKS

Mother Goose. New York: Heritage Press, 1936.
Pied Piper of Hamelin. [Robert Browning]. New York: Grosset, 1936.
Feast of Lamps. [Charlet Root]. Chicago: Albert Whitman, 1938.
Soomoon, Boy of Bali. [Kathleen Elliot]. New York: Alfred A. Knopf, 1938.
Jo-Yo's Idea. [Kathleen Elliot]. New York: Alfred A. Knopf, 1939.
Rhamon, a Boy of Kashmir. [Heluiz Washburne]. Chicago: Albert Whitman, 1939.
Tales of the Pampas. [William Hudson]. New York: Alfred A. Knopf, 1939.
Dog Cantbark. [Marjorie Fischer]. New York: Random House, 1940.
At Our House. [John McCullough]. Reading, Mass.: W. R. Scott, 1943.
Mother Goose. new ed. New York: Heritage Press, 1943.
Child's Garden of Verses. [Robert L. Stevenson]. New York: Limited Editions Club, 1944.
Jumpy, the Kangaroo. [Janet Howard]. New York: Lothrop, Lee & Shephard, 1944.
Happy Time. [Robert Louis Fontaine]. New York: Simon & Schuster, 1945.
I Won't, Said the King. [Mildred Jordan]. New York: Alfred A. Knopf, 1945.
At Daddy's Office. [Robert Misch]. New York: Alfred A. Knopf, 1946.
Daddies, What They Do All Day. [Helen Puner]. New York: Lothrop, Lee & Shephard, 1946.
Robinson Crusoe. [Daniel Defoe]. Cleveland: World, 1946.
Successful Secretary. [Margaret Pratt]. New York: Lothrop, Lee & Shephard, 1946.
Moustachio. [Douglas Rigby]. New York: Harper, 1947.
White Snow, Bright Snow. [Alvin Tresselt]. New York: Lothrop, Lee & Shephard, 1947.
Christmas Pony. [William Hall]. New York: Alfred A. Knopf, 1948.
Johnny Maple Leaf. [Alvin Tresselt]. New York: Lothrop, Lee & Shephard, 1948.
Steam Shovel That Wouldn't Eat Dirt. [Walter Retan]. New York: Aladdin Books, 1948.

Little Whistler. [Frances Frost]. New York: McGraw-Hill, 1949.
Man Who Could Grow Hair. [William Attwood]. New York: Alfred A. Knopf, 1949.
Sitter Who Didn't Sit. [Helen Puner]. New York: Lothrop, Lee & Shephard, 1949.
Sun Up. [Alvin Tresselt]. New York: Lothrop, Lee & Shephard, 1949.
Christmas Forest. [Louise Fatio]. New York: Aladdin Books, 1950.
Dozens of Cousins. [Mabel Watts]. New York: McGraw-Hill, 1950.
Follow the Wind. [Alvin Tresselt]. New York: Lothrop, Lee & Shephard, 1950.
Hi, Mister Robin. New York: Lothrop, Lee & Shephard, 1950.
Love and Dishes. [Niccolo De Quattrociocchi]. Indianapolis, Ind.: Bobbs Merrill, 1950.
Vavache, the Cow Who Painted Pictures. [Frederic Attwood]. New York: Aladdin Books, 1950.
Anna the Horse. [Louise Fatio]. New York: Aladdin Books, 1951.
Autumn Harvest. [Alvin Tresselt]. New York: Lothrop, Lee & Shephard, 1951.
Camel Who Took a Walk. [Jack Tworkov]. New York: Aladdin Books, 1951.
Amahl and the Night Visitors. [Frances Frost]. New York: McGraw-Hill, 1952.
Busby and Co. [Herbert Coggins]. New York: McGraw-Hill, 1952.
Chef's Holiday. [Idwal Jones]. New York: Longmans Green, 1952.
Talking Cat, and Other Stories of French Canada. [Natalie Carlson]. New York: Harper & Row, 1952.
Follow the Road. [Alvin Tresselt]. New York: Lothrop, Lee & Shephard, 1953.
Tell Me Little Boy. [Doris Van Liew Foster]. New York: Lothrop, Lee & Shephard, 1953.
Flash of Washington Square [Margaret Pratt]. New York: Lothrop, Lee & Shephard. 1954.
I Saw the Sea Come In. [Alvin Tresselt]. New York: Lothrop, Lee & Shephard, 1954.
Night Before Christmas. [Clement Moore]. New York: Garden City Books, 1954.
Sophocles, the Hyena. [James Moran]. New York: McGraw-Hill, 1954.
Happy Lion. [Louise Fatio]. New York: McGraw-Hill, 1954.
Happy Lion in Africa. [Louise Fatio]. New York: McGraw-Hill, 1955.
Little Red Nose. [Miriam Schlein]. New York: Abelard Schuman, 1955.
One Step, Two. [Charlotte Zolotow]. New York: Lothrop, Lee & Shephard, 1955.

Ride With the Sun. [Harold Courlander]. New York: McGraw-Hill, 1955.

Wake Up, Farm. [Alvin Tresselt]. New York: Lothrop, Lee & Shephard, 1955.

Bennie the Bear Who Grew Too Fast. [Beatrice and F. L. Fraser]. New York: Lothrop, Lee & Shephard, 1956.

Christmas on the Mayflower. [Wilma Hays]. New York: Coward-McCann, 1956.

Tigers Don't Bite. [Jack Tworkov]. New York: Dutton, 1956.

Does Poppy Live Here? [Arthur Gregor]. New York: Lothrop, Lee & Shephard, 1957.

Doll for Marie. [Louise Fatio]. New York: McGraw-Hill, 1957.

Happy Lion Roars. [Louise Fatio]. New York: McGraw-Hill, 1957.

Not a Little Monkey. [Charlotte Zolotow]. New York; Lothrop, Lee & Shephard, 1957.

Sweet Patootie Doll. [Mary Calhoun]. New York: Morrow, 1957.

Wake Up, City. [Alvin Tresselt]. New York: Lothrop, Lee & Shephard, 1957.

Frog in the Well. [Alvin Tresselt]. New York: Lothrop, Lee & Shephard, 1958.

Little Church on the Big Rock. [Hazel Hershberger]. New York: Scribner, 1958.

Wait Till Sunday. [Susan Dorritt]. New York: Abelard Schuman, 1958.

Winkie's World. [William Hall]. New York: Doubleday, 1958.

Wobble the Witch Cat. [Mary Calhoun]. New York: Morrow, 1958.

Favorite Fairy Tales Told in France. [Virginia Haviland, ed.]. Boston: Little, Brown, 1959.

Fish is not a Pet. [May Tabak]. New York: McGraw-Hill, 1959.

Houn' Dog. [Mary Calhoun]. New York: Morrow, 1959.

Pointed Brush. [Patricia Martin]. New York: Lothrop, Lee & Shephard, 1959.

Three Happy Lions. [Louise Fatio]. New York: McGraw-Hill, 1959.

Angelique. [Janice Brustlein]. New York: McGraw-Hill, 1960.

In My Garden. [Charlotte Zolotow]. New York: Lothrop, Lee & Shephard, 1960.

Please Pass the Grass. [Leone Adelson]. New York: McKay, 1960.

Timothy Robins Climbs the Mountain. [Alvin Tresselt]. New York: Lothrop, Lee & Shephard, 1960.

The Happy Lion's Quest. [Louise Fatio]. New York: McGraw-Hill, 1961.

The Nine Lives of Homer C. Cat. [Mary Calhoun]. New York: Morrow, 1961.

The Wishing Well in the Woods. [Priscilla and Otto Friedrich]. New York: Lothrop, Lee & Shephard, 1961.

The Hungry Leprechaun. [Mary Calhoun]. New York: Morrow, 1962.

Lisette. [Adelaide Holl]. New York: Lothrop, Lee & Shephard, 1962.

The Miller, His Son, and the Donkey. [Aesop]. New York: McGraw-Hill, 1962.

Under the Trees and Through the Grass. [Alvin Tresselt]. New York: Lothrop, Lee & Shephard, 1962.

Red Bantam. [Louise Fatio]. New York: McGraw-Hill, 1963.

Happy Lion and the Bear. [Louise Fatio]. New York: McGraw-Hill, 1964.

Poodle Who Barked at the Wind. [Charlotte Zolotow]. New York: Lothrop, Lee & Shephard, 1964.

Teddy. [Grete Janus]. New York: Lothrop, Lee & Shephard, 1964.

Hide and Seek Fog. [Alvin Tresselt]. New York: Lothrop, Lee & Shephard, 1965.

The Rain Puddle. [Adelaide Holl]. New York: Lothrop, Lee & Shephard, 1965.

Around the Corner. [Jean Showalter]. New York: Doubleday, 1966.

The Life and Adventures of Robinson Crusoe. [Daniel Defoe]. New York: Franklin Watts, 1966.

Mrs. McGarrity's Peppermint Sweater. [A. Holl]. New York: Lothrop, Lee & Shephard, 1966.

Nubber Bear. [William Lipkind]. New York: Harcourt Brace, 1966.

The Happy Lion's Vacation. [Louise Fatio]. New York: McGraw-Hill, 1967.

Poems from France. [William Smith, ed.]. New York: T. Y. Crowell, 1967.

The Old Bullfrog. [Bernice Freschet]. New York: Scribner, 1968.

The Remarkable Egg. [Adelaide Holl]. New York: Lothrop, Lee & Shephard, 1968.

Earth and Sky. [Mona Dayton]. New York: Harper & Row, 1969.

It's Time Now. [Alvin Tresselt]. New York: Lothrop, Lee & Shephard, 1969.

The Beaver Pond. [Alvin Tresselt]. New York: Lothrop, Lee & Shephard, 1970.

The Happy Lion's Treasure. [Louise Fatio]. New York: McGraw-Hill, 1971.

EMBERLEY, ED

AUTHORED & ILLUSTRATED WORKS

The Wing on a Flea. Boston: Little, Brown, 1961.

The Parade Book. Boston: Little, Brown, 1962.

Cock a Doodle Doo. Boston: Little, Brown, 1964.

Punch and Judy. Boston: Little, Brown, 1965.

Rosebud. Boston: Little, Brown, 1966.
London Bridge is Falling Down. Boston: Little, Brown, 1967.
Green Says Go. Boston: Little, Brown, 1968.
Drawing Book of Animals. Boston: Little, Brown, 1970.

ILLUSTRATED WORKS

Big Dipper. [Franklyn Branley]. New York: T. Y. Crowell, 1962.
Colonial Life in America. [Margaret Farquhar]. New York: Holt, Rinehart & Winston, 1962.
White House. [Mary Phelan]. New York: Holt, Rinehart & Winston, 1962.
American Inventions. [Leslie Waller]. New York: Holt, Rinehart & Winston, 1963.
Birds Eat and Eat and Eat. [Roma Gans]. New York: T. Y. Crowell, 1963.
Story of Paul Bunyan. [Barbara Emberley]. Englewood Cliffs. N.J.: Prentice Hall, 1963.
Flash, Crash, Rumble and Roll. [Franklyn Branley]. New York: T. Y. Crowell, 1964.
Columbus Day. [Paul Showers]. New York: T. Y. Crowell, 1965.
Flag Day [Dorothy Les Tina]. New York: T. Y. Crowell, 1965.
Rhinoceros, Preposterous. [Letta Schatz]. Austin, Tex.: Steck-Vaughn, 1965.
Yankee Doodle. [Richard Schackburg]. Englewood Cliffs, N.J.: Prentice Hall, 1965.
American West. [Leslie Waller]. New York: Holt, Rinehart & Winston, 1966.
Bottom of the Sea. [Augusta Goldin]. New York: T. Y. Crowell, 1966.
One Wide River to Cross. [Barbara Emberley]. Englewood Cliffs, N.J.: Prentice-Hall, 1966.
Straight Hair, Curly Hair. [Augusta Goldin]. New York: T. Y. Crowell, 1966.
Drummer Hoff. [Barbara Emberley]. Englewood Cliffs, N.J.: Prentice Hall, 1967.
Ladybug, Ladybug, Fly Away Home. [Judy Hawes]. New York: T. Y. Crowell, 1967.
Fifty First Dragon. [Heywood Broun]. Englewood Cliffs, N.J.: Prentice Hall, 1968.
Pelo Lacio, Pelo Rizo. [Augusta Goldin]. New York: T. Y. Crowell, 1968.
Clothing. [Leslie Waller]. New York: Holt, Rinehart & Winston, 1969.
Simon's Song. [Barbara Emberley]. Englewood Cliffs, N.J.: Prentice Hall, 1969.
What is Symmetry. [Mindel & Harry Sitomer]. New York: T. Y. Crowell, 1970.

ETS, MARIE HALL

AUTHORED & ILLUSTRATED WORKS

Mister Penny. New York: Viking Press, 1935.
Story of a Baby. New York: Viking Press, 1939.
In the Forest. New York: Viking Press, 1944.
My Dog Rinty. [with Ellen Tarry]. New York: Viking Press, 1946.
Oley, the Sea Monster. New York: Viking Press, 1947.
Little Old Automobile. New York: Viking Press, 1948.
Mr. T. W. Anthony Woo. New York: Viking Press, 1951.
Beasts and Nonsense. New York: Viking Press, 1952.
Another Day. New York: Viking Press, 1953.
Play With Me. New York: Viking Press. 1955.
Mister Penny's Race Horse. New York: Viking Press, 1956.
Cow's Party. New York: Viking Press, 1958.
Nine Days to Christmas. [with Aurora Labastida]. New York: Viking Press, 1959.
Mister Penny's Circus. New York: Viking Press, 1961.
Gilberto and the Wind. New York: Viking Press, 1963.
Automobiles for Mice. New York: Viking Press, 1964.
Just Me. New York: Viking Press, 1965.
Bad Boy, Good Boy. New York: T. Y. Crowell, 1967.
Beasts and Nonsense. reissue. New York: Viking Press, 1968.
Talking Without Words. New York: Viking Press, 1968.
Rosa. Minneapolis: University of Minnesota Press, 1970.

FOSTER, GENEVIEVE

AUTHORED & ILLUSTRATED WORKS

George Washington's World. New York: Scribner, 1942.
Abraham Lincoln's World. New York: Scribner, 1944.
Augustus Caesar's World. New York: Scribner, 1947.
George Washington. New York: Scribner, 1949.
Abraham Lincoln. New York: Scribner, 1950.
Andrew Jackson. New York: Scribner, 1951.
Birthdays of Freedom. New York: Scribner, 1952.

Theodore Roosevelt. New York: Scribner, 1954.
When and Where in Italy. Chicago: Rand McNally, 1955.
Birthdays of Freedom. Book 2. New York: Scribner, 1957.
World of Captain John Smith. New York: Scribner, 1959.
The World of Columbus and Sons. New York: Scribner, 1965.
Year of Columbus, Fourteen Ninety-Two. New York: Scribner, 1969.
Year of the Pilgrims, Sixteen Twenty. New York: Scribner, 1969.
Year of Independence, 1776. New York: Scribner, 1970.
Year of Lincoln, 1861. New York: Scribner, 1970.

ILLUSTRATED WORKS

Children of the White House. [Frances Cavanah]. Chicago: Rand McNally, 1936.

GATES, DORIS

Sarah's Idea. New York: Viking Press, 1938.
Blue Willow. New York: Viking Press, 1940.
Sensible Kate. New York: Viking Press, 1943.
Trouble for Jerry. New York: Viking Press, 1944.
North Fork. New York: Viking Press, 1945.
My Brother Mike. New York: Viking Press, 1948.
River Ranch. New York: Viking Press, 1949.
Little Vic. New York: Viking Press, 1951.
Becky and the Bandit. Boston: Ginn, 1955.
The Cat and Mrs. Cary. New York: Viking Press, 1962.
The Elderberry Bush. New York: Viking Press, 1967.
Blue Willow. new ed. New York: Viking Press, 1969.
Sensible Kate. new ed. New York: Viking Press, 1970.

GEISEL, THEODOR SEUSS

AUTHORED & ILLUSTRATED WORKS

And to Think That I Saw It on Mulberry Street. New York: Vanguard Press, 1937.
Five Hundred Hats of Bartholomew Cubbins. New York: Vanguard Press, 1938.
King's Stilts. New York: Random House, 1939.
Seven Lady Godivas. New York: Random House, 1939.
Horton Hatches the Egg. New York: Random House, 1940.

Boners Omnibus. Garden City, N.Y.: Sun Dial Press, 1942.
McElligot's Pool. New York: Random House, 1947.
Thidwick, the Big-Hearted Moose. New York: Random House, 1948.
Bartholomew and the Oobleck. New York: Random House, 1949.
If I Ran the Zoo. New York: Random House, 1950.
Scrambled Eggs Super! New York: Random House, 1953.
Horton Hears a Who! New York: Random House, 1954.
On Beyond Zebra. New York: Random House, 1955.
If I Ran the Circus. New York: Random House, 1956.
Cat in the Hat. New York: Random House, 1957.
How the Grinch Stole Christmas. New York: Random House, 1957.
Cat in the Hat Comes Back! New York: Random House, 1958.
Yertle the Turtle, and Other Stories. New York: Random House, 1958.
Happy Birthday to You. New York: Random House, 1959.
Green Eggs and Ham. New York: Random House, 1960.
One Fish, Two Fish, Red Fish, Blue Fish. New York: Random House, 1960.
The Sneetches, and Other Stories. New York: Random House, 1961.
Ten Apples Up on Top. New York: Random House, 1961.
Sleep Book. New York: Random House, 1962.
Dr. Seuss's ABC. New York: Random House, 1963.
Hop on Pop. New York: Random House, 1963.
The Cat in the Hat Dictionary. [with P. D. Eastman]. New York: Random House, 1964.
The Cat in the Hat Beginner Book Dictionary in French. [with P. D. Eastman]. New York: Random House, 1965.
Fox in Socks. New York: Random House, 1965.
I Had Trouble in Getting to Solla Sollew. New York: Random House, 1965.
I Wish That I Had Duck Feet. New York: Random House, 1965.
The Cat in the Hat Beginner Book Dictionary in Spanish. [with P. D. Eastman]. New York: Random House, 1966.
Come Over to My House. New York: Random House, 1966.
The Cat in the Hat Songbook. New York: Random House, 1967.

The Eye Book. New York: Random House, 1968.
The Foot Book. New York: Random House, 1968.
I Can Lick 30 Tigers Today! and Other Stories. New York: Random House, 1969.
My Book About Me. [with Roy McKie]. New York: Random House, 1969.
I Can Draw It Myself. New York: Random House, 1970.
Mr. Brown Can Moo! Can You? New York: Random House, 1970.
I Can Write. New York: Random House, 1971.
The Lorax. New York: Random House, 1971.

GRAMATKY, HARDIE
AUTHORED & ILLUSTRATED WORKS
Little Toot. New York: Putnam, 1939.
Hercules. New York: Putnam, 1940.
Loopy. New York: Putnam, 1941.
Creeper's Jeep. New York: Putnam, 1948.
Sparky. New York: Putnam, 1952.
Homer and the Circus Train. New York: Putnam, 1957.
Bolivar. New York: Putnam, 1961.
Nikos and the Sea God. New York: Putnam, 1963.
Little Toot on the Thames. New York: Putnam, 1964.
Little Toot on the Grand Canal. New York: Putnam, 1968.
Happy's Christmas. New York: Putnam, 1970.

ILLUSTRATED WORKS
Skwee-Gee. [Darwin L. and Hildegarde T. Teilhet]. New York: Doubleday, 1940.

HADER, BERTA AND ELMER
AUTHORED & ILLUSTRATED WORKS
Picture Book of Travel. New York: Macmillan, 1928.
Coming, Two Funny Clowns. New York: Coward-McCann, 1929.
What'll You Do When You Grow Up? New York: Longmans Green, 1929.
Berta and Elmer Hader's Picture Book of Mother Goose. New York: Coward-McCann, 1930.
Lions and Tigers and Elephants Too. New York: Longmans Green, 1930.
Under the Pig-Nut Tree: Spring. New York: Alfred A. Knopf, 1930.
Farmer in the Dell. New York: Macmillan, 1931.
Tookey. New York: Longmans Green, 1931.

Under the Pig-Nut Tree: Summer. New York: Alfred A. Knopf, 1931.
Picture Book of the States. New York: Harper & Row, 1932.
Chuck-a-Luck and His Reindeer. Boston: Houghton Mifflin, 1933.
Spunky. New York: Macmillan, 1933.
Midget and Bridget. New York: Macmillan, 1934.
Jamaica Johnny. New York: Macmillan, 1935.
Billy Butter. New York: Macmillan, 1936.
Green and Gold. New York: Macmillan, 1936.
Stop, Look, Listen. New York: Longmans Green, 1936.
Tommy Thatcher Goes to Sea. New York: Macmillan, 1937.
Whiffy McMann. New York: Oxford, 1937.
Cricket. New York: Macmillan, 1938.
Cock-a-Doodle-Do. New York: Macmillan, 1939.
Cat and the Kitten. New York: Macmillan, 1940.
Little Town. New York: Macmillan, 1941.
Stop, Look, Listen. new ed. New York: Longmans Green, 1941.
Story of Pancho and the Bull with the Crooked Tail. New York: Macmillan, 1942.
Green and Gold. reissue. New York: Macmillan, 1943.
Mighty Hunter. New York: Macmillan, 1943.
Berta and Elmer Hader's Picture Book of Mother Goose. new ed. New York: Coward-McCann, 1944.
Jamaica Johnny. reissue. New York: Macmillan, 1944.
Little Stone House. New York: Macmillan, 1944.
Cat and the Kitten. reissue. New York: Macmillan, 1945.
Little Town. reissue. New York: Macmillan, 1945.
Rainbow's End. New York: Macmillan, 1945.
Skyrocket. New York: Macmillan, 1946.
Big City. New York: Macmillan, 1947.
Big Snow. New York: Macmillan, 1948.
Little Appaloosa. New York: Macmillan, 1949.
Spunky. reissue. New York: Macmillan, 1950.
Squirrely of Willow Hill. New York: Macmillan, 1950.
Lost in the Zoo. New York: Macmillan, 1951.
Little White Foot. New York: Macmillan, 1952.

Friendly Phoebe. New York: Macmillan, 1953.

Wish on the Moon. New York: Macmillan, 1954.

Home on the Range. New York: Macmillan, 1955.

Runaways. New York: Macmillan, 1956.

Ding Dong Bell, Pussy's in the Well. New York: Macmillan, 1957.

Little Chip of Willow Hill. New York: Macmillan, 1958.

Reindeer Trail. New York: Macmillan, 1959.

Mister Billy's Gun. New York: Macmillan, 1960.

Quack Quack. New York: Macmillan, 1961.

Little Antelope. New York: Macmillan, 1962.

Snow in the City. New York: Macmillan, 1963.

Two is Company, Three's a Crowd. New York: Macmillan, 1965.

ILLUSTRATED WORKS

Monkey Tale. [Hamilton Williamson]. New York: Doubleday, 1929.

Baby Bear. [Hamilton Williamson]. New York: Doubleday, 1930.

Big Fellow at Work. [Dorothy Baruch]. New York: Harper & Row, 1930.

Little Elephant. [Hamilton Williamson]. New York: Doubleday, 1930.

Bingo is My Name. [Anne Stoddard]. New York: Century, 1931.

Good Little Dog. [Anne Stoddard]. New York: Century, 1931.

Lion Cub. [Hamilton Williamson]. New York: Doubleday, 1931.

Here, Bingo! [Anne Stoddard]. New York: Century, 1932.

Play-Book of Words. [Prescott Lecky]. New York: Frederick Stokes, 1933.

Story of Mr. Punch. [Octave Feuillet]. New York: Dutton, 1933.

Jimmy the Groceryman. [Jane Miller]. Boston: Houghton Mifflin, 1934.

Smiths and Rusty. [Alice Dalgliesh]. New York: Scribner, 1936.

Farmer. [Henry Lent]. New York: Macmillan, 1937.

Humpy, Son of the Sands. [Hamilton Williamson]. New York: Doubleday, 1937.

Marcos, a Mountain Boy of Mexico. [Melicent Lee]. Chicago: Albert Whitman, 1937.

Visit from St. Nicholas. [Clement Moore]. New York: Macmillan, 1937.

Who Knows. [Julia Hahn]. Boston: Houghton Mifflin, 1937.

Wings· for the Smiths. [Alice Dalgliesh]. New York: Scribner, 1937.

Banana Tree House. [Phillis Garrard]. New York: Coward-McCann, 1938.

Stripey, a Little Zebra. [Hamilton Williamson]. New York: Doubleday, 1939.

Sonny Elephant. [Madge Bigham]. Boston: Little, Brown, 1940.

Marcos, a Mountain Boy of Mexico. new ed. [Melicent Lee]. Chicago: Albert Whitman, 1942.

Timothy Has Ideas. [Miriam Mason]. New York: Macmillan, 1943.

Mr. Peck's Pets. [Louise Seaman]. New York: Macmillan, 1947.

Sonny Elephant. rev. ed. [Madge Bigham]. Boston: Little, Brown, 1956.

HAMILTON, VIRGINIA

Everybody Duck. New York: McGraw-Hill, 1962.

Zeely. New York: Macmillan, 1967.

The House of Dies Drear. New York: Macmillan, 1968.

The Time-Ago Tales of Jahdu. New York: Macmillan, 1969.

Planet of Junior Brown. New York: Macmillan, 1971.

HAYWOOD, CAROLYN

AUTHORED & ILLUSTRATED WORKS

B is for Betsy. New York: Harcourt Brace, 1939.

Two and Two Are Four. New York: Harcourt Brace, 1940.

Betsy and Billy. New York: Harcourt Brace, 1941.

Primrose Day. New York: Harcourt Brace, 1942.

Back to School with Betsy. New York: Harcourt Brace, 1943.

Here's a Penny. New York: Harcourt Brace, 1944.

Betsy and the Boys. New York: Harcourt Brace, 1945.

Penny and Peter. New York: Harcourt Brace, 1946.

Little Eddie. New York: Morrow, 1947.

Penny Goes to Camp. New York: Morrow, 1948.

Eddie and the Fire Engine. New York: Morrow, 1949.

Betsy's Little Star. New York: Morrow, 1950.

Eddie and Gardenia. New York: Morrow, 1951.

Mixed-Up Twins. New York: Morrow, 1952.

Eddie's Pay Dirt. New York: Morrow, 1953.

Eddie and His Big Deals. New York: Morrow, 1955.

Betsy and the Circus. New York: Morrow, 1956.

Betsy's Busy Summer. New York: Morrow, 1956.

Eddie Makes Music. New York: Morrow, 1957.

Betsy's Winterhouse. New York: Morrow, 1958.

Eddie and Louella. New York: Morrow, 1959.

Annie Pat and Eddie. New York: Morrow, 1960.

Snowbound with Betsy. New York: Morrow, 1962.

Here Comes the Bus. New York: Morrow, 1963.

Eddie's Green Thumb. New York: Morrow, 1964.

Robert Rows the River. New York: Morrow, 1965.

Eddie, the Dog Holder. New York: Morrow, 1966.

Betsy and Mr. Kilpatrick. New York: Morrow, 1967.

Every-Ready Eddie. New York: Morrow, 1968.

Taffy and Melissa Molasses. New York: Morrow, 1969.

Merry Christmas from Betsy. New York: Morrow, 1970.

Eddie's Happenings. New York: Morrow, 1971.

ILLUSTRATED WORKS

Dot for Short. [Frieda Friedman]. New York: Morrow, 1947.

Sundae with Judy. [Frieda Friedman]. New York: Morrow, 1949.

HENRY, MARGUERITE

Auno and Tauno. Chicago: Albert Whitman, 1940.

Dilly Dally Sally. Akron, Ohio: Saalfield, 1940.

Alaska in Story and Pictures. Chicago: Albert Whitman, 1941.

Argentina in Story and Pictures. Chicago: Albert Whitman, 1941.

Brazil in Story and Pictures. Chicago: Albert Whitman, 1941.

Canada in Story and Pictures. Chicago: Albert Whitman, 1941.

Chile in Story and Pictures. Chicago: Albert Whitman, 1941.

Mexico in Story and Pictures. Chicago: Albert Whitman, 1941.

Panama in Story and Pictures. Chicago: Albert Whitman, 1941.

West Indies in Story and Pictures. Chicago: Albert Whitman, 1941.

Alaska in Story and Pictures. 2nd ed. Chicago: Albert Whitman, 1942.

Argentina in Story and Pictures. 2nd ed. Chicago: Albert Whitman, 1942.

Birds at Home. Northbrook, Ill.: M. A. Donohue, 1942.

Brazil in Story and Pictures. 2nd ed. Chicago: Albert Whitman, 1942.

Canada in Story and Pictures. 2nd ed. Chicago: Albert Whitman, 1942.

Chile in Story and Pictures. 2nd ed. Chicago: Albert Whitman, 1942.

Geraldine Belinda. New York: Platt & Munk, 1942.

Mexico in Story and Pictures. 2nd ed. Chicago: Albert Whitman, 1942.

Panama in Story and Pictures. 2nd ed. Chicago: Albert Whitman, 1942.

West Indies in Story and Pictures. 2nd ed. Chicago: Albert Whitman, 1942.

Their First Igloo on Baffin Island. [with Barbara True]. Chicago: Albert Whitman, 1943.

A Boy and a Dog. Chicago: Follett, 1944.

Justin Morgan Had a Horse. Chicago: Follett, 1945.

Little Fellow. New York: Holt, Rinehart & Winston, 1945.

Robert Fulton, Boy Craftsman. Indianapolis, Ind.: Bobbs Merrill, 1945.

Australia in Story and Pictures. Chicago: Albert Whitman, 1946.

Bahamas in Story and Pictures. Chicago: Albert Whitman, 1946.

Bermuda in Story and Pictures. Chicago: Albert Whitman, 1946.

British Honduras in Story and Pictures. Chicago: Albert Whitman, 1946.

Dominican Republic in Story and Pictures. Chicago: Albert Whitman, 1946.

Hawaii in Story and Pictures. Chicago: Albert Whitman, 1946.

New Zealand in Story and Pictures. Chicago: Albert Whitman, 1946.

Virgin Islands in Story and Pictures. Chicago: Albert Whitman, 1946.

Always Reddy. New York: McGraw-Hill, 1947.

Benjamin West and His Cat, Grimalkin. Indianapolis, Ind.: Bobbs Merrill, 1947.

Misty of Chincoteague. Chicago: Rand McNally, 1947.

King of the Wind. Chicago: Rand McNally, 1948.

Little-or-Nothing from Nottingham. New York: McGraw-Hill, 1949.

Sea Star, Orphan of Chincoteague. Chicago: Rand McNally, 1949.

Born to Trot. Chicago: Rand McNally, 1950.

Album of Horses. Chicago: Rand McNally, 1951.
Portfolio of Horses. Chicago: Rand McNally, 1952.
Brighty of the Grand Canyon. Chicago: Rand McNally, 1953.
Justin Morgan Had a Horse. reissue. Chicago: Rand McNally, 1954.
Wagging Tails. Chicago: Rand McNally, 1955.
Cinnabar. Chicago: Rand McNally, 1956.
Black Gold. Chicago: Rand McNally, 1957.
Muley-Ears, Nobody's Dog. Chicago: Rand McNally, 1959.
Gaudenzia. Chicago: Rand McNally, 1960.
Misty, the Wonder Pony. Chicago: Rand McNally, 1961.
All About Horses. New York: Random House, 1962.
Five O'Clock Charlie. Chicago: Rand McNally, 1962.
Stormy, Misty's Foal. Chicago: Rand McNally, 1963.
White Stallion of Lipizza. Chicago: Rand McNally, 1964.
Mustang. Chicago: Rand McNally, 1966.
Dear Marguerite Henry. New York: Random House, 1969.
Dear Readers and Riders. Chicago: Rand McNally, 1969.
Album of Dogs. Chicago: Rand McNally, 1970.
Shamrock Queen. New York: Scholastic Book Service, 1970.

HOLLING, HOLLING C.
AUTHORED & ILLUSTRATED WORKS
Little Big-Bye-and-Bye. Chicago: P. F. Volland, 1926.
Claws of the Thunderbird. Chicago: P. F. Volland, 1928.
Rocky Billy. New York: Macmillan, 1928.
Rum Tum Tummy, the Elephant Who Ate. Akron, Ohio: Saalfield, 1928.
Twins Who Flew Around the World. New York: Platt & Munk, 1930.
Book of Indians. New York: Platt & Munk, 1935.
Book of Cowboys. New York: Platt & Munk, 1936.
Little Buffalo Boy. Garden City, N.J.: Garden City Pub., 1939.
Paddle-to-the-Sea. Boston: Houghton Mifflin, 1941.
Tree in the Trail. Boston: Houghton Mifflin, 1942.
Seabird. Boston: Houghton Mifflin, 1948.
Minn of the Mississippi. Boston: Houghton Mifflin, 1951.

Pagoo. Boston: Houghton Mifflin, 1957.
Book of Cowboys. rev. ed. New York: Platt & Munk, 1968.
ILLUSTRATED WORKS
Little Folks of Other Lands. [Watty Piper, ed.]. New York: Platt & Munk, 1929.
Road in Storyland. [Watty Piper]. New York: Platt & Munk, 1932.
Road in Storyland. new rev. ed. [Watty Piper]. New York: Platt & Munk, 1952.

HUNTER, KRISTIN
God Bless the Child. New York: Scribner, 1964.
The Landlord. New York: Scribner, 1966.
The Soul Brothers and Sister Lou. New York: Scribner, 1968.
Boss Cat. New York: Scribner, 1971.

JUDSON, CLARA INGRAM
Flower Fairies. Chicago: Rand McNally, 1915.
Good-Night Stories. Chicago: A. C. McClurg, 1916.
Billy Robin and His Neighbors. Chicago: Rand McNally, 1917.
Junior Cookbook. Newark, N.J.: Barse, 1920.
Camp at Gravel Point. Boston: Houghton Mifflin, 1921.
Foxy Squirrel in the Garden. Chicago: Rand McNally, 1921.
Garden Adventures in Winter. Chicago: Rand McNally, 1921.
Mary Jane Series. 12 vols. Newark, N.J.: Barse, 1921.
Garden Adventures of Tommy Tittlemouse. Chicago: Rand McNally, 1922.
Jerry and Jean, Detectors. Chicago: Rand McNally, 1923.
Child Life Cookbook. Chicago: Rand McNally, 1926.
Virginia Lee. Newark, N.J.: Barse, 1926.
Alice Ann. Newark, N.J.: Barse, 1928.
Mary Jane in England. Newark, N.J.: Barse, 1928.
Billy Robin and His Neighbors. 5th ed. Chicago: Rand McNally, 1929.
Foxy Squirrel in the Garden. 3rd ed. Chicago: Rand McNally, 1929.
Mary Jane in Scotland. Newark, N.J.: Barse, 1929.
Mary Jane in France. Newark, N.J.: Barse, 1930.
Mary Jane in Switzerland. Newark, N.J.: Barse, 1931.
Mary Jane in Italy. New York: Grosset, 1933.
Mary Jane in Spain. New York: Grosset, 1937.

Play Days. New York: Grosset, 1937.
Mary Jane's Friends in Holland. New York: Grosset, 1939.
Pioneer Girl. Chicago: Rand McNally, 1939.
Virginia Lee's Bicycle Club. New York: Grosset, 1939.
Boat Builder: The Story of Robert Fulton. New York: Scribner, 1940.
People Who Came to Our House. Chicago: Rand McNally, 1940.
Railway Engineer: The Story of George Stephenson. New York: Scribner, 1941.
Soldier Doctor: The Story of William Gorgas. New York: Scribner, 1941.
People Who Work Near Our House. Chicago: Rand McNally, 1942.
They Came From Sweden. Boston: Houghton Mifflin, 1942.
Donald McKay, Designer of Clipper Ships. New York: Scribner, 1943.
People Who Work in the Country and in the City. Chicago: Rand McNally, 1943.
They Came From France. Boston: Houghton Mifflin, 1943.
They Came From Scotland. Boston: Houghton Mifflin, 1944.
Petar's Treasure: They Came From Dalmatia. Boston: Houghton Mifflin, 1945.
Michael's Victory: They Came From Ireland. Boston: Houghton Mifflin, 1946.
Lost Violin: They Came From Bohemia. Boston: Houghton Mifflin, 1947.
Reaper Man. Boston: Houghton Mifflin, 1948.
Summer Time. Nashville, Tenn.: Broadman Press, 1948.
Green Ginger Jar: The Story of the Chinese in Chicago. Boston: Houghton Mifflin, 1949.
Abraham Lincoln, Friend of the People. Chicago: Follett, 1950.
City Neighbor. New York: Scribner, 1951.
George Washington, Leader of the People. Chicago: Follett, 1951.
Thomas Jefferson, Champion of the People. Chicago: Follett, 1952.
Theodore Roosevelt, Fighting Patriot. Chicago: Follett, 1953.
Andrew Jackson, Frontier Statesman. Chicago: Follett, 1954.
Mighty Soo. Chicago: Follett, 1955.
Mr. Justice Holmes. Chicago: Follett, 1956.
Benjamin Franklin. Chicago: Follett, 1957.
Bruce Carries the Flag. Chicago: Follett, 1957.
Michael's Victory. Chicago: Follett, 1957.
Pierre's Lucky Pouch: They Came From France. Chicago: Follett, 1957.
Sod House Winter: They Came From Sweden. Chicago: Follett, 1957.

Lost Violin. Chicago: Follett, 1958.
Petar's Treasure: They Came From Dalmatia. reissue. Chicago: Follett, 1958.
St. Lawrence Seaway. Chicago: Follett, 1959.
Abraham Lincoln, Friend of the People. reissue. Chicago: Follett, 1961.
Andrew Carnegie. Chicago: Follett, 1964.
Admiral Christopher Columbus. Chicago: Follett, 1965.
Yankee Clippers: The Story of Donald McKay, reissue. Chicago: Follett, 1965.

KEATS, EZRA JACK

AUTHORED WORKS

My Dog is Lost. [with Pat Cherr]. New York: T. Y. Crowell, 1960.
The Snowy Day. New York: Viking Press, 1962.
Whistle for Willie. New York: Viking Press, 1964.
John Henry. New York: Pantheon, 1965.
God is in the Mountain. [Ezra Jack Keats, comp.]. New York: Holt, Rinehart & Winston, 1966.
Jennie's Hat. New York: Harper & Row, 1966.
Peter's Chair. New York: Harper & Row, 1967.
A Letter to Amy. New York: Harper & Row, 1968.
Goggles. New York: Macmillan, 1969.
Night. New York: Atheneum, 1969.
Hi, Cat! New York: Macmillan, 1970.
Apartment Three. New York: Macmillan, 1971.

ILLUSTRATED WORKS

Jubilant for Sure. [Elisabeth Lansing]. New York: T. Y. Crowell, 1954.
Mystery of the Isle of Skye. [Phyllis Whitney]. Philadelphia: Westminster, 1955.
Wonder Tales of Dogs and Cats. [Frances Carpenter]. New York: Doubleday, 1955.
Danny Dunn and the Anti-Gravity Paint. [Jay Williams and Raymond Abrashkin]. New York: McGraw-Hill, 1956.
Sure Thing for Shep. [Elisabeth Lansing]. New York: T. Y. Crowell, 1956.
Three Young Kings. [George Albee]. New York: Franklin Watts, 1956.
Danny Dunn on a Desert Island. [Jay Williams and Raymond Abrashkin]. New York: McGraw-Hill, 1957.
Indians Knew. [Tillie Pine]. New York: McGraw-Hill, 1957.
Pilgrims Knew. [Tillie Pine and Joseph Levine]. New York: McGraw-Hill, 1957.
Chinese Knew. [Tillie Pine and Joseph Levine]. New York: McGraw-Hill, 1958.

Danny Dunn and the Homework Machine.
[Jay Williams and Raymond Abrashkin].
New York: McGraw-Hill, 1958.
And Long Remember. [Dorothy Fischer].
New York: McGraw-Hill, 1959.
Brave Riders. [Glenn Balch]. New York:
T. Y. Crowell, 1959.
Danny Dunn and the Weather Machine.
[Jay Williams and Raymond Abrashkin].
New York: McGraw-Hill, 1959.
Grasses. [Irmengarde Eberle]. New York:
H. Z. Walck, 1960.
Nihal of Ceylon. [Eleanor Murphy]. New
York: T. Y. Crowell, 1960.
Peg-Legged Pirate of Sulu. [Lucretia Hale].
New York: Alfred A. Knopf, 1960.
Tournament of the Lions. [Jay Williams].
New York: H. Z. Walck, 1960.
Desmond's First Case. [Herbert Best].
New York: Viking Press, 1961.
In the Night. [Paul Showers]. New York:
T. Y. Crowell, 1961.
Apple Orchard. [Irmengarde Eberle]. New
York: H. Z. Walck, 1962.
The Rice Bowl Pet. [Patricia Martin].
New York: T. Y. Crowell, 1962.
Time of the Wolves. [Verne Davis]. New
York: Morrow, 1962.
What Good is a Tail. [Solveig Russell].
Indianapolis, Ind.: Bobbs Merrill, 1962.
Flying Cow. [Ruth Collins]. New York:
H. Z. Walck, 1963.
Gobbler Called. [Verne Davis]. New York:
Morrow, 1963.
Hawaii. [Juliet Swenson]. New York: Holt,
Rinehart & Winston, 1963.
Jim Can Swim. [Helen Olds]. New York:
Alfred A. Knopf, 1963.
Our Rice Village in Cambodia. [Ruth
Tooze]. New York: Viking Press, 1963.
The Peterkin Papers. [Lucretia P. Hale].
New York: Doubleday, 1963.
Tia Maria's Garden. [Ann Nolan Clark].
New York: Viking Press, 1963.
Egyptians Knew. [Tillie Pine and Joseph
Levine]. New York: McGraw-Hill, 1964.
Eskimos Knew. [Tillie Pine and Joseph
Levine]. New York: McGraw-Hill, 1964.
Speedy Digs Downside Up. [Maxine Ku-
min]. New York: Putnam, 1964.
Zoo, Where Are You? [Ann McGovern].
New York: Harper & Row, 1964.
In a Spring Garden. [Richard Lewis, ed.].
New York: Dial Press, 1965.
The Naughty Boy. [John Keats]. New
York: Viking Press, 1965.
In the Park. [Esther Hautzig]. New York:
Macmillan, 1968.
The Little Drummer Boy. [Katherine Davis
et al.]. New York: Macmillan, 1968.
Two Tickets to Freedom. [Florence Freed-
man]. New York: Simon & Schuster,
1971.

KONIGSBURG, ELAINE
AUTHORED & ILLUSTRATED WORKS
*From the Mixed-Up Files of Mrs. Basil
E. Frankweiler.* New York: Atheneum,
1967.
*Jennifer, Hecate, Macbeth, William Mc-
Kinley, and Me, Elizabeth.* New York:
Atheneum, 1967.
About the B'nai Bagels. New York: Athe-
neum, 1969.
George. New York: Atheneum, 1970.
Altogether, One at a Time. New York:
Atheneum, 1971.

KRAUSS, RUTH
Good Man and His Good Wife. New York:
Harper & Row, 1944.
Carrot Seed. New York: Harper & Row,
1945.
Great Duffy. New York: Harper & Row,
1946.
Growing Story. New York: Harper & Row,
1947.
Bears. New York: Harper & Row, 1948.
Big World and Little House. New York:
Henry Schuman, 1949.
Happy Day. New York: Harper & Row,
1949.
Backward Day. New York: Harper & Row,
1950.
Bundle Book. New York: Harper & Row,
1951.
Hole is to Dig. New York: Harper & Row,
1952.
Very Special House. New York: Harper &
Row, 1953.
How to Make an Earthquake. New York:
Harper & Row, 1954.
I'll Be You and You Be Me. New York:
Harper & Row, 1954.
Charlotte and the White Horse. New York:
Harper & Row, 1955.
Is This You? [with Crockett Johnson]. Read-
ing, Mass.: W. R. Scott, 1955.
Big World and Little House. New York:
Harper & Row, 1956.
I Want to Paint my Bathroom Blue. New
York: Harper & Row, 1956.
Birthday Party. New York: Harper & Row,
1957.
Monkey Day. New York: Harper & Row,
1957.
I Can Fly. New York: Simon & Schuster,
1958.
Somebody Else's Nut Tree. New York:
Harper & Row, 1958.

Moon or a Button. New York: Harper & Row, 1959.
Open House for Butterflies. New York: Harper & Row, 1960.
Good Man and His Good Wife. rev. ed. New York: Harper & Row, 1962.
Mama, I Wish I Was Snow. New York: Atheneum, 1962.
A Bouquet of Littles. New York: Harper & Row, 1963.
Eyes, Nose, Fingers, Toes. New York: Harper & Row, 1964.
The Cantilever Rainbow. New York: Pantheon, 1965.
The Little King, The Little Queen, The Littler Monster, and Other Stories You Can Make Up Yourself. Chicago: Albert Whitman, 1966.
This Thumbprint. New York: Harper & Row, 1967.
What a Fine Day For . . . New York: Parents Magazine, 1967.
Is This You? [with Crockett Johnson]. New York: Scholastic Book Service, 1968.
There's a Little Ambiguity Over There Among the Bluebells, and Other Theater Poems. New York: Something Else, 1968.
I Write It. New York: Harper & Row, 1970.

LAWSON, ROBERT

AUTHORED & ILLUSTRATED WORKS

Ben and Me. Boston: Little, Brown, 1939.
They Were Strong and Good. New York: Viking Press, 1940.
I Discover Columbus. Boston: Little, Brown, 1941.
Watchwords of Liberty. Boston: Little, Brown, 1943.
Country Colic. Boston: Little, Brown, 1944.
Rabbit Hill. New York: Viking Press, 1944.
Mr. Wilmer. Boston: Little, Brown, 1945.
At That Time. New York: Viking Press, 1947.
Mr. Twigg's Mistake. Boston: Little, Brown, 1947.
Robbut. New York: Viking Press, 1948.
Fabulous Flight. Boston: Little, Brown, 1949.
Smeller Martin. New York: Viking Press, 1950.
McWhinney's Jaunt. Boston: Little, Brown, 1951.
Edward, Hoppy and Joe. New York: Alfred A. Knopf, 1952.
Mr. Revere and I. Boston: Little, Brown, 1953.
Tough Winter. New York: Viking Press, 1954.
Captain Kidd's Cat. Boston: Little, Brown, 1956.

Great Wheel. New York: Viking Press, 1957.
Watchwords of Liberty. new ed. Boston: Little, Brown, 1957.

ILLUSTRATED WORKS

Wee Men of Ballywooden. [Arthur Mason]. London: Heinemann, 1930.
Treasure of the Isle of Mist. [William Tarn]. New York: Putnam, 1934.
Story of Ferdinand. [Munro Leaf]. New York: Viking Press, 1936.
Unicorn With Silver Shoes. [Ella Young]. New York: Longmans Green, 1936.
Four and Twenty Blackbirds. [Helen Fish, ed.]. Philadelphia: Lippincott, 1937.
From the Horn of the Moon. [Arthur Mason]. New York: Garden City Publishing Co., 1937.
Hurdy-Gurdy Man. [Margery Bianco]. New York: Oxford, 1937.
The Prince and the Pauper. [Samuel Clemens]. Philadelphia: John C. Winston, 1937.
Wee Men of Ballywooden. [Arthur Mason]. New York: Garden City Publishing Co., 1937.
Mr. Popper's Penguin. [Richard and Florence Atwater]. Boston: Little, Brown, 1938.
One Foot in Fairyland. [Eleanor Farjeon]. Philadelphia: Frederick A. Stokes, 1938.
Wee Gillis. [Munro Leaf]. New York: Viking Press, 1938.
Pilgrim's Progress. [John Bunyan]. Philadelphia: Lippincott, 1939.
Gaily We Parade. [John Brewton, comp.] New York: Macmillan, 1940.
Just For Fun. Chicago: Rand McNally, 1940.
Aesop's Fables. [Munro Leaf, ed.]. New York: Heritage Press, 1941.
Story of Simpson and Sampson. [Munro Leaf]. New York: Viking Press, 1941.
Adam of the Road. [Elizabeth Gray]. New York: Viking Press, 1942.
Crock of Gold. [James Stephens]. New York: Limited Editions Club, 1942.
Poo-Poo and the Dragons. [Cecil Forester]. Boston: Little, Brown, 1942.
Prince Prigio. [Andrew Lang]. Boston: Little, Brown, 1942.
Little Woman Wanted Noise. [Valentine Teal]. Chicago: Rand McNally, 1943.
Aesop's Fables. new ed. [Munro Leaf, ed.]. New York: Heritage Press, 1945.
Shoelace Robin. [William Hall]. New York: T. Y. Crowell, 1945.
Greylock and the Robins. [Thomas Robinson]. New York: Viking Press, 1946.

Haven's End. reissue. [John Marquand]. Boston: Little, Brown, 1950.
Wee Men of Ballywooden. [Arthur Mason]. New York: Viking Press, 1952.
Unicorn With Silver Shoes. [Ella Young]. New York: McKay, 1957.
Golden Horseshoe. [Elizabeth Coatsworth]. New York: Macmillan, 1968.

LENSKI, LOIS

AUTHORED & ILLUSTRATED WORKS

Jack Horner's Pie. New York: Harper & Row, 1927.
Skipping Village. New York: Frederick Stokes, 1927.
Alphabet People. New York: Harper & Row, 1928.
Little Girl of Nineteen Hundred. New York: Frederick Stokes, 1928.
Two Brothers and Their Animal Friends. New York: Frederick Stokes, 1929.
Wonder City. New York: Coward-McCann, 1929.
Spinach Boy. New York: Frederick Stokes. 1930.
Washington Picture Book. New York: Coward-McCann, 1930.
Benny and His Penny. New York: Alfred A. Knopf, 1931.
Grandmother Tippytoe. New York: Frederick Stokes, 1931.
Arabella and Her Aunts. New York: Frederick Stokes, 1932.
Johnny Goes to the Fair. New York: Minton, 1932.
Little Family. New York: Doubleday, 1932.
Gooseberry Garden. New York: Harper & Row, 1934.
Little Auto. New York: Oxford, 1934.
Surprise for Mother. Philadelphia: Lippincott, 1934.
Little Baby Ann. New York: Oxford, 1935.
Sugarplum House. New York: Harper & Row, 1935.
Easter Rabbit's Parade. New York: Oxford, 1936.
Phoebe Fairchild, Her Book. Philadelphia: Lippincott, 1936.
A-Going to the Westward. New York: Frederick Stokes, 1937.
Baby Car. New York: Oxford, 1937.
Little Sail Boat. New York: H. Z. Walck, 1937.
Little Airplane. New York: Oxford, 1938.
Ocean-Born Mary. Philadelphia: Lippincott, 1939.
Blueberry Corners. Philadelphia: Lippincott, 1940.
Bound Girl of Cobble Hill. Philadelphia: Lippincott, 1940.

Little Train. New York: H. Z. Walck, 1940.
Animals for Me. New York: H. Z. Walck, 1941.
Indian Captive. Philadelphia: Lippincott, 1941.
Little Farm. New York: Oxford, 1942.
Bayou Suzette. Philadelphia: Lippincott, 1943.
Davy's Day. New York: Oxford, 1943.
Let's Play House. New York: H. Z. Walck, 1944.
Puritan Adventure. Philadelphia: Lippincott, 1944.
Spring is Here. New York: Oxford, 1945.
Strawberry Girl. Philadelphia: Lippincott, 1945.
Blue Ridge Billy. Philadelphia: Lippincott, 1946.
Little Fire Engine. New York: H. Z. Walck, 1946.
Judy's Journey. Philadelphia: Lippincott, 1947.
Surprise for Davy. New York: H. Z. Walck, 1947.
Boom Town Boy. Philadelphia: Lippincott, 1948.
Mr. and Mrs. Noah. New York: T. Y. Crowell, 1948.
Now It's Fall. New York: H. Z. Walck, 1948.
Cotton in My Sack. Philadelphia: Lippincott, 1949.
Cowboy Small. New York: H. Z. Walck, 1949.
I Like Winter. New York: H. Z. Walck, 1950.
Texas Tomboy. Philadelphia: Lippincott, 1950.
Papa Small. New York: H. Z. Walck, 1951.
Prairie School. Philadelphia: Lippincott, 1951.
Peanuts for Billy Ben. Philadelphia: Lippincott, 1952.
We Are Thy Children. New York: T. Y. Crowell, 1952.
We Live in the South. Philadelphia: Lippincott, 1952.
Mama Hattie's Girl. Philadelphia: Lippincott, 1953.
On a Summer Day. New York: H. Z. Walck, 1953.
Corn Farm Boy. Philadelphia: Lippincott, 1954.
Project Boy. Philadelphia: Lippincott, 1954.
Songs of Mr. Small. New York: Oxford, 1954.
We Live in the City. Philadelphia: Lippincott, 1954.
Dog Came to School. New York: H. Z. Walck, 1955.

San Francisco Boy. Philadelphia: Lippincott, 1955.

Berries in the Scoop. Philadelphia: Lippincott, 1956.

Big Little Davy. New York: H. Z. Walck, 1956.

Flood Friday. Philadelphia: Lippincott, 1956.

We Live By the River. Philadelphia: Lippincott, 1956.

Davy and His Dog. New York: H. Z. Walck, 1957.

Houseboat Girl. Philadelphia: Lippincott, 1957.

I Went for a Walk. New York: H. Z. Walck, 1958.

Little Sioux Girl. Philadelphia: Lippincott, 1958.

Songs of the City. New York: E. B. Marks, 1958.

At Our House. New York: H. Z. Walck, 1959.

Coal Camp Girl. Philadelphia: Lippincott, 1959.

Davy's Day. New York: H. Z. Walck, 1959.

The Little Airplane. New York: H. Z. Walck, 1959.

The Little Farm. New York: H. Z. Walck, 1959.

We Live in the Country. Philadelphia: Lippincott, 1960.

When I Grow Up. New York: H. Z. Walck, 1960.

Davy Goes Places. New York: H. Z. Walck, 1961.

Policeman Small. New York: H. Z. Walck, 1962.

We Live in the Southwest. Philadelphia: Lippincott, 1962.

Shoo-Fly Girl. Philadelphia: Lippincott, 1963.

Spring is Here. New York: H. Z. Walck, 1963.

The Life I Live. New York: H. Z. Walck, 1965.

The Little Auto. New York: H. Z. Walck, 1965.

We Live in the North. Philadelphia: Lippincott, 1965.

Adventures in Understanding. Tallahassee, Fla.: Friends of the Florida State University Library, 1966.

High Rise Secret. Philadelphia: Lippincott, 1966.

The Lois Lenski Collection in the Florida State University Library. Tallahassee, Fla.: Friends of the Florida State University Library, 1966.

Debbie and Her Grandma. New York: H. Z. Walck, 1967.

Songs of Mr. Small. New York: H. Z. Walck, 1967.

To Be a Logger. Philadelphia: Lippincott, 1967.

Deer Valley Girl. Philadelphia: Lippincott, 1968.

Lois Lenski's Christmas Stories. Philadelphia: Lippincott, 1968.

Susie Mariar. New York: H. Z. Walck, 1968.

Debbie and Her Family. New York: H. Z. Walck, 1969.

Debbie Herself. New York: H. Z. Walck, 1969.

Debbie and Her Dolls. New York: H. Z. Walck, 1970.

Debbie Goes to Nursery School. New York: H. Z. Walck, 1970.

City Poems. New York: H. Z. Walck, 1971.

Debbie and Her Pets. New York: H. Z. Walck, 1971.

ILLUSTRATED WORKS

Chimney Corner Stories. [Veronica Hutchinson, comp.]. New York: Putnam, 1925.

Chimney Corner Poems. [Veronica Hutchinson, comp.]. New York: Putnam, 1926.

Book of Princess Stories. [Kathleen Adams and Frances Atchinson]. New York: Dodd, Mead, 1927.

Fireside Stories. [Veronica Hutchinson, comp.]. New York: Putnam, 1927.

Candlelight Stories. [Veronica Hutchinson, comp.]. New York: Putnam, 1928.

A Hat Tub Tale. [Caroline Emerson]. New York: Dutton, 1928.

Golden Tales of Our America. [May Becker, ed.]. New York: Dodd, Mead, 1929.

Dream Days. [Kenneth Grahame]. Menlo Park, Calif.: Lane, 1930.

Little Rag Doll. [Ethel Phillips]. Boston: Houghton Mifflin, 1930.

Mr. Nip and Mr. Tuck. [Caroline Emerson]. New York: Dutton, 1930.

Twilight of Magic. [Hugh Lofting]. New York: Frederick Stokes, 1930.

Golden Tales of New England. [May Becker, ed.]. New York: Dodd, Mead, 1931.

Golden Tales of the Prairie States. [May Becker, ed.]. New York: Dodd, Mead, 1931.

Scotch Circus. [Tom Powers]. Boston: Houghton Mifflin, 1934.

Golden Tales of Canada. [May Becker, ed.]. New York: Dodd, Mead, 1937.

Edgar. [Philip Stong]. New York: Farrar, Straus & Giroux, 1938.

Once on Christmas. [Dorothy Thompson]. New York: Oxford, 1938.

Golden Tales of the Southwest. [May

Becker, ed.]. New York: Dodd, Mead, 1939.

Betsy-Tacy. [Maud Lovelace]. New York: T. Y. Crowell, 1940.

Mother Makes Christmas. [Cornelia Meigs]. New York: Grosset & Dunlap, 1940.

Betsy-Tacy and Tib. [Maud Lovelace]. New York: T. Y. Crowell, 1941.

First Thanksgiving. [Lena Barksdale]. New York: Alfred A. Knopf, 1942.

Letter to Popsey. [Mabel La Rue]. New York: Grosset & Dunlap, 1942.

Over the Big Hill. [Maud Lovelace]. New York: T. Y. Crowell, 1942.

Betsy and Tacy Go Downtown. [Maud Lovelace]. New York: T. Y. Crowell, 1943.

Five and Ten. [Roberta Whitehead]. Boston: Houghton Mifflin, 1943.

They Came from France. [Clara Judson]. Boston: Houghton Mifflin, 1943.

Donkey Cart. [Clyde Bulla]. New York: T. Y. Crowell, 1946.

Pinocchio. [Carlo Lorenzini]. New York: Random House, 1946.

Read to Me Storybook. [Child Study Association of America]. New York: T. Y. Crowell, 1947.

Mother Goose Rhymes. [Watty Piper, ed.]. New York: Platt & Munk, 1956.

LESTER, JULIUS

Look Out, Whitey! Black Power's Gon' Get Your Mama! New York: Dial Press, 1968.

To Be a Slave. New York: Dial Press, 1968.

Black Folktales. New York: Richard W. Baron, 1969.

Revolutionary Notes. New York: Richard W. Baron, 1969.

Search for the New Land. New York: Dial Press, 1969.

Folksinger's Guide to the 12-String Guitar as Played by Leadbelly. [with Pete Seeger]. New York: Oak Publications.

LEWIS, CLIVE STAPLES

Dymer. New York: Dutton, 1926.

Pilgrim's Regress. London: Dent, 1933.

Allegory of Love. New York: Oxford, 1936.

Personal Heresy. [with E. M. W. Tillyard]. New York: Oxford, 1939.

Rehabilitations and Other Essays. Folcroft, Pa.: Folcroft, 1939.

Out of the Silent Planet. London: John Lane, 1940.

Problem of Pain. London: Geoffrey Bles, 1940.

Broadcast Talks. London: Geoffrey Bles, 1942.

Hamlet, the Prince or the Poem. New York: Oxford, 1942.

Preface to Paradise Lost. New York: Oxford, 1942.

Screwtape Letters. New York: Macmillan, 1942.

Case for Christianity. New York: Macmillan, 1943.

Christian Behavior. New York: Macmillan, 1943.

Out of the Silent Planet. New York: Macmillan, 1943.

Perelandra. New York: Macmillan, 1944.

Problem of Pain. New York: Macmillan, 1944.

That Hideous Strength. London: John Lane, 1945.

George Macdònald. London: Geoffrey Bles, 1946.

Great Divorce. New York: Macmillan, 1946.

Abolition of Man. New York: Macmillan, 1947.

Beyond Personality. New York: Macmillan, 1947.

Miracles. New York: Macmillan, 1947.

That Hideous Strength. reissue. New York: Macmillan, 1949.

Transposition and Other Essays. London: Geoffrey Bles, 1949.

Weight of Glory, and Other Addresses. New York: Macmillan, 1949.

Dymer. new ed. New York: Macmillan, 1950.

The Lion, the Witch and the Wardrobe. New York: Macmillan, 1950.

Prince Caspian. New York: Macmillan, 1951.

Mere Christianity. rev. ed. New York: Macmillan, 1952.

Voyage of the Dawn Treader. New York: Macmillan, 1952.

Silver Chair. New York: Macmillan, 1953.

English Literature in the Sixteenth Century Excluding Drama. New York: Oxford, 1954.

Horse and His Boy. New York: Macmillan, 1954.

Magician's Nephew. New York: Macmillan, 1955.

Last Battle. New York: Macmillan, 1956.

Surprised by Joy. New York: Harcourt Brace, 1956.

Till We Have Faces. Grand Rapids, Mich.: William B. Eerdmans, 1956.

Pilgrim's Regress. 3rd ed. Grand Rapids, Mich.: William B. Eerdmans, 1958.

Reflections on the Psalms. New York: Harcourt Brace, 1958.

Four Loves. New York: Harcourt Brace, 1960.

Preface to Paradise Lost. rev. ed. New York: Oxford, 1960.

Studies in Words. New York: Cambridge, 1960.

World's Last Night and Other Essays. New York: Harcourt Brace, 1960.

An Experiment in Criticism. New York: Cambridge, 1961.

They Asked for a Paper. London: Geoffrey Bles, 1962.

The Screwtape Letters [and] *Screwtape Proposes a Toast.* New York: Macmillan, 1962.

A Grief Observed. New York: Seabury Press, 1963.

The Discarded Image. New York: Cambridge, 1964.

Letters to Malcolm. New York: Harcourt Brace, 1964.

Poems. [Walter Hooper, ed.]. New York: Harcourt Brace, 1965.

Letters. [W. H. Lewis, ed.]. New York: Harcourt Brace, 1966.

Of Other Worlds. [Walter Hooper, ed.]. New York: Harcourt Brace, 1966.

Letters to an American Lady. [Clyde S. Kilby, ed.]. Grand Rapids, Mich.: William B. Eerdmans, 1967.

Studies in Words. 2nd ed. New York: Cambridge, 1967.

A Mind Awake. [Clyde S. Kilby, ed.]. London: Geoffrey Bles, 1968.

Narrative Poems. [Walter Hooper, ed.]. London: Geoffrey Bles, 1969.

Selected Literary Essays. [Walter Hooper, ed.]. New York: Cambridge, 1969.

LINDGREN, ASTRID

Britt Mari Opens Her Heart. New York: Viking Press, 1944.

Pippi Longstocking. New York: Viking Press, 1950.

Bill Bergson, Master Detective. New York: Viking Press, 1952.

Bill Bergson Lives Dangerously. New York: Viking Press, 1954.

Mio, My Son. New York: Viking Press, 1956.

Pippi Goes on Board. New York: Viking Press, 1957.

Eric and Karlson-on-the-Roof. New York: Oxford, 1958.

Noriko-San, Girl of Japan. London: Methuen, 1958.

Pippi in the South Seas. New York: Viking Press, 1959.

Sia Lives on Kilimanjaro. New York: Macmillan, 1959.

My Swedish Cousins. New York: Macmillan, 1960.

Rasmus and the Vagabond. New York: Viking Press, 1960.

Brenda Brave Helps Grandmother. London: Burke, 1961.

Kati in Italy. Leicester, Eng.: Brockhampton, 1961.

Kati in Paris. Leicester, Eng.: Brockhampton, 1961.

Lilibet, Circus Child. New York: Macmillan, 1961.

The Tomten. New York: Coward-McCann, 1961.

The Children of Noisy Village. New York: Viking Press, 1962.

Christmas in the Stable. New York: Coward-McCann, 1962.

Mischievous Meg. New York: Viking Press, 1962.

Dirk Lives in Holland. New York: Macmillan, 1963.

Happy Times in Noisy Village. New York: Viking Press, 1963.

Lotta on Troublemaker Street. New York: Macmillan, 1963.

Madicken. London: Oxford, 1963.

Marko Lives in Yugoslavia. [with Anna Riwkin-Brick]. New York: Macmillan, 1963.

The Six Bullerby Children. London: Methuen, 1963.

Cherry Time at Bullerby. London: Methuen, 1964.

The Children on Troublemaker Street. New York: Macmillan, 1964.

Christmas in Noisy Village. New York: Viking Press, 1964.

Kati in America. Leicester, England: Brockhampton Press, 1964.

Bill Bergson and the White-Rose Rescue. New York: Viking Press, 1965.

Happy Days at Bullerby. London: Methuen, 1965.

Randi Lives in Norway. New York: Macmillan, 1965.

Simon Small Moves In. London: Burke Publishing Co., 1965.

Springtime in Noisy Village. New York: Viking Press, 1966.

The Tomten and the Fox. Harlow, Eng.: Longmans, 1966.

A Day at Bullerby. London: Methuen, 1967.

Noy Lives in Thailand. London: Methuen, 1967.

The Mischievous Martens. London: Methuen, 1968.

Scrap and the Pirates. Edinburgh: Oliver & Boyd, 1968.

Lotta Leaves Home. London: Methuen, 1969.

Matti Lives in Finland. New York: Macmillan, 1969.

Seacrow Island. New York: Viking Press, 1969.
Skrallan and the Pirates. New York: Doubleday, 1969.
Emil in the Soup Tureen. Chicago: Follett, 1970.
Emil's Pranks. Chicago: Follett, 1971.
Karlsson-on-the-Roof. New York: Viking Press, 1971.

LIONNI, LEO

AUTHORED & ILLUSTRATED WORKS

Little Blue and Little Yellow. New York: Astor-Honor, 1959.
Inch By Inch. New York: Astor-Honor, 1960.
On My Beach There Are Many Pebbles. New York: Astor-Honor, 1961.
Swimmy. New York: Pantheon Books, 1963.
Tico and the Golden Wings. New York: Pantheon Books, 1964.
Frederick. New York: Pantheon Books, 1967.
The Alphabet Tree. New York: Pantheon Books, 1968.
The Biggest House in the World. New York: Pantheon Books, 1968.
Alexander and the Wind-Up Mouse. New York: Pantheon Books, 1969.
Fish is Fish. New York: Pantheon Books, 1970.
Theodore and the Talking Mushroom. New York: Pantheon, 1971.

MC CLOSKEY, ROBERT

AUTHORED & ILLUSTRATED WORKS

Lentil. New York: Viking Press, 1940.
Make Way for Ducklings. New York: Viking Press, 1941.
Homer Price. New York: Viking Press, 1943.
Blueberries for Sal. New York: Viking Press, 1948.
Centerburg Tales. New York: Viking Press, 1951.
One Morning in Maine. New York: Viking Press, 1952.
Time of Wonder. New York: Viking Press, 1957.
Burt Dow, Deep Water Man. New York: Viking Press, 1963.

ILLUSTRATED WORKS

Man Who Lost His Head. [Claire Bishop]. New York: Viking Press, 1942.
Trigger John's Son. [Tom Robinson]. New York: Viking Press, 1949.
Journey Cake, Ho! [Ruth Sawyer]. New York: Viking Press, 1953.

Junket. [Anne Hitchcock White]. New York: Viking Press, 1955.
Henry Reed, Inc. [Keith Robertson]. New York: Viking Press, 1958.
Henry Reed's Journey. [Keith Robertson]. New York: Viking Press, 1963.
Henry Reed's Baby-Sitting Service. [Keith Robertson]. New York: Viking Press, 1966.
Henry Reed's Big Show. [Keith Robertson]. New York: Viking Press, 1970.

MILHOUS, KATHERINE

AUTHORED & ILLUSTRATED WORKS

Lovina. New York: Scribner, 1940.
Herodia. New York: Scribner, 1942.
Corporal Keeperupper. New York: Scribner, 1943.
First Christmas Crib. New York: Scribner, 1944.
Snow Over Bethlehem. New York: Scribner, 1945.
Egg Tree. New York: Scribner, 1950.
Patrick and the Golden Slippers. New York: Scribner, 1951.
Appolonia's Valentine. New York: Scribner, 1954.
With Bells On. New York: Scribner, 1955.
Through These Arches. Philadelphia: Lippincott, 1964.

ILLUSTRATED WORKS

Once on a Time. [Alice Dalgliesh]. New York: Scribner, 1938.
Happily Ever After. [Alice Dalgliesh]. New York: Scribner, 1939.
Book for Jennifer. [Alice Dalgliesh]. New York: Scribner, 1940.
Wings Around South America. [Alice Dalgliesh]. New York: Scribner, 1941.
They Live in South America. [Alice Dalgliesh]. New York: Scribner, 1942.
Little Angel. [Alice Dalgliesh]. New York: Scribner, 1943.
Silver Pencil. [Alice Dalgliesh]. New York: Scribner, 1944.
Along Janet's Road. [Alice Dalgliesh]. New York: Scribner, 1946.
Brownies. [Juliana Ewing]. New York: Scribner, 1946.

NORTON, MARY

Magic Bed-Knob. New York: Putnam, 1944.
Bonfires and Broomsticks. London: Dent, 1947.
Borrowers. New York: Harcourt Brace, 1953.
Borrowers Afield. New York: Harcourt Brace, 1955.

Bed-Knob and Broomstick. reissue. New York: Harcourt Brace, 1957.
Borrowers Afloat. New York: Harcourt Brace, 1959.
Borrowers Aloft. New York: Harcourt Brace, 1961.
The Complete Adventures of the Borrowers. New York: Harcourt Brace, 1967.
Poor Stainless. New York: Harcourt Brace, 1971.

O'DELL, SCOTT
Man Alone. [with William Doyle]. Indianapolis, Ind.: Bobbs Merrill, 1953.
Country of the Sun. New York: T. Y. Crowell, 1957.
Sea is Red. New York: Holt, Rinehart & Winston, 1958.
Island of the Blue Dolphins. Boston: Houghton Mifflin, 1960.
The King's Fifth. Boston: Houghton Mifflin, 1966.
The Black Pearl. Boston: Houghton Mifflin, 1967.
Psychology of Children's Art. [Rhoda Kellogg]. CRM Books, 1967.
The Dark Canoe. Boston: Houghton Mifflin, 1968.
Journey to Jericho. Boston: Houghton Mifflin, 1969.
Sing Down the Moon. Boston: Houghton Mifflin, 1970.

POLITI, LEO
AUTHORED & ILLUSTRATED WORKS
Little Pancho. New York: Viking, 1938.
Pedro, the Angel of Olvera Street. New York: Scribner, 1946.
Juanita. New York: Scribner, 1948.
Song of the Swallows. New York: Scribner, 1949.
Boat for Peppe. New York: Scribner, 1950.
Little Leo. New York: Scribner, 1951.
Mission Bell. New York: Scribner, 1953.
Butterflies Come. New York: Scribner, 1957.
Saint Francis and the Animals. New York: Scribner, 1959.
Moy, Moy. New York: Scribner, 1960.
All Things Bright and Beautiful. New York: Scribner, 1962.
Rosa. New York: Scribner, 1963.
Lito and the Clown. New York: Scribner, 1964.
Piccolo's Prank. New York: Scribner, 1965.
Mieko. San Carlos, Calif.: Golden Gate, 1969.
Emmet. New York: Scribner, 1971.

ILLUSTRATED WORKS
Least One. [Ruth Sawyer]. New York: Viking, 1941.
Angelo, the Naughty One. [Helen Garrett]. New York: Viking, 1944.
Three Miracles. [Catherine Blanton]. New York: John Day, 1946.
At the Palace Gates. [Helen Rand Parish]. New York: Viking, 1949.
Magic Money. [Ann Nolan Clark]. New York: Viking, 1950.
Looking-for-Something. [Ann Nolan Clark]. New York: Viking, 1952.
Columbus Story. [Alice Dalgliesh]. New York: Scribner, 1955.
Noble Doll. [Elizabeth Coatsworth]. New York: Viking Press, 1961.

PRIETO, MARIANA
His Cuban Wife. Daytona Beach, Fla.: College Publishing Co., 1954.
The Wise Rooster. New York: John Day, 1962.
Ah Ucu and Itzo. New York: John Day, 1964.
A Kite for Carlos. New York: John Day, 1966.
Tomato Boy. New York: John Day, 1967.
Johnny Lost. New York: John Day, 1969.
When the Monkeys Wore Sombreros. Irvington-on-Hudson, N.Y.: Harvey House, 1969.
Raimundo, the Unwilling Warrior. Irvington-on-Hudson, N.Y.: Harvey House, 1971.

REY, H. A.
AUTHORED & ILLUSTRATED WORKS
How the Flying Fishes Came Into Being. London: Chatto, Boyd & Oliver, 1938.
Raffy and the Nine Monkeys. London: Chatto, Boyd & Oliver, 1939.
Au Clair de la Lune, and Other French Nursery Songs. New York: Greystone Press, 1941.
Curious George. Boston: Houghton Mifflin, 1941.
How Do You Get There? Boston: Houghton Mifflin, 1941.
Anybody at Home? Boston: Houghton Mifflin, 1942.
Cecily G. and the Nine Monkeys. Boston: Houghton Mifflin, 1942.
Christmas Manger. Boston: Houghton Mifflin, 1942.
Elizabite. New York: Harper & Row, 1942.
Tit for Tat. New York: Harper & Row, 1942.
Uncle Gus's Circus. Boston: Houghton Mifflin, 1942.

Uncle Gus's Farm. Boston: Houghton Mifflin, 1942.

Humpty Dumpty and Other Mother Goose Songs. New York: Harper & Row, 1943.

Tommy Helps, Too. Boston: Houghton Mifflin, 1943.

Where's My Baby? Boston: Houghton Mifflin, 1943.

Feed the Animals. Boston: Houghton Mifflin, 1944.

We Three Kings, and Other Christmas Carols. New York: Harper & Row, 1944.

Anybody at Home? new ed. Boston: Houghton Mifflin, 1945.

Feed the Animals. new ed. Boston: Houghton Mifflin, 1945.

Look for the Letters. New York: Harper & Row, 1945.

Where's My Baby? new ed. Boston: Houghton Mifflin, 1945.

Curious George Takes a Job. Boston: Houghton Mifflin, 1947.

Curious George Rides a Bike. Boston: Houghton Mifflin, 1952.

The Stars. Boston: Houghton Mifflin, 1952.

Find the Constellations. Boston: Houghton Mifflin, 1954.

See the Circus. Boston: Houghton Mifflin, 1956.

Curious George Gets a Medal. Boston: Houghton Mifflin, 1957.

The Stars. enl. ed. Boston: Houghton Mifflin, 1962.

Curious George Learns the Alphabet. Boston: Houghton Mifflin, 1963.

The Stars. 3rd ed. Boston: Houghton Mifflin, 1967.

ILLUSTRATED WORKS

Polite Penguin. [Margaret Wise Brown]. New York: Harper & Row, 1941.

Don't Frighten the Lion. [Margaret Wise Brown]. New York: Harper & Row, 1942.

Katy No-Pocket. [Emmy Payne]. Boston: Houghton Mifflin, 1944.

Park Book. [Charlotte Zolotow]. New York: Harper & Row, 1944.

Pretzel. [Margret Elisabeth Rey]. New York: Harper & Row, 1944.

Spotty. [Margret Elisabeth Rey]. New York: Harper & Row, 1945.

Curious George Flies a Kite. [Margret Elisabeth Rey]. Boston: Houghton Mifflin, 1958.

REY, MARGRET AND H. A.

Pretzel and the Puppies. New York: Harper & Row, 1946.

Billy's Picture. New York: Harper & Row, 1948.

Curious George Goes to the Hospital. Boston: Houghton Mifflin, 1966.

SENDAK, MAURICE

AUTHORED & ILLUSTRATED WORKS

Kenny's Window. New York: Harper & Row, 1956.

Very Far Away. New York: Harper & Row, 1957.

Sign on Rosie's Door. New York: Harper & Row, 1960.

Where the Wild Things Are. New York: Harper & Row, 1963.

Hector Protector. New York: Harper & Row, 1965.

Higglety Pigglety Pop. New York: Harper & Row, 1967.

Alligators All Around. London: William Collins, 1968.

Chicken Soup With Rice. London: William Collins, 1968.

One Was Johnny. London: William Collins, 1968.

Pierre. London: William Collins, 1968.

Chicken Soup With Rice. New York: Scholastic Book Service, 1970.

In the Night Kitchen. New York: Harper & Row, 1970.

In the Night Kitchen Coloring Book. New York: Harper & Row, 1971.

ILLUSTRATED WORKS

Good Shabbos Everybody. [Robert Garvey]. New York: United Synagogue Book Service, 1951.

Wonderful Farm. [Marcel Ayme]. New York: Harper & Row, 1951.

Hole is to Dig. [Ruth Krauss]. New York: Harper & Row, 1952.

Maggie Rose. [Ruth Sawyer]. New York: Harper & Row, 1952.

Giant Story. [Beatrice De Regniers]. New York: Harper & Row, 1953.

Hurry Home, Candy. [Meindert De Jong]. New York: Harper & Row, 1953.

Shadrach. [Meindert De Jong]. New York: Harper & Row, 1953.

Very Special House. [Ruth Krauss]. New York: Harper & Row, 1953.

I'll Be You and You Be Me. [Ruth Krauss]. New York: Harper & Row, 1954.

Magic Pictures. [Marcel Aymé]. New York: Harper & Row, 1954.

Mrs. Piggle-Wiggle's Farm. [Betty MacDonald]. Philadelphia: Lippincott, 1954.

Wheel on the School. [Meindert De Jong]. New York: Harper & Row, 1954.

Charlotte and the White Horse. [Ruth Krauss]. New York: Harper & Row, 1955.

Little Cow and the Turtle. [Meindert De Jong]. New York: Harper & Row, 1955.

What Can You Do With a Shoe? [Beatrice De Regniers]. New York: Harper & Row, 1955.

House of Sixty Fathers. [Meindert De Jong]. New York: Harper & Row, 1956.

I Want to Paint my Bathroom Blue. [Ruth Krauss]. New York: Harper & Row, 1956.

Birthday Party. [Ruth Krauss]. New York: Harper & Row, 1957.

Happy Rain. [Jack Sendak]. New York: Harper & Row, 1957.

Little Bear. [Else Minarik]. New York: Harper & Row, 1957.

Along Came a Dog. [Meindert De Jong]. New York: Harper & Row, 1958.

Circus Girl. [Jack Sendak]. New York: Harper & Row, 1958.

No Fighting, No Biting. [Else Minarik]. New York: Harper & Row, 1958.

Somebody Else's Nut Tree. [Ruth Krauss]. New York: Harper & Row, 1958.

What Do You Say, Dear? [Sesyle Joslin]. Reading, Mass.: W. R. Scott, 1958.

Father Bear Comes Home. [Else Minarik]. New York: Harper & Row, 1959.

Moon Jumpers. [Janice Udry]. New York: Harper & Row, 1959.

Seven Tales. [Hans Christian Andersen]. New York: Harper & Row, 1959.

Dwarf Long-Nose. [Wilhelm Hauff]. New York: Random House, 1960.

Little Bear's Friend. [Else Minarik]. New York: Harper & Row, 1960.

Open House for Butterflies. [Ruth Krauss]. New York: Harper & Row, 1960.

Let's Be Enemies. [Janice Udry]. New York: Harper & Row, 1961.

Little Bear's Visit. [Else Minarik]. New York: Harper & Row, 1961.

Mr. Rabbitt and the Lovely Present. [Charlotte Zolotow]. New York: Harper & Row, 1962.

Singing Hill. [Meindert De Jong]. New York: Harper & Row, 1962.

Griffin and the Minor Canon. [Frank Stockton]. New York: Holt, Rinehart & Winston, 1963.

Sarah's Room. [Doris Orgel]. New York: Harper & Row, 1963.

She Loves Me, She Loves Me Not. [Robert Keeshan]. New York: Harper & Row, 1963.

Bat-Poet. [Randall Jarrell]. New York: Macmillan, 1964.

Bee-Man of Orn. [Frank Stockton]. New York: Holt, Rinehart & Winston, 1964.

How Little Lori Visited Times Square. [Amos Vogel]. New York: Harper & Row, 1964.

Pleasant Fieldmouse. [Jan Wahl]. New York: Harper & Row, 1964.

Animal Family. [Randall Jarrell]. New York: Pantheon, 1965.

Lullabies and Night Songs. [William Engvick, ed.]. New York: Harper & Row, 1965.

Zlateh the Goat and Other Stories. [Isaac B. Singer]. New York: Harper & Row, 1966.

The Golden Key. [George MacDonald]. New York: Farrar, Straus & Giroux, 1967.

Big Green Book. [Robert Graves]. New York: Macmillan, 1968.

A Kiss for Little Bear. [Else Minarik]. New York: Harper & Row, 1968.

The Light Princess. [George MacDonald]. New York: Ariel Books, 1969.

Osito. [Else Minarik]. New York: Harper & Row, 1969.

SEREDY, KATE

AUTHORED & ILLUSTRATED WORKS

Good Master. New York: Viking Press, 1935.

Listening. New York: Viking Press, 1936.

White Stag. New York: Viking Press, 1937.

Who is Johnny? New York: Viking Press, 1939.

Singing Tree. New York: Viking Press, 1940.

Tree for Peter. New York: Viking Press, 1941.

Open Gate. New York: Viking Press, 1943.

Chestry Oak. New York: Viking Press, 1948.

Gypsy. New York: Viking Press, 1951.

Philomena. New York: Viking Press, 1955.

Tenement Tree. New York: Viking Press, 1959.

A Brand-New Uncle. New York: Viking Press, 1961.

Lazy Tinka. New York: Viking Press, 1962.

ILLUSTRATED WORKS

Caddie Woodlawn. [Carol Brink]. New York: Macmillan, 1935.

Selfish Giant, and Other Stories. [Wilhelmina Harper, comp.]. New York: McKay, 1935.

With Heart and Lute. [Blanche Thompson]. New York: Macmillan, 1935.

Young Walter Scott. [Elizabeth Gray]. New York: Viking Press, 1935.

Gunniwolf, and Other Merry Tales. [Wilhelmina Harper, comp.]. New York: McKay, 1936.

Winterbound. [Margery Bianco]. New York: Viking Press, 1936.

Ear for Uncle Emil. [Eva Gaggin]. New York: Viking Press, 1939.

Michel's Island. [Mabel Hunt]. New York: Frederick Stokes, 1940.

Bible Children. [Blanche Thompson, ed.]. New York: Grosset & Dunlap, 1941.

Oldest Story. [Blanche Thompson]. Milwaukee, Wis.: Bruce, 1943.

Christmas Anna Angel. [Ruth Sawyer]. New York: Viking Press, 1944.

Candle Burns for France. [Blanche Thompson]. Milwaukee, Wis.: Bruce, 1946.

Hoot-Owl. [Mabel La Rue]. New York: Macmillan, 1946.

Wonderful Year. [Nancy Barnes]. New York: Julian Messner, 1946.

Adopted Jane. [Helen Daringer]. New York: Harcourt Brace, 1947.

Mary Montgomery. [Helen Daringer]. New York: Harcourt Brace, 1948.

House for Ten. [Miriam Mason]. Boston: Ginn, 1949.

Pilgrim Kate. [Helen Daringer]. New York: Harcourt Brace, 1949.

Little Vic. [Doris Gates]. New York: Viking Press, 1951.

Finnegan II. [Carolyn Bailey]. New York: Viking Press, 1953.

TUNIS, JOHN

American Girl. New York: John Day, 1928.

Was College Worth While? New York: Harcourt Brace, 1936.

Iron Duke. New York: Harcourt Brace, 1938.

Duke Decides. New York: Harcourt Brace, 1939.

Champion's Choice. New York: Harcourt Brace, 1940.

Choosing a College. New York: Harcourt Brace, 1940.

Kid from Tomkinsville. New York: Harcourt Brace, 1940.

Sport for the Fun of It. New York: A. S. Barnes, 1940.

Democracy and Sport. New York: A. S. Barnes, 1941.

This Writing Game. New York: A. S. Barnes, 1941.

World Series. New York: Harcourt Brace, 1941.

All American. New York: Harcourt Brace, 1942.

Million-Miler. New York: Julian Messner, 1942.

Keystone Kids. New York: Harcourt Brace, 1943.

Lawn Games. New York: A. S. Barnes, 1943.

Rookie of the Year. New York: Harcourt Brace, 1944.

Yea! Wildcats! New York: Harcourt Brace, 1944.

City for Lincoln. New York: Harcourt Brace, 1945.

Kid Comes Back. New York: Morrow, 1946.

High Pockets. New York: Morrow, 1948.

Son of the Valley. New York: Morrow, 1949.

Young Razzle. New York: Morrow, 1949.

Sport for the Fun of It. rev. ed. New York: A. S. Barnes, 1950.

Other Side of the Fence. New York: Morrow, 1953.

Go, Team, Go! New York: Morrow, 1954.

Buddy and the Old Pro. New York: Morrow, 1955.

American Way in Sport. New York: Duell, Sloan & Pearce, 1958.

Schoolboy Johnson. New York: Morrow, 1958.

Sport for the Fun of It. rev. ed. New York: Ronald, 1958.

Silence Over Dunkerque. New York: Morrow, 1962.

A Measure of Independence. New York: Atheneum, 1964.

His Enemy, His Friend. New York: Morrow, 1967.

WARD, LYND

AUTHORED & ILLUSTRATED WORKS

God's Man. London: Jonathan Cape, 1930.

Madman's Drum. London: Jonathan Cape, 1930.

Wild Pilgrimage. New York: Harrison Smith, 1932.

Prelude to a Million Years. New York: Equinox, 1933.

One of Us. New York: Equinox, 1935.

Song Without Words. New York: Random House, 1936.

Vertigo. New York: Random House, 1937.

Biggest Bear. Boston: Houghton Mifflin, 1952.

Nic of the Woods. Boston: Houghton Mifflin, 1965.

God's Man. Cleveland: World, 1966.

Wild Pilgrimage. reissue. Cleveland: World, 1967.

ILLUSTRATED WORKS

Ballad of Reading Gaol. [Oscar Wilde]. New York: Vanguard Press, 1928.

Prince Bantam. [May McNeer Ward]. New York: Macmillan, 1929.

Cat Who Went to Heaven. [Elizabeth Coatsworth]. New York: Macmillan, 1930.

Children of the New Forest. [Frederick Marryat]. New York: Macmillan, 1930.

Faust. [Goethe]. New York: Robert Ballou, 1930.

Jockeys, Crooks and Kings. [Winfield O'Connor]. London: Jonathan Cape, 1930.

Midsummernight. [Carl Wilhemson]. New York: Farrar, Straus & Giroux, 1930.

Stop Tim! [May McNeer Ward]. New York: Farrar, Straus & Giroux.

Impassioned Clay. [Llewelyn Powys]. New York: Longmans Green, 1931.

Christmas Poem. [Thomas Mann]. New York: Equinox, 1932.

Now That the Gods Are Dead. [Llewelyn Powys]. New York: Equinox, 1932.

Flutter of an Eyelid. [Myron Brinig]. New York: Farrar, Straus & Giroux, 1933.

Cadaver of Gideon Wyck. [Alexander Laing]. New York: Farrar, Straus & Giroux, 1934.

Frankenstein. [Mary Shelley]. New York: Harrison Smith, 1934.

Nocturnes. [Thomas Mann]. New York: Equinox, 1934.

Topgallant, a Herring Gull. [Marjorie Medary]. New York: Random House, 1935.

Haunted Omnibus. [Alexander Laing, ed.]. New York: Farrar, Straus & Giroux, 1937.

Story of Odysseus. [Homer]. New York: Modern Age Books, 1937.

Birds Against Men. [Louis Halle]. New York: Viking Press, 1938.

House by the Sea. [Hildegarde Swift]. New York: Harcourt Brace, 1938.

Les Miserables. [Victor Hugo]. New York: Limited Editions Club, 1938.

Porpoise of Pirate Bay. [F. M. Howard]. New York: Random House, 1938.

Runner of the Mountain Tops. [Mabel Robinson]. New York: Random House, 1939.

Last Hunt. [Maurice Genevoix]. New York: Random House, 1940.

Le Comte de Monte-Cristo. [Alexandre Dumas]. New York: Limited Editions Club, 1941.

Primer of Economics. [Stuart Chase]. New York: Random House, 1941.

Gargantua and Pantagruel. [Francois Rabelais]. New York: Heritage Press, 1942.

Little Red Lighthouse and the Great Gray Bridge. [Hildegarde Swift]. New York: Harcourt Brace, 1942.

Sangamon. [Edgar Lee Masters]. New York: Farrar, Straus & Giroux, 1942.

Fog Magic. [Julia Sauer]. New York: Viking Press, 1943.

Johnny Tremain. [Esther Forbes]. Boston: Houghton Mifflin, 1943.

The Praise of Folly. [Desiderius Erasmus]. New York: Limited Editions Club, 1943.

Gold Rush. [May McNeer Ward]. New York: Grosset & Dunlap, 1944.

Innocent Voyage. [Richard Hughes]. New York: Heritage Press, 1944.

Reunion in Poland. [Jean Karsavina]. New York: International Publishers, 1945.

America's Paul Revere. [Esther Forbes]. Boston: Houghton Mifflin, 1946.

Robinson Crusoe. [Daniel Defoe]. New York: Grosset & Dunlap, 1946.

Golden Flash. [May McNeer Ward]. New York: Viking Press, 1947.

Many Mansions. [Jessie Jones]. New York: Viking Press, 1947.

North Star Shining. [Hildegarde Swift]. New York: Morrow, 1947.

Kidnapped. [Robert Louis Stevenson]. New York: Grosset & Dunlap, 1948.

America's Ethan Allen. [Stewart Holbrook]. Boston: Houghton Mifflin, 1949.

Swiss Family Robinson. [Johann Wyss]. New York: Grosset & Dunlap, 1949.

California Gold Rush. [May McNeer Ward]. New York: Random House, 1950.

America's Robert E. Lee. [Henry Steele Commager]. Boston: Houghton Mifflin, 1951.

John Wesley. [May McNeer Ward]. Nashville, Tenn.: Abingdon-Cokesbury, 1951.

Black Sombrero. [Nanda Ward]. New York: Farrar, Straus & Giroux, 1952.

Conquest of the North and South Poles. [Russell Owen]. New York: Random House, 1952.

Mr. Wicker's Widow. [Carley Dawson]. Boston: Houghton Mifflin, 1952.

Story of Ulysses S. Grant. [Jeannette Nolan]. New York: Grosset & Dunlap, 1952.

Up a Crooked River. [May McNeer Ward]. New York: Viking Press, 1952.

Arabian Nights Entertainments. [Padraic Colum, ed.]. New York: Macmillan, 1953.

Martin Luther. [May McNeer Ward]. Nashville, Tenn.: Abingdon-Cokesbury, 1953.

Mexican Story. [May McNeer Ward]. New York: Farrar, Straus & Giroux, 1953.

Horn That Stopped the Band. [Arthur Parsons]. New York: Franklin Watts, 1954.

Little Baptiste. [May McNeer Ward]. Boston: Houghton Mifflin, 1954.

Sign of the Seven Seas. [Carley Dawson]. Boston: Houghton Mifflin, 1954.

War Chief of the Seminoles. [May McNeer Ward]. New York: Random House, 1954.

Dragon Run. [Carley Dawson]. Boston: Houghton Mifflin, 1955.

Santiago. [Ann Nolan Clark]. New York: Viking Press, 1955.

America's Abraham Lincoln. [May Mc-

Neer Ward]. Boston: Houghton Mifflin, 1957.

Armed with Courage. [May McNeer Ward]. Nashville, Tenn.: Abingdon Press, 1957.

Edge of April. [Hildegarde Swift]. New York: Morrow, 1957.

Canadian Story. [May McNeer Ward]. New York: Farrar, Straus & Giroux, 1958.

Cat Who Went to Heaven. new ed. [Elizabeth Coatsworth]. New York: Macmillan, 1958.

Bible Readings for Boys and Girls. Camden, N.J.: Thomas Nelson, 1959.

Gaudenzia. [Marguerite Henry]. Chicago: Rand McNally, 1960.

My Friend Mac. [May McNeer Ward]. Boston: Houghton Mifflin, 1960.

The Bible Story. Camden, N.J.: Thomas Nelson, 1961.

Rights of Man. [Thomas Paine]. New York: Heritage Press, 1961.

America's Mark Twain. [May McNeer Ward]. Boston: Houghton Mifflin, 1962.

From the Eagle's Wing. [Hildegarde Swift]. New York: Morrow, 1962.

Hi Tom. [Nanda Ward]. New York: Hastings House, 1962.

American Indian Story. [May McNeer Ward]. New York: Farrar, Straus & Giroux, 1963.

Give Me Freedom. [May McNeer Ward]. Nashville, Tenn.: Abingdon, 1964.

Peculiar Magic. [Annabel and Edgar Johnson]. Boston: Houghton Mifflin, 1965.

Brady. [Jean Fritz]. New York: Coward-McCann, 1966.

Dream of the Blue Heron. [Victor Barnouw]. New York: Dial Press, 1966.

The Master of Ballantrae. [Robert Louis Stevenson]. New York: Heritage Press, 1966.

Early Thunder. [Jean Fritz]. New York: Coward-McCann, 1967.

The Wolf of Lamb's Lane. [May McNeer Ward]. Boston: Houghton Mifflin, 1967.

The Secret Journey of the Silver Reindeer. [Lee Kingman]. New York: Doubleday, 1968.

Stories from the Bible. [Alvin Tresselt]. New York: Coward-McCann, 1971.

Stranger in the Pines. [May McNeer Ward]. Boston: Houghton Mifflin, 1971.

WHITE, E. B.

Is Sex Necessary? [with James Thurber]. New York: Harper & Row, 1929.

Lady is Cold. New York: Harper & Row, 1929.

Alice Through the Cellophane. New York: John Day, 1933.

Everyday is Saturday. New York: Harper & Row, 1934.

Fox of Peapack, and Other Poems. New York: Harper & Row, 1938.

Quo Vadimus? New York: Harper & Row, 1939.

Subtreasury of American Humor. [with K.S.A. White]. New York: Coward-McCann, 1941.

One Man's Meat. New York: Harper & Row, 1942.

Stuart Little. New York: Harper & Row, 1945.

Wildflag. Boston: Houghton Mifflin, 1946.

Here is New York. New York: Harper & Row, 1949.

Charlotte's Web. New York: Harper & Row, 1952.

Second Tree from the Corner. New York: Harper & Row, 1954.

Elements of Style. [with William Strunk]. New York: Macmillan, 1959.

The Points of My Compass. New York: Harper & Row, 1962.

Subtreasury of American Humor. abr. ed. [with K.S.A. White]. New York: Putnam, 1962.

The Trumpet of the Swan. New York: Harper & Row, 1970.

WILDSMITH, BRIAN

AUTHORED & ILLUSTRATED WORKS

ABC. New York: Franklin Watts, 1963.

Brian Wildsmith's 1, 2, 3's. New York: Franklin Watts, 1965.

Brian Wildsmith's Birds. New York: Franklin Watts, 1967.

The Hare and the Tortoise. New York: Franklin Watts, 1967.

Brian Wildsmith's Wild Animals. New York: Franklin Watts, 1967.

Brian Wildsmith's Fishes. New York: Franklin Watts, 1968.

Brian Wildsmith's Circus. New York: Franklin Watts, 1970.

Brian Wildsmith's Puzzles. New York: Oxford, 1970.

Brian Wildsmith's Months. New York: Franklin Watts, 1971.

The Owl and the Woodpecker. New York: Franklin Watts, 1972.

ILLUSTRATED WORKS

The Lion and the Rat. [Jean de la Fontaine]. New York: Franklin Watts, 1963.

Fifer for the Union. [Lorenzo Allen]. New York: Morrow, 1964.

Myths of the Norsemen. [Roger Green]. Chester Springs, Pa.: Dufour, 1964.

The North Wind and the Sun. [Jean de la

Fontaine]. New York: Franklin Watts, 1964.

Oxford Book of Poetry for Children. [Edward Blishen, ed.]. New York: Franklin Watts, 1964.

Havelok the Dane. [Kevin Crossley-Holland]. New York: Dutton, 1965.

Mother Goose. New York: Franklin Watts, 1965.

Rich Man and the Shoemaker. [Jean de la Fontaine]. New York: Franklin Watts, 1965.

Barnaby Rudge. [Charles Dickens]. Boston: Ginn, 1966.

A Child's Garden of Verses. [Robert Louis Stevenson]. New York: Franklin Watts, 1966.

Queens Brooch. [Henry Treece]. New York: Putnam, 1967.

The Bible Story. [Philip Turner]. New York: Oxford, 1968.

The Miller, the Boy, and the Donkey. [Jean de la Fontaine]. New York: Franklin Watts, 1969.

WOJCIECHOWSKA, MAIA

Market Day for Ti Andre. [Maia Wojciechowska Rodman]. New York: Viking, 1952.

Shadow of a Bull. New York: Atheneum, 1964.

A Kingdom in a Horse. New York: Harper & Row, 1965.

Odyssey of Courage. New York: Atheneum, 1965.

The Hollywood Kid. New York: Harper & Row, 1966.

A Single Light. New York: Harper & Row, 1968.

Tuned Out. New York: Harper & Row, 1968.

Hey, What's Wrong With This One? New York: Harper & Row, 1969.

Don't Play Dead Before You Have To. New York: Harper & Row, 1970.

The Rotten Years. New York: Doubleday, 1971.

YATES, ELIZABETH

Gathered Grace. Cambridge, England: W. Heffer, 1938.

High Holiday. London: Adam & Charles Black, 1938.

Climbing Higher. London: Adam & Charles Black, 1939.

Hans and Frieda in the Swiss Mountains. New York: Thomas Nelson, 1939.

Piskey Folk. New York: John Day, 1940.

Quest in the Northland. New York: Alfred A. Knopf, 1940.

Haven for the Brave. New York: Alfred A. Knopf, 1941.

Around the Year in Iceland. Boston: D. C. Heath, 1942.

Doll Who Came Alive. New York: John Day, 1942.

Under the Little Fur, and Other Stories. New York: Coward-McCann, 1942.

Mountain Born. New York: Coward-McCann, 1943.

Patterns on the Wall. New York: Alfred A. Knopf, 1943.

Wind of Spring. New York: Coward-McCann, 1945.

High Holiday. 2nd ed. London: Adam & Charles Black, 1946.

Joseph. New York: Alfred A. Knopf, 1947.

Nearby. New York: Alfred A. Knopf, 1947.

Once in the Year. New York: Coward-McCann, 1947.

Beloved Bondage. New York: Coward-McCann, 1948.

Young Traveller in the U.S.A. Letchworth, England: Phoenix House, 1948.

Christmas Story. New York: Aladdin Books, 1949.

Princess and the Goblin. New York: Dutton, 1949.

White Ring. New York: Harcourt Brace, 1949.

Amos Fortune, Free Man. New York: Aladdin Books, 1950.

Children of the Bible. New York: Aladdin Books, 1950.

Guardian Heart. New York: Coward-McCann, 1950.

Brave Interval. New York: Coward-McCann, 1952.

Place for Peter. New York: Coward-McCann, 1952.

Hue and Cry. New York: Coward-McCann, 1953.

Patterns on the Wall. New York: Aladdin Books, 1953.

Princess and Curdie. New York: Macmillan, 1954.

Rainbow Round the World. Indianapolis, Ind.: Bobbs Merrill, 1954.

Your Prayers and Mine. Boston: Houghton Mifflin, 1954.

Prudence Crandell, Woman of Courage. New York: Aladdin Books, 1955.

Carey Girl. New York: Coward-McCann, 1956.

Pebble in a Pool. New York: Dutton, 1958.

Lighted Heart. New York: Dutton, 1960.

Light Princess. New York: T. Y. Crowell, 1962.

The Next Fine Day. New York: John Day, 1962.

Someday You'll Write. New York: Dutton, 1962.

Amos Fortune, Free Man. New York: Dutton, 1963.

Sir Gibbie. New York: Dutton, 1963.

At the Back of the North Wind. New York: Macmillan, 1964.

Carolina's Courage. New York: Dutton, 1964.

Howard Thurman. New York: John Day, 1964.

Sam's Secret Journal. New York: Friendship Press, 1964.

Is There a Doctor in the Barn? New York: Dutton, 1966.

Up the Golden Stair. New York: Dutton, 1966.

An Easter Story. New York: Dutton, 1967.

Golden Key. New York: Farrar, Straus & Giroux, 1967.

With Pipe, Paddle, and Song. New York: Dutton, 1968.

On That Night. New York: Dutton, 1969.

New Hampshire. New York: Coward-McCann, 1970.

Sarah Whitcher's Story. New York: Dutton, 1971.